Dear Fred,
with my respect,
[illegible]

CRIME, PROCEDURE AND EVIDENCE IN A COMPARATIVE AND INTERNATIONAL CONTEXT

This book aims to honour the work of Professor Mirjan Damaška, Sterling Professor of Law at Yale Law School and a prominent authority for many years in the fields of comparative law, procedural law, evidence, international criminal law and Continental legal history. Professor Damaška's work is renowned for providing new frameworks for understanding different legal traditions. To celebrate the depth and richness of his work and discuss its implications for the future, the editors have brought together an impressive range of leading scholars from different jurisdictions in the fields of comparative and international law, evidence and criminal law and procedure. Using Professor Damaška's work as a backdrop, the essays make a substantial contribution to the development of comparative law, procedure and evidence. After an introduction by the editors and a tribute by Harold Koh, Dean of Yale Law School, the book is divided into four parts. The first part considers contemporary trends in national criminal procedure, examining cross-fertilisation and the extent to which these trends are resulting in converging practices across national jurisdictions. The second part explores the epistemological environment of rules of evidence and procedure. The third part analyses human rights standards and the phenomenon of hybridisation in transnational and international criminal law. The final part of the book assesses Professor Damaška's contribution to comparative law and the challenges faced by comparative law in the twenty first century.

Crime, Procedure and Evidence in a Comparative and International Context

Essays in Honour of Professor Mirjan Damaška

Edited by
John Jackson, Máximo Langer
and Peter Tillers

·HART·
PUBLISHING

OXFORD AND PORTLAND, OREGON
2008

Published in North America (US and Canada) by
Hart Publishing
c/o International Specialized Book Services
920 NE 58th Avenue, Suite 300
Portland, OR 97213–3786
USA
Tel: +1 503 287 3093 or toll-free: (1) 800 944 6190
Fax: +1 503 280 8832
E-mail: orders@isbs.com
Website: http://www.isbs.com

Hart Publishing, 16C Worcester Place, Oxford, OX1 2JW
Telephone: +44 (0)1865 517530 Fax: +44 (0)1865 510710
E-mail: mail@hartpub.co.uk
Website: http://www.hartpub.co.uk

British Library Cataloguing in Publication Data

Data Available

ISBN: 978-1-84113-682-0

Typeset by Columns Design Ltd, Reading
Printed and bound in Great Britain by
CPI Antony Rowe, Chippenham, Wiltshire

For my family: Kathy, Jane and Alex. John Jackson
For my family: Ariel and Mateo. Máximo Langer
For Ilga and Kurt. Peter Tillers

Acknowledgements

When Peter Tillers first proposed the idea of a collection of essays in honour of Mirjan Damaška, there was a very enthusiastic response from many quarters of the academic legal community. We knew that Damaška's work had influenced scholars working in different fields but we did not expect quite such an overwhelming expression of interest in the project. We decided that the best way to honour his work would be to edit a book that was more than just a collection in his honour but would also make a positive contribution to scholarship in its own right. In order to do this, we proposed to focus the book on certain themes that were central to Damaška's work and to ask contributors to address these themes in their essays. Our authors responded very positively to this idea. We thank them for providing such a stimulating set of essays and for being so accommodating towards various editorial demands and suggestions.

When we sent the proposal to Richard Hart, he also responded enthusiastically to our proposal and we would like to thank him and the staff of Hart Publishing for all their work in the production of the book.

We would like to thank Harold Koh, Dean of Yale Law School, for his support for the project and to Yale Law School for facilitating the presentation of the book to Professor Damaška at a conference to be held in honour of his work at Yale in the fall of 2008.

John Jackson would like to thank the European University Institute and members of the Department of Law there for providing an ideal environment in which to work on the book. Máximo Langer would like to thank David Sklansky for his advice on this project, and the UCLA School of Law Hugh & Hazel Darling Law Library and Jordan Blair Woods for their assistance in the editing process. Peter Tillers would like to thank Roger Park and Ugo Mattei.

Finally, the collection bears testimony to the influence that Professor Damaška has had on a whole generation of scholars. We would like to express our personal appreciation for the inspiration and encouragement he has given to us. We feel particularly privileged to have edited this book in his honour.

John Jackson
Máximo Langer
Peter Tillers
March 2008

Contents

List of Contributors

Ronald J Allen: John Henry Wigmore Professor of Law, Northwestern University School of Law; Fellow, Procedural Law Research Center, and Chair, Board of Foreign Advisors, Evidence Law and Forensic Sciences Institute, China Political Science & Law University

Georgia N Alexakis: JD Northwestern University School of Law

M Cherif Bassiouni: Professor of Law and President, International Human Rights Law Institute, DePaul University College of Law; President of the International Association of Penal Law

Craig R Callen: Professor of Law, Michigan State University College of Law

Mireille Delmas-Marty: Professor, Chair of Comparative Legal Studies and Internationalisation of Law, Collège de France

Richard S Frase: Benjamin N Berger Professor of Criminal Law, University of Minnesota Law School

Richard D Friedman: Ralph W Aigler Professor of Law, University of Michigan Law School

Elisabetta Grande: Professor of Comparative Law, Piemonte Orientale University

John Jackson: Professor of Public Law, Queen's University Belfast; Fernand Braudel Fellow, European University Institute, 2007–2008

Harold Hongju Koh: Dean and Gerard C and Bernice Latrobe Smith Professor of International Law, Yale Law School

Davor Krapac: Professor of Law, University of Zagreb; Judge of the Constitutional Court of the Republic of Croatia

Máximo Langer: Professor of Law, University of California, Los Angeles

Richard O Lempert: Eric Stein Distinguished University Professor of Law and Sociology, University of Michigan Law School

Luca Marafioti: Professor of Law, University of Roma Tre

John Henry Merryman: Nelson Bowman Sweitzer and Marie B Sweitzer Professor of Law, Emeritus and Affiliated Professor in the Department of Art, Emeritus, Stanford University

William T Pizzi: Professor of Law, University of Colorado School of Law

Paul Roberts: Professor of Criminal Jurisprudence, University of Nottingham School of Law

Stephen C Thaman: Professor of Law, Saint Louis University School of Law

Peter Tillers: Professor of Law, Benjamin N Cardozo School of Law, Yeshiva University

Thomas Weigend: Professor of Law, University of Cologne

James Q Whitman: Ford Foundation Professor of Comparative and Foreign Law, Yale Law School

1

Introduction: Damaška and Comparative Law

JOHN JACKSON AND MÁXIMO LANGER

FOR OVER 35 years Mirjan Damaška's work has shone like a beacon over those who try to make sense of the similarities and differences between national legal systems. As someone who was a professor of law at the University of Zagreb Law School before coming to the United States to teach at the University of Pennsylvania and then at Yale, his work reflects an unparalleled range of erudition and a deep understanding of the common law and civil law traditions born of personal experience. From such a unique comparative vantage point, Professor Damaška has acted in the role of what Harold Koh describes in chapter two as a 'comparative law bridge' between different cultures.[1] In this role he has inspired an entire generation of scholars immersed in these cultures and helped them to understand the different points of contrast and perspective contained within them.

This book has two aims. First, it aims to honour the depth and richness of Damaška's work through a collection of essays by leading scholars across the dominant common law and civil law traditions. Damaška kindly agreed to speak to us directly about his life and work, and an interview with him conducted by Máximo Langer in April 2007 is reproduced in the Appendix. Second, the book aims to make a positive contribution to comparative scholarship in its own right. The book does not simply aim to be a work of hagiography in the tradition of many *Festschriften*. We consider that Damaška's work is best honoured by a series of reflective and critical essays organised around certain key themes relevant to comparative law.

The tributes to Damaška's work are led in chapter two by Harold Koh, Dean of Yale Law School, who has taught with Damaška in the Yale law faculty for more than two decades. Koh offers a personal and moving

[1] Harold Hongju Koh, ch 2.

account of how Damaška rose to the top of the legal academy both in his native Croatia and in his adopted United States and pays homage to Damaška's personal qualities and intellectual achievements. He marks out three particular areas in which Damaška has served as an 'intellectual bridge'[2] between different legal cultures – comparative and foreign procedure, the law of evidence and international criminal law – and it is fitting that many of the essays warmly praise his work in these fields. Thus his scholarship has 'elegantly illuminated' the 'vast field' of the law of procedure,[3] displaying 'a unique breadth of comparative and historical erudition'.[4] As an 'intellectual master' of Continental law and American law, 'his 1986 masterpiece *The Faces of Justice and State Authority*'[5] has given us 'the single finest answer we possess' to 'the differences in culture, history and social traditions that account for the contrast between America and the Continent'.[6] The impact of his work in comparative criminal procedure is 'difficult to overstate'[7] and his contribution to this field is variously described as 'enormous'[8] and 'seminal'.[9] Within the field of Anglo-American evidence law, no one

> could fail to admire his dissections of the common law and civil law systems … They are pellucid, concise and nuanced, with insights based on research in other disciplines, including history and … psychology.[10]

In fact, some 'view Professor Damaška as an outstanding evidence scholar, who has managed the all too rare accomplishment of bringing truly new ideas to the study of evidence and procedure'.[11] As if his illumination of these fields were not enough, in more recent years his interest has turned to the 'fast-moving field' of international criminal law, where his 'rare knowledge of both the common law and civil law systems makes him the logical scholar and lawyer to help shape this critically important, quickly evolving' area.[12] He is, in sum, 'one of the most inventive, incisive and influential voices in the comparative study of legal process, procedure and

[2] Harold Hongju Koh, ch 2, 30.
[3] John Henry Merryman, ch 15, 275.
[4] Thomas Weigend, ch 3, 39.
[5] MR Damaška, *The Faces of Justice and State Authority* (New Haven, Yale UP, 1986), hereafter referred to as '*Faces of Justice*'.
[6] James Q Whitman, ch 19, 389.
[7] William T Pizzi, ch 4, 65.
[8] Davor Krapac, ch 7, 121 n 5.
[9] Elisabetta Grande, ch 8, 145.
[10] Craig R Callen, ch 9, 165.
[11] Richard Lempert, ch 20, 395.
[12] Harold Hongju Koh, ch 2, 34–5.

evidence over the last three decades',[13] whose 'substantial contributions to the understanding of western legal systems' are 'of the sort to which the rest of us can only aspire'.[14]

The remainder of this chapter addresses the second and main aim of the book, which is to examine and develop themes arising from his work and its implications for comparative law in the 21st century. It seems particularly fitting that his contribution to comparative law is considered at this time, when it has been claimed that the subject finds itself at 'something of a crossroads',[15] pulled in two competing directions, between being viewed on the one hand as a practical endeavour aimed at encouraging judges to learn about solutions in other jurisdictions or helping legislators to promote harmonisation between them, and being viewed on the other hand as an autonomous branch of social science in its own right, reaching towards what has been called 'comparative legal studies'. These debates are unfolding at a time when considerable challenges and opportunities are posed to the subject by the increasing interaction between legal cultures as globalisation drives different parts of the world to become more interdependent.[16]

The contributors to this collection were asked to relate their essays to issues arising from the major comparative themes in Damaška's work. Perhaps his single most outstanding contribution was to provide us with new theoretical tools to explain the substantial differences that exist in the laws of procedure and evidence of different countries across the world. In order to show the links between procedure, the organisation of authority and political goals, he articulated two pairs of opposing ideal-types.

The first pair opposes the hierarchical ideal to the co-ordinate ideal, as two different ways to organise authority in the administration of justice. The hierarchical ideal is familiar to readers of Weber on bureaucracy.[17] It assigns the administration of justice to professional decision-makers, who are part of a hierarchical structure and who apply technical standards in their decisions. The co-ordinate ideal is a new theoretical device that Damaška described in an article in the 1970s.[18] This ideal-type assigns the

[13] Paul Roberts, ch 16, 295.

[14] Ronald J Allen and Georgia N Alexakis, ch 17, 329.

[15] D Nelken, 'Comparative Law and Comparative Legal Studies' in E Örücü and D Nelken (eds), *Comparative Law – A Handbook* (Oxford, Hart Publishing, 2007) 3. See also P Legrand and R Munday, *Comparative Legal Studies: Traditions and Transitions* (Cambridge, CUP, 2003); E Örücü, *The Enigma of Comparative Law: Variations on a Theme for the Twenty-First Century* (The Hague, Martinus Nijhoff, 2004).

[16] See W Twining, *Globalisation and Legal Theory* (London, Butterworths, 2000) and W Twining, 'Globalisation and Comparative Law' in Örücü and Nelken, *ibid* 69.

[17] See M Weber, *Economy and Society* (Berkeley, Los Angeles, London, University of California Press, 1978).

[18] M Damaška, 'Structures of Authority and Comparative Criminal Procedure' (1975) 84 *Yale Law Journal* 480.

administration of justice to lay decision-makers who are in a horizontal relationship of power and who apply community standards of justice in their decisions.

The second pair of opposing ideal-types refers to two types of states – reactive and activist – that set two different ends for the administration of justice and the legal process: conflict-solving and policy-implementing. In the conflict-solving model of the reactive state, the purpose of the administration of justice is to provide a framework for social interaction by solving conflicts among citizens. In the policy-implementing model of the active state, the purpose of the administration of justice is to manage society by implementing the conception of the good life that the state embraces.

It is hard to overstate the importance of these two pairs of opposing ideal-types for comparative studies. The first opposition provides an account of how the form of the organisation of authority in the administration of justice may both historically explain and provide a rationale for features of the Anglo-American and Continental legal process as diverse as – respectively – the concentration of proceedings at trial *versus* the methodical succession of procedural stages, reliance on oral communication and live testimony *versus* reliance on a written dossier, the legitimacy of private procedural action *versus* the exclusivity of the official process, and the use of bending *versus* unbending rules to regulate the legal process.[19]

The opposition between the conflict-solving and policy-implementing models also provides an account of how the political goals of the administration of justice may affect procedure and provide a rationale for many differences between legal processes in Anglo-American and Continental jurisdictions.[20] To be sure, Damaška was not the first to establish a link between types of political states and types of legal processes.[21] But the novelty and genius of Damaška's opposition was in linking the two types of political goals of the legal process to modern political theory: his conflict-solving and policy-implementing types of states can be traced back to the opposition between liberal political conceptions versus anti-liberal conceptions of the state, an opposition that has been crucial for theoretical political debates to this day.[22]

In addition, the combination of the organisation-of-authority and political-goal axes creates a bi-dimensional framework of analysis that

[19] See *Faces of Justice,* above n 5, 16–70.
[20] *Ibid* 71–180.
[21] See, eg, Montesquieu, *The Spirits of the Laws* (Cambridge, UK, CUP, 1989).
[22] See, eg, Rawls, *Political Liberalism* 2nd edn (New York, Columbia University Press, 2005); Holmes, *The Anatomy of Antiliberalism* (Harvard University Press, 1993).

offers a more nuanced and flexible alternative than the adversarial-inquisitorial dichotomy.[23] For instance, from the perspective provided by Damaška, Continental civil procedure is not simply less adversarial than Continental criminal procedure, but fits into a conflict-solving process before a hierarchical officialdom.[24]

Aided by these theoretical models, Damaška proceeded, in *Faces of Justice*, in his later articles and in his *Evidence Law Adrift*,[25] to make a number of important claims about the administration of justice:

(1) The institutional environment and the political purposes of the administration of justice are central for an understanding of the current configuration and the potential evolution of the laws and practices of procedure and evidence.

(2) Damaška's two axes for characterising (a) the organisation of authority (co-ordinate *versus* hierarchical) and (b) the political purposes of the administration of justice (conflict-solving *versus* policy-implementing) are crucial for understanding the current configuration and evolution of the law of procedure.

(3) These two variables capture most differences between the administration of justice and procedure in Anglo-American and Continental-European jurisdictions and indeed allow us to classify and shed light on all kinds of procedures (administrative, civil and criminal) all over the world, including places and times as diverse as the Soviet Union, Mao's China and absolutist Prussia.

(4) The institutional environment is also central in predicting how the law of evidence has evolved over time. In particular the structure of the court (bifurcated *versus* unitary), the concentration or non-concentration of proceedings at trial, and adversarial *versus* inquisitorial procedures are central to understanding the current configuration and the potential evolution of the law of evidence and methods of proof.

(5) This environment – in particular, adversarial and inquisitorial procedural forms – is linked to broad conceptions about the political purposes of the state and the administration of justice – conflict-solving *versus* policy-implementing.

(6) These institutional factors and political purposes also provide an analytical rationale for the laws and practices of procedure and evidence. In other words, they not only contribute to historically explaining the

[23] Paul Roberts, ch 16.
[24] See *Faces of Justice,* above n 5, 206–12.
[25] MR Damaška, *Evidence Law Adrift* (New Haven, Yale, 1997).

current configuration and potential evolution of the laws of procedure and evidence, but also give an institutional and political rationale to these bodies of law.

(7) While these institutional factors and political purposes can result in legal procedures expressing different levels of commitment to the search for truth and can even impede and shape the way we reason about evidence, there is a limit to the extent to which they can interfere with 'natural' processes of reasoning.

It is important to make the point that we are not claiming that all of Damaška's work can be reduced to this general framework. Damaška has written in areas totally unrelated to these themes such as his recent examination of command responsibility in international criminal law.[26] Even when operating within this framework, however, Damaška's work is full of erudite, creative and illuminating analyses and remarks.

We are also not suggesting that there are not other reasonable alternative readings of Damaška's work. What we do suggest is that this general framework helps to give coherence to much of his work and raises significant questions for comparative procedural and evidentiary scholarship. For example, what is it that shapes our procedural and evidentiary environments and what are the implications for concepts such as 'justice' and 'truth'? To what extent are the laws of procedure and evidence driven by the institutional environments and political purposes of the administration of justice, and to what extent do these laws shape or impede our reasoning about evidence? To what extent is it possible to merge procedural and evidentiary practices that have arisen from different legal traditions, either within nation states or at an international level? What are the implications of Damaška's focus on institutional and political factors for comparative scholarship and how valuable is his characterisation of ideal types and his use of dichotomies for the method of 'doing' comparative scholarship? Is his work on comparative procedure relevant to other fields such as philosophy and criminology?

While our contributors were not bound to accept this framework, and the questions arising from it, they responded thoughtfully and imaginatively to our invitation to relate their essays to these themes. After Professor Koh's personal tribute in chapter two, the book is divided into four parts. In the first part, contributors analyse current trends in criminal procedure in five regions – Germany, United States, Italy, the former Soviet Republics and South-Eastern Europe – highlighting differences in the institutional environment and in the political goals of the administration of

[26] M Damaška, 'The Shadow Side of Command Responsibility' (2001) 49 *American Journal of Comparative Law* 455.

criminal justice, with reference in particular to the tendency to borrow or 'transplant' features from one system to another. In the second part, using a number of insights from Damaška's work, contributors analyse epistemological issues related to evidence and procedure. In the third part of the book, contributors move from the national to the international arena by analysing current trends in transnational and international criminal law and procedure and international human rights. The fourth and final part focuses on the challenges that comparative law is currently facing as a discipline and the extent to which Damaška's method of comparative scholarship addresses these challenges. The collection concludes with an 'epilogue' by Richard Lempert, which analyses the relationship between legal systems and social integration from a functionalist perspective and emphasises that despite obvious, and in certain respects deep, differences, Continental and Anglo-American legal systems face similar challenges and largely operate under similar post-Enlightenment constraints.

The first part of this book looks more directly at the changes that have been taking place in the procedural landscape. It is undeniable that during the span of Damaška's writings there have been many changes in the criminal procedural landscape throughout the world, and the pace of these changes seems to be accelerating rather than declining. Some of these changes seem to be mainly due to internal pressures within national systems – although the rise in transnational crime means that some of these pressures may come from beyond a state's national boundaries. Other changes may be the result of external influence or transnational networks. The break-up of the Soviet Union and the former Yugoslavia has also forced countries in these regions to re-examine their procedural systems.[27]

An initial question presented by the chapters in Part I is how well Damaška's fundamental distinction between co-ordinate and hierarchical models of justice and between active and reactive states accounts for these changes. Paul Roberts points out in his essay that Damaška himself was at pains to stress that real life processes do not evolve precisely in accordance with the 'blueprints of procedural ideals'.[28] An ideal-type approach deals with changes in procedure by moving the changed procedures along the continuum created by the ideal-types. For instance, if a procedure moves away from the conflict-solving model, the ideal-type framework would account for that development by characterising the new procedures as being closer to the policy-implementing model. Another related question that the chapters in Part I raise is how the increasing hybridisation of

[27] On the different reasons why and how rules, norms and policies may diffuse among states, see M Langer, 'Revolution in Latin American Criminal Procedure' (2007) 55 *American Journal of Comparative Law* 617, 621–26.

[28] Paul Roberts, ch 16, 306.

procedures should be viewed. Damaška himself claimed that 'some adaptation of pristine arrangements will occur and ... mixtures of activist and reactive forms will emerge'.[29] An ideal-type methodology deals with this hybridisation phenomenon by placing the hybrid procedures at different points within the ideal-type continuum.

In chapter three Thomas Weigend examines the 'astonishing' rise of plea bargaining justice in Germany over the last 30 years.[30] Within an ideal co-ordinate model of justice where the justice system is directed at resolving conflict, an outcome negotiated between the parties is regarded as the ideal way of solving a case. But within an 'activist state' and a hierarchical model of justice exemplified by the inquisitorial process, so long associated with the Continental tradition, 'it is not for the parties to determine the outcome of the process through negotiation and consent' and the idea of plea bargaining or 'equal-level negotiations' between the defendant and state officials appears as an 'even more extravagant aberration', striking fundamentally at the values of 'finding the truth' and arriving at a 'just' decision.[31] Yet plea bargaining and 'its functional equivalents' are 'omnipresent' in today's Continental systems,[32] even in Germany where there is as yet no legislation on the subject and it has been grudgingly accepted by appellate courts.

As well as examining how this phenomenon has arisen, Weigend considers why plea bargaining has come into existence at this moment in history and why it has managed to infiltrate the system. He puts to one side any desire to transplant the procedural practices of the United States and considers that it is to be explained more by the rise of an active defence bar, the weakening of the rule of mandatory prosecution and the rise in time-consuming cases involving drugs and economic crime. As the recent attempts to regulate the practice by statute have shown, plea bargaining is still controversial in Germany, where the two most prestigious organisations of defence lawyers have disputed 'the respective roles of truth and consent in lending legitimacy to criminal judgements'.[33] Weigend cautions against viewing the expansion of plea bargaining as representing any dramatic turn in a conflict-solving or co-ordinate direction, as the great majority of negotiated judgments are more a means of making defendants submit to punishment without trial and with the minimum of cost. He concludes pessimistically that the dilution of the inquisitorial ideal that protected the defendant against abuse and unjust sentencing through the barrier of truth finding has not been replaced by any equitable

[29] *Faces of Justice*, above n 5, 93.
[30] Thomas Weigend, ch 3, 43.
[31] *Ibid*, 41.
[32] *Ibid*.
[33] *Ibid*, 58.

allocation of power in the criminal process and instead of the inquisitorial ideal we are left with a system of justice that has no basis in law or in procedural principle.

While Weigend charts the rise of plea bargaining within a traditionally inquisitorial system, William Pizzi in chapter four points to the persistence of an inquisitorial feature within the United States, which quite self-consciously sees its criminal justice system as 'rigorously adversarial' yet appears, somewhat schizophrenically, to tolerate an inquisitorial mode of procedure at the sentencing stage.[34] Moreover, unlike plea bargaining in Germany and other Continental countries, this has been a traditional feature of the United States's adversarial system.

In his essay Pizzi discusses a recent clash between adversarial and inquisitorial values in attempts to reform sentencing by requiring judges to follow guidelines. Under these guidelines, judges who wish to impose a sentence at the high end of the sentencing range must support such a decision with specific factual findings. According to Pizzi, this restriction on sentencing was intended to protect defendants from harsh sentences by requiring that judges justify such sentences. But in *Blakely v Washington* the Supreme Court has thwarted this reform by ruling that such factual findings need to be made by a jury, not a judge.[35] While the debate has focused on whether such a reform usurps the role of the jury in finding facts, Pizzi argues that the issue in reality is who should control sentencing – the judge or the parties – as so many 'jury convictions' are in fact based on plea bargains. Like Weigend, Pizzi argues for giving the court an independent role to dispense justice irrespective of what is bargained between the parties. The implications of this argument for Damaška's two pairs of opposing ideal types are important. Pizzi's essay, like Weigend's, aptly illustrates Damaška's insight that his ideal types are not replicated, feature by feature, in real-life systems, and its example of inquisitorial sentencing demonstrates Damaška's observation that 'inquisitorial features, sometimes quite conspicuous, can be found in Anglo-American lands'.[36] Pizzi's final conclusion that this is no coincidence, as those features may be necessary as a counterbalance to other extremely adversarial features of the same system, however, raises similar questions as Weigend's essay as to how far inroads into the features of ideal types can be tolerated without them losing all their explanatory force.

One of the implications of Damaška's theory, which puts so much store on the influence of different forms of authority on procedural systems, is that change can be met with cultural resistance – with the result that attempts to 'transplant' processes from one legal culture into another are

34 William T Pizzi, ch 4, 66.
35 542 US 296 (2004).
36 *Faces of Justice*, above n 5, 6.

'translated' into a very different form.[37] The controversy over plea bargaining, which is highlighted in Weigend's chapter, provides an example of such a phenomenon. In chapter five Luca Marafioti examines the difficulties Italy has experienced by incorporating significant adversarial procedures into what had previously been an inquisitorial system. One of the innovations he describes is the way in which the new Italian Code of Criminal Procedure parts company with civil tradition by limiting the written materials which a court may consider at trial. In what he calls a 'counter-reformation', the Constitutional Court permitted the statements of co-defendants made to prosecutors, and even to the police, to be included in the written file and used in the trial. In response, the legislature made a change in a criminal co-defendant's right of silence by requiring co-defendants who make declarations against others to give evidence at trial. Another point of tension he points to is the role played by appeals under the new Code. Unlike the adversarial stance that was applied by the Code to the pre-trial and trial phases of procedure, the Code retained the system of broad appellate review characteristic of civil law systems, and a battle followed between the courts and the Italian legislature over the retention of the prosecutor's right of appeal.

Beyond these specific issues which were played out between the courts and the Italian legislature, Marafioti points to an erosion of the Italian Code at three levels: in the challenges in the Constitutional Court to various articles of the Code; in the steps taken by the Italian legislature to change the Code to make the fight against organised crime more effective; and, finally, in the specific practices of the courts. Although the latter development has been difficult to quantify it has perhaps been the most significant because, according to Marafioti, it is very difficult to graft adversarial party-driven procedures onto a system in which judges retain ultimate responsibility for the verdict and sentencing. He concludes by pointing to common problems facing all Western countries: ever-increasing case loads and limited resources to deal with them – which together inevitably confer considerable factual discretion on prosecutors – and a deep crisis in the liberal ideal of the trial based on oral confrontation between the parties before an impartial judge.

The tone of pessimism on which Marafioti and Weigend conclude their essays on the direction of criminal procedure is echoed by Stephen Thaman in chapter six, which examines the impact of the attempts to reform the criminal procedural systems of the 15 republics of the former Soviet Union. According to Thaman, the Soviet criminal justice system fitted squarely into the hierarchical, policy-implementing and traditionally inquisitorial

[37] On the importance of 'translation', see M Langer, 'From Legal Transplants to Legal Translations: The Globalization of Plea Bargaining and the Americanization Thesis in Criminal Processes' (2004) 45 *Harvard International Law Journal* 1.

model elaborated by Damaška in *Faces of Justice*. A number of reforms introducing adversarial procedure, plea bargaining and jury trial would appear on their face to move these systems in the direction of the co-ordinate and conflict-solving model of justice.

But Thaman demonstrates that many of the reforms have failed to have this effect, and that police and prosecutors have been able to turn many of the new rules to their advantage. Although the constitutions of a number of the post-Soviet republics prescribe an 'adversarial procedure', any moves in this direction are limited to the trial stage, as none of the new codes accords the defence broad adversarial rights at the preliminary investigation. At trial the written investigative dossier continues to play a central role, acting, in Damaška's words cited by Thaman, 'in the wings of the trial like the prompter of an amateur play'.[38] As a result, the 'no-acquittal' policy so dominant during the Soviet era still exists in Russia and the trial remains largely a mere sentencing court. The 'pseudo-oral and pseudo-immediate trial' based on the dossier at least permits some semblance of adversarial testing and requires a written judgment.[39] But trials have been largely replaced by new consensual procedures, because a one-third sentencing discount acts as a strong incentive for a defendant to waive his right to a trial in which he faces a very high probability of being convicted. One of the hopes of promoters of jury trial was that the use of juries would sometimes lead to acquittals in systems that previously had been so disposed towards convictions. But jury trial has thus far only been introduced in Russia and there only for certain serious crimes. In addition, while there is evidence of a much higher acquittal rate in jury cases, the system is subverted by an appeals process that results in large numbers of acquittals being reversed. Thaman's gloomy conclusion is that, far from achieving a successful transplantation or translation of 'co-ordinate' institutions, the new reforms seem only to provide democratic legitimation for systems that are reluctant to allow these institutions to be catalysts for real change.

By contrast Davor Krapac in chapter seven paints a picture of relatively 'successful procedural transplants' in the countries experiencing transition following the break up of the former Yugoslavia.[40] In the early 1990s a number of these states launched major legislative reforms of their criminal law and procedure. Although many of the new codifications of criminal procedure law that were put in place retained a number of features inherited from the old Yugoslav or Austrian-Croatian codes dating to the end of the 19th century, major modifications were made to the provisions on preliminary proceedings and the trial.

[38] *Faces of Justice*, above n 5, 50.
[39] Stephen C Thaman, ch 6, 118.
[40] Davor Krapac, ch 7, 141.

Krapac discusses three general trends arising from these changes: the constitutionalisation of the procedural rights of participants in proceedings, the 'self-reduction' of criminal justice and the 'hybridisation' of the procedural model. Constitutionalisation enabled individuals to bring constitutional complaints before a constitutional court to vindicate their constitutional rights to liberty and fair trial. The latter right has resulted in the previous inquisitorial model being adjusted to the postulate of ever greater participation of procedural participants in proceedings. 'Self-reduction' refers to the means used to by-pass or speed up criminal proceedings, means that include giving prosecutors discretion to drop cases and institute various 'summary' and consensual forms of procedure. Finally, 'hybridisation' has resulted in a reconstruction of criminal procedure around the principles of 'contradictoriness' and the equality of arms. Krapac refers to a particular reform in Croatia inspired by Damaška, whereby defendants should only be interrogated in the customary inquisitorial manner at the beginning of the trial when they indicate that they are guilty of the charges against them. Citing a survey of Croatian judges designed to assess the impact of this reform and another reform, the purpose of which was to give the parties a greater role in the examination and cross-examination of witnesses in criminal proceedings, he suggests that implanting elements of core adversarial procedure into the traditional mixed procedure is not impossible and concludes that the reforms have provided a fairly high level of human rights protection and defence rights in criminal procedure.

But Krapac ends on a cautionary note by reminding us that changes in criminal procedure cannot be divorced from the wider policy aims they are designed to fulfil, and by warning about the dangers of not paying sufficient regard to the need for criminal procedure to be an effective instrument of social control. He points to two paradoxes which accompanied the reforms. First, the reforms were introduced with high standards of human rights protection at a time when these countries were experiencing a significant increase in crime. The second paradox is a chilling reminder of the limitation of 'ideal' procedures: Although the increase in crime did not lead legislatures to change these new procedures, the new procedures were subverted on the ground by the police who resorted to various 'pseudo-procedures' that included violations of human rights that the 'ideal' reforms were meant to protect.[41]

Besides showing the vitality of Damaška's categories to describe recent criminal procedure changes and to account for the resistance to legal transplants, the chapters in Part I raise the issue of the predictive value of Damaška's framework. If the political purpose of the administration of

[41] *Ibid*, 122.

justice is central for understanding the potential evolution of procedure, it is legitimate to ask whether the procedural changes described by these chapters were brought about by changes in the political goals of the domestic states. The chapters do not explicitly address this issue. But interestingly enough, many of the changes described in these chapters were introduced in the context of transitions to democracy in places like South-Eastern Europe and the former Soviet Republics. We do not think, though, that cases in which there has not been a change in state goals preceding the reforms – such as the introduction of plea bargaining in Germany – disproves Damaška's framework. This framework provides an institutional and political rationale for procedural rules and practices and it provides a testable hypothesis about how changes within institutions and in state goals may bring about procedural changes. But Damaška's framework does not assume that these are the only factors that may bring about procedural changes, or that changes in institutional factors and political purposes will automatically bring about procedural changes.

Part II of this book analyzes epistemological issues related to evidence and procedure. In chapter eight, Elisabetta Grande raises questions as to what truth and justice mean, and how they are interpreted in different criminal justice systems. Her essay begins by re-visiting one of Damaška's most influential and most cited articles, an article published in the *University of Pennsylvania Law Review* in 1973. In this article Damaška argued that the common law jury trial presents greater evidentiary barriers to conviction than the Continental criminal trial. He linked this difference to the dichotomy between adversarial and inquisitorial procedures.[42] Arguing that the core contrast between these two procedural styles was one of a party-controlled contest as against an officially-controlled inquest and that the role assigned to the parties as opposed to officials was the focal point of differentiation, he maintained that these contrasting patterns of distributing procedural control explained why Continental proceedings were more committed to searching for the truth than common law ones.

In her essay Grande uses this polarisation to argue, somewhat differently, that far from one procedural type being more committed to the truth than the other, the contrast is to be found in a different attitude towards the search for the truth and in different assumptions about what type of truth is discoverable in the criminal process. While Continentals search for what she calls 'ontological truth' based on a belief that an objective reconstruction of reality is attainable, the adversarial system rests on the assumption that such truth is unattainable and the adversarial system is therefore prepared to settle instead for what she calls 'interpretive truth', a

[42] M Damaška, 'Evidentiary Barriers to Conviction and Two Models of Criminal Procedure: A Comparative Study' (1973) 121 *University of Pennsylvania Law Review* 506.

truth that emerges from opposing views of reality in a 'fair contest'. Tracing the roots of interpretive truth in the common law to the lawyerisation of proceedings and to laissez-faire Lockean values, she uses an intriguing metaphor to suggest that the 'relational' nature of truth finding in the adversarial system produces a 'tango' idea of justice where it 'takes two – and only two – to dance'.[43] On the Continent by contrast the secret, unilateral inquiry has transformed the search for truth from a unilateral inquiry into a collective enterprise resembling a 'rumba' dance in which many dancers in different capacities dance together in the common enterprise of discovering the truth.

This dancing metaphor suggests a somewhat different polarity from the contest/inquest models advanced by Damaška in *Evidentiary Barriers*. Models of procedure are not centered around different endeavours – contest and inquest. Rather, procedures are conceptualised around the common endeavour of truth-finding, which is achieved, however, through different means or dances. The idea of the rumba dance furthermore modifies the tendency to view Continental procedure through the prism of a unilateral inquiry, updating this idea of inquest to reflect the plurality of perspectives that are to be seen at play in the recent reforms of Continental procedure. The different attitudes towards the search for truth that are at the heart of this polarity also convey different meanings of justice, with adversarial systems equating justice to fairness between the parties and Continental justice equating it to the discovery of the 'ontological' truth. She concludes that these different conceptions of truth and justice can pose a challenge to the study of comparative law and she echoes the lesson from Damaška's scholarship that it is essential to look deep into the fundamental matrix of different systems.

Although Damaška advances the view that non-adversarial modes of procedure are more committed to truth finding than adversarial modes of procedure, he was careful in *Evidentiary Barriers* not to make the claim that this means that non-adversarial factual findings are ipso facto more reliable.[44] In *Evidence Law Adrift* he highlighted the cognitive disadvantages which fact-finders encounter in both systems. In one of the most vivid metaphors ever advanced to portray the truth distorting effect of the adversarial system, he likened the evidence that is presented to adjudicators in such a system to that of a world illuminated by 'two narrow beams' of a car driving at night.[45] Yet as Craig Callen reminds us in chapter nine, Damaška has also been critical of some aspects of Continental procedure, particularly the risk in such judge-driven systems that triers of fact will form hypotheses about reality prematurely. The question as to which

[43] Elisabetta Grande, ch 8, 148.
[44] Damaška, above n 42, 588.
[45] *Evidence Law Adrift*, 92.

system is better able to render reliable verdicts is one that has been the subject of much debate. Damaška argued that only the behavioural sciences, especially psychology, can lay this debate to rest, and he made certain observations on how research might be designed to do this.[46]

Callen sets out to illustrate how psychology can illuminate a different question that Damaška raised in a recent article, where he made the observation that what is truly intriguing about different systems is

> not how perfect or imperfect they are, but why they operate tolerably well, despite numerous departures from cognitively optimal arrangements.[47]

Callen draws attention to the fact that a number of cognitive scientists disagree with the very idea of cognitively optimal methods: He argues that we cannot follow 'unbounded rationality' as we never have unlimited resources (including memory capacity) or time when we make decisions.

Callen argues that research on bounded rationality helps to explain how our systems of evidence succeed tolerably well despite their less than optimal cognitive arrangements. He discusses three particular cognitive strategies used by fact-finders in the forensic process to offset these limitations as well as the risks that these cognitive strategies entail. First, we use a 'story model' when fact-finding to assist in the organisation and evaluation of evidence. Second, we form beliefs at an early stage in the search for information which are cognitively difficult to reverse once they are accepted. Third, we tend to believe that we are given evidence for good reason and we may therefore give it greater probative value than it is worth. Callen argues that cognitive research should have a place among the tools that we use in comparative analysis, because such research can help us understand features of different evidentiary systems. While the story model and belief formation theory reinforce Damaška's observation that judge-driven systems may lead to hypotheses being formed too early, these theories draw attention to the compensating importance of narrative testimony, reasoned judgments and *de novo* review in such systems. Conversely, communication theory, Callen argues, highlights the compensating importance of exclusionary rules in bifurcated common law systems which can offset the tendency to give too-ready acceptance to evidence.

Callen's emphasis on how our cognitive strategies are used to cope with the limitations imposed by the institutional environment draws attention to the relationship between institutional factors and different modes of reasoning. Damaška took the view that, while these factors can influence whether we adopt certain modes of reasoning – for example whether we

[46] See, eg, M Damaška, 'Presentation of Evidence and Factfinding Precision' (1975), 123 *University of Pennsylvania Law Review* 1083.

[47] M Damaška, 'Epistemology and legal regulation of proof' (2003) 2 *Law, Probability & Risk* 117, 121.

engage in atomistic or holistic reasoning[48] – the extent to which legal systems can place constraints on proof processes is limited. Damaška thus argued that, throughout the history of the law of evidence, apparently irrational methods of proof, such as trial by oath-swearing, and highly regulated systems, such as the roman-canon system, had only a limited impact on the natural reasoning processes of fact-finders.[49]

In chapter 10 Peter Tillers builds upon another important insight provided by Damaška that there are different types of fact which may involve different mental operations.[50] Damaška drew a particular distinction between 'external facts', which in a manslaughter charge arising out of reckless driving would involve questions such as the speed of the car, the condition of the road and the driver's identity, and 'internal facts', which would involve questions of the defendant's knowledge and volition in order to apply the legal standard. Tillers considers whether there is one universal model of evidential inference. Evidential inference is often assumed to be best viewed as a network or web of inferences, whereby propositional 'atoms' are linked together by nomological entities which are sometimes called generalisations.

But there are circumstances when this model of evidential inference may have little to say about the relationship between evidence and hypotheses. He gives three examples of 'nonstandard' evidential inference. First, there are situations in which fact-finders are not concerned with the occurrence or non-occurrence of some event or events, but are concerned to determine the meaning of that event or events to some person or persons. In his view, 'meaning' questions cannot be adequately addressed merely by considering comparative probabilities about the occurrence or non-occurrence of an event, because solutions to puzzles about human meaning do not depend solely on judgments about the existence or non-existence of a specific state of mind. Answers to questions about the meaning attached to events by other persons involve reading other people's minds, and depend as well on judgments and inferences about the structure of meanings and families of meanings, which call for the 'imaginative reconstruction of meaning'. The other examples he gives of non-standard inference are the unconscious inferences that are at play in perception and the inferences that are involved in special sciences such as quantum mechanics or genetics. From these exceptions to the contemporary standard model of inference, Tillers concludes that human inference does not just involve explicit ratiocinative

[48] See M Damaška, 'Atomistic and Holistic Evaluation of Evidence' in R Clark (ed), *Comparative and Private International Law: Essays in Honour of John Merryman* (Berlin, Duncken and Humblot, 1990).

[49] See, eg, M Damaška, 'The Death of Legal Torture' (1987) 87 *Yale Law Journal* 860; M Damaška, 'Rational and Irrational Proof Revisited' (1997) 5 *Cardozo Journal of International & Comparative Law* 25.

[50] Damaška, above n 49, 'Rational and Irrational Proof Revisited', *ibid.*

processes but is mostly hidden from human sight. This insight amounts to a rejection of the dichotomy between mind and body and restores in modern guise the Aristotelian notion of organism. An important function of explicit ratiocination is to

> have the human organism wrest out of itself and its encounters with the 'world' ... some principles and logics (forms of reasoning) that the organism can hold consciously in mind

and enable it to improve its inner logic[51]. But we need to remember that many or most of the logical operations of the human organism will nevertheless remain hidden from our sight and comprehension.

If so many of the inferences we make in handling evidence are beyond the reach of explicit ratiocination this would seem to render the efforts of legal systems to regulate our reasoning processes extremely problematic. Damaška has pointed out how Continentals long ago gave up the effort to impose legal 'chains' in analysing evidence.[52] The common law by contrast was never averse to using instruments aimed at constraining the fact-finder's freedom in processing evidence. Yet one of the central themes in *Evidence Law Adrift* is the extent to which the common law system of evidence is changing and drifting apart, not it would seem as a result of any declining faith in the system's ability to curtail the fact-finder's freedom in evaluating evidence but, according to Damaška, as a result of the weakening of the institutional mechanisms that give support to its evidentiary doctrines.

The third part of this book analyses changes and challenges that criminal procedure is facing at the transnational and international levels. Since the end of World War II, human rights standards have been articulated and interpreted at the international and regional levels. In addition there have been external pressures on states to find common solutions to problems of organised crime, drug smuggling, people trafficking and, most recently and urgently, international terrorism. On top of this, acts of barbarity arising out of conflicts in a number of regions of the world have led the international community to make efforts to bring to justice, through international criminal tribunals, those who have engaged in war crimes and crimes against humanity, thus requiring common procedures to be agreed at an international level.

These developments have presented scholars and policy-makers with challenges about the best ways to arrange criminal law and procedure to deal with criminal offences in these transnational and international arenas. Damaška himself has concentrated a substantial part of his work in recent

[51] Peter Tillers, ch 10, 197.

[52] M Damaška, 'Freedom of Proof and its Detractors' (1995) 43 *American Journal of Comparative Law* 343.

years in analysing problems in these areas.[53] The next four chapters address these issues by turning towards attempts to reach agreement on common standards of criminal law and procedure at the international level. While Krapac's essay draws attention at the national level to the perils of devising 'ideal' procedures without regard to whether they are effective for what they are intended to do, Cherif Bassiouni in chapter 11 draws attention to the danger of the failure to agree on a coherent criminal justice policy at the international level. In recent years international criminal justice has engaged the attention of policy makers, diplomats and legislators. Much attention has been given to the International Criminal Court created by the Rome Treaty in 1998 and to the rise in the number of international criminal tribunals. These dramatic developments have tended to divert attention from the vitally important role that national courts play in enforcing international crimes. As Bassiouni reminds us, international criminal tribunals rely on national states' co-operation in order to function effectively and under the ICC's complementarity regime national courts have a major role to play in enforcing international criminal law. This is likely to lead to an expansion in claims made by states to exercise extraterritorial jurisdiction for international crimes. As well as this, states are increasingly perceiving threats to their interests outside their territory and as a result of the globalisation of crime there are likely to be increasing demands made for exercising extraterritorial jurisdiction. Yet as Bassiouni points out, there has never been a clear international policy establishing a priority of jurisdictional theories nor an international convention that would provide norms or guidelines to address conflicts that arise when more than one state claims extraterritorial jurisdiction.

The problem is particularly acute when it comes to terrorism offences. When these offences are carried out there is likely to be acute anxiety when states for whatever reason are unable or unwilling to carry out effective prosecutions on their territory and there is a particular need in these cases for a coherent policy on how extraterritorial jurisdiction is to be exercised. Although there is a multiplicity of terrorism conventions, all catalogued in this chapter, these do not consistently posit, either explicitly or implicitly, a duty to prosecute or to extradite, they provide no order of priority as to these obligations and they do not address the problem of jurisdictional conflict. Bassiouni points to the fact that a more coherent policy would contribute to improved co-operation between states in prosecuting or extraditing persons charged with terrorism and would also help to give such prosecutions greater legitimacy. The present diversity of forum

[53] M Damaška, 'The Shadow of Command Responsibility', above n 26; 'Negotiated Justice', below n 57; 'Assignment of Counsel and Perceptions of Fairness' (2005), 3 *Journal of International Criminal Justice*, 3; '*L' incerta identità delle Corti penali internazionali*' (2006) *Criminalia: Annuario di Scienze Penalistiche* 9.

choices reduces the certainty of the applicable law and it thus raises questions about substantive and procedural legality, including the requirement of notice of what precise law is applicable and what procedural rights may be available. Bassiouni is not very explicit about the risks involved if the international community continues to ignore this issue; but he alludes to the fact that when extradition fails states sometimes engage in questionable or illegal practices such as 'disguised extradition' or even outright abduction in violation of international law, and on this point Bassiouni cites the Eichmann abduction from Argentina.[54] In the more recent aftermath of 9/11 there has been a regrettable tendency for certain states to engage in illegal acts. The lack of a more effective system for combating international terrorism does not excuse such illegality but it may increase the risk of it continuing to happen.

Bassiouni's reference to the variation in the procedural rights that may be available in different legal fora to individuals charged with terrorism offences draws attention to the diversity of evidentiary and procedural standards that apply in such cases, a diversity that could be considered a failing in the application of criminal law at the international level. Although countries have ratified a number of human rights treaties, these are minimal standards and there are considerable variations as to the manner in which they are applied across different regimes. John Jackson in chapter 12 returns to the theme of procedure and considers two international attempts to develop common standards of process and procedure: the effort by the European Court of Human Rights to apply human rights standards of fair trial laid down by Article 6 of the European Convention on Human Rights across the different criminal justice systems of the member states of the Council of Europe, and the international community's attempt to develop a set of rules and procedures for prosecuting those charged with international crimes.

While it has been suggested that Damaška's work gives us much reason to be sceptical about attempts to transplant processes from one national system to another,[55] the difficulties would seem to be even more formidable at the international level where the challenge is not just to ensure that any change is translated effectively into the particular legal tradition of the nation state but to meet a number of traditions across national boundaries to the mutual satisfaction of all parties concerned. However, Jackson suggests that the European Court of Human Rights has been relatively

[54] M Cherif Bassiouni, ch 11.

[55] However, Damaška has pointed out that certain legal transplants inspired in Anglo-American systems have the potential to truly transform Continental jurisdictions. See M Damaška, '*Aspectos Globales de la Reforma del Proceso Penal*' in Fundación para el Debido Proceso Legal (ed), *Reformas a la Justicia Penal en las Américas* (Washington DC, The Due Process of Law Foundation, 1999).

successful in using human rights standards to develop a vision of defence participation by means of autonomous concepts such as the principles of equality of arms and adversarial procedure that have been able to reach across the common law and civil law traditions within the Council of Europe. How successful the ECHR has been in ensuring that this vision is translated across the different systems of the member states is, of course, a different question. Chapters six and seven in this collection suggest its success has been mixed. On the one hand, Thaman's picture of the state of criminal procedure in the former Soviet republics suggests there is a long way to go before the Court's vision of defence participation will take root there. On the other hand, Krapac refers to the positive role that principles such as the equality of arms have had in enabling countries with a Continental tradition to adjust their procedures toward greater participation of the parties.

Jackson paints a different picture with regard to the international criminal tribunals. Although these too are bound by international human rights standards, he argues that their procedures have evolved in a pragmatic rather a principled manner, with a tendency to mix procedures from both the dominant legal traditions together with scant regard to Damaška's warning that a mixing of procedures can produce

> a far less satisfactory fact finding result in practice than under either Continental or Anglo-American evidentiary arrangements in their unadulterated form.[56]

Yet Jackson considers that such unadulterated procedures would also not be appropriate to the context in which these tribunals operate and that a better approach would be to develop the human rights standards developed by the European Court in a suitably contextual manner.

Mireille Delmas-Marty in chapter 13 points to further kinds of analysis that should be applied in the new 'jobs' for comparative law that arise from the internationalisation and globalisation of criminal justice. She argues that comparative law can act here not only as a cognitive tool but also as an instrument which can assist in the process of constructing and criticising normative integration. Comparative law can provide a link between national and international law, and when supranational jurisdiction becomes necessary only comparative study can help develop truly 'common' norms defined not by the unilateral transplantation of a dominant system but by building a common 'grammar' from general international law principles, human rights instruments and a comparison of criminal justice systems.

Delmas-Marty provides an example of how comparative law can perfect the process of 'hybridisation' involved in the mixing of legal traditions. She

[56] M Damaška, 'The Uncertain Fate of Evidentiary Transplants: Anglo-American and Continental Experiments' (1997) 45 *American Journal of Comparative Law* 839, 852.

draws on her own experience with the Corpus Juris project, which attempted to design a European criminal code to regulate fraud in the European Union. She explains that the method used to develop this code was broken down into four phases. The first cognitive phase involved analysing the criminal procedure of each European country by using a common language to identify the various 'actors' and 'powers' that determine how a trial unfolds and identifying how these are linked together in each system. The project found that there was a considerable degree of common ground, which paved the way for hybridisation. The second phase involved formulating guiding principles. Here the principles of the European Court of Human Rights referred to in other essays proved helpful. The third phase of critical analysis by the member states was followed by a fourth 'political' phase of carrying the project through to completion. This final phase has proved the most difficult to achieve and has yet to be realised.

Delmas-Marty then turns to the process of hybridisation within international criminal tribunals. Although she demonstrates that a process of constructive hybridisation has begun there, she indicates that there are a number of issues yet to be resolved such as plea bargaining between the prosecution and defence. Through the work that Damaška has brought to bear in this area,[57] she illustrates how comparative law can play a significant role in helping to work out a 'common grammar' which takes into account the specificities of international criminal justice.

While Delmas-Marty's essay illustrates how, by emulating Damaška's work, comparative law can act as a 'bridge' between international and national systems of justice and as a catalyst for hybridisation across different traditions, in chapter 14 Richard Friedman illustrates the difficulty in applying human rights standards in a consistent manner across different legal cultures by considering the different conceptions which the United States Supreme Court and the European Court of Human Rights have taken towards the right to confrontation. Having traced the origins of the right to confrontation in the common law system of criminal jurisprudence down to the recent Supreme Court decision in *Crawford v Washington*,[58] he considers how the right has been developed in the jurisprudence of the European Court and he makes a number of points of comparison between the two systems. First, whereas in the common law the right has had to be disentangled from the hearsay rule, the European Court has never developed any concept of hearsay. Second, whereas the European Court has linked the right to the principle of the equality of arms, the conception in the common law is not based on a concept of equality

[57] See M Damaška, 'Negotiated Justice in International Criminal Courts' (2004) 2 *Journal of International Criminal Justice* 1018.

[58] 541 US 36 (2004).

between prosecution and defence but rather on a deep-seated belief that an essential condition to making prosecution testimony acceptable is that the accused has a choice to confront and examine the witness. Third, the right under *Crawford* is categorical, whereas within the European conception the denial of confrontation is merely a factor to be taken into account in considering whether an accused has had a fair trial.

Friedman also suggests that differences in the approaches of the two systems may be justifiable because of the institutional differences mentioned by Damaška in *Evidence Law Adrift*. An adversarial system which revolves around party control of questioning suggests a stronger need for cross-examination than in the Continental system, where it is enough to provide the defence with an opportunity to call the witness to testify before the court. Similarly, the common law emphasis on the concentrated trial suggests that the right of cross-examination should be one that can be exercised at trial whereas in the less concentrated European institutional environment the ability to cross-examine at other stages of the process should be sufficient. As a result of the institutional factors identified by Damaška and the greater emphasis on individual rights in the common law tradition, Friedman doubts whether these differences will diminish in the foreseeable future. He ends by raising a question mark over the United Kingdom, where the right has its origin but where it has been subsumed by hearsay rules that have been greatly diluted by recent legislation. This produces the result that the right in the UK is now apparently kept alive only by the European jurisprudence. He suggests that the UK may yet rediscover the right in the manner that *Crawford* has reinvigorated the right in the US. But for the moment the UK presents an interesting case study on how rights strongly rooted in a political culture can weaken over time almost to the point of extinction.

The emphasis in the last four essays on international systems of justice that extend beyond the nation state is an illustration of the new challenges that have arisen for comparative law. As in other areas of law, globalisation is raising questions about the 'jobs' that comparative law should do and how they should be done. The fourth part of the book turns to consider Damaška's legacy to comparative law at this exciting time in its development. In chapter 15 John Merryman discusses a problem that has long preoccupied comparativists working within the traditional territory of municipal private law, but that is now increasingly engaging the attention of the international community, as it tries to protect cultural property against theft and destruction, namely: what attitude should be taken towards the question whether the owner of stolen property should be able to recover it from a good faith purchaser. In American law and some other common law countries the prevailing rule is that the owner can recover the

stolen object and need not compensate the purchaser, but in the civil law world the law is significantly more generous towards the good faith purchaser.

Taking the fascinating example of stolen art, Merryman examines the competing arguments for each approach through the different perspectives of theft deterrence, economic analysis and corrective justice and considers whether there are additional considerations that need to be taken into account for works of art. He goes on to consider the merit of alternative approaches such as splitting the loss and whether there should a different approach as time goes by. He argues that the need to preserve valuable works of art and cultural property argues more strongly for a rule that more effectively deters theft. This suggests that a rule protecting the good faith purchaser would provide an incentive for owners to increase their precautions against theft. But he acknowledges that the American bias towards ownership would make it difficult for any such rule to be accepted and instead advances a solution that would require owners to register their loss of stolen property in an accessible record when it is stolen.

In the course of his essay Merryman refers to a doomed comparative law project which had recommended back in 1961 a rule protecting the good faith purchaser on the basis that this was the position supported in the majority of laws. But the project overestimated the degree of consensus that could be reached and 'joined legal history's catalogue of lost causes'.[59] This example of 'doing' comparative law without digging below the surface of the rules to uncover the values that underlie them stands in marked contrast to Damaška's method of making connections between law, political culture and forms of authority. This method is explored in depth by Paul Roberts in chapter 16. Taking *Faces of Justice* as an example, he launches a strong defence of Damaška's methodology of 'comparative modelling'. In answer to the challenge that model-building in the mode of 'ideal types' is a distraction from detailed study of the world around us, Roberts cites Damaška's reference to Weber that such a world cannot be understood 'without constructing analytical models through which to organise and interpret the empirical data which bombard our senses'.[60]

Roberts goes on to identify four strengths in Damaška's methodology. First, the link to political theory offered an approach that enabled us to learn much more about the distinctive character of the legal process. Second, the sophisticated approach of using intersecting models contrasting styles of government and structures of authority was better able to encapsulate the complexities of real legal processes than one-dimensional

59 John Henry Merryman, ch 15, 281.
60 Paul Roberts, ch 16, 300.

models such as 'adversarial' and 'inquisitorial' legal processes. Third, the 'modular flexibility' of his models enabled nuances to be observed that might be overlooked in a more rigid dichotomy. Fourth, his approach brought a perspectival approach to comparative study indicating how the same structures can be viewed in different ways according to one's perspective so that processes that might appear 'inquisitorial' within a common law perspective may appear markedly 'adversarial' when set against a Soviet or Maoist perspective.

Whether one agrees, as Roberts suggests, that Damaška's models breathe new life into the 'staid dichotomy between "inquisitorial" and "adversarial" legal process'[61] or whether instead they serve to raise questions whether this dichotomy has any longer real heuristic value, it is hard to disagree that they provide a framework of analysis that is likely to live well into the 21st century despite the tide of 'postmodern doubt' that Roberts sees as infecting some recent legal scholarship. Something of that doubt which was noticeably absent in *Faces of Justice* is to be seen, he suggests, in *Evidence Law Adrift* which concludes that the common law rules of evidence are facing near extinction. In the second part of the chapter he takes issue with this 'almost apocalyptic' conclusion suggesting that some of the visible symptoms of what Damaška sees as weakening the three pillars that support the rules – a bifurcated trial court, concentrated proceedings and adversarial process – can be matched by countervailing indications of continued vitality. At the end of the chapter he provides a vivid example which has assumed particular importance since *Evidence Law Adrift* was written, namely how supranational judicial institutions have incorporated 'adversarial' features into the notion of a fair trial thereby lending support to the pillar of adversary process that Damaška saw in decline.

While Roberts defends the continuing relevance and importance of conceptual analysis and modelling in comparative law, he acknowledges that 'constructing ideal-typical models should be a starting point, rather than the ultimate destination, of comparative legal analysis'.[62] In chapter 17 Ron Allen and Georgia Alexakis, although not purporting to be comparativists, point to the importance of another dimension of comparative method, namely the need to engage in empirical study. Like Roberts' essay, their chapter is a tale in two parts. In the first part they praise *Faces of Justice* for bringing conceptual clarity to the diversity of arrangements and institutions through which justice is administered. As a work whose objective was utility, the best evidence of its success can be seen in the number of scholars who have found it useful.

[61] *Ibid*, 325.
[62] *Ibid*.

By the time Damaška came to write *Evidence Law Adrift*, however, he had changed direction away from classifying, towards explaining and predicting the demise of the common law rules of evidence. According to Allen and Alexakis, this different enterprise called for a different method which relies far less on conceptual analysis and far more on empirical data; yet his method did not change. Like Roberts, who points to empirical trends against the claim that the three supporting pillars of the common law rules are in decline, Allen and Alexakis are also sceptical of this claim. They provide empirical evidence to question two central propositions in *Evidence Law Adrift* – the vanishing jury trial and the rise in managerial judging – and they proceed to take issue with the description of the American evidentiary process as a 'legion' of exclusionary rules, pointing out how over the course of the last century fact-finders have been progressively freed from the constraints of rules like the hearsay rule and the character/propensity rules.[63] They also point to examples of the neglect of the work of economists in the treatment of the American litigation process and Continental systems and ask why if the American approach to litigation is being eroded it would appear to be making substantial inroads into Continental legal systems and international tribunals. They conclude by giving credit, nevertheless, to Damaška for pointing comparative law in a new direction, moving beyond conceptual work, so well exemplified in *Faces of Justice*, towards empirical work, a movement they see as part of a general transformation in legal scholarship which is both positive and inexorable.

The final two essays take Damaška's work as an example of how comparative law can reach across different academic disciplines and provide inspiration in other fields. One of their themes is how little exchange there has been between comparative law and other disciplines, pointing by way of example to how sentencing theorists and legal philosophers have passed comparative law by, rather as ships in the night, failing to take on board the insights it has to offer. Richard Frase in Chapter 18 shows how comparative sentencing scholars have focused their work on sentencing purposes and severity and given very little attention to sentencing procedure, unaware it would seem of the theories of Damaška and other comparative procedure scholars. In the first part of his essay

[63] It is important to mention that, as Allen and Alexakis partly acknowledge, Damaška has not been alone in claiming that trials are vanishing in the United States and that managerial judging is an important phenomenon before US courts. See, eg, M Galanter, 'The Vanishing Trial: An Examination of Trials and Related Matters in State and Federal Courts' (2004) 1 *Journal of Empirical Legal Studies* 459; TE George & AH Yoon, 'Chief Judges: The Limits of Attitudinal Theory and Possible Paradox of Managerial Judging' (2008) 61 *Vanderbilt Law Review* 1; AR Miller, 'The Pretrial Rush to Judgment: Are the "Litigation Explosion," "Liability Crisis," and Efficiency Clichés Eroding Our Day in Court and Jury Trial Commitments?' (2003) 78 *New York University Law Review* 982.

Frase brings Damaška's comparative criminal procedure models to bear on sentencing theory and considers how well these models explain or predict traditional differences and changes. While Damaška's models explain or predict some difference and changes, they fail to do so in respect of others because of the powerful effects which sentencing goals have on sentencing procedure. As Pizzi's example of 'inquisitorial' processes in sentencing also suggests, it would seem that the choice of sentencing processes is driven by factors independent of the dominant systemic purposes that drive criminal procedures as a whole.

In the second part of his chapter Frase turns to examine comparative sentencing theories and argues that in pointing to socio-political factors to examine differences in sentencing severity and purposes between different countries and at different times, these theories might be improved by incorporating insights from Damaška's models. He concludes, however, on a somewhat sceptical note by questioning the value of modelling cross-national differences and changes in sentencing: Critical data is often non-existent or non-comparable, and even where it is available

> the value of global models may become increasingly limited; the growing complexity and hybridisation of modern criminal justice systems tend to undercut the simplicity needed for models to serve their descriptive, explanatory, predictive and normative functions.[64]

As one of the sentencing theorists referred to by Frase, James Whitman would seem well placed to examine Damaška's contribution to the field of sentencing but in chapter 19 he turns his attention instead to the contribution which comparative law can make to legal philosophy with reference in particular to how Damaška's work illuminates the 'no right answer' debate that has consumed the attention of legal philosophers so much since Dworkin's article in 1977.[65] Whitman points to an early article by Damaška in 1968 where he argued that while the Continental will seek the right solution, his American counterpart 'will display a liberal agnosticism about "right" answers',[66] thereby providing an 'intriguing contrast' to Dworkin's claim that there must always be a right answer to any given question of law.[67] Taking Damaška's scholarly lead, Whitman argues that by limiting themselves to the Anglo-American tradition, Anglo-American philosophers have tended to miss the point that different cultures tend to conceive of 'right answers' differently: 'Continental systems tend to seek answers that are not only *correct* but also *definitive*', while

[64] Richard S Frase, ch 18, 369.

[65] R Dworkin, 'No Right Answer? in P M S Hacker and J Raz (eds), *Law, Morality and Society: Essays in Honour of HLA Hart* (Oxford, OUP, 1977), 58.

[66] M Damaška, 'A Continental Lawyer in an American Law School: Trials and Tribulations of Adjustment' (1968) 116 *University of Pennsylvania Law Review* 1363, 1375.

[67] James Q Whitman, ch 19, 371.

> [o]ther legal traditions, including the American, tend to devote themselves to the search for *correct* answers in a way that largely excludes the possibility that those answers could be *definitive*'.[68]

Whitman argues that, while there is now a consensus among legal philosophers within the Anglo-American and Continental traditions that it is impossible to give definitive answers to all legal questions, lawyers within the two traditions differ considerably in their commitment to the pursuit of definitive correct answers. As Damaška demonstrated in his 1968 article, Americans are content to seek the best arguments for a given case, whereas Continentals seek for the right answer to the problem at hand. Whitman points to a number of examples which illustrate this contrast in attitude towards the pursuit of right answers, a contrast that cannot be accounted for by philosophy but that arises from differences in culture, history and social traditions. Although he considers that Damaška's distinction in *Faces of Justice* between co-ordinate and hierarchical forms of authority goes much of the way to explaining these differences, he suggests that there are other avenues of inquiry which are worth exploring, such as differences in attitude towards individual autonomy and differences in religious traditions. He concludes that the value of comparative law is that it forces us to recognise that legal systems are different value systems, and it is these different value commitments that must be the topic of any ultimately persuasive legal philosophy of right answers.

This introduction has attempted to demonstrate how highly the scholars in this collection regard Damaška's scholarship and why they regard his work as hugely influential within the field of comparative law and elsewhere. It is now time to let them have their own voice. We hope that the collection will encourage those who have not already done so to read Damaška's work for themselves. As the debates within comparative law continue as to where it is going in a world where different cultures increasingly intersect with each other, the importance of trying to understand these differences from outside our immediate field of vision, demonstrated so well by Damaška's scholarship, becomes all the greater. We may not be able to perfect his ability to 'look at things from the outside'.[69] But we can all be inspired by his example.

[68] *Ibid*, 373.
[69] *Faces of Justice*, above n 5, 15.

2

Mirjan Damaška: A Bridge Between Legal Cultures

HAROLD HONGJU KOH *

HOW MANY PEOPLE ascend the highest mountains in both their native and adopted countries? In law, I know of only one: Mirjan Damaška, Sterling Professor of Law at Yale Law School. Professor Damaška rose to the top of the legal academy of Croatia during the first half of his life, uprooted himself to the United States and then rose to the top of the legal academy in his new country. The University of Zagreb Law School, where Mirjan Damaška served as Acting Dean nearly four decades ago, is 230 years old; Yale Law School, of which I am proud to be Dean, is nearly 200 years old. But in those two centuries, only one individual has scaled the heights of the legal academies of both the United States and the former Yugoslavia. Only one scholar has received the Ruđer Bošković Award for Legal Science in Croatia and the Sterling Professorship of Law at Yale University. Only one lawyer has been elected a Fellow of both the American Academy of Arts and Sciences and the Croatian Academy of Arts and Sciences.

What would be a stunning accomplishment for any scholar has been made particularly poignant by Mirjan's unique scholarly role as a 'comparative law bridge' between the United States and Europe. Damaška has divided his life between two legal cultures. After his student days studying for his basic law degree at the University of Zagreb in Croatia, he earned

* This chapter grew out of remarks delivered in November 2006 at the 230th Anniversary Ceremony for the Faculty of Law, University of Zagreb, at the awarding of the Ruđer Bošković Prize in Legal Science to Professor Mirjan Damaška, in conjunction with the International Conference on Global Legal Trends in Comparative Perspective. I am grateful to Dean Josip Kregar and Vice Deans Ivan Šimonović and Ksenija Turković of the Faculty of Law, University of Zagreb for their extraordinary hospitality; to Kate Desormeau and Nicole Hallett of Yale Law School for their outstanding research assistance; and to Mirjan Damaška for including me in an unforgettable event in which Croatia's President, Prime Minister, and his two law schools honoured his lifetime of achievement.

his Diploma in Comparative Law from Luxembourg and his PhD from the University of Ljubljana in what is now Slovenia. Soon thereafter, he began his professorial career at the University of Zagreb Faculty of Law, where he taught for 11 years, two of them as Acting Dean of the Faculty. His integrity was legendary. When the son of Yugoslavia's President Josip Broz Tito presented him with a failing examination, Professor Damaška forthrightly awarded him a failing grade. How many of us would have had the courage to do the same?

In 1971, when he saw his own students being beaten and arrested, Damaška made a heart-wrenching decision: To leave his native land and accept a tenured professorship at the University of Pennsylvania School of Law. There he taught for six years,[1] before moving to Yale in 1976, where he has graced our faculty for the past three decades, first as Ford Foundation Professor of Foreign and Comparative Law and then as Sterling Professor of Law.

As a scholar who has spent his life between two cultures, Mirjan Damaška has never turned his back on the past. He became a mentor to many young scholars, whose tributes appear in this *festschrift*. Seeing in me another child of immigrants, he has shown me special kindness as his junior colleague. In the more than two decades we have taught together on the Yale law faculty, he and his lovely wife Marija have been the most gracious friends and faculty colleagues. He served on the appointments committee that voted me a junior professorship at Yale. He reassured me during my tenure process. When I was asked to serve as Assistant Secretary of State for Democracy, Human Rights and Labor, he advised me on the likely challenges and rewards. And as a former Dean himself, he has confided wise secrets on how best to survive and thrive as a law school dean.

For all of his personal graciousness, Mirjan's greatest contribution has been as an intellectual bridge between the two cultures he has inhabited. His greatness is measured best, not just by his academic achievements, but by the pathbreaking ideas he has contributed to legal thought. He has written six books and published over 80 articles, in eight countries, regarding comparative law, criminal law, criminal and civil procedure, evidence, constitutional law, and Continental legal history. Proficient in eight languages, he has served on boards of editors of journals all over the

[1] For a thoughtful account of his early years in the United States, see M Damaška, 'A Continental Lawyer in an American Law School: Trials and Tribunals of Adjustment' (1968) 116 *University of Pennsylvania Law Review* 1363

world;[2] and he has served as an intellectual bridge particularly in three areas: comparative and foreign procedure, the law of evidence, and international criminal law.

In comparative procedural law, his deepest influence has come from his pathbreaking book *The Faces of Justice and State Authority: A Comparative Approach to the Legal Process*.[3] Rejecting the traditional dyad of comparative procedure, which equates common law with adversarial process and civil law with inquisitorial process, Damaška offered a more nuanced descriptive framework, organised along two different axes. Damaška's 'hierarchical – co-ordinate' axis reflects the way a state has organised its judicial officials, with hierarchic states structuring their judicial branches with stratified authority and rigid role definition, in contrast to co-ordinate states, who organise their judges loosely, with overlapping spheres of authority and concentrated, informal decision-making processes. Damaška's second, 'state activism' axis considers as 'activist' those states that seek to implement substantive values through many vehicles, including the judicial process, while reactive states endorse no specific substantive vision of the good life, with their judiciary playing the role of neutral arbiter of private disputes, enforcing contestants' bargains, and deferring to party autonomy.

Any procedural system, Damaška argued, can be located along these two axes. Viewed in this light, the classic Anglo-American trial is co-ordinate/reactive, while the classic Continental approach is hierarchic/activist. Within these frameworks, procedural rules evolve to carry out the work that they are doing. The particular rules of procedure that develop within these systems reflect an organisational structure that captures the society's preferred view of the state. Thus, Damaška views particular procedural rules as reflections of complex sociopolitical attitudes and choices about the social ends that trials are designed to achieve. By viewing procedural rules as components of larger legal systems, he builds holistic interpretive frameworks, without lapsing into reductionism or oversimplification.

Damaška's reframing of comparative procedure has been hugely influential, by shifting the explanatory weight from narrow policies designed to

[2] Professor Damaška has served on the Board of Editors of the American Journal of Comparative Law; on the Board of Editors of the International Journal of Evidence & Proof in London; on the Boards of Editors of Zbornik Pravnog, at the Faculty of Law in Zagreb and of Hrvatski Ljetopis za Kazneno Pravo in Zagreb; and on the Advisory Board of the Journal of International Criminal Law.

[3] M Damaška, *The Faces of Justice and State Authority: A Comparative Approach to the Legal Process* (New Haven, Yale University Press, 1986). He is also the co-author of a leading comparative law casebook. See M Damaška *et al*, *Comparative Law*, 5th edn (Mineola, NY, The Foundation Press, 1988).

explain particular rules toward broader cultural attitudes toward governance and state authority. Under Damaška's two-by-two matrix, for example, the distrust of hearsay in Anglo-American procedure (as opposed to the relative tolerance of hearsay by civil law procedure) does not simply reflect distrust of the cognitive limitations of lay juries. More fundamentally, the more restrictive hearsay rule in common law countries is a functional antidote to the nonhierarchical, co-ordinate structure of decisionmaking in those countries, a structure that increases the risk that derivative evidence will be entered in error.[4]

Damaška's second seminal book, *Evidence Law Adrift,* expanded upon his cultural enquiry into comparative procedure.[5] Asking why Anglo-American common law rules of evidence have evolved into their current form, Damaška offered a characteristically systemic and cultural answer. He isolates the bifurcated jury trial, the temporal concentration of the hearing, and the adversarial system of dispute resolution as three distinctive institutional pillars supporting our modern Anglo-American system of evidence. Yet each pillar, he notes, is fast eroding. Jury trials are disappearing; the stages of trial are proliferating; and the rise of managerial judging, plea bargaining, settlements, administrative procedures, and alternative dispute resolution have all diluted the traditional party-driven adversarial system. As Anglo-American common law trials have begun to resemble Continental, civil law trials, Damaška writes:

> with jury trials marginalised, procedural concentration abandoned, and the adversarial system somewhat weakened, the institutional environment appears to have decayed that supplied distinctive features of common law evidence with a strong argumentative rationale. ... Therefore, the rules of evidence 'face the danger of becoming antiquated period pieces, intellectual curiosa confined to an oubliette in the castle of justice.[6]

At the same time, however, Damaška explains that common law jurisdictions will not simply converge into civil law systems, because they lack the professionalised civil service bureaucracy and activist mentality needed to support the activist enforcement of civil law rules. Instead, he predicts, common law jurisdictions will produce 'indigenous remedies' to reflect

[4] See M Damaška, 'Of Hearsay and Its Analogues' (1992) 76 *Minnesota Law Review* 425, 427–29. Damaška notes that Anglo-American courts typically have juries deliberating *in camera*, left to their own devices outside the judge's earshot, while Continental courts allow factfinders to sit side by side with professional judges. Civil law trials are only one stage in an ongoing sequence of hearings; thus, if a witness reproduces an out-of-court statement in a civil law trial, the factfinder can usually find the original declarant in time to secure his testimony in court during the next phase in proceedings. Thus, the unhurried pace of the civil law system, made possible by the *hierarchical* organisation of its judicial system, permits hearsay to be vetted more easily and hence entered into evidence with less risk of error.

[5] M Damaška, *Evidence Law Adrift* (New Haven, Yale University Press, 1997).

[6] *Ibid* 142 (internal citations omitted).

their judicial systems' changing demands on the rules of evidence.[7] In the end, Damaška suggests, the strong Anglo-American adversarial system is more committed to dispute resolution than to truthfinding, elevating

> considerations of disputational fairness – such as the balancing of advantages between the litigants – to the status of values capable of interfering with the search for the truth. And it is the primacy of the conflict-resolving vision that explains why the competitive fact-finding system appears acceptable – or even desirable – in Anglo-American countries, despite the departures it entails from ordinary fact-finding practices.[8]

Like *The Faces of Justice*, *Evidence Law Adrift* has been hugely influential, and these two works have become canonical works in the field of comparative procedure.[9] Damaška has been celebrated not simply for his ability to bring order to complexity, but for his prodigious 'wealth of learning and ... richness of detail,'[10] his 'sterling record of scholarship'[11] and his stature as a 'historian of great breadth and ability.'[12] Beyond his erudition, Damaška has been praised for his 'finesse,'[13] and his unusually

> graceful English, ... [marked by] remarkable precision and ease ... [which] conveys a sense of fascination with the language and what it can do.[14]

But what most inspires his admirers – one of whom calls his work 'spell-binding'[15] – is his ability, like Linnaeus, to catalogue phenomena and, by cataloguing, to illuminate their places in a larger ecosystem[16] and, like a chess grandmaster, to understand and illuminate complex systems

[7] *Ibid* 151–52.

[8] *Ibid* 124. See also M Damaška, 'Truth and Its Rivals: Evidence Reform and the Goals of Evidence Law' (1998) 49 *Hastings Law Journal* 289 (elaborating upon the goals of fact-finding in common law proceedings, particularly the diminution of the goal of truth-finding).

[9] For just a sampling of the academic praise for Damaška's work, see, eg, RD Friedman, 'Anchors and Flotsam: Is Evidence Law "Adrift"'? (1998) 107 *Yale Law Journal* 1921 (book review); M Reimann, 'The Faces of Justice and State Authority: A Comparative Approach to the Legal Process' (1988) 82 *AJIL* 203 (book review); NV Demleitner, 'More Than "Just" Evidence: Reviewing Mirjan Damaška's Evidence Law Adrift' (1999) 47 *Am J Comp L* 515 (book review); I Markovits, 'Playing the Opposites Game: On Mirjan Damaška's "The Faces of Justice and State Authority"' (1989) 41 *Stanford Law Review* 1313 (book review); RC Park, 'An Outsider's View of Common Law Evidence: Evidence Law Adrift' (1998) 96 *Michigan Law Review* 1486.

[10] Markovits, above n 9, at 1316.

[11] HT Edwards, 'Comments on Mirjan Damaška's *Of Evidentiary Transplants*' (1997) 45 *Am J Comp L* 853, 853.

[12] Friedman, above n 9, at 1923.

[13] Reimann, above n 9, at 204.

[14] Park, above n 9, at 1506.

[15] Demleitner, above n 9, at 515.

[16] See Markovits, above n 9, at 1315: 'Like that great classifier, Carl von Linne, who brought order into the bewildering richness of plant life by devising a consistent hierarchy of plant properties that allows botanists to name and group every conceivable species, Damaška

with multiple moving parts.[17] Indeed, it is precisely because Damaška has enough distance from both his home and adopted legal systems that he can grasp the deep structure of both systems and see their commonalities and convergences.

Damaška's scholarly approach emphasises three demands: careful attention to context; resisting oversimplification; and the need for legal systems to adjust to revolutionary change. He argues, for example, that evidentiary rules are so rooted in their historical and cultural context that they cannot be transplanted piecemeal from common law to civil law jurisdictions. 'The score may be the same, so to speak,' he once said, 'but if the instruments and players are not, the legal music will sound differently.'[18] For the same reason, Damaška calls for restraint from those scholars who would simplistically call for transplanting certain procedural rules from one jurisdiction to another. Yet at the same time, Damaška recognises that, as jury trials disappear, concentration of procedural hearings diffuses and the adversarial system weakens, the common law procedural and evidentiary system will undergo real, revolutionary change, which our legal policymakers will need to address.

A third and final area of Damaška's interest has been the fast-moving field of international criminal law.[19] Since 1995, he has periodically advised the Croatian government in its relations with the International War Crimes Tribunal for the Former Yugoslavia and the International Court of Justice in The Hague, and he has studied legal issues facing the International Criminal Court as well. He has counseled leading law firms on matters of foreign law, conflict of laws, and international criminal law, and served on the advisory board of the *Journal of International Criminal Law*. As we have seen in recent years, international criminal justice serves multiple functions in a global system of human rights: deterrence; truth-telling; retribution for the victims; and enunciation of emerging global norms,[20] as well as delegitimation of political actors – such as Slobodan Milošević, Radovan Karadžić, or Charles Taylor – who might otherwise

wants to construct procedural archetypes that will allow us to name the components of the most diverse existing procedural styles and group them into recogni[s]able and meaningful patterns'.

[17] Markovits, above n 9, at 1314 (comparing *The Faces of Justice and State Authority* to 'a grandmaster's opposites game').

[18] Edwards, above n 11, at 853, quoting Mirjan Damaška.

[19] See, eg, M Damaška, 'Negotiated Justice in International Criminal Courts' (2004) 2 *JICJ* 1018–1039; M Damaška, '*Boljke Zajedničkog Zločinačkog Pothvata* [The Malady of Joint Criminal Enterprise]' (2005) 12 *Hrvatski Ljetopis za Kazneno Pravo i Praksu* [*Croatian Annual of Criminal Law and Procedure*] no 1, 3–11; M Damaška; *L'incerta identita delle Corti penali internazionali* [The uncertain self-identity of international criminal courts], (Criminalia, Annuario di scienze penalistiche, 2006) 9–55.

[20] See, eg, *Prosector v Kunarac et al*, Judgment (22 Feb 2001), Case No IT-96–23/1, *available at* <http://www.un.org/icty/foca/trialc2/judgment/index.htm> accessed 13 June 2008 (holding that rape and sexual enslavement in wartime are crimes against humanity).

seek to play a future role in the political life of an embattled country. Damaška's rare knowledge of both the common law and civil law systems makes him the logical scholar and lawyer to help shape this critically important, quickly evolving field.

In short, although Mirjan Damaška has accomplished a great deal in his two lifetimes, the crises of our times gives him much work still to do. In this essay, I have deployed an array of metaphors to describe Mirjan Damaška's intellectual gifts and scholarly role. I have called him variously a mountaineer, a botanist of the law's ecosystem, and a grandmaster of the law of procedure. But in the end, perhaps the most lasting image of Mirjan will be as an intellectual bridge between legal cultures. For as globalisation proceeds, Mirjan Damaška's ideas will only grow in importance, as the rapid development of transnational and international law create multiple channels for dialogue among diverse legal cultures in a globalising world.

I

Diverging and Converging Procedural Landscapes, Changes in the Institutional and Political Environment and Legal Transplants

3

The Decay of the Inquisitorial Ideal: Plea Bargaining Invades German Criminal Procedure

THOMAS WEIGEND

I. PLEA BARGAINING IN CONTINENTAL CRIMINAL PROCEDURE: A PRACTICE THAT CANNOT BE

In 2004, Mirjan Damaška offered this diagnosis:

> [T]he full adjudicative process is everywhere in decline ... [T]he novel mode is for authorities to offer concessions to defendants in exchange for an act of self-condemnation which permits avoidance of the adjudicative process or at least its facilitation.[1]

Anyone attentive to recent changes in procedural legislation and jurisprudence worldwide is bound to agree with this statement.[2] Whether the diagnosis calls for a cure, however, or whether it states a welcome progressive step toward efficiency and economy in criminal justice – that question is still subject to controversy, at least among scholars of the 'Continental' tradition.[3]

Although the advance of negotiations in criminal justice is an open secret, it takes a scholar with Damaška's unique breadth of comparative and historical erudition to adequately place this development in perspective. We owe him an analysis that traces the latest changes of procedural

[1] M Damaška, 'Negotiated Justice in International Criminal Courts' (2004) 2 *International Journal of Criminal Justice* 1018, at 1019 (hereinafter *Negotiated Justice*).

[2] For a broad comparative study of negotiated criminal justice based on information from a multitude of legal systems, see S Thaman, 'Plea-Bargaining, Negotiating Confessions and Consensual Resolution of Criminal Cases' in K Boele-Woelki and S van Erp (eds), *General Reports of the XVIIth Congress of the International Academy of Comparative Law* (Utrecht, 2007), p 951 (hereinafter *Plea Bargaining*).

[3] For critical assessments of the advance of negotiated criminal justice, see, eg, B Schünemann, '*Die Absprachen im Strafverfahren*' in E Hanack, H Hilger, V Mehle and G Widmaier (eds), *Festschrift für Peter Rieß* (Berlin, 2002) 525; E Weßlau (2004) '*Absprachen im Strafverfahren*' 116 *Zeitschrift für die gesamte Strafrechtswissenschaft* 150.

law back to the great divide between English and Continental procedure law evolving in the 12th and 13th centuries, when on the Continent the influence of Canon law and reminiscences of Roman law transformed the ancient, party-driven, public Germanic criminal process (which indeed did not differ significantly from what we would now term civil process) into an official, unilateral, secret investigation of acts deemed sins as well as challenges to public authority.[4]

In his seminal works on criminal justice,[5] Damaška has painted an even larger panorama, relating procedural styles back to differing concepts of state and power and to distinct systems of allocating authority. In that grand picture, plea bargaining appears as closely related to the ideal type of a co-ordinated polity, in which power does not emanate from one single centre but is distributed among various entities interacting with and at the same time controlling each other.[6] In such a system, as Damaška has shown, criminal justice is not the result of a state-centred, administrative effort directed at finding 'the truth'; rather, the justice system as a whole – its civil as well as its criminal branch – is directed at resolving conflict where it arises.[7] Consequently, when the parties concerned (the representative of the state, the alleged offender, and possibly the private victim) find a consensus as to the proper resolution of the case, the court's role need not go beyond that of a notary public: The judge will formally ratify the agreement but will not question its content.[8] A negotiated outcome, in this system, is not regarded as an aberration from the regular process but as the ideal way of solving the case: quick, economical and satisfactory to all concerned.

[4] Damaška, *Negotiated Justice*, above n 1, at 1020.

[5] M Damaška, *The Faces of Criminal Justice and State Authority: A Comparative Approach to the Legal Process* (New Haven 1986) (hereinafter *The Faces of Justice*); M Damaška, 'Structures of Authority and Comparative Criminal Procedure' (1975) 84 *Yale Law Journal* 480; M Damaška, 'Evidentiary Barriers to Conviction and Two Models of Criminal Procedure' (1973) 121 *University of Pennsylvania Law Review* 507. I may note here that I had the good luck, as a young man, to come into personal contact with Mirjan Damaška during his stay in Freiburg in 1974 and to get a first glimpse of his scholarship when translating one of his articles into German: see M Damaška, '*Strukturmodelle der Staatsgewalt und ihre Bedeutung für das Strafverfahren*' (1975) 87 *Zeitschrift für die gesamte Strafrechtswissenschaft* 713. I have since benefited again and again from his immense knowledge of law, history, language and culture, his deep insight and the graceful elegance both of his personal and his writing style.

[6] For a succinct description of the 'co-ordinate ideal', see Damaška, *The Faces of Justice*, above n 5, at 23–28.

[7] See Damaška, *The Faces of Justice*, above n 5, at 109 *ff*.

[8] Damaška explains, however, that practice in Anglo-American systems of justice sometimes deviates from the ideal: parties in criminal cases often need the consent of the judge to withdraw 'their' contest once they have submitted it to the court. Damaška suggests that this may be so because 'the prestige of the state adjudicative system is now at stake'. *The Faces of Justice*, above n 5, at 110.

It does not come as a surprise, then, that criticism of plea bargaining in the common law system is rare – and where it exists, critics do not usually remonstrate against the principle of resolving cases without trial but against abuses that have crept into the system as a consequence of case overload and a resulting inequitable pressure on the accused to waive his right to trial.[9]

Contrast that with the 'activist state' and its hierarchical model of justice, exemplified by the inquisitorial process under the *ancien régime*. Where the state provides a system of (criminal) justice not for the purpose of resolving inter-individual conflicts but in order to improve the economic or moral welfare,[10] it is not for the parties to determine the outcome of the process through negotiation and consent. The notion of the criminal defendant disposing of the process by offering a plea of guilty is alien to this system. Or, as Damaška puts it:

> The question 'are you guilty?' ('how do you plead?'), if it is asked at all, is not a vehicle to ascertain whether a process-sustaining controversy exists, as it is in the conflict-solving mode. Instead the question is no more than an invitation addressed to the defendant to confess to the facts of the crime. Whether his confession is credible ... is for the judge and not the defendant to decide.[11]

The idea of plea bargaining – that is, equal-level negotiations between the defendant and state officials on the charge or sentence – must appear as an even more extravagant aberration. Even if some sort of bargaining might be regarded as practically useful, Damaška writes, it is unacceptable in an hierarchically ordered system because it is contrary to the intrinsic non-instrumental values of activist government.[12] In criminal justice, these values can be defined as 'finding the truth' and arriving at a 'just' decision.

And yet, plea bargaining and its functional equivalents are omnipresent in today's criminal justice systems. This applies not only to those Continental legal systems that have introduced negotiated judgments by statute, such as Italy[13], France[14], Spain[15] or Poland[16], but also to countries such as Germany where a practice of bargaining has silently and surreptitiously

[9] For criticism of plea bargaining from US scholars, see A Alschuler, 'Implementing the Criminal Defendant's Right to Trial: Alternatives to the Plea Bargaining System' (1983) 50 *University of Chicago Law Review* 931; S Schulhofer (1984) 'Is Plea Bargaining Inevitable?' 97 *Harvard Law Review* 1037; S Schulhofer (1992) 'Plea Bargaining as Disaster' 101 *Yale Law Journal* 1979.

[10] Cf. Damaška, *The Faces of Justice*, above n 5, at 85.

[11] Damaška, *The Faces of Justice*, above n 5, at 95.

[12] Damaška, *The Faces of Justice*, above n 5, at 86 n 26; see also Damaška, *Negotiated Justice*, above n 1, at p 1020.

[13] Arts 444 *ff Codice di procedura penale.*

[14] Arts 495–7 *ff Code de procédure pénale.*

[15] Arts 652, 688, 694 *Ley de enjuiciamiento criminal.*

[16] Arts 335, 343, 387 *Kodeks postępowania karnego.*

undermined the statutory arrangement and has eventually been – grudgingly – accepted by appellate courts.[17]

Damaška and other commentators have correctly pointed out that there exist obvious differences between US-style plea bargaining and the new schemes to be found on the Continent,[18] and those new schemes also differ considerably amongst each other. But such variations do not significantly detract from the overall picture: The outcome of criminal cases is not determined unilaterally by the court but results from interactions between the parties (and often the court), aiming at a sanctioning decision that the defendant is willing to accept without seeking further legal recourse. En route to the agreed-upon outcome, the facts of the case as well as potentially applicable provisions of substantive and procedural law are reduced to mere arguments, none of them dispositive and each of them subject to being outweighed by competing considerations of fact or law or utility.[19] By using a strictly utilitarian approach to resolving criminal cases (what result best satisfies all participants?), the new system strongly deviates from the (by now ancient) inquisitorial ideal, which strove for 'truth and justice' regardless of cost and time constraints and irrespective of the parties' subjective desires.

It seems, then, that practice in Continental systems of justice has been severed from its theoretical moorings. How can that be? Is there something wrong in principle with inquisitorial theory? Does it have to be abandoned, adapted or adjusted? Or should we react as Hegel is said to have done when a student remarked that practice did not reflect his theory: 'So much worse for practice'?

Let me begin by explaining in some more detail the German experience with negotiated criminal justice. To some extent, the history of 'plea bargaining' in Germany is similar to its American counterpart: it went through the stages of secrecy and denial, recognition in lower-court practice, public and scholarly debate, and finally acceptance and partial regulation by appellate courts. But the fact that negotiated dispositions

[17] For details, see Section 2 below. For a similar development in Austria, see R Moos, '*Absprachen im Strafprozess*' 2004 *Österreichische Richterzeitung* 56.

[18] Damaška, *Negotiated Justice*, above n 1, at 1025–26; M Langer (2004) 'From Legal Transplants to Legal Translations: The Globalization of Plea Bargaining and the Americanization Thesis in Criminal Procedure' 45 *Harvard International Law Journal* 1, at 62 (hereinafter *Legal Transplants*) (based on a comparative analysis of developments in Argentina, France, Germany and Italy).

[19] For example, in a case involving an assault on a police officer: the facts that the officer was injured, that the defendant was drunk, and that the police officer may have initiated the altercation by using excessive force; statutory enhancements for assaulting police officers; difficulties of proving or disproving self-defence; the availability of witnesses; the questionable admissibility of the defendant's incriminatory statements; the extent of the prosecutor's and the court's case dockets; financial interests of defence counsel; and many other factors can be part of the discussions. All these considerations are exchangeable and negotiable bargaining chips.

represent a radical break from the theoretical foundations of German criminal procedure raises questions beyond those that have determined the Anglo-American debate. While plea bargaining in the United States and England has mainly been discussed as a practical problem (how can the plea process be designed to be fair and reliable, and how is actual power amongst participants to be allocated?), in Germany the advent of negotiated justice has led to a 'Second Code' of criminal procedure, a set of norms quite independent of and in some respects contrary to the tenets of the 'official' Code of Criminal Procedure.

II. THE ASTONISHING CAREER OF NEGOTIATED JUSTICE IN GERMANY

A. Plea Bargaining *à l'Allemand*

Less than 30 years ago, well-known comparatist John Langbein called Germany a 'Land without Plea Bargaining'.[20] There was then good reason to assume that Germany was and would remain immune to the practice of plea bargaining. Not only was there no empirical indication in the 1970s of anything resembling judgment-oriented negotiations between the parties in German courts;[21] there was generally very little interaction between judges, prosecutors and defence lawyers except in the courtroom at trial.

Moreover, the basic principles of German criminal procedure law seemed to create a firm bulwark against any invasion of plea bargaining. According to the inquisitorial principle (*Amtsermittlungsgrundsatz*) as embodied in the German Code of Criminal Procedure of 1877 (*Strafprozessordnung*), the court, upon receiving a formal accusation from the public prosecutor, is obliged at trial to conduct a full enquiry into the relevant facts of the case.[22]

The defendant does not plead but is invited (though not obliged) to make a statement in open court. Even if he comes forward with a confession at the beginning of the trial, that does not relieve the court of the duty to 'discover the truth'. According to paragraph 244 sec 2

[20] J Langbein, 'Land without Plea Bargaining: How the Germans Do It' (1979) 78 *Michigan Law Review* 204.

[21] A legal sociologist's report about American plea bargaining KF Schumann, *Der Handel mit Gerechtigkeit* (Frankfurt, Suhrkamp, 1977) was widely received with incredulity and shock about the mores of a very different legal culture.

[22] According to para 261 *Strafprozessordnung*, the court's judgment must be based exclusively on the 'truth' as determined by the court at the trial.

Strafprozessordnung,[23] the court is responsible for ascertaining that all evidence needed to discover the truth about the case is produced at trial.[24] Hence, even when the defendant has confessed, the court may have to call witnesses and take other evidence in order to find out to what extent the defendant correctly and completely related the facts of the case.

Nor is it for the parties to determine the kind of evidence that goes into the court's decision-making: It is the presiding judge who calls and interrogates witnesses and experts and also introduces documentary and real evidence.[25] The court remains, moreover, unfettered by the legal 'charges' cited in the accusatory instrument (*Anklageschrift*): The court's inquiry cannot go beyond the defendant's conduct as described in the *Anklageschrift*, but the court can determine that that conduct corresponds to crime definitions different from those suggested by the prosecution.[26] How could anyone expect that plea bargaining might thrive in such adverse climate?

And yet, the times of full-scale trials for each case are long past. Today, a substantial part of criminal cases, especially of those involving white-collar crime, are no longer resolved by trial – at least not by a trial in the traditional sense – but on the basis of negotiations carried out behind closed doors (or on the telephone) among the judge, the defence lawyer, and the public prosecutor.[27] The subject of such discussions is, as in any

[23] See para 244 sec 2 *Strafprozessordnung*: 'In order to discover the truth, the court has to extend, *ex officio*, the taking of evidence to all facts and pieces of evidence that are relevant to its decision'.

[24] The prosecution will usually suggest relevant pieces of evidence in the accusatory instrument, and both the defence and the prosecution can make formal motions requesting the court to take specified additional evidence. With respect to witnesses, the court can reject such motions only when the proposed evidence is clearly irrelevant or redundant (para 244 sec 3 *Strafprozessordnung*).

[25] Para 238 sec 1 *Strafprozessordnung*.

[26] If, eg, the defendant has been charged with larceny the court can convict him of robbery when the evidence taken at the trial shows that he took the goods by force or threat of force (para 249 *Strafgesetzbuch*). The prosecutor's consent is not required, but the court must give the defendant advance warning that his conduct may warrant conviction of a crime not cited in the indictment, and the defendant can ask for a continuance to give him sufficient time to adjust his defence (para 265 *Strafprozessordnung*). The court is bound, however, by the time and place of conduct designated in the *Anklageschrift*: If the defendant has been accused of stealing a wallet in Berlin on 29 December, the court cannot – even when there is sufficient evidence at the trial – convict him of a larceny committed in Munich, or on 31 December. Only with the consent of the defendant can the prosecutor by oral declaration extend the indictment to additional incidents (para 266 *Strafprozessordnung*).

[27] According to a recent survey conducted in the German state of Northrhine-Westphalia, more than half of all judges, prosecutors and defence lawyers involved in white-collar criminal cases said that they resolved the majority of their cases through negotiations. K Altenhain, H Hagemeier, M Haimerl and KH Stammen, *Die Praxis der Absprachen in Wirtschaftsstrafverfahren* (Baden-Baden, 2007), p 54. For a recent qualitative empirical study of 'plea bargaining' in Germany, see J I Turner, 'Judicial Participation in Plea Negotiations' (2006) 54 *American Journal of Comparative Law* 199, at 217 *ff* (hereinafter *Judicial Participation*).

plea bargaining, a *quid pro quo*: The defence offers the possibility of a confession, and the court offers the possibility of a lenient sentence.

Since the issue of sentencing is addressed directly and not treated indirectly through prosecutorial charging decisions or sentence recommendations,[28] the main bargaining partners in the German system are the court (in practice, the presiding judge[29]) and defence counsel. The prosecutor sometimes plays an active part in the deal, for example, by offering not to bring charges on unrelated offences allegedly committed by the defendant; more frequently, the prosecutor's role is that of a mere control agent representing the public interest in adequately sanctioning offenders. The prosecutor can effectively play that role because he has a factual veto power: Since negotiated judgments do not exactly follow the rules prescribed by the Code of Criminal Procedure, an appeal the prosecutor might file against the sentence would inevitably lead to a reversal of the judgment. If negotiations are successful the court eventually commits itself to a maximum sentence that it will not exceed if the defendant comes forward with a confession to (some of) the charges.

A trial will still be held, but in most cases the 'trial' will only serve to formally ratify and announce the deal made earlier behind closed doors. When negotiations have been concluded before the date set for trial, the 'trial' is typically reduced to an empty ritual. After the opening of the court's session, the prosecutor will read out the formal charges consisting of a very brief description of the defendant's alleged criminal conduct and a recitation of the applicable sections of the Criminal Code. The presiding judge then asks the defendant if he wishes to make a statement. The defendant (or counsel speaking for him) admits to crucial facts of the prosecution case or simply declares that he does not contest (some of) the charges.[30] The court should then announce on the record that negotiations

[28] Since the prosecutor's charges are not binding upon the court (see text at n 26 above) and the court has exclusive sentencing discretion, it would make little sense to engage in 'charge bargaining'; it is hence the court that the defendant and his lawyer need to win over in order to obtain the desired result. Because of the court's active (even pro-active) role in plea bargaining, parties do not have to guess at the effect their actions may have on the court's sentencing decision. For a general argument in favour of a more active judicial role in plea bargaining, see Turner, *Judicial Participation*, above n 27, at 256 *ff*.

[29] Criminal cases in Germany are adjudicated by a single professional judge or by a combination of professional and lay judges. The most serious cases fall within the jurisdiction of *Große Strafkammer* (Grand criminal chamber), consisting of two or three professional judges and two lay justices sitting together (cf paras 24, 25, 28, 74 *Gerichtsverfassungsgesetz*). Informal negotiations before or during trial are typically conducted by the presiding judge, ie the panel's most senior professional judge.

[30] In one case involving repeated sexual assault, all the defendant ever said was 'yes' in response to the presiding judge's question of whether he did what the prosecutor accused him of. The ensuing conviction was upheld by the Federal Court of Appeals. *Bundesgerichtshof*, Judgment of 10 June 1998, 1999 *Neue Zeitschrift für Strafrecht* 92; but see, *contra*, *Bundesgerichtshof*, Judgment of 10 April 2004, 2004 *Neue Juristische Wochenschrift* 1885,

had been held before trial and that the court had committed itself to a maximum sentence in case of a confession. The parties make perfunctory closing statements, and the court then formally convicts the defendant and announces the agreed-upon sentence.[31]

If negotiations take place after the trial has begun, a successful conclusion of talks between the parties and the court often leads to the 'sudden death' of a trial that may previously have dragged on for weeks or months, typically with the defendant relying on his right to silence: To the surprise of the public, the parties who had theretofore bitterly fought every inch of the way on matters of evidence and law will one morning appear in court with a smile on their faces, and the trial is concluded within a few minutes, as described above.

The German practice of negotiating criminal judgments has several important implications. First, deals and lenient sentencing are not available to everyone. A defendant who was caught *in flagrante* or who made an early (admissible) confession has little or nothing to bargain with. German 'plea bargaining', as any other, favours system-wise defendants who know and insist on their right to remain silent and who have lawyers that can make life difficult for the court.[32]

Second, the German system of negotiated judgments is based on differential sentencing: A co-operative defendant receives, *ceteris paribus*, a lesser sentence than a defendant who offers no confession but is convicted after a full trial. Although German sentencing law[33] makes no reference to a confession as a mitigating circumstance, courts routinely use this factor

at 1886 (defendant's declaration that he does not contest the indictment and accepts the sanction suggested by the judge is not sufficient evidence for conviction).

[31] In the German criminal process, the issues of guilt and sentence are treated together and there are no separate sentencing hearings.

[32] Defence motions for additional evidence (cf n 24 above) are powerful weapons that can endlessly prolong a trial. Some attorneys also have developed great skill in repeatedly demanding court rulings on minor points of procedure and in repeatedly questioning the court's neutrality and moving for a recusal of the judge.

[33] The relevant provision is para 46 sec 1 *Strafgesetzbuch*, which demands that the sentence be determined according to the offender's culpability and that the impact of the sentence on his future life in society be taken into account. Para 46 sec 2 *Strafgesetzbuch* mentions as one sentencing factor the offender's 'conduct after the offence'. The courts and some commentators have taken that phrase to be a reference to the offender's subsequent co-operation with the justice system or to a confession. See, eg, *Bundesgerichtshof*, Judgment of 28 August 1997, 43 *Entscheidungen des Bundesgerichtshofes in Strafsachen* 195, at 209 (1997); W Theune, in HW Laufhütte, R Rissing-van Saan and K Tiedemann (eds), 2 *Strafgesetzbuch: Leipziger Kommentar* (12th edn, Berlin 2006), § 46 nn 205, 206. It is more likely, however, that the legislature meant this phrase to refer to cases of immediate compensation on one hand and of obstruction or concealment on the other, because only such conduct can be indicative of the degree of the offender's 'culpability'. For a thorough discussion, see F Streng, in U Kindhäuser, U Neumann and HU Paeffgen (eds), 1 *Nomos-Kommentar Strafgesetzbuch*, (2nd edn, 2005), § 46 nn 75–81.

in sentencing. As in any other plea bargaining system, sentence differentials are the carrot (and at the same time the stick) with which defendants are coaxed into co-operation.

The pressure on German defendants is even more intense than in other systems because it is the presiding judge who conducts the negotiations. It is the same judge who will – together with his colleagues – later be responsible for determining the sentence. The judge's 'guess' of a sentence that might await the defendant if he refuses to confess therefore carries great weight. The statutory sentencing ranges, and thus the 'play' for the court in sentencing, in Germany are typically very broad. For example, sentences for offences such as forgery of documents (paragraph 267 *Strafgesetzbuch*) or extortion (paragraph 253 *Strafgesetzbuch*) can vary between a small fine and 10 or 15 years imprisonment. The larger the sentence differential suggested by the court, the greater the pressure on the suspect to cooperate – and this refers to guilty defendants as well as to those who are innocent or against whom the evidence is too weak to establish guilt beyond a reasonable doubt.

Third, plea bargaining typically involves only the lawyers and reduces others affected by the case to marginal roles. Neither the defendant nor the victim will normally be present during negotiations. The defendant will later be informed – and often persuaded to give his consent – by his lawyer, and the victim, if he gets involved at all,[34] may at best try to voice his opinion to the prosecutor. Lay judges officially play an essential part in the German criminal justice system,[35] but typically learn about plea bargains only after they have been concluded. Negotiating judgments thus turns a process that was meant to be a public affair involving everyone with an interest in the case into a secretive administrative proceeding.

B. Roots and Causes

Astonishingly, the German version of plea bargaining has developed from the grass roots, without any support in the written law. Although there may have been instances of negotiations earlier,[36] the first clear signs of the

[34] The victim, who generally plays a marginal role in German criminal procedure, is normally not involved in plea bargaining. Only when the victim of an offence against the person has joined in the case as a 'complementary prosecutor' (*Nebenkläger*) does he need to be consulted (because the victim may then file an appeal against the negotiated judgment; para 400 *Strafprozessordnung*).

[35] Above n 29.

[36] For an early case of a (failed) 'deal' between the court and the defendant (and his lawyer), see *Bundesgerichtshof*, Judgment of 1 April 1960, *14 Entscheidungen des Bundesgerichtshofes in Strafsachen* 189. In that case, the presiding judge had encouraged the defendant to make a confession by stating in open court that he would consider a confession as a mitigating circumstance. He then adjourned the trial, and defence counsel told the

practice appeared in the early 1980s. The first article on 'settlements in the criminal process' in a professional journal appeared in 1982, published by a well-known defence lawyer who used a pseudonym because evidently the topic was considered too 'hot',[37] and a few publications discussing the legality of the practice followed.[38]

For several years, the existence of plea bargaining in German courts remained the elephant in the room: lawyers knew that it existed but hesitated to openly discuss the practice and its possible legal consequences. In 1990, the topic of *Absprachen* (negotiated judgments) was placed on the agenda of the biannual conference of German lawyers (*Deutscher Juristentag*). That conference witnessed a clash between academics fervently opposed to the new practice,[39] and lower court judges, prosecutors and defence lawyers who mostly favoured negotiations because of their potential to shorten the process.

The appellate courts, especially the Federal Court of Appeals (*Bundesgerichtshof*), hesitated to deal head-on with the legality of negotiated judgments. They were able to avoid the issue because parties content with the bargained-for outcome of their cases would not normally file an appeal.[40] Only in 1997 had the *Bundesgerichtshof* an opportunity to rule

defendant that he could avoid high-security prison (*Zuchthaus*) if he made a confession. The defendant confessed, and the court sentenced him to *Zuchthaus*. The Federal Court of Appeals held that the defendant's confession was admissible evidence, explaining that the judge had not made any promise as to the kind of prison sentence and the defendant was not to rely on counsel's interpretation of the judge's words.

37 'Detlev Deal', 'Der strafprozessuale Vergleich' 1982 *Strafverteidiger* 545.

38 See, eg, W Schmidt-Hieber, *Verständigung im Strafverfahren* (Munich, 1986); E Hanack, *Vereinbarungen im Strafprozeß, ein besseres Mittel zur Bewältigung von Großverfahren?*, 1987 *Strafverteidiger* 500; F Dencker and R Hamm, *Der Vergleich im Strafprozeß* (Frankfurt 1988). Mirjan Damaška entered the German debate early with a thoughtful comparative analysis of the role of plea bargaining. See M Damaška, '*Der Austausch von Vorteilen im Strafverfahren: Plea-Bargaining und Absprachen*' 1988 *Strafverteidiger* 398.

39 The most vocal critic of plea bargaining, Bernd Schünemann of the University of Munich, wrote an extensive expertise for the 1990 session of *Deutscher Juristentag*. Based on a comprehensive study including empirical, process-theoretical, psychological and comparative considerations, Schünemann came to the conclusion that judgment negotiations as they had come to be practised not only violated basic tenets of German procedure law but that lawyers involved in those practices also committed criminal offences. B Schünemann, '*Absprachen im Strafverfahren? Grundlagen, Gegenstände und Grenzen. Gutachten B zum 58. Deutschen Juristentag*' in *Ständige Deputation des Deutschen Juristentages* (ed), 1 *Verhandlungen des 58. Deutschen Juristentages* (Munich, 1990) B1.

40 A few 'plea bargaining' cases reached the Federal Court of Appeals in the early 1990s, but in each of them something had gone wrong, eg, one party had not been properly involved in negotiations or the bargain had not been kept. The *Bundesgerichtshof* dealt with those cases on the basis of regular fair trial standards. For an overview of the court's jurisprudence, see T Weigend, '*Der BGH vor der Herausforderung der Absprachenpraxis*' in C Roxin and G Widmaier (eds), IV *50 Jahre Bundesgerichtshof: Festgabe aus der Wissenschaft* (Munich 2000), p 1011, at 1017 *ff*. The Federal Constitutional Court (*Bundesverfassungsgericht*) was confronted with a negotiated criminal judgment very early but limited itself to emphasising general standards of fair trial and equitable sentencing. A three-judge panel of the court pointed out that there must not be any 'bargaining with justice' (*Handel mit Gerechtigkeit*)

on the legality of negotiated judgments as such: A defendant brought an appeal although he had received exactly the sentence he had bargained for, claiming that the procedure violated basic tenets of German criminal procedure law.

The *Bundesgerichtshof* ruled that negotiations between the court and the parties before or during the trial were not *per se* illegal but that certain ground rules had to be observed lest the procedure violate principles of fairness.[41] The Court demanded inter alia: that negotiations (but not their exact contents) be made public at the time of the trial and that their result be put on the trial record; that any agreement needed the consent of the prosecutor, lay judges and the defendant (but that it was sufficient to inform them after a provisional agreement had been reached between defence counsel and the presiding judge); that the court could not promise a fixed sentence but was limited to indicating a sentence 'cap' in case the defendant made a confession;[42] that no undue pressure must be exerted upon the defendant to come forward with a confession; that the sentence must reflect the seriousness of the offence and the defendant's guilt (but the fact of a confession could be taken into account as a mitigating factor); and that the defendant or his lawyer must not, in the course of negotiations, be induced or even asked to promise not to file an appeal against the judgment.[43]

Lower courts more or less complied with these guidelines, at least they did not openly rebel against them. Surprisingly, it was the least conspicuous of the conditions imposed by the *Bundesgerichtshof*, that is, the prohibition for the court to elicit an advance waiver of appeal, that caused serious conflict even within the Federal Court of Appeals. The matter was eventually placed before the Grand Panel in Criminal Matters (*Großer Strafsenat*)[44], which in 2005 confirmed both the legality of negotiated

but refrained from squarely approving or condemning negotiated judgments as such. *Bundesverfassungsgericht*, Decision of 27 Jan 1987, 1987 *Neue Zeitschrift für Strafrecht* 419.

41 *Bundesgerichtshof*, Judgment of 28 August 1997, 43 *Entscheidungen des Bundesgerichtshofes in Strafsachen* 195.

42 This requirement was meant to leave open the possibility of imposing a lesser sentence when evidence at the trial indicated that the defendant's guilt was not as serious as anticipated.

43 Under German law, the defendant as well as the prosecution have the right to appeal against the sentence (paras 296, 318 *Strafprozessordnung*). Either party can waive the right to appeal but can technically do so only after the court has announced the sentence (para 302 *Strafprozessordnung*). If there is an informal advance agreement between the court and the parties on a particular sentence to be announced, the court of course expects the parties to accept that sentence and not to file an appeal. Yet the *Bundesgerichtshof* in its 1997 judgment (above n 41) expressly prohibited judges from demanding an advance promise of a waiver, arguing that such an advance commitment would deprive the defendant of any remedy in case the court violated the agreement.

44 The Federal Court of Appeals, the highest court in criminal matters, has five panels (*Senate*) that adjudicate criminal matters. Each panel sits with five judges when hearing and deciding cases. Individual judges of the Federal Court of Appeals held (and still hold) widely

judgments in general and the need to protect the defendant from being coerced into waiving his right to appeal in advance.[45] The Grand Panel based its acceptance of negotiated judgments mainly on pragmatic considerations: The system of criminal justice no longer had the means and staff to provide a full-scale trial in each case, and therefore certain deviations from the procedural model as devised in the 19th century had to be accepted.

The short history of German 'plea bargaining' as sketched above fails to explain why negotiated judgments came into existence at a certain moment of legal history and why they managed to infiltrate the system – which, as has been explained above, was anything but fertile ground for their growth – with such impressive velocity. The answer is still not fully known.[46] Most plausibly, a number of unrelated factors are responsible for the amazing advance of negotiated judgments. For one, in the 1970s a professional, active defence bar learned how to use the rules of criminal procedure law to the advantage of their clients, no longer limiting themselves to asking the court for lenient punishment at the end of the trial (as had been the practice before), and often surprising courts by being confrontational as well as inventive.[47]

Another factor was the weakening of the strictly 'legal' orientation of the prosecution, which the original version of the Code of Criminal Procedure had bound to a rule of mandatory prosecution: Whenever there was suspicion of criminal wrongdoing strong enough to make conviction

differing views as to the legitimacy of negotiated judgments in general and as to necessary preconditions for accepting 'bargains' in particular. When two *Senate* disagree on a point of law relevant to the decision of cases before them, they must place the issue before the *Großer Senat*, which consists of eleven judges representing each of the five panels, and the *Großer Senat* will then render the final decision (which in fact often is a compromise between conflicting views).

[45] *Bundesgerichtshof*, Judgment of 3 March 2005, 50 *Entscheidungen des Bundesgerichtshofes in Strafsachen* 40. The Grand Panel in fact demanded that the trial judge, after announcing the judgment and passing sentence, specifically inform the defendant that he is not bound by any promise of his lawyer or himself not to appeal against the judgment. For a comment on this decision, see F Saliger, '*Absprachen im Strafprozess an den Grenzen der Rechtsfortbildung*' 2006 *Juristische Schulung* 8.

[46] One factor that can be excluded as promoting 'plea bargaining' is a desire to emulate US procedural practices. While the American example may have played a role in establishing 'plea bargaining' rules in Italy and formerly Socialist countries (see Damaška, *Negotiated Justice* above n 1, at 1024), the spirit of the 1970s and 1980s in Germany did not favour imitation of American practices, which were regarded as rather alien. For a closer analysis of this issue see M Langer, 'Legal Transplants', above n 18, at 62–64.

[47] One commentator has associated the development of an active professional defence with the trials of terrorism suspects in the 1970s. E Hanack, '*Vereinbarungen im Strafprozeß, ein besseres Mittel zur Bewältigung von Großverfahren?*' 1987 *Strafverteidiger* 500. Another, probably more important factor may have been the increase of criminal prosecutions for white-collar crime, which generated a new class of well-to-do defendants able to demand and pay for high-level and active defence counsel.

probable, prosecutors were obliged by law to file charges.[48] This rule had been relaxed for the first time in 1923, but it was in 1974 that the legislature introduced the possibility for the suspect to 'buy off' a criminal prosecution, on the prosecutor's initiative, by making a payment to the victim, a charitable organisation, or the state (see paragraph 153a *Strafprozessordnung*). In some cases, this new rule led to negotiations between prosecutors and defence lawyers representing wealthy clients and thus opened up lines of communication between the prosecution and the defence that had not theretofore existed. The introduction of 'settlements' also put an end to the traditional idea that the criminal process was invariably bound by hard and fast rules; instead, it became possible for the defence to 'make a deal' with the prosecution and thus to avoid a criminal conviction.[49]

At the same time, the courts and prosecution offices came under pressure by an increase of complex, time-consuming cases involving drug and economic crime. The Code of Criminal Procedure of 1877 was not designed to accommodate the speedy trial of cases that involved extensive paper trails, a multitude of potential witnesses, or conflicting expert opinion. Faced with an aggressive defence, some courts saw the alternative only between a trial 'by the rules' that could drag on for a long time and the offer of sentencing concessions to a defendant willing to be 'co-operative', that is, to come forward with a confession.[50]

[48] The rule of mandatory prosecution is still embodied in para 170 sec 1 *Strafprozessordnung*: 'The public prosecutor files an accusatory instrument (*Anklageschrift*) with the competent court whenever the investigation has yielded sufficient cause for public accusation'. But this rule is subject not only to the prosecutor's assessment of what constitutes 'sufficient cause' in a given case but also to a long list of statutory exceptions (see paras 153 *ff Strafprozessordnung*).

[49] Similar opportunities for bargaining had long existed in connection with the 'penal order' (*Strafbefehl*), a written proceeding initiated and dominated by the prosecutor leading to a criminal conviction (paras 407 *ff Strafprozessordnung*). Because the defendant could render that simple, non-public proceeding futile by subsequently demanding a trial, it seemed useful for the prosecution and the defence to enter into advance negotiations about what sentence might be acceptable to the defendant. An American observer was quick to perceive the parallel between this practice and plea bargaining; see WF Felstiner, 'Plea Contracts in West Germany' (1979) 13 *Law & Society Review* 309. Damaška has also pointed out that parallel while emphasizing crucial differences. *The Faces of Authority*, above n 5, at 193.

[50] There may also be a (rather tenuous) connection between the enhanced recognition of procedural rights of defendants and the felt need to circumvent those very rights by dispensing with trial altogether. Cf Damaška, *Negotiated Justice*, above n 1, at 1023; Thaman, *Plea bargaining*, above n 2, at 951, 953. But the evidence for this connection in Germany is not strong because there was no discernible 'defendants' rights revolution' in this country comparable to the watershed in the late 1960s jurisprudence of the US Supreme Court. It is rather that those rights had always been inherent in the (fairly liberal) German Code of Criminal Procedure of 1877, just waiting to be discovered and used by defence lawyers. It is noteworthy, however, that the German Federal Court of Appeals tends to grant defendants sentence discounts to compensate them for a disregard of their procedural rights, eg, in cases of a violation of speedy trial or fair trial rights. See, eg, *Bundesgerichtshof*, Judgment of 10 Nov 1999, 45 Entscheidungen des Bundesgerichtshofes in Strafsachen 308; Judgment of 18

Once the spirit of strict 'legality' of criminal proceedings had been weakened, the professional actors quickly discovered that taking short cuts to judgment might be to their personal advantage. It is obvious that resolving a complicated and potentially time-consuming case without trial (or through a perfunctory caricature of a trial) creates great savings for judges, prosecutors and defence counsel alike.

Who has the most to gain is difficult to determine, however. Many defence lawyers initially embraced the new option, which seemed to hold the promise of a more active role for counsel as well as a lesser sentence for his (co-operative) client. In recent years defence lawyers' euphoria has waned:[51] frequently, sentence 'negotiations' seem to turn into unilateral sentence impositions by the judge, who knows only too well how to handle what Germans call *Sanktionsschere* (sentencing scissors), with the sentence for a confession on one side and the (much more severe) sentence for an unco-operative defendant on the other.[52] It seems that what used to be a discount offer for defendants who come forward with a confession has quickly become the 'regular' sentence, whereas those who insist on having their guilt proved in court will receive a hefty add-on when it comes to sentencing. It is thus not the defendant who benefits from negotiated judgments but the professional 'players' in the criminal justice system – and that very fact guarantees that negotiated judgments will be here to stay, regardless of whether they fit into the remainder of Germany's procedural system.[53]

Nov 1999, 45 Entscheidungen des Bundesgerichtshofes in Strafsachen 321, at 324 *ff*. The *quid pro quo* between a loss of procedural rights and a sentence discount is thus not alien to the German courts' thinking.

[51] See *Strafrechtsausschuss des Deutschen Anwaltvereins*, *'Soll der Gesetzgeber Informelles formalisieren?'* 2006 *Strafverteidiger Forum* 89.

[52] For cases involving a fourfold difference between the sentence offered in case of a confession and the sentence imposed after a full trial, see *Bundesgerichtshof*, Judgment of 6 September 2004, 2004 *Strafverteidiger* 636, and Judgment of 12 January 2005, 2005 *Strafverteidiger* 201. For further reports on this practice see HJ Weider, *Vom Dealen mit Drogen und Gerechtigkeit*, (Mönchengladbach, 2000), p 176 *ff*; HJ Weider, '*Revisionsrechtliche Kontrolle bei gescheiterter Absprache?*', 2002 *Neue Zeitschrift für Strafrecht* 174, at 177; G Widmaier, '*Die Urteilsabsprache im Strafprozess – ein Zukunftsmodell?*' 2005 *Neue Juristische Wochenschrift* 1985, 1986.

[53] Numerous articles and dissertations have been written on the question whether negotiated judgments violate German procedural law or can be reconciled with the Code of Criminal Procedure. For recent critical analyses, see eg, C Nestler, '*Gibt es Neues? Schünemanns Gutachten zu den Absprachen im Strafverfahren von 1990*' in R Hefendehl (ed), *Empirische und dogmatische Fundamente, kriminalpolitischer Impetus* (Cologne 2005), p. 15; E Weßlau, '*Absprachen im Strafverfahren*', (2004) 116 *Zeitschrift für die gesamte Strafrechtswissenschaft* 150; G Duttge, '*Möglichkeiten eines Konsensualprozesses nach deutschem Strafprozessrecht*', (2003) 115 *Zeitschrift für die gesamte Strafrechtswissenschaft* 539; B Schünemann, '*Die Absprachen im Strafverfahren*' in E Hanack, H Hilger, V Mehle and G Widmaier (eds), *Festschrift für Peter Rieß* (Berlin 2002), p 525. The question whether negotiated judgments in Germany are *praeter legem* or *contra legem* is a moot question, however 'plea bargaining' is so alien to the normative framework on which German procedure law was built in the second half of the 19th century that the practice cannot even be said to 'violate' the Code – it is totally outside its purview.

Powerful support for 'consensual' criminal justice comes from those responsible for funding and administering the justice system. Disposal of criminal cases without trial evidently saves system resources and thus appears as a much more efficient alternative to the old-fashioned search for the truth through taking and evaluating evidence. Thrift, or 'economy', has indeed become the key word in the German debate on negotiated judgments. On one level, 'economy' refers to the process and denotes its efficiency: The end result – in most cases, the conviction of the defendant – is to be achieved with as little effort and in as little time as possible. On a second level, 'economy' translates into fiscal savings: when many criminal cases can be disposed of without a full trial, the state can maintain the number of judges and prosecutors in spite of an increasing caseload, or even reduce staff when input remains about even. Given the attractiveness of negotiated justice not only to those actively involved in the criminal process but also to administrators, it is no wonder that the shrinking group of those opposed to the brave new world of consensual criminal procedure has no real chance of reversing the tide.[54]

C. Legislating Negotiated Judgments?

What is still missing in a system relying on legislation as heavily as the German system does is statutory recognition of and authority for the new system; and that final step is likely to be taken before long. When the Grand Panel of the Federal Court of Appeals in 2005 declared the practice of negotiating judgments compatible with the German system of criminal justice[55] the Court in very explicit terms appealed to the legislature to take action.[56] According to German tradition and constitutional law, the courts' task is only to interpret the law, not to make it. There certainly exist areas – for example, the law of labour contracts – in which statutory law only provides broad guidelines and the courts have devised the rules necessary for practical application. But basic issues affecting civil rights, such as the

[54] Thaman, *Plea Bargaining*, above n 2, at 1003, suggests that 'academicians' tend to be sceptical because the new style of proceeding violates 'cherished principles of criminal procedure they studied in school'. While a certain amount of structural conservatism may well be found among lawyers (academicians as well as others), adherence to 'cherished principles' may be more than just that. Principles represent value judgments such as the importance of truth-orientation in deciding on guilt and innocence and the relevance of voluntariness when rights are being waived. Those favouring a more 'efficient' and less costly criminal justice system are often ready to dispose of the very foundations on which the credibility of this system rests. For a more extensive argument for indispensable principles governing the criminal process, see T Weigend, '*Unverzichtbares im Strafverfahrensrecht*' (2001) 113 *Zeitschrift für die gesamte Strafrechtswissenschaft* 271.

[55] See text at nn 44 and 45 above.

[56] *Bundesgerichtshof*, above n 45, at 63–64.

way the criminal process is to be conducted, should under German law not be left to judicial law-making but must be considered and ultimately decided by the legislature.[57]

Although the German legislature has not so far amended the Code of Criminal Procedure to legitimise 'plea bargaining', there exist several drafts for statutory regulation of the practice. In 2006, the Federal Ministry of Justice made public a draft – hereinafter referred to as 'Ministry Draft' – that would integrate 'understandings' (*Verständigungen*) between the court and the parties into the Code of Criminal Procedure.[58] The Ministry Draft follows, with small variations, the rules set up by the Federal Court of Appeals. It aims at legalizing the present practice while at the same time professing adherence to the 'traditional principles of German criminal procedure'.[59]

The Ministry Draft would insert into the Code of Criminal Procedure a new paragraph 257c. According to that new provision, the court 'can' during trial[60] enter into an 'understanding' with the parties. With the defendant's consent, the court can define maximum and minimum limits for the sentence that it will impose conditional on parties' 'procedural conduct' or their 'actions with respect to the proceedings' (*verfahrensbezogene Maßnahmen*). By these vague terms, the Ministry Draft refers to a confession made by the defendant in open court, but also to other procedural activities, such as waiving motions for taking additional evidence or (on the part of the prosecution) dismissing unrelated charges against the defendant.[61] If none of the parties objects, the provisional proposal becomes binding upon the court. Yet the court can withdraw from the 'understanding' if the parties fail to fulfil the court's expectations with respect to their 'procedural conduct' or if the court arrives at a different evaluation of the factual or legal situation (paragraph 257c sec 4 Ministry Draft). If the sentence is within the limits previously announced by the court, the judgment can be appealed only on limited grounds.

[57] See, eg, *Bundesverfassungsgericht*, Judgment of 9 May 1972, 33 *Entscheidungen des Bundesverfassungsgerichts* 125, at 158–9; Judgment of 14 July 1998, 98 *Entscheidungen des Bundesverfassungsgerichts* 218, at 251.

[58] The draft of May 2006 (hereinafter referred to as 'Ministry Draft') can be found on the website of the Federal Ministry of Justice: <http://www.bmj.bund.de/files> accessed 13 June 2008. A draft similar to that of the Federal Ministry has been published by the State of Lower Saxony (*Bundesrats-Drucksache* 235/06), and the Attorneys General of the 16 German States published a common statement entitled *Eckpunkte für eine gesetzliche Regelung von Verfahrensabsprachen vor Gericht* (published in 2006 *Neue Juristische Wochenschrift*, Special Issue '*Der Deal im Strafverfahren*', p 9).

[59] Ministry Draft, above n 58, at 12–13.

[60] The Draft does not contain rules as to negotiations before (rather than during) trial except for a general authorisation for the prosecutor and the court to discuss the state of the proceedings with the parties (paras 160a, 202a Ministry Draft, above n 58).

[61] Ministry Draft, above n 58, at 23.

The Ministry Draft, although proclaiming adherence to 'traditional principles', provides a blank cheque to the courts and does very little to regulate the new practice. Several features of the Ministry Draft point into the direction of unrestricted judicial discretion: For one, the defendant is accorded no right to an offer of an 'understanding' by the court – it is left to the court's discretion whether to enter into negotiations with the parties, what sentence range to offer and what conditions to impose. There is no explicit obligation on the court to take evidence even when the defendant's confession is obviously incomplete.[62]

Nor does the Ministry Draft oblige judges to keep their word after they have ostensibly committed themselves to an 'understanding'; instead, it shifts the risk of any unexpected turn of the events to the defendant. Not only can judges impose a more severe sentence when they find the defendant's confession to be less extensive than they had anticipated; they can also deviate from the 'understanding' if, for whatever reason, they determine that the facts[63] or the law (!) are different from what they had thought. This would create only a limited risk for the defendant if he were able to withdraw his confession in case the court reneges on the deal. In the German system, however, a confession is not a procedural declaration but a factual statement – once made it cannot easily be undone. The Ministry Draft in fact declares any statement the defendant has made in court to be admissible against him even when the 'understanding' has failed, provided that the defendant had been informed of that possibility (paragraph 257c sec 5 Ministry Draft).

In short, the Ministry Draft creates a judge's paradise: The court can make use of its broad sentencing authority to pressurise the defendant into co-operation whenever (and if) the court wants; and the court still has free reign even after the defendant has irretrievably incriminated himself by making a confession in open court.[64]

Nor does the Ministry Draft meaningfully circumscribe the contents of bargained-for judgments. The Draft emphasises that 'understandings' can only refer to sanctions, not to the offence of which the defendant is to be convicted (paragraph 257c sec 2 Ministry Draft). But there are no substantive guidelines as to how much weight the sentencing court can (or

[62] The general rule that the court is responsible for taking all 'necessary' evidence (para 244 sec 2 *Strafprozessordnung*) continues to apply, but it would have been useful to clarify that this rule is not made obsolete by a prior 'understanding' as to the disposition of the case.

[63] 'New facts' can of course derive from the defendant's confession. This means that the defendant must be extremely careful not to say too little (which could be interpreted as an insufficient 'procedural conduct') or too much (which might provide the court with 'new facts' on which to base a more severe sentence).

[64] For an extensive critical assessment of the Ministry Draft, see K Altenhain, H Hagemeier and M Haimerl, '*Die Vorschläge zur gesetzlichen Regelung der Urteilsabsprachen im Lichte aktueller rechtstatsächlicher Erkenntnisse*' 2007 *Neue Zeitschrift für Strafrecht* 71.

must) give to the defendant's confession, and the court does not have to indicate that weight in the judgment. The court's judgment is not based on evidence taken at the trial, and it is not based on spelled-out considerations of substantive justice – all that legitimises the court's pronouncement of the verdict and sentence is the consent of the parties. This marks a radical deviation from basic tenets of German criminal procedure, a shift from a judgment based on truth and justice to a judgment based on the defendant's submission. His submission is in turn brought about by the threat of harsher punishment if he refuses to confess.

D. Consent or Truth?

Although this shift is clearly apparent in the Ministry Draft, its authors still claim to adhere to the traditional principles of German criminal procedure (the search for the truth, the completeness of evidence, the guilt-orientation of punishment).[65] More radical voices in German legal literature would go one step further and replace the old-fashioned foundations of 'truth and justice' by a new 'consent principle'.[66] According to that principle, the consent of the prosecution and the defence provides a sufficient basis for the court's decision; if the parties have agreed on a disposition, the court can ratify that agreement without examining its basis. The court would thus be relegated to the role of a notary public with very limited supervisory functions.

It can hardly be denied that the 'consent principle' would mean nothing less than 'system change' for Germany: the German criminal process would no longer be tied to the inquisitorial model but would be better compatible with the adversarial, party-oriented model prevalent in the common law world.

An influential organisation of lawyers, the Federal Chamber of Lawyers (*Bundesrechtsanwaltskammer*)[67], has published a draft law (hereinafter

[65] Ministry Draft, above n 58, at 12–13.

[66] See, eg, M Jahn (2006) '*Die Konsensmaxime in der Hauptverhandlung*' 118 *Zeitschrift für die gesamte Strafrechtswissenschaft* 427; C Weichbrodt, *Das Konsensprinzip strafprozessualer Absprachen* (Berlin, 2006) 75 *ff*. For criticical analyses of the 'consent principle' see E Weßlau, *Das Konsensprinzip im Strafverfahren* (Baden-Baden, 2002) 66 *ff*; S Sinner, *Der Vertragsgedanke im Strafprozeßrecht*, (Frankfurt, 1999) 179 *ff*.

[67] In Germany, every practising attorney must be a member of the local Chamber of Lawyers (*Rechtsanwaltskammer*). Chambers of Lawyers have a head organisation formally representing all German practicing attorneys, the Federal Chamber of Lawyers (*Bundesrechtsanwaltskammer*). For policy making, the Federal Chamber has several committees consisting of prominent attorneys and guest members (often high-ranking judges and law professors). The Draft law mentioned in the text has been proposed by the Criminal Law Committee of the Federal Chamber of Lawyers.

'Chamber Draft')[68] that would explicitly base negotiated judgments on the 'consent principle', which is to be limited only by the 'general fairness of punishment'.[69] The most important consequence of the 'consent principle', according to the Chamber Draft, is the fact that a consensual disposition does not require a confession. Because the court no longer needs to base the judgment on the 'truth', the defendant can offer any concession in exchange for a lenient sanction; the Chamber Draft mentions a waiver of his right to ask for (additional) evidence or of his right to challenge the admission of illegally obtained evidence.[70]

In line with its guiding principle, the Chamber Draft suggests that negotiations should not initiate from the court but (jointly)[71] from the prosecution and the defence; the court, can, however, flatly refuse to accept any bargain and decline to make a sentence offer.[72] If the judges think that a consensual disposition is desirable they can enter into joint or separate negotiations with the parties to determine their positions on sentencing. It is eventually for the court to propose a (maximum) sentence and to indicate the conditions that the parties need to fulfil in order to avail themselves of the court's offer; in that context, the court can demand that the defendant make a confession, pay compensation to the victim or take any action to speed up the criminal process.[73]

As with the Ministry Draft (see above), the court is 'normally' bound by the proposed sentence unless one of the parties objects. Yet the court can still impose a heavier sentence for a broad range of reasons, including aggravating sentencing factors that the court had not known or had 'overlooked' before proposing the sentence.[74] Yet the Chamber Draft at least offers the defendant the possibility of withdrawing from his part of the deal: If the court is no longer bound by the sentence proposal, any

[68] The Chamber Draft has been published in 2006 *Neue Juristische Wochenschrift*, special issue '*Der Deal im Strafverfahren*' 3.

[69] Chamber Draft, above n 68, at 3–4. The 'general fairness of punishment' is said to require a balancing between the needs of the criminal justice system, the legitimate interests of the accused and those of the victim. It remains unclear, however, in what respect the interests of the criminal justice system could be in conflict with the legitimate (!) interests of the accused.

[70] Chamber Draft, above n 68, at 7. This means that the defendant can consent to be convicted on the basis of inadmissible evidence, gaining a sentence discount for his co-operation in violating the rules of evidence.

[71] The requirement of a joint initiative means that the prosecution can effectively block any negotiations.

[72] Chamber Draft, above n 68, at 6.

[73] Chamber Draft, above n 68, at 4.

[74] Chamber Draft, above n 68, at 4–5.

procedural or factual declaration the defendant had made in reliance on the bargain becomes void and inadmissible at trial.[75]

In spite of its pragmatism, the Chamber Draft has met with heavy criticism, not only from legal scholars but also from defence lawyers. As a matter of principle, 'consent' has been said to be insufficient to legitimise criminal judgments. Edda Weßlau, a leading academic expert in procedural law, argues that parties can to some extent consensually determine how much evidence is needed to support the court's verdict[76] but that they cannot dispose of the basic issue of the criminal process as such. The criminal process, Weßlau maintains, is not about finding an acceptable resolution to a legal dispute but aims at the determination of the necessary consequences of a norm violation; these consequences, affecting all of society, cannot be left to an agreement between the prosecutor and the defendant.[77]

Defence lawyers, on the other hand, fear that 'consent'-oriented proposals would cast defence counsel in the role of a double agent and would put at risk the unconditional loyalty to his client's cause, while at the same time undermining the necessary trust between client and lawyer.[78] On a more fundamental basis, an influential association of defence lawyers has argued that the defendant has nothing to gain from the suggested 'consent principle' because he will always be in an inferior position vis-à-vis the State; it is thus only strict adherence to formal rules, not the informality of criminal proceedings that can help the defendant avoid an unfair conviction or sentence.[79]

The rift that appears between the two most prestigious German organisations of defence lawyers concerns one of the foundations of criminal procedure law: that is, the respective roles of truth and consent in lending legitimacy to criminal judgments. The Federal Chamber of Lawyers

[75] Chamber Draft, above n 68, at 5. There is however an important exception to the principle mentioned in the text: A confession remains admissible when aggravating circumstances appear after the court has made its sentence offer. This would include the defendant's subsequent confession. If he confesses 'too much', his self-incriminating declaration would thus be admissible evidence.

[76] Parties can influence the quantum of evidence to be produced in court in various ways. For example, the defendant can, by credibly admitting to certain facts, reduce the court's duty to adduce evidence to prove the factual basis of the judgment. The parties can, moreover, acquiesce in the court's evidence-taking and refrain from demanding that additional evidence be heard.

[77] E Weßlau, '*Konsensprinzip als Leitidee des Strafverfahrens*' 2007 *StrafverteidigerForum* 1.

[78] R Hamm, '*Ist Strafverteidigung noch Kampf?*' 2006 *Neue Juristische Wochenschrift* 2084, at 2088.

[79] *Strafrechtsausschuss des Deutschen Anwaltvereins, 'Soll der Gesetzgeber Informelles formalisieren?'* 2006 *StrafverteidigerForum* 89. The authors of this article are well-known defence lawyers. They form the Criminal law committee of the German Lawyers' Association (*Deutscher Anwaltverein*), a nation-wide private organisation of attorneys.

assumes that the consensus of the parties carries with it a specific guarantee that the outcome of the bargaining process is correct (*eine spezifische Richtigkeitsgewähr des ... Verfahrensergebnisses*).[80] If that assumption were well-founded, the consensual settlement of criminal cases through negotiations would indeed be preferable to the cumbersome trial process, much like settling civil disputes is to be preferred over taking them to trial. Yet the 'guarantee' suggested by the authors of the Chamber Draft is backed neither by theory nor by reality.

In reality, that assumption overlooks the vast power differential between the court and the defendant – the defendant can at best delay the process by weeks, but the court can add years to the defendant's time in prison.[81] As a matter of procedural theory, the outcome of the bargaining process (that is the verdict and sentence) can be 'correct' only if it reflects the 'true' seriousness of the crime the defendant has culpably committed and the need (if any) to impose crime-preventive measures on him. The fact that both the prosecution and the defence are (for different reasons) 'happy' with the result of their negotiations does not mean that that outcome fulfils the requirements of criminal 'justice'. On the contrary, it is more likely than not that the bargained-for sentence fails adequately to reflect the defendant's guilt because it is either too lenient (when the defence has managed to extract unwarranted concessions) or too severe (when the defendant has submitted to a compromise judgment in light of an adverse evidentiary situation).

Those who draw a parallel between the virtue of compromise in civil and criminal matters overlook the crucial difference between those two areas of law: In a typical civil case, any outcome that subjectively satisfies both parties is a 'correct' outcome because it is only their individual (and in most cases financial) dispute that is to be resolved.[82] In criminal matters, by contrast, the accusing 'party' (in most cases: the public prosecutor) does not bring suit to vindicate his personal interest but that of society at large. Society's interest in criminal matters is twofold. First, crimes are events that cause public concern sufficient to trigger an official enquiry, and the purpose of that enquiry is to authoritatively determine what happened and who is responsible for any harm that occurred. Secondly, society is interested in having social peace restored by imposing adequate sanctions as well as in having future harm averted by minimizing the risk emanating from dangerous persons.

[80] Chamber Draft, above n 68, at 4.

[81] This point has also been made by Damaška, *Negotiated Justice*, above n 1, at 1028, citing 'asymmetrical positions of negotiating partners'.

[82] There may well be exceptions, eg, in family law matters where a public interest is involved.

None of these purposes can be achieved by the mere fact that two or three individuals have arrived at a compromise (for example, that the suspect should make a payment or spend some time in detention). The public interest aroused by a suspected crime requires an independent determination of what happened, why it happened and what the appropriate consequences should be; and the public interest in restoring peace requires a sanction that 'truly' reflects the harm that the offender has culpably caused. The public is rightfully incensed when it learns that a suspected offender, who may or may not have committed a grievous wrong, had his attorney strike a deal for him – a deal under which the suspect may pay a sum of money or receive a suspended jail sentence on the basis of just a formal acceptance of the indictment. In some countries, the public may have learned to accept this special kind of 'justice' because the state claims to be unable to afford to bring all suspects to trial, but that nevertheless remains an uneasy compromise between the requirements of justice and fiscal necessity.

Whatever practical compromise may have invaded the administration of justice, 'consent' theories are insufficient to legitimise criminal convictions and sentences. Such legitimacy can be had only when an ostensibly honest attempt has been made to bring out the truth – be it through an 'inquisitorial' judicial investigation, be it through a trial mechanism that relies on adversarial parties to challenge each other's versions of 'the truth'.

But isn't the quest for 'truth', suggested here as the 'true' meaning of the criminal process, an elusive chase for a multi-coloured butterfly that can never be caught? Can we ever know what 'really' happened and, if so, can we find out by using the crude methods of a judicial enquiry mostly relying on witness testimony, or by conducting a public trial with all its contingencies and formalities? That is a philosopher's question, and I will not even try to answer it (although I suspect that the answer has to be negative).[83] The simple and practical reply to the doubts about the chances of ever 'finding the truth' is that of Sisyphus – we must make our best effort even if we cannot succeed. Nothing less is required when the state claims the power of inflicting punishment on one of its citizens.[84]

[83] For elaborate answers, see M Damaška, 'Truth in Adjudication' (1998) 49 *Hastings Law Journal* 289; T Hörnle, '"Justice as Fairness" – *ein Modell auch für das Strafverfahren?*' (2004) 35 *Rechtstheorie* 175. Both authors come to the conclusion that we should not fall into the trap of accepting 'transactional truth', ie any outcome of a regular formalised process, as 'the truth' in criminal matters. One of the reasons for the insufficiency of 'transactional truth' in the crime context is the irreversible power differential between the participants in the process, and hence the obvious absence of a domination-free discourse in the sense of Jürgen Habermas' theory.

[84] For a more extensive statement of this thesis, see T Weigend, 'Is the Criminal Process about Truth? A German Perspective' (2003) 26 *Harvard Journal of Law & Public Policy* 157.

That does not mean that every case requires a full trial with evidence being presented on every fact that might conceivably be relevant. No criminal justice system demands 'full proof' with respect to uncontested issues. Even in systems that adhere to the inquisitorial model, the fact-finder takes certain matters for granted and concentrates his efforts on those issues that the defence and the prosecution present in a different light. One of the (informal) purposes of the pre-trial investigation in inquisitorial systems is a preliminary assessment of the evidence and the definition of issues that will have to be proved (or contested) at the trial.[85] The same effect is reached in the adversarial process by letting the parties define the conflict: There will not be any evidence offered or taken on facts the parties have agreed on.

Most procedural systems have ways of dealing with uncontested cases without a trial. In Germany, for example, the majority of criminal cases not rejected or diverted by the prosecutor are resolved by a 'penal order' procedure,[86] that is a criminal judgment drafted by the prosecutor and signed by the judge after a summary *ex parte* examination of the facts presented by the prosecutor. The defendant need not be asked in advance for his consent to the issuance of a penal order; but when he receives a penal order he can file an objection and will then automatically be granted a trial. In Italy, there exists the option for the defendant to submit to a single judge's decision based on the file of the pre-trial investigation.[87] The judge can hear additional evidence if he deems it necessary to reach a decision. The defendant is rewarded for his waiver of a full trial by a sentence reduction by one third.

Such simplified, abbreviated procedures are unobjectionable when used for totally or largely uncontested cases. Their outcome is not based on a 'consent principle' but on pre-trial proceedings, ideally with full participation rights of the defence, that both parties and the decision-making judge agree to have sufficiently determined the relevant facts. Such abbreviated trials need not be limited to petty offences but have a large potential field

[85] Although inquisitorial theory may demand that the court take 'all evidence' at the trial, both economy and reason limit that duty to issues that have not satisfactorily been cleared up in the course of the pre-trial investigation. Some procedural systems, such as the Dutch and to some extent the French, permit a transfer of the results of the pre-trial investigation into the trial by introduction of the file of the pre-trial investigation as trial evidence. Other systems, such as the German and Italian, restrict such transfers, at least as long they might interfere with the defence right to confront adverse witnesses (cf European Convention on Human Rights, art 6, s 3(d)). Yet even in those systems the result of the pre-trial investigation ordinarily informs the trial court's concept of the case before the trial even starts.

[86] Paras 407–412 *Strafprozessordnung*. Penal orders are mostly used to impose fines. The maximum punishment that can be imposed by penal order is a prison term of one year, suspended.

[87] *Giudizio abbreviato*, arts. 438–443 *Codice di Procedura Penale*. A similar procedure exists in Polish law. See art 335 *Kodeks postępowania karnego*.

of application.[88] They may blend into special short-track trials for confession cases as envisaged by Damaška in the context of international criminal justice.[89] Such mini-trials involving a re-affirmance of the basic facts of the case have great theoretical appeal as a middle ground between a full-scale trial and a merely formal assent of the parties to the court's decision. Whether they also thrive in practice will depend on a variety of factors, most prominently the incentives given to parties for choosing the middle ground over trial or informal negotiations.

III. PRACTICE WITHOUT A THEORY?

I would like to close by addressing the question of how – if at all – the triumphant advance of negotiated judgments in Continental Europe can be reconciled with inquisitorial theory.[90] There are two possible answers to that query. Optimists could argue that the ancient hierarchical model of state has everywhere made room for a more 'democratic', co-ordinate organisation of authority, with an ensuing shift from court-imposed judgments to party-controlled proceedings. The expansion of plea bargaining to Continental Europe would thus be indicative of a much broader tectonic change, of nothing less than the demise of the remnants of autocratic rule and the victory of the co-ordinate ideal.[91] Pessimists might, by contrast, claim that the hierarchical model of criminal justice as such has not been abandoned; negotiated judgments would then have to be viewed as pragmatic aberrations from theory and may even reinforce the unilateral sentencing power of the courts at a lesser cost.

The optimist view can point to remarkable changes in the 'grand' picture, especially since the disappearance of socialist and other authoritarian regimes from Europe. The *ancien régime* has become a very faint reminiscence, and concepts of state that subjugate the individual and his interests to overriding concerns of 'the whole' have likewise been relegated to the care of historians. But it would be a misinterpretation of Damaška's sophisticated concept to identify the 'hierarchical' model of justice with authoritarianism: Damaška in fact explicitly refuses to specify the political or social 'profile of officialdom' in the 'policy-implementing' ideal type of

[88] Cf Thaman, *Plea Bargaining*, above n 2, at 956: 'The more comprehensive and two-sided the pre-trial investigation and the more adversarial the taking of evidence in the pre-trial stages, the more the consensual modes of trial … will be able to make claims to truth-approximation'.

[89] Damaška, *Negotiated Justice* above n 1, at 1037–38.

[90] See text after note 19 above.

[91] For a description of that ideal, see Damaška, *The Faces of Justice*, above n 5, at 24 *ff*. Thaman, *Plea Bargaining*, above n 2, at p 963 interprets plea bargaining as the result of 'more communitarian notions of compromise and restoring the judicial peace'. This interpretation fits well with the 'optimist' thesis referred to in the text.

procedural arrangements.[92] If the distinctive feature of that ideal type is the pursuit of activist goals in the administration of justice,[93] most criminal justice systems in Europe (and beyond) fall into that category, regardless of their overall democratic affiliation. Nor could it be said that the adoption of plea bargaining as such represents a 'co-ordinate' turn within a system of justice.

One might associate the practice of negotiating judgments with the conflict-solving type of proceedings, which Damaška regards as characteristic of a laissez-faire government.[94] But as Damaška correctly points out, the conflict-solving ideal type presupposes 'arrangements intended to afford equal chance of victory to the contestants'.[95] Plea bargaining would thus reflect the conflict-solving type of proceedings only if 'bargaining' indeed occurred on an equal level, between equally strong parties and with an open end. None of these conditions applies when the prosecutor or the court dominate 'negotiations' through their sanctioning authority, and the defendant's sole choice is between accepting the sentence offered to him and forgoing trial, or running the high risk of a much more severe punishment. In the harsh reality of the courthouse, the great majority of judgment negotiations are not instances of a co-ordinate distribution of authority but a technique to make the defendant submit to punishment without trial and thus to save the state money.

We are left, then, with the pessimist interpretation of recent developments. The advance of plea bargaining in Germany and elsewhere does not signify a more equitable allocation of power in the criminal process but a deplorable dilution of the inquisitorial ideal. That ideal had protected the defendant against abuse and unjust sanctioning through the barrier of truth-finding: Only if conscientious and independent officials are convinced, on the basis of a comprehensive and serious inquisition of the relevant facts, that the defendant is guilty can he be subjected to criminal punishment proportional to his proven guilt.[96]

When truth-finding is replaced by mechanisms designed to coerce the defendant into giving his 'consent' to a proposed judgment, this may in individual instances lead to the same or even a more lenient sanction than would have been imposed after an 'old style' trial – but the principle that had protected defendants against being overwhelmed by a powerful state system fails to operate, and the defendant is left to fend for himself in a fight that lacks rules other than the law of the marketplace. Many judges

[92] Damaška, *The Faces of Justice*, above n 5, at p 147.
[93] *Ibid.*
[94] Damaška, *The Faces of Justice*, above n 5, at 97 *ff*.
[95] Damaška, *The Faces of Justice*, above n 5, at 103.
[96] This ideal is, of course, not limited to 'inquisitorial' procedure – adversary procedure does not differ with respect to the goal of truth-finding but only with respect to the preferred methods of reaching that goal.

and prosecutors, to be sure, will refrain from abusing their power and will endeavour to treat defendants fairly. But that is not the point. The problem is that the practice of negotiating for justice does not have a basis in law (even if a savings clause should be inserted into the Code of Criminal Procedure) or in procedural principle. Its basis is expediency only – and that, I am afraid, is not a proper foundation of a system of criminal justice.

4

Sentencing in the US: An Inquisitorial Soul in an Adversarial Body?

WILLIAM T PIZZI*

INTRODUCTION

IT IS DIFFICULT to overstate the impact that Mirjan Damaška has had in comparative criminal procedure, because he gave us not only powerful templates through which to understand Continental and common law systems – his archetypes of the hierarchical ideal and the co-ordinate ideal – but he took us even into the minds of lawyers in the two traditions to show us how common law lawyers or a Continental lawyers think about procedural stages in their system. The result is so rich that those of us working in the field often feel that we are simply elaborating and unpacking insights that were unearthed by Professor Damaška.

In this chapter, I intend to elaborate on a point that Professor Damaška made at the start of his seminal work, *The Faces of Justice and State Authority*.[1] In the passage I am referring to, Professor Damaška explains the difficulties one encounters when one tries to characterise a national system as either adversarial or inquisitorial.[2] The problem he observes is that there is no single set of features that one finds uniformly among countries we would likely describe as adversarial. Even more confounding is the fact that in the process of looking closely at a national system, one is likely to come upon opposing traits in the system so that one finds adversarial traits in systems that we might consider almost reflexively to be

* The author wishes to thank Morris Hoffman, John Jackson and Máximo Langer for their comments on an earlier version of this chapter.

[1] M Damaška, *The Faces of Justice and State Authority: A Comparative Approach to the Legal Process* (New Haven, Yale University Press, 1986).

[2] *Ibid* 5–6.

inquisitorial, while, borrowing Professor Damaška's words, 'inquisitorial features, sometimes quite conspicuous, can be found in Anglo-American lands.'[3]

It is this last point of Professor Damaška's that I wish to build on – the idea that even in an Anglo-American land, there can be a quite conspicuous inquisitorial feature. In this chapter I want to convince readers that the United States, despite a self-image that sees its criminal justice system as rigorously adversarial, has traditionally embraced features at sentencing that are strongly inquisitorial. By sharply separating 'trial' in the United States from sentencing, it is amazing how comfortably the US has been living in a world that is somewhat schizophrenic not only as to the roles of the lawyers and judge as a criminal proceeding shifts from trial to sentencing, but even as to the values that are emphasised at the two phases.

But in the last several years, there has emerged a clash between adversarial and inquisitorial values. The clash has to do with attempts to reform sentencing by requiring judges to follow guidelines. Under these guidelines, judges who wish to impose a sentence at the high end of the sentencing range must support such a decision with specific factual findings. This restriction on sentencing was intended to protect defendants from harsh sentences by requiring that judges justify such sentences. But the Supreme Court has thwarted this reform by ruling that such factual findings need to be made by a jury, not a judge. I will suggest that the real issue is not whether judges or juries make such findings, but rather who should control sentencing – the judge or the parties?

TRIALS IN THE US

It is a fundamental tenet of the belief system of American lawyers and judges that our trial system is strongly adversarial and that such a system is to be preferred over Continental systems, which are often referred to as 'inquisitorial', with some disparagement sometimes intended. The Supreme Court itself has made reference on many occasions to the fact that the US system 'is the accusatorial as opposed to the inquisitorial system.'[4]

One of the hallmarks of an adversarial system is the fact the trial judge often knows less about the case than either of the lawyers. There is no common 'dossier' containing the results of the police investigation that is shared by the prosecutor, the defence lawyer, and the trial judges, such as one would usually find on the Continent. An American judge does not

[3] *Ibid* 6.

[4] *Moran v Burbine*, 475 US 412, 434 (1986). See also *Miller v Fenton*, 474 US 104, 110 (1985); *Minnesota v Murphy*, 465 US 420, 450 (1984); *Watts v Indiana*, 338 US 49, 54 (1949).

need access to such evidence because judges in the US have a much weaker role to play with respect to both the charging decision and the conduct of the trial. Even if a judge in the US disagrees with the charging decision of the prosecutor, there is no authority vested in a trial judge to question the charging decision as long as there is evidence to support the charge that has been filed. As the Supreme Court has explained,

> so long as the prosecutor has probable cause to believe that the accused committed an offense defined by statute, the decision whether or not to prosecute, and what charge to file ... generally rests entirely in [the prosecutor's] discretion.[5]

Similarly, a trial judge in the US does not need a full grasp of the evidence that has been gathered because the judge does not have responsibility for calling witnesses at trial. Though US judges have the power to ask questions of witnesses and theoretically could call their own witnesses, the system strongly discourages judges from doing either of these things.[6] Part of the reason for the reluctance of judges to intervene with the development of evidence is that there is no affirmative mandate on judges in the US to see that justice is done in their courtrooms. Instead, ethics codes emphasise the need for judges to be 'impartial' in their rulings,[7] which usually is interpreted to mean that the judge should be passive.[8] The role of the trial judge in the United States is frequently analogised to that of a 'neutral referee' in the world of sport, meaning that the judge is not one of the players, but rather someone who makes sure the contest is fair and played according to the rules, but who should be indifferent to the outcome.[9]

Even among common law countries that also share an adversarial trial tradition, the US is more extreme in both the amount of control the parties are permitted in presenting evidence as well as the degree of passivity thought desirable for the trial judge. Thus England, for example, does not want barristers to rehearse their witnesses prior to their giving testimony at

[5] *Bordenkircher v Hayes*, 434 US 357, 364 (1978).

[6] See CM Bradley, 'United States' in CM Bradley (ed), *Criminal Procedure: A Worldwide Study* (Durham, Carolina University Press, 1999) 395, 421–22.

[7] Center for Professional Responsibility, Model Code of Judicial Conduct (Chicago, American Bar Association, 2007) Canon 2 A.

[8] One critic worries that when judges come to view impartiality as synonymous with passivity this 'can make a judge the unwitting abettor of intolerable injustice.' See F Strier, *Reconstructing Justice: An Agenda for Trial Reform* (Westport, Quorum, 1994) 83.

[9] See M Langer, 'From Legal Transplants to Legal Translations: The Globalization of Plea Bargaining and the Americanization Thesis in Criminal Procedure' (2004) 45 *Harvard International Law Journal* 1, 12, 21–22. See also Bradley, above n 6, at 421–22.

trial and considers it ethically improper to do so.[10] But it is perfectly ethical for lawyers in the US to rehearse witnesses and 'polish' their testimony for adversary advantage. (It might even be considered ineffective assistance of counsel were a defence attorney in an important case not to prepare witnesses for trial in this way.) This process of preparing witnesses by rehearsing their projected testimony and preparing them for the rigors of cross-examination is usually referred to, somewhat pejoratively, as the 'wood shedding' of witnesses,[11] the idea being that sometimes one needs to take a witness to the shed outside the courthouse in order to prepare the witness for his appearance inside.

The US system also prefers that judges assume a much more passive role with respect to the development of evidence at trial than judges in other common law countries. One indication of this phenomenon is the near abandonment in the US of the traditional common law responsibility of judges to summarise the evidence for the jury at the end of the trial.[12] In other common law countries, the summation for the jury is an important feature of the trial and it takes place after the lawyers have finished their closing arguments and just before the jury begins its deliberations. Even if the trial has only lasted a few days, the trial judge in other common law countries systems will use the notes taken during the trial to provide the jury a short summary of the testimony of each witness to help the jury recall how the trial has unfolded.

In the United States, the tradition of summarising the evidence for the jury has gradually died out, so that it is rare today for a judge to summarise the evidence.[13] It is a measure of American populism that in many states, state law specifically prohibits judges from summarising the evidence.[14] But even in jurisdictions in which the practice is still permitted, such as the federal system, judges do not exercise this power.[15]

That a judge after a complicated and protracted criminal trial would not be permitted or would prefer not to summarise the evidence is symptomatic of the weak role that is preferred for judges in the United States. The

[10] Rule 705 of the Bar Council's Code of Conduct for Barristers states that a barrister must not 'rehearse practice or coach a witness in relation to his evidence.' The Code of Conduct is available online at the Bar Council's website: <http://www.barcouncil.org.uk> accessed 13 June 2008.

[11] See JW McElhaney, *McElhaney's Trial Notebook*, 2nd edn (Chicago, American Bar Association, 1987) 31–32.

[12] See R Pattenden, *Judicial Discretion and Criminal Litigation* (New York, Oxford, 1990) 182–83.

[13] See JB Weinstein, 'The Power and Duty of Federal Judges to Marshall and Comment on the Evidence in Jury Trials and Some Suggestions on Charging Juries' (1988) 118 *West's Federal Rules Decisions* 161 (1988).

[14] See, eg., AR Const Art 6 s 27; CO Rev Stat s 13–2–108; FL Stat s 90.106.

[15] See WT Pizzi, *Trials without Truth* (New York, New York University Press, 1999) 143–44.

trial system puts control of the evidence in the hands of the parties and it is up to each of the lawyers, not the judge, to make sure the jurors understand and recall the evidence. If a lawyer fails in that task, she may suffer the consequences when the jury returns its verdict. But it is not the job of the judge to step between the parties and assist the jury with the evidence. This explains not only why judges do not summarise the evidence, but also why questions to a witness will be few or, often, none; it is up to the lawyers, not the judge, to bring out the evidence in a clear and understandable way for the jury.

INQUISITORIAL SENTENCING IN THE US: THE BROAD DISCRETION STATES

Sentencing statutes vary considerably from jurisdiction to jurisdiction in the US and so painting with a broad brush is necessary. But although individual details will vary, state by state, this overview captures the two main types of sentencing statutes that predominate in the US

The sentencing world in the United States divides into two groups which I will refer to as the 'broad discretion states' and the 'sentencing guidelines states'. The group of states vesting broad discretion in the sentencing judge is the much larger group.[16] In this section I will discuss the broad discretion states and in the next section discuss states with guidelines systems.

Broad discretion is relative, of course, and the amount of discretion vested in a judge at sentencing will vary in broad discretion states. In some states, a judge may have the discretion to sentence, for example, an armed robber anywhere within a range of 30 or 40 years. Many progressive states like California, New Jersey and Colorado, have cut back on these draconian sentencing ranges. But even in these states, it would not be unusual for a judge to have discretion to sentence an armed robber to a sentence somewhere within a range of 10, 15 or 20 years.

This sort of tremendous sentencing power vested in the trial judge (and traditionally unreviewable on appeal)[17] indicates how suddenly the role of the judge changes from trial to sentencing. Gone is the neutral referee with no responsibility for the trial outcome and in her place is a judge with full responsibility for imposing the proper sentence on the defendant.

[16] For a chart of all state sentencing systems, see Bureau of Justice Assistnce, US Dept of Justice, National Assessment of Structured Sentencing, 20 (1996), available at <http://http://www.ncjrs.gov/pdffiles/strsent.pdf> accessed 13 June 2008.

[17] See AW Campbell, *Law of Sentencing*, s 14.4, (Eagan, MN, Thomson/West, 2004) 579: 'Despite significant sentencing reforms in the late 20th Century, the dominant principle of appellate sentence review has remained unchanged: Unless trial court discretion was abused, sentences within constitutional and statutory boundaries are not reviewable.'

As the judge shifts from neutral and passive referee at trial to the central decision-maker at sentencing, the roles of the prosecutor and the defence lawyer correspondingly change. Much like lawyers in the Continental tradition, they play a supplementary role. They may perhaps suggest reasons for a certain sentence and perhaps recommend a specific sentence. But the final decision belongs to the judge. There is no necessity that the judge follow the recommendations of either attorney, and thus it is possible that a judge might impose a sentence more severe than that suggested by the prosecutor or less severe than that urged by the defence attorney.

Similarly, the language about the prosecution's 'burden of proof,' so strongly associated with the trial phase, is missing from sentencing. A prosecutor may 'recommend' a certain sentence, but there is no obligation on the prosecutor to 'prove' this sentence appropriate. It is up to the judge to impose the proper sentence, whether recommended or not.

A judge needs evidence to make a sentencing decision as there will often be little information brought out about the defendant at trial. Here again, there is a sharp divergence between trial and sentencing. At trial, powerful hearsay rules require that important witnesses give their testimony orally at trial and prior statements in the prosecutor's file serve mainly to predict what the future testimony of a witness is likely to be. The file itself is not evidence. By contrast, as Professor Damaška notes, in Continental trial systems investigators are able to generate competent evidence out of court in advance of trial as the dossier itself has considerable evidentiary significance.[18]

When it comes to sentencing in the United States, the system switches gears so that the file with sentencing materials in it – referred to as the pre-sentence report – comes to dominate the sentencing decision.[19] Witnesses are rare at sentencing hearings (except in capital cases which are tried to a jury) and instead the trial judge relies heavily on the evidence assembled in the pre-sentence report which the probation officer has put together.

The pre-sentence report is the result of an extensive out-of-court investigation into the crime and the defendant's background conducted by a probation officer on behalf of the sentencing judge.[20] To understand the scope of the crime, the probation officer will usually interview the prosecutor and perhaps examine the police reports in the prosecutor's file. She will also try to talk to the defendant, the defence attorney, and perhaps the victim or the investigating officer. To better understand the defendant, the probation officer will usually interview the defendant's friends, family,

[18] See Damaška, above n 1, at 57–58.

[19] See Campbell, above n 17, at 11:1, 482; 'No single document has greater impact on criminal offenders than the pre-sentence report.'

[20] See Campbell, above n 17, at s 9:6, 367

former employers, etc, to try to understand his character, work habits, or personal problems. The probation officer will also indicate the prior convictions of the defendant and any facts about his prior crimes that might be relevant to sentencing.

When the report is complete it will go to the judge along with a recommendation for a particular sentence from the probation officer. This recommendation will often carry considerable weight with the judge.[21]

Note that the probation officer has a stature at sentencing analogous to the neutral experts appointed by the judges in Continental trial systems. While the adversarial tradition in the US is highly sceptical of the concept of a 'neutral expert', at sentencing the system changes gears and a neutral expert, working in the background, will have a tremendous impact on the defendant's sentence.

THE CLASH OF ADVERSARIAL AND INQUISITORIAL VALUES IN SENTENCING GUIDELINES STATES

The picture I have described of the relationship between trial and sentencing in the US is a very extreme example of the way that a national system embraces strong adversarial values at times, yet has, within the same system, features that are deeply inquisitorial.

We have lived for many years with this Janus-faced approach to central features of the system, such as party control of evidence, judicial passivity, and the insistence that important witness testify under oath. At times, the system smiles proudly at these features, but at other times, the system scowls at them and treats them dismissively. But recently a clash between adversarial and inquisitorial values has emerged in some sentencing situations.

Interestingly, this clash has not occurred in those many states that continue to vest broad discretion in judges at sentencing. Rather, the clash of values has emerged in those states that have tried to restrain the sentencing power of judges to make sentencing fairer, less harsh, and more predictable. These are the states – approximately 16 in number – that have adopted system that follow the sentencing guidelines model.[22]

The sentencing guidelines model was developed roughly two decades ago as a way to prevent the obvious abuses that can occur under the broad discretion model: judges in the same court who give very different punishments to similarly situated defendants, judges who have idiosyncratic views on certain crimes, and judges whose conscious or unconscious

[21] *Ibid.*

[22] See generally American Bar Association, 'Introduction' *ABA Standards for Criminal Justice Sentencing*, 3rd edn (Washington, American Bar Association, 1994) xxi–xxv .

racism or other bias may result in far harsher sentences for minority or other defendants. Minnesota created and put into place the original sentencing guidelines system in 1980, and since that time reform groups, such as the American Bar Association and the American Law Institute, have put forward versions of the sentencing guidelines model and have tried to get states to adopt this approach to sentencing.

In contrast to traditional sentencing systems, where judges are given a broad sentencing range and asked to decide in each case what punishment should be imposed, under the sentencing guidelines model judges are given a narrow sentencing range for each crime that is considered appropriate for an 'ordinary' offender who has committed a certain crime. The sentencing guidelines model thus provides a presumed starting point for judges at sentencing. From this starting point, the guidelines require judges to increase or decrease the sentence, depending on factors which the guidelines enumerate. Thus the fact that the offence did minimal damage or that the offender immediately expressed remorse after the crime might be factors that would decrease a sentence under a particular state guidelines system, while the fact that the offender had a previous conviction or did an unusual amount of damage would increase the sentence.

One big improvement of guidelines systems is that they clarify what judges should and should not consider as sentencing factors. For example, should a judge in sentencing consider it to be a mitigating fact that the defendant is the sole parent of young children, is elderly, or made restitution for some of the damage caused? These are the sorts of policy issues that are usually resolved when drawing up and adopting guidelines but these are exactly the sorts of issues that are left to the whim of individual judges in states with broad discretion sentencing systems.

The constitutional problems for guidelines systems have developed around one specific aspect of the guidelines model, namely, the ability of a judge under the guidelines to depart above the sentencing range in the guidelines when a judge concludes that there are strong aggravating reasons for doing so. The idea behind these provisions allowing a judge to depart above or below the guideline range stems from the fact that not every factor that might influence a sentence can be anticipated and provided for in guidelines systems. Thus, judges need the ability to depart in where there are strong aggravating or mitigating reasons for doing so.

Studies have shown that these departures are uncommon – usually between 10 and 20 per cent with most of these departures being mitigating departures that favour defendants.[23] But it was a departure above the normal range that led to constitutional problems.

23 *Ibid* xxiii.

The case that raised the issue of whether a judge had the constitutional authority to increase a sentence above the normal range in a guidelines system was *Blakely v Washington*.[24] *Blakely* stemmed from a sad and vicious domestic crime in which the defendant – upset that his wife had filed for divorce – went to his wife's home, abducted her at knifepoint, bound her with duct tape, and forced her into a coffin-like box in the back of his truck.[25] When his 13-year old son returned from school, Blakely ordered him to follow the truck in another car, threatening to harm his mother with a shotgun if the son did not do as he was ordered. The son managed to escape along the route when they stopped at a gas station, but Blakely continued with the kidnapping and took his wife to the home of a friend in Montana, where Blakely was arrested. Blakely was charged with the first-degree kidnapping, but he pled guilty to second degree kidnapping with a firearm.

The constitutional problems arose at Blakely's sentencing. Under Washington's guidelines system, the starting point for sentencing an ordinary offender convicted of second-degree kidnapping with a firearm is 49 to 53 months in prison and this was the sentence range recommended by the prosecutor.[26] But the guidelines permit a judge to impose a sentence above the standard range if the judge finds 'substantial and compelling reasons justifying such an exceptional sentence.'[27] After hearing testimony from Blakely's wife, the judge imposed a sentence of 90 months, which was 37 months longer than the maximum sentence in the standard range, because the judge concluded that the crime had been committed with deliberate cruelty.[28]

The Supreme Court struck down this sentence. The Court ruled that when a judge imposes a sentence beyond that which the jury's verdict alone allows, those additional facts – in the case of Blakely, his deliberate cruelty – must be found by a jury.

Blakely only involved one aspect of the sentencing guidelines model – the ability to depart above the normal sentencing range where there was a substantial and compelling reason for a higher sentence – and these departures are not common. In Washington, the departure rate was 10 per cent or less, and most of these were mitigating departures which would

[24] 542 US 296 (2004).

[25] 542 US at 298.

[26] 542 US at 299.

[27] WA Stat Ann ss 9.94A.120(2). Washington law at the time of *Blakely* provided that any reason thought to justify an exceptional sentence can be considered only if it has not been used in computing the standard range sentence and, in addition, any such sentence will be reversed if the record is insufficient to support the reason given for the exceptional sentence. See *State v Gore*, 143 Wash 2d 288, 315–16, 21 P 3d 262, 277 (2001).

[28] 542 US at 300.

take the sentence below the normal range.[29] Moreover, it would be easy for Washington (or any other guidelines state) to revise its statutes to avoid this problem by, for example, simply raising the maximum sentence in the normal sentencing range.

But a rough idea of the philosophical impact of *Blakely* on sentencing reform can be garnered from the metaphors used to describe the decision. *Blakely* has been variously described as 'a force 10 earthquake',[30] 'a bombshell',[31] or 'a bull in a china shop'.[32]

The reason that *Blakely* has so upset sentencing reformers is that the decision does not affect those jurisdictions that continue to place enormous sentencing discretion in the hands of the judge, be the sentencing range 0–15 years, 0–20 years, or 0–40 years. These jurisdictions are not affected because the jury verdict alone supports a sentence of up to the maximum in the sentencing range. But when a progressive jurisdiction tries to moderate punishment and better protect defendants from disparate and unjust sentences by setting out a range for 'ordinary' offenders of the crime and then requiring specific reviewable findings before a judge can sentence outside of that range,[33] the system is declared unconstitutional by the Court.

Blakely is not the end of the world for sentencing reform as it is possible to find ways around the decision. Indeed, a year after *Blakely*, the Supreme Court in *United States v Booker*,[34] 'saved' the federal sentencing guidelines by striking down the provision that made them mandatory so that the guidelines were only 'advisory.'[35] This means, according to *Booker*, that a federal judge ultimately has discretion whether to follow the sentence called for by the guidelines, subject to appellate review for reasonableness.[36] But this model is hardly attractive to sentencing reformers because voluntary state guideline systems have been tried and they were not

[29] See *American Bar Association*, above n 22, at xxiii n 12.

[30] Justice Sandra O'Connor, one of the dissenting justices in *Blakely*, used this metaphor when speaking to members of the judiciary about Blakely's likely impact on state sentencing systems. See J Chorney, 'O'Connor to Judges: Meet with Congress Members' (23 Aug 2004) 25 *National Law Journal*, S9 (Col 1).

[31] See K Reitz, 'The New Sentencing Conundrum: Police and Constitutional Law at Cross-Purposes' (2005) 105 *Columbia Law Review* 1082, 1083.

[32] *Ibid.*

[33] Unfortunately, most lawyers who are not sentencing specialists have a negative view of sentencing guidelines because the federal sentencing guidelines were intended to increase the harshness of sentences and that has been their effect. See Kevin R. Reitz, above note 31 at 1105 (2005). But most of the states that have adopted sentencing guidelines systems have seen much slower rates of prison growth than states without guideline systems. *Ibid* 1104.

[34] 543 US 220 (2005).

[35] *Booker* had two majority opinions, one written by Justice Stevens, 543 US 220, ruling that the federal sentencing guidelines were unconstitutional under the Sixth Amendment, and a second majority opinion written by Justice Breyer, 543 US 245, ruling that the guidelines could be saved by striking their mandatory requirement.

[36] 543 US 245 (Breyer J).

effective in reducing disparities or the harshness in sentencing.[37] What assurance then could sentencing reformers give a legislature that an "advisory" system on the Washington model would achieve the goals of a fairer sentencing system? Not surprisingly, sentencing reform is stalled for the moment.

SHOULD SENTENCING CONFORM TO THE ADVERSARIAL MODEL?

Viewed from an adversarial perspective, *Blakely* makes perfect sense. The US is deeply committed to jury trials and the Supreme Court has extended the right even to very minor cases as long as there is a possible sentence of more than six months in jail in the event of a conviction. While this is obviously expensive, the Court sees a jury as a necessary protection against 'the compliant, biased or eccentric judge'.[38] Deeply distrusting judicial power, as we do at trial, it seems only logical that a jury stand between a defendant and a possible increase of several years to a defendant's sentence.

Piously trumpeting the importance of juries in the American system, the Court in *Blakely* intoned that a jury conviction cannot be 'a mere preliminary to a judicial inquisition into facts of the crime the State *actually* seeks to punish.'[39]

There are problems with this statement. The first is that sentencing has always been a way to bridge the gap between the offence of conviction and the real offence(s) committed by the defendant. This is the frustration of *Blakely*: a sentencing system that carefully controls what can be considered by a judge in deciding whether to enhance a conviction is condemned, even though there was a hearing and a carefully reasoned decision tied to the facts surrounding the crime. Yet, in the overwhelming majority of jurisdictions in the US, a judge is permitted to increase a sentence based on hearsay evidence about other alleged crimes or reports of the defendant's character with not a witness being presented at the sentencing hearing. Thus judges in broad discretion states will often give a defendant a longer sentence if the judge concludes, usually based only on the pre-sentence report, that the defendant has not shown any remorse, that the defendant is a gang member, or that defendant has done similar crimes on other occasions (though not convicted of any of these).

Moreover, the Court in other cases has been comfortable affirming sentences that not only expand on a jury's verdict, but that actually are based on a view of the crime that conflicts with the jury verdict. In *United*

37 See Reitz, above n 31 at 1114–15.
38 *Duncan v Louisiana*, 391 US 145, 156 (1968).
39 542 US at 307 (emphasis in original).

States v Watts,[40] a dealer in cocaine base (referred to commonly as 'crack') was charged with possessing more than 500 grams of crack and with using a firearm in connection with the drug offence. (The police had found the crack in the kitchen and had found two loaded guns and ammunition in a bedroom closet of Watts' home.) Watts was convicted by a jury of the drug charge but acquitted of the gun charge. Yet, at sentencing, the judge added four years to Watts' sentence because he found that Watts had possessed the gun in connection with the drugs. The Supreme Court had no trouble affirming the enhanced sentence.

In short, the strongly adversarial values that predominate up to the point of conviction have always been tempered by inquisitorial values at sentencing that place a much higher value on truth. We are in the habit in the US of speaking about a defendant's 'conviction offence' and his 'real offence' and, at sentencing, as *Watts* shows, judges often sentence based on the defendant's real offence.

This is not a comfortable situation and one can well ask whether a trial system should permit a gap, sometimes a large gap, between a defendant's conviction offence and his real offence or offences. But this raises an aspect of the US system that has to be considered – namely, the system's overwhelming reliance on plea bargaining.

A second problem with the Court's pious pronouncement in *Blakely* that a judge should not expand upon a *jury conviction* to find facts that increase the defendant's sentence ignores the fact that there was no jury and no jury conviction at the trial level. Instead, there was a plea bargain.

Scholars used to say that to say that 90 per cent of the system's criminal convictions came from guilty pleas. But today in most jurisdictions that number is too low – it would be 95 per cent or even higher in most jurisdictions.[41] The trend away from trials has not gone unnoticed: there are often articles in law journals lamenting the fact that criminal trials are 'vanishing' in the US.[42] In federal court, for example, fewer criminal trials take place today than forty years ago, despite the fact that there are many more judges and many more prosecutors.[43]

Plea bargaining takes many forms, but in one form of plea bargaining, referred to as a 'charge bargain', the prosecutor agrees to dismiss certain

[40] 519 US 148 (1997).

[41] In the latest year for which these statistics are available, 2003, the federal plea bargaining rate was 96.3%. There were 74,850 federal criminal cases were filed (and not dismissed) and 72,110 of them were disposed of by guilty plea. See Bureau of Justice Statistics, 'US Dept of Justice, Sourcebook of Criminal Justice Statistics Online,' tbl 5.22, at <http://www.albany.edu/sourcebook/pdf/t522.pdf> accesed 15 June 2008. In state systems, the average plea bargaining rate is 95%: *Ibid*.

[42] See, eg, JW Keker, 'The Advent of the "Vanishing Trial": Why Trials Matter' (Sept/Oct 2005) *The Champion* 32.

[43] *Ibid* 36–37.

charges if the defendant agrees to admit guilt to other charges.[44] This will usually narrow the sentencing range within which the judge may sentence the defendant. *Blakely* involved a form of charge bargaining in which the prosecution dismissed the first-degree kidnapping charge against Blakely in exchange for Blakely's plea of guilty to second-degree kidnapping.

Plea bargaining fits comfortably into the system's strong adversary tradition – if the two sides to the dispute are able to reach a settlement, what is the authority of the judge to stand in the way of its implementation? But this is why sentencing has always been strongly inquisitorial in the US. The judge at sentencing is expected to study the pre-sentence report and see exactly what crimes the defendant committed, what the defendant's character and prior record are, the amount of injury that resulted from the crime, and any other facts that should bear on the proper punishment.

Blakely is an example of the way adversarial values at trial clash with inquisitorial values at sentencing. Blakely pled guilty to second-degree kidnapping, but this crime does not adequately describe the extent of the crimes Blakely committed. Blakely was originlly charged with first-degree kidnapping (which requires that a defendant intentionally abduct a person with the intent to inflict mental distress on that person or a third person[45]), and could have been convicted of that charge and probably another charge of kidnapping when he forced his son to accompany him by threatening to kill the boy's mother with a shotgun.

Not surprisingly, when the matter came for sentencing, the trial judge saw the case as one that might demand a sentence beyond the normal range for a conviction to a single count of second-degree kidnapping. This is the inquisitorial judge who feels an obligation to make the sentence fit the actual crime and the background and individual circumstances of the defendant.

It might be argued that the problems in *Blakely* could have been avoided had the judge refused to accept the original charge bargain. But while the rules of criminal procedure require that a plea bargain be brought before the trial judge and that the judge approve the bargain, this moment in the procedure finds the judge whipsawed between adversarial and inquisitorial responsibilities. For the neutral referee, who should not involve herself in the contest and dare not even summarise the evidence at trial, what is the theory that permits such a referee to reject a proposed settlement? It is also procedurally awkward – how does the neutral referee step into an inquisitorial role and reject a plea bargain in a serious case, but then return to the role of the neutral referee, indifferent to the outcome at the ensuing trial?

[44] See J Dressler, *Understanding Criminal Procedure* (Newark, Lexis Nexis, 2002) s 31.05[B].

[45] See WA Stat s 9A 40 020(1) (2000).

Thus, it is at sentencing that the judge serves as inquisitorial check on the plea bargain by imposing a sentence that attempts to punish a defendant for his actual criminal conduct whether or not the prosecutor wishes or agree to such a sentence. Recall that in *Blakely*, the prosecutor recommended a sentence within the normal range.

CONCLUSION

Some may suggest that it is too late in the day in the US to worry that a defendant be punished fairly and justly for the crime the defendant actually committed. The US is a plea bargaining system today and if the parties can resolve their 'dispute' through a plea bargain, a judge should accept what they have done just as the judge would accept a negotiated settlement in a civil dispute.

But serious criminal cases are not two-sided in the way that a contract dispute or an employment dispute may have two sides. There are interests in a criminal case that diverge from those of the two disputants in civil cases, such as the interest of victims past and future, the interest in seeing that similar defendants be treated similarly, and the interest in seeing that a defendant receives a punishment for his crime that is just and fair. There needs to be some independent check on the parties and sentencing in the US has been a control on plea bargaining.

The Supreme Court swings wildly on sentencing issues and thus provides very poor guidance. The Court sees no problem when a judge enhances a sentence based on a crime for which the defendant was acquitted but at other times insists that a jury play a central role if a sentence is to be enhanced. This failure to face up to the clash of the values involved at sentencing has stalled sentencing reform. Those jurisdictions which leave judges with extremely broad sentencing discretion are fine. Even though extravagant judicial fact-finding takes place at sentencing in those broad discretion systems, the absence of legal constraints on the fact-finder seems to insulate those sentencing decisions from constitutional problems.

But a state sentencing system that limits judicial sentencing discretion, by (i) specifying the enhancing factors that permit a judge to depart and impose a longer than normal sentence, (ii) requiring that judges conduct a hearing and hear evidence on such factors, and (iii) requiring specific findings in support of any enhanced sentence, offends the right of a defendant to a jury trial.

In *Blakely*, the Court missed what should have been the central issue. It is not whether a judge or a jury should be finding facts that would support an enhanced sentence, but rather who should control the decision to seek

such a sentence: the prosecutor or the judge. To remove the judge as an independent control, especially in a system so reliant on plea bargaining, would be a mistake.

As Professor Damaška's observed, 'inquisitorial features, sometimes quite conspicuous, can be found in Anglo-American lands.'[46] This chapter suggests that sometimes this is no coincidence: those features may be necessary as a counterbalance to other extremely adversarial features of the same system.

[46] See Damaška, above n 1, at 6.

5

Italian Criminal Procedure: A System Caught Between Two Traditions

LUCA MARAFIOTI

I

A WRITER ALWAYS faces challenges when asked to complete a paper in a language that is not his native tongue. These become even more formidable when he is writing on a subject which is very difficult to describe. It is certainly not at all easy to explain in plain terms what has been happening in the field of Italian criminal justice.[1] Yet we draw a lesson from a comparative analysis of Italian criminal justice that may contribute to the debate that Mirjan Damaška's work inspired on comparative criminal procedure. In particular, the analysis could help illuminate the criminal procedure general trend away from strict evidential concerns, and some of the convergences that are taking place beyond the traditional '*summa divisio*' of adversarial/inquisitorial and common law/civil law systems.

On October 24, 1989, the Republic of Italy adopted a new Code of Criminal Procedure, incorporating significant adversarial features into what had previously been an inquisitorial system.[2] There is no doubt that the reform of Italian criminal procedure was long overdue. The former system was a relic of the Fascist era, dating back to the 1930s. As originally conceived, the 1930 Code of Criminal Procedure envisioned a

[1] Among other things, it is hard to try to describe or popularise the subject without making a personal evaluation of the principles that should be respected by a system that outline fair procedures and trials. In other words, it is hard to say how things are really going without saying how they should be going.

[2] Italy faced the same problem as that faced by post-revolutionary France: the new Code of Criminal Procedure has attempted to build an adversarial trial system in institutions that remain strongly rooted in the tradition and ideology of civil law. The result is a system caught between the two traditions.

mixed system. During a secret pre-trial inquisitorial phase, evidence was gathered to determine if a crime had been committed and, if so, by whom. A judge controlled the pre-trial examination phase (*istruzione formale*), performing the roles of both judge and investigator, but the investigative function clearly dominated. A public trial followed the examination phase, where all the evidence on which the defendant could be convicted was supposed to be produced. In practice, however, the examination phase grew in importance at the expense of the trial, and the trial became a purely formal exercise. The traditional principles of orality and immediacy were abandoned, and records and materials collected during the investigative phase became the basis of the verdict and sentence. In short, the trial merely confirmed what had taken place during the pre-trial examination phase.

The need for major reforms became painfully clear following the adoption of a constitution in 1947. Some reforms did occur in the post-war period. Parliament enacted criminal procedure reforms in 1955. A series of decisions by the *Corte Costituzionale* (Constitutional Court) in the period from 1965–1972 had the cumulative effect of allowing the defence more participation in the pre-trial phase. But while these decisions provided greater protection to the defendant in the pre-trial phase (*garantismo inquisitorio*), they did nothing to temper the system's exclusive focus on the pre-trial phase.

II

There are a number of features that are worth highlighting in the new 1989 Italian Code. First of all, it places the public prosecutor, rather than the police, in control of the pre-trial investigation of a crime,[3] although the police are at the prosecutor's disposal.[4] The prosecutor functions to some extent as an advocate, but the Code also places on him an obligation of fairness that requires him to investigate exculpatory as well as inculpatory evidence.[5] As a matter of principle, statements obtained from defendants under police questioning are not admissible at trial unless defendants had their counsel present during questioning or they waived their right to silence.

After the introduction of the new code, the legislature took notice of the unequal balance of power between the prosecution and defence during the

[3] Italian Criminal Procedure Code, art 327.

[4] A victim's report of a crime places the police under a tight deadline: they must inform the public prosecutor of the crime without delay and send him all the information they have gathered. Upon learning of the crime, the public prosecutor must record the crime in the crime register.

[5] Italian Criminal Procedure Code, art 358.

pre-trial phase. Thus, in 2000, the legislature introduced new regulations[6] which enabled the defence to engage in its own investigations.[7] It is now possible for counsel, paralegals and investigators acting on behalf of the defence to search for evidence, contact and interview potential witnesses and even obtain written statements from witnesses in the form of an affidavit.[8] The defence may present these statements before the judge or use them for impeachment purposes during the trial.[9]

In common with other civil law countries, Italy is wary of broad prosecutorial discretion in deciding whether or not to charge a suspect. The Italian Constitution reflects this distrust by mandating compulsory prosecution.[10] Nevertheless, the Code provides a method for disposing of weak cases. A prosecutor may ask the judge for a judgment of dismissal (*decreto di archiviazione*) whenever the evidence is insufficient to prove that a crime was committed or was committed by a particular defendant.[11]

The *incidente probatorio*, a deposition-like procedure, is an important investigatory device that can be employed at any time before trial. This procedure allows either the prosecutor or the defence to request the hearing of testimony from a witness if there is a compelling reason for the request, such as the need to protect a witness from physical harm or to obtain the testimony of a witness who may die before trial.[12] The *incidente probatorio* thus serves to 'freeze' the testimony of a witness, as the evidence which is obtained is included in the file which the judge receives at the start of the trial.[13]

A judge is assigned specifically to supervise all preliminary investigations. This judge determines matters such as bail and preserves the impartiality of the investigation. While control of the investigation is largely in the hands of the public prosecutor, the judge serves as a check on his power.

The Italian Code also provides for a preliminary hearing (*udienza preliminare*), which is essentially a document review by the judge, designed to determine whether the case should proceed to trial.[14] The public prosecutor requesting a preliminary hearing sends the judge a file containing all documents and reports collected during the investigation.[15] At the hearing which is held in camera, the prosecutor does not present any

6 L 7 December 2000, no 397, amending the Code.
7 Italian Criminal Procedure Code, art 327-*bis*.
8 Italian Criminal Procedure Code, arts 391-*bis* to 391-*decies*.
9 Italian Criminal Procedure Code, art 391-*decies*.
10 Italian Constitution, art 112.
11 Italian Criminal Procedure Code, art 408.
12 Italian Criminal Procedure Code, art 392.
13 Italian Criminal Procedure Code, arts 403, 431 (f).
14 Italian Criminal Procedure Code, arts 416–429.
15 Italian Criminal Procedure Code, arts 416, 417.

witnesses but instead outlines the investigation and its results using the documents gathered in the investigation. The defence, also working from the investigation file or from its own defence file, has the opportunity in turn to argue against setting the case for trial. In addition, the defendant may ask the judge to interrogate him, though he may not be cross-examined. The judge may ask the parties to gather any additional evidence he considers necessary.[16] At the conclusion of the hearing, the judge will then decide whether or not to send the case to trial.[17] A judge's decision to dismiss the charges against a suspect at the preliminary hearing amounts to a declaration that the defendant must be acquitted immediately without a trial.[18]

During the first years of the Code's life, the preliminary hearing was to a large extent a formality because judges applied an extremely lenient standard to the prosecutor's case. A weak case against the accused was not a basis for dismissal. A reform in 1999,[19] however, has made it more difficult for cases to proceed to trial. A judge may now reject charges at the preliminary hearing if the case does not seem strong enough or does not appear to meet the standards of proof that are applied at trial, or if the incident charged does not constitute a criminal offence, the defendant is not criminally responsible for it or the offence may not be legally prosecuted.[20]

In addition, the judge has been given powers to complete the dossier *sua sponte*, if some relevant evidence has not been gathered by the prosecution.[21] This could have opened up a new era for the preliminary hearing: but, as ever, much depends on the individual judges and their attitude towards these new powers. Most judges do not like a mini-trial taking place before them and still prefer to send cases to trial where there is any doubt about the outcome.

While the preliminary hearing permits the judge to make use of a dossier based on the entire investigative file, the new Code parts company with civil law tradition by limiting the written materials a court may consider at trial. The file sent to the trial judges is limited to the charging documents, physical evidence connected with the crime, evidence gathered using the *incidente probatorio* and the records collected by the prosecutor concerning evidence which can no longer be presented at open trial (the so-called *prove irripetibili*).[22] The rest of the evidence must be presented orally at the trial unless the parties agree to use written materials collected during

16 Italian Criminal Procedure Code, arts 421-*bis*, 422.
17 Italian Criminal Procedure Code, art 424.
18 Italian Criminal Procedure Code, arts 425, 426.
19 L 16 December 1999, no 479.
20 Italian Criminal Procedure Code, art 425 as amended.
21 Italian Criminal Procedure Code, art 422.
22 Italian Criminal Procedure Code, art 431.

party-investigations. These written materials constitute an alternative mode of proof to oral testimony but the evidence contained in them may still be disputed at trial.[23]

III

For trial judges educated and trained in the civil law tradition, the changes described above are significant. Given the civil law's distaste for excluding probative evidence, judges have been inclined to give a broad interpretation to the exceptions contained in the Code for admitting written evidence. Furthermore, as a result of changes that the *Corte Costituzionale* and the legislature introduced in the 1990s, what was intended by the Code to be exceptional is becoming in some cases a rule as some of the statements made by witnesses and co-defendants before the prosecutor or – even worse – the police are included in the written file considered by the judge and used as evidence at trial.

The 1990s witnessed something of a counter-reformation to the changes introduced by the Code in 1989. The main elements in the *fil rouge* of this counter-reformation were the re-assertion of the search for truth as a procedural value and, in order to achieve this, a more extensive use of pre-trial evidence than was envisaged under the Code. In this counter-reformation, tensions arose between the legislature and the Constitutional Court.

An example may be seen in the treatment of the testimony of co-defendants. It is difficult to find a satisfactory balance between the accused's right to confrontation and a co-defendant's right to silence when the co-defendant has made accusations against the accused. This problem may be exacerbated in those civil law jurisdictions like Italy that have traditionally been permissive about the use of pre-trial statements at trial, and in which the prosecution may not grant use or transactional immunity to witnesses. As a consequence, the prosecutor may use at trial the statements that a co-defendant made against a defendant in the pre-trial phase, but the co-defendant may also raise his right to silence and avoid being subjected to cross-examination by the defendant at trial. In fact, given the absence of immunity regulations, if the co-defendant did not use his right to silence, he could be prosecuted on the basis of his own trial testimony. (In common law systems, by contrast, the oral tradition has prevented prosecutors from using at trial the statements of co-defendants against defendants; and prosecutors may lift the co-defendant's right to silence by giving him immunity to testify at trial.)

[23] Italian Criminal Procedure Code, arts 431, 493.

In Decision no 361 of 1998, the Italian Constitutional Court resolved this tension in the following way. First, it drew a sharp distinction between '*dichiarazioni sul fatto proprio e dichiarazioni sul fatto altrui*' (that is, declarations on one's own actions and declarations on other people's actions), and held that a co-defendant witness does not have the same rights to defence and against self-incrimination once he has co-operated with the prosecution. But the Constitutional Court also said that the prosecutor could use at trial statements made by a co-defendant before the police or prosecutor. This undermined the rule against hearsay and the right to confrontation that the Criminal Procedure Code of 1989 had established as it meant that these statements could not be impeached directly by the accused, who could only draw attention to the weak probative value of those statements.

In order to give greater weight to the principle of orality and cross-examination at trial, the legislature amended Article 111 of the Constitution by stating a number of principles inspired by the 'due process of law' clause. The effect has been – under some amendments to the Italian criminal procedure code[24] – requiring persons who make statements against others to assume the role of witnesses who must undergo examination at the trial and cannot invoke the right to silence. The only concession made to such persons was to grant them a sort of 'use immunity' whereby any statements that they made could not be used against them.[25]

The trial itself begins with opening statements by the public prosecutor, the lawyers representing any civil parties, and the defence attorney. Parties call witnesses in the same order, and each party is granted an opportunity to cross-examine the others' witnesses. Closing statements then follow in the same order. After the closing statements, each of the advocates is entitled to present a rebuttal of the other summations. The defence always has the opportunity to speak last.

The defendant traditionally plays an active role in a civil law trial. The new Code continues the tradition by permitting the defendant to speak at any point in the trial in order to challenge a witness's testimony. While the defendant has the right to refuse to take the witness stand and to refuse to answer any question, such refusals are exceptional. A defendant may theoretically remain silent, but a defendant who wishes to present mitigating facts relevant to sentencing must do so during trial. Despite the new trial procedures and the right of the defendant to remain silent, the assumption in civil law systems that the defendant should cooperate with the trial judge and fully answer any questions has in practice undermined the right to silence.

[24] See L 1 March 2001, no 63.

[25] Italian Criminal Procedure Code, art 197-*bis*.

Following trial, the court must explain its decision in an opinion that evaluates the evidence and explains in detail the grounds for the decision (*motivazione*).

IV

Another point to be made about the Code has been the role played by appeals. For several years, the new Code left this final phase of Italian criminal procedure almost untouched for a number of reasons. First, reformers were so preoccupied with the radical changes concerning pre-trial investigations, preliminary hearings and the trial phase that there was little time to focus on appeals. In fact there was no meaningful debate on the best mode of appellate review within the new model. A more subtle reason was that leaving the traditionally broad scope for appellate review untouched created a kind of safety net for the new reforms. Even the reformers used to such a tradition within the inquisitorial model would have been nervous about restricting appellate review as they did not completely trust the new system and were worried about the risk of judicial errors. So it was thought preferable to keep a mixed model combining the elements of a new adversarial trial and a more traditional appellate system.

The new Code thus retains the broad appellate review characteristic of civil law systems. The appellate process centres on the formal opinion of the court, which sets out the evidence relied upon to reach the verdict and explains the reasoning behind the decision. All parties, including civil parties injured by the crime, may appeal against the decision of the trial court. The appellate court may change any aspect of the decision, including the sentence, either in part or completely and it even has the power to take new evidence if appropriate.

The lamentable delays caused to the criminal process by such a broad appellate system process which led to the expiry of statute of limitations in many cases called for some change to be made. First, in 2001 some procedural rules were introduced to allow the Supreme Court (*Suprema Corte di Cassazione*), through its president and a special court, to make it easier to declare *ricorsi* (that is appeals of third instance) inadmissible.[26] This was intended to curb the huge number of third instance appeals which were declared inadmissible (over 60 per cent) and, indirectly, to limit access to the highest Court which is much broader than in other Western countries.

In addition, steps were taken through Law no 46/2006 – which amended the Code to require proof 'beyond any reasonable doubt' before there

[26] Italian Criminal Procedure Code, art 610.1 as amended by L 26 March 2001, no 128.

could be a verdict of guilty[27] – to restrict the prosecution's right to appeal against trial acquittals. Under Article 593 of the Italian Criminal Procedure Code, prosecutors could only appeal against acquittals where it was alleged that there was new 'fresh evidence' for a conviction.

Commentators celebrated these amendments as they seemed to shed revolutionary new light on the role of the parties, standards of proof, the presumption of innocence and the traditional conception of appeals in Italy. The apparent higher standard of proof appeared to make it more difficult to obtain convictions. In addition, it seemed that prosecution appeals on the merits should now be the exception rather than the rule. A recent decision of the Constitutional Court, however, has cast a shadow over these changes. In Decision no 26/2007 the Court held that the denial of the prosecution's right to have cases reviewed on the merits was unconstitutional on the ground that it violated the principle of 'equal protection' between the parties and the principle of proportionality. Although this decision has put an early end to the new balance of power between the parties that the reforms were designed to achieve, there is still scope for debate on what further changes should be made in appeal phases following the first instance trial.[28]

V

All western criminal justice systems increasingly face the problem of judicial backlog. The new Code was intended in large part to provide the Italian criminal justice system with new, efficient procedures to combat its perennial case backlog. The Italian approach is a flexible one. Instead of requiring all cases to proceed down a single path, there are a number of different avenues along which a case may proceed to resolution, governed by factors such as the seriousness of the crime and the strength of the

[27] Under Art 533, '*il giudice pronuncia sentenza di condanna se l'imputato risulta colpevole del reato contestato al di là di ogni ragionevole dubbio.*'

[28] In Italy, as in other civil law countries, injured persons are entitled to participate through representatives as parties to a criminal case, from the pre-trial hearing to the appeal. Injured parties have both an interest in 'seeing justice done' to the defendant and the possibility of obtaining monetary compensation. Injured parties may recover damages from criminals by drawing upon either tort law or a specific Criminal Code provision, making convicted criminals liable for restitution and reparation. As full participants, injured parties are able to protect these interests by examining and cross-examining witnesses, presenting evidence, requesting further investigations and opposing motions to dismiss. The role of the *parte civile* on appeal was much discussed in the light of reform no. 46/2006 because it was not at all clear whether or not it retained the right of the *parte civile* to appeal acquittals. Judicial decisions have been unclear and inconsistent on this crucial point. In a decision which was issued at the same time as its ruling on prosecution appeals, the *Corte Costituzionale* has held that the right of appeal for the *parte civile* never disappeared from the Italian justice system: see Decision no 32/2007.

evidence. Defendants are also offered significant sentence reductions in exchange for selecting some of the simplified procedures.

The new Code makes provision for simplified procedures in two different ways: by circumventing the need for a preliminary hearing in the interest of expediting the case for trial and by offering alternatives to trial altogether.

When the investigation of a crime is concluded and the public prosecutor believes there is enough evidence to merit prosecution, he makes a request to the judge for a preliminary hearing. In cases where there is strong evidence against the accused, however, the preliminary hearing may be circumvented and the case set for immediate trial under two different procedures: the *giudizio direttissimo*[29] (accelerated trial) and the *giudizio immediato*[30] (immediate judgment).[31]

A number of alternatives to trial are provided for under the new Code. First of all there is the *procedimento per decreto penale*, (proceeding by penal decree),[32] available only for minor crimes for which a fine is sufficient punishment. It is, in essence, a unilateral offer by the public prosecutor to resolve the case by means of a discounted fine. The defendant is free to accept or reject the offer.

Secondly, Italy has also adopted a mild form of plea bargaining in the new Code which is called the *applicazione della pena su richiesta delle parti* ('application of punishment upon the request of the parties').[33] At the preliminary hearing or before the trial begins, the public prosecutor and the defence attorney may agree upon a particular sentence and ask the judge to impose it. The normal sentence can be reduced by as much as one-third, so long as the final negotiated sentence is not more than five years. Prosecutors can agree to defer the sentence up to a period of two years.[34]

[29] Italian Criminal Procedure Code, arts 449–452.

[30] Italian Criminal Procedure Code, arts 453–458.

[31] The *giudizio direttissimo* is available in four types of situations, each involving strong evidence of the defendant's culpability. The defendant is permitted a full trial, but it is straightforward and takes place quickly because the evidence is clear and overwhelming. The other procedure for bypassing the preliminary hearing is the *giudizio immediato*, for situations in which the evidence against a defendant is very strong, though falling short of the standards of the *giudizio direttissimo*. The defendant may also request the *giudizio immediato*, which is analogous to waiving the preliminary hearing in the US system.

[32] Italian Criminal Procedure Code, arts 459–464.

[33] Italian Criminal Procedure Code, arts 444–448.

[34] Although Italian-style plea bargaining may appear similar to US plea bargaining – and is even referred to by Italian lawyers as a *patteggiamento*, which is the Italian word for 'bargaining' – certain limitations differentiate it from the US practice. First, in the Italian system, the public prosecutor and the defendant do not bargain over the nature of the crime to which the defendant will plead guilty. Secondly, the fixed maximum reduction of up to one-third of the normal sentence, coupled with the restriction that the final sentence may not exceed five years, considerably limits the range of cases that qualify for plea bargaining. Thirdly, the defence may ask the judge for up to one-third reduction in sentencing under the

A third alternative to a trial is the *giudizio abbreviato* or 'summary trial'.[35] This procedure grants a defendant a quick resolution of his case based solely upon the investigative file (plus any investigation that is presented by the defence) in return for a substantial reduction in sentence should he be found guilty. It is not a US-style plea bargain, because the issue of guilt remains open, nor is it a trial, because the evidence is limited to the materials in the investigative files. Thus, the *giudizio abbreviato* has aspects of both plea bargain and trial – it is like a plea bargain in that the defendant obtains a reduced sentence in exchange for choosing an expedited resolution of the case, and it is like a trial in that the issue of guilt must still be decided by the judge. In the event that the defendant is found guilty, the judge may reduce the normal sentence (taking into account aggravating and mitigating circumstances) by up to one-third. The *giudizio abbreviato* procedure may also be used to reduce a sentence of life imprisonment – the highest level of punishment available in Italy – to a sentence of 30 years.[36]

statute, even if the prosecutor refuses to join in such a request. In such cases, the prosecutor must state his reasons for refusing the proposed disposition. The intent of the Italian Code is to make reduced sentences available to all defendants who wish to plea bargain, whether or not the prosecutor agrees. This arrangement reflects the traditional civil law distrust of prosecutorial discretion and a commitment to uniform treatment of defendants as the idea that prosecutors should set different sentences for defendants is anathema to civil law. The final difference between US and Italian plea bargaining is perhaps more one of form than of substance. The Italian variant involves no actual plea of guilty. It is thus still possible for a judge who is asked to approve a plea bargain to conclude that the defendant is not guilty when he has reviewed the records as he is required to do prior to approving the agreement. The fact that a person can go to prison for up to five years when there is neither an admission nor a formal finding of guilt illustrates Italy's difficulty in reconciling plea bargaining with its civil law tradition.

[35] Italian Criminal Procedure Code, arts 438–443.

[36] Before 1999, the *giudizio abbreviato* procedure could only be granted when a defendant had made a request and the public prosecutor had joined in it. Once he received a request for a *giudizio abbreviato*, the judge decided whether the case could be adjudicated on the basis of the preliminary hearing documents. Under an amendment introduced to the Code in 1999, the *giudizio abbreviato* has, however, become almost a right for the defendant. Once he makes his request, consent by the prosecutor is no longer needed and the judge must proceed under this summary mode of trial. Judges can only exercise discretion where the defendant wants to introduce evidence or where the case is not yet ready for a decision. In the former instance, the judge may refuse a motion for *abbreviato*; in the latter instance, the judge may ask the parties for additional evidence or introduce evidence *sua sponte* before issuing his abbreviated judgment. Even where a request to introduce additional evidence is permitted, the *giudizio abbreviato* continues to be regarded as a special procedure for a very straightforward case and may be viewed as a 'soft' form of plea bargaining. It could be argued that the *giudizio abbreviato* procedure could be expanded further by loosening some of the evidentiary restrictions that are built into it. If the *giudizio abbreviato* were to be turned into almost a full trial, the efficiency gains for which the procedure was designed would be significantly reduced. If defendants were permitted to add additional written evidence to the file, however, in order to mitigate punishment before the *giudizio abbreviato*, with the prosecution retaining the right to submit any written evidence in rebuttal, the procedure's efficiency would be only slightly impaired. With the *giudizio abbreviato* undergoing a 'second youth', it is difficult at this point in time to gauge how well the procedure is working.

These expedited procedures were supposed to allay Italy's backlog problem by making it more attractive for defendants to opt for such procedures rather than insisting on a full adversarial trial. However, the success of these procedures has been hindered by a lack of certainty as to what will happen in a full trial. For reduced sentences to persuade defendants to forego their right to trial, the threat of a full sentence for those on trial must be credible. Unfortunately, this is not the case. Today's defendants realise that the delays inherent in the system may result in an acquittal, as evidence is lost, witnesses become unavailable, memories and emotions fade and amnesties are declared. While a one-third sentencing reduction may seem attractive to a defendant facing trial and conviction in the near future, it has less appeal for a defendant who has been freed on bail and whose trial may be years away.

Furthermore, if alternatives to trial are to be made attractive, defendants must have some assurance in the accuracy of the charging document. While overcharging encourages negotiation in the US system, in Italy it has precisely the opposite effect. In order to bring the charges down to a realistic level, the overcharged defendant is forced to undergo a full trial.[37]

VI

The new Italian Code of Criminal Procedure has attempted to graft adversarial procedures on to a fundamentally inquisitorial legal system. The result is a system caught between two different traditions. When we refer to the new Italian code of criminal procedure, however, we can no longer regard it as the original code which came into force in 1989.

The original model has been gradually eroded at three different levels. First of all, from the inception of the new Code, the Constitutional Court has had to adjudicate upon a number of constitutional claims against various of the Code's articles. Secondly, the legislature has introduced reforms to fight organised crime more effectively which have modified

[37] Since Italian trials determine both guilt and sentencing, a guilty defendant may not opt for a *giudizio abbreviato* if the file does not contain all the mitigating evidence that could lower his base sentence. The benefits of the one-third sentence reduction are diminished when the file does not contain such evidence. It might appear that this problem could be solved by vigilant defence efforts to ensure that exculpatory and mitigating evidence are placed in the defendant's file prior to requesting a *giudizio abbreviato* or by a faith in the judge's determination to ensure that the file is based on complete information. But in Italy this is not as simple as it seems, since the defence counsel's role has traditionally been largely passive. Defence counsel are normally lawyers appointed to handle cases for little remuneration. As such lawyers can usually devote only a minimal amount of time to the case, and they rarely perform an investigative role prior to trial. This constraint was not a weakness under Italy's former inquisitorial system, in which the defence lawyer played a subsidiary role in the gathering and presentation of evidence. The move to an adversarial trial system, however, places new responsibilities on defence counsel which they are not well placed to assume.

some of the fundamental articles of the Code. Thirdly, the original model has been eroded by practice at every court level. This phenomenon is obviously the most difficult to quantify as it does not arise as a result of specific reforms but through everyday judge-made law.

It is impossible to give any detailed explanation of this process of erosion. To understand it, it is necessary to notice that from the beginning there was never a full correspondence between the model and its practice in the pre-trial investigation phase. Recording a crime in the register takes much more time than expected and the prosecutor's obligation to assemble a complete file during the investigation is hardly ever fulfilled. This dysfunction obviously has an effect upon later stages of the process such as the screening function during the preliminary hearing, the roles of the parties facing the alternative procedures and – last but not least – the adjudication during a public adversarial trial.

It may be said that there are two particular respects in which the adversarial model prescribed by the Code has not been translated into practice on the ground. First of all, judges have continued to assume a dominating position in the criminal process. While this can help balance any supposed inequality between the parties, it does not sit easily with the adversarial model in which the parties usually hold control and bear responsibility for the selection and presentation of evidence. This can be illustrated by decisions of the Constitutional Court which have restricted some of the adversarial powers of the parties that were considered to be too broad and by the increasingly managerial view of the judge's role.[38] Another example is to be seen in the legislature's extension of the judges' powers to acquit defendants after the preliminary hearing on the ground that the evidence is too weak to take the case to trial.

In addition, over the years, both the *Corte di Cassazione* and then the *Corte Costituzionale* have given a very extensive interpretation to the judge's power to call *sua sponte* witnesses at trial. Originally, the judge could call witnesses only after the parties had presented their evidence and only in exceptional situations in which he could not decide the case on the evidence presented.[39] Today, things have changed to such an extent that the judge can call witnesses and receive evidence not only when the prosecutor

[38] See, eg, Constitutional Court no 88/1991 (prohibiting any discretion in a decision not to prosecute), no 81/1991, no 23/1992 (permitting judicial control over the content of the prosecution's dossier after a request for a giudizio abbreviato), no 313/1990 (granting greater judicial control over the merits of plea bargaining including sentencing reduction). All these decisions appear to be examples, on the one hand, of a greater judicial responsibility for the outcome of criminal procedures and, on the other hand, of a narrowing of adversarial managing of cases by parties.

[39] Italian Criminal Procedure Code, art 507.1.

has delayed in filing a motion to hear a witness[40] but also when he has not filed any motion at all.[41] This broad interpretation of what was designed to be an exceptional power can in theory be attributed to the need to search of the truth. In reality, however, it has had the effect of counter-balancing weaknesses in the prosecution case and reversing the onus on it to prove its case.

The second respect in which the original adversarial model has been subverted is in the tendency to consider as evidence the results of the prosecutor's investigations. The results of these investigations have tended to dominate the trial to the detriment of oral presentation of evidence in open court and of the right to full confrontation. Although changes made to Article 111 of the Constitution and to the Code of Criminal Procedure[42] were designed to promote orality and confrontation at trial, they do not seem to have offset this tendency.[43]

There are also many examples to be found in court practice which illustrate how the new Code of Criminal Procedure has been rejected by those who are instrumental in implementing it. In general terms, it is this author's view that prosecutors and judges have been dissatisfied with the limiting, exclusionary rules governing the collection of evidence for trial. In addition, the extension of maximum time limits for the investigation has become a rule instead of an exception. The resulting time gap between the crime and the ascertainment of truth at trial has the logical and implicit consequence of putting pressure on prosecutors to use investigation material (and particularly statements of witnesses before the prosecutor) as trial evidence.

All this demonstrates the practical difficulties that there are in escaping the old 'inquisitorial nightmare'. There is one simple explanation why the judge has remained so dominant in Italian criminal procedure. In common law systems, it is the jury which decides the verdict while the judge is left

[40] Italian Criminal Procedure Code, art 468.1: parties have the duty to file a list of witnesses to be introduced and examined at trial at least seven days before the trial's date. Oral witness presented at trial should be based on that list.

[41] For such an extension of the Code's provisions, see Cass Sez Un, 21 November 1992, Martin, in *Riv It Dir e Proc Pen*, 1993, 822; Cass Sez Un, 17 October 2006, Greco, in Cass Pen, 2007, 952.

[42] L 1 March 2001, no 63.

[43] More reforms were introduced in the aftermath of the emotional trauma caused by appalling mafia murders (see DL 8 June 1992, n 306, L 7 August 1992, n 356). Most of these reforms have been repealed by new provisions introduced in 2001 (L 16 March 2001, n 63) to limit the admission of written evidence against defendants which has been obtained from defendants in other trials. Now prosecutors may only admit these records where the witnesses are available for oral examination. But the rights of prisoners convicted of organised crime have been strongly limited as they cannot be admitted to probation or given benefits if they fail to co-operate with the system. Although this law does not formally concern the criminal trial as it is a restriction on prisoners' rights, in reality, it has the inevitable effect of coercing prisoners into making statements against their accomplices in organised crime.

merely to direct the jury. In civil law systems, by contrast, the judge both directs the trial and determines the guilt and sentencing. He thus feels responsible for the verdict and ends up playing a very active role instead of simply responding to what the parties present and accepting that a weak prosecution case should lead to a 'not guilty' verdict.

The two features we have outlined that have continued to dominate criminal procedure despite the introduction of the Code – the increasing role of the judge and the pressure to consider the prosecutor's file as evidence for trial – are not independent of each other. The managerial role played by the judge has increased the pressure to admit the prosecutor's file as evidence with the result these two features together have transformed the original adversarial Code into a post-adversarial one. The Code has become such a patchwork that some have compared it to a 'harlequin suit'; others would prefer to return to the former Code.

VII

Italy did not err in grafting adversarial procedures on to a civil law system. The failure of some of its efforts merely demonstrates that procedures cannot be adapted easily from one system to another. Different legal traditions and cultures foster different responsibilities within a system, thus encouraging different expectations.

One explanation for the difficulties that have been encountered is that an adversarial culture and tradition cannot be manufactured 'out of the blue'. But this is not the whole story and there are much deeper reasons. Beyond the particular criminal procedures, authority structures and state powers of each system, there are two basic kinds of problem facing all western countries and not just Italy: problems relating to the prosecution function and problems relating to the trial.

We can summarise the first set of problems by saying that in any western justice system the gap between caseloads and the resources of justice simply cannot be filled. As legislatures have increasingly resorted to overcriminalisation, justice systems have borne an enormous burden, especially prosecutors who have to find methods of screening out the bulk of cases they are faced with. The result is that the principle of compulsory prosecution has become nothing more than a mere slogan. On the pretext of dismissing weak cases, prosecutors have been given a broad discretion to reduce their caseloads according to professionally devised criteria or, even worse, on the basis of their own personal, political and cultural prejudices.

In Germany, the solution to this problem has been dealt with by a constellation of legal provisions which authorise the prosecutor to dismiss cases where there are evidential weaknesses or where there is a lack of

public interest in favour of prosecution. More generally, there is a hierachical control of the prosecutor's conduct. The US system also grants broad discretion to prosecutors. Because trials are highly adversarial, prosecutors are typically reluctant to pursue a full trial if they think the chances of conviction are poor. A substantial percentage of cases are also kept out of court through deferred prosecutions and pre-trial diversion programmes which provide offenders with treatment or vocational training. Broad prosecutorial discretion also permits selective prosecution in order to maximise the deterrent value of those cases that are filed. However, in the US, this policy is applied in a co-ordinated rather than a hierachical manner through internal guidelines which determine local priorities of crime prevention and through a system of informal control which is supervised often by elected prosecutors or their professional assistants.

Both solutions are deeply rooted in the cultural and political tradition of each country. They each have their own strengths and weaknesses but they are at least attempts to deal with the problem of case overload. Italy follows neither of these two systems. Under the continuing shadow of compulsory prosecution which is little more than a dogma, prosecutors exercise discretion without any checks and balances at a hierarchical or political level. The medicine (that is, the principle of compulsory prosecution) is worse than the disease (that is, the risk that the prosecutor does not act independently) that we would like to cure.

The new Italian system seeks efficiency by avoiding a full adversarial trial through a series of special procedures, including variants of plea bargaining. An adversarial system is not an essential prerequisite for expedited procedures or negotiated settlements. But negotiated settlements are more easily made in a system that assigns control over the presentation of evidence to the parties and recognises that the parties have a right to dispose of a case without trial. However, the proper functioning of an adversarial system depends on the parties' ability and willingness to function as adversaries.

The role of the office of the prosecutor (*pubblico ministero*) poses the most difficult institutional challenge to the attempts of the new Code of Criminal Procedure to introduce an adversarial system. Although the prosecutor presents the state's case against the defendant at trial, as in common law systems, this masks a tremendous difference between common-law and Italian systems in both outlook and tradition. The Italian prosecutor is in reality a judicial figure who has passed the same examinations as the judge and who enjoys the same salary and career options. Both are members of the judiciary (*magistratura*). A person holding the position of *pubblico ministero* may go from that position to being a judge, and vice versa.

Over time, however, the institution of *pubblico ministero* has lost the advantages of the civil law model: it lacks an effective hierarchical structure, strong internal guidelines and internal controls as well as a strong sense of professionalism. The Italian prosecutor is a career bureaucrat with a lifelong position of almost complete autonomy. A mechanism for automatic wage increases keeps the salaries of the judges and prosecutors at the top of the payscale for public employees. In short, the *pubblico ministero* seems to occupy a unique position which has evolved to retain all the bureaucratic disadvantages of the civil law model, becoming an entrenched, well-paid civil service position. The Italian Constitution mandates the prosecution of cases, yet it creates no correlative pressure on prosecutors to properly deal with them.

Thus, one of the major shortcomings of the reform of Italian criminal procedure is the Code's failure to move the *pubblico ministero* away from the inquisitorial tradition. Although in 1987 the Italian Parliament asked the government to organise the judiciary so that it could function consistently with the new Code, it issued practically no specific directives on the subject. Since the *magistratura* is such a powerful political force in Italy – indeed, a substantial number of those who drafted the new Code came from within the *magistratura* – only cosmetic reforms were made in the organisation of the judiciary and this seems set to continue. Even the most recent parliamentary debate that there has been on a more radical reform of the court system does not involve any effective and sharp separation of careers between judges and prosecutors. This is symptomatic of the Italian anomaly whereby the most radical changes can be made to all aspects of criminal procedure except to the institution of the *pubblico ministero*.

There are also symptoms of a deep crisis in the ideal of the criminal trial as a model for determining guilt in a fair manner.[44] In Italy the introduction of procedures for negotiating justice and the tendency to regard the

[44] The United States deals with swelling criminal dockets in two main ways. First, as mentioned above, through broad prosecutorial discretion. Secondly, US prosecutors rely on plea bargaining to dispose of the vast majority of cases prosecuted. The overwhelming use of plea bargaining is symptomatic of the trial crisis. Generally, trials are criticised because they are too dependent on juries, too contest-driven, too 'lawyerised' and too dominated by complicated rules of evidence to be a good method for ascertaining the truth. Even in Germany, generally considered the classic civil law country in which the 'written law' is strictly applied to each case, a practice of 'informal justice' has developed. This practice seriously challenges the basic tenets of the system and demonstrates the pressure to avoid full trials. Despite limited prosecutorial discretion, informal deals between the judge and the defence counsel (with or without the prosecutor's consent) often result in shorter, less contested trials, in exchange for sentencing discounts. Different labels are applied to this shadow practice – *Absprache*, *Verständigung*, *Vergleich* – but the effect is the same. The defendant receives sentencing assurances for keeping the trial simple. This practice continues within Germany while there is periodic discussion as to how a new model of criminal procedure oriented to forms of justice by consent might be achieved. See Thomas Weigend, ch 3.

dossier filed by the prosecutor as the evidence in the case are symptomatic of this crisis. More generally, as investigations into organised crime, political corruption and white-collar crimes have become the norm, public opinion in Italy has become increasingly intolerant towards due process of law clauses and is inclined to consider the accused guilty from the very first crime report and before the verdict is pronounced. This emotional anticipation of guilt has resulted in a complete lack of trust in the trial as the correct method for resolving criminal allegations. But this is only symptomatic of a deeper crisis which is revealing a truly frightening reality.

In Italy, like many other criminal justice systems, the law of evidence as practiced in the criminal courts is moving in a new direction. Everyday the criminal trial becomes less the kingdom of oral and direct witness testimony and more the venue where evidence has already been moulded and shaped into a fixed form by pre-trial exhibits. On the one hand, we are witnessing the growing use of technical evidence, expert evidence, presumptions and circumstantial evidence; on the other hand, video, computer and all types of wiretapping and technological evidence are playing an increasing role that the 'father founders' of adversarial criminal procedure simply could not have forecast.

Another aspect to consider is the difficulty in proving certain essential elements of modern criminal law and liability that are increasingly expressed in terms of concepts such as 'conduct', 'harm', 'danger', 'duty to perform in case of omission', 'complicity' and 'intention' or 'recklessness'. A worrying picture emerges when we combine these difficulties with the increasing role of party control in the management of evidence.[45] On the one hand, we could see many possible short-cuts in fact-finding which could result in punishment without proof or through a 'consensual', stipulated or bargained proof. On the other hand, we could see a spreading decline in responsibility for judgment which involves careful handling of evidence and critical understanding.

Criminal justice systems differ even within western experience as they are based on specific historical and political traditions. Nevertheless, it would seem that the ideal of determining guilt through a criminal trial that evolved from a common liberal tradition and was strongly based upon the notion of oral confrontation between the parties before an impartial judge is in decline today and is undergoing an almost terminal crisis of confidence before it has been given the chance to work as effectively and

[45] This increasing role of party control in the management of evidence is leading to a 'consensually' arranged kind of fact-finding that goes beyond any classical common law fact-finding and even any corruption of this model through inquisitorial borrowing in the direction of a third model of procedure – a brand-new post-modern 'neo-inquisitorial' one.

completely as it should. This crisis is showing different symptoms in various western legal systems but we need to tackle it seriously without succumbing to dogmatism.

6

The Two Faces of Justice in the Post-Soviet Legal Sphere: Adversarial Procedure, Jury Trial, Plea-Bargaining and the Inquisitorial Legacy

STEPHEN C THAMAN

I. INTRODUCTION

> Our obtuse, our blinkered, our hulking brute of a judicial system can live only if it is infallible.
>
> Alexander Solzhenitsyn, *The Gulag Archipelago*.[1]

THE SOVIET CRIMINAL justice system fits squarely into the hierarchical, policy-implementing (and traditionally inquisitorial) model that Mirjan Damaška elaborated in his book *The Faces of Justice and State Authority*.[2] The overarching policy of Communist Party officialdom was one of no acquittals. This policy was dutifully carried out by its cadre of criminal justice officials from the police, criminal investigator (*sledovatel*), prosecutor (*prokuror*), and trial and appellate judge, as the raw material of the case, the *dossier*, made its way along the assembly line.[3]

The 15 republics which became independent after the collapse of the Soviet Union in 1991[4] inherited this system and are attempting to reform it

[1] A Solzhenitsyn, *The Gulag Archipelago* vol 3 (London, Fontana, 1979) 520.

[2] MR Damaška, *The Faces of Justice and State Authority* (New Haven, Yale University Press, 1986) 11–17.

[3] Many innocent suffered. According to a 1986 study, approximately 2,500 citizens were 'illegally arrested' and more than 3,000 wrongfully prosecuted each year. T Foglesong, 'Habeas Corpus or Who Has the Body? Judicial Review of Arrest and Pretrial Detention in Russia' (1996) 14 *Wisconsin International Law Journal* 541, 547–48.

[4] I will use the first two letters of these republics when referring to their codes and constitutions, which are listed in Appendix A: Armenia (AR), Azerbaijan (AZ), Belarus (BE),

by introducing institutions from what Damaška calls the co-ordinate, problem-solving (and largely non-inquisitorial, that is, adversarial) systems of justice modeled upon Anglo-American criminal procedure.[5]

This essay will focus on three of these institutions, adversary procedure, plea bargaining, and jury trial. Jury trial and adversary procedure were already articulated as principles for criminal justice reform during the Soviet *perestroika* period[6] and became the keystones of the 1991 Concept of Judicial Reform of the Russian Republic,[7] the most comprehensive blueprint for judicial reform to be drafted in post-Soviet lands. They sought to improve the quality of the evidence presented to the trier of fact through adversarial testing, and to liberate the trial judge from dependence on the prosecutor and executive organs. Juries would enable the court to acquit when the evidence was clearly insufficient to overcome the presumption of innocence. Plea-bargaining and guilty pleas were part of a later reform agenda and were introduced for reasons of procedural economy.[8] We will discuss the impact of these reforms and assess whether they have led to an improvement in the quality of the evidence presented to the trier of fact, a liberation of the trial and appellate judges from the juggernaut of hierarchical Soviet 'crime control' policies, and the development of a culture where acquittals of guilty and innocent will be tolerated when the evidence lacks credibility or is insufficient to constitute proof beyond a reasonable doubt.

II. FROM INQUISITORIAL TO ADVERSARIAL TRIAL?

The Preliminary Investigation and the Preparation of the Dossier

The Lack of Adversariality in the Preliminary Investigation

The raw material of the Soviet inquisitorial assembly line of pre-determined justice was the dossier, which each official inspected, added value to, and stamped for quality as it passed to the next stage of production. Each official, from police to trial and appellate judge, had the same duty: to 'take all measures provided by law for the all-sided, complete

Estonia (ES), Georgia (GE), Kazakhstan (KA), Kyrgyzstan (KY), Latvia (LA), Lithuania (LI), Moldova (MO), Russia (RU), Tajikistan (TA), Turkmenistan (TU), Ukraine (UK), and Uzbekistan (UZ). I will also refer to the Model Code of Criminal Procedure for the Commonwealth of Independent States (1996), which had a great influence on the reforms in all but the Baltic Republics of Estonia, Latvia and Lithuania.

5 Damaška, above n 2, at 11–17.

6 See SC Thaman, 'The Resurrection of Trial by Jury in Russia' (1995) 31 *Stanford Journal of International Law* 61, 70.

7 See *Ibid* 72–74, for a discussion of the 'Concept of Judicial Reform.'

8 MR Damaška, 'Models of Criminal Procedure' (2001) 51 *Zbornik (collected papers of Zagreb Law School)* 477, 485.

and objective investigation of the circumstances of the case' – that is, to ascertain the truth, the quintessential goal of inquisitorial justice.[9]

Today, the constitutions of several[10] and the Codes of Criminal Procedure of nearly all post-Soviet republics[11] prescribe 'adversarial procedure' (*sostiazatel'nost'*) and equality of arms as governing principles, but commentators tend to limit them to the trial stage of procedure.[12] No post-Soviet codes accord the defence broad adversarial rights at the preliminary investigation, and, in particular, do not allow the defence to be present when witnesses are being interviewed or other evidence gathered.[13] Few of the post-Soviet republics[14] have instituted pre-trial procedures to preserve witness testimony which guarantee the right to confrontation required by international conventions to which the post-Soviet republics are parties.[15]

[9] S 20 Ugolovno-protsessual'nyy kodeks RSFSR, Affirmed by Supreme Soviet of the RSFSR. 27 Oct 1960 published in *Zakony RSFSR I Postanovleniia Verkhovnogo soveta RSFSR* (Moskva, Verkhovnyy Sovet RSFSR, 1960). The CCP-RSFSR, virtually identical to the codes in force in the other 14 Soviet Republics, will be used as the Soviet-era model. Similar language is still found in CCP-TA s 15(1); CCP-draft-TU s 23; CCP-UZ s 15. The judge, as last in line, was obligated to ratify the results of the officials who preceded him. TG Morshchakova, *Rossiyskoe pravosudie v kontekste sudebnoy reformy* (2004) 178.

[10] Art 123(3) Const-RU provides that 'court procedure is realised on the basis of adversary procedure and equality of the parties.' For similar sections, see Art 148, Const-AZ, Art 115, para 1, Const-BE, Art 85(3) Const-GE, Art 129(3) Const-UK.

[11] CCP-AR s 23(1); CCP-AZ s 32(1); CCP-BE s 24(1); CCP-ES s 14(1); CCP-GE s 49; CCP-KA s 23(1); CCP-KY s 18(1); CCP-LI s 7(1); CCP-RU s 15; CCP-Draft-TU s 22(1); CCP-UK s 16–1.

[12] See IF Demidov, 'Proekt UPK v svete ego osnovnykh poniatiy' in *Sudebnaia reforma v Rossii: problemy sovershenstvovaniia protsessual'nogo zakonodatel'stva* (Moskva, R Valent, 2001) 230, 236. On the inquisitorial nature of the American pre-trial, see *McNeil v Wisconsin*, 501 US 171, 181 (1991). Soviet theorists felt that the investigator could incorporate the roles of accuser, defender and judge within himself and maintain complete neutrality. Mikhaylovskaia, below n 52, at 9–10.

[13] A right to participate is usually granted only with 'permission' of the investigator: see Model Code s 104(1)(3), as well as CCP-AR s 73(1)(3); CCP-KA s 69(2); CCP-KY s 40(1)(11); CCP-UK s 48(4). In RU there is also no express right to counsel during confrontations between witnesses, CCP-RU s 192, or line-ups involving the defendant, CCP-RU s 193.

[14] For exceptions, see CCP-LI ss 179, 234; CCP-MO s 109(3). For a discussion on the trend to 'adversarialise' the preliminary hearing see SC Thaman, *Comparative Criminal Procedure: A Casebook Approach* (Durham, NC, Carolina Academic Press, 2002) 37–38.

[15] Art 6(3)(d) of the European Convention on Human Rights (hereafter ECHR) and Art 14(3)(e) of the International Covenant on Civil and Political Rights (hereafter ICCPR) guarantee the right to confront the state's witnesses. Armenia, Azerbaijan, Estonia, Georgia, Latvia, Lithuania, Moldova, Russia and Ukraine are bound by the ECHR and all the republics are bound by the ICCPR.

'Long Live the Queen!' Confessions as the Queen of Evidence

The coerced confession was traditionally the centerpiece of nearly all Soviet-era prosecutions despite its inherent unreliability.[16] This has changed little in post-Soviet times.[17] The investigator assembles the rest of the dossier – witness statements, expert opinions, reports of investigative acts – to corroborate the 'truth' of the confession.

The move from inquisitorial to adversary procedure should signify a demotion of the search for truth, to the level of other important values protected by modern constitutions such as the right to privacy, the right to human dignity, the right to due process, etc.[18] Many of the post-Soviet republics have paid lip service to these rights by making exclusion of illegally gathered evidence a constitutional command;[19] and by enacting provisions broader than those in most countries, excluding evidence gathered in violation of constitutional[20] as well as mere statutory norms.[21]

But although the right to remain silent is guaranteed in nearly all the post-Soviet republics,[22] and defendants must be advised of this right and

[16] R Conquest, *The Great Terror: A Reassessment* (New York, OUP, 1990) 121–24. *Vyshinskiy* and others have called the confession the 'queen of evidence'. SC Thaman, 'Miranda in Comparative Law' (2001) 45 *Saint Louis University Law Journal* 581.

[17] In Russia, it has been estimated that up to 50% of all criminal defendants, and 80% of those who refuse to admit guilt, are subject to torture or ill-treatment. The practices include asphyxiation, beatings, electroshock, threats and use of fellow prisoners to mistreat uncooperative suspects. D Lohman, *Confessions at any cost: police torture in Russia* (New York, Human Rights Watch, 1999) 1, 21, 36. On the use of coerced confessions in Azerbaijan, Georgia and Ukraine, see NP Kovalev, *Lay Adjudication Reforms in the Transitional Criminal Justice Systems of the Commonwealth of Independent States* (Doctoral Dissertation, Belfast, Queen's University, 2007) 136, 139, 347. For evidence that this practice exists in all post-Soviet republics, see 'US State Department Country Reports on Human Rights Practices' (2006), available at <http://www.state.gov/g/drl/rls/hrrpt/2006/> accessed 15 June 2008.

[18] On exclusionary rules related to the determination of truth, and those based in other important values, see MR Damaška, 'Evidentiary Barriers to Conviction and Two Models of Criminal Procedure' (1973) 121 *University of Pennsylvania Law Review* 506,513.

[19] Art 42(2) Const-AR; Art 71(3) Const-AZ; Art 27(2) Const-BE; Art 42(7) Const-GE; Art 77(3)(9) Const-KA; Art 89(2) Const-KY; Art 50 Const.-RU; Art 62(3) Const-UK.

[20] In CCP-LA s 130(2,3), the court will weigh whether a violation was 'substantial' and decide admissibility based thereon, unless the procedure involved use of force, threats, coercion, or violation of basic principles of criminal procedure.

[21] For provisions including mere statutory violations: CCP-BE s 105(4); CCP-GE s 7(6); CCP-KA s 116(4); CCP-KY s 6(3); CCP-LI s 19(4); CCP-RU s 75(1). For a comparison of modern approaches, see SC Thaman, 'Wahrheit oder Rechtsstaatlichkeit: die Verwertung von verfassungswidrig erlangten Beweisgegenständen im Strafverfahren' in J Arnold *et al* (eds), *Menschengerechtes Strafrecht: Festschrift für Albin Eser zum* 70. *Geburtstag* (München, CH Beck, 2005) 1042–44.

[22] Art 42(1) Const-AR; Art 74 Const-AZ; Art 27, para 1, Const-BE; Art. 22(3) Const-ES; Art. 42(8) Const.-GE; Art. 77(3)(7) Const-KA; Art. 51 Const-RU; Art. 63, para 1, Const-UK. It is statutorily guaranteed in: Model Code s 25(1) and CCP-AR s 20(1); CCP-AZ s 20(1); CCP-BE s 10(4); CCP-GE s 73(1)(b); CCP-KY s 12(2); CCP-MO s 21; CCP-RU s 47(4)(3); CCP-draft-TU s 25(1); CCP-UK s 63, para 1.

the right to counsel before being interrogated,[23] the right may be waived and police and investigators routinely use illegal methods to obtain such waivers. This fact led Russia to introduce a strict exclusionary rule which applies to confessions taken in the absence of counsel, if the defendant retracts the confession at trial.[24] Nevertheless, Russian police and investigators have found a way around this protection by using the so-called 'pocket lawyer' (*karmanyy advokat*), who actively work with the investigator or police in encouraging the suspect to confess and on occasion watch while the suspect is tortured.[25]

The File at Trial: Undermining the Presumption of Innocence and the Right to Confrontation

Today, as in Soviet times, the trial judge is either the sole trier of fact, or clearly calls the shots as part of a collegial mixed court of 'people's assessors' (commonly known as 'nodders'), who are responsible for deciding all questions of fact, law, guilt and sentence.[26] The only exceptions are the tiny amount of jury trials provided for in Russian law.[27]

In Soviet theory, adversary procedure could co-exist with an active trial judge who was obligated to ascertain the truth[28] and this position still finds support today.[29] However, the predominant theory now entrenched in

[23] CCP-AR s 211(3); CCP-AZ ss 90(7)(10), 232(4); CCP-ES ss 34, 75(2); CCP-GE s 310(2,3); CCP-KA ss 114, 216(3), 217(2); CCP-KY s 191(2); CCP-LA ss 150, 265(1); CCP-MO ss 64(2), 104(1); CCP-RU ss 173, 47(4)(3,8); CCP-draft-TU s 255(3). See also Model Code ss 252(3), 253(8). Only in CCP-TA ss 53.1, 412.11 and CCP-UZ s 47, para 2, does one find the old Soviet admonition which is limited to the 'right to give evidence'. Cf CCP-RSFSR s 47, para 2.

[24] CCP-RU s 75(2)(1). Kommentariy (2002), below n 49, at 206.

[25] The lawyer will then be a witness for the prosecution that no torture was used. *Confessions at any cost: police torture in Russia*, above n 17, at 66. Many 'pocket lawyers' actually share their fees with the investigators who invite them to perform such a role. Marogulova, above n 12, at 54.

[26] Thaman, above n 6, at 67. 'People's assessors' have also been called 'pawns in the hands of the judge' and 'wordless judges'. VV Mel'nik, *Iskusstvo dokazazyvaniia w sostiazatel'nom ugolovnom protsesse* (Moskva, Delo, 2000) 19. On the 'ritual' of lay participation on the European Continent, see Damaška, above n 2, at 33. On how the Belarussian and Uzbek mixed courts have not been perceived to have gained independence since Soviet times, see N Kovalev, 'Lay Adjudication of Crimes in the Commonwealth of Independent States: An Independent and Impartial Jury or a "Court of Nodders"?' (2004) 11 *Journal of East European Law* 123, 136, 153–54.

[27] It has been estimated, following the Russian abolition of the mixed court and turn to jury trial, that there will be lay participation in only 0.8% of criminal cases. S Pashin, 'Who Needs a Dependent Judge?' *Moscow Times*, 2 July 2001, 10.

[28] This was the position of *A. Ya. Vyshinskiy*, Minister of Justice during the late Stalinist period. IB Mikhaylovskaia, *Tseli, funktsii i printsipy Rossiyskogo ugolovnogo sudoproizvodstva* (Moskva, Prospekt, 2003) 69.

[29] VI Zazhitskiy, '*Istina i sredstva ee ustanovleniia v UPK RF: teoretiko-pravovoy analiz*' (2005) 6 *Gosudarstvo i Pravo*, at 67. According to a commentary edited by, among others,

Russia and the majority of the post-Soviet republics is that a tri-partite division of labour between prosecution, defence and court, is the crucial factor in achieving adversariality.[30] This theory, of course, requires a passive judge no longer responsible for the ascertainment of truth in the matter.[31]

The turn to adversary procedure, however, has not led to a change in the trial role of the judge sufficient to guarantee the required neutrality in most of the new codes. It is still the trial judge, who in nearly all trials is also the trier of the facts, who is obligated to read the entire dossier of the preliminary investigation and certify that the evidence is sufficient legally and factually for the trial court to potentially return a guilty judgment.[32] This procedure undermines the presumption of innocence by requiring a 'pre-judging' of the merits of the case which should disqualify the judge as a trier of fact at the trial.[33]

Today the parties decide which evidence is presented at trial, whereas in Soviet times this role was carried out by the judge, who was in effect an ersatz prosecutor in more than half of all criminal cases because the prosecutor was not obligated to appear.[34] Most codes no longer require the trial judge to ascertain the truth, but rather to 'create the necessary conditions for the fulfillment by the parties of their procedural duties and the realisation of the rights accorded them.'[35] Observers in Russia,

the presidents of the Supreme Court and Constitutional Council of Kazakhstan, one can even have adversary procedure if the prosecutor does not appear in court and the defendant must defend himself alone in front of the judge! II Rogov, '*St 23-Osushchestvlenie sudoproizvodstva na osnove sostiazatel'nosti i ravnopraviia storon*' in II Rogov, SF Bychkova and KA Mami (eds), *Ugolovno-protsessual'nyy kodeks Respublika Kazakhstan (Obshchaia chast') Kommentariy* (Almaty, Zheti Zharfy, 2002) 67–8.

[30] Model Code s 28; CCP-AR s 23; CCP-BE s 24; CCP-KA s 23; CCP-Draft-TU s 22; CCP-UK s 16–1. The separation of powers aspect is stressed in CCP-ES s 14(1), CCP-LA s 17, CCP-LI s 7(2); CCP-MO s 24; CCP-RU s 15. The phrase 'adversary procedure' is not mentioned in the codes of LA and MO.

[31] Damaška, above n 2, at 3.

[32] CCP-RSFSR s 222. This procedure was recommended in Model Code s 221(1) and still is found in CCP-AR s 292; CCP-LI s 228(1); CCP-RU ss 227–231; CCP-TA s 222; CCP-draft-TU s 330(2); CCP-UK s 245.

[33] On this 'preconceived opinion as to guilt' imbued by study of the dossier, see KJ Mittermaier, *Das Volksgericht in Gestalt der Schwur- und Schöffengerichte* (Berlin, CG Lüderitz, 1866) 22. As to whether Continental European systems take the presumption of innocence 'somewhat less seriously' due to such trial arrangements, see Damaška, above n 8, at 491. There was no question of this in the USSR, where the presumption of innocence was impugned as 'bourgeios.' IL Petrukhin, *Teoreticheskie osnovy reformy ugolovnogo protsessa v Rossii: Part II* (Moskva, Prospekt, 2005) 122. On how this 'file prejudice' poisoned the Soviet-Russian trial, see LM Karnozova, *Vozrozhdennyy Sud Prisiazhnykh* (Moskva, Nota Bene, 2000) 155.

[34] Thaman, above n 6, at 67.

[35] See Model Code s 28(4), and CCP-AR s 23(4); CCP-BE s 24(5); CCP-GE s 15(5); CCP-KA s 23(6); CCP-KY s 18(6); CCP-MO s 314(2); CCP-RU s 15; CCP-draft-TU s 22(1)(6); CCP-UK s 16–1; CCP-UZ s 25, para 6.

however, report that judges still do the lion's share of questioning of defendants and witnesses in patent disregard for the new procedure.[36]

The trial still opens in most post-Soviet republics by asking the defendant whether he admits the charges, and wants to testify; usually preceded by an admonition of the right to remain silent.[37] This procedure is problematic in light of the defendant's presumption of innocence[38] and the prosecution's burden to prove guilt. In Soviet times the defendant nearly always testified, either admitting guilt and hoping for lenience in sentencing in the unified guilt and penalty phase proceedings[39] or retracting his pre-trial confession and contesting the charges.[40] Little has changed in this respect.[41] The often coerced pre-trial confession of the defendant is read in court, whether or not the defendant remains silent or contests its validity,[42] because trial courts uniformly refuse to suppress them despite the widely-acknowledged use of torture and other coercion.[43] In Russia, the defence may not even attack the credibility of the prior statement at trial by alleging unlawful methods, for the Supreme Court of Russia (SCRF) has ruled that such allegations are grounds for reversing acquittal judgments.[44]

As in Soviet times, the new codes do not treat the reading of the written material in the investigative dossier as a violation of the otherwise-guaranteed principles of an 'oral' and 'immediate' trial.[45] All reports of

[36] *Basmannoe pravosudie: Uroki samooborony. Posobie dlia advokatov* (2004) 25 (a study of one Moscow court in October 2003).

[37] CCP-RSFSR s 278. CCP-AR s 334(2); CCP-GE s 472; CCP-KA s 346; CCP-LI ss 267, 268; CCP-RU ss 273–275; CCP-TA s 280, para 3; CCP-draft-TU s 388; CCP-UK s 299. On this tradition of inquisitorial procedure, see Damaška. above n 18, at 506, 525.

[38] The presumption of innocence has constitutional and statutory protection in most republics. See Art 41, Const-AR; Art 71(1,2) Const-AZ; Art 40 Const-GE; Art 77(3)(1) Const-KA; Art 92 Const-LA; Art 31(1) Const-LI; Art 21 Const-MO; Art 49(1) Const-RU; Art 62 Const-UK; and CCP-BE s 16; CCP-ES s 7; CCP-KY s 15; CCP-draft-TU s 18(1).

[39] On how the pressure of a single phase trial leads nearly all continental European defendants to testify at trial, see Damaška, above n 18, at 527.

[40] The typical Russian trial consisted in the defendant's confession to investigative authorities and his subsequent retraction thereof at trial: H Franz, *Die Hauptverhandlung im russischen Strafverfahren* (Berlin, Verlag Dr. Köster, 2000) 70–72.

[41] *Basmannoe pravosudie*, above n 36, at 76.

[42] See for example, CCP-AR s 337(1); CCP-KA s 349(1); CCP-KY s 289(1); CCP-MO s 368(1); CCP-RU s 276(1); CCP-Draft-TU s 391.

[43] Kovalev, above n 17, at 136. As to this practice in Armenia, Azerbaijan, Tajikistan, see USDOS, above n 17; *Confessions*, above n 17, at 7, 68, 76. Judges have estimated that at least one-third and probably more of all convictions are based on coerced confessions. P Finn, 'For Russians, Police Rampage Fuels Fear' *Washington Post*, 27 Mar 2005, available at http://www.washingtonpost.com/wp-dyn/articles/A4009–2005Mar26.html.

[44] On the massive reversal of acquittals on this basis, *see* SC Thaman, 'The Nullification of the Russian Jury: Lessons for Jury Inspired Reform in Eurasia and Beyond' (2007) 40 *Cornell International Law Journa* 357, at 377–78*l*; See Karnozova, above n 33, at 352 n 19; For a similar ruling regarding commenting on coercion used against witnesses to induce their pre-trial statements, *Kovalev*, above n 17, at 347.

[45] CCP-RSFSR s 240, para 1. Compare CCP-BE s 286; CCP-GE s 440(1); CCP-KA s 311(1); CCP-KY s 253(1); CCP-LA s 449(3); CCP-LI s 237(1); CCP-RU s 240; CCP-TA

investigative acts (arrests, searches, etc) and documents may be read to the trier of fact,[46] along with statements of witnesses who do not appear in court.[47] This unreformed approach to the use of hearsay and written evidence which has been prepared in inquisitorial secrecy by law enforcement organs appears to violate the rights to equality of arms and confrontation.[48]

In 2001 the CCP-RU 2001 took a hopeful step by excluding all prior statements of witnesses or victims if they failed to appear at trial, unless both parties stipulated otherwise,[49] but pressure by the procuracy led to a return to the old Soviet rule.[50] The file thus continues to act 'in the wings of the trial like the prompter at an amateur play.'[51]

Returning the Case for Supplementary Investigation to Avoid Acquittals

Under the Soviet-era codes a judge could refuse to acquit when there was clearly insufficient evidence of guilt if he/she was not convinced of the defendant's innocence and felt further investigation was required for an 'all-sided, complete and objective investigation of the circumstances necessary and sufficient to decide the case.' The case would then be returned to the investigator to look for such hypothetical evidence.[52] The issue was

s 241; CCP-draft-TU s 351; CCP-UZ s 26. This is also the approach of German law, see C Roxin, *Strafverfahrensrecht* 24 edn (München, Beck, 1995) 335. 'Immediacy means that the trier of fact should directly hear the evidence. *Ibid.*

[46] See CCP-RSFSR ss 69, para 2, 87, 88, 292, which was included in Model Code ss 142(2), 156(2), 396 and is virtually replicated in: CCP-AR ss 104(2)(8,9), 121(2); CCP-AZ ss 124(2)(4,5), 134(2); CCP-BE ss 88(2), 338; CCP-GE s 110(2)(f,g); CCP-KA ss 122(1), 357; CCP-KY ss 81(2)(4,5), 89, 90, 299; CCP-LA ss 135, 137, 229(1); CCP-LI ss 92(1)(1), 286; CCP-MO ss 93(2)(4,5), 373; CCP-RU ss 83, 84; CCP-TA ss 62, 295; CCP-draft-TU ss 124(2)(4,5), 400; CCP-UZ ss 81, 443.

[47] See Model Code s 391(1), and CCP-AR ss 337(1), 342(1); CCP-AZ s 329(1) CCP-BE s 333; CCP-ES s 291 CCP-GE s 481(1); CCP-KA s 353; CCP-KY s 294 CCP-LA s 501; CCP-LI s 272; CCP-MO s 371; CCP-RU s 281; CCP-TA s 289; CCP-draft-TU s 395(1); CCP-UK s 306; CCP-UZ s 104.

[48] Which the ECHR and ICCPR make binding on all republics. See above n 15. The US also prohibits the reading of prior statements that have not been subject to cross-examination by the defence. *Crawford v Washington*, 541 US 36 (2004).

[49] CCP-RU s 281 (2001), in DN Kozak & YB Mizulina (eds), *Kommentariy k ugolovno-protsessual'nomu kodeksu Rossiyskoy Federatsii* (Moskva, Yurist', 2002) 309.

[50] CCP-RU s 281(2). See S Pomorski, 'Modern Russian Criminal Procedure: The Adversarial Principle and Guilty Plea' (2006) 17 *Criminal Law Forum* 129, 144, who calls the changes a 'throwback to the Soviet past'.

[51] Damaška, above n 2, at 50, 53. Pomorski, above n 50, at 142, calls it the 'backbone' of the trial.

[52] See PH Solomon Jr, 'The Case of the Vanishing Acquittal: Informal Norms and the Practice of Soviet Criminal Justice' (1987) 39 *Soviet Studies* 531. For a characterisation of the practice as a 'fetishisation' of truth-finding obliging the court to redo that which the organs of

phrased as an 'insufficiency of evidence' upon which to acquit a defendant.[53] Acquittals were seen as a blemish on the work of law enforcement organs and required compensation of those acquitted for unlawful pre-trial detention,[54] so cases with insufficient evidence either disappeared upon return to the investigative stage, or ended with guilty judgments for unfounded lesser offences.[55]

The Criminal Code of Procedure of Russia of 2001 eliminated the return of the case for supplementary investigation in its traditional form,[56] inspired by an April 1999 decision of the Russian Constitutional Court (CCRF) which declared that, among other principles, it violated the presumption of innocence and the right to adversary procedure.[57] In December 2003, however, the CCRF backed off its earlier ruling and declared the unconstitutionality of the new provision on the grounds that it violates the victim's right to access to justice.[58] Now the victim or prosecutor may seek to remove a case from the trier of fact to 'restore rights of the victim or the accused violated by law enforcement agencies.'[59] This was a clear victory for the prosecutor's office, which has finally succeeded in giving priority to the rights of the victim over those of the defendant.[60] Law enforcement organs can now intentionally violate the

the preliminary investigation were unable to do properly do. IB Mikhaylovskaia, '*Sotsial'noe naznachenie ugolovnoy yustitsii i tsel' ugolovnogo protsessa*' (2005) 5 *Gosudarstvo i pravo*, 111, 116.

[53] This language is still found in: CCP-BE s 302(5); CCP-GE ss 426(1)(a), 501. For an excellent discussion of the Soviet concept of doubts 'that cannot be eliminated during the pre-trial investigation and trial (*neustranimye somneniia*)' see *Kovalev*, above n 17, at 351–53.

[54] In the 'system of statistical evaluation of judicial activity' which dominated in the USSR and Russia, an acquittal was seen as a 'defect.' Morshchakova, above n 9, at 178.

[55] In more than half of the cases returned for further investigation judges find the defendant guilty on clearly insufficient evidence but sentence them to credit for time served, resulting in their release. See *Confessions* ..., above n 17, at 120–22.

[56] CCP-RU s 237 limited such motions to the stage of the preliminary hearing and restricted the substance of such motions to the correction of errors which prevent a valid judgment from being rendered, or to cases where the accusatory pleading was not handed to the accused. The procurator was given five days to cure these defects.

[57] See Thaman, above n 14, at 181–83.

[58] Now that Russia's reform has been aborted, the procedure, found in Model Code ss 348, 362, continues to exist in CCP-AR ss 297, 311, 363; CCP-BE s 302(5); CCP-GE ss 426(1)(a), 501; CCP-KA ss 303, 323(1); CCP-KY s 244(3); CCP-LA s 462(3) (when prosecutor wants to amend charges during trial to detriment of defendant); CCP-TA ss 233, 260, 310; CCP-UK s 281; CCP-UZ s 419. The European Court of Human Rights condemned Ukraine for violating the ECHR right to a fair trial, in part on a complaint that returning the case for further investigation violated the right to a fair trial. *Salov v Ukraine*, paras 78–98 (decision of 6 Sept 2005).

[59] Decision of 8 Dec 2003, reprinted in VG Strekozov (ed) *Konstitutsionnyy sud Rossiyskoy Federatsii, Postanovleniia, Opredeleniia* (Moskva, Yurist', 2003) 4–5.

[60] On the long-time quest of a noted professor in the institute of the procuracy to establish the priority of the rights of the victim over those of the defendant and for maintaining the returning of the case for further investigation. See Franz, above n 40, at 141–44.

rights of the victim and then rely on the victim to reassert those rights during trial, after it becomes clear that the evidence will be insufficient for a conviction.

The Acquittal-Free Post-Soviet Landscape

A 'no-acquittals' policy still exists in Russia, and effectively converts the trial court into a mere sentencing court which imposes the judgment sanctioned in advance by the prosecutor in the accusatory pleading.[61] This turn away from the spirit of the Concept of Judicial Reform could be a result of the nearly total domination of Russian democracy by the executive branch under President Putin and its 'power ministries' (*siloviki*) such as the FSB (successor to the KGB), and, for purposes of criminal procedure, the procuracy, and the unwillingness or incapacity of the judiciary to buck this trend.

In the first three years following passage of the CCP-RU in 2001, the overall acquittal rate (including jury trials) rose from 0.3 per cent to 0.9 per cent.[62] Acquittal rates are likely not higher in other post-Soviet republics.[63] Since post-Soviet reform efforts to bolster the independence of the judiciary from executive organs and the procuracy have largely proved unsuccessful,[64] and because the Soviet-era mixed courts with their 'nodding' people's assessors are an ineffective counterweight to politically dependent judges, the classic jury still appears to be the only means to facilitate acquittals in cases which lack sufficient credible evidence of guilt.

[61] S Pomorski, 'Justice in Siberia: a case study of a lower criminal court in the city of Krasnoyarsk' (2001) 34 *Communist and Post-Communist Studies* 447, 456–58. Three-judge panels in Russia, an alternative to trial by jury, acquitted none of the 1,564 persons coming before them in the years 1994–1998. Mel'nik, above n 26, at 42. To enforce this 'no-acquittals' policy, the SCRF routinely reverses a much higher percentage of acquittals (which constitute less than 0.5 % of all judgments) than they do of convictions. For instance, in 1996 it reversed 29.4% of acquittals and only 2.2% of convictions and in 1997, 33.1% of acquittals and only 2.5% of convictions. *Confessions*, above n 17, at 118–19.

[62] Petrukhin, above n 33, at 101.

[63] For some sample acquittal rates: 0.25% in Armenia in 2003, 0.27% and 0.26% in Ukraine in 2002 and 2003: less than 0.5% in Belarus in 1998; 0.57% and 0.81% in Kazakhstan in 2002 and 2003; 0.45%, 0.47%, 0.67% and 0.74% in Georgia in the years 2000–2003, see Kovalev, above n 17, at 135. A no acquittal policy is also rigidly enforced in Turkmenistan. *Ibid* 125.

[64] USDOS, above n 17, report on nearly universal corruptness of the judiciary and its dependence on the executive branch and/or procuracy in all except the Baltic republics, and problems with corruption in Latvia. Compare, Kovalev, above n 17, at 123–25.

III. PLEA BARGAINING: EMPOWERMENT OF THE DEFENCE OR INQUISITORIAL INDUCEMENT TO CONFESS?

Introduction

As Damaška has noted, the inducement of confessions through procedural arrangements in the hierarchical inquisitorial procedures of the European continent, made it unnecessary for those countries to engage in American style bargaining for guilty pleas.[65] The procedurally induced confession was only 'evidence,' from which the court could infer guilt, for a defendant in the civil law realm could not herself usurp the judicial role by stamping herself as guilty with a plea. Yet, now, many of the post-Soviet republics have introduced new consensual procedures designed to waive their new, albeit flawed, adversarial trial procedures. Are they a natural result of the move to adversarial procedure,[66] or a procedural replacement of inquisitorial truth-seeking judge with his confession-inducing procedural arsenal?

Avoiding the Trial through Confession or Stipulation to the Truth of the Charges

On the European continent, the first inroads into the principle of legality, which required the judge to determine the correct legal qualification of the charged criminal acts and the legal appropriateness of the sentence based strictly on the adduced evidence, were allowed only in the adjudication of minor crimes. Several of the post-Soviet republics have followed this trend and permit conditional dismissals (diversion),[67] penal orders,[68] and victim-offender conciliation (which usually applies only in relation to minor crimes subject to private prosecution).[69] But our emphasis will be on the procedures relating to more serious criminal offences.[70]

[65] MR Damaška, 'Negotiated Justice in International Criminal Courts' (2004) 2 *Journal of International Criminal Justice* 1018, 1022.

[66] See M Langer, 'From Legal Transplants to Legal Translations: The Globalization of Plea Bargaining and the Americanization Thesis in Criminal Procedure' (2004) 45 *Harvard International Law Journal* 1, 6, 10, who traces this common law adversarial institution through its 'translation' into the inquisitorial language of erstwhile inquisitorial countries.

[67] CCP-MO ss 510–511 (requiring a confession); CCP-ES s 202(1).

[68] CCP-ES s 261 ff; CCP-LI s 425 *ff*.

[69] It was already included in the CCP-RSFSR s 5(6), relating to cases initiated by complaint of the victim; see also Model Code s 36(1)(6)); CCP-AR s 36; CCP-BE ss 26(2), 29(1)(5), 30(1)(2); CCP-LA ss 536–38; CCP-LI ss 207, 420; CCP-RU ss 20(2), 319(5); CCP-TA ss 5, para 1, (3); CCP-UZ ss 582–86 CCP.

[70] For a comprehensive analysis of the genesis and application of these forms throughout Europe and America, see SC Thaman, 'Plea-Bargaining, Negotiating Confessions, and

In more serious cases, the first clear turn to consensual procedures in modern Europe,[71] came with the Italian Code of Criminal Procedure of 1988 with the introduction of the 'application for punishment upon request of the parties', which provided for up to one third discount on punishment if the bargained sentence was no longer than two years deprivation of liberty. The *patteggiamento* was the model for Russia's new form of guilt-stipulation.[72] There is a tendency, however, to extend the new consensual procedures to more serious criminal offences. The *patteggiamento* was extended in 2003 to cases punishable by up to five years (after the up to one-third sentence reduction).[73] The Russian provision, applicable to crimes punishable by no more than five years in the CCP-RU of 2001, was extended in 2003 to apply to crimes punishable by up to 10 years imprisonment.[74] Guilty plea procedures also apply to all but the most serious crimes in Estonia and Moldova.[75]

However, more wide-open, American-style negotiation of charge and sentence between prosecution, defence and victim, without statutory discounts, exists in the new Estonian 'settlement proceedings.'[76] American-inspired 'co-operation agreements,' which link plea or sentence bargaining to the defendant's aid in the prosecution of others, have found their way into Georgia, Latvia and Moldova.[77] Estonia and Latvia have also adopted a procedure similar to the *giudizio abbreviato* introduced in Italy in 1988,[78] where the maximum sentence in the event of conviction is reduced by one-third if the defendant agrees to a 'trial' based in the written material in the investigative dossier. This 'trial' is an ironic replica of the classic written inquisitorial trial of the late Middle Ages, mitigated only by the

Consensual Resolution of Criminal Cases' in K Boele Woelki & S Van Erp (eds), *General Reports of the XVII Congress of the International Academy of Comparative Law* (2007) 951, 964–71.

[71] Since the 19th century Spain has allowed a defendant to express his or her conformity (*conformidad*) with the pleadings and be punished without trial if the threatened punishment did not exceed six years. See SC Thaman, 'Spain Returns to Trial by Jury' (1998) *Hastings International Comparative Law Review* 309–16.

[72] I included a procedure based on the Italian model in a chapter on consensual procedures I drafted for the authors of the CCP-RU of 2001, which was eventually adopted in modified form. The one-third discount model exists in Russia and Lithuania. CCP-RU s 316(7); CCP-LI s 440(1).

[73] Langer, above n 66, at 49–50.

[74] CCP-RU s 314.

[75] CCP-ES s 239; CCP-MO s 504(2).

[76] CCP-ES ss 245, 248.

[77] In CCP-GE s 679–1 'co-operation' in the prosecution of corruption and other serious crimes can lead to reduction or even dismissal of charges. See also CP-LI s 210; CCP-MO s 505(1)(1).

[78] Thaman, above n 14, at 159–61.

right given to the defendant, subject to rebuttal by prosecutor and judge, to testify or to introduce supplementary evidence.[79]

In Belarus, Kazakhstan, Lithuania and in the Turkmenistan-draft, if the defendant admits the charges when questioned by the judge, the court, depending on the seriousness of the charge, may truncate the evidence to a questioning of the defendant and the victim, move directly to closing arguments, or even directly to the imposition of sentence.[80]

Consensual Procedures in Practice

By 2002, 59.8 per cent of all cases in Estonia were handled with the 'simplified proceedings' which were in force from 1996 until 2004.[81] The use of the Russian consensual procedure has also grown exponentially since it was introduced in mid-2002 and has 'taken root'.[82] The same can be said for Moldova, where plea bargaining resolved around 8.6 per cent of cases in 2004, 35 per cent in 2005 and 49 per cent in 2006.[83]

Wide-open American-inspired plea bargaining in Georgia, has been, however, an unmitigated disaster. An American advisor who worked on reforming the Georgian law has called it an 'institutionalised form of bribery.'[84] After the 'Rose Revolution' the new government of Mikheil Saakashvili began targeting members of the *ancien regime* on corruption charges and would routinely dismiss charges under the new law if the accused paid a large amount of money to the government, without even requiring a guilty admission, much less any kind of 'co-operation' which the original law was intended to encourage.[85] A condition of many 'plea

[79] In Estonia, a 1/3 discount is possible in all cases except those punished by life imprisonment. CCP-ES ss 233, 238. In Latvia, the accused may 'agree to not require the taking of evidence during the trial,' but without statutory discount. CCP-LA s 71(6).

[80] CCP-BE s 326(1); CCP-KA s 363; CCP-LI s 269; CCP-draft-TU s 406. Prior to the 2004 CCP-ES, Estonian 'proceedings' followed this model. M Sillaots, 'Admission and Confession of Guilt in Settlement Proceedings under Estonian Criminal Procedure' (2004) 9 *Juridica International* 116, 117–18. A similar provision was introduced in the 1993 Russian jury law but was seldom used and disappeared in the CCP-RU of 2001. Thaman, above n 6, at 103–104.

[81] Sillaots, above n 80, at 115–16.

[82] It was applied in 0.9% of all criminal cases in 2002 rising to 14.3% in 2003 and 2004. Pomorski, above n 50, at 141. In 2005 the procedure was used in 37.5% of peace court (misdemeanor) cases, 30% of district court and 2.4% of jury court cases. 'Statisticheskaia spravka o rabote sudov obshcheiy yurisdiktsii za 2005 god' available at http://www.cdep.ru/material.asp?material_id=90.

[83] 'Statistics of the Procurator General of the Republic of Moldova,' conveyed to the author by Alla Panici per e-mail.

[84] JD Reichelt, 'A Hobson's Experiment: Plea Bargaining in the Republic of Georgia' (2004) 11 *Journal of East European Law* 159, 185.

[85] *Ibid* 170–177.

agreements' was also the abandonment of allegations of torture or other unlawful coercion during the preliminary investigation.[86]

III. THE JURY AS ACQUITTAL CATALYST

The ice is breaking, ladies and gentlemen of the jury! The ice is breaking.[87]

Juries and Mixed Courts in the Post-Soviet Republics

For the authors of the Concept of Judicial Reform, the logical answer to the subservient Soviet judiciary and the 'nodding' lay assessors, was the classic jury which would relieve the judge of the duty of determining guilt, provide the foundation for adversary procedure, and make acquittals possible. They suggested juries be used in all cases punishable by more than one year deprivation of liberty,[88] and that the 'nodding' mixed courts be abolished.

A number of former Soviet republics eliminated the lay assessors in the years after independence.[89] Constitutional provisions providing for trial by jury were adopted in Russia, Armenia, Kazakhstan and Ukraine.[90] Provisions for jury trial were also contained in a 'concept of judicial reform' in Belarus in 1992 and were included in the 1999 CCP-BE, only to be removed later at the behest of authoritarian President Alekxander Lukashenka.[91] Other than Russia, only Azerbaijan has actually enacted legislation providing for trial by jury, but its implementation continues to be postponed, allegedly on fiscal grounds.[92] There is, however, new interest in jury trial since the 'colour' revolutions in Georgia ('rose'),[93] Ukraine ('orange'),[94] and Kyrgyzstan ('tulip').[95]

[86] *Ibid* 180–81. See also USDOJ, above n 17.

[87] Famous winged phrase of the rogue Ostap Bender in the 1928 Soviet novel *The Twelve Chairs*, see *Il'ia Il'f & Yevgeniy Petrov, Dvenadtsat' stul'ev* (Moskva, Eksmo, 2005) 49.

[88] '*O kontseptsii sudebnoy reformy*' (1991) 44 *Vedomosti RSFSR*, Item No 1435, reprinted in *Kontseptsiia sudebnoy reformy v Rossiyskoy Federatsii* (Moskva, Verkhovnyy Sovet Rossiyskoy Federatsii, 1992) 41.

[89] The mixed court has been abolished in Armenia, Azerbaijan, Georgia, Kazakhstan, Kyrgyzstan, Lithuania and Moldova. JD Jackson and NP Kovalev, 'Lay Adjudication and Human Rights in Europe' (2006) 13 *Columbia Journal of European Law* 83, 94.

[90] Art 92, para 2, Const-AR; Art 75(2) Const-KA; Art. 47 Const-RU; Arts 124, para 4, 127 para 1, 129, para 2, Const-UK.

[91] Kovalev, above n 26, at 132–33.

[92] *Ibid* 129.

[93] Art 82(5) Const-GE providing for jury trial was added by law in 6 Feb 2004 and a draft CCP providing for an American style jury system has been submitted to parliament.

[94] Jackson and Kovalev, above n 89, at 120.

[95] I have recently received a new draft law proposing the introduction of a classic jury system: *Proekt. Zakon Kyrgyzskoy Respubliki* '*O vnesenii izmeneniy i dopolneniy v nekotorye zakonodatel'nye akty Kyrgyzskoy Respubliki po vprosam uchastiia prisiazhnykh zasedateley v ugolovnom sudoproizvodstve*' (hereafter: Draft Jury Law-KY-2007).

Kazakhstan has taken a path of compromise by introducing a 'jury court,' which began functioning in January of 2007[96] and is patterned on the French *cour d'assise*, consisting in a 'jury' of nine presided over by two professional judges, but in which 'jurors' and judges deliberate together as in a mixed court.[97]

Based on the successes and failures of the Russian jury system, which functioned in nine of its regions and territories from 1993 through 2003 and now exists everywhere except in Chechnya, we can attempt to predict the viability of the future post-Soviet jury systems if they do finally become a reality.

Avoidance of the Jury in Russia

In Russia and in the prospective systems in other republics, jury trials are substantively limited to cases of aggravated murder and a smattering of other crimes.[98] In Russia and in all systems, the right to trial by jury belongs to the defendant and may be waived.[99] Despite the virtual impossibility of obtaining an acquittal in the non-jury courts, a majority of eligible Russian defendants have waived jury trial, choosing ineluctable conviction before professional judges. In the years 1994–2001, only 23 per cent of those eligible proceeded to judgment before the jury court.[100] Since the expansion of jury trial to the rest of the republic defence motions to have their cases heard by juries have declined to around 18 per cent in 2003[101] and to even lower percentages in 2004 and 2005.[102] It is clear that investigators, prosecutors and even defence lawyers pressure defendants to

[96] *Sud prisiazhnykh v Kazakhstane: pervyy god ne vyshel komom*, TSENTRASIA 19 June 2008 http://www.centrasia.ru/newsA.php?st=1213858500 mentions the passage of the law, its going into effect on 1 Jan 2007 and some news of its success.

[97] CCP-KA ss 544, 568, 569.

[98] CCP-RU s 31(3); CCP-AZ s 362; CCP-KY s 240, as amended by Draft Jury Law-KY (2007).

[99] CCP-RU ss 217(5), 325; CCP-KA s 546, ss 402–5, 402–6 Draft Jury Law-KY (2007); CCP-AZ s 24(1), and s 13 Draft Jury Law-GE (2005). Trial by jury was mandatory in pre-revolution Russia, *MV Nemytina, Rossiyskiy sud prisiazhnykh* 24 (Moskva, Bek, 1995), as it is in Spain's new jury system. SC Thaman, *Spain Returns to Trial by Jury*, 21 Hastings Int'l & Comp L Rev 241, 256–58 (1998).

[100] In the years 1997–2001 only 39.2% of eligible cases ended up in the jury courts. *Obzor sudebnoy praktiki rossmotreniia ugolovnykh del s uchastiem prisiazhnykh zasedateley*, Biulleten' verkhovnogo suda Rossiyskoy Federatsii, No. 7 (29 July 2002) http://www.supcourt.ru/vscourt_detale.php?id=2098.

[101] '*Obzor po delam rassmotrennym sudami s uchastiem prisiazhnykh zasedateley v 2003 godu*,' <http://www.supcourt.ru/vscourt_detale.php?id=165> accessed 15 June 2008 (SCRF-Jury Review-2003).

[102] 10.7% in 2004 and 12% in 2005. '*Statisticheskaia spravka o rabote sudov obshcheiy yurisdiktsii za 2005 god*' http://www.cdep.ru/material.asp?material_id=90.

waive jury trial.[103] Cases have also been undercharged, so that they will not be subject to the jurisdiction of the jury courts.[104]

The raising of the maximum punishability to ten years under the Russian consensual procedures will not affect trials for aggravated murder or other grievous offences, but a large swath of lesser crimes will now be subject to the new consensual procedures, facilitating the avoidance of jury trial.[105]

Judicial Nullification of the Jury's Power to Determine Guilt

The Russian legislator rejected the Anglo-American general verdict of 'guilty' or 'not-guilty,' in favour of a special verdict consisting in a list of questions, which was adopted by most Continental European countries in the 19th century.[106] The CCP-RU requires that three basic questions be asked with respect to each crime charged by the public prosecutor: (i) has it been proved, that the charged offence was committed; (ii) has it been proved, that the offence was committed by the defendant; and (iii) is the defendant guilty of having committed the offence. After the trifurcated guilt question, questions may be asked which modify guilt.[107]

Such special verdicts fit well in a Continental European system which requires reasoned judgments, for they compel professional judges, in writing the judgment, to adhere to the logic of the jurors' decision.[108] They also make juries more accountable, especially when rendering a guilty verdict in a serious case.[109] The Russian and Azerbaijani codes and the Georgian and Kyrgyz drafts allow the jury to compel lenience in sentencing

[103] Thaman, above n 6, at 87–88. Sergey Pashin, chief author of the 1993 Russian jury law, shares this view. L Nikitinskiy, '*Prestuplenie i opravdanie*' *Moskovskie novosti*, 8 Apr 2003. Defence lawyers' reluctance to insist on the procedural form more likely to result in an acquittal can only be explained by: (1) fear that a conviction will be interpreted as an indication of their lack of skill as a lawyer, which would hurt their career; (2) their succumbing to pressure on the part of the investigator; or (3) the fact that they are 'pocket lawyers.'

[104] SC Thaman, 'Europe's New Jury Systems: The Cases of Spain and Russia' in N Vidmar (ed), *World Jury Systems* (New York, OUP, 2000) 319, 325–26.

[105] For an estimate that more than 200 criminal offences are now subject to the consensual procedures, *Petrukhin*, above n 33, at 105.

[106] Thaman, above n 104, at 338.

[107] CCP-RU s 339. The identical verdict form may be found in CCP-KA s 566; and s 402–22 Draft Jury Law-KY (2007).

[108] SC Thaman, 'Japan's New System of Mixed Courts: Some Suggestions Regarding Their Future Form and Procedures' (2001–2002) *St Louis-Warsaw Transatlantic Law Journal* 89, 110.

[109] JD Jackson, 'Making Juries Accountable' (2002) 50 *American Journal of Comparative Law* 477, 520 (2002).

by the judge which encourages guilty verdicts instead of jury nullification when jurors fear Draconian judges or sentencing schemes.[110]

Unfortunately, the SCRF has undermined the jury's authority to decide guilt by interpreting the law to restrict jurors to answering questions related to the factual aspects of *actus reus*, and thus arrogating to the professional bench the power to decide *mens rea* and thereby, the question of criminal guilt.[111] It has also articulated such a confused and contradictory line of cases on which 'factual' questions the jury may answer and which 'legal' questions are for the professional judge, that errors in formulating the question list have been the main reason for reversals of jury judgments, especially of acquittals.[112]

The Azerbaijani jury law has abandoned the complicated Russian question list in favour of two simple questions, one of guilt and another as to whether the defendant should receive a lenient sentence; and the parties may request supplemental questions related to lesser-included offences and mitigating circumstances.[113] The most recent draft of the future Georgian CCP goes the furthest, however, in introducing an American style general verdict of 'guilty' or 'not guilty' as to each charge.[114] The Georgian draft also follows American law in making jury acquittals final and not subject to appeal.[115]

Post-Soviet juries will never function autonomously, as true juries, unless their (acquittal) verdicts are not subject to arbitrary reversal by the higher courts. Unlike in the US, the procurator and the victim may appeal judgments of acquittal.[116] Since errors need not be raised in the trial court to preserve them for appeal, a number of prosecutors and judges have

[110] CCP-RU ss 349(2); CCP-AZ s 379(6)(2) allow sentencing below the statutory minimum; whereas CCP-draft-GE s 248 and s 402–31(3) CCP-KY, as amended by Draft Jury Law-KY(2001), prohibit sentencing to more than 2/3 of the statutory maximum. For a return to jury sentencing in the US, see A Lanni, 'Jury Sentencing in Noncapital Cases: An Idea Whose Time Has Come (Again)?' (1999) 108 *Yale Law Journal* 1775.

[111] Thaman, above n 104, at 339–40. For a detailed account of the court's methodology in doing so, see Thaman, above n 44.

[112] *Ibid*. See also Karnozova, above n 33, 168–260 at 43% of all reversals were related thereto in the first three years of jury trial and the trend has continued through 2003. SCRF, above n 101.

[113] CCP-AZ ss 369–370. The Ukrainian draft has also followed this model. See Jackson and Kovalev, above n 89, at 120.

[114] The most recent draft of the 'Special Part' of the proposed CCP includes such a verdict in CCP-draft-GE s 243.

[115] CCP-draft-GE s 251.

[116] Victims can universally lodge appeal whether for review on the facts (*appellatsiia*) or in cassation (ie, on mistakes in the application of the law or on procedural errors). For some of the provisions, see Model Code § 468(1)(3). See also CCP-AR s 404; AR-AZ s 409(1)(2); CCP-BE s 370(1); CCP-KA s 396(2); CCP-KY s 332(2); CCP-LA s 562(2); CCP-LI s 365(1); CCP-RU ss 354(1), 370(1), 385; CCP-TA s 329; CCP-draft-TU s 436(2); CCP-UK s 498.

intentionally committed errors at the pre-trial and trial stage so that, in the event of an acquittal, the errors may be later raised on appeal.[117]

Despite the serious nature of the crimes tried in the jury courts, there has been a much higher rate of acquittals (around 15 per cent) in those courts than in the regular courts (less than 1 per cent).[118] Yet the SCRF has reversed acquittals at an astonishingly high rate in comparison to convictions: from 1997–2001 it reversed approximately 50 per cent of all acquittals and only 16–17 per cent of convictions.[119] The trend continued in 2004 with the SCRF reversing 45.8 per cent of all acquittals which were appealed as opposed to 3.9 per cent of convictions.[120]

Russian courts have cleverly turned the new rules of adversarial procedure, introduced to protect defendants from Soviet-era abuses, into vehicles for overturning acquittals and other defence-favourable verdicts. Thus when a defendant successfully suppresses illegally gathered evidence under the new Russian exclusionary rule it is not infrequent that the prosecutor or the victim appeals on grounds that their adversary rights have been violated.[121] Once the victim is granted 'equality of arms' in an adversary trial,[122] the prosecution has a Trojan horse it can send into the arena to undermine the adversarial rights of the defendant. The SCRF has not hesitated to reverse jury acquittals when the aggrieved party has complained of a supposed violation of his or her rights.[123]

CONCLUSION

> Our social life is like swampy, shaky ground. No matter how wonderful a building is erected on this ground, it vanishes in an unseen manner into this ground, little by little it is sucked up by this soil.
>
> *VD Spasovich*[124]

[117] Judges have admitted doing this in Russia. Karnozova, above n 33, at 152.

[118] Thaman, above n 104, at 348.

[119] W Burnham (ed), *The Russian Federation Code of Criminal Procedure* (2004) 67.

[120] '*Obzor kassatsionnoy praktiki sudebnoy kollegii po ugolovnym delam verkhovnogo suda Rossiyskoy Federatsii za 2004 god*,' <http://www.supcourt.ru/vscourt_detale.php?id=2759> accessed 15 June 2008.

[121] For at least 14 acquittal-reversals on this ground, see Thaman, above n 44.

[122] For some of the provisions giving victims the same adversarial rights as defendants, see Model Code ss 91,358 CCP-BE ss 50,292; CCP-KY s 50; CCP-LA ss 97, 99, 454(2),455; CCP-LI s 27(2); CCP-MO ss 59(7–13), 315; CCP-RU s 42; CCP-TA s 54; CCP-Draft-TU s 351; CCP-UK s 267.

[123] Typically, the SCRF will reverse acquittals when law enforcement organs or the court have not notified the aggrieved party of the day of the trial or have not allowed them to engage in some procedural acts. Thaman, above n 44.

[124] Quote of famous pre-revolution Russian lawyer, in AM Bobrishchev-Pushkin, *Empiricheskie zakony deiatel'nosti Russkogo suda prisiazhnykh* (Moskva, AI Snegirova, 1896) 13.

Can one change the hierarchic, inquisitorial Soviet system of justice by introducing alien institutions from the co-ordinate common law legal sphere? Is a process of 'Americanisation' going on, especially in light of the many American advisers[125] who have been involved in the reforms in many of the former Soviet republics? Can we talk of transplants or translations of these co-ordinate institutions,[126] or merely of their use as democratic legitimisation for systems reluctant to allow these institutions to be catalysts for real change? Will the face of justice in these countries reveal in the end an adversarial American smile, or the 'two-faced' smirk of the entrenched bureaucrats dressed in their new democratic clothes?[127]

The fact that Russia, where all decry the abysmal quality of criminal investigations,[128] can maintain its acquittal-free system despite the introduction of adversary procedure and jury trial leads one to ask whether this 'co-ordinate' edifice is actually only a *Potemkin* village behind which the coerced confession and the perfunctory benediction of contents of the file and accusatory pleading will continue to shape Russia's criminal justice reality.[129] More frightening is the notion that, with the expansion of guilty pleas, the charade of an oral, immediate trial will also be dispensed with and adjudication will recede behind closed doors as in the times of Stalinist terror. If Russian defendants can be coerced or inveigled into waiving a 15–20 per cent chance of getting an acquittal for the inevitable conviction, there is no reason to believe that their waivers of trial and acceptance of the discounted sentence upon guilty plea will be any more voluntary.

A plea bargaining system can only reach just and verifiable results in the post-Soviet world if it is based on evidence gathered pre-trial that has been subject to adversarial testing, which can really provide a factual basis for guilt.[130] The post-Soviet codes provide the framework for exclusion of

[125] The author has consulted on law reform efforts in Russia, Georgia, Latvia, Kyrgyzstan, Kazakhstan and Uzbekistan in relation to jury trial, plea-bargaining and adversary procedure. For criticisms that reforms were instituted just to 'please foreign experts,' see Pomorski, above n 50, at 136.

[126] On the 'Americanization' thesis and the notion of 'translations' in relation to plea-bargaining, Langer, above n 66, at 4–5.

[127] Will the 'internal dispositions' among the organs responsible for implementing the reforms lead to distortion of the original meaning. See Langer, above n 66, at 12.

[128] Thaman, above n 6, at 66–68; Pomorski, above n 50, at 146.

[129] See Damaška, above n 18, at 544. See B Schünemann, '*Reflexionen uber die Zukunft des deutschen Strafverfahrens*' in *Strafrecht, Unternehmensrecht, Anwaltsrecht: Festschrift fur Gerd Pfeiffer* (Köln, C Heymann, 1988) 482–83, for the opinion that Germany's trial is a 'Potemkin facade,' an 'orchestrated blessing of the results of the preliminary investigation.'

[130] For a provocative model of making an adversarial preliminary investigation the centerpiece of a consensual based model of adjudication, see. J Wolter, *Aspekte einer Strafprozessreform bis 2007* (München, CH Beck, 1991) 79–91; T Weigend, *Die Reform des Strafverfahrens: Europäische und deutsche Tendenzen und Probleme* (1992) 104 Zeitschrift der gesamten Strafrechtswissenschaft 486, 506–11. For a similar suggestion, see Bernd Schünemann, '*Reflexionen über die Zukunft des deutschen Strafverfahrens*' in *Strafrecht, Unternehmensrecht, Anwaltsrecht. Festschrift für Gerd Pfeiffer* (1988) 482.

illegally seized evidence but have in no way changed the inquisitorial pre-trial pre-packaging of the evidence by the prosecuting organs, despite token and ineffectual grants to the defence of the right to collect evidence by themselves.[131] Although the one-third discount model of consensual procedure is not as inherently coercive as the wide-open American model,[132] defendants will have no 'bargaining chip' until juries become autonomous co-ordinate decision-makers, not just decoration at an intermediate step in the hierarchical juggernaut of conviction.

The pseudo-oral and pseudo-immediate trial based on the dossier and guided by its truth-seeking judicial trier of fact, and its procedural inducements of confessions, which itself has been characterised by some writers as a form of plea or sentence bargaining,[133] at least requires an in-court confession subject to adversarial testing and a written judgment founded in the materials of the investigative dossier.[134] The more perfunctory the guilty plea and the review of its factual basis, the more risk that innocent persons will end up at the other end of the conveyor belt.[135]

[131] Kovalev, above n 17, at 319–20.

[132] For a discussion on how the latent coerciveness of a 'bargain' grows with the greater gap between maximum punishment and tendered offer see Damaška, above n 65, at 1027–28.

[133] In relation to Japan, see DT Johnson, 'Plea Bargaining in Japan' in M M Feeley & Setsuo Miyazana (eds), *The Japanese Adversary System in Context: Controversies and Comparisons* (New York, Palgrave Macmillan, 2002) 142–45.

[134] Modern German confession-bargains (*Absprachen*), are a more honest recognition of how the inquisitorial trial was really a form of such bargaining. See Thaman, above n 14 at 144–52. See also Langer, above n 66, at 39–46.

[135] For a view that negotiation of an in-court confession, rather than a perfunctory American-style guilty plea better serves the interests of justice in international criminal tribunals, see Damaška, above n 65, at 1037–38.

7

Some Trends in Continental Criminal Procedure in Transition Countries of South-Eastern Europe

DAVOR KRAPAC

INTRODUCTION

THE LAST DECADE of the 20th century saw intense legislative activity in Europe in the field of criminal procedure. This activity can scarcely be summarised in a few general words. The requirements of national criminal policy bounded each European legislature. But each legislature was also exposed to various foreign influences, starting from those emanating from international law (created, for instance, within the Council of Europe or the European Union) to those generated by the requirements of respective national theory and practice.

In the spirit of post-modernist eclecticism of social dialogue and culture, the 1990s contributed to the erosion of clear-cut borders between strictly defined schools and theoretical hierarchies that had previously existed in criminal law sciences. On the one hand, repressive tendencies were on the rise in criminal policy – influenced by conservative policies (encouraged by the Reagan Administration in the USA); on the other hand, there was greater emphasis on human rights protection, especially in the context of the definition of criminal procedure concepts.[1]

A summary account of the complexities of Continental procedure is impossible without generalised and abstract criteria that make it possible to conduct a functional and horizontal comparison of procedural concepts, as legal and non-legal phenomena of particular procedural systems.[2] It has been suggested that a set of eleven criminal policy trends during the last

[1] T Weigend, '*Strafrecht und Zeitgeist*' in Sieber/Albrecht (eds), *Strafrecht und Kriminologie unter einem Dach, Kolloquium zum 90 Geburtstag von Professor Dr Dr hc mult Hans-Heinrich Jescheck*, (Berlin, Duncker and Humblot, 2006) 59–60.

[2] U Sieber, 'Strafrechtsvergleichung im Wandel,' in above n 1, at 112–114.

decade can serve as such criteria for studying Polish criminal law.[3] These trends include *constitutionalisation*, *'self-reduction' of criminal justice*, *'hybridisation' of procedural models*, *internationalisation* of criminal law in general, as well as what is called *Europeanisation* of substantive and procedural criminal law. Another trend has been the *specialisation* of criminal procedure, because the emergence of new forms of crime calls not only for organisational changes in criminal justice, but also for its functional adaptation. In Continental criminal procedure juvenile and military criminal justice have been examples of such specialisation; and lately there has also been some talk of a special criminal justice system for organised crime cases and for cases involving the criminal liability of legal entities.[4]

If we wish to use such trends as criteria for functional comparisons of procedural systems, we must bear in mind two limitations. First, the trends mentioned earlier are actually *criminal policy trends*, for example, an expression of practical legislative activity aimed at resolving issues raised by the task of combating modern forms of crime by coercive measures. Second, however, each of these trends can also be matched with a corresponding *criminal procedure principle*, whose features best express the requirements of the given policy trend. For example, the constitutionalisation of criminal procedure can be linked to the principle of fair trial in criminal cases; the 'self-reduction' of criminal justice can be linked to the principle of economy; whereas the 'hybridisation' of procedural models can be attached to the restraining of official control over the progress of lawsuits, or the principle of contradictoriness.

We should study criminal procedure principles with caution, because this area still lacks standardisation. Indeed, there are many terminological differences and variable contents of the requirements the legislator aims to meet by accepting criminal policy trends and incorporating these principles into statutory texts. Hence, we should not use the principles mentioned as criteria for assessing whether a specific criminal procedure law is better or

[3] Compare S Waltoš, '*Die neue polnische StPO im Vergleich mit dem deutschen Strafprozessrecht*' in T Weigend and G Küpper (eds), *Festschrift für HJ Hirsch zum 70 Geburtstag* (Berlin, W de Gruyter 1999) 996. It is possible to use other criteria to compare procedural systems, such as criteria based on the relationship of criminal procedure towards state authority, substantive criminal law or proof-taking methods in proceedings (see, amongst many other sources: H Jung, '*Der Strafprozess: Konzepte, Modelle und Grundannahmen*' in J Czapska, A Gaberle, A Swiatlowski, and A Zoll (eds), *Zasady procesu karnego wobec wyzwań współczeności* (Warsaw, Wydawnictwa Prawnicze PWN, 2000) 27–35).

[4] See, eg, for Croatia, Z Djurdjević, 'Problems regarding procedural law in the implementation of the Act on Criminal Responsibility of Legal Entities' (2005) 12 *Croatian Annual of Criminal Law and Practice* 739–62; D Novosel, 'Financial investigations and processing economic crime perpetrators' (2007) 14 *Croatian Annual of Criminal Law and Practice* 739–83.

worse than another, but only as a magnifying glass through which we can take a look at the internal organisation of criminal procedure's ideas and structures.[5]

It is also important to note that for an evolutionary diagnosis of national criminal procedure law, no matter how suitable the statements on criminal policy trends seem to be, the starting point for studying the criminal procedures of what are called 'transition countries'[6] in the preceding decade is the fact that these countries experienced 'labour pains' in producing their 'new' criminal procedure systems, which, on the one hand, had to be based on the principles of the rule of law and, on the other hand, had to respond to the increasing need for efficiency in criminal procedure because of new dangerous forms of crime, in particular, organised crime.

These developments produced two paradoxes in almost all transition countries. The first paradox is that these countries introduced criminal

[5] Professor Damaška, to whose enormous contribution to comparative criminal procedure law this paper is dedicated, emphasised a long time ago that the first step in every piece of comparative research is to find out which 'procedural ideas and structural patterns are embraced by classificatory labels of a particular procedural type' (M Damaška, 'Evidentiary Barriers to Conviction and Two Models of Criminal Procedure: A Comparative Study' (1973) 123 *University of Pennsylvania Law Review* 508–9) and later on used this precept to develop his nominalistic theory of the types of judicial proceedings on the basis of their interaction with the hierarchical or co-ordinated organisation of state authority on the one hand, and with the regulatory or dominative objectives of the state on the other (M Damaška, *The Faces of Justice and State Authority* (New Haven, Yale University Press, 1986). Otherwise, for the importance of the comparative method in 'globalised' law, see B Markesinis and J Fedtke, 'The Judge as Comparatist' (2005) 80 *Tulane Law Review* 11, 76–109. For differences between criminal procedures, arising not from the structure of state authority but from elements of social culture, see T Hörnle, '*Unterschiede zwischen Strafverfahrensordnungen und ihre kulturellen Hintergründe*' (2005) 117 *Zeitschrift für die gesamte Strafrechtswissenschaft* 801–838.

[6] According to the definition given by Wikipedia (*Transition economy; Countries in transition,* <http://en.wikipedia.org/wiki/Transition_economy> accessed 16 June 2008), transition economy covers a wider range of countries than merely in Continental and Eastern Europe, which emerge from a socialist-type command economy towards a market based economy and which attempt to change their basic constitutional elements towards market-style fundamentals. This attempt at a definition, however, should refer to different periods in particular countries. Namely, although this global process started in the 1990s, in some countries it is still going on, because the initial crises in the respective societies and economies have not only remained unresolved, but have even deepened (for instance the crisis that ensued from the break-up of the former Socialist Federal Republic of Yugoslavia and the wars in the Balkan area, which led to the creation of the first *ad hoc* international criminal tribunal since the international military tribunals after the Second World War for grave violations of international humanitarian law). In the majority of the former members of the Soviet bloc, the transition is not over yet. The end of transition can only be said for those which joined the European Union on 1 May 2004 (the Czech Republic, Estonia, Hungary, Latvia, Lithuania, Poland, Slovakia, Slovenia). At the time of writing this paper, Croatia, the native country of Professor Damaška, has still not managed to accomplish this, even though in 2005 it opened accession negotiations with the European Union, and transition indicators measuring the performance of its economy show that it is at the same level as some of the countries which joined the European Union in 2004, or is even superior to them.

procedures with high human rights standards while simultaneously experiencing a significant increase in serious crime. This made the public in these countries draw the frustrating conclusion that there was a causal link between these two phenomena, which generated the second paradox in criminal policy. On the one hand, after the adoption of liberal criminal procedure regulations, lawmakers, aware of the bitter experiences of recent, totalitarian history, were reluctant to reduce once again fundamental rights and liberties in criminal procedure for the sake of increasing criminal justice efficiency. On the other hand, law enforcement authorities, primarily the police – who were facing chronic financial and staff shortages in situations where they were expected to ride donkeys in chase of the Ferraris' of experienced criminals while (new) procedural formalities tied their hands– expressed their helplessness and frustration not only through poor work performance, but also by being more brutal towards citizens and petty 'ordinary' criminals. Statistics on police disciplinary procedures in many transition countries can easily substantiate this fact.

As Damaška said in his lectures at Zagreb Law School in 2004 and 2005, when it comes to criminal policy, the law enforcement system exhibited 'neurotic' behaviour. Freud asserted that when an individual's super-ego is too strong he or she behaves neurotically. By analogy, if criminal procedure focuses only on the protection of human rights and neglects imposing efficient punishment on real culprits, or if the legislator has created an ideal procedure, that is not implemented in practice, this may lead to the emergence of various pseudo-procedures by means of which law enforcement bodies aim to accomplish their tasks, which in turn cause various forms of 'neurosis' (including violations of the human rights they are actually supposed to protect).

In transition countries, this situation will persist until it becomes widely accepted in society that procedural guarantees, which were established after the structural 'reversal' of the early nineties, can and must be legitimately restricted in order to combat crime. Those due to take part in this process will probably also include citizens' associations, which previously supported the idea of maximum liberalisation of criminal justice, and will now have to offer greater support to the victims of criminal offences. In criminal legislation and criminal policy, this will be reflected in demands to broaden the legislative framework and introduce new criminal offences, and in court practice in attempts to toughen the severity of the sentences imposed.[7]

[7] Croatia's new criminal legislation, adopted in 1997, initially resisted this tendency, but eventually 'gave in' with the adoption of the 6th amendments to the Criminal Code, which entered into force on 1 October 2006. See, Proceedings of the XIXth Annual Conference of the Croatian Association of Criminal Sciences and Practice, published in *Croatian Annual of Criminal Law and Practice*, vol 13, no 2 (2006) 381–990.

A number of the trends of contemporary criminal procedural law in transition countries[8] should be considered with an eye to the two paradoxes mentioned. In the early nineties these countries, in addition to constitutional reforms,[9] adopted major reforms of their criminal law and procedure.[10] These legislative reforms took place at different speeds.

Among the successor states of the former Socialist Federal Republic of Yugoslavia, Slovenia was the first (Criminal Procedure Act 1994), followed by Croatia and Macedonia (Criminal Proceure Act 1997), the Federation of Bosnia and Herzegovina (Criminal Procedure Act 1998) and (the former) Federal Republic of Yugoslavia, now Serbia and Montenegro (Criminal Procedure Act 2001).

Even though these laws constitute new codifications of the criminal procedure law, they have largely retained the solutions 'inherited' from the Yugoslav or Austrian/Croatian criminal procedure law dating back to the end of the 19th century. These solutions include the division of the law into normative wholes that include general provisions that apply to all procedural phases; provisions on pre-trial proceedings, the trial, appeals and special proceedings; provisions on court jurisdiction, recusal of judges, and procedural powers of the prosecutor, the injured party and the private prosecutor; provisions on the computation of time and the service of court subpoenas; and so on. Major changes were introduced to the provisions on pre-trial proceedings and the trial, where the previously mentioned 'hybridisation' of procedural models originated the largest differences among the countries' regulations.

It is interesting to note two things regarding these reforms. First, the legal tradition and standardised drafting methods greatly influenced the process of formulating procedural law provisions in these countries. In fact, in spite of the very different social circumstances in which the reforms

[8] Here we do not mean transition countries whose state and legal structures were completely destroyed in war conflicts (see R Teitel, 'Transitional Justice: Postwar Legacies' (2006) 27 *Cardozo Law Review* 1615–1631). Neither are we interested in Western European countries with 'old' democracies (for a comparison of the criminal procedure systems in France, Italy, Germany and the United Kingdom, see the comprehensive work M Delmas-Marty/J Spencer (eds), *European Criminal Procedures* (Cambridge, CUP, 2002). Descriptions of criminal procedures in several European countries in the period from 1986–1996 can be found in Feiburg (ed), Eser/Huber (eds), *Strafrechtsentwicklung in Europa, Landesberichte 1993/1996 über Gesetzgebung, Rechtsprechung und Literatur,* vol 5.1 (1997), vol 5.2 (1999).

[9] For comparative constitutional law, see the excellent comparative study by H Roggemann (ed), *Die Verfassungen Mittel- und Osteuropas*, (Berlin, Berlin Verlag Arno Spitz, 1999) 45 *ff*, 61 *ff*, 73–76, 84 *ff*, 110 *ff*.

[10] An extensive comparative law study of criminal procedure systems of 22 transition countries is contained in: B Pavišić and D Bertaccini, *Le altre procedure penali. Transizioni dei sistemi processuali penali*, vol 1 (Turin, 2002) and B Pavišić (ed), *Transition of Criminal Procedure Systems*, vol 2, (Rijeka, Croatia, 2004).

were passed and the new emphases in their criminal policies, there were not many changes in the new laws regarding 'procedural and technical' institutions.

Second, there were tensions and conflicts between the due process and the law enforcement approach to criminal policy: in all these countries, new laws were subject to amendments very soon after their adoption (Slovenia 1999, Croatia 2002, proposed amendments of the Criminal Procedure Act in Macedonia 1999). This shows that the legislatures' initial choices were not completely realistic and that law makers did not adequately weigh Herbert Packer's two models of criminal procedure – the 'crime control' and the 'due process' model.[11]

A similar situation took place in some other transition countries. For instance, the Polish Criminal Procedure Act 1997 was amended in 2000 and 2003;[12] the Hungarian Criminal Procedure Act 1973 was replaced in 1998 by a new law that went through several changes before being adopted by Parliament; the Russian Criminal Procedure Act 1960 was replaced by a new law of 18 December 2001, which had been prepared for four years, and was already amended in 2002 and 2003;[13] and in the period from 1989 until the end of 2001 the Czech Criminal Procedure Act 1961 was amended as many as 16 times.

THREE TRENDS IN SOUTHEASTERN EUROPEAN COUNTRIES

Now let us look at several key features of the new criminal procedure legislation in transition countries in this part of Continental Europe, which can be illustrative of three criminal procedure trends. This overview will be very general in nature; it will be only a brief outline. It will be so general that we shall disregard some issues that are relevant for functional comparative overviews – such as issues that relate to the principal subjects of criminal procedure (such as issues regarding the position of the defendant and the defence counsel, the rights of injured parties, etc), the position of the court (and the extremely important issue of keeping judicial independence safeguards in place while frequent judicial reform take place), important procedural features (especially regarding the sequence of

[11] H Packer, 'Two Models of the Criminal Process' (1964) 113 *University of Pennsylvania Law Review* 1.

[12] 'The goal of [these] amendments was to conduct criminal procedure much more effectively' (P Hofmanski and E Kunštek, 'Poland' in Pavišić, above n 10, at 216.

[13] N Sidorova, 'Russia' in Pavišić, above n 10, at 260.

steps in progress of the pre-trial procedure, and the role of the police), evidence law (especially regarding illegal evidence and legal sanctions against their use),[14] etc.

We shall concentrate solely on the elements of the three general trends of the criminal procedure law of these countries: the constitutionalisation of the procedural rights of participants in proceedings, in particular the defendant; the self-reduction of criminal justice; and what is called the 'hybridisation' of the procedural model.

Constitutionalisation

Constitutionalisation is one of the main development trends in the field of criminal procedure law. As about thirty years ago, the prevailing American view that criminal procedure law was nothing more than a collection of detailed constitutional norms about the relationship between individuals and law enforcement authorities was quite a shock for Continental procedure theory.[15] However, after the constitutional reforms in transition countries – reforms that, in almost all cases, established constitutional courts as supreme guardians of the constitutional order[16] and entrusted such courts with abstract constitutional review and with dealing with individual constitutional complaints – this viewpoint gained wide acceptance.[17]

In Slovenia, the constitutionalisation of criminal procedure was strongly advocated by Professor Zupančić, who viewed constitutional criminal

[14] For these issues, see the useful juxtaposing of two classic models of criminal procedure, the adversarial and inquisitorial in S Thaman, *Comparative Criminal Procedure, A Casebook Approach* (Durham, Carolina Academic Press, 2002).

[15] This was so especially because in the mid sixties the case law of the Supreme Court of the United States under Chief Justice Earl Warren considerably extended the reach of the Fourth, Fifth and Sixth Amendments by making them application to the various states of the United States, thus opening the door to constitutionalisation of criminal procedure law. For more details on this, see AK Pye, 'The Warren Court and Criminal Procedure' (1968) 67 *Michigan Law Review*, 249. Since them most American standard textbooks on criminal procedure have mainly consisted of major cases of the Supreme Court – with some exceptions, such as the M Miller and R Wright, *Criminal Procedures: Cases, Statutes and Executive Materials*, 2nd edn (New York, Aspen Publishers, 2003). For a critical analysis of the state of constitutional criminal procedure, see AR Amar, *The Constitution and Criminal Procedure: First Principles* (New Haven, Yale University Press, 1997).

[16] Compare Roggemann, above n 9.

[17] One of the first countries in Western Europe to introduce the constitutionalisation of criminal procedure law was the Federal Republic of Germany in the early 1970s, when its federal constitutional court, the *Bundesverfassungsgericht,* dealt with specific criminal procedure issues raised in criminal proceedings against members of the terrorist group Baader/Meinhof. The eminent German criminal justice scholar K. Tiedemann wrote that he was sure that German constitutional courts would experience 'what some authors call the constitutionalisation of the criminal procedure law' ((1994) *Revue de science criminelle et de droit penal comparé* 1).

procedure as jurisprudence which aims to achieve demonstrably correct answers to difficult legal (procedural) questions through the interpretation of constitutional principles, such as the rule of law, equality before the law.[18] This type of jurisprudence came into play soon after independence, in two decisions by the Constitutional Court delivered before the amendments to the Criminal Procedure Act 1999.

In the first decision (U-I-18/93 of 11 April 1996), the Constitutional Court of Slovenia repealed on constitutional grounds the provisions on obligatory pre-trial detention and the risk of committing new offences pending charges. The Court found that the provisions on the procedure for ordering pre-trial detention were not compatible with the Constitution because of their vagueness. It also repealed the entire set of measures to ensure the defendant's presence at trial based on the absence of less restrictive measures to achieve that goal. In the second decision (U-I-25/95 of 27 November 1997), the Court repealed, on constitutional grounds, the entire statutory arrangement regulating the use of what are called 'special investigatory methods and means' (for example, clandestine surveillance and recording of the private lives of individuals) in criminal proceedings.

Both decisions ordered the Slovenian legislature to remove the provisions found unconstitutional within a one year; and adopt new provisions on pre-trial detention and modify in part the provisions for securing the defendant's presence at trial and for the use of special investigatory methods and means.

The Croatian Constitutional Court took a similar path when it adjudicated constitutional complaints about pre-trial detention, which is the procedural coercive measure most restrictive of individual liberty. It was in a decision of 1998 that the Constitutional Court for the first time took the position that a constitutional complaint challenging a pre-trial detention warrant based on the violation of the constitutional right to personal freedom is allowed even before criminal proceedings have ended. In that decision, the Court articulated a legal view on the manner in which courts should interpret the statutory notion of 'risk of re-offending' (for example, the risk of the defendant committing new offences pending charges), as the legal basis for ordering detention, and applied it in particular cases (U-III-1162/1997 of 2 December 1998).

In another decision the Croatian Constitutional Court criticised courts' practice of ordering pre-trial detention by sweeping decisions and without sufficiently articulating the reasons for keeping defendants in pre-trial detention. It also ruled that these reasons were to be established pursuant to the provisions of the Constitution of the Republic of Croatia, the

[18] BM Zupančić *et al*, *Ustavno kazensko procesno pravo* (Constitutional Criminal Procedure Law) 3rd edn, (Ljubljana, Atlantis Publishing, 2000).

European Convention on Human Rights[19] and the Criminal Procedure Act (CPA) safeguarding the fundamental right to personal freedom.

The Constitutional Court of the Republic of Croatia derived the latter opinion from three normative requirements, which are based on the postulate of the rule of law. The rule of law requires that in every instance in which personal freedoms are restricted it is necessary to assess in advance whether in that particular case the protection of a specific *public* interest is so important that it outweighs the constitutional principle of inviolability of the individual's freedom and the principle of the presumption of innocence.

These three normative requirements are as follows. First, pre-trial detention is 'an especially sensitive measure of deprivation of liberty' because it is imposed before the person concerned is found guilty by a *res iudicata* decision. According to the principle of presumption of the innocence, pre-trial detention should not be turned into punishment for the defendant, but should remain a measure for ensuring the application and conduct of criminal proceedings. Thus, it should only be applied where there is a high degree of probability that the defendant would be found guilty and sentenced to serve time in prison.

Second, the principle of proportionality referred to in Article 16, paragraph 2 of the Constitution of the Republic of Croatia, together with the principle of proportionality in criminal proceedings (Criminal Procedure Act, Article 87) and the principle of proportionality in ordering pre-trial detention (Criminal Procedure Act, Article 10, paragraph 3), are particularly important in considering whether it is justified and well-founded to prolong pre-trial detention after the expiration of the time limit provided for by law. This is because 'it is only detention which deprives a person of his or her liberty, whereas all other measures only limit this liberty.'

Third, in giving a limited explanation for prolongation of detention a court disregards the safeguards of the detainee's other constitutional rights – such as the right to be acquitted or convicted 'within a statutory time limit' (Art 25, para 2 of the Constitution of the Republic of Croatia) – because a court fails to consider the reasonableness of the length of criminal proceedings when it authorises deprivation of the liberty of a person whose guilt has not been established by a *res iudicata* decision (U-III-3698/2003 of 28 November 2004).

The constitutionalisation of criminal procedure law provides citizens and the state with commensurate procedural footing when the state initiates

[19] A detailed and critical analysis of the influence of the European Court of Human Rights case law on constituting procedural rights of participants in Continental criminal procedure is given by K Ambos, '*Der Europäische Gerichtshof für Menschenrechte und die Verfahrensrechte*' (2003) 115 *Zeitschrift für die gesamte Strafrechtswissenschaft* 583–637.

criminal proceedings against citizens. Regardless of the theoretical question whether and to what extent the constitutional court's supervision of the constitutionality of laws, subordinate regulations and individual legal acts in a specific country violates the principle of supremacy of the legislative assembly over other state bodies, transition countries will continue to apply constitutionalisation in practice. This will result in the implementation of the fair trial principle in criminal cases.

The fair trial principle is the most important new legal value of Continental criminal procedure. All countries with a Continental legal tradition still face considerable difficulties in defining this principle's 'open textured' contents.[20] But the principle makes it possible for such countries[21] to gradually adjust their criminal procedures – without having to abruptly stop using the previous inquisitorial criminal procedure model – to make them conform to the postulate of ever greater participation of procedural participants in the proceedings. The principle also allows these countries to strike an acceptable balance between the need to protect society from crime and the need for human rights protection, in order to prevent the state's efforts in criminal proceedings to establish the 'truth' in criminal proceedings from going too far.[22]

'Self-reduction' of Criminal Justice

Some theoreticians use the term 'self-reduction' of criminal justice to refer to the expansion of the principle of opportunity of criminal prosecution in

[20] The *fair trial* principle in Continental law is not equivalent to the American *due process* principle, although, as regards its ethical foundations, it derives from the same postulate of distributive justice *suum quique tribuere*. However, it is known that American interpretations encouraged the introduction of this principle in international human rights conventions, from which it exerted increasing influence on the national criminal procedures of the states parties to the European Convention on Human Rights of 1951, especially through the case law of the European Court of Human Rights regarding Art 6 of this Convention, first of all the countries of 'western democracy' (eg, Germany starting from a 1969 decision by the Federal Constitutional Court: D Steiner, *Das Fairnessprinzip im Strafprozess*, (Frankfurt, Peter Lang, 1995) 35 *ff*), and then also the transition countries, so it can even be said to represent a normative basis for the standardisation of different procedural systems in Europe, in the same way as the normative contents of the notion of *due process* had an impact on the case law of the US federal Supreme Court (cf JH Israel, 'Free-Standing Due Process and Criminal Procedure: The Supreme Court's Search for Interpretive Guidelines' (2001) 45 *Saint Louis Law Journal* 303–431).

[21] By means of components such as the principle of 'equality of arms,' the party's right of access to an independent judge who must bring the proceedings to an end within a reasonable time by a reasoned judgment, etc (compare R Clayton and H Tomlinson, *Fair Trial Rights* (Oxford, OUP, 2001).

[22] See an informative article by H Jung, '*Der Grundsatz des fair trial in rechtsvergleichender Sicht*' in (H Prütting/H Rüssman (eds), '*Verfahrensrecht am Ausgang des 20. Jahrhunderts*', *Festschrift für G. Lüke zum 70 Geburtstag* (Munich, CH Beck, 1997) 323–336.

Europe[23] and the introduction of numerous procedural forms that are designed to simplify and speed up criminal proceedings and to encourage consensual resolution of criminal proceedings. According to Eser, new legal devices that are designed to facilitate such consensual resolution lead to what is called 'reprivatisation' of criminal proceedings.[24] Under the indisputable influence of American law, here we can find various forms of *plea bargaining*, such as the Italian *patteggiamento* or the Spanish *conformidad* in proceedings for offences prosecuted *ex officio*.[25]

Opportunity Principle

Following the model of Article 162 of the Criminal Procedure Act of the Republic of Slovenia, Croatia introduced into Article 175 of the Croatian Criminal Procedure Act two more situations in which the state attorney decides according to the principle of purposefulness (opportunity), and these two situations are in addition to the previously existing exemptions from the principle of legality of criminal prosecution. Interestingly, when it comes to the seriousness of criminal offences liable to prosecution, these two new situations are at opposite ends of the spectrum.

At one end there are cases involving 'negligible offences.' The Croatian legislature has expressed its willingness to relieve courts of the burden of negligible crime, not only by allowing courts to render an acquitting judgment on the basis of the substantive law provision on what is called 'insignificant' offence, but also by authorising the state attorney, by means of a procedural norm, to find that the insignificant character of an offence constitutes a procedural obstacle to the initiation of criminal proceedings.

In Croatia, the state attorney may temporarily postpone the institution of criminal proceedings for an offence punishable by a fine or imprisonment for up to three years – a type of offence that involves a low degree of guilt – when the extent of the harmful consequences of such an offence does not justify the public benefit of criminal prosecution, provided that the defendant has agreed to fulfil one or more of the six obligations

[23] For example, see P Tak, *The Legal Scope of Non-Prosecution in Europe* (Helsinki, Helsinki Institute for Crime Prevention and Control, 1986).

[24] A Eser, '*Funktionswandel strafrechtlicher Prozessmaximen: Auf dem Weg zur "Reprivatisierung" des Strafverfahrens?*' (1992) 104 *Zeitschrift für die gesamte Strafrechtswissenschaft* 361.

[25] Plea bargaining is of particular interest to German legal theory, as even a cursory glance at a standard textbook on German criminal procedure law reveals a sizeable body of literature on this issue. In Germany, Damaška also exerted influence in this matter with his article '*Der Austausch von Vorteilen im Strafverfahren: Plea-Bargaining und Absprachen*' (1988) 8 *Strafverteidiger* 398–402. See also: T Weigend, '*Eine Prozessordnung für abgesprochene Urteile?*' (1999) 19 *Neue Zeitschrift für Strafrecht*, 57–63; F Meyer, '*Zurück zur gesetzlichen Beweistheorie?*' (2007) 119 *Zeitschrift für die gesamte Strafrechtswissenschaft* 633–63; T Weigend, ch 3.

prescribed. A (tacit) agreement by the court to postpone criminal prosecution was previously obligatory under the law, but in 2002 amendments to the Criminal Procedure Act of Croatia abolished this arrangement, which brought Croatian law in this area even closer to the Slovene law.

Article 145 of the Macedonian Criminal Procedure Act provides that the state attorney may, with the agreement with the injured party, postpone criminal prosecution for an offence punishable by imprisonment for less than three years or by a fine, if the defendant is willing to behave according to instructions given by the state attorney and fulfil certain obligations which reduce or remove the harmful consequences of the offence.

Article 236 of the Criminal Procedure Act of the former Federal Republic of Yugoslavia provided that the state attorney could postpone criminal prosecution for offences punishable by a fine or imprisonment for less than three years if the suspect accepted one or more of four 'measures': removal of harmful consequences, payment of a monetary sum into a humanitarian or public fund, community service and fulfilment of maintenance obligations. However, the state attorney was allowed to immediately reject a crime report if the suspect, 'who feels genuine regret, prevented the occurrence of damage or has already made good the damage,' so the state attorney considers that, in such circumstances, the imposition of a criminal sanction would not be 'fair' (Art 237).

Does this necessarily constitute 'reprivatisation' of criminal procedure, as Eser believes? Not always: reprivatisation occurs only when the state attorney applies the principle of opportunity, using completely unstructured discretion, and thereby arbitrarily prefers the public interest at the expense of the private interest. However, the provisions of the mentioned procedural laws are apparently designed to prevent this sort of neglect of the public interest and to avert this sort of 'privatisation' to a greater or lesser extent.

At the other end of the spectrum there are the gravest offences, usually those related to organised crime, where the state attorney bargains with 'repentant offenders' about desisting from criminal prosecution in return for help in detecting offences or disclosing the names of other members of the criminal groups to which they belong. In Croatia, these matters were until recently governed by only one regulation: Article 176 of the Criminal Procedure Act which authorised the Chief State Attorney to issue a decision dismissing a crime report or desisting from criminal prosecution

> against a person who was a member of a criminal organisation if this is of importance for the discovery of offences and of members of the criminal organisation, in proportion to the gravity of the offences committed and the importance of that person's statement.

In practice, these provisions have raised many issues of interpretation. The legislature tried to solve them through detailed regulatory arrangements contained in the Act on the Office for the Suppression of Corruption and Organised Crime of 2001.[26]

Summary Procedures

New criminal procedures in transition countries show a strong tendency toward 'self-reduction' of criminal justice through a variety of summary procedures. Their popularity is undoubtedly attributed to the desire to speed up proceedings and reduce the backlog of cases in the criminal justice system, as poor in resources and personnel as that system is.

In Croatia, proceedings for issuing a so-called penal order were introduced into the summary procedure system. Croatia was thus following the Austrian tradition in this respect (Arts 446–450). Unless the defendant files an objection against the judgment containing a penal order, such proceedings by penal order are ended by the imposition of a fine of ten to one hundred average daily incomes, a judicial admonition, confiscation of pecuniary benefit obtained in consequence of the commission of an offence, prohibition to operate a motor vehicle for up to two years or seizure of objects. Articles 449–53 of the Criminal Procedure Act of the Federal Republic of Yugoslavia ('proceedings for imposing punishment before the trial') provided for a similar arrangement. Past research in Croatia has shown that the application of the penal order considerably varies from one state attorney's office to another: some use it frequently, others rather seldom, so the Chief State Attorney has a lot of work to do to standardise the practice in this area.

A novelty in Croatia is, for instance, Article 18, para 3 of the Criminal Procedure Act. This novelty, reminiscent of the Italian *giudizio abbreviato*, was introduced by the 2002 Amendments. It provides that the parties may agree before the commencement of the trial about the form of the proceedings; for example, the parties are allowed to agree that the trial in criminal proceedings for offences punishable by imprisonment for up to ten years shall be conducted by the president of the chamber as a single judge, unless the composition of the chamber is prescribed by a special law.

[26] Pursuant to Arts 29–38 of this Act, the Chief State Attorney may, after entering into an agreement with the 'repentant offender' about giving testimony in court, request the court to permit him or her to examine this witness as a 'crown witness'. If a decision is issued to grant this request (this decision is issued if certain substantive and formal requirements have been met), the witness enjoys immunity from criminal prosecution for the offences he or she committed as a member of the criminal organisation against which he or she testifies. The protection of a 'crown witness' is implemented according to the provisions of the Criminal Procedure Act (part of criminal proceedings) and of the special Witness Protection Act (not a part of criminal proceedings). The latter was drafted on the model of similar US federal legislation.

(The parties are not allowed to revoke their consent to this type of proceeding, a proceeding before a single judge.) This change, together with numerous simplified procedural forms in summary proceedings introduced by these Amendments, should – the legislature believed – significantly accelerate proceedings in these kinds of criminal cases and thereby reduce the burdens on the criminal justice system.

Consensual Procedures

'Self-reduction' of criminal justice also results from various methods for resolving criminal proceedings consensually. According to many specialists in criminal procedure, such consensual arrangements represent a fundamental novelty. No novelty in European Continental criminal procedure has perhaps been so strongly advocated or so strongly disputed, as the idea that parties in criminal proceedings should be allowed to reach a settlement.

Since its creation in the mid-19th century, European criminal procedure has been built on the postulates of the rule of law (for example, liberty, equality, the autonomy of the individual). These postulates define the framework for imposing public punishment on perpetrators of criminal offences, and they presuppose the state's monopoly on the use of force and that the legitimation of the exercise of such force is by the legal system, rather than by the procedural participants' consent to punishment.

This is why traditional Continental criminal procedure is hardly compatible with procedures for consensual resolution of criminal proceedings; such consensual arrangements acknowledge that parties have a public interest in deciding not only about the type of proceedings to be conducted, but also about the very functionality of the punishment that the state administers. Regardless of the consensual form involved, whether this be, for instance, the extension of the principle of opportunity of criminal prosecution, or what are called 'diversion' proceedings in juvenile criminal justice, mediation between parties in proceedings instituted upon a private charge, proceedings for issuing a criminal order, settlement reached between the perpetrator and the victim of the offence, the figure of a 'crown witness' or other similar forms – it is beyond doubt that these forms are hardly compatible with Continental criminal procedure, which is focused on determining the perpetrator's guilt or innocence and imposing a legally appropriate criminal sanction on the perpetrator.[27]

[27] It is for this reason that consensual elements should be introduced with caution in the procedure, as, for example, it is done through the case law of the German Federal Supreme Court. S Sinner, *Der Vertragsgedanke im Strafprozessrecht,* (Frankfurt, Peter Lang Verlag, 1999) 187.

Nonetheless, we are witnessing the successful march of these forms into the territory of our criminal procedure law. For example, with its 2002 Amendments to its Criminal Procedure Act Croatia went a step further than Slovenia had gone in 1997, when it had authorised a state prosecutor to dismiss the charges conditionally subjected to the fulfilment of certain obligations by the defendant (Art 162 of the Slovenian Criminal Procedure Act). Article 190a of Croatia's Criminal Procedure Act now authorises 'the rendering of judgment at the request of the parties to the investigation', a procedural form that closely resembles the Italian *patteggiamento*. Parliamentary debates on this procedural form revealed that Members of Parliament had fears about these novelties: one argument was that such a procedural form was contrary to the presumption of the defendant's innocence. But none of these Parliamentary debates about this procedural form had any bearing on the law adopted by Parliament because none of the Members of Parliament attempted to modify or delete the proposed regulations about this procedural form from the legislative proposal submitted to the Croatian Parliament.

The Criminal Procedure Act of the former Federal Republic of Yugoslavia of 2001 prescribed a model similar to the Croatian one. In Articles 455–458, the former Act provided for 'proceedings for punishment and imposition of conditional sentences by the investigating judge', and they provided that when the defendant enters an unconditional guilty plea in the presence of his or her defence counsel, the investigating judge may impose a fine or conditional sentence or imprisonment for less than one year, accompanied by seizure of objects, prohibition to operate a motor vehicle or confiscation of pecuniary benefit at a separate hearing, either at the request of the state attorney filed immediately after the completion of the investigation into an offence punishable by imprisonment of less than five years, or a fine or at the motion of the defendant after the indictment was issued. No appeal may be made against this judgment on grounds of erroneous or incomplete establishment of facts.

The diffusion[28] march of *patteggiamento* will probably continue. However, *patteggiamento* requires the development of a new model of Continental criminal procedure. In contrast to the old model, which was directed towards public punishment within the framework of state authority, the new model should be directed towards introducing a procedure that consists of a preparatory stage as well as a trial, and also includes between them a gradual array of procedural measures and devices for the resolution of proceedings as early as possible and by mutual agreement, with clearly

[28] A factor behind this diffusion is probably the expansion of the American school of thought known as 'philosophical pragmatism' and its epistemological tenets calling for the replacement of 'supreme principles' in cognition by flexible decision-making rules, which are situationally defined and provide for an individual prognosis (Hörnle, above n 5, at 810).

regulated performances and counter-performances of the parties.[29] Ultimately, acceptance of this new model would imply that the current procedural norms, whereby the state attorney and the defendant may only formulate a *consensus* (in the final analysis, only a provisional one) on how to solve a particular situation in criminal proceedings, should be upgraded to make such a consensus legally mandatory, and even actionable.

'Hybridisation'

'Hybridisation' of procedural models in national criminal procedure produces more extensive intermingling of adversary and inquisitorial procedural forms than was found when modern Continental criminal procedure first emerged after the French Revolution. Hybridisation is now visible in preliminary proceedings. (In the territory of the former Yugoslavia, the Criminal Procedure Act of the Republic of Slovenia of 1994, in Article 178, paragraphs 1 and 7, set an example by authorising a 'mini replica' of the trial.)

But hybridisation is generally most clearly evident in the trial. The trial provides particularly fertile ground for the reconstruction of criminal procedure in accordance with the principles of contradictoriness and 'equality of arms.' Subsequently, in 1997, the Criminal Procedure Act of the Republic of Croatia: (a) reorganised the concept of the defendant's declaration, which is made at the beginning of the trial, to allow a defendant to use the declaration to question whether the charge or charges against him or her are well-founded; and (b) restructured the presentation of evidence at the trial by introducing cross-examination of witnesses and expert witnesses to strike a new balance between the adversarial elements of the trial (its public nature, oral presentation, directness, contradictoriness) and the strong inquisitorial elements of the trial. (In Croatia, the president of the chamber previously played a prominent role in collecting and introducing the evidence.)

Now, we shall consider several features of these two 'hybrid' solutions, especially the second one, which involves cross-examination. John H Wigmore, the American evidence scholar, considered the original form of cross-examination in the Anglo-American procedural tradition to be

[29] Sinner, above n 27, at 296.

'beyond any doubt the greatest legal engine ever invented for the discovery of truth.'[30] According to Damaška, it represents one of the *naturalia* of the adversary procedural style.[31]

Defendant's Declaration at Trial

Admittedly, the old Croatian criminal procedure law, ever since its origins in the Criminal Procedure Act 1875, did contain an original model for the interrogation of the defendant at trial. This model first called for 'the defendant's plea to each count of the indictment', and then for 'the presentation of defence', which was intended to allow the defendant an opportunity to take a general stand on the charges against him or her. After this – and only after this – could 'the interrogation of the defendant' take place. This interrogation took the form of an evidentiary proceeding conducted by the president of the chamber and by members of the chamber, if necessary, (the inquisitorial element) and then by the parties (the accusatorial element).

However, the opportunity for the defendant to 'plead to the charges' – as provided for by the 1875 Act – was not used in practice. Rather, the defendant was immediately subjected to interrogation with the intention of using him or her as a source of evidence – before any evidence was presented against him or her. This practice pretty much nullified the guarantees arising from the presumption of the defendant's innocence – a legal principle that not only serves as guidance for judges when they are required to resolve any doubts regarding the facts which are in legal terms relevant to the question of guilt or innocence, but also constitutes a burden-of-proof rule, according to which the defendant is not required either to carry the burden of requesting the production of evidence beneficial to his or her defence or to shoulder the burden of persuading the court of his or her innocence.

In addition, in this interrogation *ad personam*, questions addressed to the defendant often made references to the defendant's previous convictions and such interrogation often delved into information that was relevant only to the court's sentencing decision. According to legal principle known as the presumption of innocence, information that is pertinent only to the sentencing question should not influence the court before it has

[30] See Tillers (ed), JH Wigmore, *Evidence in Trials at Common Law* (Boston, Little Brown, 1983) 608.

[31] The procedural form of the bilaterally submission of evidence through direct and cross-examination is not necessarily implied by the concept of an adversary procedural system. The principal feature of an adversary system is a contest between parties, a contest conducted for the purpose of settling a legal dispute precipitated by an allegation of the commission of crime. These are the real *essentialia* of the adversary style. Compare Damaška, *Evidentiary Barriers*, above n 5, at 564 and Damaška, *The Faces of Justice*, above n 5, at 96.

made a finding of the existence or non-existence of the defendant's guilt. It is therefore clear that interrogations conducted in this way produced results that were contrary to the original purpose of this regulation: namely, given the defendant's testimony during the interrogation – and, in particular, given the information made available to the court in the written dossier about the defendant's prior record – a court with the responsibility of deciding a defendant's guilt or innocence generally would be willing to find the defendant guilty on the basis of less evidence than it would have otherwise have required.

Criminal procedure theorists attempted to solve this 'chronic' problem of all Continental criminal procedures, hybrid in nature, in various ways. Very radical solutions were sometimes proposed, ranging from proposals from dividing the trial into two stages – in the first stage the court would make a decision on the defendant's guilt after holding an oral and adversary hearing, in the second stage the court would make a decision on the sanction after holding a separate hearing – to proposals for the complete revamping of trials on the basis of the accusatorial model.

Professor Damaška suggested the 'revitalisation' of the idea of an initial procedural phase in which the defendant would be expected to take position on the charges against him or her. This suggestion, not unknown in comparative law,[32] was embraced by Croatia in the Croatian Criminal Procedure Act 1997. Under this Act the position taken by the defendant determines the subsequent course of the trial: (1) if, after the reading of the indictment, the defendant states that he or she challenges all or some parts of the indictment, the trial continues with the presentation of evidence and the defendant may not be interrogated before its completion (Art 320, para 7), whereupon the court may, amongst other things, be informed about the defendant's criminal record; however, (2) if, after the indictment has been read, the defendant states that he or she pleads guilty[33] to all counts of the charge, the trial immediately continues by interrogating the defendant with a view to taking his or her testimony and after that with the presentation of evidence.

In this connection, it should be pointed out that in cases where the defendant's affirmative statement contains a full confession of the offence, confirmed by the evidence already gathered, the law provides that the court shall introduce only evidence that is relevant to the court's decision about the sentence (Art 320, para 6). In this way, no discussion is actually

[32] Compare M Damaška, 'On Mixing the Inquisitorial and Accusatorial Procedural Models' (1997) *Croatian Annual of Criminal Law and Practice* 387.

[33] To protect the rights of the defendant without a defence counsel, the law initially allowed him or her to withdraw his or her affirmative statement on the well-foundedness of the charge before the commencement of the presentation of evidence, but this provision was abolished by the 2002 Amendments.

held on the defendant's culpability and the trial moves to the stage in which the only discussion is about the type of sentence and its length. This manner of proceeding constituted a departure from previous procedural forms for the implementation of governmental policy, which preferred the 'officially controlled inquest', as Professor Damaška put it, to agreements between parties.

Direct- and Cross-Examination at Trial

Inspired by some other European Continental systems of criminal procedure, the Croatian legislature, in the Croatian Criminal Procedure Act 1997, restructured the procedures for examination of persons for the purpose of obtaining testimony for use as evidence at trial. This Act specifies that this kind of examination is primarily conducted by parties and only subsequently by the president and other members of the chamber, and that examination by the chamber only occurs only if the chamber finds that this is necessary, as part of its duty to 'take care that the case is thoroughly discussed' (Art 297, para 3).[34]

In this way, in the case of the interrogation of the defendant – either immediately after his or her affirmative statement on the well-foundedness of the charge (Art 320, para 4) or after the presentation of evidence is completed (Art 335) – and in the case of the examination of witnesses and expert witnesses (Art 326), the procedure follows the model of what is called direct and cross examination. In this context, the defendant is always first interrogated by his or her defence counsel, whereas questions are addressed to witnesses and expert witnesses first by the party who moved for the introduction of this evidence, then by the counter-party, and afterwards by the president and members of the chamber, unless otherwise agreed by the parties. However, if the court *ex officio* orders the introduction of evidence, questions will first be put by the president of the chamber, then by members of the chamber, and finally by the prosecutor, the defendant and the defence counsel. The purpose of these rules is in part to

[34] No parliamentary debates were held on the introduction of the new method for presentation of evidence at the trial, according to which the initiative for the presentation of evidence is placed in the hands of the parties. Such quick acceptance of the cross-examination of witnesses and expert witnesses, a principle that is diametrically opposed to the previous method of presenting evidence, may be attributable not only to the desire to restrict the inquisitorial maxim and avoid the partiality of the judge – by strengthening the parties' initiative in the presentation of evidence – but also to a wider, politically-motivated reason: after the disappearance of the policy-implementing state of socialism in which the judge had a noticeable search-finding function, normative principles, such as the principle of legality, came to the foreground. The more this principle is assimilated in general culture, the greater the emphasis laid on the understanding that what matters in adjudication is not so much the judge's capabilities, but the procedural options the parties have at their disposal to influence its outcome (Hörnle, above n 5, at 819).

restrict excessive initiative of the president and members of the chamber in the establishment of facts, which can undermine objectivity.[35]

Evaluation of the Results of the Two Hybridising Reforms

Although lack of space precludes detailed consideration, we can say that the results of the application of both procedural solutions described above – even though they diverge to a certain extent from their original form in the Anglo-American procedural tradition – show that they are 'successful legal transplants':[36] with the passage of time after their implementation in the national procedural system, they achieved a consensus among participants in the criminal procedure in practice and have thus passed the test of time – which is an operational concept of truth within the meaning of Popper's philosophy of science.[37] A survey conducted among Croatian judges in the two largest Croatian cities – Zagreb and Split – on the application of these two 'hybrid' procedural solutions showed that implanting elements of the 'pure' adversarial procedure into the traditional, for example, mixed, procedure is not impossible and that during the three years after the introduction of these new procedural forms, these were applied almost faultlessly.[38] Only in some respects was their 'integration' with the old tissue questionable.[39]

The survey found that Croatian judges are very careful when taking testimony from the defendant about the well-foundedness of the charge (Art 320, para 3); it was found that judges take care that the defendant understands the relevance of this testimony for the further course of the trial (for the course of what is called 'bifurcated trial'). Judges have

[35] The Croatian Criminal Procedure Act 1997 also attempts to restrict excessive judicial initiative in proof-taking by attaching greater legal significance to motions for the introduction of evidence put forward by parties, by providing that such motions are legally mandatory for the court, and can only be rejected based on public interest exemptions. See, Croatian Criminal Procedure Act 1997, Art 322 (modelled after some foreign laws, such as the German and the Polish). This regulation increases legal certainty not only in the presentation of evidence at the trial, but also in rendering a judgment, because in its Statement of Reasons for a written judgment the court must precisely indicate why it rejected a particular motion for the introduction of evidence (Art 359, para 7).

[36] For the phrase 'legal transplants', see D Nelken and J Feest (eds), *Adapting Legal Cultures*, (Oxford, Hart Publishing, 2001).

[37] See RA Posner, 'The Jurisprudence of Skepticism' (1988) 86 *Michigan Law Review* 857.

[38] The statistics on appellate cases at the Supreme Court of Croatia in 1999 and 2000 reveal an almost negligible number of appeals on the grounds of substantial violation of criminal procedure relating to breaches of Criminal Procedure Act provisions. This led to a reform of the trial in 1997. Incidentally, statistics on courts kept by the Ministry of Justice of Croatia show that in Croatia the intervention of appellate courts against first instance judgments stands at about 50% on average, where the erroneous or incomplete establishment of facts was found to be the reason for such intervention in about 60% and procedural violations in about 30% of the cases where the first instance judgment had been quashed.

[39] See D Krapac and M Mrčela, 'The New Practice of the Criminal Procedure Trial' (2000) 7 *Croatian Annual of Criminal Law and Practice* 803.

correctly interpreted the defendant's silence at that critical moment as challenging the well-foundedness of the charge. When judges had doubts as to whether the defendant had fully understood the meaning of his or her testimony, they would repeat the substance of the charge and clarify the circumstances which raised these doubts. Yet, in doing so, judges would very rarely or never use the option of holding a special hearing provided for by the law for this purpose.

The survey found that the common situations in which the defendant who had previously pleaded guilty to any of the counts of the charge afterwards changed his or her original statement when giving testimony about the facts of the case (the so-called 'vague defence') is handled properly by the majority of the surveyed judges: they interrupt the defendant's testimony and state for the record that the testimony clearly indicated that the defendant is challenging the charge. They would then shift to the presentation of evidence and interrogate the defendant only after the presentation of the evidence against the defendant has been completed. However, the surveyed judges divided over the appropriate treatment of co-defendants who take different positions on the question of the well-foundedness of the charge: the majority of judges would start interrogating a defendant who pleads guilty to the indictment, and 'leave' the co-defendants, who challenged the indictment, for the end of the presentation of evidence, thus keeping them present in the courtroom during the whole trial.

The survey found that interrogations of the defendant were conducted unevenly, regardless of the fact that the law gives priority to cross-examination by the defence counsel and the prosecutor before the president and members of the chamber. Some judges would, after the defendant's statement and in agreement with the parties, immediately interrogate the defendant by themselves and would then give the floor to other participants in the proceedings. Other judges would – again with the parties' consent – intervene in the defendant's free presentation with questions and secondary questions, to fill gaps of meaning and eliminate contradictions. And finally, there were also judges (about one third of those surveyed) who would ask questions only after the parties had completed their cross-examination. Only the conduct of this latter group of judges is in the spirit of the new model of the criminal trial in Croatia.

As regards the process of presentation of evidence at the trial, the survey showed that judges in Croatia still embody the spirit of 'initiative' in evidence taking. Although the majority of them first invited the parties to propose[40] the introduction of their evidence and then decide which of the

[40] These motions are, in general, much less frequent than motions for the introduction of evidence filed by parties in the 'pure' adversarial procedural system because in the Croatian criminal procedure, much as in other Continental procedures, which are based on a different,

proposed items of evidence would actually be introduced (referring in this regard to the statutory grounds for rejecting motions for the introduction of evidence referred to in Article 322, paragraph 4 of the Criminal Procedure Act), generally speaking the control of fact-finding remains in the hands of the president of the chamber, who still has the duty to

> take care that the case is thoroughly discussed and that matter which delays the proceedings without contributing to the clarification of the case is removed.
>
> (Criminal Procedure Act, Art 297, para 2)

Finally, the survey indicates that one of the most important novelties in the law – the cross-examination of witnesses and expert witnesses during the presentation of evidence – does not present any major difficulties in technical terms for the majority of judges: less than three years after the entry into force of the CPA, the new model was followed by 62.5 per cent of municipal (that is those with jurisdiction over lesser offences) and 84.62 per cent of county (that is those with jurisdiction at the first instance over serious offences) judges participating in the survey. This means that cross-examination has taken hold in practice.[41]

In this regard, the survey revealed two important pieces of data: that 20.83 per cent of municipal judges would always first examine witnesses or expert witnesses, regardless of whether the parties had reached an agreement to that effect or whether they had consented to this; and that in 15.38 per cent of proceedings before county judges, parties would always surrender to the president of the chamber the right to be the first to examine witnesses or expert witnesses.

As a result, it was suggested, first, that for trials before municipal courts the model of the cross-examination of witnesses or expert witnesses should be prescribed as an option for parties, rather than as obligatory, and, secondly, that special procedural *incentives* should be found and introduced to better prepare parties, especially in regard to the public prosecutor's burden to gather evidence and examine it before the court.

Of these two initiatives, the Croatian legislature only accepted the first when, by amendments to the Criminal Procedure Act of May 2002, it simplified summary trials by removing the division, that is the 'bifurcation' of the course of the trial on the basis of how the defendant pleads. (The law provides that the defendant is always interrogated at the beginning of the presentation of evidence, no matter how he pleads, and that questions

eg, 'inquisitorial' paradigm, the trial is preceded by *ex officio* police and judicial inquiries aimed at supplying the court with evidence, unimpeded by party allegations and proof offers. See MR Damaška, *Evidence Law Adrift* (New Haven, Yale University Press, 1997) 118.

41 This is also confirmed by the 'control' piece of information showing that procedural violations of methods of the cross-examination of witnesses or expert witnesses did not appear as grounds for an appeal in proceedings before county courts.

are addressed to the defendant first by the judge and then by the parties – and that he or she is first interrogated by the defence counsel and only then by the prosecutor.) However, the majority of the provisions governing the trial remain unchanged in these amendments.

CONCLUSION

So what can be said in conclusion about this brief outline of development trends in criminal procedure in some European countries in transition? The first conclusion reached by those familiar[42] with the developments surrounding criminal procedure law in countries in transition is undoubtedly that the reform of this branch of law has actually become an ongoing process. On one hand, reform has provided a fairly high level of protection of human rights and defence rights in criminal procedure, a level of protection that, when taken as a whole, meets international standards. This success in reform includes the cases of 'successful procedural transplants.'

However, we should keep in mind the considerations mentioned in the introductory part of this paper – that in the eyes of the public criminal procedure has become too complicated, too long and inefficient to deal effectively with certain types of crime. This public sentiment is particularly strong in relation to the growing problem of organised crime; it is widely believe that participants in organised crime do not expose themselves to a significant risk of detection and punishment, and that for them crime thus pays. Such sentiments and beliefs naturally cause dissatisfaction and frustration among the public, and also among law enforcement authorities.

These worries, however, are not adequately addressed by the leading political figures: political personalities generally either place too much emphasis on the need for the protection of human rights or offers sweeping criticisms of the inability of the criminal justice system to deal with complicated cases without making serious attempts to resolve many issues in the field of crime definition, policing and adjudication.[43] This political ineptitude justifies the question which is often posed: are criminal law and criminal procedure law in transition countries at all capable of being regarded as appropriate and useful instruments of social control? The

[42] Compare J Musil, 'Grundlinien der Strafverfolgung und praktische Umsetzung' in A Eser, J Arnold and J Trappe (eds), *Strafrechtsentwicklung in Osteuropa*, (Berlin, Duncker and Humblot, 2005) 283–295.

[43] For serious criticism of the political system, and in particular the concepts of constitutional law, which in the USA have a significant influence on the politics of crime by shaping political rhetoric and introducing overpunitiveness and undermining liberty and autonomy interests, compare WJ Stuntz, 'The Political Constitution of Criminal Justice,' (2006) 119 *Harvard Law Review* 780–850.

answer to this question should be left to theory and practice, working together with the goal of finding the right track for criminal policy in each particular country.

II

Re-Exploring the Epistemological Environment

8

Dances of Criminal Justice: Thoughts on Systemic Differences and the Search for the Truth

ELISABETTA GRANDE

I. OBSERVING PROCEDURES FROM THE SHOULDERS OF DAMAŠKA

MORE THAN THIRTY years ago, Mirjan Damaška offered his seminal contribution to comparative criminal procedure by demonstrating that serious comparative understanding, for the purpose of fruitful communication among legal traditions and of a better grasp of domestic procedural systems, requires a simple analytical tool.[1] Damaška moved beyond the old taxonomy based on the over-used dichotomy of '*accusatorial v inquisitorial*' procedures, which carries with it a multiplicity of referents, and as a result proving itself incapable of a clear contraposition between the two types of procedure. Damaška articulated the core contrast between contemporary common law and Continental criminal procedures as involving alternative patterns of distributing procedural control. His observation of the systems in action located the essence of the common law style, that is of the *adversary* model, in the allocation of control over the proceeding to the conflicting parties of the dispute. He thus pointed to a sharp contrast with the fundamental matrix of the Continental style, that is of the *non-adversary* model, where that same control is allocated to non-partisan officials. Where parties monopolise procedural action, the process takes the form of a contest between the prosecution and the defence; on the contrary, where the judge or some other official is in charge, the process turns into an enquiry into the alleged commission of a crime.

Organising the two rival procedural models around the basic idea of a party-controlled contest as opposed to an officially-controlled inquest,

[1] MR Damaška, 'Evidentiary Barriers to Conviction and Two Models of Criminal Procedure: A Comparative Study' (1973) 121 *University of Pennsylvania Law Review* 506.

provided the intellectual framework for grasping the intimate essence of the two procedural styles and a fresh understanding of their different structural arrangements. In a new light, many features, which according to the old taxonomy were considered as essential characteristics of one of the two contrasting models, proved to be comparatively irrelevant. Thus, many procedural arrangements historically associated with the inquisitorial or the accusatorial models, such as for example – in relation to the former – a career judiciary, secrecy, and written evidence, or – concerning the latter – jurors, publicity and oral testimony, appeared compatible with both models of procedure when approached in practice. Thus '[f]orensic contest can' indeed

> unfold in secrecy, before career judges, with disputation centring on documentary evidence, while an official inquiry can be conducted in public, by lay persons who rely on oral testimony.[2]

The inquisitorial versus accusatorial opposition was consequently comparatively sterile; the fundamental difference between common law and civil law procedures had to be grasped elsewhere. In the new alternative perspective, presented by Damaška, the focal point capable of differentiating the common law proceeding from the Continental one is the role assigned to the parties as opposed to the officials in the fact-finding process: a common law model of fact-finding managed by two contestants, who shape the extension of their dispute, as opposed to a Continental model where fact-finding responsibilities are assigned to court officials.

At the core of this polarisation lies a very different attitude toward the search for the truth characterising the two procedures. In this chapter I submit that, far from one procedural type being more committed to the truth than the other,[3] the systemic difference, clarified by using Damaška's framework, is to be located in the paths that the systems follow in searching for the truth and in the assumptions about what type of truth is deemed discoverable through the criminal process.[4]

Starting from the idea that a third party ascertainment of the truth is possible, the non-adversarial system pursues the discovery of an objective truth (the 'revered Continental concept of substantive truth'[5] as opposed to

[2] MR Damaška, 'Models of Criminal Procedure' (2001) 51 *Zbornik PFZ* (Collected Papers of Zagreb Law School) 477, 484.

[3] For a strong argument in support of the thesis that one procedural type is more committed to the truth than the other, see MR Damaška, *Evidence Law Adrift* (New Haven, Yale UP, 1997) 120 *ff* and Damaška, above n 1, 578 *ff*.

[4] For a deep discussion as to whether aspiring to objective truth is realistic, see MR Damaška, 'Truth in Adjudication' (1998) 49 *Hastings Law Journal* 289. Even if one deems that in the abstract an objective truth is discoverable, it still remains open to question how in concrete terms the objective truth is attainable in the criminal process. However, this chapter does not dare tackle the major philosophical debate about the nature of 'truth'.

[5] Damaška, above n 1, 581, n 199.

the procedural truth), which I will call *ontological truth*, based as it is on the belief that an objective reconstruction of reality is attainable. For this purpose, the enquiry is assigned to non-partisan officials. Being responsible for the ultimate decision on the issue of guilt or innocence, they are committed to the completeness of the evidentiary data-base and to the accuracy of factual findings. In this sense, the discovery of the 'ontological' truth follows the ordinary patterns of everyday life. As Damaška explains:

> In their personal and business affairs, people are in the habit of actively taking part in obtaining knowledge about facts on which their decisions turn. As students, they ask questions in wrestling with ideas expressed in professional lectures. And in specialised fields of inquiry – such as history – they cherish their freedom actively to inform themselves about the subject of their study.[6]

Consequently, justice in the non-adversary model is believed to be served when the ascertainment of the *objective*, *substantive, ontological,* truth has been accomplished.

By way of contrast, the adversarial system adopts the perspective that there is no such ontological truth that can be ascertained by a neutral party, because neutrality is simply impossible to achieve. Even genuinely disinterested third parties inevitably form early hypotheses of the reality they seek to reconstruct. 'Because people assimilate information selectively',[7] their initial hypothesis makes them more receptive to evidence confirming it. Consequently, they will interpret in an unconsciously biased way the information they assume in order to ascertain the truth. As a result of the recognition of these cognitive limitations, adversarial systems deem any third party reconstruction of the facts as biased and non-objective and a truly non-partisan approach in searching for the truth as unachievable in the human world. The search for the truth in a legal process needs therefore to depart from ordinary cognitive practices, and has to be pursued through a fair confrontation of two parties, each one promoting her side of the story in front of a passive adjudicator. What results is a different notion of truth that, short of being 'ontological', is indeed the product of a contest between two interpretations of reality.

In this chapter I will call this conception of truth *interpretive truth* to point to its scepticism towards an objective reconstruction of reality. In this perspective, the only realistically discoverable truth is a 'second-best' one, compared to the 'ontological' truth pursued by non-adversarial systems. This 'interpretive' truth emerges from the parties' opposing views of reality, provided – of course – that fair rules are established and respected. Justice and fairness are thus inevitably strictly equated in the adversary model

[6] Damaška, above n 3, 90.
[7] *Ibid* 95.

because only a fair contest can bring about just results.[8] The 'relational' nature of the truth-discovering enterprise in an adversarial system produces what I would call a 'tango' idea of justice. As in tango, where it takes two – and only two – to dance, in an adversarial conception it takes two to produce a reconstruction of reality that can be equated to truth.[9] I will later develop an alternative notion of justice based on the metaphor of the rumba dance. As in the dance, in 'rumba justice' a variety of dancers (the parties, the victim, and the officials) perform together in a collective search for the 'ontological' truth.

To sum up and restate my argument, the historical truth that the two models assume is discoverable through the criminal process is different: an 'ontological' (or 'objective', or 'substantive') as opposed to an 'interpretive' truth. I argue that the Continental idea of justice, or 'rumba justice', reflects the notion of an 'ontological' truth, while 'tango justice' reflects the notion of an 'interpretive' truth. This is not an essay on the relationship between justice and truth in general. Rather, I wish here only to show that discrete notions of truth might carry different notions of justice. When justice is located within an adversary framework of 'interpretive truth', it equates to fairness. When, on the contrary, it is located within a Continental framework of 'ontological truth', it differs from the notion of fairness and is a thicker concept.

II. THE RECENT ROOTS OF INTERPRETIVE TRUTH IN THE COMMON LAW

The divergence between non-adversary and adversary models outlined above, that is between non-partisan and dialectical searches for the truth in the criminal process, does not reach far back into the history of legal systems. On the contrary, as with many relevant systemic differences, it is relatively recent. According to John Langbein, its origins can be traced back to the end of the eighteenth and the beginning of the nineteenth centuries.[10]

After the abandonment of trial by battle, as early as the thirteenth century, common law lawyers deployed a criminal procedure system where the search for the truth was largely entrusted to a trier of fact who actively

[8] For a philosophical point of view on the subject, see J Rawls, *A Theory of Justice* (Cambridge, Mass, Harvard University Press, revised edn 1999).

[9] In this sense, the dispute-solving goal does not seem at odds with a truth-finding goal. In fact, the former is the essence of the latter, because in the adversary system solving the dispute is the method to ascertaining the truth.

[10] JH Langbein, 'The Criminal Trial before the Lawyers' (1978) 45 *University of Chicago Law Review* 263, 316 ('Adversary procedure cannot be defended as part of our historic common law bequest').

intervened in the fact-finding process. This was so, not only during Angevin times, when juries were self-informing,[11] but also until much later.

To be sure, by the late fifteenth century, 'it had become expectable that jurors would be ignorant of the crimes they denounced and determined'.[12] But still well into the end of the 18th century, despite the celebrated 'altercation' between citizen accuser and citizen accused described by Sir Thomas Smith,[13] the normal absence of prosecution and defence counsel (except than in cases of treason) pressed the judge, as a third party, to assume an active role in the fact-finding process.

As Langbein explains, reporting on the unfolding of the Old Bailey trials:

> To the extent that evidence was not adduced spontaneously in the altercation of accuser and accused, it was the trial judge who examined the witnesses and the accused, and it was he who, like the modern Continental presiding judge, dominated the proceedings.[14]

> It was the task of the trial judge to help the accuser establish the prosecution case as well as to be 'counsel for the defendant'.[15]

> The common practice clearly was for the judge to take the victim and any accusing witnesses through their testimony line by line, acting as both examiner and cross examiner, until he was satisfied that the fullest possible case had been presented.[16]

The trial judge, moreover, relentlessly questioned the accused, who was urged to speak, in a truth finding effort that mirrored ordinary cognitive practices.[17] Throughout the 18th century, consistent with the goal of the criminal process being to discover the 'ontological' truth, guilty pleas were virtually non-existent and judicially rejected on the grounds that they were

[11] 'In the thirteenth century "it is the duty of the jurors, so soon as they have been summoned, to make inquiries about the facts of which they will have to speak when they come before the court. They must collect testimony; they must weigh it and state the net result in a verdict." Medieval juries came to court more to speak than to listen': JH Langbein, 'The Origins of Public Prosecutor at Common Law' (1973) 17 *The American Journal of Legal History* 313, 314, quoting F Pollock and FW Maitland, *The History of English Law before the Time of Edward I* vol 2 2nd edn (Cambridge, CUP, 1898) 624–25.

[12] *Ibid* 315.

[13] T Smith, *De Repubblica Anglorum* (Mary Dewar, ed, Cambridge, CUP, 1982, 1st edn, 1583), bk 2, ch 23.

[14] Langbein, above n 10, 315.

[15] JH Langbein , 'The Historical Origins of the Privilege against Self Incrimination at Common Law' (1994) 92 *Michigan Law Review* 1047, 1051.

[16] *Ibid* n 16, quoting JM Beattie, *Crime and the Courts in England: 1600–1800* (Princeton, Princeton UP, 1986) 342.

[17] '[T]he very Speech , Gesture and Countenance, and Manner of Defense of those who are Guilty, when they speak for themselves, may often help to disclose the Truth, which probably would not so well be discovered from the artificial Defense of others speaking for them': W Hawkins, 2 *A Treatise of the Pleas of the Crown* (Garland Publishing, 1978, London 1721) ch 39, §2 as quoted by Langbein *ibid* 1053.

not voluntarily given.[18] In common with both the old and the modern Continental judge, the common law trial judge before the late 18th century combined the task of fact-finding with the task of fact adjudication:

> The Old Bailey judge was a real participant in adjudication, and in this sense his role was closer to that of the Continental judge than to that of the passive traffic controller who presides over modern Anglo-American adversarial system.[19]

The judge used to maintain an informal communication with jurors, which enabled him to control their deliberations. The close interaction between judge and jury

> allowed the trial judge to get some insight into jurors' thinking before they left for deliberations; further, the judge could also discover the reasons for a proffered verdict when the jury returned from deliberations, because in many cases the jury either volunteered the information or supplied it under questioning by the judge.[20]

In fact,

> [i]f the jury attempted to return a verdict (whether of guilt or innocence) that displeased the judge, the judge had the power to reject it provisionally. He would then question the jurors about their thinking, explain to them why he differed with them (be it on matters of law or fact), and require them to deliberate and decide again. It took a determined jury to resist such pressure.[21]

Jury verdicts were in sum, 'collaborative products, impounding deep judicial involvement on the merits'[22] and the pursuit of the truth was very much a matter of judicial enquiry.[23]

Common law and Continental proceedings were consequently not distinguishable at this time along the lines of the *party-controlled contest/officially-controlled inquest* alternative suggested by Damaška, although

[18] JH Langbein, 'The English Criminal Trial Jury on the Eve of the French Revolution' in A P Schioppa (ed), *The Trial Jury in England, France, Germany 1770–1900* (Berlin, Duncker and Humblot, 1987) 29.

[19] Langbein, above n 10, 315.

[20] JH Langbein, 'Historical Foundations of the Law of Evidence: A View from the Ryder Sources' (1996) 96 *Columbia Law Review* 1168, 1190.

[21] Langbein, above n 18, 36.

[22] Langbein, above n 20, 1195.

[23] Even before John Langbein's research, conducted on the Old Bailey Session Papers, produced strong evidence of it, Professor Damaška pointed out how common law criminal proceedings before the 19th century were fundamentally non-adversary. 'The adversarial style of processing criminal matters is largely a product of the early 19th century. Until the middle of that century, the pre-trial phase of the process was essentially a type of judicial investigation along inquisitorial lines conducted by justices of the peace. Nor was the trial an adversary battle of counsel. Lawyers would seldom appear for the prosecution and defence counsel were not admitted in ordinary felony cases until 1837. In this situation the judge called witnesses and examined them, and in the century prior, had also interrogated the defendant.': MR Damaška, 'Structure of Authority and Comparative Criminal Procedure' (1975) 84 *Yale Law Journal* 480, 542, n 156.

there were a number of contrasting features between them, many of which were associated with the repressive arrangements of the Continental criminal procedure prior to the French revolution.

The revolutionary change that accounts for the modern polarisation between non-adversary and adversary models has its roots in more than one factor. What made the common law depart from a searching style for the ontological truth, which was up to then shared with its Continental counterpart?

Certainly, the lawyerisation of the proceedings, that is the advent of an era in which lawyers both for the prosecution and the defence became the main actors in the common law criminal process, can be held accountable for the rise of the new style. Prosecuting counsel had always been permitted, but rarely employed until the early 18th century. English courts allowed felony defendants to have the assistance of counsel as early as the 1730s but solely for the purpose of examining and cross-examining witnesses. In 1836 a statute finally allowed defence counsel to make a closing address to the jury. Beginning in the 1780s, defence representation at trial became the rule. By the end of the 18th century, the regular presence of opposing counsel pressed the judge to become passive while counsel conducted the trial.[24]

The novel posture of the trial judge as a mere umpire of the forensic contest was certainly made easier by the very fact of the existence of the jury as a separate body accountable for fact determination. Released from the ultimate decision on the issue of guilt or innocence – a task that jurors now exclusively had to bear on their shoulders – the trial judge could easily divest himself of the authority over the fact-finding process. The absence of a bureaucratic pre-trial procedure, of the sort that was in place on the Continent with its emphasis on a judicial search for the truth as opposed to the English system of private prosecution, helped the transition to the adversarial style as well.[25]

Another important factor accounting for the common law adversarial style was the strong impact of *laissez-faire* Lockean values on English institutional arrangements in general and, for the purpose of the present argument, on procedural choices in particular. The narrowing of judicial functions was indeed germane to the ambition of classic English liberalism to limit state intervention. The government was to be kept out of the citizen's life as much as possible and the role of the judge was to be limited in the criminal process. The classic liberal urge to keep the state at arms length required the restructuring of the criminal process as a dispute

[24] For bibliographical support on all these points see Langbein, above n 15, 1048, 1057 *ff*.

[25] On this point see more extensively Langbein, above n 10, 316. Professor Langbein's thoughts on the origins of the adversarial style in criminal matters are to be found in JH Langbein, *The Origins of Adversary Criminal Trial* (Oxford, OUP, 2003).

between two sides – the prosecution and the defence (very much conceived as private parties) pursuing their opposing interests in front of a passive state official who was given virtually no involvement in the investigation of the actual facts.

In the classic liberal framework, any intervention of the judge in shaping the proceeding – by raising matters, adducing or supplementing parties' evidence, examining or cross-examining witnesses, raising *ex officio* questions of admissibility or inadmissibility, rejecting parties' stipulations, and so forth – was perceived as an unacceptable invasion of individual freedom by the state. As a result any official control over fact-finding had to be removed. Henceforth, the search for the truth was assigned to the battle between the adversaries and, in order to make the battle a fair contest, the law of evidence, only applicable on request by the parties, was developed. Underlying the new procedural style was a general attitude of scepticism toward objectivity: 'Since no belief or idea regarding human affairs' was considered 'exclusively or demonstrably true',[26] a third party factual enquiry was regarded as an imposition upon the parties of an arbitrary single-sided reconstruction of reality. Thus, according to classical liberal ideology, neutrality and objectivity, viewed as unattainable in the human world, were even more suspect if vested in the much distrusted state officials.

In the common law perspective, a change of view of what promoted veracity occurred. The new order substituted the previous reliance upon a third party factual enquiry with the faith in the truth-detecting efficacy of a fair contest between two parties. An 'interpretive' truth, stemming from an equally-balanced confrontation between two one-sided accounts of reality (neither one of them possessing the complete truth), took the place of the 'ontological' truth as ascertained through a neutral enquiry. In light of this transformation, fairness became the cipher of justice, substituting the 'impossible' discovery of the 'objective' truth. To borrow from Damaška's words:

> Transplanted to America, the classic liberal ethos fell upon fertile soil. Such circumstances as the frontier society, the natural abundance of resources, and the religious legacies of 17th century Protestantism, facilitated the introduction of liberal disposition toward authority into the American political culture to an extent astonishing even to English 19th century liberals.[27]

[26] Damaška, above n 23, 532.
[27] *Ibid* 542.

III. THE CONFIRMATION OF THE ONTOLOGICAL TRUTH IN CONTINENTAL EUROPE

To be sure, the attack launched by the classic liberal credo against the very idea of a 'neutral' enquiry in the search for the truth did not spare the Continent either. Over time, changes in Continental procedural arrangements show the desire of Continental systems to cope with the 'lack of neutrality' problem. Nevertheless, they never went so far as to provoke the Copernican revolution that occurred in the common law world. Continental lawyers refused in fact to renounce the idea of searching for a 'substantive' (or 'objective' or 'ontological') truth in the criminal process.

Starting from the beginning of the 19th century, the secret, unilateral, and official enquiry that had dominated previous Continental criminal proceedings for more than half of a millennium came increasingly under attack. Over the next 200 years, Continental criminal procedure was relentlessly modified in order to make its features compatible with the changed political and social climate that followed the French Revolution.

Continental systems seeking to protect defendants against governmental oppression abandoned for good negative features like the absence of specific charges, unlimited pre-trial detention, the presumption of guilt, coerced and unreliable confessions, unbridled searches and the absence of right to defence counsel. Changes in Continental procedural arrangements were also aimed at coping with the problem of the possible lack of neutrality of the official truth seeker. It became clear that the more the enquiry was unilateral, the higher the risk of undermining the truth seeker's impartiality. From this perspective, the introduction in the French *Code d'instruction criminelle* of 1808 of two additional figures – the prosecutor and the defence counsel – within the new, so-called, 'mixed' system of criminal procedure was the first step in the move towards making the official enquiry more pluralistic and unbiased overall. The prosecutor was given the novel function of limiting the power of the investigative judge in setting the boundaries of his inquiries in the investigative phase and the defence counsel became entitled to participate in proof-taking and to offer through argument and debate a contrasting point of view to the inquirer in the trial phase.[28]

After World War II, many changes aimed at increasing the official truth seeker's neutrality occurred in the various Continental criminal procedures. The traditional investigative monopoly of state officials was everywhere abandoned for a multilateral approach. In this spirit, defence attorneys were granted a role in the investigative phase of the proceeding, acquiring the right not only to inspect the dossier freely but also to be present when many procedural activities were taking place and to offer counter-proof

[28] Damaška, above n 23, 535; F Cordero, *Procedura penale* (Milano, Giuffré, 1998) 64.

and counter-arguments. Moreover, in many countries the defence (and in some countries, like France and Italy, also the victim), were allowed to ask for the performance of investigative steps and in case of refusal were entitled to a formal reply subject to review.[29] By granting the defence (and sometimes the victim) a greater input into officially conducted investigations, European systems transformed the search for the truth from unilateral inquiries into a sort of collective enterprise. They increased the plurality of perspectives and as a consequence the impartiality of the official in charge of the enquiry. Italy went even further legitimating, after December 2000, a system of two parallel (but interrelated) investigations, an official and a private one, the latter conducted by the defence.[30] The enhanced right of the defence to oppose all incriminating evidence in the trial phase and to have exculpatory evidence produced also provided for a more serious pluralistic approach to the overall official search for the truth.

In the same effort to enhance the neutrality of the official search for truth, other reforms took place in Continental European countries. The prohibition against the investigative judge also being a member of the trial court panel (for example, in France) helped to fragment the official authority in charge of the enquiry and led to a plurality of perspectives within the very decision making process.[31] The sharp severance of the investigative and judicial functions, achieved by abolishing the investigating judge altogether in Germany in the 1970s and in Italy after 1988, served the same goal.

Other reforms limiting the use of evidence from the official file of preliminary investigative activities favoured a fresh understanding of the facts by the trial judge. The strongest severance between investigation and adjudication in order to safeguard the truth seeker's impartiality was accomplished by the Italian system in 1988. In order to insulate the trial judge completely from the approach taken by the public official during the pre-trial phase, the Italian Code does not permit the previously gathered

[29] See generally, M Chiavario (ed), *Procedure penali d'Europa* (Padova, Cedam, 2002). Regarding France, see *ibid* 148; regarding Italy, see O Vannini and G Cocciardi, *Manuale di diritto processuale penale italiano* (Milano, Giuffré, 1986) 368.

[30] See Law of December 7, 2000 '*Disposizioni in materia di indagini difensive*', *Gazzetta Ufficiale* n 2, 3 January 2001. The defence, conducting her own investigation, is still allowed to be present when most prosecutorial activities are under way. Freely permitted to contact 'her own' witnesses in the pre-trial phase, the defence may make the prosecutor interview potentially favourable witnesses on her behalf or seize materials in her interest (thus obtaining help from him with her own investigation). In the same vein the defence can also ask the prosecutor, at the end of the prosecutor's investigation, to gather new exculpatory evidence. Both parties, moreover, are allowed to freely inspect each other's dossiers before the trial begins.

[31] See *Procedure penali d'Europa* above n 29, 118; see also art 61 of the previous Italian Criminal Procedure Code (1930).

investigatory product to be made available to him. Thus the Italian trial judge today approaches the case as a *tabula rasa*. [32] In Continental systems the old tradition of appellate supervision of criminal trial courts provides, moreover, for a further fragmentation of the official authority in charge of the enquiry, enhancing the plurality of perspectives.

The transformation of Continental procedure from an official unilateral enquiry into a pluralistic one, accomplished by increasing the plurality of perspectives upon which judgments could be based, made Continental justice – in a dancing metaphor – resemble the 'rumba' dance, in which many dancers in different capacities dance together in the common enterprise of discovering the truth. This was the reply to the 'lack of neutrality' problem raised since the end of the seventeenth century by English classic liberalism. Therefore, in the Continental world neutrality is still considered attainable in the criminal process, and the search for an 'objective' truth has never been replaced with a search for an 'interpretive' truth. Officials, made as impartial as possible, are still charged with the task of searching for it, and this is so even in Italy (the most 'revolutionary' country among all European Continental countries) where the convergence toward the adversary model has reached a highpoint. In the Continental criminal process, justice – never equated to fairness – continues to be associated with the neutral search for a substantive, 'ontological' truth.

IV. 'TANGO' AND 'RUMBA' JUSTICE

Different ideas about justice convey different images that can be captured by a dancing metaphor. The adversarial system can be associated with the idea of a 'tango justice'; the non-adversary one with that of a 'rumba justice'. 'Tango' can be performed by two dancers and only by those two, acting together in the venture of establishing the adversarial truth. 'Rumba', on the contrary, is performed by a variable number of dancers occasionally alone and occasionally in groups with many shifts and continuous substitutions of dancers and roles. It is a genuinely communal performance in the collective search of an objective truth. The two dances associated with the two systems lead to different procedural arrangements consistent with their underlying tenets. Let me point to some of them.

As already mentioned, the different role assigned to the adjudicator as an active searcher for the 'ontological' truth, as opposed to a passive spectator of a dialectical confrontation producing the 'interpretive' truth, provides for the most obvious clash of procedural arrangements. An adjudicator's 'neutrality' acquires a different meaning in the two systems.

[32] Art 431 of the current Italian Criminal Procedure Code.

In the adversarial system, neutrality is synonymous with passivity; in the non-adversary one, the same concept is equated to impartiality.

This in turn implies that in the Continent the adjudicator, as a *super partes* (as much as possible non-biased) agent has the duty to conduct his factual enquiry both against and in favour of the accused, raising matters and adducing evidence whenever this initiative appears to him important to the discovery of 'objective' truth. As the truth seeker, the impartial adjudicator in Continental criminal procedure needs control over the fact-finding process and even where – as in Italy – the legislator attempted to limit his factual enquiry powers, in a very short period of time he regained full authority.[33] Continental faith in the 'ontological' truth, discoverable by a neutral, that is, impartial, adjudicator, therefore prevailed in Italy over the adversarial approach toward an 'interpretive' truth. In order to discover the 'ontological' truth, it is essential to ensure that the evidentiary material is as complete as possible.

The completeness of the evidentiary material is, however, irrelevant to the ascertainment of an 'interpretive' truth; what matters is that procedures are fair, the only device capable of bringing about just results within that conception of truth. This is why, provided that fair rules are established and respected, parties in the adversarial system are allowed to dominate the fact-finding process and freely determine what facts shall be presented and be subject to proof at trial, as well as what sources of information will be produced as evidence. This is so, even if their choices – as is very often the case[34]– produce a limited picture of reality. Through an adversarial lens, the full picture that emerges from the completeness of the evidentiary material available is in fact as illusory as the existence of the 'ontological' truth. Differently stated, in the adversarial perspective, a broader picture, attained through the activity of a third party, will not necessarily be more accurate. This attitude is explained by an underlying scepticism towards the notion of third party neutrality.

In the search for an interpretive truth, the adversarial system gives the defendant a monopoly over most defence issues and permits him to discharge them whenever he so decides. In contrast, 'as part of his official duties the Continental judge must raise all defence issues for which there is some support in the case. Any other arrangement is viewed as risking the conviction of an innocent person',[35] and therefore inherently unjust.

[33] See, more extensively, E Grande, 'Criminal Justice: the Resistance of a Mentality' in JS Lena and U Mattei (eds), *Introduction to Italian Law* (The Hague, Kluwer, 2002), 181, 201 *ff*.

[34] As extensively demonstrated by Professor Damaška: see above n 3, especially 92 and 100.

[35] Damaška, above n 23, 535, n 137.

Provided they are voluntary and knowingly given, guilty pleas (even if they are the result of a bargain) are accepted in the adversarial perspective as consistent with the parties' freedom to shape proceedings and to establish the existence and the borders of their contest. They are part of the tango of justice, which can be danced by two and only those two together, as much as any other fair adversarial posture. The adjudicator's passivity in watching this tango justice accounts for the regular acceptance of party stipulations as well. With no duty and willingness to intervene in the fact-finding enterprise, should the trial judge reject the stipulation 'the resulting procedural action [would be] bound to be lifeless or anemic.'[36]

On the contrary, guilty pleas and plea bargaining are in principle extraneous to Continental legal consciousness. The achievement of justice through the discovery of the ontological truth requires the adjudicator to proceed in his enquiry even if the defendant declares that he is guilty; the prosecutor in the same vein can be judicially obliged to prosecute. Judicial activism will compensate for both parties' inactivity.[37] To be sure, the trend to converge towards the adversary model, recently experienced by some Continental systems (for example, in France and Italy), pressed them to introduce a very limited sort of plea bargaining. Justified on efficiency grounds, this new kind of 'bargained justice' is, however, very much at odds with the Continental idea of achieving justice; rather perceived as a *dismissal* of justice, it has consequently been adopted with a limited scope.[38]

The law of evidence in the adversarial system plays the key role of establishing the rules that provide for a fair contest, allowing the tango to be successful in its production of the 'interpretive' truth. This law evens the playing field of the dispute by assuring the balancing of advantages between litigants in proof-taking activity, thereby giving the parties equal opportunities to present their view of reality. Should parties not be granted even chances in presenting their side of the story, a neutral – that is passive in the adversarial perspective – adjudicator would not be able to ascertain

[36] Damaška, above n 3, 104.

[37] For a historical review of different attitudes toward plea bargaining in Continental and common law traditions and for an analysis of negotiated justice in the international setting, see MR Damaška, 'Negotiated Justice in International Criminal Courts' (2004) 2 *Journal of International Criminal Justice* 1018.

[38] The Law of March 9, 2004 which introduces in France the '*procédure de comparution sur reconnaissance préalable de culpabilité*' limits the applicability of the procedure to crimes (délits) punishable with a maximum of 5 years of imprisonment, permitting a 'bargained sentence' not heavier than one year of imprisonment (and in any event not heavier than half of the sentence statutorily provided). In Italy the heaviest 'bargained sentence' was two years' imprisonment before the Law of June 12, 2003 was enacted. Today it is five years' imprisonment. For an account of the informal plea bargaining mechanisms in the German system, usually within a very much limited maximum penalty, see MD Dubber, 'American Plea Bargains, German Lay Judges, and the Crisis of Criminal Procedure' (1997) 49 *Stanford Law Review* 547, 558 *ff*. See also Thomas Weigend, ch 3.

the 'interpretive' truth. Therefore, adversarial fairness underlies the truth-discovery process in the Anglo-American perspective. Cross-examination, hearsay prohibition, corroboration rules, the privilege against self-incrimination, compulsory process and many exclusionary rules are all designed to such an end. Consistent with the tenets of an adversarial approach, most evidence law is, however, only conditionally applicable: it comes to life only if the parties invoke its rules.[39] Since litigants are presumed to know what is best for them, and since no one else can establish better knowledge, no one, and especially not the distrusted state official, can impose his view on the parties.[40] The dancers draft their own script. Even intrinsic exclusionary rules which exclude material of dubious probative value apt to mislead the fact-finder[41] and thus serving the purpose of safeguarding the accuracy of factual determination can normally be displaced by unilateral waiver, or party stipulations. This strikes the Continental observer as a perversion of justice.

In non-adversarial systems by and large, evidentiary regulation is the province of the judge not of the parties, and this is especially so with regard to evidence rules meant to protect the accuracy of fact-finding.[42] The duty to search for an 'ontological' truth prevents the adjudicator from taking into consideration information deemed to be insufficiently reliable. Such unreliable information is expunged from the evidentiary material that is used as the basis for the judgment, irrespective of whether or not the rule is invoked by the side adversely affected by the production of the prohibited material. Even in the Italian system, where the convergence toward the Anglo-American procedure has reached its zenith among all Continental countries, parties do not have control over the application of exclusionary evidence rules; their violation can in fact always be officially raised at any stage or level of the proceedings.[43]

In non-adversarial systems the desire to meet the adjudicator's investigative needs is a priority. Consequently, even if non-adversarial systems have gradually implemented the parties' right to confront all adverse evidence, these systems still permit the admission of both hearsay evidence and

39 Damaška, above n 3, 87.

40 Damaška , above n 23, 535.

41 Such as for example, rules excluding gruesome or inflammatory evidence, or prohibiting character evidence or excluding certain types of statistical and scientific information.

42 Like for example rules prohibiting a testimony obtained in a way likely to modify the declarant's self-determination (via lie detectors, narco-analysis, and so forth), that one finds in a variety of civil law jurisdictions. For a further discussion: see Damaška, above n 3, 87, and G Aimonetto, '*L'acquisizione della prova dichiarativa nei principali sistemi processuali europei: riflessioni di sintesi*' in Bologna Conference Proceedings, '*La prova dichiarativa nello spazio giudiziario europeo: mutuo riconoscimento e prospettive di armonizzazione*' 18–19 April 2007.

43 Art 191 n 2 of the Italian Code of Criminal Procedure. For a more extensive treatment: see Grande, above n 33, 203 *ff*.

out-of-court secretly gathered declarations of witnesses, whenever they are not available in court because of intervening death, mental illness, or some other reason that makes their previous declaration impossible to repeat.[44]

This would probably strike the common law observer as a perversion of justice. Yet in the Continent, where justice and fairness do not overlap, the former can be preferred to the latter in order to enable the fact-finder to consider the broadest picture of reality. In non-adversarial systems, the fact-finder has to provide a fully reasoned judgment in writing which is always subject to supervision by an appellate court. This prevents the fact-finder from overweighing the value of the evidence that the parties have not confronted. Thus, from a Continental jurist's perspective, the sacrifice of fairness – brought by the use of written testimony that the parties have not confronted – does not preclude a just decision by the trial fact-finder.

It is obvious at this point that these divergent conceptions of justice and their implementation lead to contrasting procedural arrangements that are occasionally shocking from the opposite perspective. An additional example can illustrate the issue.

The conception that equates justice to fairness assumes that fair trial adjudication is final. The limited scope of appeals in common law jurisdictions – particularly in the United States, where appeals are restricted to questions of law[45] and only against convictions – can thus be explained as a consequence of the internal logic of the adversarial system. True, since the jury's verdict gives no reasons for its conclusions, there is little to review in appeal. But we can offer another explanation which is consistent with the adversarial 'interpretive' conception of truth: whenever fair rules have been applied in the trial contest between adversaries, the result is necessarily just.

In America today, as with the *appeal of felony* of medieval times, when a fair battle is over, *rien ne va plus*. In many American jurisdictions this is the case to the great astonishment of the Continental observer, even when a review of the factual basis of the judgment would be necessary on the ground that fresh evidence has emerged after the trial is over.[46] In 1993 the Supreme Court of the United States affirmed that: 'a claim of actual innocence is not itself a constitutional claim' and refused to find in violation of due process the very limited period permitted by one state for appealing a conviction which barred defendants from filing for a new trial

[44] See arts 512 and 195 n 3 of the Italian Code of Criminal Procedure, or, in Germany, §§ 251 I, 252, 252 II StOP (*Strafprozessordnung*).

[45] Leaving aside cases in which a directed verdict of acquittal is improperly denied.

[46] For a vivid description of what this means in real life, see B Scheck, P Neufeld and J Dwyer, *Actual Innocence* (New York, Doubleday, 2000). For an overview of some recent changes in American law regarding post-conviction DNA testing see <http://www.innocenceproject.org/news/National-View.php> accessed 16 June 2008.

based on newly discovered evidence.[47] Within a strict adversarial perspective, the legal system is not equipped to redress the actual innocence of convicted defendants. The vindication of innocence based on newly discovered evidence is administered by executive clemency. In this way, the question is assigned to the political domain, rather than to the legal domain.

On the contrary, equating justice with the discovery of the 'ontological' truth implies the need for direct reconsideration of the trial adjudication by a higher court.[48] In this sense, appeal review is part of the 'rumba justice.' The review enables the supervision of the trial fact-finder's use of the evidentiary material, the rationality of his enquiry into the facts, and whether the data that his judgment is based on are complete. This supervision is necessary for the sake of assuring that in the official enquiry, neutrality – in the non-adversarial meaning of impartiality – is respected so that the 'ontological' truth is actually discovered.

In non-adversarial systems written reasons, given in support of the trial adjudicating decision, provide the basis for appellate courts' supervision. Issues both of law *and* of fact are subject to appeal and this is normally so – to the bewilderment of the common law observer – even in the case of acquittals,[49] although double jeopardy provisions prevent the re-opening of criminal proceedings against defendants who have been definitively acquitted.[50] An ideal of justice in search of a 'substantive' truth, moreover, forces the legal system to give redress to actual innocence. The extraordinary remedy of re-opening criminal proceedings is always available after the trial to the innocent wrongfully convicted even where the defence were in possession of evidence pointing to innocence during the trial but failed to bring it to the attention of the trial court.[51]

Many other different procedural arrangements in the two systems, mirroring different dances of justice, can be enumerated. Another interesting example is the different approach taken towards the imposition of *res judicata* upon civil suits arising out of criminal adjudication. In adversarial

[47] *Herrera v Collins* (1993) 506 US 390. 'Claims of actual innocence based on newly discovered evidence have never been held to state a round for habeas corpus relief absent an independent constitutional violation occurring in the underlying state criminal proceeding ... This rule is grounded in the principle that federal habeas courts sit to ensure that individuals are not imprisoned in violation of the Constitution – not to correct errors of fact.' (400).

[48] After 2000, this is so in France even for assize courts' guilty pronouncements, previously not subject to appeal on any question of fact. However some restrictions still apply in Germany, particularly with regard to 'mixed' courts with lay assessors: see § 312 StPO.

[49] This is also true in the Italian system after the Italian Constitutional Court held to be unconstitutional a statute (Law February 20, 2006 n 46 art 1) which, in the wake of the American system, provided that acquittals could not be appealed on factual grounds. See Decision no 26/2007 of January 24, 2007.

[50] See, eg, arts 629 and 649 of the Italian Criminal Procedure Code.

[51] See, eg, art 630 of the Italian Criminal Procedure Code.

systems the sceptical attitude toward the type of truth attainable in the criminal process (only a second-best, 'interpretive' truth) prevents the imposition of *res judicata* upon civil proceedings that are issued for damages arising out of the offence; whereas it is often the opposite in non-adversarial systems, where criminal proceedings are deemed to achieve the 'ontological' truth even when the victim did not participate as a 'civil party' in the criminal proceedings.

V. WHEN SHOULD 'TANGO' BEGIN?

I hope I have been able to demonstrate that adversary and non-adversarial systems reflect two different approaches toward the search for the truth, both equally valid from their own theoretical point of view. I would like to address an additional question regarding the 'tango' vision of justice: when should 'tango' with its fair rules of the game begin? Differently stated: in which phase of the criminal proceeding should fairness, that is equal opportunities for the dancers to present their view of reality, take place? If we follow Langbein in thinking that 'in matters of criminal procedure, pre-trial … shap(es) trial',[52] we must conclude that offering equal opportunities to the parties in the pre-trial phase is essential for the truth discovery enterprise.

Yet, unfortunately this is often not the case in adversarial systems, especially in the United States. In the pre-trial phase indeed, disparities of power are very strong between the individual and the powerful state, and the balancing of advantages is far from assured. Only the prosecutor in fact can make inspections, searches and seizures, or intercept conversations and communications or compel participation in line ups. The prosecution, moreover, 'starts with the great investigative manpower of the police and adds to that the far greater investigative legal authority of the grand jury's subpoena power'.[53] The state is able to force witnesses to speak or third parties to produce documents or accomplices to waive their privilege against self incrimination through the use of the immunity grant.

No similar opportunities are given to the defence, 'who frequently find avenues of enquiry closed by a reluctance of witnesses to assist the accused',[54] and whose chances to obtain a trial court order for the production of documents and other tangible items in possession of third parties is very limited.

[52] JH Langbein, 'The Prosecutorial Origins of Defence Counsel in the Eighteenth Century: the Appearance of Solicitors' (1999) 58 *Cambridge Law Journal* 314, 319.

[53] Y Kamisar, WR Lafave, JH Israel, NJ King, *Modern Criminal Procedure* (St. Paul Minn., West Group, 2005), 1221 quoting Justice Brennan, 'The Criminal Prosecution: Sporting Event or Quest for Truth?' (1973) 1963 *Washington University Law Quarterly* 279.

[54] *Ibid*.

> Prosecution's investigators usually arrive first at the scene of the crime and begin their investigation when the trail is fresh, whereas defence counsel typically enters the picture at a much later date.[55]

Forced by the lack of technical means to renounce a proactive defence (that is, a defence aimed at proving innocence), the American defendant generally cannot even effectively engage in a reactive one (that is, a defence merely aimed at disproving the inculpatory material gathered and presented in court by the prosecutor). The lack of extensive pre-trial discovery justified on fairness grounds as a correlative of the right to remain silent, gives a great advantage to the only litigant that in the pre-trial phase had the opportunity to gather the evidence, that is the prosecutor. Thus a principle grounded in fairness even precludes the preparation of a defence which is merely aimed at disproving the charge.

In addition to the lack of technical means, almost 90 per cent of American defendants are disadvantaged by a lack of economic means.[56] 'The financial advantages of the State will overpower' irreparably the defendant, 'and leave (him) effectively at the mercy of prosecutorial whim'.[57] With no means to pay investigators, forensic experts, or skilful counsel to search for the evidentiary material, and to sift it and prepare it, the defendant is deprived of a level playing ground with the prosecution in his trial contest. The strong disparity of power between litigants in the pre-trial phase then runs over into their battle at trial, severely undermining the trial's fairness, as well as its capability of discovering the truth, if only an interpretive one.

As Damaška observes,

> Two one-sided accounts can be expected somehow to cancel out and expose the truth only on condition that the contestants can disburse roughly equal resources in readying their cases for trial. Absent this condition, the resultant force of the two partisan vectors, so to speak, is likely to deviate from the correct view of reality.[58]

Even judging the system in its own terms, the comparativist can observe that the tango of justice must start before trial in order that trial parties have more equal opportunities to 'dance', that is to prepare their trial case. Otherwise, the adversarial system's ideological tenets of justice, fairness

[55] *Ibid.*

[56] Innocence Project, Subcommittee on Crime, and Homeland Security Advancing Justice through the use of Forensic DNA Technology 2003, 'Testimony of Peter Neufeld' in http://www.inocenceproject.org/docs/Neufeld_Congressional_Testimony.html, 3.

[57] JH Langbein, 'Money Talks, Client Walks' (1995) *Newsweek*, April 17, 33.

[58] Damaška, above n 3, 101.

and the search for an 'interpretive' truth are at risk of being seriously undermined together with their democratic image of an arms length model.[59]

VI. CONCLUSION

A final observation needs to be stated in the conclusion to this chapter, which is fondly dedicated to Professor Mirjan Damaška.

To the extent that fairness and justice are equated to each other in adversarial systems, but remain two different concepts in non-adversarial ones, their alternate use in the context of legal transplants and legal translations poses a challenge to the study of comparative law.[60] Notions of fairness and justice, when used outside the common law world, assume a different meaning from the one assumed at home which is consistent with the new institutional context. Lack of awareness of this transformation can bring about ambivalence and confusion.[61] As an example, when the notion of fairness is adopted in the Continental world – as in the case of Article 6 of European Convention on Human Rights which introduced the concept of '*procès équitable*' – its deep meaning seems to be that of justice in a Continental perspective, therefore implying the view of a search for the 'substantive' truth, rather than that of fairness in an adversarial perspective. This is why, for instance, procedural arrangements incompatible with the adversarial idea of fairness, such as the admissibility of anonymous witnesses declarations, can be to some extent congenial with the European notion of a 'fair' trial. In the new setting – characterised by a rumba idea of justice – the notion of fairness, as the European Court of Human Rights noticed, involves in fact not only a fair treatment to the defendant and to the prosecutor, but also to the victim and to the witnesses.[62]

[59] See also Rudolf Schlesinger's observation that at the end of the day as a guilty defendant he would prefer to be tried under the common law system, but as an innocent one he would much rather be tried under a civil law one. See RB Schlesinger, HW Baade, PE Herzog, EM Wise, *Comparative Law, Cases-Text-Materials* 6th edn (New York, Foundation Press, 1998) 531.

[60] On legal transplants and on the need to take into consideration the different institutional context of the system of production from that of destination, see MR Damaška, 'The Uncertain Fate of Evidentiary Transplants: Anglo-American and Continental Experiments' (1997) 45 *American Journal of Comparative Law* 839. On legal transplants and legal translations, see M Langer, 'From Legal Transplants to Legal Translations: The Globalisation of Plea Bargaining and the Americanization Thesis in Criminal Procedure' (2004) 45 *Harvard International Law Journal* 1.

[61] For a deep exploration of the connection between language and legal thought, see GP Fletcher, *Basic Concepts of Legal Thought* (New York, OUP, 1996); GP Fletcher, *Loyalty: An Essay on the Morality of Relationships* (New York, OUP, 1993).

[62] '[P]rinciples of fair trial also require that in appropriate cases the interests of the defence are balanced against those of witnesses or victims called upon to testify': *Doorson v Netherlands*, ECtHR, March 26, 1996, § 70.

In sum, legal translations pose to comparative lawyers the problem of adjusting legal language to the cultural specific legal values of the context in which the language is used, and for the accomplishment of this task a deeper understanding of the fundamental matrix of each system, following Professor Damaška's lesson, is essential.

9

Cognitive Strategies and Models of Fact-Finding

CRAIG R CALLEN*

WHENEVER I READ Professor Damaška's comparative analyses of evidence law I come away with admiration of his work – particularly *Evidence Law Adrift*. I do not always agree with his ultimate conclusions about matters of Anglo-American evidence law. Even so, I do not see how anyone in the field could fail to admire his dissections of the common law and civil law systems. They are pellucid, concise and nuanced, with insights based on research in other disciplines, including philosophy, history and (most important for this essay) psychology.[1]

One of his psychological concerns is the degree to which the passive fact-finding role in party-driven common law systems, or the more active role of fact-finding judges in judge-driven civil law systems, serves the cognitive needs of fact-finders.[2] In a recent article, Professor Damaška observed that

> What is truly intriguing about both [party- and officially dominated fact-finding] styles is not how perfect or imperfect they are, but why they operate tolerably well, despite numerous departures from cognitively optimal arrangements.[3]

* I am grateful to Franklin Boster, Emma Haas, Norbert Kerr, Barbara O'Brien and Charles Ten Brink for suggestions, to Jane Edwards, Matthew Hodges and Adam Keith for research, and Michigan State University College of Law for a grant that supported the preparation of this essay.

[1] See, eg, M Damaška, 'Assignment of Counsel and Perceptions of Fairness' (2005) 3 *Journal of International Criminal Justice,* 3, 3; M Damaška, 'Epistemology and legal regulation of proof' (2003) 2 *Law, Probability and Risk* 117, 119; M Damaška, 'Truth in Adjudication' (1998) 49 *Hastings Law Journal* 289, 300; M Damaška, 'Free Proof and its Detractors' (1995) 43 *American Journal of Comparative Law* 343, 349–50.

[2] See, eg, MR Damaška, *Evidence Law Adrift* (New Haven, Yale UP, 1997) 94–103. It is not possible to discuss all of the variations on the classic common law and civil law systems here, so I will confine myself to the typical features of each system.

[3] M Damaška, 'Epistemology and legal regulation of proof' (2003) 2 *Law, Probability and Risk,* 117, 121.

This chapter is an essay, not only in form, but, in the terms of dictionary definitions, an attempt or experimental effort. It suggests that theories of bounded rationality, as Herbert Simon conceived it, can help us to understand how our systems achieve the 'tolerable' success that intrigues Professor Damaška.

Professor Damaška recognises that no 'single fact-finding method could possess the same accuracy-generating capacity' for all questions of fact that might arise in litigation.[4] That suggests that his concern in referring to 'cognitively optimal arrangements' was accuracy, rather than compliance with some formal protocol without reference to its practical results.[5]

That distinction is important. Futile efforts to adhere to particularly demanding conceptions of rationality can distract us from the ways in which common law and civil law systems can function 'tolerably well' despite the constraints under which human fact-finders operate. No one argues that we should prefer falsity or random choice over truth. Nor would anyone be likely to argue that we should forsake an apparently good decision-making practice for a seemingly worse one, other things being equal. Nevertheless idealised conceptions of inquiry can be enemies (for practical purposes) of decision-making processes that are, in practice, more successful.

Humans act rationally when they rely on cognitive strategies from everyday life in fact-finding. The key to success in both common law and civil systems is exploitation of the potential benefit from fact-finders' use of cognitive strategies, and limitation of the harmful effects.

THE UTILITY OF COGNITIVE STRATEGIES

Cognitive strategies enable us to make good decisions in everyday life despite our limitations. Humans will be the fact-finders in litigation for the foreseeable future. The information, time, material and cognitive resources we can devote to decisions in our own lives are limited. We must make decisions despite those limitations. In order to do so, we develop strategies that help us to identify critical data and employ those data in making decisions without incurring unreasonable cognitive costs. Those strategies are very useful, but they are not perfect – they tolerate the possibility of certain errors in order to keep demands on our limited resources within reasonable bounds.

[4] Damaška, above n 2, 130.

[5] G Gigerenzer and PM Todd, 'Fast and Frugal Heuristics: The Adaptive Toolbox' in G Gigerenzer *et al* (eds), *Simple Heuristics that Make Us Smart* (New York, OUP, 1999) 3, 8–12.

Essentially, they guide the search process (accumulation and evaluation of evidence) by: (i) identifying critical information and facts; (ii) setting limits on the process of gathering evidence through establishing standards for searches that are adequate; and (iii) in the process delineating risks of erroneous decision that are worth running in the context in which the strategies typically apply. Even mechanisms with seemingly more computing power than humans can benefit from them. For example, the chess computer Deep Blue could not have won its chess match with Kasparov without strategies that guided its search process.[6]

To regulate the search process at the trial level, the common law system primarily relies on the parties to gather and offer evidence, and to trigger enforcement of the rules of evidence, assigning fact-finders an outwardly passive role.[7] The typical Continental system allocates fact-finding responsibility to judges, who themselves guide the accumulation of evidence and evaluate it. Professor Damaška has analysed the cognitive shortcomings of each. And Judge Posner has argued that a judge-driven system may give judges insufficient incentives for adequate search.[8] When we view rationality, or human decision-making, in light of constraints on resources, information and time, there seems to be a subtle, yet important shift in our view of each system.

A number of cognitive scientists would disagree with the very idea of cognitively optimal methods, arguing that we cannot follow 'unbounded rationality', decision-making methods that assume we have unlimited cognitive resources (including memory capacity) and time, since both are obviously limited. Nor, given the limitations on our cognitive resources, can we calculate the marginal benefits and costs of all items of evidence to ensure that we only gather and evaluate evidence to the point where its marginal benefits equal its marginal costs (in time, resources and foregone opportunities), sometimes called 'optimisation under constraints'.[9] Instead, often the best we can do is to rely on our experience (or information from others) to develop heuristics or other cognitive strategies to help us identify critical information that we can employ to make good decisions despite our limitations. In other words, those strategies can lead us to consider evidence when, and only when, we believe its likely contribution to

[6] See WD Hillis, *The Pattern on the Stone: The Simple Ideas That Make Computers Work* (New York, Basic Books, 1998) 83–87.

[7] The reasons that it does so may be cognitive in part, as with the avoidance of pre-trial influences, or political, as with a preference for decentralised authority. They are beyond the scope of this paper, so that allocation of fact-finding responsibility will be taken as given.

[8] His primary purpose might have been opposition to proposals for a judge-driven system in the United States. See RA Posner, *Frontiers of Legal Theory* (Cambridge, Mass, Harvard UP, 2001) 351 (mentioning American political culture and skepticism about administrative agencies as arguments that search incentives in judge-driven systems may be inadequate).

[9] Gigerenzer and Todd, above n 5, 8–12; G Gigerenzer and DG Goldstein, 'Betting on One Good Reason: The Take the Best Heuristic', *Ibid* 75, 75.

resolution of the issue justifies the effort and resources needed to evaluate it. As the perfect may be the enemy of the good, so the effort to optimise may be the enemy of accuracy.

Three cognitive strategies, taken together, suggest a response to a number of questions that Professor Damaška and others have raised – including why it makes sense to exclude evidence that is prejudicial, even though we suspect that judges, sitting as fact-finders, would not be wholly immune to the effect of that evidence. The story model explains how fact-finders organise and exploit data to reach decisions about historical fact. Professor Gilbert's work on belief formation suggests that judge-driven search for evidence may be affected by formation of beliefs about the case before evidence is presented. As for admissibility rules in party-driven proceedings, Professor Grice's work suggests an explanation for exclusion of evidence in common law courts other than lack of respect for the cognitive abilities of the jury – avoidance of miscommunication resulting from jurors' rational reliance on a cognitive strategy that is critical for communication.

THE STORY MODEL, BELIEF FORMATION AND THE JUDGE-DRIVEN SYSTEM

Finders of fact in adversarial systems may not gather evidence or ask questions, but they do bring to bear a great deal of information from their own experience. Accordingly, although 'passive' is not an inaccurate description of their role, lack of action to gather evidence does not entail psychological inaction. The common law system asks jurors to bring their everyday decision-making experience to bear.[10] It would be difficult, for example, for jurors to decide whether a reasonable person would have acted as the plaintiff did, or whether defendant's behavior indicated that she meant to harm the defendant, without relying on their experience with the actions of people in everyday life.

Empirical research suggests a global mechanism through which jurors bring their experience to bear in fact-finding. Jurors receive a significant amount of information about the facts at trial. They seem to use a strategy for organising and evaluating evidence, called the 'story model', to assist them in the search process, that is, organisation of the evidence and

[10] See, eg, *Sioux City & Pac R R v Stout,* 84 US (17 Wall) 657, 664 (1873); Comm on Pattern Jury Instructions, Judges Assn, 5th Cir, *Pattern Jury Instructions (Civil Cases)* (1997 edn) s 2.18, 22.

evaluation of whether and to what extent it supports the parties' contentions.[11] If cognitive scientists are right that comprehension of discourse is 'a constructive process',[12] then it is probably inevitable that fact-finders, whether judge[13] or jury, rely on the construction of stories to deal with the evidence they receive at trial. Without the organisational structure and links to prior experience that stories provide, triers would find the evidence at trial either cumbersome or overwhelming – given its quantity and the 'disconnected' manner (at least on the common law side) in which they receive it.[14] They do not limit themselves to the evidence at trial when constructing stories. Instead, they rely on knowledge about similar events, and the nature of explanations of such events, and inferences from that knowledge to fill out the story as best they can.[15] In a common law system, the parties may suggest those inferences, or the jurors may make them on their own initiative.[16]

Triers use the stories to reach a verdict.[17] The experience that triers have with respect to stories in everyday life allows them to assess the stories they construct. The story each juror constructs to account for the evidence (or 'best' story if she constructs alternatives) is the basis of her verdict.[18] When information needed to flesh out a story is lacking, or there are no plausible inferences that will complete the story, the trier's confidence in the story will be decreased.[19] In common law systems, where the burden of persuasion is particularly important, jurors who believe that the party on whom that burden rests has offered inadequate evidentiary support for an aspect of a story necessary to support its claim will find against that party, relying on the default rule.[20] Otherwise, when the evidence is such as to make jurors confident in their judgment, and to fill in necessary elements of the story, they reach a verdict by comparing the likelihood of stories.[21]

The story model raises issues in regard to both party-driven and judge-driven search processes. Judge Posner questions whether judges in

[11] See, eg, N Pennington and R Hastie, 'A Cognitive Theory of Juror Decision Making: The Story Model' (1991) 13 *Cardozo Law Review* 519.

[12] *Ibid* 523 and fn 11.

[13] See, eg, J Jackson and S Doran, *Judge Without Jury: Diplock Trials in the Adversary System* (Oxford, OUP, 1995) 217–21.

[14] Pennington and Hastie, above n 11, 523.

[15] *Ibid* 522.

[16] *Ibid* 527.

[17] *Ibid* 522–23.

[18] R Hastie and N Pennington, 'The OJ Simpson Stories, Behavioral Scientists' Reflections on *The People of The State of California v Orenthal James Simpson*' (1996) 67 *University of Colorado Law Review* 957, 959–60.

[19] *Ibid* 527–28.

[20] Pennington and Hastie, above n 11, 530–31. Jurors will similarly decide in favour of the default if the story does not coincide with one or more elements of the claim or defence: *Ibid.*

[21] N Pennington and R Hastie, 'Evidence Evaluation in Complex Decision-Making' (1986) 51 *J Personality & Social Psychology* 242, 245, 254.

the prototypical civil law system have adequate incentives to engage in the search process. His argument is, essentially, that the party-driven adversarial system privatises the process. He contends that parties have incentives to gather and present evidence until the cost of doing so is equivalent to the likely benefit. Accurate fact-finding is socially valuable in that it makes punishment less random, and deterrence more effective. Evidence is socially useful to the extent that it contributes to fact-finding, and, when the benefit of search for the parties equals its social benefit, then, his argument goes, a party-driven system will be efficient, or at least tend to be so.[22]

He contrasts the process of search in an adversarial system with that of a judge-driven system. Posner questions whether a judge in a judge-driven system will conduct an adequate search, given that: (i) the degree to which a correct outcome benefits the judge is uncertain, and the judge's time might make gathering evidence particularly costly;[23] and (ii) professional judges are more likely to be case-hardened than juries, and so less willing to entertain novel hypotheses, or arguments for non-typical results.[24] To put the point in terms of the story model, the concern is that the judge may be too unwilling to believe stories out of the norm, or in favour of criminal defendants, and too unwilling to hear evidence suggesting unusual findings, or the innocence of defendants. In other words, the story model, as a cognitive strategy, may encourage the court to become passive, to stop the search process, when a further search would be socially beneficial.

That is closely related to a concern that Professor Damaška mentions in *Evidence Law Adrift*. Presiding judges in judge-driven systems have primary responsibility for exposition of evidence at trial, and they prepare for their examination and evaluation of evidence by consulting the dossier prepared in advance of trial. Even though the presiding judge is prohibited from explicitly communicating the contents of the file to the other members of the panel, the panellists may gather much from any number of subtle cues, such as tone of voice. Moreover, the presiding judge's questions may reveal ideas triggered by the file, without giving the other panellists the opportunity to assess them against that file.[25] As the professor notes, one of the risks inherent in that aspect of judge-driven systems is the risk that the triers of fact will form hypotheses about reality too early. Even tentative early formulation of such theories, he thought, will make the triers view evidence confirming those hypotheses more favorably than they otherwise might.[26]

22 Posner, above n 8, 340–41, 346–47.
23 *Ibid* 346.
24 *Ibid* 350–51.
25 Damaška, above n 2, 72.
26 *Ibid* 95–96.

Research in social and cognitive psychology confirms Professor Damaška's observation. In fact, it suggests that he might have been a bit conservative. In his article *How Mental Systems Believe,* Professor Gilbert argued that, as Spinoza suggested, comprehension and evaluation of a proposition are not separate mental operations.[27] Based on a great deal of research on perception and the mechanics of belief, Professor Gilbert argued that comprehension of an idea involves the formation of a belief in that idea – if only for a short time. Once having comprehended the idea, the decision maker is free to reverse the acceptance, or to maintain or reinforce the belief. Reversing the acceptance is more cognitively difficult than the initial acceptance of the idea.[28] Research into how subjects dealt with 'mere possibilities' presented to them showed that they tended to search for information to confirm those possibilities. That tendency was reversed when the subjects were led to consider both a proposition and its negation.[29] In explaining that result, Professor Gilbert argued that engaging in a confirmatory search for information when one believes the proposition makes more sense than conducting other sorts of searches. A confirmatory search would be subjectively more informing than a neutral search, given, for example, an initial suspicion that the defendant was angry immediately before the victim was injured. First, such a search would help one to determine how angry the defendant seemed to be. Second, if one believed that the defendant was angry, asking him about details of his lack of anger would not seem well calculated to gather useful information. On the other hand, when led to question the initial surmise, dissipating the effect of an initial belief, the tendency to engage in confirmatory searches disappeared.

Professor Gilbert theorised how nature, as 'an inveterate jury-rigger', might have eventuated in the Spinozan process. Animals believe what they see, and only seldom question the accuracy of what they see – their percepts. There is little need to question percepts, because they are generally accurate. Gilbert surmised that the cognitive systems developed on the model of perception, which resulted in a strong tendency to believe what that system comprehends, as well as what the visual system perceives. Human societies consider lying blameworthy, which gives rise to a tendency to communicate accurate information, and for the audiences of communications to regard them as accurate. We may be enabled to act on our perceptions, he thought, by capitalising on their generally accuracy. Accordingly, cognition may facilitate our actions by capitalising on the general accuracy of communications. Indeed, he suggested that cognition involved a trade-off of resources and accuracy. 'One might even argue that

27 DT Gilbert, 'How Mental Systems Believe' (1991) 46 *American Psychologist* 107, 108.
28 *Ibid* 110–13.
29 *Ibid* 115–16.

the savings of time and energy outweighs the intellectual deficits of inaccurate beliefs.'[30] In that light, it is what I have been calling a cognitive strategy, a decision making technique that enables us to make good decisions despite limits on our time and resources.

Gilbert's work does suggest that the dossier may influence the presiding judge in civil law courts to limit the search process, which underscores the concerns that Professor Damaška and Judge Posner raised. In comparison, the common law systems give each side the incentives and the ability to challenge beliefs that fact-finders have formed that might otherwise go unchallenged. Professor Gilbert's research on belief formation would suggest that advocacy of an alternative theory would dissipate the effect of initial belief formation on the search process. Judge-driven systems seem to have no explicit requirement for development of alternative theories. Some of the features of adversarial systems most likely to lead to the development of alternative hypotheses that will offset the initial beliefs are missing from judge-driven systems. Professor Damaška observes that examination of witnesses in a Continental jurisdiction is not as searching as an adversarial cross-examination.[31] Among other things, the parties may be very reluctant to open a new line of questioning with the witness, for fear of offending the court.

The possible influence of the dossier is not untroubling to those of us trained in the adversarial tradition, but some features of judge-driven systems which Judge Posner ignores and Professor Damaška does not mention in regard to the effect of the dossier give civilian courts incentives to engage in a more thorough search than a judge motivated only by economic self-interest might.

Judges in a judge-driven system must prepare written findings of fact – primarily the responsibility of the presiding judge.[32] Those findings are subject to *de novo* review[33] so that evidence can later be analysed from entirely new angles. Reviewing courts in judge-driven systems do make 'authoritative statements' on the adequacy of evidentiary support for findings at trial. It may be difficult to synthesise rules from those statements, given that they may be highly contextualised, but Professor Damaška reports that trial judges do observe the standards in those statements.[34] Moreover, there may be protocols requiring the court to search for specific information. For example, a German judge who fails to examine an original declarant and simply relies on the testimony of a

[30] *Ibid* 116.
[31] M Damaška, 'The Uncertain Fate of Evidentiary Transplants: Anglo-American and Continental Experiments' (1997) 45 *American Journal of Comparative Law* 839, 846–47.
[32] Damaška, above n 2, 45, 50.
[33] *Ibid* 64.
[34] Damaška, above n 2, 22–23.

hearsay witness will face a real challenge to justify that action in findings of fact that satisfy a reviewing court.[35]

It would be too much to assume that presiding judges would record the court's unconscious decision making processes in their findings of fact, and Professor Damaška reports that they do invoke boilerplate formulas as a common law judge might in her opinions. Nevertheless, the finding requirement requires that the court show that its findings have evidentiary support, and facilitates review of those findings by the reviewing court.[36] While Judge Posner may be right that Continental judges may not have an immediately ascertainable stake in the correctness of their results, it is rarely, if ever, in a judge's interest to have a decision overturned.

Moreover, while the record of a common law court might be limited to responses to relatively narrow questions posed by each side, the record in a judge-driven proceeding will typically include free testimonial narratives from the witnesses, which the presiding judge invites prior to more specific questioning.[37] The conventional requirement for those narratives provides the judge with information to evaluate that the judge might not seek out independently, which will become part of the record on appeal.

Of course, it would be impossible to flesh out all of the incentives for search in a legal system, let alone all of the processes involved in fact-finding under uncertainty. Gilbert's work, Judge Posner's arguments and the story model do suggest that the dossier may have a more inhibitory effect on search in the Continental system than champions of that system might acknowledge. That is not to enter what may be a bottomless pit in our current state of knowledge: arguing that one system is superior to another. It is simply to suggest that research on bounded rationality should have a place among the tools that we use in comparative analysis of the Continental system, and, as the next section suggests, of common law evidentiary doctrine.

THE EFFECT OF COMMUNICATION ON JURORS

The common law system poses a problem related to the story model and to Professor Gilbert's work on belief formation, but with features of its own. Triers of fact in a common law jurisdiction, and particularly jurors, depend on the evidence they receive from the parties to construct a story or stories. Exclusionary rules deny them evidence that they might otherwise use to construct stories. For example, evidence of prior convictions might be

[35] M Damaška, 'Of Hearsay and its Analogues' (1992) 76 *Minnesota Law Review* 425, 454.

[36] Damaška, above n 2, 45.

[37] *Ibid* 93.

particularly likely to trigger use of a story in which the defendant is a dangerous person whose mistaken incarceration the jury might be relatively unlikely to regret.[38] Even so, Professor Damaška makes the point that jurors might not be inherently more vulnerable to the effects of prejudicial influences (or to overweighing evidence) than a judicial trier of fact would be.[39]

The communicative environment of a trial may make the critical difference. Professor Damaška points out that bifurcation of fact-finding responsibility in adversarial trials makes exclusionary rules workable. Otherwise such rules would ask someone who had heard the evidence in ruling on the exclusion to unring the bell, and exclude the information from his or her memory. Research on the strategies we use in communication suggests that bifurcation of fact-finding between a professional judge and a lay person may produce a strong inclination to exclusionary rules. Submission of evidence to a trier of fact is, at bottom, a communication. Passive recipients of a communication are, almost by definition, dependent on those who communicate information to them. Empirical research confirms that speakers and hearers rely on a strategy to convey or gain more information from a communication than the words or actions necessarily convey.

Professor Grice first delineated that strategy in his maxims of co-operation,[40] which Professors Wilson and Sperber have recently simplified.[41] In order to convey information in a short period of time, in light of limitations on both speakers' and hearers' cognitive capacities, communicators expect audiences to rely on certain conventions, which audiences in turn expect them to follow. We tend to focus on information to the extent it produces positive effects (new data, revision of old assumptions or suggestions of new conclusions) and to the extent that we can achieve positive effects with relatively low expenditure of resources, including cognitive effort.[42] Communication depends on two implicit assumptions: (i) that the communicator will only impart information when its positive effects warrant the expenditure of resources to understand and evaluate it; and (ii) that the communicator will convey information in a form that will produce the largest surplus of positive effects over costs with respect to

[38] D Menashe and M E Shamash 'The Narrative Fallacy' (2005) 3 *International Commentary on Evidence,* article 3, at 13–14, <http://www.bepress.com/ice/vol3/iss1/art3/> accessed 16 June 2008; RO Lempert, 'Modeling Relevance' (1977) 75 *Michigan Law Review* 1021, 1038–41.

[39] Damaška, above n 2, 31–32; M Damaška, 'Propensity Evidence in Continental Legal Systems' (1994) 70 *Chicago-Kent Law Review* 55, 65.

[40] See, eg, P Grice, *Studies In The Way of Words* (Cambridge, Mass, Harvard UP, 1991) 26–27.

[41] D Wilson and D Sperber, 'Truthfulness and Relevance' (2002) 111 *Mind* 583, 604.

[42] *Ibid* 601–3.

that information, given the communicator's abilities and interests.[43] Recipients who are the targets of communication expect communicators to comply with the conventions. Those who violate the conventions run the risk of being misunderstood, if their targets do not wholly fail to comprehend them, ignore them, or even decide to ignore or discount the communicator's information in the future.[44]

The argument is not that the conventions would lead jurors to assume that all evidence offered would be true – that would be inconsistent with the court's interest in having the jury resolve questions of fact. Yet jurors would tend to assume, at the least, that the evidence admitted was worth their time and effort – a consequence of the passivity of their role and the allocation of fact-finding power among the judge and jury. That assumption could well cause jurors to draw two types of mistaken inferences. One would affect their opinion of evidence, the other, their understanding of the law.

A good example of the effect on jurors' opinion of the probative value of evidence is research on their evaluation of redundant witnesses. Jurors in Professor Sanders' studies of Bendectin cases seemed to believe that the relative number of expert witnesses on causation reflected the actual division of opinion in the scientific community – an inaccurate assumption that was notably robust.[45] The most likely source of that assumption is a belief that the court would not admit information that was simply redundant, drawn from the conventions of communication. Testimony from an expert on each side would have sufficed to merely set out the substance of the opposing views. The conventions would suggest that the trial process (and particularly the judge) would not provide them with more information on scientific opinion than necessary. Reliance on the conventions would mislead them to the conclusion that the number of witnesses reflected opinion in the scientific community.[46]

Moreover, there is the dilution effect. Addition of irrelevant information to relevant information can adversely affect subjects' decision making. One

[43] *Ibid* 604. Professors Wilson and Sperber expressed this in terms to which they gave their own technical definition, which could be very confusing in a discussion of evidence law: 'Every utterance conveys a presumption of its own optimal relevance.' *Ibid.*

[44] The point is centuries old. See, eg, B Jonson, 'Timber: or, Discoveries" in *The Workes* (1641) 122, cited in ER Tufte, *Visual Explanations: Images and Quantities, Evidence and Narrative* (Cheshire, Conn, Graphics P, 1997) 26: 'Negligent speech doth not only discredit the person of the Speaker, but it discrediteth the opinion of his reason and judgment; it discrediteth the force and uniformity of the matter, and substance.'

[45] J Sanders, 'From Science to Evidence: The Testimony on Causation in the Bendectin Cases' (1993) 46 *Stanford Law Review* 1, 39–41 and fn 199 (a defence witness who testified to the contrary had little or no effect upon it).

[46] Other studies confirm that jurors may accord substantial significance to the relative number of witnesses the parties call: eg, N Pennington & R Hastie, 'Explaining the Evidence: Tests of the Story Model of Juror Decision Making' (1992) 62 *J Personality & Social Psychology* 189, 194.

explanation for the dilution effect is that the subjects believe that the researchers would not give them information that they should ignore. Jurors might be particularly inclined to defer to what they perceive as the judge's opinion of the worth of evidence when the judge overruled an objection to it, or when doing so would conform to their pre-existing opinions.[47] While the theory is relatively new, the conclusion is not. Wigmore, for example, thought that, without the requirement of authentication, jurors would readily assume that an object was authentic after being presented with it, ignoring the possibility that parties might offer evidence of less than certain origin.[48] Similarly, foundation requirements (which courts in adversarial systems seldom enforce on their own) provide triers of fact with information tending to show that proffered evidence warrants the effort to evaluate it, or to make evaluation of the evidence less demanding, all in service of accurate fact-finding and dissipation of confusion.[49]

Judges are, of course, more sophisticated consumers of evidence, and less likely to be unduly impressed with their own decisions to admit it, so the conventions of communication do not suggest that exclusionary rules should operate as rigorously in bench trials as with juries.[50] Moreover, while it would be impractical for Continental judges, having heard evidence, to exclude it from their memories, evidence law may have the effect of prohibiting them from referring to technically inadmissible evidence in group deliberations or in findings.[51] So, technical inadmissibility on the Continent amounts, at least, to a weight requirement: more evidence is necessary to reach the conclusion to which the inadmissible evidence points. And judge-driven systems may require explanations for reliance on troublesome evidence such as hearsay or uncharged prior bad acts.[52] (Requiring such an explanation from a jury would be awkward, if not unworkable.) Keeping in mind that exclusionary rules in Anglo-American systems compensate for a problem in communication that systems with a unitary fact-finder do not have, Continental treatment of inadmissible evidence and common law exclusionary rules do seem to reflect some of the same cognitive concerns.

[47] E Beecher-Monas, 'Heuristics, Biases, and the Importance of Gatekeeping' [2003] *Michigan State Law Review* 987, 1003–06.

[48] JH Wigmore, *Wigmore on Evidence* vol 7, 3rd edn (Boston, Little, Brown, 1940) § 2129, 564–65.

[49] Eg, C Callen, 'Rationality and Relevancy: Conditional Relevancy and Constrained Resources' [2003] *Michigan State Law Review* 1244, 1282.

[50] Of course, application of exclusionary rules in bench trials is also fairly impractical. Damaška, above n 2, 48.

[51] Damaška, above n 2, 50–51.

[52] *Ibid* 16; Damaška, 'Propensity Evidence', above n 39, at 62.

As to law, while it is a commonplace to say that jurors do not decide questions of law, they must interpret the legal criteria (sometimes somewhat vague or cryptic) in the court's instructions to them.[53] Suppose, for example, that the jury would usually understand the court's ambiguous or cryptic instructions[54] to say that they are to apply legal standard *A*, rather than standard *B*. If the court admits evidence with no apparent bearing on *A*, but a great deal of significance on *B*, the jury might well take that as indicating that the should interpret the instructions to permit or require them to consider *B*. Assume that evidence tending to show a criminal propensity was admissible in common law courts. There is little reason to conclude that evidence that shows the defendant has a greater than normal propensity to commit crimes in general is very probative of guilt of a specific crime.[55] Nevertheless, reception of the evidence may: (i) encourage jurors to over-weigh it based on the conventions of communication; or (ii) to suggest that they apply a rule of decision encouraging conviction of the defendant based on general dangerousness or blameworthiness.

As another example of the effect of admitting evidence on legal interpretation, consider admission of evidence that the alleged victim in a rape case had non-marital intercourse with persons other than the defendant. In light of the low probative value of that evidence with respect to the elements of rape, jurors might conclude from the admission of the evidence that: (i) the court's appraisal of utility of the evidence was much more favourable than the jurors'; and therefore (ii) that the evidence was useful for a purpose the jurors had not considered, to show that the victim's prior sexual activity deprived her of some legal protection.[56] When lay people participate in fact-finding on the Continent, in contrast, they deliberate in a group with a judge or judges, who can tutor them on questions of law[57] obviating the need for instructions or reinforcement through exclusion of evidence.

Once again, setting aside the bifurcation of fact-finding, party- and judge-driven systems seem to reflect the same concerns: the effect of cognitive strategies on the fact-finding function.

[53] On the jury's role in legal interpretation, see eg, AAS Zuckerman, 'Law, Fact or Justice' (1986) 66 *Boston University Law Review* (1986) 487, 492–94.

[54] Jurors may be well aware that they do not understand all of the legal criteria. Cf RLWinslow, 'The Instruction Ritual' (1962) 13 *Hastings Law Journal* 456, 467–68 (discussing jurors' difficulties in understanding proximate cause instructions).

[55] Damaška, above n 39, 58.

[56] See JH Wigmore, *Evidence in Trials at Common Law* vol 1A (Boston, Little, Brown, P Tillers rev, 1983) s 62.1, 1327; A Althouse, 'Thelma and Louise and the Law: Do Rape Shield Rules Matter?' (1992) 25 *Loyola Law Review* 757, 766–68.

[57] Damaška, above n 2, 52.

CONCLUSION

Research on bounded rationality helps to explain how our systems of evidence and procedure manage to succeed reasonably well, even though the participants in them do not have unlimited time, resources or cognitive ability. That is not to suggest that all questions about evidentiary doctrine boil down to questions about bounded rationality – the absence of reductionist theories is a hallmark of Professor Damaška's work, and an admirable one. He brings theories from a number of disciplines to bear, with striking and insightful results. The links among the story model, Gilbert's work on belief formation, and Wilson and Sperber's simplification of Grice's work on communication are interesting in themselves. The research they link offers useful tools for the continuing effort to understand the law of evidence through understanding human cognition.

10

Are There Universal Principles or Forms of Evidential Inference? Of Inference Networks and Onto-Epistemology

PETER TILLERS*

> [I]magine a manslaughter charge arising out of reckless driving. The decision-maker must determine the truth of a certain number of propositions regarding 'external facts', such as the speed of the automobile, the condition of the road, the traffic signals, the driver's identity and so on. The mental operations required to ascertain such 'external facts' belong primarily to the sphere of sensory experience. The inquiry here appears to be relatively objective, and the 'truth' about such facts does not seem to be too elusive.
>
> But many 'internal facts' will also have to be established in the imagined case. They regard aspects of the defendant's knowledge and volition, to the extent to which these are important for the application of the relevant legal standard. The ascertainment of such facts is already a far less objective undertaking than the ascertainment of facts derived by the senses: processes of inductive inference from external facts are the most frequently traveled cognitive road. Even so, we do not hesitate to accord roughly the same cognitive status to findings regarding these internal facts as we do to findings of external facts. The characterisations 'true' and 'false' retain their respective meanings.
>
> The situation changes, however, when the facts ascertained must be assessed in the light of the legal standard. Whether a driver has deviated from certain standards of care-and if so to what degree-are problems calling for a different type of mental operation than that used in dealing with external facts. It is, of course, a matter of free semantic choice whether to characterise the outcome of

* Part of this paper was given as a lecture at the British Academy, for the conference 'Evidence, Enquiry and Facts', 13–14 December 2007, <http://www.britac.ac.uk/events/2007/evidence/index.html> accessed 19 June 2008. I am grateful for the comments and suggestions made by Jim Franklin, Lothar Philipps, Mike Redmayne and William Twining. The paper's errors and flaws, however, are entirely mine.

legal evaluation as 'true' or 'false', or to use some other pair of symbols. But if one decides to stick with the former, he must recognise that these symbols acquire a different meaning in the new context. In essence they convey the idea that the result of the activity is either correct (coherent) or incorrect (incoherent) within a given framework of legal reference.

Mirjan Damaška[1]

A POWERFUL NEW MODEL OF FACTUAL INFERENCE: WEBS OF INFERENCES HELD TOGETHER BY NOMOLOGICAL GLUE

DURING THE LAST several decades there has been a veritable explosion of scholarship and research about evidential inference. Although the models of inference generated in this latest wave of scholarship and research are varied, one thread does run through many of those models: Many contemporary accounts of evidential (or 'factual') inference emphasise the multi-stage, or hierarchical, nature of evidential inference; it is now commonly argued or assumed that evidential inference is best viewed as a network or web of inferences.[2]

[1] M Damaška, 'Presentation of Evidence and Factfinding Precision' (1975) 123 *University of Pennsylvania Law Review* 1083, 1085–86 (footnotes omitted; punctuation and spelling Anglicised).

[2] John Henry Wigmore began the parade toward inference networks many years ago. See JH Wigmore, *The Principles of Judicial Proof, or, The process of proof as given by logic, psychology, and general experience and illustrated in judicial trials* (Boston, Little, Brown & Co, 1931); JH Wigmore *The Science of Judicial Proof, or, The process of proof as given by logic, psychology, and general experience and illustrated in judicial trials* (Boston, Little, Brown & Co, 1937). Wigmore's approach was nonmathematical. In any event, he had few if any followers before the 1970s. In the 1970s and in the early 1980s David Schum led the way in making inference networks an important topic in probability theory. See, eg, D Schum and C Kelly 'A problem in cascaded inference: Determining the inferential impact of confirming and conflicting reports from several unreliable sources' (1973) 10 *Organizational Behavior and Human Performance* 404. Schum quickly extended his work into law. See, eg, D Schum and A Martin 'Formal and Empirical Research on Cascaded Inference in Jurisprudence' 17 *Law & Society Review* 105. Other scholars, both legal scholars and scholars in fields such as probability and decision theory, then took up serious study of inference networks. See, eg, RA Howard, *Influence Diagrams* (unpublished report) (1980); RA Howard, 'From Influence to Relevance to Knowledge' in RM Oliver and JQ Smith (eds), *Influence Diagrams, Belief Nets and Decision Analysis* (New York, John Wiley, 1990) 3; J Pearl, 'Reverend Bayes on Inference Engines: a Distributed Hierarchical Approach' in *Proceedings, AAAI National Conference on AI, Pittsburgh Pennsylvania* (August 1982) 133–36; P Tillers, 'Webs of Things in the Mind: A New Science of Evidence' (review essay) 87 *Michigan Law Review* 1225 (1989); T Anderson and WL Twining, *Analysis of Evidence* (Boston, Little, Brown & Co., 1991; paperback edn, Evanston, Illinois, Northwestern University Press, 1998); J Pearl, *Bayesian Networks*, UCLA Cognitive Systems Laboratory, Technical Report (R-216), Revision I, published in M Arbib (ed), *Handbook of Brain Theory and Neural Networks* (Cambridge, Mass, MIT Press, 1995) 149; B Robertson and G Vignaux, *Interpreting Evidence* (New York, John Wiley, 1995). Schum continued his work on inference networks both by himself and in collaboration with others. See, eg, D Schum, *Evidential Foundations of Probabilistic Reasoning* (New York, John Wiley, 1994; Evanston, Illinois, Northwestern University Press, 2001); T Anderson, D Schum and WL Twining, *Analysis of Evidence* 2nd edn (Cambridge, CUP, 2005).

Although the proponents of such models of evidential inference sometimes disagree (in important ways) about the properties or structure of multistage evidential inference, it is fair to say that such models generally rest on the compound proposition that real-world evidential inference usually or always consists of propositional 'atoms' (that is, relatively granular propositional statements about states of the world) that are linked together (in some way) by nomological entities of some kind, entities that are often – but not always – called 'generalisations'.[3] In this chapter I refer to these sorts of models or representations of evidential inference as 'NAGs', which is my shorthand for 'network-and-generalisation' models of evidential inference.

THE UNIVERSALITY OR NON-UNIVERSALITY OF THE NAG MODEL OF EVIDENTIAL INFERENCE

The case for the NAG model is a powerful one: NAGs seem to capture important properties of much evidential inference. However, even if NAGs are 'valid' representations of evidential inference, an important question (or family of questions) remains: Is a network-and-generalisation model or representation of evidential inference 'universal'? Does every problem of evidential inference take the form of a NAG? Does a network-and-generalisation model capture the essence of all inferential inferential problem; or – in any event – does (some version of) the NAG model capture an important ingredient of every problem of factual inference?

This question (or family of questions) arose recently within the transdisciplinary research programme and community known as 'Enquiry, Evidence and Facts'. Debate about the question of the universality or non-universality of the NAG model was provoked by a lecture given by David Schum at University College, London, in 2005[4]. In that lecture Schum argued that that there is such a thing as a science of evidence and that evidential inference in the form of a NAG is applicable – at least in principle – to any investigation into the truth or falsity of any proposition

[3] William Twining has a perceptive discussion of varieties of generalisations in WL Twining, 'Narrative and Generalizations in Argumentation about Questions of Fact' (1990) 40 *South Texas Law Review* 351. Some theorists believe that the nomological glue ought to be part of the inference network itself whereas other theorists (including most legal theorists) think that entities such as generalisations should be viewed as ancillary to an inference network. This is an important disagreement. An even more important division is between people who believe (eg, Judea Pearl) that inference networks represent causal connections (among events in time) and those who reject this view (eg, David Schum). The difference of opinion on this point may reflect a fundamental epistemological disagreement about the possibility of knowledge based on associations in the absence of knowledge or plausible hypotheses about causal connections.

[4] D Schum, Thoughts about a Science of Evidence (29 December 2005) (research report), at http://www.evidencescience.org/pubs/pubs_detail.asp?pubID=70.

about a state of the world.[5] Participants in Enquiry, Evidence and Facts raised a variety of questions and objections to Schum's thesis. Schum responded to those questions and objections.[6] However, the question of the reach of the NAG model of evidential inference remains unresolved – as does the question of whether any model or representation of evidential inference can achieve 'universality'.

I believe that the question of universality or non-universality of NAGs is literally unanswerable. In this chapter I argue – once again[7] – that the only genuinely general thing that can be said about the structure of problems of evidential inference is that when human beings (or other agents) configure problems of evidence in a certain way, inference networks (of some sort) are ineluctable and do describe the structure of the problem at hand but that when problems of evidence are perceived – that is, configured – only or mainly in some other ways, representations of an inferential process as a web of factual hypotheses connected by generalisations are of little or no use. In short, I take the arguably 'wishy-washy' position that sometimes NAGs have little or no epistemic value because in some situations web-like patterns of reasoning do not accurately portray the way that an observer, investigator or fact-finder configures, or perceives, a problem of inference, together with the evidence that seemingly pertains to the problem that the observer, investigator or fact-finder perceives.

I support and illustrate my thesis about the relationship between (evidential) argument and configuration (or perception) by examining three situations in which network-and-generalisation representations of evidential inference – 'NAGs' – seem to have little to say about the relationship between evidence and hypotheses. The first is a situation in which there is a question about the meanings that human beings attach to actions or events. The second is a situation in which tacit or unconscious inference – that is non-explicit inference – is at work. The third is a situation in which the (complex) inferential methods (strategies) employed by a 'special science' such as physics, chemistry or genetics seem to address best the inferential problem at hand. After discussing these three examples of 'non-standard' evidential inference I conclude by pointing out some features of man and mind that are suggested by a proper understanding of inference and inferential theory.

[5] Schum's belief in the existence of a science of evidence is longstanding. See P Tillers, 'Webs of Things in the Mind: A New Science of Evidence' (review essay) (1989) 87 *Michigan Law Review* 1225.

[6] D Schum, A Reply to the 'Schum challenge' at UCL (6 September 2006), available at <http://www.evidencescience.org/pubs/pubs_detail.asp?pubID=52> accessed 16 June 2008.

[7] The general theoretical underpinnings of the argument in this chapter were anticipated in P Tillers 'Mapping Inferential Domains' (1986) 66 *Boston University Law Review* 883, reprinted in P Tillers and E Green (eds), *Probability and Inference in the Law of Evidence: The Uses and Limits of Bayesianism* (Dordrecht, Boston and London, Kluwer Academic Publishers, 1988) 277.

THREE EXAMPLES OF 'NON-STANDARD' EVIDENTIAL INFERENCE

1. Inference about Human Meaning – IRM

In some situations an investigator or fact-finder does not focus on the question of the occurrence or non-occurrence of some event or events. Sometimes an investigator instead assumes (if only provisionally) the occurrence (or non-occurrence) of some event or events and seeks to determine the meaning or meanings of those events (or the absence of some events) to some person or persons. For example, an investigator might reasonably believe or assume (provisionally, for example) that, as expected, the sun appeared in the sky in the morning of some particular day or that a comet unexpectedly became visible to the naked eye a few weeks ago – and ask, 'What did that mean to Peter Tillers?' or 'What did that mean to the Pope?' Hence, in the hypothesised type of situation, instead of asking whether evidence such as $\mathbf{E_L}$ – the appearance of some new light in the sky, some apparent new light in the sky – supports the hypothesis **A**, the appearance (or seeming appearance) of the sun or of a comet,

$$\mathbf{E_L} \rightarrow \mathbf{A}$$

Expression 1

the actor or observer assumes the occurrence of some event such as **A** and seeks to determine **M**, the meaning of some event **A** (whether in the eyes of Peter Tillers, the Pope or some other person or persons).

The manner in which Expression 1 portrays the relationship between some evidence $\mathbf{E_L}$ and some event **A** may suggest that it is both possible and appropriate to depict the relationship between some event or events **A** and some meaning or meanings **M** in precisely the same way: If so, perhaps the question of **M** given **A** involves nothing more and nothing other than the question of whether and the extent to which a mental state such as **M** is supported by evidence such as **A**. If so, questions about the meanings attached to events or circumstances – I shall sometimes refer to such questions as MQs – are merely problems or questions that take the form

$$\mathbf{E} \rightarrow \mathbf{A} \rightarrow \mathbf{M}$$

Expression 2

In some situations it is appropriate to conceive of the relationship between a meaning **M** and an event such as **A** in this manner. However, in many instances this way of framing the relationship between some possible meaning **M** and some possible event such as A is inappropriate. In many situations the problem confronting an investigator or trier of fact is

whether or not a meaning such as **M** is wrapped around or attached to an event such as **A**. Conceived in this way, judgments about the meaning or meanings of acts are better pictured in the following way:

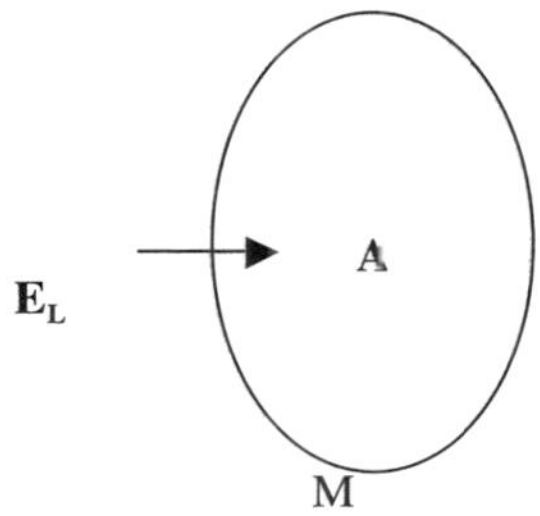

M = Concept having meaning M

Figure 1

Consider two possible visions of the meaning of the structure of the cosmos and one or two of its major parts. This is one vision:

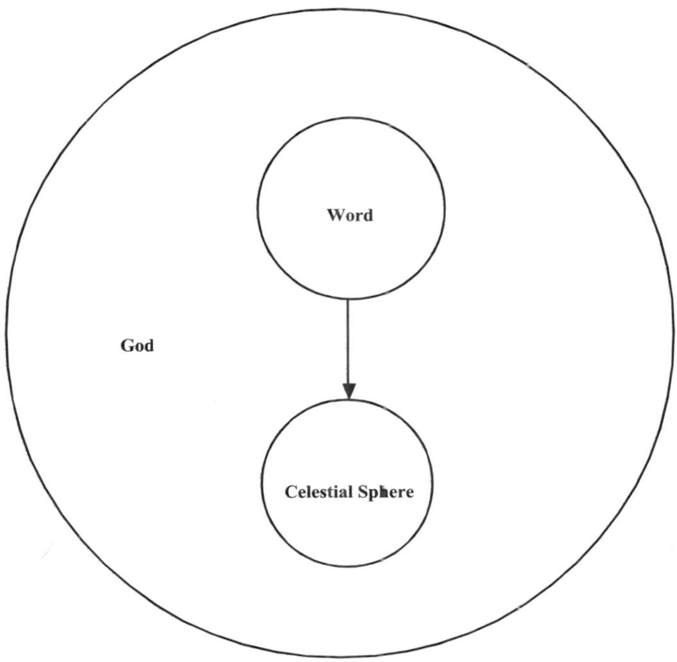

Figure 2

Here is another vision:

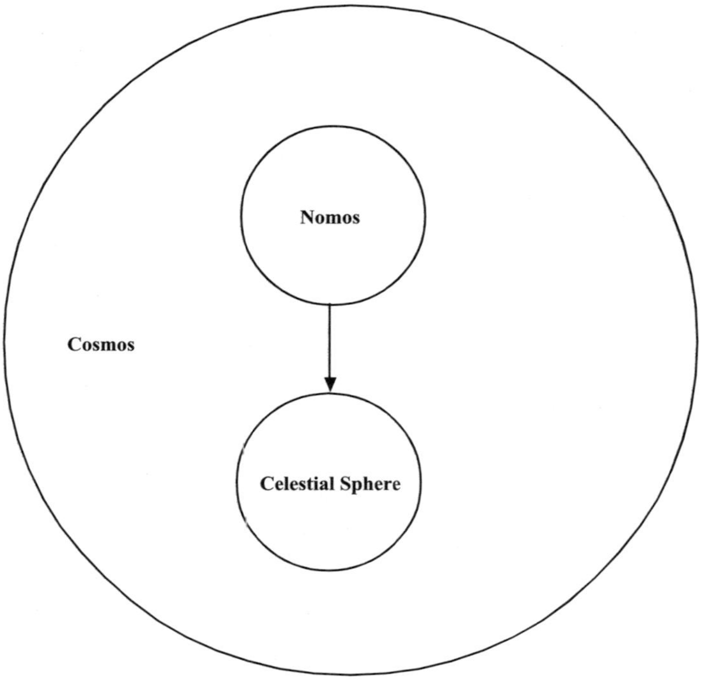

Figure 3

Although these two visions (that is, those reflected in Figures 2 and 3) are very general and lack detail, they suffice to illustrate the different ways that different people might think about the meaning or meanings of the same event. These two visions suggest, for example, that a religious person might view the appearance of a comet in the night sky as a manifestation or expression of God's Word in the cosmos, while another person might believe that celestial phenomena are manifestations of underlying natural laws that reign in the cosmos.[8]

The attempt to determine the meaning or meanings that some person or persons attach to various events and circumstances in the world is an intellectual activity that involves imagination and reconstruction. (I will occasionally refer to this sort of creative and constructive intellectual activity as the 'imaginative reconstruction of meaning', or IRM.) The effort to infer meanings that 'reside' in the minds of others (at certain times)

[8] Note that despite their differences, both of these imaginary people might accept scientific accounts such as special relativity and quantum theory. If you doubt this, it is worth recalling that Isaac Newton believed in the existence of God.

involves the attempt to read other minds.[9] If done explicitly rather than intuitively, this sort of effort to discern the meanings that are at work in the minds of others perhaps must be done in a particular way.

The 'meanings' that human beings attach to events and circumstances usually involve complex concepts (or complexes of concepts) rather than only simple, or irreducible, concepts. Moreover, individual meanings (such as lust, anger, jealousy, and respect) belong to families of concepts (such as 'infidelity', 'spouse', 'love', 'children', 'class' 'chastity'). Hence, when an investigator makes a serious attempt at an IRM – that is when an investigator, or enquirer, makes an attempt to put together a reconstruction that that has at least a remote chance of being representative of some actual state of affairs or some actual series of events – the investigator must try to formulate a complex of concepts (and also the complex of principles that governs the relationships among that complex of non-primitive, or decomposable, concepts) that depicts and reconstitutes, to at least some degree, the meanings that some other persons actually attach (at some point or interval in time) to events and acts that those persons think they encounter in the sort of world that they believe they inhabit.

When evidential inference takes the form of a NAG, evidence plays a role much like the role that symptoms play in the diagnosis of a physical disease such as cancer. In such an investigation, evidence is of interest to an investigator (or 'fact-finder') because the evidence, it is thought, may speak to the truth or falsity of some proposition about the occurrence or non-occurrence of some event or condition in the world. But in investigations of MQs evidence regularly serves a very different epistemic purpose. In an enquiry about MQs an investigator may look to events and circumstances mainly or exclusively to see if she can find in some events or circumstances the footprint, or imprint, of some human mind or minds. In this kind of enquiry the investigator wants to see if some circumstance, such as a person's conduct, harbours a trace of – some evidence of – the structure of the thinking and beliefs of some person or persons.

An investigator who looks at evidence for this purpose and in this way – to reconstruct the meaning or meanings in the head of another person or persons – often views evidence virtually in a medieval or scholastic fashion.

[9] Human beings have no 'direct' access to the minds of other human beings; they cannot directly perceive the minds of other human beings. Philosophers' awareness of this point has made them question – philosophers are wont to raise seemingly strange questions – the existence of other minds. However, one should be wary about making too much of any argument based on our lack of direct access to others' minds. The logic of the argument for doubting the existence of other minds quite possibly implies that one must doubt the existence of anything – since, after all, there is good reason to think that human beings have no 'direct' epistemic access to anything in the world, except perhaps (but only perhaps!) to their own perceptions of the world. (There is good reason to doubt that human beings know even their own perceptions directly.)

An investigator or fact-finder who looks to events such as human conduct for traces of the content and structure of an actor's thinking may view evidence such as human conduct as an almost literal *sign*: such an investigator may believe that circumstances in the world can embody bits of meanings, intentions, beliefs and similar matters, and that circumstances sometimes do so because fragments of human minds can be deposited in the world by the deliberate actions of intelligent beings.

Although it is rational and sensible to believe that events and circumstances in the world can echo the workings of the human mind and the human heart, the model of evidential inference as a NAG – as a network or web of web of inferences accompanied by generalisations or law-like statements of some kind – is, I believe, a powerful and compelling one. A person enchanted by inference network model of evidential inference – and I count myself as such a person – might try to shoehorn all deliberation about human meaning into the form of a NAG. For example, I can imagine that a dedicated proponent of inference networks might take the position that a question about what species of meaning **M** some actor attaches to some event or action (at some point or interval in time) is a question of fact like any other question of fact and that the possible relationships between evidence and a proposition about a fact of type **M** are the same as between evidence and a proposition about any other type of fact. Hewing to this line of thinking, one might then take the position that the question of whether an actor attached some specific meaning **Mi** to some event or act amounts to the question whether the actor did or did not have a state of mind **S** containing the specific meaning **Mi**. Schematically stated, then, the issue before the trier would be

$$\{S_{Mi} \mid {\sim}S_{Mi}\}$$

Expression 3

The relationship of this question to evidence such as evidence of the actor's possible irritation $\mathbf{E}_i$ could then be visualised thus:

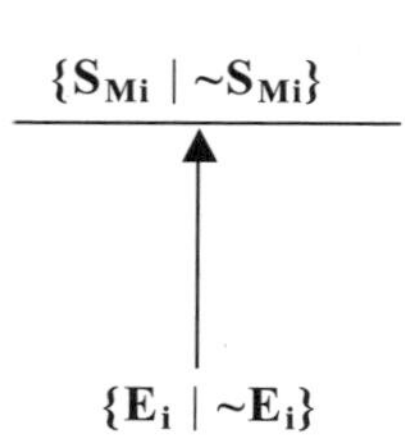

Figure 4

If one grants or assumes that all questions and arguments about the meanings that human actors attach to events and circumstances can and

should be formulated in this way, one can then apply the particular type of inference network that one prefers to any given question about human meaning. For example, if one has Bayesian inclinations one can follow Bayesian convention and reverse the direction of the arrow in the diagram in Figure 4, and then compare (i) the probability of **Ei** given **SMi** with (ii) the probability of **Ei** given **~SMi** and consider what impact this ratio has on one's pre-existing judgment about the probability of **SMi**. Alternatively,[10] one can ask whether and to what extent evidence such as **Ei** supports the hypothesis of **SMi** (the state of mind **S** harbouring the meaning **Mi**). And then if one also believes that some possible glue connecting **SMi** with **Ei** must be separately considered in any rational argument about the inferences supported by any evidence, any potentially-pertinent ancillary generalisations can and should be made to envelop or to be enveloped by the sort of inference structure shown in Figure 4.

But the ability of a person to shoehorn deliberation about human meaning into the form of a NAG proves little. It might be possible to give pigs wings and to enable them to fly. But a flying pig with wings would be an unnatural and ungainly spectacle. Similarly, it might also be possible to make all deliberation about human meaning take the form of an inference network. But to do so would sometimes create an unedifying spectacle as well as an unnatural and ungainly one. As explained earlier, in many investigations (or parts of investigations) of the meanings that actors attach to events and circumstances in the world – in many investigations of 'M-assignments' – the central question is not whether some state of mind **S** harbouring **Mi** did or did not occur and the main task at hand is instead to ascertain the structure of **M** and the family of concepts **F** to which **M** belongs. NAGs do not elucidate or facilitate this latter sort of enquiry because the latter sort of activity is a creative and imaginative activity – I call it the imaginative reconstruction of meaning, or IRM – and a NAG does not elucidate or facilitate this sort of imaginative or creative activity.

When proceeding in an IRM mode, an investigator is engaged in hypothesis-formation. Arguments in the form of NAGs do not directly facilitate hypothesis-formation because NAGs are principally devices for assessing the strength or weight of evidence on defined – that is either known or assumed – hypotheses.[11] (Hypotheses are formed within inference networks, but the hypotheses that are formed are so formed in the

[10] It is possible this alternative formulation is not essentially or necessarily different from a Bayesian formulation.

[11] P Tillers and D Schum, 'A Theory of Preliminary Fact Investigation' (1991) 24 *University of California at Davis Law Review* 931 (discussing the difference between the role of evidence in argument about stated factual hypothesis and the role of evidence in the formation of factual hypotheses; the article also suggests why abduction in the form of 'inference to the best explanation' does not adequately explain or promote the formation of epistemically fertile hypotheses). For an illuminating analysis of varieties of abductive

interstices between the two poles of inference networks, foundational evidence and ultimate hypotheses.) Furthermore, in the case of IRM the formation of hypotheses about human meanings is not provoked or suggested by the presence of some sensory event whose appearance seems more probable given some one possible meaning (or set of meanings) rather than some other possible meaning (or set of meanings). In much IRM the enquirer creates hypotheses about complexes of meanings by examining properties of events that, in the eyes of the enquirer, seem to constitute marks that are expressive or indicative of – that seem to echo – some complex of meaning-concepts and meaning-rules. In an IRM mode an investigator proceeds in much the way that a cryptographer proceeds: the investigator's focus is on the logic that may be partially displayed in some marks that appear in some events or circumstances in the world.

The analysis presented here of the kind of reasoning that is ordinarily (and properly) used in IRM is, in its broad contours, in harmony with a well-established philosophical and intellectual tradition that also holds that a distinctive method of argument, reasoning and thinking must be used to

inference, see D Schum 'Species of Abductive Reasoning in Fact Investigation in Law' (2001) 22 Cardozo Law Review 1461. By arguing that NAGs do not portray the workings of IRM I am not suggesting that IRM in legal proceedings should proceed without the benefit of evidence. In IRM as in any other type of deliberation, the formation of hypotheses that are completely unrooted in evidence is likely to lead to production of propositions about the world that may be entertaining but have little chance of being true. Legal adjudication of rights and duties cannot rest on entirely speculative propositions about events in the world. By arguing that NAGs do not capture the workings of IRM, I am not suggesting that propositions generated by IRM need not be supported by evidential argument. Moreover, I am not intimating that any judgments generated by IRM cannot be a constituent of an argument that takes the form of a NAG. Perhaps it goes without saying that although deliberation in the form of IRM and deliberation in the form of NAGs are different, IRM can be an ingredient of evidential argument and inference that takes the form of a network. If this is indeed already obvious to every reader, it is possible that the main service performed by this chapter is to remind students of forensic proof that not only are meaning assignments – eg, 'the pulling of this trigger is intended to cause death and destruction' – often the ultimate *facta probanda* in legal proceedings, but that meaning assignments – eg, 'Switzerland is a lovely country with courteous people' – are also often part of the foundation for an argument about some ultimate *factum probandum* in a case. (The common use of M-assignments as a basis for further inference raises a variety of knotty inferential issues that US and UK scholarship in the law of evidence has yet to examine in a systematic fashion. For example, perhaps actors' judgments of meaning are ordinarily quite fuzzy; ie perhaps actors' concepts about what makes this or that event or condition or property good, lovely, vile, rotten, etc., are ordinarily very fuzzy. Moreover, perhaps the rules that actors use to reason about their fuzzy concepts of meaning tend to be fuzzy; eg, if an actor thinks that being loud-mouthed is generally bad but that being outspoken in the defence of oppressed minorities is generally good, what sort of judgment should the actor make about a loud-mouthed defender of the rights of Italian-Americans? Furthermore, the concepts and rules that actors use to attach meanings to events and circumstances in the world may be quite unstable and changeable. If all of these baleful possibilities turn out to be true, how can investigators and fact finders draw rational or epistemically-defensible inferences from the meaning-complexes that reside or seem to reside in the heads and hearts of actors? Is the attempt to infer action from thought always a game of blind man's buff? I am not sure of the answers to these questions.)

investigate the meaning or meanings that human beings attach to events in the world and states of the world. I am referring to the intellectual approach founded or resurrected by Wilhelm Dilthey (1833–1911). Dilthey maintained that a special method of knowing – he called it *Verstehen* – is required in the human sciences, in the *Geisteswissenschaften*.[12] However, Dilthey's thesis about a special way of knowing and studying social and cultural phenomena never quite achieved the prestige in the United States that it enjoyed on much of the European Continent.[13] Perhaps this is one reason why for the larger part of the 20th century 'official' legal discourse about factual inference rarely even hints at the existence of even a suspicion that courtroom investigations into matters such as cultural practices or an actor's intentions might call for the use of evidentiary processes that differ substantially from those that are employed in courtroom investigations of so-called 'physical' or 'external' facts or events.[14]

[12] W Dilthey, *Der Aufbau der geschichtlichen Welt in den Geisteswissenschaften* (Stuttgart, BG Teubner, 1958, 1992) (VII Band, *Gesammelte Schriften*) 205.

[13] Dilthey's notion of *Verstehen* had its roots in Kant's philosophy of law and, more broadly speaking, in the philosophical and intellectual tradition that we now call German Idealism. Although German Idealism was not wholly unknown in American intellectual circles in the 20th century – eg, John Dewey was influenced by German Idealism – the influence of German Idealism in American intellectual circles for most of the 20th century was not nearly as great as it was on the European Continent.

[14] However, there have been exceptions to this general indifference to or unawareness of Diltheyesque claims about the importance of using distinctive methods of investigation when studying matters such as mental processes, moral beliefs, cultural values, cultural practices, aesthetic sensibilities and religious practices and predilections. One intriguing exception is Jerome Bruner. Jerome Bruner is a renowned psychologist. He is nominally not a legal scholar. However, in recent years and decades he has taken to writing about legal matters. Bruner expressly embraces the general theoretical tradition or perspective that Dilthey sired or resurrected. In his book *Acts of Meaning*, Bruner states, 'Very early on, emphasis [in cognitive science] began shifting from "meaning" to "information," from the *construction* of meaning to the *processing* of information. These are profoundly different matters'. J Bruner, *Acts of Meaning* (Cambridge, Mass and London: Harvard UP, 1990) 4. A bit later in the same book Bruner adds that 'to understand man you must understand how his experience and acts are shaped by his intentional states'. (*Ibid* 33) Among the methods of investigation and deliberation that Bruner favours for getting at the meaning of individual and social acts and arrangements – eg, for ascertaining the intentions and purposes that individual acts and social practices and arrangements may embody or reflect – is story-telling. It is clearly no coincidence that Bruner – a refugee from a Nazifying Europe – received his education on the European Continent.

It is tempting to treat Mirjan Damaška – another European immigrant who received his university education on the European Continent – as another exception that proves the general rule: Like Bruner, Damaška has had an interest in 'soft' and 'holistic' methods of proof. See, eg, Damaška, *Evidence Law Adrift* (New Haven and London, Yale 1997), 34–36. However, unlike Bruner, Damaška has never unequivocally embraced a purely epistemological argument for the superiority of soft or holistic proof processes – or, for that matter, of any other mode of proof. It is, however, quite plain that Damaška was always acutely aware of Diltheyesque (and, surely, also Marxian and Marxist) epistemological arguments in favour of this or that method of investigating 'factual' questions involving the 'inner world' (or worlds) of individuals or groups. This sort of awareness of various ways of thinking about 'truth' and

Unconscious Inference

Hermann von Helmholtz noticed more than a century ago that perception is a form of 'unconscious inference'.[15] One likely reason why we usually refer to perceptual inference with the singleton 'perception' rather than with the phrase 'perceptual inference' is that we usually have little understanding of the underlying principles that lead biological mechanisms (for example, perceptual organs such as eyes, ears, and so on) to generate the inferences that they do. Perhaps in the 'fullness of time' it will be shown that the underlying logic takes the form of, say, a NAG. Or perhaps not! Or perhaps it will be shown that multiple logics are at work. (This seems more likely.) But regardless of how such difficult intellectual puzzles are eventually resolved, it remains true for the time being – even though in recent decades there have been great advances in our understanding of the workings of perception (visual perception, aural perception, etc) – that we human beings generally can do little more than marvel at the workings of our perceptual organs and at present have relatively little ability to make healthy sense organs work better than they naturally do. But perhaps human beings sometimes can do just a bit more than this; perhaps I exaggerate. For example, perhaps empirical studies can identify some types of situations – generalisable situations – in which error rates of various kinds are comparatively high (or low). However this may be, the simple fact is the logical workings of much subconscious inference remain elusive and cannot yet be explicitly described in a systematic fashion. (The fact that the 'intelligence' of some or much human inference is largely impervious to explicit restatement by human beings does not mean that perceptual intelligence and inference do not exist. Quite the contrary: Much unintelligible subconscious inference is extraordinarily intelligent.[16])

various kinds of 'facts' has lent Damaška's ruminations about evidentiary, inferential and proof processes a subtlety and a depth that were usually missing in the work of 'mainstream' American Evidence scholars of his day.

[15] HE Adler, 'Hermann Ludwig Ferdinand von Helmholtz: Physicist as Psychologist' in 4 GA Kimble and M Wertheimer (eds), *Portraits of Pioneers in Psychology* (Lawrence Erlbaum, 2000) 15; G Hatfield, *Perception as Unconscious Inference* (University of Pennsylvania Institute for Research in Cognitive Science Technical Report No IRCS-01–04, 1 April 2001): available at <http://repository.upenn.edu/ircs_reports/9/>, posted 7 August 2006, accessed 17 June 2008, and in D Heyer and R Mausfeld (eds), *Perception and the Physical World: Psychological and Philosophical Issues in Perception* (Oxford, OUP, 2002) 115–145. Helmholtz was not the first person to suggest the notion of unconscious inference; Hatfield traces the notion to antiquity. Hatfield observes that today there is some disagreement about whether sensory or perceptual processing of sensory information should be called 'inference'. For present purposes it makes eminent sense to do so.

[16] This premise is the basis of much contemporary research in fields such as artificial intelligence, cognitive science, and neuroscience. This is not just a matter of believing that human thought rumbles somewhat below the plane of conscious thought and is therefore hard to grasp. The underlying premise is that some kind of logic or logics animate practically all or all aspects of human cognition. For example, Marvin Minsky, one of the founders of

Inference in the Special Sciences

Certain problems of evidence and inference present or are thought to present inferential issues that only a special science such as quantum mechanics or genetics can adequately address. The extent to which representations in the form of NAGs illuminate the logic that is deployed to address such problems depends on the presuppositions and methods of the special science that are thought to hold the key to the inferential riddles that are presented. Not all sciences – not even all 'hard' sciences – use logic and methods that NAGs usefully represent.

Consider a very abstract example. Suppose that the following network of inferences along with certain ancillary generalisations correctly represents the structure of an inferential problem as understood by a scientist such as a physicist or metallurgist:

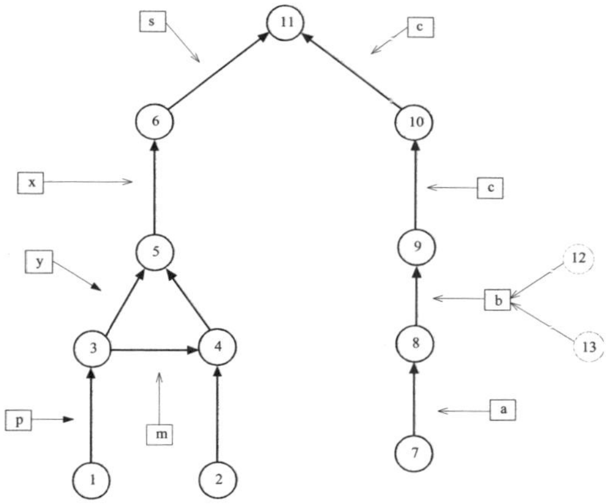

Figure 5A

modern AI, rejects the suggestion that there are some perceptions, sensations, sensory signals or sense *qualia* that are just whatever they are. He wrote:

[S]ome people … think that the qualities of such sensations [such as the sensation of a colour such as 'red'] are so basic and irreducible that they will always remain inexplicable. However, I prefer to take the opposite view – that what we call sensations are complex reflective activities. They sometimes involve extensive cascades in which some parts of the brain are affected by signals whose origins we cannot detect – and therefore, we find them hard to explain. So, I see no exceptional mystery here: we simply don't yet know enough about what is actually happening in our brains. But when you think enough about anything, then you see this is also the case with everything.

M Minsky, *Interior Grounding, Reflection, and Self-Consciousness*, <http://web.media.mit.edu/~minsky/papers/Internal%20Grounding.html> accessed 23 Nov 2007; paper originally published in *Brain, Mind and Society, Proceedings of an International Conference on Brain, Mind and Society* (Graduate School of Information Sciences, Brain, Mind and Society, Tohoku University, Japan, September 2005).

where node b in the above diagram represents the following equation:

$$x = \frac{s + (m/2)}{y^b}$$

Earlier I said that the diagram in Version A of Figure 5 accurately represents the structure of an inferential problem as understood by some scientist. So what is there to talk about? We have a NAG, don't we?

Yes. But the diagram in Figure 5, Version A may nevertheless fail to represent the way the scientist 'sees' the problem at hand. For example, although my hypothesised scientist concedes that the NAG in Figure 5, Version A accurately represents the logical structure of the problem she believes she faces, she may in fact envision the problem she faces in the way depicted in Figure 5, Version B:

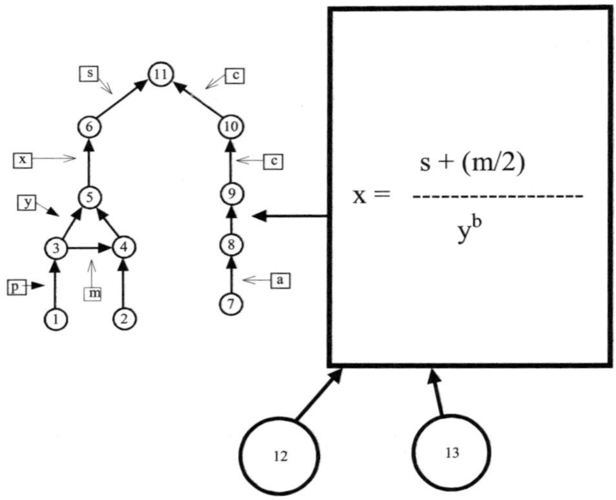

Figure 5B

The two versions of Figure 5 are, from some logical points of view, identical. For example, from the standpoint of a graph theorist, despite the differences in the sizes and locations of some of the nodes and arrows, the problems in the two versions have the same structure and they are therefore identical. But, of course, in one version of the problem (Figure 5, Version B) one ingredient of the problem is much 'bigger' – visually – than in the other version (Figure 5, Version A). This difference in shape and size (but not in structure and content) is designed to suggest and represent a difference in my hypothesised scientist's attitude toward or view of the problem. Although this difference might be characterised as a 'psychological' one, the fact

remains that my hypothesised scientist believes that the calculations, computations and reasoning called for by node b are the 'really important' part of the procedure for attacking the question or problem represented by node 11; that is, she believes that the calculations and reasoning referenced and represented by node b are likely to be decisive for the solution of the ultimate inferential question designated by node 11. Given this belief and assumption (an assumption that may be well-grounded), the node-and-arrow-with-ancillary-generalisations scheme – a NAG – that appears in both versions of Figure 5 adds nothing useful (in her eyes) to the part of the problem – the equation – that node b designates.

Now it is true – as the structure of Version B of Figure 5 effectively acknowledges – that the upshot of the computations, calculations, and meditations required by or involved in node b may be affected by the other propositions and calculations represented by the entire NAG. But the diagram I have drawn (Figure 5, Version B) asserts (so I proclaim!) that in the mind of the scientist the ingredients of the inference problem outside of node b may be ignored; she knows or believes she knows what the upshot is for hypothesis 11 once she has properly done the calculations represented by node b. And what she believes is also what someone else (for example, the trier of fact in a legal trial) may rationally and reasonably believe!

A REBIRTH OF ARISTOTELIAN EPISTEMOLOGY AND ONTOLOGY?

The root of these 'exceptions' to NAGs (and of other 'exceptions' that remain to be identified) is a fundamental onto-epistemological premise or hypothesis. This hypothesis begins with a firm denial that rational inference involves only explicit logic. Although human inference is a rational and logical activity, human inference – that is, the inferential activity of the human organism – involves not just (let alone only, or even mainly) explicit ratiocinative processes. Inference is one of the activities of a sentient human organism. (The same is true of non-human organisms.) The human organism, though sentient, is 'rational' to its core: Logic – a complex logic or a set of logics – is embedded in the human organism and regulates its activities.[17] It is true that many (and probably most) indwelling human

[17] As already noted, even the human organism's sentient activities are fundamentally and deeply logical, and they are, in that sense, 'rational'. Among students of the mind and the brain – cognitive scientists, neuroscientists and others of this ilk – the debate today is not whether some tacit logic guides subconscious processes such as vision and memory. The debate is largely about the nature of such tacit logics and their precise source. Some scholars stress the physiological or biological roots of indwelling logics. Others stress that the nature of the indwelling logic is what matters and that human intelligence can be embedded in various kinds of material structures. But whatever position scholars take on this general

logics are still poorly understood.[18] But however imperfectly we understand the subconscious logics within us, there is good reason to think that such logics are nevertheless 'there' – that a variety of indwelling logics are at work in the human organism. The bottom line is that although it is true that human beings are inferential reasoners, much human inferential reasoning – a vast amount of it – is hidden from human sight.

Since the dawn of modern artificial intelligence – and even before – man (AKA his mind, AKA his brain, AKA his neural system, AKA woman, etc, etc) has been analogised to a mechanical computer.[19] This analogy (which

question, all or almost all of them agree that: (i) subconscious logics embedded in human biological material process information – such inbred logics do inference; and (ii) most human information processing – inference – occurs at a subconscious level. Sciences such as genetics are making it increasingly plain that logical forms, or information, such as the 'genetic code', drive the development – and thus the very existence – of humanity as a species and of individual human beings. But to hypothesise that matters such as the genetic code ensure the rationality of the human animal may be taking the argument for inbred human rationality a bit too far. For example, I can imagine that a 'rational' genetic code (and any other similar 'codes' that shape or influence the development of organisms) can produce 'irrational' and inept creatures – creatures, for example, who manage to survive only because some of their biological 'friends', who do a better job of processing information, throw their inept companions a life-line. Cf J Fodor, 'Why Pigs Don't Have Wings' (18 October 2007) 29 *London Review of Books* No 20 (discussing, in part, why Mother Nature, the notion of evolutionary adaptation and similar ideas do not explain why organisms have properties that are analogous to spandrels, which serve no purpose in architecture but accompany and must accompany certain architectural designs).

[18] That the subconscious logics at work in the human animal remain poorly understood should not occasion surprise. Although human intelligence may or may not be synonymous with the physical architecture of the human animal, almost all observers agree that the workings of tacit human intelligence do depend in a fundamental and necessary way on physical architecture of the human organism, on matters such the properties and design of human eyes and the properties and workings of the neural system (including constituents such as neurons and axons). Hence, if a full understanding of subconscious inference (including matters such as vision, hearing, taste) is ever to be possible, our knowledge of a vast multiplicity of sciences probably has to be perfected – sciences such as genetics, physics, electro-mechanics, signal detection, neural science, chemistry, biochemistry, quantum mechanics and who knows what else. But it is possible that even comprehensive knowledge about the mechanics or physical structure of the human brain and the human organism would not fully reveal the indwelling logics that are at work in human cognition and inference. This is because one must still consider the possibility that the environment feeds information and logic and (so to speak) processing power and capacity into a human organism with a receptive architecture. So I do not mean to intimate or suggest that the logic or logics that dwell within a developed human organism in the 21st century are necessarily in any sense synonymous with the physical architecture of the brain, the human nervous system or any yet broader swath of the human organism. Fortunately, except for the hypothesis that the human mind is not separate from human matter (but is, rather, embedded in human matter), the argument in this chapter does not depend on any particular solution to the vexing question of the relationship between human mind and human matter.

[19] See the exhaustive survey of the history of this idea in M Boden, Mind as Machine: A History of Cognitive Science vols 1 and 2 (Oxford, Clarendon Press, 2006). There is excellent reason to think the analogy is significantly inexact. First, there appears to be widespread agreement that the brain uses parallel rather than serial processing. Hence, if the brain is like a computer, its operations are not isomorphic to the operations of a typical digital computer, which (I gather) performs operations sequentially. Second, some studies of the neural system

is often taken very seriously) amounts to an ontological-epistemological revolution; it amounts to a rejection of the dichotomy between mind and body, thought and matter,[20] and it restores, in modern guise, the Aristotelian notion of organism. To think in terms of organisms is to think in terms of purposes and functions.[21]

The emerging reversion to an Aristotelian ontology is, in my view, a lovely revolution; this 'new' – but ancient – way of thinking about man tends in the right direction. However, the contemporary turn in fields such as AI towards functional and teleological accounts of man frequently suffers from a serious defect. The ruling image, model or analogy of man (or human mind) as computer does not always sufficiently stress that the 'human computer' is a developing computational creature.

What sort of evolution does the human inferential computer undergo? Common sense, the presuppositions of the study of evidence and inference in legal settings, and a great deal else (for example, thermostats) suggest or

suggest that signals are not transmitted only at synapses – the junctions between nerve cell extensions – but that signals are also transmitted 'along the entire length of [nerve cell] extensions and, in this way, excite the neighbouring cells' and this – one study suggests – may mean that neural information processing works 'chaotically'. See 'Brain works more chaotically than previously thought', Science Blog (27 February 2007), at <http://www.scienceblog.com/cms/brain-works-more-chaotically-than-previously-thought-12682.html> accessed 17 June 2008.

[20] S Pinker, *How the Mind Works* (New York and London, WW Norton, 1997) 24:

'This book is about the brain, but I will not say much about neurons, hormones, and neurotransmitters. That is because the mind is not the brain but what the brain does, and not even everything it does, such as metabolizing fat and giving off heat ... The brain's special status comes from a special thing the brain does ... That special thing is information processing, or computation.

Information and computation reside in patterns of data and in relations of logic that are independent of the physical medium that carries them ...

This insight...is now called the computational theory of mind. It is one of the great ideas in intellectual history, for it solves one of the puzzles that make up the "mind-body problem": how to connect the ethereal world of meaning and intention, the stuff of our mental lives, with a physical hunk of matter like the brain'.

[21] It may seem a bit odd – but it seems to be a fact – that some of the best-known AI adherents to the proposition that the mind is what the brain does, to the proposition that fundamental to an understanding of the workings of the mind is an understanding of the functional logic that is embedded in the brain – are people who style themselves 'materialists' of one kind of another – people such as Daniel Dennett and Paul and Patricia Churchland, who at one time or another have favoured some kind of 'functionalism'. See, eg, Boden, above n 19, vol 2, 1362–69 (on Dennett) and 1376–1379 (on the Churchlands). In my view such theorists have moved in the direction of an organic and neo-Aristotelian view of the relationship between man and human thought. In any event, the world of AI and cognitive science is replete with people who view human physiology and the various material parts of the human organism as being only the 'substrate' of a logical architecture, an architecture that can in principle be embedded within different material substrates – except, of course, to the extent that differences in the substrate prevent replication or installation of the necessary logical architecture. See, eg, the amusing statement in GM Edelman, *Second Nature, brain science and human knowledge* (New Haven and London, Yale UP, 2006) 127 that '[t]he position that the proposed artifact [having an intelligence equal to that of the human organism] must be made of biochemical components is known as biological chauvinism'.

suppose that it is possible, here and there, for tacit human inference – or, if you prefer, inference simpliciter – to emerge into the light, to become explicit. Such considerations and such examples of the victories of relatively complete explicit ratiocination (that is, examples of a fairly high degree of inferential automation) suggest, more broadly, that the human organism has some capacity (the full extent of which is as yet necessarily undetermined) to force at least some its tacit, or subconscious, logical processes into the light of consciousness and to make previously tacit inference explicit or, in any event, to make relatively tacit inferences more explicit and thus more subject to some explicit logical analysis and argument. This latter function is, in my view, frequently (but not always) precisely the central function of mental crutches and representations such as NAGs. (Sometimes – but only sometimes – inbred human logics will manage to emerge from the human animal and escape from the clutches of their creator. An example is to be seen in Isaac Asimov's *I, Robot*.[22] Less dramatically, consider once again the lowly thermostat – or the flying drones now used by the military for surveillance and even for combat operations.)

On this view of things – on my neo-Aristotelian view of the general relationship between the logic(s) in (wo)man and (wo)man's explicit ratiocination about the world (including him- or herself) – an important function of explicit reflection, analysis, argument and reason is to have the human organism wrest out of itself and its encounters with the 'world' (including its encounters with itself) some principles and logics (forms of reasoning) that the organism can hold consciously in mind or, in any event, that can be recorded and stored elsewhere, by means of marks made in the world, as in readable computer scripts and programs. The aim of such explicit expression and formulation is in part to enable the organism to facilitate and, perhaps paradoxically, improve the workings of at least some of the logics that dwell – hitherto unseen – in the human organism (and in its environment).

When such victories of explicit ratiocination (either victories that facilitate inference or those that automate inference) are achieved, they ought to be celebrated. And whenever possible, the human organism should use its emergent logic to improve its immanent logic. But on my view of things, humility about human inferential capacity – humility, that is, about the power of explicit inferential calculation – has the status of a virtual first principle. It must not be forgotten that many or most of the logical operations of the human organism remain hidden from the human organism's sight and comprehension. In many situations, therefore, (unless we share the wild-eyed – and seductive! – optimism of a Marvin Minsky)

[22] I Asimov, *I, Robot* (New York, Gnome, 1950).

the only reasonable expectation we can have of deliberation about evidence is that such deliberation will bring some shards of our indwelling logical processes to light. But we should remain alert: (i) to the possibility that sometimes we will just have to trust our unanalysed hunches; and (ii) to the perverse possibility that it is not always the case that explicit analysis of evidence will improve our inferential performance.

III

Human Rights Standards and Hybridisation in the Transnational and International Prosecution of Crime

11

Extraterritorial Jurisdiction: Applications to 'Terrorism'

M CHERIF BASSIOUNI*

I. INTRODUCTION

THEORIES OF EXTRATERRITORIAL jurisdiction, whether applicable to civil or criminal matters, reflect the state-centric system of international relations. This explains why the exercise of proscriptive and enforcement criminal jurisdiction[1] is deemed almost exclusively a manifestation of state sovereignty.[2]

Extraterritorial criminal jurisdiction refers to the power of a state to proscribe conduct taking place outside its territory with respect to conduct which causes harm to occur within its territory, which has an impact upon its interests, or which is committed by or against its nationals; and, to the power of a state to enforce such proscriptions within its domestic legal system. It primarily reflects states' interests and to a lesser extent, collective states' interests.

Enforcement of collective states' interests is based on the international community's shared interests, values and goals, which in turn give rise to

* This essay was completed on 14 May 2007.

[1] For a description of criminal jurisdiction theories, see MC Bassiouni, *International Extradition: US Law and Practice*, 5th edn (New York, OUP, 2007) ch VI (hereinafter Bassiouni, *International Extradition*); MC Bassiouni, 'Universal Jurisdiction for International Crimes: Historical Perspectives and Contemporary Practice' (2001) 42 *Virginia Journal of International Law* 81 (hereinafter Bassiouni, *Universal Jurisdiction*); CL Blakesley, 'Extraterritorial Jurisdiction' in MC Bassiouni (ed), 2 *International Criminal Law: Procedural and Enforcement Mechanisms* 33, 2nd rev edn (Ardsley, NY, Transnational, 1999) (hereinafter Bassiouni, *ICL*). For an earlier approach, see HD de Vabres, *Les Principles Modernes du Droit Pénal International* (Paris, Recueil Sirey, 1928).

[2] Inter-governmental organisations also have such powers. The Security Council established the International Criminal Tribunals for the former Yugoslavia, SC Res 827, UNSCOR, 48th Sess, 3217th mtg., UN Doc S/RES/827 (1993) and Rwanda, SC Res 955, UNSCOR, 49th Sess, UN Doc S/RES/955 (1994). The International Criminal Court was established by treaty (ICC Statute, A/Conf.183/9 (1998)), thus in accordance with the political will of states. See MC Bassiouni (ed), *The Legislative History of the International Criminal Court* (3 vols, edn 2005).

jurisdictional conceptions and applications to matters affecting common concerns.[3] Nonetheless, enforcement jurisdiction of international crimes is essentially through domestic jurisdiction, which includes extraterritorial applications whenever national legislation provides for it.

Resort by states to extraterritorial criminal jurisdiction, whether for domestic or international crimes enforcement, faces problems due to their overlapping and competing applications with other states endeavoring to do the same; and, with international tribunals. With respect to national systems, the problem is in part due to the absence of an internationally recognised hierarchy among these theories, and the absence of mechanisms to resolve conflicts of competence. This situation contributes to the reduction of state enforcement capabilities which in turn negatively impacts on the effectiveness of inter-state co-operation in penal matters.[4]

A state's power to prescribe and to enforce does not imply an ability to secure *in personam* jurisdiction over an alleged offender or convicted person whenever such a person is within the jurisdiction of another state. To secure *in personam* jurisdiction over such a person, the state desirous of exercising its extraterritorial criminal jurisdiction must rely on the co-operation of other states, which is essentially by means of extradition.[5] It is in this respect that priorities in criminal jurisdiction theories are particularly important.[6] However, when extradition fails because extraterritorial jurisdiction cannot be lawfully exercised, states sometimes engage in questionable or illegal practices, such as disguised extradition and even outright abduction, thus violating international law.[7]

One of the purposes of exercising extraterritorial national criminal jurisdiction is to maintain domestic public order. Another purpose is to assist friendly states seeking to accomplish the same goal. Presumably, in this era of globalisation, these interests extend to all members of the international community. This notion is embodied in the Grotian maxim

[3] See below nn 8 & 9 and accompanying text.

[4] For a number of contributions on the various modalities of inter-state co-operation in penal matters, see MC Bassiouni (ed), 2 *International Criminal Law: Procedural and Enforcement Mechanisms*, 3rd edn (Ardsley, NY, Transnational, 2008).

[5] See Bassiouni, *International Extradition*, above n 1.

[6] As they are with respect to other modalities of international co-operation in penal matters such as mutual legal assistance.

[7] This was the case with the Eichmann abduction from Argentina. See MH Cardozo, 'When Extradition Fails, is Abduction the Solution?' (1961) 55 *American Journal of International Law* 127. But see for the Alvarez-Machain abduction from Mexico, *US v Alvarez-Machain*, 504 US 655 (1992). See also Bassiouni, *International Extradition*, above n 1, ch IV.

aut dedere aut judicare,[8] which is predicated on an unarticulated premise, namely the existence of an international *civitas maxima*.[9]

The value-oriented goal of *aut dedere aut judicare* is to enhance national law enforcement capability to the benefit of the international community as a whole. In turn, this presupposes that the international community has well defined shared values and interests, as well as identified goals designed to preserve world public order.[10] Thus, whereas the enforcement of national criminal law reflects the interests of the enforcing state, and the enforcement of other states' criminal law reflects the interests of interstate co-operation in penal matters which are essentially bilateral, the enforcement of international criminal law reflects a broader world community interest. It can therefore be said that the recognition of an international legal obligation either to prosecute or extradite or to both prosecute and extradite, and cooperate with other states in the prevention, control and suppression of certain international crimes reflects the collective interests of the international community. 'Terrorism'[11] is one of these international crimes, though it is more of a category of international crimes than a single crime, which falls within the purview of this international obligation.

II. SOME POLICY CONSIDERATIONS

Territorial jurisdiction has been historically linked to sovereignty and mutatis mutandi sovereignty is, par excellence, manifested on a state's territory.[12] Extraterritorial national criminal jurisdiction theories have developed as an extension of state sovereignty interests. The applications of such such theories of extraterritorial jurisdiction, however, are subject to

[8] See MC Bassiouni and EM Wise, *Aut Dedere Aut Judicare: The Duty to Extradite or Prosecute in International Law* (Dordrecht, The Netherlands, Martinus Nijoff Publishers, 1995).

[9] See GOW Mueller, 'International Criminal Law: *Civitas Maxima*' (1983) 15 *Case Western Reserve Journal of International Law* 1.

[10] See MS McDougal & FP Feliciano, *Law and Minimum World Public Order: The Legal Regulation of International Coercion* (New Haven, CT, Yale University Press, 1961).

[11] See MC Bassiouni, 'Legal Controls of International Terrorism: A Policy-Oriented Perspective' (2002) 43 Harvard International Law Journal 83; MC Bassiouni, 'Terrorism: The Persistent Dilemma of Legitimacy' (2004) 36 *Case Western Reserve Journal of International Law* 298; MC Bassiouni, *International Terrorism: Multilateral Conventions 1937–2001* (Ardsley, NY, Transnational, 2001); MC Bassiouni (ed), *International Terrorism: A Compilation of UN Documents* (2 vols, Ardsley, NY, Transnational, 2001).

[12] This does not exclude the exercise of jurisdiction by international judicial entities established by an international organisation having such legal competence as in the cases of the International Criminal Tribunal for the former Yugoslavia and the International Criminal Tribunal for Rwanda; or by the collective will of states as in the case of the International Criminal Court. See above n 2.

the rights and interests of other sovereign states.[13] To exercise extraterritorial criminal jurisdiction, a state must evidence the existence of a nexus between the conduct committed outside its territory and that state's national interests which includes the control of some of its nationals' conduct beyond its borders, as well as the protection of its nationals abroad.

Thus, there are three major theories of extra-territorial criminal jurisdiction: active personality (that is, the power of a state to proscribe conduct taking place outside its territory which is committed by its nationals, and to enforce such proscriptions); passive personality (that is, the power of a state to proscribe conduct taking place outside its territory which is committed against its nationals, and to enforce such proscriptions); and protected interest (that is, the power of a state to proscribe conduct taking outside its territory which has an impact upon its interests, and to enforce such proscriptions).[14]

It is hard to say whether historically states' practices have favored the passive or active personality theory or vice-versa.[15] However, after World War II, states have consistently expanded their extraterritorial criminal jurisdiction with respect to their national security, as well as with respect to their economic interests.[16] This legislative and enforcement policy approach has been broadened particularly since the late 1960s with respect to 'terrorism', as discussed below. As harmful conduct – including 'terrorism' – increases against nationals who are outside the territorial jurisdiction of their respective States, States tend to extend their jurisdiction extraterritorially.[17] Necessarily, however, the extension of the passive

[13] *SS Lotus* (*France v Turkey*), 1927 PCIJ (ser A) No 10, at 95–96 (Sept 7) (Altamira J, dissenting), reprinted in 2 MO Hudson, *World Court Reports* (Washington, DC, Carnegie Endowment for International Peace, 1935) 20, 83–84. Judge Altamira also pointed out: 'In regard to criminal law in general, it is easy to observe that in municipal law, with the exception of that of a very small number of States, jurisdiction over foreigners for offences committed abroad has always been very limited: It has either (1) been confined to certain categories of offences; or (2) been limited, when the scope of the exception has been wider, by special conditions under which jurisdiction must be exercised and which very much limit its effects.' *Ibid* 99, reprinted in 2 MO Hudson, *World Court Reports* 20, 86.

[14] See, eg, above n 1.

[15] See above n 13.

[16] This is the case with respect to anti-trust, securities violations, export-import restitutions, trade and banking laws. See VP Nanda & MC Bassiouni (eds), *International Criminal Law: A Guide to US Practice and Procedure* (Ardsley, NY, Transnational, 1987). See also below n 20.

[17] For judicial applications of the 'passive personality' doctrine, see *US v Layton*, 509 F Supp 212, 215–16 (ND Cal), *appeal dismissed*, 645 F 2d 681 (9th Cir 1981); *US v Benitez*, 741 F 2d 1312, 1316 (11th Cir. 1984); *US v Yunis*, 681 F Supp 896, 901–03 (DDC 1988). See also *Restatement (Third) of the Foreign Relations Law of the US* § 402 cmt g, § 403 (1987) (hereinafter *Restatement (Third) of Foreign Relations*). Cf Act for the Prevention and Punishment of the Crime of Hostage-Taking, 18 USC § 1203 (1994 & Supp IV 1998); Act for the Prosecution of Terrorist Acts Abroad Against United States Nationals, 18 USC § 2331 (1994); 18 USC § 7(1), 7(8) (1994); 18 USC § 1653 (1994).

personality theory makes this theory more likely to collide with the recognised historic priority given to territorial jurisdiction and other high ranking jurisdictional priorities such as active personality jurisdiction.[18]

Presumably, the expansion of active and passive personality theories reflects a policy of deterrence through the strengthening of a worldwide jurisdictional net that reduces the opportunity for perpetrators to escape criminal prosecution. This hypothesis is predicated on another assumption borne out of experience, namely that some states are, in whole or in part, unable or unwilling to carry out effective prosecution of crimes committed on their territory. This outcome may also be due to other factors such as the foreign nationality of the perpetrators or victims, or because of the perceived 'political' character of the crimes committed.[19] Based on the above, it can be argued that in cases of 'terrorism', extraterritorial criminal jurisdiction theories based on the active and passive personality theories are necessary to fill the gap created by the failure of the territorial state in carrying out its obligation to prosecute, no matter what the reason may be.

Contemporaneous with the expansive extraterritorial approach described above, states have also extended their extraterritorial criminal jurisdiction as a manifestation of their perceived need to protect certain national interests from the harmful consequences of conduct performed outside the state. This is reflected in the protected interest theory. Originally that theory was intended to protect the strategic and economic interests of states.[20] However, the protected interest theory, like the other extraterritorial jurisdictional theories, has been expanded extraterritorially without regard to the other national competing jurisdictional claims.

In addition to the traditional reasons advanced for extraterritorial criminal jurisdiction, the manifestations of globalisation have brought about new threats to states' interests which thereby justify new approaches to extraterritorial legislative reach and to their enforcement. These threats include, in addition to 'terrorism', such new international, or as some

[18] See W Estey, Note, 'The Five Bases of Extraterritorial Jurisdiction and the Failure of the Presumption Against Extraterritoriality' (1997) 21 *Hastings International and Comparative Law Review* 177.

[19] For the 'political offence' exception to extradition, see CM Bassiouni, *International Extradition*, above n 1, at ch VIII.

[20] By 1947 the United States and NATO countries had elaborated administrative export controls designed to prevent the then-Eastern Block from receiving weapons and advanced technology from the Western Block. This was followed by measures designed to protect national security from threats by non-state actors, leading to the post 9/11 PATRIOT Act and other legislation on terrorism. From 1947 to date, all of these laws' jurisdictional features include extraterritorial criminal jurisdiction based on the protected interest doctrine, as well as the passive and active personality doctrines. See above n 16.

prefer to call them, transnational crimes, such as inter-state cyber-crime,[21] transnational organised crime,[22] corruption of foreign public officials,[23] and trafficking in human beings.[24]

Universal jurisdiction, which applies only to certain international crimes,[25] could be deemed a form of extraterritorial jurisdiction, but it has another origin, as well as other value-oriented goals. The theory of universal jurisdiction can be said to be based on the Roman legal concept of *actio popularis*. Its nature reflects the values embodied in the concept referred to as a *civitas maxima*. In contemporary terms, the theory of universal jurisdiction reflects both an idealistic conception and a utilitarian approach designed to enhance compliance with and accountability for certain international crimes.[26] In accordance with this rationale, universal jurisdiction becomes the last resort jurisdictional mechanism to prosecute the perpetrators of certain international crimes who would otherwise evade accountability. The assumption is that universal jurisdiction enhances accountability, which in turn assumes enhanced compliance with the norms of international criminal law. This, in turn, is based on the assumption that a certain level of general deterrence is attained by making enforcement jurisdiction more effective and, thus, prosecutions more likely.

Prescinding from the validity of such assumptions on general deterrence, it nevertheless remains true that if universal jurisdiction is only a theory of last resort, it is subject to the hierarchical priorities of the other theories of national criminal jurisdiction, which do not necessarily reflect collective international interests, but only individual states' interests. A utilitarian

[21] For cyber-terrorism, see FJ Cilluffo, PB Pattack, & GC Salmaoiraghi, 'Bad Guys and Good Stuff: When and Where Will the Cyber Threats Converge?' (1999) 12 *DePaul Business Law Journal* 131; DR Johnson & D Post, 'Law and Borders – The Rise of Law in Cyberspace' (1996) 48 *Stanford Law Review* 1357; M Sheehan, 'International Terrorism: Trends and Responses' (1999) 12 *DePaul Business Law Journal* 45.

[22] United Nations Convention Against Transnational Organised Crime, GA Res 25, annex I, UN GAOR 55th Sess, Supp No 49, at 44, UN Doc A/45/49 (Vol I) (2001), entered into force 29 September 2003.

[23] United Nations Convention Against Corruption, UN Doc A/58/422, entered into force 14 December 2005.

[24] Protocol to Prevent, Suppress and Punish Trafficking in Persons, Especially Women and Children, Supplementing the United Nations Convention Against Transnational Organized Crime, G A Res 25, annex II, UN GAOR, 55th Sess, Supp No 49, at 60, UN Doc A/45/49 (Vol I) (2001), entered into force 25 December 2003.

[25] See Bassiouni, *Universal Jurisdiction*, above n 1, at 96–101. Universal jurisdiction, according to Principle 1 of the Princeton Principles on Universal Jurisdiction, is 'criminal jurisdiction based solely on the nature of the crime, without regard to where the crime was committed, the nationality of the alleged or convicted perpetrator, the nationality of the victim, or any other connection to the state exercising such jurisdiction.' See MC Bassiouni, 'The History of Universal Jurisdiction and Its Place in International Law' in S Macedo (ed), *Universal Jurisdiction. National Courts and the Prosecution of Serious Crimes Under International Law* (Philadelphia, University of Pennsylvannia Press, 2003) 39, 42.

[26] See *Princeton Project on Universal Jurisdiction* (Princeton University Program in Law and Public Affairs, 2001). These principles, however, do not contain such a hierarchy.

policy-oriented approach to universal jurisdiction may be advanced as being akin to a collective states' interests approach because it achieves the goals of enhancing international accountability, which serves the collective interests of all states and ultimately the individual interests of states. However universal jurisdiction is perceived, it is nonetheless subject to certain national and international legal limitations,[27] not to mention the obstacles posed by *realpolitik*.[28]

Based on the utilitarian and idealistic rationales described above, universal jurisdiction should be applicable to 'terrorism' crimes. So far, however, there is little support for this proposition in the applicable treaties or in the practice of states.[29]

Notwithstanding all of the above, there is no evident interest on the part of the international community to develop an international convention on the inter-state priorities of extraterritorial jurisdictional theories or on how to address inter-state jurisdictional conflicts.

III. NORMATIVE CHARACTERISATION AND ITS IMPACT ON ENFORCEMENT JURISDICTION

Enforcement jurisdiction necessarily starts with the identification of the applicable legal norm, whether it be international or national. The proscribing norm is therefore the basis of the enforcement jurisdiction. The process of characterisation of the applicable norm is undertaken by a state's judicial or political body or by an international judicial body or international legal authority.[30]

[27] In the *Case Concerning the Arrest Warrant of 11 April 2000 (Democratic Republic of Congo v Belgium)*, 2002 I C J Rep (Feb 14), *available at* <http://www.icj-cij.org/docket/files/121/8126.pdf>, the International Court of Justice (hereinafter 'ICJ') ruled that Belgium's universal jurisdiction law of 1993 for genocide, crimes against humanity and war crimes violated international law, in that it was held to apply to an incumbent minister of foreign affairs who was protected by the 1969 Vienna Convention on the Law of Diplomatic Immunity. Thus, the ICJ upheld the temporal immunity of diplomats and heads of state under conventional and customary international law, upholding the non-applicability of such immunity in the substantive sense. The ICJ also recognised that organs established by the Security Council, like the International Criminal Tribunal for the former Yugoslavia and the International Criminal Court and the International Criminal Tribunal for Rwanda, could derogate from such conventional and customary rules as could states by virtue of a treaty with respect to the International Criminal Court's Art 27.

[28] See MC Bassiouni, 'The Perennial Conflict between International Criminal Justice and *Realpolitik*' (2006) 22 *Georgia State University Law Review* 541; MC Bassiouni, 'International Criminal Justice in the Era of Globalization: Rising Expectations' in *The Global Community, Yearbook of International Law & Jurisprudence* (2006) p 3; MC Bassiouni, 'Combating Impunity for International Crimes' (2000) 71 *University of Colorado Law Review* 409.

[29] See *Princeton Project on Universal Jurisdiction*, above n 26.

[30] This applies to the Security Council which established the International Criminal Tribunal for the former Yugoslavia and the International Criminal Court, above n 2.

The considerations that go into making a particular characterisation necessarily derive from legislative policy, but also from judicial and political interpretation. For example, a given act of 'terrorism' may be characterised by a judicial or political body as falling within the context of the law of armed conflict. Thus it could be within the competence of the ICC, an ad hoc international tribunal, a domestic military tribunal, or another similar organ.[31] In turn, this may give rise to a question of whether such an act constitutes a war crime or whether it could be deemed lawful use of force by a combatant. If the act is characterised as being outside the scope of the law of armed conflict, it could be considered as falling within the meaning of 'crimes against humanity',[32] depending upon its magnitude, or it could be deemed a violation of one of the international conventions prohibiting certain specific acts of 'terrorism.'[33]

However, the same conduct can also be characterised as a crime under domestic criminal law. In that case, the crime's label, definition and elements may be significantly different from its counterpart international crime. Thus, what could be charged as one of the 'terrorism' crimes, or a 'war crime' or 'crimes against humanity', would be charged as murder or manslaughter. From a pure accountability perspective, there is no difference, but from a technical legal charging perspective, there is a notable distinction between these crimes.

The outcome of legal characterisation determines the appropriate jurisdictional forum and, in some cases, the priority of that forum over others.[34] Within national legal jurisdictions, a given conduct may be characterised as a violation of the national criminal laws of more than one state, namely the territorial state or the one invoking active or passive personality jurisdiction, or protected interest, or the state invoking universal jurisdiction. If the state invoking jurisdiction is relying on an international criminal law convention, the invocation of jurisdiction on that legal basis will depend on the relevant provision contained in the applicable treaty.

31 See for example the President of the United States enacting an Executive Order establishing special military commissions for persons declared 'enemy combatants'. See below n 39.

32 See MC Bassiouni, 'Crimes Against Humanity' in MC Bassiouni (ed), 1 *International Criminal Law: Crimes*, 2nd rev edn (Ardsley, NY, Transnational, 1999). For an author supporting the proposition that 'terrorism' could be encompassed within 'crimes against humanity' in Art 7 of the International Criminal Court Statute, above n 2, see R Arnold, *The ICC as a New Instrument for Repressing Terrorism* (Ardsley, NY, Transnational, 2005).

33 See under heading 'The Normative Structure of 'Terrorism' Offences' below.

34 The jurisdiction of the International Criminal Court is subject to the principle of complementarity stated in Art 7, above n 2. With respect to the jurisdiction of an ad hoc international criminal tribunal established by the Security Council as in the cases of the International Criminal Tribunal for the former Yugoslavia and the International Criminal Tribunal for Rwanda, these organs' jurisdiction supersedes national jurisdictions. See 2 Bassiouni, *ICL*, above n 2.

National prosecutions for international crimes are based on national criminal law. However, crimes defined under national criminal laws are for the most part differently defined under international criminal law conventions. The incorporation of international criminal law in national criminal law is also subject to jurisdictional distinctions in the domestic legal order. This is particularly the case with respect to international humanitarian law, which is included in almost all countries of the world in their domestic military law. The latter, however, does not usually extend to civilians or former military personnel. Thus, persons not subject to military law and who violated international humanitarian law are subject to domestic criminal laws which may define crimes differently than their domestic military counterpart.

Another example is 'crimes against humanity'.[35] Nearly all domestic criminal laws do not include 'crimes against humanity' in their domestic criminal laws as this category of international crimes is defined in customary international law.[36] Assuming that certain acts of 'terrorism' can be deemed to fall within the meaning of 'crimes against humanity'[37] or 'war crimes',[38] they would likely be subject to prosecution under this label before the International Criminal Court or before a national judicial organ based on domestic criminal laws. In the latter case, as stated above, the crime would not be characterised as 'crimes against humanity'.

As described above, there are multiple legal regimes at the international and national levels which are susceptible of addressing the various manifestations of crimes of 'terrorism'. Which one of these legal regimes is selected for initiating a 'terrorism' prosecution is likely to affect the outcome of the prosecution. This is due to the fact that different legal regimes have different requirements as to the elements of the crime that need to be proven and as to evidentiary and procedural standards.[39]

[35] See Bassiouni, *Crimes Against Humanity*, above n 32.

[36] *Ibid.*

[37] One author argues that the International Criminal Court's Art 7 definition of 'crimes against humanity' could include 'terrorism' when committed by non-state actors. See Arnold, above n 32.

[38] See HS Levie, *Terrorism in War: the Law of War Crimes* (Dobbs Ferry, NY, Oceana Publications, 1993).

[39] For example, military justice in almost every country in the world offers fewer rights to the defendants, and specially tailored military commissions as in the US offer even fewer rights than under the Uniform Code of Military Justice, 10 USC §§ 801–941 (2000) or under the Geneva Conventions, which are binding on the United States. This led the US Supreme Court in *Hamdan v Rumsfeld,*126 S. Ct. 2749 (2006) to hold that the Presidential Executive Order establishing these special military commissions in Guantanamo was unconstitutional. As a result, Congress adopted a statutory basis for these military commissions the Military Commission Act of 2006, Pub L No 109–266, and when challenged, the Supreme Court in *Boumediene et al v Bush*, 127 S Ct 1478 (2 April, 2007) refused to grant the petition for a writ of certiorari. Presumably, the Court is hoping that the Military Commissions will correct their defects before accepting certiorari. The selection of any of these options also involves policy choices as to certain principled considerations, which may be in contrast with

The diversity of forum choices also reduces the certainty of the applicable law and raises questions about substantive as well as procedural legality. This includes the lack of notice of what substantive law and penalties are applicable[40] and what procedural rights[41] may be available in the course of prosecution. While this uncertainty may suit certain political and practical purposes in prosecuting persons charged with acts of 'terrorism', it also undermines the certainty of the law and its legitimacy. Undermining the process of legality (or the rule of law) as a whole lends credibility and support to those who violate the law under the guise of a higher legitimacy.[42]

Thus, legal characterisation has an impact on enforcement jurisdiction and is therefore often outcome-determinative, not only as to inter-state jurisdiction, but also with respect to intra-state jurisdiction.[43]

The alternative to technical legal characterisation is to rely on the social interest sought to be protected and the harmful means and methods sought to be prevented.[44] On its face, this is a value-neutral approach. However, what such an apparently neutral conception fails to address with respect to 'terrorism' is a realistic consideration. Perpetrators of terror-violence rely on this violent strategy because of the asymmetry of forces existing between state and non-state actors. This causes the latter to resort to terror-violence as a way of redressing the respective forces' imbalance. Moreover, this approach also fails to address the enforcement monopoly of domestic and international organs. The monopoly of states over making and applying criminal law norms gives primacy to states over non-state

expedient or pragmatic alternative jurisdictional mechanisms. The former include issues of procedure and what have now been established as international norms of due process of law, as well as substantive principles, such as the right of an accused to be tried before his/her 'natural judge', and the higher principle of certainty of the law, embodied in the 'principles of legality' *nulla poena sine lege* and *nullum crimen sine lege*.

40 See MC Bassiouni, *Substantive Criminal Law* (Springfield, IL, Charles C Thomas, 1978) 25–26; MC Bassiouni, 'The Principles of Legality' in MC Bassiouni (ed), 1 *International Criminal Law: Crimes*, 3rd edn (in print, Ardsley, NY, Transnational, 2008).

41 See MC Bassiouni (ed), *The Protection of Human Rights in the Administration of Justice: a Compendium of United Nations Norms and Standards* (Ardsley, NY, Transnational, 1994); C Gane & M Mackarel (eds), *Human Rights & the Administration of Justice: International Instruments* (London, Kluwer, 1997); A Bayefsky, *The UN Human Rights Treaty System: Universality at the Crossroads* (London, Kluwer, 2001).

42 See MC Bassiouni, 'Terrorism: Reflections on Legitimacy and Policy Considerations' in W McCormack (ed), *Values and Violence* (New York, Springer Publishing Company, forthcoming 2008).

43 While attention is usually focussed on the operational aspects deriving from enforcement jurisdiction, in particular on whether or not prosecution or extradition are carried out, limited attention is given to the primary sources of law under which enforcement jurisdiction arises, except insofar as the 'double criminality' principle in extradition law and practice. See MC Bassiouni, *International Extradition*, above n 1, ch VI.

44 This is the approach of the European Convention on Terrorism, Council of Europe: European Convention on the Suppression of Terrorism, ETS No 90, 15 ILM 1272 (27 Jan 1977).

actors. Thus, non-state actors who confront this dual asymmetry in their conflicts with states resort to terror-violence in part to redress the scales of the forces' asymmetry and in part as a challenge to states' control of national and international institutions.

The recognition of *aut dedere aut judicare* as based on a *civitas maxima*, whether because of the more idealistic premise that there exist globally-shared values and interests or whether it is premised on a pragmatic and utilitarian policy-oriented basis, produces the same result, namely the tightening of the net of international criminal accountability to prevent the perpetrators of international and transnational crimes, including 'terrorism' from benefiting from impunity.[45]

The theories of criminal jurisdiction described above fall within the meaning of enforcement jurisdiction and are relevant to the national and international strategies of prevention and suppression of crime. However, there is no correlation between these theories and normative provisions on the specific crimes deemed within the purview of 'terrorism' – an elastic label applied to a broad category of crimes and to a large category of offenders and jurisdictional theories.[46]

III. THE NORMATIVE STRUCTURE OF 'TERRORISM' OFFENCES

'Terrorism' is a value-laden term, which can be defined as 'a strategy of violence designed to instill terror in a segment of society in order to achieve a power-outcome, propagandize a cause, or inflict harm for vengeful political purposes'.[47] Consequently, 'terrorism' can be committed by states, acting through their agents; individuals who are part of non-state actors' ideologically motivated groups; and individuals acting on their own for ideological or other reasons.[48] If the focus of the definition of 'terrorism' would be exclusively on the human and material harm it produces, it would be immaterial who commits the crime or for what purpose it was committed. However, this is not what the conventions listed below reveal.

[45] MC Bassiouni, 'Searching for Peace and Achieving Justice: The Need for Accountability' (1996) 59 *Law and Contemporary Problems* 9.

[46] See MC Bassiouni, *International Terrorism: Multilateral Conventions 1937–2001* (Ardsley, NY, Transnational, 2001). While these conventions deal directly with specific means of terror violence, other international treaties also apply indirectly to violent acts associated with terrorism. For example, the Universal Postal Union, an agency mainly concerned with the licit international regulation, standardisation and co-operation of mail delivery, included prohibitions against the unlawful use of the mails for bombings. The Universal Postal Union Convention and the Postal Parcels Agreement, since 1964, prohibit the insertion of any explosive, flammable, or other dangerous substance in letter-post items.

[47] MC Bassiouni, 'Legal Controls of International Terrorism: A Policy-Oriented Perspective' (2002) 43 *Harvard International Law Journal* 83.

[48] MC Bassiouni, *International Terrorism: Multilateral Conventions 1937–2001* (Ardsley, NY, Transnational, 2001) 1–67.

There is so far no comprehensive convention on 'terrorism'.[49] Instead, the relevant conventions listed below apply to different means employed in the course of terror-violence activities.[50] This piecemeal approach, as opposed to having a single comprehensive convention, is the result of states' interests in applying these proscriptions to individuals, thus excluding state-action. The international conventions which specifically pertain to the suppression, control, or prevention of 'terrorism' are[51] 1958 Convention on the High Seas;[52] 1963 Convention on Offences and Certain Other Acts Committed on Board Aircraft;[53] 1970 Convention for the Suppression of Unlawful Seizure of Aircraft;[54] 1971 Convention for the Suppression of Unlawful Acts Against the Safety of Civil Aviation;[55] 1973 Convention on the Prevention and Punishment of Crimes Against Internationally Protected Persons, Including Diplomatic Agents;[56] 1979 Convention Against the Taking of Hostages;[57] 1980 Convention on the Physical Protection of Nuclear Material;[58] 1982 Convention on the Law of the Sea;[59] 1988 Protocol for the Suppression of Unlawful Acts of Violence at Airports Serving International Civil Aviation;[60] 1988 Convention for the Suppression of Unlawful Acts Against the Safety of Maritime Navigation;[61] 1988 Protocol for the Suppression of Unlawful Acts Against the Safety of Fixed

[49] See however, Draft Comprehensive Convention against International Terrorism, the consolidated text as contained in UN Doc A/59/894 of 12 August 2005, Appendix II.

[50] There are also seven regional instruments addressing the issue of terrorism, including the OAS Convention to Prevent and Punish the Acts of Terrorism Taking the Form of Crimes Against Persons and Related Extortion that are of International Significance (1971); European Convention on the Suppression of Terrorism (1977); SAARC Regional Convention on Suppression of Terrorism (1987); The Arab Convention on the Suppression of Terrorism (1998); Treaty on Cooperation among the States Members of the Commonwealth of Independent States in Combating Terrorism (1999); Convention of the Organisation of the Islamic Conference on Combating International Terrorism (1999); and the OAU Convention on the Prevention and Combating of Terrorism (1999).

[51] The United Nations, however, only lists twelve. See *International Instruments Related to the Prevention and Suppression of International Terrorism* (United Nations, 2001).

[52] Convention on the High Seas, UN Doc A/Conf. 13/L. 52–55 or 52 & 56 (1958).

[53] Convention on Offences and Certain Other Acts Committed on Board Aircraft, *opened for signature* 14 September 1963, 704 UNT S 219.

[54] Convention for the Suppression of Unlawful Seizure of Aircraft, opened for signature 16 December 1970, 860 UNT S 105.

[55] Convention for the Suppression of Unlawful Acts Against the Safety of Civil Aviation, *opened for signature* 23 September 1971, 974 UNT S 177.

[56] Convention on the Prevention and Punishment of Crimes Against Internationally Protected Persons, including Diplomatic Agents, *opened for signature* 14 December 1973, 1035 UNT S 167.

[57] Convention Against the Taking of Hostages, UN Doc A/Res/34/146 (1979).

[58] Convention on the Physical Protection of Nuclear Material, IAEA Doc FCIRC/25 (3 March 1980), 1456 UNT S 125.

[59] Convention on the Law of the Sea, UN Doc A/Conf. 62/122 or 13/51 & 45 (1982).

[60] Protocol for the Suppression of Unlawful Acts of Violence at Airports Serving International Civil Aviation, ICAO Doc 9518 (24 Feb 1988).

[61] Convention for the Suppression of Unlawful Acts Against the Safety of Maritime Navigation, IMO Doc Sua/Conf/15/Rev 1 (1988).

Platforms Located on the Continental Shelf;[62] 1991 Convention on the Marking of Plastic Explosives for the Purpose of Detection;[63] 1994 Convention on the Safety of United Nations and Associated Personnel;[64] 1998 Convention for the Suppression of Terrorism Bombings;[65] 1999 Convention for the Suppression of Financing of Terrorism;[66] and 1999 Convention on the Suppression of Acts of Nuclear Terrorism.[67] In addition, the law of armed conflicts applies to manifestations of terror-violence. Conventional international law embodied in the Geneva Conventions refers to these crimes as 'grave breaches', while customary international law refers to them as 'war crimes'.[68]

These international conventions do not consistently posit, explicitly or implicitly, the duty to prosecute and/or to extradite;[69] none provides for an order of priority as to these obligations,[70] and none addresses the most common enforcement problem, namely jurisdictional conflicts.[71]

[62] Protocol for the Suppression of Unlawful Acts Against the Safety of Fixed Platforms Located on the Continental Shelf, IMO Doc Sua/Conf/16/Rev2 (1988).

[63] Convention on the Marking of Plastic Explosions for the Purpose of Detection, UN Doc S/22393 & Corr.1, 30 ILM 721 (1 March 1991).

[64] Convention on the Safety of United Nations and Associated Personnel, UN Doc A/Res/49/59, 17 February 1995 (1994).

[65] Convention for the Suppression of Terrorism Bombings, G A Res 164, UN GAOR, 52nd Sess, Supp No 49, at 389, UN Doc A/52/49 (1998), entered into force 23 May 2001.

[66] Convention for the Suppression of the Financing of Terrorism, G A Res 109, UN GAOR, 54th Sess, Supp No 49, UN Doc A/54/49 (Vol I) (1999), S Treaty Doc No 106–49 (2000), 39 ILM 270 (2000), *adopted* 9 Dec. 1999, entered into force 10 April 2002.

[67] Convention on the Suppression of Acts of Nuclear Terrorism, UN Doc A/Res/59/290, 13 April 2005.

[68] See HS Levie, *Terrorism in War: the Law of War Crimes* (Dobbs Ferry, NY, Oceana Publications, 1993); MC Bassiouni (ed), *A Manual on International Humanitarian Law and Arms Control Agreements* (Ardsley, NY, Transnational, 2000).

[69] The jurisdictional provisions and penal characteristics of the 'terrorism' conventions are listed in MC Bassiouni (ed), *International Criminal Law Conventions and Their Penal Provisions* (Ardsley, NY, Transnational, 1997) at pp 777–882.

[70] *Ibid.*

[71] For example, the 1971 Montreal Convention for the Suppression of Unlawful Acts Against the Safety of Civil Aviation is imprecise and ambiguous about the duties to prosecute or extradite. Read together, Arts 7 and 8 do not clearly state which of the two duties, to prosecute or to extradite, has precedence over the other. Likewise, these articles do not state the unarticulated premise that both prosecution in the custodial State and extradition to a requesting State must have effective and fair jurisdictional safeguards. This lack of specificity resulted in the problem between Libya, on one side, and the United States and the United Kingdom, on the other, over the prosecution of those accused of the explosion of Pan Am Flight 103 over Lockerbie, Scotland. *Case Concerning Questions of Interpretation and Application of 1971 Montreal Convention Arising from Aerial Incident at Lockerbie* (*Libya v UK*), 1992, ICJ 3 (April 14); (*Libya v US*), 1992 ICJ 114 (Apr. 14); 1992 ICJ 234 (June 19); 1992 ICJ 231 (June 14); 1995 ICJ 90 (Sept 22); 1995 ICJ 282 (Sept 22); PHF Bekker, 'Questions of Interpretation and Application of the 1971 Montreal Convention Arising From the Aerial Incident at Lockerbie, Preliminary International Court of Justice, February 27, 1998' (1998) 92 *American Journal of International Law* 503; J Crawford, 'Current Developments: The ILC Adopts a Statute for an International Criminal Court' (1995) 89 *American Journal of International Law* 404; MS Simmons, 'A Review of Issues Concerned

Almost all of these conventions contain an express or implied obligation to prosecute or extradite. All of them recognise the territoriality principle, and relevant conventions recognise the law of the flag (ships and aircraft), which is deemed an extension of the territoriality principle. The active and passive personality theories are less recurring – in fact, they are few if one goes by explicit provisions.[72]

Universality only arises in connection with the above-listed conventions with regard to piracy and war crimes. What is also significant is that the provisions on jurisdiction in these conventions are seldom identified in a specific provision. Instead, they are part of provisions addressing questions that are not exclusively jurisdictional. Even so, there is no consistency, let alone uniformity, in the treaty language employed in connection with jurisdiction. This is explained by the fact that each convention is the subject of political negotiations, by different negotiators, most of whom are diplomats or individuals not very familiar with international criminal law.

This significant lack of consistency may also be due to the assumption made by the negotiators that these conventions' obligations will be incorporated in the domestic laws of states who will then do whatever is legislatively needed at the national level to address any weaknesses in the said conventions. For inexplicable reasons, the UN member states most interested in this question have even refused to have a single convention that incorporates all the twelve UN conventions so as to avoid inconsistencies and so as to harmonize the difference in language used to refer to some questions such as jurisdiction.

The last three conventions of 2005, 1999 and 1997, and the pending draft convention merit more careful consideration than their predecessors in connection with their respective jurisdictional provisions. These provisions are an improvement over those contained in conventions adopted in the thirty years between 1969 and 1989.[73] We can summarise their jurisdictional contents as follows:

1) Each of these four international instruments (partially) excludes its

with Aerial Hijacking and Terrorism: Implications for Australia's Security and the Sydney 2000 Olympics' (1998) 63 *Journal of Air Law and Commerce* 731; HE Reser, Comment 'Airline Terrorism: The Effect of Tightened Security on the Right to Travel' (1998) 63 *Journal of Air Law and Commerce* 819; S Sucharitkul, 'Procedure for the Protection of Civil Aircraft in Flight' (1944) 16 *Loyola International and Comparative Law Journal* 513; SS Evans, 'The Lockerbie Incident Cases: Libyan Sponsored Terrorism, Judicial Review and the Political Question Doctrine' (1994) 18 *Maryland Journal of International Law and Trade* 21; Note, '*Libya v US*: The International Court of Justice and the Power of Judicial Review' (1993) 33 *Virginia Journal of International Law* 899. The 10-year stalemate was broken when the parties agreed to a change of venue to The Hague, The Netherlands. See MC Bassiouni, 'Policy Considerations on Inter-State Cooperation in Criminal Matters' in 2 Bassiouni, *ICL*, above n 1, 3.

[72] See Bassiouni, above n 69.

[73] See Bassiouni, above n 69.

own applicability when an offence is committed within a single State, and the offence has no nexus to any other State.[74]

2) All of these international instruments stipulate that States shall take the necessary measures to establish jurisdiction based on the territoriality principle, including a vessel flying the flag of that State or an aircraft registered under the laws of that State at the time of the offence.[75]
3) All of these international instruments stipulate that States shall take necessary measures to establish jurisdiction based on the active personality principle.[76]
4) All of these international instruments contain the possibility for States of voluntarily broadening the jurisdictional scope ('A State Party may also establish jurisdiction …'):
   a) based on the passive personality principle;
   b) if the offence is committed against a State or government facility abroad;
   c) if the offence is committed by a stateless person who has his or her habitual residence in the territory of that State;
   d) if the offence is committed in an attempt to compel that State to do or abstain from doing any act; and
   e) if the offence is committed on board an aircraft which is operated by the Government of that State.[77]

[74] See International Convention for the Suppression of Acts of Nuclear Terrorism, New York, 13 April 2005 (opened for signature 14 September 2005–31 December 2006) UN Doc A/59/766 of 4 April 2005, Annex, art 3; International Convention for the Suppression of the Financing of Terrorism, adopted by the General Assembly of the United Nations on 9 December 1999, open for signature from 10 January 2000– 31 December 2001, 39 ILM 268 (2000), art 3; International Convention for the Suppression of Terrorist Bombings, adopted by the General Assembly of the United Nations on 15 December 1997, opened for signature 12 January 1998, 37 ILM 249 (1998), art 3; Draft Comprehensive Convention against International Terrorism, the consolidated text as contained in UN Doc A/59/894 of 12 August 2005, Appendix II, art 4.

[75] See International Convention for the Suppression of Acts of Nuclear Terrorism, above n 74, art 9 (1) (a) and (b); International Convention for the Suppression of the Financing of Terrorism, above n 74, art 7 (1) (a) and (b); International Convention for the Suppression of Terrorist Bombings, above n 74, art 6 (1) (a) and (b); and Draft Comprehensive Convention against International Terrorism, above n 74, art 7 (1) (a) and (b).

[76] See International Convention for the Suppression of Acts of Nuclear Terrorism, above n 74, art 9 (1) (c); International Convention for the Suppression of the Financing of Terrorism, above n 74, art 7 (1) (c); International Convention for the Suppression of Terrorist Bombings, above n 74, art 6 (1) (c); and Draft Comprehensive Convention against International Terrorism, above n 74, art 7 (1) (c).

[77] See International Convention for the Suppression of Acts of Nuclear Terrorism, above n 74, art 9 (2); International Convention for the Suppression of the Financing of Terrorism, above n 74, art 7 (2) (establishing in a different order these potential bases for broadening a State's jurisdictional scope, and establishing as an additional basis 'if the offence was directed towards or resulted in the carrying out of an offence in the territory … of that State); International Convention for the Suppression of Terrorist Bombings, above n 74, art 6 (2); and Draft Comprehensive Convention against International Terrorism, above n 74, art 7 (c)

5) All of these international instruments instruct States to take measures to establish jurisdiction if the alleged offender is present on their territory and the State does not extradite that person to any of the States Parties which have established their jurisdiction in accordance with paragraph 1 or 2 of the respective article of the international instrument.[78]
This could be understood to give the custodial State priority, rather than instituting a hierarchy based on where, by whom or against whom the offence was committed. This is supported by the provision included in all of these international instruments that contain a duty to inform other State Parties having jurisdiction if the custodial State intends to exercise jurisdiction.[79]
6) The International Convention for the Suppression of Terrorist Bombings contains a dispute resolution mechanism calling for initial negotiations, then arbitration and the option of a referral to the ICJ, if the parties are unable to agree on the organisation of the arbitration.[80]
In the case of a dispute concerning its interpretation or application (which would include situations in which several States wish to exercise jurisdiction simultaneously), the International Convention for the Suppression of Acts of Nuclear Terrorism contains a dispute resolution mechanism calling for arbitration and in the case of a failure to agree on the organisation of the arbitration, the option of a referral to the International Court of Justice.[81]
In contrast, the International Convention for the Suppression of the Financing of Terrorism and the Draft Comprehensive Convention against International Terrorism contain a provision for the occurrence of multiple jurisdictions, calling for coordination and co-operation without, however, offering a resolution of the problem: 'the relevant

(establishing in a different order these potential bases for broadening a State's jurisdictional scope, and establishing as an additional basis 'if the offence is committed wholly or partially outside its territory, if the effects of the conduct or its intended effects constitute or result in, within its territory, the commission of an offence set forth in article 2).

78 See International Convention for the Suppression of Acts of Nuclear Terrorism, above n 74, art 9 (4); International Convention for the Suppression of the Financing of Terrorism, above n 74, art 7 (4); International Convention for the Suppression of Terrorist Bombings, above n 74, art 6 (4); and Draft Comprehensive Convention against International Terrorism, above n 74, art 7 (4).

79 See last sentence of International Convention for the Suppression of Acts of Nuclear Terrorism, above n 74, art 10 (6); International Convention for the Suppression of the Financing of Terrorism, above n 74, art 9 (6); International Convention for the Suppression of Terrorist Bombings, above n 74, art 7 (6); and Draft Comprehensive Convention against International Terrorism, above n 74, art 11 (6).

80 See The International Convention for the Suppression of Terrorist Bombings, above n 74, art 20 (1).

81 See International Convention for the Suppression of Acts of Nuclear Terrorism, above n 74, art 23.

States Parties shall strive to co-ordinate their actions appropriately, in particular concerning the conditions for prosecution and the modalities for mutual legal assistance'.[82] But these two instruments also contain a dispute resolution mechanism calling for arbitration and in the case of a failure to agree on the organisation of the arbitration, the option of a referral to the ICJ.[83]

7) Finally, the International Convention for the Suppression of Acts of Nuclear Terrorism, and Draft Comprehensive Convention against International Terrorism, contain the duty to prosecute if a State does not extradite;[84] while the International Convention for the Suppression of the Financing of Terrorism, and International Convention for the Suppression of Terrorist Bombings, contain a duty to prosecute or extradite.[85]

IV. CONCLUSION

There has never been an internationally agreed upon policy for the development of international criminal law. More specifically, the United Nations in its work on the elaboration of international criminal law conventions has not reflected the existence of a coherent international criminal justice policy. The nearly 300 international criminal law conventions adopted between 1815 and 2005 fall into 28 different categories of international crime,[86] but they have few jurisdictional provisions.[87]

[82] International Convention for the Suppression of the Financing of Terrorism, above n 74, art 7 (5); and Draft Comprehensive Convention against International Terrorism, above n 74, art 7 (5).

[83] International Convention for the Suppression of the Financing of Terrorism, above n 74, art 24 (1); and Draft Comprehensive Convention against International Terrorism, above n 74, art 20 (1).

[84] See International Convention for the Suppression of Acts of Nuclear Terrorism, above n 74, art 11 (see also art 10 (1) and (2)); and Draft Comprehensive Convention against International Terrorism, above n 74, art 12 (1) (see also art 11 (1) and (2)).

[85] See International Convention for the Suppression of the Financing of Terrorism, above n 74, art 10(1) (see also art 9(1), (2); International Convention for the Suppression of Terrorist Bombings, art 8(1) (see also art 7 (1), (2).

[86] They are (1) aggression, (2) genocide, (3) crimes against humanity, (4) war crimes, (5) unlawful possession or use or emplacement of weapons, (6) theft of nuclear materials, (7) mercenarism, (8) *apartheid*, (9) slavery and slave-related practices, (10) torture and other forms of cruel, inhuman or degrading treatment, (11) unlawful human experimentation, (12) piracy, (13) aircraft hijacking and unlawful acts against international air safety, (14) unlawful acts against the safety of maritime navigation and the safety of platforms on the high seas, (15) threat and use of force against internationally protected persons, (16) crimes against United Nations and associated personnel, (17) taking of civilian hostages, (18) unlawful use of the mail, (19) attacks with explosives, (20) financing of terrorism, (21) unlawful traffic in drugs and related drug offences, (22) organised crime, (23) destruction and/or theft of national treasures, (24) unlawful acts against certain internationally protected elements of the

The international legal regime of enforcing international criminal law is essentially an indirect enforcement scheme[88] because it relies on states to criminalise under domestic law the international prohibited conduct and to enforce it by means of prosecution or extradition. Thus, national jurisdictional theories are the primary mechanism for claiming a state's right to enforce. Even internationally established judicial organs such as the International Criminal Tribunal for the former Yugoslavia, the International Criminal Tribunal for Rwanda and the International Criminal Court depend on states' co-operation based on the same modalities which are used in inter-state co-operation in penal matters.

In turn, prosecutions, whether at the national or international levels, will be affected by the legal regime chosen and under which prosecution is initiated. Each regime has its own jurisdictional basis and that includes extraterritorial jurisdictional mechanisms based on the three recognised theories of extraterritorial criminal jurisdiction. Considering the expansion of states' applications of these extra-territorial jurisdictional theories, the potential for competing and conflicting applications intra-state and between states and international tribunals increases. Yet, there is neither an international convention establishing a priority of jurisdictional theories, nor one providing for norms or guidelines to address conflicts between these theories when claimed by more than one state in the pursuit of the same person for prosecution.

With respect to 'terrorism', these problems are compounded because the relevant conventions are directed to the same end but employ different jurisdictional mechanisms. The lack of an international legislative policy based on coherence and sound technical drafting is regrettably evident. The consequences are that international and national legal systems lack effective complementarity and that national legal systems tend to engage in unlawful and unfair practices as a way of palliating their jurisdictional difficulties.

The absence of an international legislative policy designed to enhance effective and complementary national and international criminal jurisdictions is also reflected in the absence of norms or guidelines on jurisdictional priorities as well as in the lack of articulation of certain conditions for the exercise of jurisdiction by means of either prosecution or extradition, namely effectiveness and fairness.

environment, (25) international traffic in obscene materials, (26) falsification and counterfeiting, (27) unlawful interference with submarine cables, and (28) bribery of foreign public officials. See MC Bassiouni, *Introduction to International Criminal Law* (Herndon, VA, Transnational, 2003) 117.

87 See Bassiouni, above n 69.

88 See MC Bassiouni, *Introduction to International Criminal Law*, above n 86, 29, 333–386.

As extraterritorial criminal jurisdiction laws have proliferated in the last half-century, they have not evidenced concerns with respect to the need for having a hierarchy or priority of these theories aimed at avoiding conflicts of jurisdiction,[89] or providing for norms or guidelines to resolve criminal jurisdictional conflicts. Clearly this would have contributed to improved international co-operation between states in prosecuting or extraditing persons who are charged with acts of 'terrorism'.[90]

Another indication of the absence of an international criminal justice policy is the inconsistency in the inclusion of specific extraterritorial criminal jurisdiction bases in various international criminal law conventions, including the conventions that deal with specific manifestations of 'terrorism'.[91]

There has also been a historic and consistent failure to articulate either the conditions for and limitations on the exercise of extraterritorial criminal jurisdiction or the criteria for the resolution of jurisdictional conflicts between a state having custody, albeit the territorial state, of a person charged with acts of 'terrorism' and another state seeking the extradition of that person for the same acts.[92]

[89] But see 'Harvard Research in International Law: Jurisdiction with Respect to Crime', 29 *Am J Int'l L* 443 (Supp 1935).

[90] See above n 71.

[91] See under heading 'The Normative Structure of 'Terrorism' Offences' above.

[92] *Ibid.*

12

Transnational Faces of Justice: Two Attempts to Build Common Standards Beyond National Boundaries

JOHN JACKSON*

Even a cursory look at the administration of criminal justice in our time reveals that multidirectional changes are in progress. Entangled convergences and differences arise among national systems, eluding conventional points of reference. Many of the large scale concepts by means of which we had been accustomed to sorting out the world of procedure have begun to come apart. Even the venerable frontier between Anglo-American and Continental European criminal procedures has become increasingly ill-marked, open and transgressed. ... The confusing complexity of the legal landscape has recently been heightened by the emergence of international criminal courts whose architects, in shaping procedural arrangements, decided to hybridize and blend Anglo-American and Continental procedural rules.

Mirjan Damaška[1]

I. INTRODUCTION

ONE OF THE enduring legacies of Mirjan Damaška's scholarship has been to provide the conceptual tools for us to understand the differences that are evident in common law and civil law systems of justice. Until Damaška comparative criminal procedure was depicted in

* This essay was prepared during the course of a British Academy research leave fellowship from October 2006–September 2008 and while I was a Fernand Braudel Fellow at the European University Institute in Florence from October 2007–June 2008. Many thanks are due to Máximo Langer for his comments on a first draft of this article.

[1] M Damaška, 'Negotiated Justice in International Criminal Courts' (2004) 2 *Journal of International Criminal Justice* 1018, 1018–9.

well worn and often misleading terms as a contrast between adversarial and inquisitorial systems. It is a tremendous achievement of Damaška's scholarship that he was able to enrich and deepen our conceptions of the different ways of dispensing justice by linking different procedural systems to broader issues of state structure and authority, demonstrating how the institutional and political environment of the administration of justice are central to understanding different procedural styles. Rather than engage in the task of trying to match procedural styles to actual systems and thereby become intertwined in an endless debate as to what features are characteristic of one form or another, Damaška moved the comparative debate on to a search for what lies at the essence of the different systems and the underlying institutional and political forces that divide them.

Thus in his landmark article, 'Evidentiary Barriers to Conviction', Damaška explained the different evidentiary styles in common law and civil law criminal procedure in terms of a contrast between arranging proceedings around the notion of a dispute or contest between two sides in a position of theoretical equality before a court and arranging them around the notion of an official and thorough inquiry driven by court proceedings.[2] In his later article, 'Structures of Authority', he developed differences in the organisation of authority by contrasting two ideals of officialdom which he labelled 'hierarchical' and 'co-ordinate', the former exaggerating certain features of Continental judicial organisation with its emphasis on officials organised in a hierarchy applying technical norms and the latter based on certain tendencies within Anglo-American justice to hand over decision making to lay persons applying community norms.[3] In his path-breaking masterpiece, *The Faces of Justice and State Authority*,[4] he advanced another pair of opposing 'ideal-types' around different conceptions about the purpose to be served by the administration of justice: one seeing the end of justice as conflict-resolution within a reactive state which 'is limited to providing a framework within which citizens can pursue their chosen goals';[5] the other seeing justice as implementing policy within an activist state dedicated to the 'material and moral betterment of its citizens'.[6]

While these opposing ideal types provide much stronger lenses for understanding the machinery of justice on the European continent and in the lands of the Anglo-American tradition, they concentrate very much

[2] M Damaška, 'Evidentiary Barriers to Conviction and Two Models of Criminal Procedure' (1973) 121 *University Pennsylvania Law Review* 506.

[3] M Damaška, 'Structures of Authority and Comparative Criminal Procedure' (1975) 85 *Yale Law Journal* 480.

[4] MR Damaška, *The Faces of Authority and State Authority* (New Haven, Yale UP, 1986).

[5] *Ibid* 73.

[6] *Ibid* 80.

more on the differences between these procedural traditions than on any similarities. Damaška's emphasis on structural difference in the organisation of authority and on different perceptions of the ends of justice and the role of the state indeed reveals a world of difference not only in the form of procedures but also in deeper institutional, ideological and cultural traditions. Thus although we can agree that the criminal process is about convicting the guilty, an ideology which is distrustful of the state and is fearful of governmental abuse of power tends to reinforce the need for criminal proceedings to be arranged around the notion of a contest giving the accused every opportunity to challenge the manner in which the criminal investigation was carried out. By contrast, an ideology which is less distrustful of the state tends to reinforce the view that criminal proceedings should be arranged around the notion of an inquiry and that the defence ought to be given less opportunity to make 'technical' objections to the criminal investigation. These differences draw attention to the difficulties of transplanting processes from one tradition into another as institutional and cultural resistance may prove too strong to achieve the impact intended. Damaška himself has illustrated this by reference to the attempt to transplant the English criminal jury on to the Continent after the French Revolution and, more recently, the attempt to impose adversarial traits into the new Italian Code of Criminal Procedure.[7]

Yet while Damaška was exposing in his scholarship good reasons as to why we should be wary of attempts to combine common law and civil law approaches to evidence and procedure, there have been considerable pressures over the last 30 years or so to do precisely this. At an inter-state level, there have been pressures on states to find common solutions and processes to deal with the problems of transnational crime, organised crime, drug trafficking and most recently international terrorism.[8] This has been particularly evident in Europe where supranational institutions such as the Council of Europe and the European Union have been driving change.[9] The emergence of international criminal tribunals to try persons responsible for international crimes has also required the international community to develop a set of rules of procedure and evidence acceptable to both traditions.[10] One message that might be taken from Damaška's

[7] M Damaška, 'The Uncertain Fate of Evidentiary Transplants: Anglo-American and Continental Experiments' (1997) 45 *American Journal of Comparative Law* 839. See also Luca Marafioti, ch 5.

[8] See D Amann, 'Harmonic Convergence? Constitutional Criminal Procedure in an International Context' (2000) 75 *Indiana Law Journal* 809.

[9] See M Delmas-Marty and JR Spencer, *European Criminal Procedures* (Cambridge, CUP, 2002).

[10] M Findlay, 'Synthesis in Trial Procedures? The Experience of International Criminal Tribunals' (2001) 50 *International Comparative Law Quarterly* 26. For an excellent account of how the international community came to re-develop international criminal justice in the

scholarship may be that we should be pessimistic about such an endeavour. Trapped as we are within the confines of our own respective traditions, there is the evident danger that we lose our way when we are required to build *sui generis* procedures beyond these traditions and become, as Damaška has suggested, 'mariners on the ocean without compass, star or landmark'.[11] Yet his work also bears witness to the fact that procedures can evolve to produce a mix of arrangements to meet the social and political demands of the day even when such changes do not appear to sit comfortably with the way in which the machinery of justice has been traditionally organised. The 'mixed' type of procedure that European scholars developed in the 19th century in order to instil accusatorial features into the old inquisitorial processes that dominated Continental European countries from the thirteenth century may be viewed as a positive example of the ability of European procedure to adapt to the changed political and social climate of the time even though there continued to be a mismatch between aspiration and reality.[12] Another example which Damaška also draws attention to would appear to be the attempts in the United States and England in the late 20th century to instil greater judicial activism into conflict-solving civil procedures as the civil process was seen to include greater policy-implementing aspects.[13]

Inspiring as these examples may be, the challenge to develop common standards and procedures would seem to be even more formidable when jurists look beyond the nation state and try to develop common procedures beyond national boundaries. The challenge here is not just to meet the particular procedural tradition which has been developed within the nation state but to meet a number of traditions across national boundaries, of which the common law and civil law traditions have been the most dominant.

This chapter compares and contrasts two attempts to develop common standards of process and procedure across these two traditions. The first example examines the efforts made by the European Court of Human Rights to apply the human rights standards laid down by Article 6 of the European Convention of Human Rights (ECHR) across the different criminal justice systems of the member states of the Council of Europe.[14]

1990s, 50 years after Nuremberg, see G Robertson, *Crimes Against Humanity: The Struggle for Global Justice* 2nd edn (London, Penguin Books, 2002).

[11] Above n 1, 1019.

[12] See Damaška, above n 4, 189–194 and above n 2, 558–560. For an examination of the contribution made by European jurists of the 19th century towards this development, see SJ Summers, *Fair Trials: The European Criminal Procedural Tradition and the European Court of Human Rights* (Oxford, Hart Publishing, 2007).

[13] See Damaška, above n 4, 237–238. For further discussion, see MR Damaška, *Evidence Law Adrift* (New Haven, Yale UP, 1996) 134–8.

[14] Although the member states are bound by the Statute of the Council of Europe to safeguard and realise the democratic ideals and principles of individual freedom, political

The second example looks at the international community's attempt over a number of years to develop a common set of rules and procedures for prosecuting those charged with genocide, war crimes and crimes against humanity at an international level.[15]

These enterprises are different in nature. One seeks to regulate the behaviour of states towards their nationals while the other seeks to exercise jurisdiction over individuals charged with international crimes. While the first enterprise is therefore concerned with state conduct in national criminal justice systems, the second is entirely international in character. Another difference is that while the European Court seeks to set common standards, the various international tribunals are set the more ambitious task of drawing up detailed rules of procedure to apply the norms of international criminal law.

The greater ambition of the international criminal law enterprise also adds to greater complexity. While the European system had to establish a secretariat and appoint judges for the court, the international criminal systems had to establish other institutions such as an Office of the Prosecutor. In addition to this, the European system has been set one fairly simple objective – compliance with the Convention, although there has been increasing debate as to how this should be achieved with the rise in the number of individual applications as a result of the enlargement of the Council of Europe.[16] By contrast the international criminal tribunals are said to have multiple objectives beyond the traditional objective of national systems of criminal justice of convicting those guilty of criminal conduct.[17] The Security Council resolution which announced the establishment of an international tribunal for the former Yugoslavia stated that the tribunal would prosecute persons responsible for serious violations of humanitarian law which 'would contribute to the restoration and maintenance of

liberty and the rule of law, they each have a different history of protecting human rights and democracy, with almost half of the states having a communist background.

[15] Within the last 15 years, international tribunals have been established in the former Yugoslavia, Rwanda, East Timor, Sierra Leone and Cambodia. The crowning achievement of international criminal justice, however, has been the establishment of a permanent International Criminal Court as a result of a multilateral treaty agreed in Rome in 1998. See A Cassese, P Gaeta and JRWD Jones (eds), *The Rome Statute of the International Criminal Court: A Commentary* (Oxford, OUP, 2002).

[16] As of 30 September 2007, there were 47 members of the Council of Europe, almost half of which, from former communist countries, have joined since 1989. This has put increasing pressure on the case load of the Court. At the end of September 2007, the Court had 103,606 cases pending. See M O'Boyle, 'On Reforming the Operation of the European Court of Human Rights' (2007), available at <http://www.qub.ac.uk./schools/SchoolofLaw/> accessed 17 June 2008. The Council of Europe introduced reforms under Protocol 11 to deal with the growing volume of individual applications to the Council and Protocol 14 proposes further changes – although Russia has refused to ratify this Protocol. See generally SC Greer, *The European Convention on Human Rights* (Cambridge, CUP, 2006).

[17] See WA Schabas, *The UN International Criminal Tribunals: The Former Yugoslavia, Rwanda and Sierra Leone* (Cambridge, CUP, 2006) 67–73.

peace'.[18] This suggests the need for active trial management to ensure that cases are dealt with expeditiously. But beyond this other objectives have been canvassed for international criminal tribunals which would seem to require a more drawn out process such as the need to give victims a forum for telling their stories, to aid the process of national reconciliation after conflict and to produce a reliable account of atrocities that have taken place.

This chapter makes no conclusions about how successful each enterprise has been in achieving its objectives. While there are considerable difficulties in measuring national Convention compliance across the member states of the Council of Europe, there would seem to be much scope for improvement across the member states, especially in a number of the former Soviet republic and Balkan states.[19] International criminal justice for its part is still arguably a 'fledging discipline [which] has barely been conceptualised, or elaborated',[20] with the result that it is very difficult as yet to carry out any assessment of how successful it has been. The chapter instead focuses on one common aspect of the work of each system which has been the need for actors within it to reach across their national legal traditions and develop a common approach towards procedural and evidentiary standards of criminal justice. Although it would not be appropriate to make direct comparisons between the work of such different institutions, it will be argued that the European Court of Human Rights has been able to use common human rights standards to develop a model that can reach across the dominant common law and civil law traditions without being drawn into applying the norms of one tradition or the other. The international criminal tribunals and courts, by contrast, have tended instead to mix aspects of each tradition in an uneasy compromise without giving enough thought as to whether the objectives of the tribunals are served thereby.

[18] UN Doc S/RES/827 (1993), preamble.

[19] See Greer, above n 16, ch 2. A number of these countries have been plagued by human rights defects in their criminal justice systems such as incommunicado detentions, torture and abuse of suspects by police. See *2008 Human Rights Watch World Report*, available at http://www.hrw.org/wr2k8/ accessed 17 June 2008; *Amnesty International Report 2008*, available at http://thereport.amnesty.org/eng/Homepage/. For the position in Russia see Stephen C Thaman, ch 6.

[20] P Roberts, 'Restoration and Retribution in International Criminal Justice: An Exploratory Analysis' in A von Hirsch (ed), *Restorative Justice and Criminal Justice* (Oxford, Hart Publishing, 2003) 115, 136.

II. THE EUROPEAN COURT OF HUMAN RIGHTS[21]

Since World War II there have been a number of attempts to build international institutions to enforce human rights.[22] The most advanced example of supra-national application of human rights norms has undoubtedly been that of the ECHR by the (now abolished) European Commission of Human Rights and by the European Court of Human Rights.[23] As an indication of the impact these institutions have achieved, it is estimated that taken together both the text of the ECHR and the jurisprudence of the Commission and Court have inspired several hundred national constitutional court decisions.[24] It has been argued that, as the Constitutional Court for Europe, the European Court of Human Rights has become a vehicle for promoting national Convention compliance, which in its turn, promotes 'greater convergence in the "deep structure" of national constitutional, legal and political (though less so economic) systems'.[25] The Convention and Court can hardly be said to have created a truly independent legal order as their role has been merely to correct rather than supplant national legal norms. But this distinction has become somewhat blurred as the jurisprudence of the Commission and Court has come to complete and enrich the often vague text of the Convention and in this manner arrive at a set of norms that seems more and more to be that of a truly supranational legal order.[26]

The key instrument that has been used to develop procedural and evidentiary human rights norms has been the fair trial right in Article 6 of the ECHR. The right to a fair trial finds its roots deep in the history of human rights and is given expression in the UN Universal Declaration of Human Rights.[27] Article 6(1) of the Convention contains a general definition of the right which closely follows Article 10 of the Declaration, whilst Article 6(2) enshrines the presumption of innocence which is contained in Article 11 of the Declaration. But Article 6 goes further than the Declaration by enumerating a number of other specific safeguards,

[21] This section draws heavily upon JD Jackson, 'The Effect of Human Rights on Criminal Evidentiary Processes: Towards, Convergence, Divergence or Realignment' (2005) 68 *MLR* 737.

[22] Thus the Inter-American Court is tasked with applying the American Convention on Human Rights, the African Commission applies the African Charter on Human and People's Rights and the UN Human Rights Committee applies the International Covenant on Civil and Political Rights.

[23] The Commission was abolished in 1998 under Protocol 11 and the Court now has sole jurisdiction to determine applications: see http://www.echr.coe.int/ECHR/EN/Header/The+Court/The+Court/History+of+the+Court/.

[24] M Delmas-Marty, *Towards a Truly Common Law* (Cambridge, CUP, 2002) 67.

[25] Greer, above n 16, 317.

[26] *Ibid* 63–64.

[27] AH Robertson and JG Merrills, *Human Rights in Europe* 3rd edn (Manchester, Manchester UP, 1993) 87.

including in Article 6(1) the right to be brought to trial within a reasonable time and in Article 6(3) a number of defence rights for those charged with a criminal offence, including the right to have adequate time and facilities for the preparation of the defence, the right to legal assistance, the right to examine or have examined witnesses against the defence and to obtain the attendance and examination of witnesses under the same conditions as prosecution witnesses.

In many respects the inclusion of these specific rights may be seen as a triumph for those British lawyers steeped in the common law tradition who argued against their civil law counterparts in favour of a more specific set of rights in preference to a mere restatement of the principles in the Universal Declaration.[28] Taken at face value, the specific rights incorporated in Article 6, drafted as they were largely by the British, naturally appeared to favour an approach which had greater resonance in the common law than in the civil law tradition. Certainly the emphasis in Article 6(3) on the rights of the defence and in particular the concern to buttress the role of the parties in presenting and challenging evidence appears to give the Convention a decidedly adversarial mould.[29] Any victory which the common law tradition was able to claim from the enumeration of defence rights in the Convention, however, was over time reined back by the interpretation that came to be given to these rights by the Commission and the Court in subsequent jurisprudence.

It may be said that the Strasbourg organs adopted two strategies to prevent the imposition of a fully-fledged adversarial system on to the member states. First of all, they gave considerable freedom in the choice of the appropriate means of ensuring that their judicial systems comply with the requirements of Article 6.[30] In particular they were unwilling to prescribe common law rules of evidence or concepts such as admissibility, a clear signal that they had no wish to impose a common law system of evidence on member states. Instead it is for the competent authorities to determine the relevance of any proposed evidence and rules on the admissibility of evidence are 'primarily a matter for regulation under national law'.[31] Secondly, the Commission and Court both said at an early stage that their task was to determine whether they can be satisfied that the

[28] AWB Simpson, *Human Rights and the End of Empire* (Oxford, OUP, 2001).

[29] B Swart and J Young, 'The European Convention on Human Rights and Criminal Justice in the Netherlands and the UK' in P Fennell, C Harding, N Jorg and B Swart (eds), *Criminal Justice in Europe: A Comparative Study* (Oxford, Clarendon Press, 1995).

[30] *Hadjianastassiou v Greece* Series A no 252-A (1993) 16 EHRR 219, para 33.

[31] *Schenk v Switzerland* Series A no 140 (1991) 13 EHRR 242, para 46, *Delta v France* Series A no 191A (1993) 16 EHRR 574, para 35.

proceedings taken 'as a whole' were fair.[32] This enabled them to give an expansive interpretation to Article 6 by looking beyond the specific rights in Article 6 and to develop their own distinctive principles of fairness.

A. The Equality of Arms Principle

Instead of adopting a fully fledged adversarial position requiring party control over the presentation of evidence, the Commission and Court from an early stage chose to develop the principle of 'equality of arms' whereby every party to the proceedings must be afforded 'a reasonable opportunity to present his case in conditions that do not place him at substantial disadvantage *vis-à-vis* his opponent'.[33] Although this is an old principle with roots in both common law and civil law traditions,[34] a number of Continental countries have had to modify their practices to ensure that, in accordance with the principle, both prosecution and defence are treated equally and that prosecutorial functions are completely separated from judicial functions.[35]

The principle has gone beyond ensuring that the parties are accorded a formal equality during the presentation of evidence at the trial and appeals process. In order to be able to contest on equal terms, the Commission and Court recognised that as a result of the disparity in the resources between prosecution and defence, the principle of the equality of arms requires that the 'facilities' which everyone charged with a criminal offence should enjoy under Article 6(3)(b) include the right of the accused to have at his disposal all relevant information that has been or could be collected by the competent authorities.[36] The Strasbourg authorities here have predicated fairness at the trial upon fair disclosure before trial. In Continental procedure this is effected through a shared dossier which is constructed by judicial or prosecutorial officials charged with gathering information in favour as well as against the accused. The notion of sharing information is not so easy to assimilate into the common law tradition with its emphasis on each side gathering and presenting 'its own' evidence. It can argued, for example, that the disclosure provisions under the UK's Criminal Procedure

[32] *Nielson v Denmark* (1957) 4 Yearbook 518, *Barberà, Messegué and Jabardo v Spain* Series A no 146 (1989) 11 EHRR 360, *Delta v France, ibid.*

[33] *Kaufman v Belgium* (1986) 50 DR 98, 115, *Foucher v France* (1998) 25 EHRR 234, para 34.

[34] The principle is an expression of the old natural law principle, *audi alteram partem*, which was first formulated by St Augustine: see JR Lucas, *On Justice* (Oxford, Clarendon Press, 1980) 84.

[35] See, eg, *Borgers v Belgium* Series A no 214 (1993) 15 EHRR 92.

[36] *Jespers v Belgium* (1981) 27 DR 61.

and Investigations Act 1996 are not fully compatible with Article 6 in as much as these do not require disclosure of all the evidence in the prosecutor's possession.[37]

Despite the significance that the principle of the equality of arms attaches to party information and party presentation, however, there are limitations in regarding it as an adversarial principle. These were illustrated in the civil case of *Feldbrugge v Netherlands*[38] where the applicant had been denied an opportunity to appear either in person or through her lawyer in making her claim for health insurance benefits. The Court held that there had been no breach of the principle of the equality of arms because Mrs Feldbrugge's opponents were equally disadvantaged under the procedures of the Appeals Board.

It is true, of course, that Article 6(3) specifically guarantees certain defence rights in criminal cases such as the right to call witnesses but even here the equality of arms principle serves to limit adversarialism as the Article provides that parties have the right to obtain the attendance and examination of witnesses on their behalf only 'under the same conditions' as their opponent. It follows that the defence have no right under this principle to call any witness of its choosing. The competent national authorities are therefore able to decide upon the relevance of the proposed evidence of each witness.[39] As well as this it would seem that where a system proceeds on the basis of experts being called by the court, parties have no right to call their own expert to challenge this evidence unless there are objectively justified fears concerning the court expert's impartiality.[40]

B. The Right to an Adversarial Trial

Towards the end of the 1980s, the Court began to develop the right to be heard and to refer not just to the principle of equality of arms but also to the principle that 'all the evidence must be produced in the presence of the accused at a public hearing with a view to adversarial argument'.[41] A number of decisions ruled that the right to an adversarial trial means, in a

[37] See *Edwards v UK* (1993) 15 EHRR 417, *Glover v UK* (2005) 40 EHRR SE 18. See also the discussion in B Emmerson, A Ashworth and A Macdonald (eds), *Human Rights and Criminal Justice* 2nd edn (London, Sweet & Maxwell, 2007) 540–45.

[38] (1986) Series A no 99.

[39] *Engel v Netherlands*, above n 61, para 91, *Vidal v Belgium* (1992) Series A 235-B.

[40] *Brandstetter v Austria* Series A no 211 (1993) 15 EHRR 378.

[41] *Barberà, Messegué and Jabardo*, above n 32, para 78.

criminal case, that the prosecution and defence must be given the opportunity to have knowledge and comment on the observations filed and the evidence adduced by the other party.[42]

It is important to see, however, that in developing this adversarial right the European Court fell short of prescribing the kind of adversarial trial that is associated with common law jurisdictions where procedural control is largely in the hands of the parties rather than the judge. Under the label of *une procédure contradictoire* it has long been considered important in Continental procedure that the defendant should be present when procedural activities are under way and should be entitled to offer counter-proofs and counter-arguments.[43] The Commission and Court have sought to 'translate' the defence rights prescribed in Article 6 into a vision of adversarialism that was as compatible with the Continental notion of *une procédure contradictoire* as with the common law adversary trial.[44] Defendants have to be guaranteed rights to legal representation, to be informed of all information relevant to the proceedings, to be present and to present arguments and evidence at trial. But this does not rule out considerable participation by judges in asking questions or even calling witnesses.

If the Strasbourg authorities have not slavishly adopted an Anglo-American conception of adversarialism, however, neither have they self-consciously tried to squeeze the Article 6 defence rights into a Continental mould and imposed this across the contracting states. The one right that would seem to stretch the notion of *une procédure contradictoire* as it has been developed in Continental procedure is the right to examine witnesses, expressly safeguarded in Article 6(3)(d). In a series of decisions beginning in 1986,[45] the European Court began to interpret Article 6(3)(d) to mean that convictions should not be substantially based upon the statements of witnesses whom the defence were unable to cross-examine.

There would seem to be little doubt that these decisions were a major factor in some of the changes that began to take effect in a number of Continental jurisdictions which were more firmly associated with the old inquisitorial tradition.[46] As a result of the *Kostovski* decision against the

[42] *Brandstetter v Austria*, above n 40, para 67, *Rowe and Davis v UK* (2000) 30 EHRR 1, para 60.

[43] Damaška, above n 2, 561.

[44] For an analysis of the concept of legal translation, see M Langer, 'From Legal Transplants to Legal Translations: The Globalization of Plea Bargaining and the Americanization Thesis in Criminal Processes' (2004) 45 *Harvard International Law Journal* 1.

[45] See, eg, *Unterpertinger v Austria* Series A no 110 (1991) 13 EHRR 175, *Kostovski v Netherlands* Series A no 166 (1990) 12 EHRR 140, *Windisch v Austria* (1991) 13 EHRR 281, *Delta v France* (1993) 16 EHRR 574.

[46] Nijboer has singled out Spain, France, Belgium and the Netherlands in this category: see J F Nijboer, 'Common Law Tradition in Evidence Scholarship Observed from a Continental Perspective' (1993) 41 *American Journal of Comparative Law* 299, 311.

Netherlands, for example, in which the Court ruled that there was a breach of Article 6 where the conviction was based to a decisive extent on the statements of two anonymous witnesses who gave evidence in the absence of the accused, the Dutch Supreme Court was forced to retreat from earlier case law that had permitted the use of anonymous hearsay evidence.[47]

In France the Court of Cassation held that Article 6(3)(d) requires the trial court to grant the defendant's request to summon and question a witness unless the witness is clearly unavailable, or his testimony would be irrelevant, or the accused has had an adequate opportunity to confront and question the witness in prior proceedings, or there is a serious risk of witness intimidation or retaliation.[48] The adversarial defence rights in Article 6 had a strong influence upon the Delmas-Marty Commission which proposed that a list of basic principles should be placed at the head of a new code of criminal procedure and in reforms in 2000 the principle that criminal procedure should be fair and 'contradictoire' was given pride of place in the list of guiding principles.[49]

In Italy the new code of criminal procedure in 1988 gave expression to these principles and Article 111 of the Italian Constitution was amended to provide that every trial should be based on giving the parties the right to offer counterproofs and counterarguments against unfavourable evidence (including *contradittorio tra le parti*) on an equal standing in front of an impartial judge.[50]

Although the right to examine witnesses would seem to have stretched the Continental notion of *une procédure contradictoire* beyond its traditional boundaries, this right has not required any full scale transition towards a party-controlled trial as the right to confrontation does not mean that in order to be used as evidence the statements of witnesses should always be made at a public hearing. So long as opportunities exist for challenging witnesses before trial, the absence of an opportunity to examine these witnesses at trial is not fatal to compliance with Article 6 standards.[51] This would seem as discomforting to traditional common law approaches, so long associated with the adversarial right of cross-examination at trial, as to civil law traditions.[52]

47 See PTC van Kampen, *Expert Evidence Compared* (Leiden, E M Meijers Institute, 1998) 105–6.

48 J Pradel, 'France' in C Van Den Wyngaert (ed), *Criminal Procedure Systems in the European Community* (London, Butterworths, 1993) 120.

49 See V Dervieux, 'The French System' in Delmas-Marty and Spencer, above n 9, 218, 220–22.

50 A Perrodet, 'The Italian System' in *ibid* 348, 368–69.

51 *Kostovski v Netherlands* (1990) 12 EHRR 140.

52 JH Langbein, *The Origins of Adversary Criminal Trial* (Oxford, OUP, 2003).

C. Towards Convergence or Realignment?

Some commentators have argued that the European Court's move towards adversarialism is promoting some sort of convergence between the two legal traditions.[53] The principle of equality of arms has required civil law countries to make a sharper differentiation between those exercising judicial functions and those exercising 'party' functions. The principle of an adversarial trial has also required such systems to give greater weight to defence rights to examine witnesses. Yet the Court's idea of adversarial proceedings does not correspond in every respect with the notion as it is understood in common law countries. The Court itself did not set out with any presumption that the common law concept of a fair trial is superior to the civil law concept, or the latter superior to the former and has steered clear of imposing any abstract model of proof on contracting parties.[54] Instead, as we have seen, it has tried to 'translate' the principles in Article 6 in such a manner as to make them amenable to accommodation within both common law and civil law traditions.

It is tempting to see in this some sort of gradual convergence of party- and court-dominated procedures towards a mixed model of proof, more party-orientated than traditional Continental criminal procedure but falling short of the party control exercised in the common law adversarial trial. But rather than attempt to piece together the various strands of both traditions, borrowing from each tradition where possible to reach a compromise between the two, the Court has developed its own distinctive brand of jurisprudence through the principles of the equality of arms and the right to an adversarial trial which is transforming rather than merely mixing together the two traditions.

Delmas-Marty has argued that the great lesson of the European jurisprudence is that *no* model of criminal procedure – accusatory, inquisitorial or mixed – has escaped censure by the Strasbourg tribunals.[55] Instead the Commission and Court have over the years developed a vision of participation in the decision-making of the justice system which is rooted both in common law principles of natural justice and due process and in what is known on the Continent as *la theorie de la procédure contradictoire*. At the heart of this vision is what Delmas-Marty has called the 'contradictory debate' – the rejection, as she has put it, 'of revealed, uncontested truth replaced by facts which are contested and only then established as

[53] See, eg, Swart and Young, above n 29.

[54] Swart and Young, above n 29, 86; M Chiavario, 'The Rights of the Defendant and the Victim' in Delmas-Marty and Spencer, above n 9, 541, 548.

[55] M Delmas-Marty, 'Toward a European Model of the Criminal Trial' in M Delmas-Marty (ed), *The Criminal Process and Human Rights: Towards a European Consciousness* (Dordrecht, Martinus Nijhoff, 1995) 191, 196. See also Fennell *et al*, above n 29, 384.

truths'.[56] Her own Commission in France went some way towards attempting to realise this ideal in practice when it recommended that defence lawyers be given enhanced rights of access to their clients in custody, access to the official dossier, a right of attendance at judicial hearings and the power to request investigative acts of a new *juge des libertés*.[57]

The Court has had to develop this vision in a piecemeal fashion, case by case, proceeding on the basis that the Convention is a living instrument that requires adaptation as circumstances change. Nevertheless, it is possible to identify four broad strands in the development of its vision of defence participation in the criminal processes of proof that require to be accommodated within national systems. First, defendants cannot be required to participate in the proof process. Although Article 6 makes no mention of the privilege against self-incrimination, the Court made it clear in 1993 that the right of anyone charged with a criminal offence to remain silent and not contribute to incriminating himself flowed directly from Article 6 of the Convention.[58] Secondly, any participation must be on an informed basis. This would seem to require the assistance of counsel at pre-trial stages when the accused is being questioned, full disclosure of relevant information to the defence and a defence right to comment on the evidence.[59] Thirdly, the defence must be given an opportunity to challenge this evidence including, as we have seen, the right to examine decisive witnesses at some stage during the proceedings. Finally, the national courts must indicate with sufficient clarity the grounds on which they base their decisions. This requires some form of reasoned judgment which can be challenged by the defence.[60]

The attempt of the Court to establish evidentiary and procedural principles which transcend the procedural traditions of common law and

[56] *Ibid* 197.

[57] M Delmas-Marty, *La mise en état des affaires pénales: Rapport de la Commission justice pénale et droits de l'homme* (Paris, La Documentation française, 1991). For recent studies on how far these participatory principles are challenging and reforming pre-trial practice in France, see J Hodgson, 'Constructing the Pre-trial Role of the Defence in French Criminal Procedure: An Adversarial Outsider in an Inquisitorial Process' (2002) 6 *International Journal of Evidence & Proof* 1; S Field and A West, 'Dialogue and the Inquisitorial Tradition: French Defence Lawyers in the Pre-trial Criminal Process' (2003) 14 *Criminal Law Forum* 261.

[58] *Funke v France* Series A no 256-A (1993) 16 EHRR 297. This does not preclude, however, taking into account an accused's silence in situations which clearly call for an explanation. See *John Murray v UK* (1996) 22 EHRR 29.

[59] The precise parameters of the right of access to counsel before trial, like the right of silence, remain uncertain. Cf *John Murray v UK* (1996) 22 EHRR 29, *Brennan v UK* (2002) 34 EHRR 507; *Öcalan v Turkey* (2003) 37 EHRR 10. A further question which is not so clear, however, relates to whether an accused person can in effect waive his right to a fair trial by refusing to participate at all in his trial.

[60] *Hadjianastassiou v Greece* (1993) 16 EHRR 219, para 33.

civil law systems may be seen as building upon the success the Court has had in using the Convention to transform the constitutional traditions of many European states.[61] While resisting the temptation to become a 'fourth instance' court,[62] in fashioning these participatory principles out of Article 6 of the Convention the Court is arguably going beyond setting a framework for individual substantive rights within the criminal process and establishing a model of procedural justice which calls upon states to provide meaningful, institutional support for the exercise of defence rights. As the Court grapples with an increasing case load, the challenge in the future will be whether it will be able to influence the Convention's present 47 contracting parties as strongly as it was able to influence the original contracting parties.

III. THE INTERNATIONAL SYSTEM OF CRIMINAL JUSTICE

The relative success with which the European organs have managed over time to develop common standards of fairness across diverse European states may be contrasted with the unease that has accompanied the attempt of the international criminal tribunals to develop common procedures for dealing with international crimes. Although this process was started after the Second World War by the Nuremberg trials, it was not until the 1990s in the wake of the atrocities in the former Yugoslavia and Rwanda that the first truly independent international criminal tribunals were established and these were followed by the establishment of the International Criminal Court in 2002.

Considerable effort has gone into developing definitions for the international crimes that come within the jurisdiction of this new international criminal justice.[63] The death of Slobodan Milošević in 2006 in the course of a trial that had been going on for four years has now led to increasing attention as to how this justice is being delivered.[64] Disquiet has been expressed about the delays that have crippled the tribunals, the large costs that have been associated with them and procedures which appear to give defendants, as one commentator has put it, 'not hours but years to strut

[61] The Court has interpreted the ECHR as a constitutional charter of Europe. See *Ireland v UK* (1979) 2 EHRR 25. On the rise of judicial activism across Europe since the establishment of the Court, see A Stone Sweet, *The Judicial Construction of Europe* (Oxford, OUP, 2004).

[62] L Wildhaber, 'A Constitutional Future of the European Court of Human Rights' (2002) 23 *Human Rights Law Journal* 161.

[63] See G Mettraux, *International Crimes and the Ad Hoc Tribunals* (Oxford, OUP, 2005).

[64] For a thorough analysis of the Milošević trial and the lessons to be learned from it, see G Boas, *The Milošević Trial* (Cambridge, CUP, 2007).

and fret upon a televised stage.'[65] All this might be forgiven if it were possible to say that the defendants received a fair trial at the end of their trial. But there has not been a consensus about this.[66]

A. The Current Mixed Model

Just as with the European system, human rights have provided the bedrock for achieving a common procedure for the international criminal tribunals. The report which the UN Security Council requested the Secretary General to prepare on the international tribunal for the prosecution of persons relating to violations of humanitarian law committed in the former Yugoslavia considered that it was axiomatic that the tribunal must fully respect internationally recognised standards regarding the rights of the accused at all stages of its proceedings.[67] Consequently Article 21 of the Statute establishing the International Criminal Tribunal for the former Yugoslavia (ICTY) and Article 20 of the Statute for the International Criminal Tribunal for Rwanda (ICTR) gave full recognition to the right to a fair trial contained in Article 14 of the International Covenant on Civil and Political Rights (ICCPR).[68] The Covenant is closely modelled on the ECHR and the tribunals themselves have increasingly applied this treaty based human rights law.[69]

When it came to drafting the rules of procedure and evidence, however, there was limited guidance to be sought from international human rights instruments. Judges of the tribunals who were assigned this task chose to adopt the pragmatic approach of working from what was available to them rather than start completely afresh to consider which rules would be best suited for the purposes of the tribunals within a human rights context. Although the rules adopted by the Nuremberg and Tokyo tribunals were too brief to provide an adequate reference point, these trials had set an

[65] G Robertson, 'General Editor's Introduction to Essays on Fairness and Evidence in War Crimes Trials' (2006) *International Commentary on Evidence*: Vol 4: Iss 1, Art 1.

[66] Cf C Francia, 'Due Process in International Criminal Courts: Why Procedure Matters' (2001) 87 *Virginia LR* 1381; M Fairlie, 'The Marriage of Common Law and Continental Law at the ICTY and its Progeny, Due Process Model' (2004) 4 *International Criminal L R* 243; P Wald, 'Fair Trials for War Criminals' (2006) *International Commentary on Evidence*: Vol 4 : Iss 1, Art 6.

[67] Report of the Secretary General pursuant to para 2 of Security Council Resolution 808 (1993), UN Doc S/25704, para 106.

[68] For a study of the origins of the right to a fair trial as articulated in the Covenant, see D Weissbrodt, *The Right to a Fair Trial* (The Hague, Kluwer, 2001) ch 3.

[69] See G Sluiter, 'International Criminal Proceedings and the Protection of Human Rights' (2003) 37 *New England Law Review* 935.

adversarial precedent, albeit one that took the form of a military commission.[70] Apart from this precedent, the judges received proposals from a number of states and organisations. The most comprehensive contribution came from the United States and the adversarial approach it adopted proved 'particularly influential'.[71] While the rules that were drafted for the tribunals did not slavishly adopt US criminal procedures, the adversarial approach adopted was clear from the manner in which the parties were made the most active actors in the proceedings, in charge of developing their own pre-trial investigations and cases at trial. Judges were given the power of their own motion to issue orders, summonses, subpoenas and warrants but it was the prosecutor who was given the responsibility for investigation.

There were, nevertheless, certain features which the new international criminal tribunals shared in common with the Nuremberg and Tokyo tribunals that were distinguishable from the classic adversarial common law trial. The most striking was the absence of detailed rules of evidence. These traits have caused a number of commentators to consider that although the international tribunals were structured in an adversarial fashion they have developed into a mixed model, which is adversarial so far as the presentation is concerned but inquisitorial as regards the admission of evidence.[72]

Rule 89(C) of the Rules of Procedure and Evidence of both tribunals states that the Trial Chamber may admit any relevant evidence which it deems of probative value although r 89(D) of the ICTY rules states that a chamber may exclude evidence if its probative value is substantially outweighed by the need to ensure a fair trial. It is true that the rules at first displayed greater bias towards oral evidence that could be tested in court than written evidence. The ICTY rules originally stated that in principle witnesses shall be heard directly by the chambers unless a chamber has ordered that the witness be heard by means of a deposition.[73]

[70] For discussion of the evolutionary history of the Nuremberg and Tokyo tribunals, see E J Wallach, 'The Procedural and Evidentiary Rules of the Post – World War II War Trials: Did They Provide an Outline for International Legal Procedure?' (1999) 37 *Columbia Journal of Transnational Law* 851.

[71] See V Morris and M Scharf, *An Insider's Guide to the International Criminal Tribunal for the Former Yugoslavia: A Documentary History and Analysis* (Irvington-on-Hudson, NY, Transnational Publishers, 1995) 177.

[72] See, eg, V Tochilovsky, 'Rules of Procedure for the International Criminal Court: Problems to Address in the light of the Experience of the Ad Hoc Tribunals' (1999) *Netherlands International Law Review* 343, 359, D A Mundis, 'From "Common Law" toward "Civil Law": The Evolution of the ICTY Rules of Procedure and Evidence' (2001) 14 *Leiden Journal of International Law* 287, S Zappalà, *Human Rights in International Criminal Proceedings* (Oxford, OUP, 2003) 22–24.

[73] See Rule 90(A) of the original ICTY rules first published in 1994. The latest version of the rules was published in July 2007.

But over time with anxieties about the length of time it was taking to process cases, pressure mounted on judges to admit written evidence in place of oral evidence and the rules were changed to permit Chambers to receive evidence 'orally or, where the interests of justice allow, in written form'.[74] Further rules imposed certain restrictions on the admission of written statements when they went to proof of the acts and conduct of the accused but after a ruling by the Appeals Chamber from the Milosevic trial permitting these statements to be admitted as evidence in chief,[75] the rules were changed again to admit such statements under certain circumstances.[76]

It has been argued that this mix of adversarial party control with free admissibility of evidence has evolved into a hybrid which is closer to the managerial system that has been adopted in US civil procedure than to elements that are found in the inquisitorial system.[77] It is true that many of the changes made to the rules were motivated by a managerial need to speed up proceedings rather than by any concerted desire to move the structure of the proceedings away from party competition towards a more truth finding tribunal. The pressure for cases to be expedited became particularly pronounced when the Security Council endorsed a Completion Strategy for both the Former Yugoslavia and Rwanda tribunals which called for an end to trials by 2008 and appeals by 2010.[78] But it would be wrong to view this shift as a consensual and effortless movement towards a managerial model.[79] Judges and other protagonists steeped in their own domestic culture still tend to view processes through adversarial and non-adversarial lenses. Although there has been little empirical research on the conduct of the trials, there is some evidence to suggest that there is considerable diversity in the way in which the trials are managed, depending on which domestic culture takes hold within the Trial Chamber, and that there can be a clash of cultures as the features of one culture come up against that of the opposing tradition.[80]

More important than the rubbing points that the present mix of legal procedures can cause for the practitioners involved is the question whether

[74] ICTY, ICTR, Rule 89(F).

[75] *The Prosecutor v Slobodan Milosević*, Decision on Interlocutory Appeal on the Admissibility of Evidence-in-Chief in the form of Written Statements. Case No IT-02–54-AR73.4 30 September 2003.

[76] See ICTY, Rule 92*bis*, 92*ter* and 92*quater*; ICTR, Rule 92*bis*.

[77] M Langer, 'The Rise of Managerial Judging in International Criminal Law' (2005) 53 *American Journal of Comparative Law* 835.

[78] Security Council Resolution (2003) 1503.

[79] Langer accepts that there has been resistance to managerial judging but argues that the managerial judging system provides the 'best account' of ICTY criminal procedure. See above n 77, 908.

[80] See FJ Pakes, 'Styles of Trial Procedure at the International Criminal Tribunal for the Former Yugoslavia' (2003) 17 *Perspectives in Law and Psychology* 309.

this mix has proved to be the best foundation for achieving the goals of international criminal justice. Although there has been considerable debate as to whether the tribunals should embrace wider goals than domestic conventional criminal justice, a key goal remains the need to reach an accurate verdict so far as the guilt of the accused is concerned in a fair and expeditious manner.[81] We have seen that one of the purposes of relaxing the rules on the admissibility of evidence has been in order to accommodate the need for expedition. There has been an assumption that this can be done without sacrificing fairness where there are experienced judges as opposed to juries who are able to give evidence its appropriate weight.[82]

This argument has not been accepted by certain common law commentators who have drawn attention to the dangers of admitting written hearsay evidence within an adversarial context and expressed bewilderment at the ease with which judges say they can assess the weight of hearsay evidence. As Patricia Wald, a former judge at the ICTY, has asked, how does one assess the credibility of a piece of paper?[83] In her time at the ICTY she had seen countless statements made years earlier by a witness that the same witness repudiates, contradicts or ignores in his or her courtroom testimony. There was no question in her view that a very different aura surrounds a witness giving live testimony to the judges in front of the accused than in an interview with a prosecution or defence representative out of court.

The dissenting judge in the Milošević Appeals Chamber case was also critical of his colleagues' decision to permit the admission of witness statements relating to the particularly sensitive issue of the acts and conduct of the accused despite the existence of Rule 92*bis* which appeared to forbid such admission.[84] In the judge's view, the prohibition of such statements prepared by the party adducing them with the possibility that they therefore put the best gloss on the evidence was based on the need to ensure the reliability of the evidence and to permit them to be admitted in chief was directly inconsistent with the policy of the rule. The decision

[81] See G Boas, 'Creating Laws of Evidence for International Criminal Law: The ICTY and the Principle of Flexibility' (2001) 12 *Criminal Law Forum* 41.

[82] According to the statement made by the President of the ICTY, Antonio Cassese, on the adoption of the rules of procedure and evidence, admissibility rules developed out of the 'ancient trial by jury system' and the absence of a jury meant 'needing to be shielded from irrelevancies or given guidance as to the weight of evidence they have heard' rendered such rules unnecessary. See *Statement by the President made at a Briefing to Members of Diplomatic Missions concerning the Adoption of the Rules of Evidence and Procedure at the ICTY* (IT/29, 11 February 1994).

[83] P Wald, 'To "Establish Incredible Events by Credible Evidence": The Use of Affidavit Testimony in Yugoslavia War Crimes Tribunal Proceedings' (2001) 42 *Harvard International Law Journal* 535, 551.

[84] *Prosecutor v Milošević*, 'Dissenting Opinion of Judge David Hunt on Admissibility of Evidence in Chief in the form of Written Statements', Case No IT-02–54-AR73.4, 21 October 2003.

could only be explained in the light of a desire to assist the prosecution to bring the Completion Strategy to a speedy conclusion and risked destroying the rights of the accused enshrined in the Tribunal's Statute.

Other judges have defended the system of admitting statements with cross-examination as an appropriate and fair way to expedite proceedings.[85] New rules, however, now make special provision for the admission of statements going to the acts and conduct of the accused even where the witness is no longer available for cross-examination.[86]

These concerns go to the heart of Professor Damaška's warning that a mixing of procedures can produce a far less satisfactory fact-finding result in practice than under either Continental or Anglo-American evidentiary arrangements in their unadulterated form.[87] Despite the relaxation of the admissibility rules, the international criminal tribunals remain fundamentally adversarial in structure as evidence is collected and presented by a prosecutor who has to prove guilt rather an independent magistrate. As with other adversarial systems there is therefore good reason to be suspicious of the manner in which that evidence has been collected.

The problem is exacerbated in international tribunals where there are a number of factors that point to the added difficulty in assessing written statements in this environment. First of all, many of the witnesses coming from one side of an armed conflict may be said to be inherently biased as they have a considerable interest in the outcome of the proceedings.[88] Secondly, there are grave dangers of errors creeping into the fact-finding process where different languages are at play.[89] In the usual case, the witnesses give their statements orally in their native tongue. These are then translated into English, prepared in written form by investigators, read back and translated for the witnesses who then sign an English written statement. Neither the interview nor the reading back is tape-recorded to ensure the accuracy of the oral translation given at each stage. A third point is that quite apart from any errors in translation there is considerable scope for fabrication and misrepresentation in this environment. There would appear to be an absence of ethical rules concerning the coaching of witnesses and the preparation of their statements by investigators from the Office of the Prosecutor. The ICTY has commented on the fact that

[85] O Kwok, 'The Challenge of an International Criminal Trial as Seen from the Bench' (2007) 5 *Journal of International Criminal Justice* 360.

[86] See ICTY RPE, 92*quater*.

[87] Above n 7, 839, 852.

[88] MP Scharf, *Balkan Justice* (Durham, Carolina Academic Press, 1997) 212.

[89] The process is described in *Prosecutor v Galić*. Decision on Interlocutory Appeal Concerning Rule 92bis (C) Case No IT-98–29 AR73.2, 7 June 2002, para 30, n 56. See also Wald, above n 83, 551; R Cryer, 'A Long Way from Home: Witnesses before International Criminal Tribunals' (2006) International Commentary on Evidence: Vol 4: Iss 1, Art 8.

questions concerning the reliability of written statements given by prospective witnesses to the Office of the Prosecutor investigators have unfortunately arisen.[90]

Relaxing the standards for the admissibility of such evidence without the possibility of cross-examination of the original source runs the risk of error. Even where witnesses are available to be cross-examined at trial, by this stage they are not likely to have as good a recollection of events as when the statements were originally taken. Errors could be better avoided if an investigating judge were able to take the statements in a proper forensic atmosphere and compile a dossier of evidence relating to the entire case which would then be passed on to the trial judges. But this cannot be done under a system which is essentially party driven with the investigation of crimes and the collection of evidence in the hands of the prosecutor and the defence.[91]

It is true that the international tribunals are not required to admit the written statements of witnesses that have been taken by the Office of the Prosecutor investigators. The judges have been given active powers to call and question witnesses themselves and to require the production of documents and other evidentiary material.[92] But here again a civil law feature was grafted on to an essentially adversarial party dominated structure. Damaška has pointed out that the difficulty with this is that judges know less about the case than counsel and risk pursuing lines of inquiry which fully informed counsel have explored and abandoned as inappropriate.[93] This intrusion risks throwing the strategies of counsel out of kilter and creating an appearance of unfairness on the part of the parties. To make judicial questioning more effective, further steps in the direction of Continental fact-finding methods would have to be contemplated in the form of providing the judge with an 'information-rich dossier' so that they could be adequately prepared for trial. But this suggests again the need for a Continental style investigating judge with the consequent diminishment of party collection and presentation of evidence.

B. Towards a Fairer and More Effective System

In some respects the very fact that an international legal community sharply divided by tradition as to the best means for conducting international criminal cases has managed to agree a set of detailed rules of procedure and evidence and brought a number of persons to justice within

[90] See *Prosecutor v Galić, ibid* para 30.
[91] See Langer, above n 77, 898–899.
[92] *Ibid* 858–9.
[93] Above n 7, 851.

the ad hoc regime of The Hague and Rwanda tribunals may be counted as a considerable success. When one considers that all this has been achieved within a relatively short period of time since 1993 the success may seem all the more remarkable. This success undoubtedly helped to encourage the establishment of the International Criminal Court under the Rome Treaty of 1998 which is presently beginning its first cases.[94]

At the same there are lessons to be learned from the ad hoc experience as the hybrid system that has been developed may be said to have led to a deficit in terms of truth finding and fairness to the accused.[95] The rationale for strict rules such as hearsay in an adversarial system is that the partisan presentation of evidence that the parties use needs to be subjected to scrutiny and cross-examination. The pre-trial briefs that the parties furnish to the court before the trial are not 'an information rich dossier' as is the case in civil law jurisdictions and often the product of partial and dubious information collecting techniques. Although the move towards such a hybrid system was motivated by the need for expedition, it is questionable whether it has produced an effective 'managerial' model.

The challenge for the International Criminal Court and for future tribunals is whether it is possible to develop a fairer and more effective system which is better suited to the context and purpose of international criminal justice. The judges in the Court have one advantage over their predecessors in the international tribunals in that they sit in a permanent court and are appointed for longer periods of time.[96] One of the criticisms levelled by Judge Hunt in his dissenting judgment in the Appeals Chamber decision in the Milošević case against his fellow judges was that as the Completion Strategy came into effect, they were too ready to give priority to the politics of expedition over fairness to the accused. Judges in the new Court are unlikely to be under the same pressures. This gives rise to the hope that together with other professional actors working for the Court, the Court will be successful over time in fashioning a system of criminal justice suitable to the conditions of international crime. This does not need to entail an entirely 'sui generis' model totally divorced from the traditional 'adversarial' and 'inquisitorial' models of justice. But it does require

[94] See SD Roper and LA Barria, *Designing Criminal Tribunals* (Aldershot, Ashgate, 2006) 14.

[95] Fairlie, above n 66, 291.

[96] Judges at the ICTY and ICTR serve terms of four years and although these are subject to renewal, re-election of the judges is by no means automatic with the result that a number only complete four years of service. *Ad litem* judges can only sit for a maximum of three years and they only work when they are assigned to a particular case. See Schabas, above n 17, 508. By contrast judges at the International Criminal Court are given set terms of nine years: see Rome Statute of the International Criminal Court, Art 36(9)(a).

that a common language is found for working together, what Delmas-Marty has described elsewhere in this collection as a 'common grammar'.[97]

The language of human rights is a useful starting point. We have seen that the importance of adhering to human rights standards was recognised in Article 21 of the ICTY Statute and in a similar manner Article 67 of the Rome Statute incorporates the standards laid down in Article 14 of the ICCPR. It is not suggested that the international community needs to follow in all respects the jurisprudence that has been developed by organs such as the European Court for national jurisdictions. The types of consideration relevant to these human rights bodies may not be appropriate for international tribunals freed from municipal considerations and acting on behalf of the international community as a whole. The context in which the tribunals operate and the purposes of the tribunal may positively require them to develop different standards. One example would seem to be the need to consider much more actively than the international jurisprudence to date the position of victims who are given special protection and participation rights in the Rome Statute.[98] The importance of context, however, should not necessarily lead international tribunals to seek to reduce the protections that have been afforded to accused persons within the existing human rights regimes and to minimise the participatory standards identified above. Rather what is needed is an approach which seeks to determine how these participatory rights can best be enhanced within the constraints that international tribunals are under and without prejudicing the purposes that have led to their establishment.

Here it may be seriously questioned whether the adversarial structure within which the ad hoc tribunals have operated to date is best suited for their purposes. We have seen that where partisan parties are responsible for collecting their own evidence there is a need for considerable regulation of the evidence at trial and that the flexible approach towards the admissibility of evidence adopted by the tribunals prevents the proper testing of this evidence. Far from the hybrid of adversarial presentation and free admissibility resulting in the best from the two dominant legal cultures, it has led instead to the admissibility of partisan evidence which cannot be tested effectively. But the answer to this is not necessarily to adopt common law rules of evidence within an unchanged adversarial structure. One concern is whether such a system can deliver a true equality of arms within the international context of criminal proceedings.[99]

[97] See Mireille Delmas-Marty, ch 13.

[98] See C Jorda and J Hemptinne, 'The Status and Role of the Victim' in Cassese *et al*, above n 15, 1387.

[99] See G MacIntyre, 'Equality of Arms – Defining Human Rights in the Jurisprudence of the International Criminal Tribunals for the Former Yugoslavia' (2003) 16 *Leiden Journal of International Law* 269.

A key difficulty for international courts is that they are unable to enforce the attendance of witnesses in the manner of domestic courts and have to rely upon the co-operation of states. Although both parties are handicapped by this incapacity, in practice prosecutors as an official organ of the Tribunal with much better resources have been able to access much more material than the defence. The problem becomes even more acute when defendants choose to conduct their own defence, as a number of defendants including Milošević have, before the ad hoc tribunals.[100] This means that the defence are heavily dependent upon prosecutors for access to information, yet although prosecutors are under a duty to disclose exculpatory material to the defence the adversarial position that they adopt does not require that they seek out such material.[101]

The drafters of the Rome Statute have tried to ameliorate this situation by imposing explicit truth finding duties upon the prosecutor. Article 54.1 of the Statute states that the Prosecutor shall in order to establish the truth extend the investigation to cover all facts and evidence relevant to an assessment of whether there is criminal responsibility under the Statute and in doing so shall investigate incriminating and exonerating circumstances equally. There was also considerable discussion during the preparatory process on what role, if any, pre-trial judges should play in reviewing the work of the prosecutor. The idea that judges should intervene in certain investigative acts to protect the rights of the suspect or accused proved particularly controversial.[102] Article 56 provides that where the prosecutor considers that an investigation presents a unique opportunity to take testimony or a statement from a witness which may not be available at the trial, the Pre-Trial Chamber may on the request of the prosecutor take such measures as are necessary including providing that the defence be present at the taking of the testimony. Article 57, moreover, grants the defence the right to request the issuance of orders as may be necessary to assist in the preparation of the defence.

Different views have been expressed as to whether these measures will effectively assist the defence. The danger yet again is that a hybrid constructed to satisfy both of the dominant legal traditions will result in achieving not the best but the worst of both traditions. From one perspective the independence of the prosecutor and the judiciary may be completely undermined 'by inviting the judiciary to take over the job of prosecuting which is incompatible with the Anglo-American adversarial

[100] See Boas, above n 64, ch 4.

[101] ICTY RPE 68(i), ICTR RPE 68(A) (requiring the Prosecutor to disclose to the Defence exculpatory material *in the actual knowledge of* the Prosecutor)(emphasis added).

[102] See SA Fernandez de Gurmendi, 'International Criminal Law Procedures' in R Lee (ed), *The International Criminal Court – Issues, Negotiations, Results – The Making of the Rome Statute* (The Hague, Kluwer, 1999) 234–235.

model upon which the Court is principally based'.[103] Viewed from another perspective, however, the changes may not go far enough in transforming the role of prosecutor from being *parti pris*.[104]

This has prompted some commentators to conclude that what is a necessary is a process that is from its inception 'fundamentally civilian in structure, and not adversarial', a process governed by judicial control in which an investigating judge is responsible for the investigation of the case, the preparation of an indictment and the collection and presentation of a dossier upon which the court proceeds with the case.[105] It has been suggested that a 'single, neutral investigation' would suit the context of international criminal justice much better than adversarial justice for a number of reasons.[106] First of all, the idea of sending in a team of prosecutor investigators and then a second defence team adds layers of complexity that cannot be afforded. Secondly, the idea of involving victims is also easier within a civil law framework as the ability of witnesses to explain their connection to the case in an uninterrupted narrative makes them more comfortable with that procedure. Thirdly, the civil law mode with its focus on truth finding is better suited within the international context for dealing with cases efficiently as some of the mechanisms for achieving efficiency in domestic trial systems such as plea bargaining or negotiated sentences cannot be easily used for international crimes.

While these radical ideas are a bold attempt to take cognisance of the actual context of international criminal tribunals and of the added purposes of involving victims and reaching a speedy verdict, the risk again is that by expressing a preference for one established model over the other, the protagonists involved are asked to think only in terms of established traditional procedures. The point has been made that it is easier for common law lawyers to adjust to the civil law tradition as there are 'inquisitorial' overtones such as sentencing hearings within common law systems.[107] But there has also been a tendency in domestic civil law systems to move away from the concept of the investigating judge as an ideal model.[108] Such a judge can all too easily become captivated by a crime

103 Robertson, above n 10, 377.

104 G Boas, 'A Code of Evidence and Procedure for International Criminal Law? The Rules of the ICTY' in G Boas and W A Schabas (eds), *International Criminal Law Developments in the Case law of the ICTY* (The Hague, Martinus Nijhoff, 2003) 1, 26.

105 *Ibid.*

106 W Pizzi, 'Overcoming Logistical and Structural Barriers to Fair Trials at International Tribunals' (2006) *International Commentary on Evidence*: Vol 4: Iss 1, Art 4.

107 *Ibid.* See also William T Pizzi, ch 4.

108 The position has disappeared from a number of European states, see Van Den Wyngaert, above n 48.

control ideology or by a construction of events that has already been set up by on-site investigators, raising questions about the concept of a 'neutral investigation'.[109]

Leaving aside truth finding considerations, it is also questionable whether a judicial inquiry model would be able to satisfy all of the objectives that have been set for international criminal justice. Damaška has argued that in view of particular need for international criminal courts to establish legitimacy in their practices, it is more important for them to give weight to the values of transparency and publicity.[110] This, together with the object of bringing about reconciliation of the groups involved in the conflict that gave rise to the proceedings would seem to argue in favour of a model of evidence that gives maximum scope for party participation both at the investigative and trial stage of proceedings rather than simply 'neutral' judicial investigation.

This suggests that it may be over-hasty to abandon the idea advanced in the Rome Statute of an investigating prosecutor, but one whose activities may be reviewed by a pre-trial chamber with every opportunity given to enable the defence to participate, so that a dossier may be compiled which is more than just a prosecution case file. Although some have been sceptical about the ability of the pre-trial chamber to make much impact on the pre-trial phase of evidence gathering given that this continues to be dominated by the parties,[111] first signs are that the chambers are keen to develop an active role in the investigative stage.[112] In the first case to be brought before the International Criminal Court involving allegations of child soldiering in the Democratic Republic of Congo, the Pre-Trial Chamber made orders of their own motion to have the prosecutor report to them on developments in his investigations.[113] It has also been active in using its powers under the Statute to guarantee the rights of the defence by making orders requesting that the UN obtain access to interview notes made by officials with witnesses which fell outside the scope of the prosecution's disclosure obligations.[114]

In truth, however, much of the time of the Pre-Trial Chamber has been spent on disclosure matters rather than on taking active investigative steps. In keeping with the more active duties imposed on prosecutors to seek

[109] See J Hodgson, *French Criminal Justice* (Oxford, Hart Publishing, 2006).

[110] Above n 1, 1031.

[111] G Sluiter, 'The Law of Domestic Criminal Procedure and Domestic War Crimes Trials' (2006) 6 *International Criminal Law Review* 605, 616.

[112] J de Hemptinne, 'The Creation of Investigating Chambers at the International Criminal Court' (2007) 5 *Journal of International Criminal Justice* 402, 414.

[113] See M Miraglia, 'The First Decision of the ICC Pre-Trial Chamber – International Criminal Procedure Rules Under Construction' (2006) 4 *Journal of International Criminal Justice* 188.

[114] *Prosecutor v Dyilo*, Decision on Defence Requests for Disclosure of Materials. Case ICC-01/04–01/06 17 November 2006.

exculpatory as well as inculpatory material, the Chamber has considered that the prosecution is under an obligation to make its utmost effort to obtain the prior statements of those witnesses on whom it intends to rely and that the rules do not limit disclosure to prior statements only in the possession or control of the prosecutor.[115] But the disclosure obligations on the prosecution remain substantially the same as those of the prosecutors in the ad hoc tribunals.[116] In another ruling the Chamber rejected a defence request for full access to the prosecutor's file on the ground that full access was fundamentally contrary to the system of disclosure set out in the Statute and the rules.[117] Neither a literal nor a contextual interpretation led to such a requirement as the provisions regulated only the manner in which the defence can access *some* of the materials in its possession, namely those that are exculpatory or material to defence preparations. But if the conditions of accessing evidence relevant to international crimes invariably put the defence at a disadvantage, the defence become particularly reliant on the prosecution for information and the equality of arms principle is not in practice achieved by disclosing merely some of the evidence that the prosecution deems to be exculpatory or useful to the defence.

The defence can always seek an order of disclosure from the Court, but the Pre-Trial Chamber is also denied full access to prosecution materials with the result that it is difficult for it to rule on disclosure motions.[118] Full access to the prosecution file would enable the chamber to rule more effectively on these motions but also allow it to exercise greater supervisory powers over the investigation.[119] At present the power to take investigative steps is limited to situations where evidence may not be available at trial. But this could be extended to situations where evidence may not be available in as good a condition as at trial including situations where the memory of witnesses may deteriorate by the time of trial. Opportunities would be given for the defence to be present and to cross-examine such witnesses. The effect of this would be to create a full

[115] *Ibid.*

[116] Cf, in particular the identical language used in ICTY, ICTR RPE 66(B) and ICC RPE 77 (requiring the Prosecutor to permit the defence to inspect materials in its possession or control which are material to the preparation of the defence.) Cf also, ICTY RPE 68(i), ICTR RPE 68(A) (requiring the Prosecutor to disclose exculpatory material *in the actual knowledge of* the Prosecutor) and Art 67(2) of the Rome Statute of the ICC (requiring the Prosecutor to disclose exculpatory material in the Prosecutor's *possession and control*)(emphasis added).

[117] *Prosecutor v Dyilo*, Decision on the Final System of Disclosure and the Establishment of a Timetable. ICC-01/04–01/06, 15 May 2006.

[118] Under ICC RPE 121(2)(b) the Pre-Trial Chamber shall hold status conferences to ensure that disclosure takes place under satisfactory conditions. Rule 121(2)(c) requires that all *disclosed* evidence should be communicated to the Pre-Trial Chamber but this falls short of providing the Chamber with full access to prosecution materials.

[119] de Hemptinne, above n 112, 416.

dossier of evidence taken under more reliable conditions than if the task of investigation were left entirely to the prosecutor. This would obviate the need for technical rules of exclusion at trial such as hearsay and reduce the number of witnesses who may have to attend trial and give oral evidence.

In many respects these changes would move the Court more in a civil law direction but with the principle of 'adversarial procedure' enabling the defence to cross-examine vital witnesses at some stage during the process. It remains to be seen how pro-active the pre-trial chambers in the Court will turn out to be. The judges in the Court do not have the same ability to change the rules of the Court as their predecessors in the ad hoc international tribunals and it may make some time before a successful accommodation is found. It took many years before the European Court of Human Rights was able to become so influential within and beyond the boundaries of Europe. It is to be hoped that in time the International Criminal Court will become as significant in setting standards of procedure for the trial of international crimes in both national and international jurisdictions.

IV. CONCLUSION

The imperatives of globalisation and the gradual dilution of national boundaries are forcing the different traditions of the common law and civil law world to come together and devise common standards and practices for national and international systems of justice. Damaška's scholarship on comparative law and evidence provides both a warning and an inspiration for this endeavour. The warning is to be found in the temptation to blend together practices from different legal traditions which can dilute rather than enhance the ends of justice they are designed to achieve. The inspiration is to be found in his analysis of the manner in which changes can evolve to produce forms of justice that might have seemed unpromising in the legal landscape from which they have arisen.

When seeking remedies for ailments that arise within national boundaries, Damaška has considered that it is prudent to begin by cultivating one's own garden rather than look to foreign transplants.[120] Those seeking to develop procedures across such boundaries, however, do not have a ready made garden to work from. It is not enough to apply those procedures that are most familiar to us. Instead we have to engage in the unpractised art of cross-fertilisation and begin with what we believe will pollinate best in the new environment. In the uncharted territory of international criminal justice, it would seem prudent to begin with values that have an appeal to all the protagonists involved – the individual victims

[120] Damaška, *Evidence Law Adrift* above n 13, 150.

and defendants who are the immediate subject matter of the proceedings, the communities and states involved in the conflict that gave rise to the proceedings and the various professional actors – investigators, prosecutors, defence lawyers and judges – charged with playing their respective roles in the proceedings. The example of the European Court of Human Rights suggests that the language of human rights can provide the necessary moral compass.

13

Reflections on the 'Hybridisation' of Criminal Procedure

MIREILLE DELMAS-MARTY*

COMPARATIVE LAW APPEARS to be the guarantor of pluralist internationalisation, a role well understood by Mirjan Damaška whom I am pleased to honour here.

The development of European and global criminal justice has greatly increased the need for comparative law: not only as a cognitive tool, but also as an instrument of normative integration and as a source of critical analysis that can provide a basis for resistance to integration that will not work.[1] But for comparative law to play this role, it must engage with the principle of subsidiarity in Europe and, in international law, complementarity, which renders the jurisdiction of the International Criminal Court (ICC) subsidiary to that of national tribunals. Only comparative studies can reveal whether or not member states can protect the goals of the European Union[2] or, at the global level, the willingness and ability of a State to adjudicate international crimes within its jurisdiction.[3] And when supranational jurisdiction seems necessary, only a comparative study makes it possible to develop truly 'common' norms, that is, norms defined not by the unilateral transplantation of a dominant system, but a pluralist combination of the best of each national tradition, through synthesis or even 'hybridisation', a metaphor that encourages prudence, because hybrids are sometimes sterile.

* The author wishes to express her sincere thanks to Naomi Norberg for this translation.

[1] See M Delmas-Marty, H Muir Watt and H Ruiz Fabri (eds), *Variations autour d'un droit commun* (Paris, SLC, 2001 and 2002). See also M Delmas-Marty (ed), *Critique de l'intégration normative, L'apport du droit comparé à l'harmonisation des droits* (Paris, PUF, 2004).

[2] Art I-11, Constitutional Treaty (CT); cf Art. 35 Corpus Juris.

[3] Art 17, ICC Statute.

I have twice had first-hand experience confronting the problems of hybridisation and have been able to measure the importance of comparative law: in 1993, as a member of the commission tasked by the United Nations Security Council to draft a statute for an international criminal tribunal, and from 1996–1999, as coordinator of the project called 'Corpus Juris'.[4] I will therefore discuss these two projects, starting with the Corpus Juris, and conclude with some general remarks on the conditions necessary for pluralist hybridisation.

THE EUROPEAN EXAMPLE OF THE CORPUS JURIS

As it turned out, the drafting of the procedural portion of the Corpus Juris was preceded by a comparative research project. I believe this initial research – which was later supplemented by a comparison of provisions of the Corpus Juris with various national legal systems, including those of EU-candidate countries[5] – improved our mutual understanding and enabled us at least to perfect a method of hybridisation, if not to propose a perfect solution. Our method was broken down into four main phases.

The first phase comprised comparison for cognitive purposes. Before the European Commission created our group of experts, a two-year university research project had been organised that, while limited to only five countries (Germany, England and Wales, Belgium, France and Italy), enabled us to develop the 'analysis grid'[6] that we used to analyse the criminal procedure of each country. This grid was our common language: it liberated criminal procedure from the confines of national systems, and thus allowed the project to identify the 'actors' and the 'powers' that determine how a criminal process unfolds.

With respect to actors, the problem was describing them in terms that made sense in all five systems. Thus, the project chose neutral terms such as 'prosecuting party' (public prosecutor or victim), accused (suspect, defendant or person under investigation), and judge (investigating magistrate, that is, the judge who supervises the investigation and orders pre-trial detention, or trial judge).

Similarly, we split the powers that determine how a criminal process unfolds into eight categories, each of them including several elements:

[4] M Delmas-Marty (ed), *Corpus juris: introducing penal provisions for the protection of the financial interests of the European Union* (Paris, Economica, 1997); M Delmas-Marty and J Vervaele (eds) *The implementation of the* Corpus juris *in the Member States*, Vols I – IV (Antwerp, Intersentia, 2000 and 2002).

[5] Accomplished in 2000–2001 under the direction of Christine van den Wyngaert.

[6] See J Spencer and M Delmas-Marty (eds), *European Criminal Procedures* (Cambridge, CUP, 2002).

—reporting of the offence (written or oral complaint, with or without the alleged victim's participation as a civil plaintiff in the criminal process (*partie civile*));
—investigation (into the facts or into the person);
—evidence (considered under different aspects according to whether or not legal rules limit its gathering and production at trial);
—accusation;
—adversariality (includes being informed of the charges, consultation of the dossier, the right to legal assistance, defence on procedure and substance, and the right to appeal);
—coercive measures (arrest, pre-trial detention, summons, and other measures restricting freedom and property rights);
—disposal of the case (unilateral or, as in the cases of mediation or plea bargaining, multilateral); and
—decision making (procedural rulings, judgment on guilt, and decision on penalty).

It was then possible to identify how each system linked these actors and powers together to arrive at its legal grammar. There were two types of legal grammar: (i) accusatory grammar, which assigns most of the powers to private parties, from reporting of the offence and gathering of the evidence to disposal of the case; and (ii) inquisitorial grammar, which assigns most of the powers to public actors, in particular to the emblematic investigating magistrate who fulfils both police and judicial functions, from pre-trial investigation and compiling the file for the trial court to deciding whether or not to detain the accused.

These divergent kinds of legal grammar made hybridisation seem impossible but the comparative study showed a movement toward convergence under the influence of repeated domestic reforms and of the European Court of Human Rights, whose jurisprudence reveals that each system has its weaknesses. Most countries on the Continent have progressively abolished the position of investigating magistrate and have given a more active role to the defence: criminal procedure in Italy is now partially accusatory, and France has instituted a judge of freedoms (Law of 15 June 2000) and a system of guilty pleas (Law of 9 March 2004).[7] In England, meanwhile, a Public Prosecution Service was introduced in 1985 and a Serious Fraud Office in 1987, and, as in the United States though by different means,[8] it is now more difficult to exclude hearsay evidence.[9] As my British colleague John Spencer put it very clearly,[10] this movement has not entirely overcome

[7] See D Charvet, 'Réflexions autour du plaider coupable' (2004) *Dalloz*, Chr 2517.
[8] See *Crawford v Washington*, 541 US 36 (2004).
[9] Criminal Justice Act 2003.
[10] See J Spencer 'Introduction', in Spencer and Delmas-Marty, above n 6, 1–75.

divergence, but has lessened it, paving the way for mixed procedures where hybridisation takes the best from each system.

The second phase, drafting the Corpus Juris,[11] highlighted the instrumental function of comparative law. Unlike a traditional code, the Corpus Juris combines: six guiding principles; 34 articles that formulate unified rules primarily concerning the conduct of investigations, rights of the parties and submission of evidence; and a final article that provides for the complementarity of national law. The novelty lies in the fact that these rules derive their coherence from three guiding principles from the European Convention on Human Rights[12] that characterise a new, hybrid 'grammar' called 'contradictoire.' These three guiding principles are:

—European territoriality, the conceptual foundation for attributing jurisdiction over the entire territory to a European prosecutor – a public prosecution office borrowed from the inquisitorial model;

—judicial guarantee, assured during the pre-trial phase by a national or European 'judge of freedoms' (not an investigating judge, but a judge who is sufficiently neutral to intercede between the prosecution and the defence, in the style of the accusatory model); and

—the principle of proceedings which are 'contradictoire', a new conception, particularly with regard to evidence, which combines a written file (from the inquisitorial model) with strict exclusionary rules (from the accusatory model).

In the third phase, comparative law fulfilled its critical function, as the first draft of the Corpus Juris was subjected to a number of comparative critiques. A study was undertaken for each of the 35 articles in each Member State (15 at the time) and candidate states. The results were synthesised into a comparative table that shows quite precisely the points of agreement and disagreement with regard to procedure.[13] The draft then became the subject of debates organised in various countries, particularly Germany and the United Kingdom.[14]

These critiques were instructive and resulted in an amended version, which was completed during meetings at the European University Institute in Florence in 2000.[15] The debate was then reopened in 2001, when the European Commission issued a Green Paper focusing on the European prosecutor.

[11] See above n 4.

[12] European Convention for the Protection of Human Rights and Fundamental Freedoms, Nov 4, 1950, 213 UNTS 221 (entered into force Sept 3, 1953).

[13] Delmas-Marty and Vervaele, above n 4, Vol I, 142–185.

[14] Select Committee on the European Communities, *Prosecuting fraud on the Communities finances, the Corpus juris* (9th Report, Session 1998–1999, House of Lords Paper 62).

[15] Delmas-Marty and Vervaele, above n 4.

The fourth and final, more political, phase of bringing the project to fruition was well underway until the rejection of the European constitutional treaty by France and the Netherlands threw the success of the project into doubt. The Constitutional Treaty provides that a European law of the Council may establish a European Public Prosecutor's Office, but the Council must act unanimously after obtaining consent from the European Parliament.[16] The treaty specifies that the law must resolve various issues raised in the Corpus Juris, such as the general rules applicable to the prosecutor's office, the conditions governing performance of its functions, the procedural rules applicable to its activities and governing admissibility of evidence, and rules applicable to judicial review of the procedural measures taken by the prosecutor's office.[17]

The question of legitimacy will no doubt be raised. It is clear that criminal procedure will not be entirely unified. Theoretically, the Constitutional Treaty limits the European Public Prosecutor's jurisdiction to the Convention on the Protection of the European Communities' Financial Interests,[18] which is understandable since the Union's financial interests are supranational by nature. However, jurisdiction may be extended to 'serious crime having a cross-border dimension', either when the European Public Prosecutor's Office is created or at a later date, upon unanimous Council approval after obtaining the consent of the European Parliament and after consulting the Commission.[19]

However, unification seems to be limited by the Constitutional Treaty, as it was by the Corpus Juris, to the preparatory phase of litigation. In the judgment phase, the European Public Prosecutor will 'exercise the functions of prosecutor in the competent courts of the Member States'.[20] The precise relationship between the national and European institutions is left for a future European law, which will have to define the relationship between the Prosecutor's Office and other European offices such as Eurojust, Europol and the European Anti-Fraud Office (OLAF) and no doubt provide for a minimum of harmonisation of national rules. This will require new comparative studies to determine which differences are compatible with the implementation of the Corpus Juris and which are not.

The process will clearly not end with legislation but will require fine tuning, as has international justice at the global level.

[16] See CT, Art III-274(1).
[17] *Ibid* Art III-274(3).
[18] OJ 95/C 316/03 27.11.95. See *Ibid* Art III-274(3).
[19] *Ibid* Art III-274(4).
[20] *Ibid* Art III-274(2).

GLOBAL CRIMINAL JUSTICE

Global criminal justice is far ahead of European criminal justice. The International Criminal Tribunal for the Former Yugoslavia (ICTY) and the International Criminal Tribunal for Rwanda (ICTR) were established more than 10 years ago and have already adopted over 20 revisions of procedural and evidentiary rules.[21] Though criticised from a separation of powers point of view, these reforms have nonetheless greatly contributed to the hybridisation that, in part, inspired the ICC Statute.

The subject of hybridisation was broached by the judges from the very beginning. In an early dissenting opinion, President Cassese insisted that '[i]nternational criminal procedure results from the gradual decanting of national criminal concepts and rules into the international receptacle.'[22] In his view, 'international criminal proceedings ... combine and fuse' the accusatorial and inquisitorial approaches and the 'mechanical importation' of concepts drawn from one nation's law into international criminal proceedings 'may alter or distort the *specificity* of these proceedings' which proceed in a very different manner from national criminal proceedings since they operate on an inter-state level and lack autonomous means of coercion.[23] The danger of domination remained strong, however, because there were many rules drawn from the common law tradition (the guilty plea, for example), so most judges tended to base their interpretation on common law principles. In a second very early case, however, the court declared that '[t]he general philosophy of the criminal procedure of the International Tribunal aims at maintaining a balance between the accusatory procedure of the common law systems and the inquisitorial procedure of the civil law systems, whilst at the same time ensuring the doing of justice.'[24]

A balance was thus struck over time, with various reforms strengthening both the equality of arms (accusatory grammar) and the active role of the judge (inquisitory grammar). A typical example of how a hybrid grammar was adopted through successive adjustments and readjustments is that a pre-trial judge was first instituted in practice, and then established in an amendment to the ICTY rules adopted in July 1998 to ensure the proper application of admissibility rules.[25] This judge thus plays a hybrid role: '[t]he purpose of Rule 47(E) ... is in effect to equate the confirming judge

[21] See the symposium 'The ICTY 10 Years On: The View from Inside' (2004) 2 *Journal of International Criminal Justice* (2004) 353–597.

[22] ICTY, *Erdemovic* case (Cassese J, dissenting), 7 October 1997.

[23] *Ibid* paras 4 and 5 (emphasis in original).

[24] ICTY, *Delalic et al* case, *Decision on the Motion of the Joint Request of the Accused Persons Regarding the Presentation of Evidence, dated 24 May 1998*, 4 February 1998, para 20.

[25] See ICTY Rules of Procedure and Evidence, Rule 65*ter*.

to the grand jury (or committing magistrate) in the common law system or to the *juge d'instruction* in some civil law systems'.[26] In creating a pre-trial chamber, the ICC statute thus expands and strengthens the international criminal tribunals' institution of a pre-trial judge.[27]

The same is true for the sensitive issue of the case file: successive reforms to the general rules of evidence at the ICTY managed eventually to give judges the power to receive oral or written depositions 'where the interests of justice allow' and eliminated the prohibition on hearsay.[28] The ICC Statute approves this hybrid model in Article 64, which makes it clear that the judges, not the parties, direct the proceedings (particularly with regard to witnesses[29]).

The ICC Statute goes even further in other respects by providing for the participation of victims. Article 68(3) provides that they may be represented by counsel and thus assimilates them to the 'parties civiles' of various Continental systems, even though their intervention here does not automatically trigger criminal proceedings.

Other areas, such as bargaining between prosecution and defence, have not yet stabilised at the ICC. At first glance, plea bargaining seems to have been excluded due to the gravity of international crimes, but it may become necessary for practical reasons. Its legal consequences have yet to be decided upon, however: while the ICC Statute provides for pleading guilty,[30] this is defined more along the lines of the Continental confession than as a guilty plea in the Anglo-American sense, and gives no indication as to possible negotiation between prosecution and defence.[31]

Noting the confusing complexity of the current legal landscape and describing criminal law specialists as 'mariners on the ocean without compass, star or landmark',[32] Mirjan Damaška states that in different models, plea bargaining obeys different, and apparently irreconcilable, rules, namely as to the role of the judge and the publicity given to bargaining.[33] He concludes that we must innovate, both because of the hybrid nature of the Statute and the pedagogical function which is more appropriate to international criminal justice. He suggests specific rules to avoid judicial bias and to make bargaining transparent. But he leaves open

26 ICTY, *Brdjanin* case, *Decision on the Motion to Dismiss Indictment,* 5 October 1999, para 13.

27 See ICTY Statute, Arts 15, 56, 57, 58.

28 See ICTY Rules of Procedure and Evidence, Rule 89 (F). See John Jackson, ch 12.

29 See ICC Statute, Art 64(6)(b).

30 *Ibid* Art 64(8).

31 *Ibid* Art 65.

32 M Damaška, 'Negotiated Justice in International Criminal Courts' (2004) 2 *Journal of International Criminal Justice* 1018, 1019.

33 See also M Langer, 'From Legal Transplants to Legal Translations: The Globalization of Plea Bargaining and the Americanization Thesis in Criminal Procedure' (2004) 45 *Harvard International Law Journal* 1.

the question of the judge's role, suggesting either a public hearing of the testimony of the prosecution's principal witnesses, according to the Anglo-American model, or questioning of the accused by the judge, as in the Continental model.

The problem is that a simple transposition of national principles governing the rights of the accused (presumption of innocence or right to confront witnesses) is not enough to guarantee the effectiveness or the legitimacy of international criminal justice, considering its specificities. Instead of defining the elements of systemic coherence on a case-by-case basis as technical questions arise, it is better to start by working out a common grammar that will guide the process of hybridisation via both legislation and judicial interpretation.

THE NEED FOR A COMMON 'GRAMMAR'

The concept of 'hybridisation' reveals the supranational character of unified legal ensembles, and thus the limits of the process of unification. Because unification profoundly changes the nature of inter-state relations, it must no doubt be limited. The debate over the jurisdiction of the future European prosecutor suggests as much through its reference to the nature of the interests to be protected and, more broadly, the principle of subsidiarity, which the Constitutional Treaty would judicialise by providing for recourse to the European Court of Justice in the event of a violation of the rules. Paradoxically, unification has already been accepted for the ICC: even if the principle of complementarity reduces the impact of the ICC statute, it provides a good opportunity to observe the process of unification and the methods of hybridisation.

To conclude, I would stress that a system of justice conceived by hybridisation will necessarily be distinguishable from its national 'parents' and will progressively become autonomous. In other words, hybridisation goes hand in hand with autonomisation.[34] Therefore the system's coherence cannot be pre-established and cannot simply be borrowed from a preexisting one, but must be built. True hybridisation, as distinct from simple transplantation, makes it easier to do so by using not only common technical rules, but also a common 'grammar', that is, the guiding, or meta principles that structure the system around general international law principles, human rights instruments and a comparison of the main

[34] J Hemptinne, '*Hybridité et autonomie du règlement de procédure et de preuve du TPIY*' in M Delmas-Marty, E Fronza and E Lambert (eds), *Les sources du droit international pénal* (Paris, SLC, 2005).

national criminal justice systems. This 'grammar' then guides the interpretation of the questions of first impression that will inevitably arise and makes it possible, when suitable, to integrate in a unified, pluralist manner.

14

The Confrontation Right Across the Systemic Divide

RICHARD D FRIEDMAN*

IN HIS NOTABLE work, *Evidence Law Adrift*, Mirjan Damaška identified three pillars of the common law system of determining facts in adjudication, and examined these through a comparative lens: the organisation of the trial court; the phenomenon of temporally compressed trials; and a high degree of control by parties and their counsel. In reviewing the book, I suggested that a strong concept of individual rights was another critical feature of the common law system, especially in its American variant and especially with respect to criminal defendants.[1]

In this essay, I will explore how these four features play out in the Anglo-American and Continental system with respect to one right that has been of particular interest to me, the right of a criminal defendant to be confronted with the witnesses against him.

This right has long been one of the central aspects of the common-law system of criminal jurisprudence. Nevertheless, for much of the last two centuries the right has been swallowed up and nearly lost in the rule against hearsay. Commentators have often regarded the hearsay rule, which has no real counterpart outside the common law system, as a product of the jury system, what Damaška calls the divided trial court. I contend, however, that the hearsay rule reflected a broadening, and in effect a dilution, of the confrontation right, which had been established long before and was entirely independent of the jury system. The great breadth of the hearsay rule was attributable to the increased role of criminal defence lawyers, an aspect of the party control discussed in depth by Damaška. But a rule so broad could not be maintained rigorously

* Many thanks to Christopher Miller, for very helpful research in unfamiliar territory.

1 'Anchors and Flotsam', Book Review of M Damaška, *Evidence Law Adrift* (1998) 107 *Yale Law Journal* 1921.

without yielding absurd results, and so the hearsay rule became relatively porous. As a consequence, the meaning of the confrontation right was virtually lost. Perhaps ironically, a basically sound conception of the right, as a critical aspect of the law governing the procedure for witnesses giving testimony, emerged in Continental Europe, under the European Convention on Human Rights, in dealing with systems unencumbered by a rule against hearsay. More recently, the decision of the United States Supreme Court in *Crawford v Washington*[2] has also established a basically sound conception of the right under the Confrontation Clause of the Sixth Amendment to the United States Constitution. Although I have described both the European and American conceptions as basically sound, they are substantially different from each other. As one might expect, the American right is more categorical in nature. Also, two of Damaška's pillars, party control and the compressed nature of the common law trial, make salient particular issues that are of less importance in the Continental system: who produces the witness to testify and the timing of confrontation.

* * *

If an adjudicative system is to be rational, it must depend on the testimony of witnesses. Once the Catholic Church withdrew its support of the irrational ordeals as a method of proof in 1215, it became virtually inevitable that the adjudicative systems of the western world would develop procedures governing how witnesses would give testimony. The courts of Continental Europe tended to take testimony in writing behind closed doors, out of the presence of the parties, to prevent intimidation by the parties.[3] But the English courts took a different path. The presence of a jury did not prescribe this path. Indeed, the English followed the course of the ancient Hebrews[4] and Romans,[5] which did not rely on juries, and took testimony out in the open, in the presence of the adverse party. In the 16th century, Thomas Smith famously described the heart of a criminal trial as an 'altercation' between accuser and accused.[6] And for centuries, English commentators and judges proclaimed the open, confrontational nature of the English criminal trial as a key superiority of their system of criminal adjudication over its Continental counterpart.[7] This principle was emphasised in numerous treason statutes that required prosecution witnesses to be brought 'face to face' with the accused. The practice of presenting the

2 541 US 36 (2004).

3 See RC Van Caenegem, 'History of European Civil Procedure' in M Cappelletti (ed) 16 *International Encyclopedia of Comparative Law* 2, 77 (Boston, Mohr, 1973).

4 See Deuteronomy 17:6, 19:15–18.

5 See Acts 25:16.

6 T Smith, *De Republica Anglorum* (1583) M Dewar ed, (Cambridge, CUP, 1982) 114.

7 Eg, *Case of the Union of the Realms*, Moore (1604) (KB) 790, 798, 72 ER 903, 913, per Popham CJ; S Emlen, Preface to *State Trials* (1730); M Hale, *History of the Common Law* (c 1670) CM Gray ed, (Chicago, Chicago UP, 1971) 163–64.

testimony of prosecution witnesses at trial, in the presence of the accused and subject to adverse questioning, was not followed with perfect regularity, but it clearly was the norm well before 1700. The practice came to America with the English settlers, and in an environment in which criminal defence lawyers played a larger role than in England, it thrived. Indeed, most of the early state constitutions established the practice as a right of the accused; some of these used the time-honoured 'face to face' formula, and others, drawing on Hale and Blackstone, used phrasing very similar to that which was later incorporated in the Sixth Amendment to the Constitution in 1791 as part of the Bill of Rights.[8] This is the Confrontation Clause, which provides: 'In all criminal prosecutions, the accused shall enjoy the right ... to be confronted with the witnesses against him.'

Notice that on its face the Clause governs how witnesses shall testify, for testifying is what witnesses do, and indeed in many languages 'testimony' and 'witness' have the same root. The Clause does *not* speak in terms of hearsay. It was not a constitutionalisation of the rule against hearsay, and it could not very well have been, because though courts and commentators had long spoken of such a rule in general terms it was still in an amorphous and embryonic state when the Clause was adopted. During the last two decades of the 18th century and the first few of the 19th, however, the rule rapidly expanded, and elaborations of it became far more sophisticated. Initially, the decisive force seems to have been the growing role of criminal defence lawyers,[9] though the doctrine soon kept pace on the civil side. Believing fervently in the value of cross-examination, lawyers did not limit their desire for it to adverse witnesses. Any time an out-of-court statement was offered against them to prove that what the statement asserted was true, they perceived the potential value of cross-examining the maker of the statement. And so the modern concept of hearsay, 'an out-of-court statement offered to prove the truth of a matter asserted in it', was first articulated.[10] And indeed, the conception went even beyond that. In the famous 1838 case of *Wright v Tatham*,[11] the scope of the hearsay rule reached its high water mark, extending not only to assertions of a proposition but also to conduct that did not assert the proposition at issue but appeared implicitly to reflect the actor's belief in that proposition.

[8] See RD Friedman and B McCormack, 'Dial-In Testimony' (2002) 150 *University of Pennsylvania Law Review* 1171, 1207.

[9] TP Gallanis, 'The Rise of Modern Evidence Law' (1999) 84 *Iowa Law Review* 499.

[10] The following passage from 1 SM Phillipps, *A Treatise on the Law of Evidence* 7th edn (London, Butterworth, 1829) 229 is not found in earlier editions (including the 6th edition of 1824): 'Hearsay is not admitted in our courts of justice, as proof of the fact which is stated by a third person'.

[11] 5 Cl & F 670, 7 ER 559, 47 Rev Rep 136 (HL 1838).

A rule so extensive could not feasibly be enforced with rigour; it would have caused the exclusion of too much evidence. Although beginning in the early 19th century there has been a tendency to attribute the hearsay rule to the presence of a jury, there is no persuasive reason to discern such a connection.[12] Indeed, there is no good basis for believing that as a presumptive matter the introduction of hearsay evidence relevant to a material proposition will lead a jury away from rather than closer to the truth; on the contrary, it appears that the exclusionary rule, shutting the eyes and ears of the trier of fact to evidence that is often highly probative, impairs, slows, and adds unnecessary expense to the truth-determining process.[13] And so over most of the 19th and 20th centuries the trend was to ease the rule against hearsay, by adding and broadening exemptions to it and by establishing the power of the trial court to except individual statements from it on a case-specific basis. This trend was fostered by the dominant evidence scholar of the first part of the 20th century, John Henry Wigmore. Lost in this development was a clear sense of the confrontation right as a relatively narrow procedural principle governing the giving of testimony by witnesses against an accused. But a flicker remained, keeping alive some intuitive sense of the ancient right so central to our system.

In the homeland of the hearsay rule, the trend towards lenience went so far, beginning with the Civil Evidence Act 1968, as to virtually eliminate the hearsay rule in civil cases. The resulting dichotomy, a body of traditional hearsay law in criminal cases but not in civil cases, has been ascribed to another dichotomy, the presence of the jury in most English criminal trials but not in civil litigation. As suggested above, however, I find that explanation unpersuasive; I believe rather that Parliament has not abolished the hearsay rule in criminal prosecutions because of some sense that at the core of the rule is a valid principle central to the common law system of criminal adjudication. And yet, because that principle is usually not well understood or even articulated, Parliament has hacked away at the rule in the criminal context as well in a manner seemingly designed to shrivel the confrontation right. Thus, for example, Criminal Justice Act 1988 s 23 allowed several categories of statements made by an unavailable declarant and embodied in a document, including a statement that 'was made to a police officer or some other person charged with the duty of investigating offences or charging offenders'. It is hard to imagine a provision better crafted to allow prosecution witnesses who might later

12 I have developed this point in R Friedman, 'No Link: the Jury and the Origins of Confrontation Right and the Hearsay Rule' in JW Cairns and G Mcleod (eds), *The Dearest Birth Right of the People of England: The Jury in the History of the Common Law* (Oxford, Hart Publishing, 2002) 93.

13 See also R Friedman, 'Thoughts from Across the Water on Hearsay and Confrontation' [1998] *Criminal Law Review* 697, 700–01.

become unavailable to give testimony in precisely the way that their ancestors three and four centuries ago prided themselves would *not* be allowed. And yet, Criminal Justice Act 2003 s 116 has since gone much further, establishing what amounts to a general exception for first-hand hearsay of statements made by a declarant deemed unavailable.

In the United States, the trend towards weakening the hearsay rule reached a culmination of sorts with the adoption of the Federal Rules of Evidence in 1975. The Rules narrowed the definition of hearsay, rejecting the rule of *Wright* so that only assertions of a proposition could be deemed hearsay; they chose broad versions of existing exceptions and incorporated others that were not yet well established; and they explicitly authorised courts to exempt statements from the exclusionary rule on the basis of case-specific factors. Although the shape of some of the exemptions appears to reflect an implicit sense of the confrontation right, the rules draw rather little explicit distinction between criminal and civil cases, or between statements that might be deemed to be the testimony of witnesses and other hearsay.

And what of the expression of the confrontation right in the Sixth Amendment? Until 1965, the Confrontation Clause could not matter very much at all with respect to out-of-court statements. It was only applicable to federal courts, and a court inclined to rule that admission of a given statement would violate the Clause could easily find that admission would violate ordinary hearsay law. But after the Supreme Court ruled that the Clause was applicable against the states,[14] the Clause had great potential significance: although the Supreme Court, or any federal court acting on a petition for *habeas corpus*, still lacked the authority to hold that a state court had violated the state's hearsay rule by admitting a statement against an accused, it could hold that the same act had violated the Confrontation Clause. The trouble, though, was that the confrontation right had become so shrouded by the hearsay rule that the Supreme Court had no clear conception of what it meant. After a decade and a half, the Court ventured to articulate a general theory, under which the Clause was meant to sort out reliable from unreliable hearsay: reliability could be inferred without more if the statement in question fitted within a 'firmly rooted' hearsay exception, and even if this condition were not met the Clause might be satisfied if the statement were deemed to have sufficient 'individualized guarantees of trustworthiness'.[15] This doctrine left the Confrontation Clause almost completely limp, as little more than an easily evaded constitutionalisation of the hearsay rule.

14 *Pointer v Texas*, 380 US 400 (1965).
15 *Ohio v Roberts*, 448 US 56 (1980).

As the millennium closed, however, there were some encouraging signs, because three justices of the Supreme Court indicated their willingness to rethink the doctrine, and to recapture the original meaning behind the Confrontation Clause.[16] And then in the *Crawford* case came the great transformation. Seven out of nine justices signed on to an opinion discarding the old rubric. No longer could the Confrontation Clause be satisfied by a judicial determination that the statement at issue was reliable. Rather, the Court interpreted the Clause in accordance with its clear language and its original meaning, as a procedural provision governing the method by which witnesses give their testimony. The Court therefore detached the meaning of the Clause from the hearsay rule; the focus of the Clause, the Court recognised, was not on all hearsay statements but only on those characterised as *testimonial*, a category the bounds of which it left undetermined for the time being.[17] Within that category, however, the Clause states a firm rule: a testimonial statement cannot be introduced against an accused unless he has had an opportunity to be confronted with and cross-examine the witness who made the statement, and even if that condition is satisfied a testimonial statement made out of court cannot be introduced against the accused unless the witness is unavailable to testify in court. The Court explicitly indicated that the accused could forfeit the confrontation right, by wrongful conduct rendering the witness unavailable, and it suggested the possibility that certain dying declarations might be admissible even absent an opportunity for confrontation, as an historically justified *sui generis* exception to the general rule, but these two qualifications, and in my view they are part of the same one,[18] were the only ones indicated by the Court.

[16] *White v Illinois*, 502 US 346, 358 (1992) (Thomas J, with Scalia J, joining, concurring in part and concurring in the judgment); *Lilly v Virginia*, 527 US 116, 140 (1999) (Breyer J, concurring), 143 (Scalia J, concurring).

[17] *Crawford* also left deliberately undecided whether the Confrontation Clause imposed any strictures at all on non-testimonial statements. In *Davis v Washington*, 126 S Ct 2266 (2006), it answered that question in the negative. This is the proper answer, in my view. (For a contrary perspective, see SJ Summers, 'The Right to Confrontation After *Crawford v Washington*: A Continental European Perspective' (2004) 2 *International Commentary on Evidence*, Issue 1, Art 3.) The confrontation right governs the manner in which prosecution witnesses give testimony. If an out-of-court statement is not testimonial in nature, then, though there may be other reasons why it should not be admitted, it is simply not within the ambit of the confrontation right. At the same time, a sensible concept of the right depends on its recognition that a statement is testimonial if made, no matter how informally or to whom, in circumstances in which a reasonable declarant would anticipate a reasonable likelihood of evidentiary or prosecutorial use. Failure to recognise this point would allow, and encourage, testimony made informally or through private intermediaries but without an opportunity for confrontation. See below n 25.

[18] The traditional justification for the dying declaration exception to the hearsay rule, that no one would wish to meet his Maker with a lie on his lips, is unpersuasive. The better reason for admitting some dying declarations is that the accused rendered the witness unavailable by striking the blow that later killed her. I have explored this idea in various places, including a

Among the questions left open by *Crawford* the most obvious, and one that the Court has already begun to answer, in *Davis v Washington*,[19] is that of what testimonial means. But there are many others as well, involving matters such as the adequacy of prior opportunities for cross-examination, the standards to be applied to child witnesses, and the substantive and procedural principles governing the determination of forfeiture.[20] It will take decades for the Supreme Court to work out these problems and develop a sound framework for the confrontation right. But at least now it is on the right course.

Unfortunately, no other country in the common-law world has yet followed the lead of the United States, though perhaps they will in time. But, and here is what, in the grand historical sweep, appears to be a large and delicious irony, in England, where the confrontation right was such a point of pride for centuries, the courts and Parliament are now constrained against ignoring the right altogether by doctrine issued by a court sitting in France.[21]

* * *

Article 6, paragraph 1 of the European Convention on Human Rights provides in general terms that litigants have a right to 'a fair and public hearing' and paragraph 3(d) more specifically guarantees the right of a criminal defendant 'to examine or have examined witnesses against him'. I will not attempt to discuss here why this latter provision was adopted, what changes in national procedures its drafters contemplated it would require,[22] or why it lay virtually dormant for several decades. The key fact is that since *Unterpertinger v Austria*,[23] in which the European Court of Human Rights first found a violation of the Convention because of the lack of an opportunity for cross-examination,[24] a steady trickle of cases

blog post entitled *Forfeiture: The Standard of Proof and the Reflexive Case*, http://confrontation right.blogspot.com/2007/08/standard-of-review-for-limitations-on.html (July 20, 2007).

19 126 S Ct 2266 (2006).

20 I have laid out some of the pending issues in a blog post, *Pending Crawford Issues*, http://confrontationright.blogspot.com/2006/11/pending-crawford-issues.html (12 November 2006), and in *Crawford, Davis, and Way Beyond*, 15 *JL & Policy* 551 (2007).

21 See C Tapper, *Cross and Tapper on Evidence* 11th edn (London, Butterworths, 2007) 645, 664–6. The tendency of courts in the United Kingdom appears to be to interpret the national statutes stringently enough and the Convention leniently enough that the two do not conflict. See B Emmerson, A Ashworth and A Macdonald, *Human Rights and Criminal Justice* 2nd edn (London, Sweet & Maxwell, 2007) 643–53.

22 Continental procedures are very diverse, a point emphasised in Summers, above n 17. While confrontations between accused and prosecution witnesses have been 'not uncommon' in some Continental systems, it is also clear that the Convention has had a significant impact in requiring confrontation. *Ibid* 2.

23 Series A, No 110, App No 9120/80 (ECHR 1986), (1991) 13 EHRR 175.

24 See M Holdgaard, 'The Right to Cross-Examine Witnesses: Case Law under the European Convention on Human Rights' (2002) 71 *Nordic Journal of International Law* 83, 83 n1.

emanating from Strasbourg has addressed the question of the circumstances in which an accused must have an opportunity to be confronted with the prosecution witnesses. Several points about this body of law, especially in comparison to its American counterpart, are significant here.

First, this is clearly a doctrine governing the procedure under which prosecution witnesses give testimony, pure and simple. To be effective, a right meant to ensure that witnesses testify in proper judicial proceedings must reach witnesses who effectively testify *outside* such proceedings; the European Court has not had difficulty recognizing this idea.[25] The doctrine developed by the Court is one of confrontation, and the Court has referred to it as such.[26] It does not purport to create a rule against hearsay, and the Court's discussion does not refer to that rule or to any doctrines from the common law countries. Indeed, it seems probable that the absence of any controlling hearsay rule left the landscape uncluttered and made it easier for the Convention and the Court to articulate a straightforward doctrine on the examination of witnesses. And so, though it is ironic it may not be surprising that the European Court began establishing this doctrine nearly two decades before *Crawford* and while law reformers in England and other parts of the common law world were dismantling the hearsay rule with little heed for the confrontation principle.

Second, the European Court perceives a 'principle of equality of arms inherent in the concept of a fair trial and exemplified in paragraph 3(d)';[27] similarly, the Court has said that Articles 6(1) and 6(3)(d) are 'aimed at securing equality between the defence and the prosecution in criminal proceedings'.[28] Although some American observers talk about a 'level playing field', the savvier ones recognise that this is a myth in criminal procedure.[29] the prosecution has some advantages, the defence has others, and the two sets are not commensurable. Equality is not a significant part of the rhetoric of the confrontation right in the common law system. The confrontation right is much older than the right to call witnesses in one's

[25] Eg, *Mild and Virtanen v Finland*, App Nos. 39481/98, 40227/98 (ECHR 26 Jul 2005). Summers, above n 17, 8–9, suggests that the European right is construed more broadly than the American right in one important respect. Statements to a doctor describing criminal activity, such as a statement by a child describing sexual abuse, are considered non-testimonial by some American courts, but Summers contends that they would be within the purview of the Convention. In my view, a statement describing a crime made to a doctor should ordinarily be considered testimonial as fully as if the statement were made to the police, because in all probability the doctor will act as a conduit to the criminal justice system.

[26] See *Saïdi v France*, App No 14647/89, [1994] 17 EHRR 251 (ECHR 1993) ('The lack of any confrontation deprived him in certain respects of a fair trial.')

[27] *Bonisch v Austria*, Series A, No 92, App No 8658/79, [1987] 9 EHRR 191 (ECHR 1985).

[28] *Asch v Austria*, Series A, No 203-A, App No 12398/86, [1993] 15 EHRR 597 (ECHR 1991).

[29] See HR Uviller, *The Tilted Playing Field: Is Criminal Justice Unfair?* (New Haven, Yale UP, 1999).

defence, which even now many defendants do not invoke. The confrontation right is based not on a concept of equality between prosecution and defence but rather on a deep-seated belief that an essential condition to make prosecution testimony acceptable is that the accused have a chance to confront and examine the witness.

Third, as suggested by the passages quoted in the last paragraph, the European Court regards the confrontation right developed under Article 6(3)(d) of the Convention as an instantiation of the general right to a fair trial under Article 6(1), and in a weak sense; that is, the overall question is whether the accused has had a fair trial, and a denial of confrontation is a factor to be taken into account in making that assessment.[30] By contrast, under *Crawford*, as discussed above, the right is categorical: if a statement is testimonial in nature, then (putting aside the possibility of forfeiture and the case of dying declarations) it cannot be admitted against an accused unless he has had an opportunity to cross-examine and the witness is unavailable. To be sure, American appellate courts will not reverse a conviction on the basis of a confrontation violation if they deem the error to be harmless, and they are often rather aggressive in so deeming. But the harmless-error doctrine does not avoid the fact of a violation, and it can only be invoked by an appellate court. An American court could *not* legitimately say, 'It is unclear whether admitting this statement, which is testimonial in nature and as to which the accused has not had confrontation, would alter the outcome of the trial, but overall the defendant has had a fair trial, so there is no violation'.

The fuzzier nature of the European right manifests itself in various ways.[31] One is that in some circumstances unavailability of the witness through the fault of neither party is deemed enough to excuse the absence of an opportunity for confrontation;[32] by contrast, under *Crawford*, only if the witness's unavailability was caused by the wrongful conduct of the accused (and, under the recent case of *Giles v California*[33], only if the conduct was designed to have that effect) can it excuse the absence of an opportunity for cross-examination. Another manifestation is that the European right is less likely than its American counterpart to be deemed violated if the witness in question does not appear to be central to the case.[34]

30 See Holdgaard, above n 24, 85.

31 Summers, above n 17, complains about insufficiently predictable 'judicial self regulation' under the decisions by the Strasbourg Court.

32 Eg, *Gossa v Poland*, App No 47986/99 (ECHR 9 Jan 2007).

33 126 S Ct 2678 (2008).

34 Eg, *Trivedi v UK*, App No 31700/96, [1997] EHRLR.521 (Eur Comm Human Rts 1997) 'The Commission ... emphasised that Mr C's statements were not the only evidence in the case to show [a critical fact].').

Fourth, because of the difference between common law and Continental systems in the role of the parties in the litigation, one of the key features stressed by Damaška, it may possibly be appropriate for the systems to adopt different attitudes towards rules allowing defendants to call witnesses to testify at trial. Under *Crawford*, if the prosecution does not provide an opportunity for confrontation, it should not be a sufficient answer that the accused could have called the witness to the stand himself.[35] An accused who puts on the stand a hostile witness whose statement has already been admitted against him runs a great risk that he will have little or nothing to show for the effort, in which case the move will almost certainly backfire. The risk is indeed so great that defence counsel virtually never do it, though if the prosecution were to put the same witness on the stand defence counsel would almost certainly ask at least a few questions on cross-examination. The opportunity to call the witness to testify, therefore, should not be regarded as an adequate substitute for the opportunity to cross-examine a prosecution witness. By contrast, in the Continental system, in which there is much less association of parties with witnesses and much less structuring and party control of questioning, perhaps it is acceptable to provide that the witness will not be brought to trial unless the accused takes the initiative to produce her.[36]

Similarly, another of the pillars emphasised by Damaška, the compressed nature of the common law trial, makes salient in the common law system another issue that may be less important in the Continental system, the timing of the opportunity for confrontation. Under *California v Green*,[37] a pre-*Crawford* decision that is presumably still good law in this respect, an opportunity to cross-examine the witness at a preliminary hearing satisfies the confrontation right if the witness is unavailable to testify at trial.[38] That is an unfortunate result, I believe, because the functions of the preliminary hearing and of the trial are so distinct that, even though the accused formally has an opportunity to pose questions at the hearing, hardly ever does defence counsel engage in a complete cross-examination; indeed, if counsel tried to do so, the judge would probably put a short stop

[35] See, eg, *Thomas v US* 914 A 2d 1 (DC 2006), and my blog posts *Pending Cert Petitions*, <http://confrontationright.blogspot.com/2007/01/pending-cert-petitions.html> (3 January 2007) accessed 18 June 2008; *Shifting the Burden, Take 2*, http://confrontationright. blogspot.com/2006/08/shifting- burden-take-2.html (2 August 2006); and *Shifting the Burden*, http://confrontationright.blogspot. com/2005/03/shifting-burden.html (16 March 2005). Some cases have, however, taken the contrary view, eg, *State v Campbell*, 719 NW 2d 374 (ND 2006), *cert denied*, 127 S Ct 1150 (2007).

[36] Note the cases discussed in Holdgaard, above n 24, 103.

[37] 399 US 149 (1970).

[38] *Crawford* explicitly reaffirmed another aspect of *Green*, that the confrontation right is not violated by introducing an earlier statement if the witness testifies at trial, even if the witness's direct testimony is inconsistent with the prior statement. I believe both these aspects of *Green* are ill-considered.

to the exercise.[39] But if one regards the Continental system as creating a less sharp functional distinction between steps in the process, then arguably it is more justifiable to hold, as the European Court does, that an opportunity for examination at a preliminary hearing satisfies the confrontation right.[40]

* * *

The American and Continental traditions are very different, not only in the institutional respects emphasised by Damaška but also in their constitutional styles, and particularly in their treatment of individual rights. For this reason, I doubt that within the foreseeable future the contours of the confrontation right as developed in the two systems will become much closer than they are now; the categorical American right will presumably remain stronger than its European counterpart.

The interesting question is what will happen in the United Kingdom. It is there that the confrontation right first flourished and reached maturity, and there that for centuries the right was a particular matter of pride. But the rule against hearsay subsumed the right, and eventually became so broad that inevitably it, along with the right, was greatly diluted; as a result the right was little understood and nearly forgotten. In the United States, the text of the Confrontation Clause provided a reminder of the nature of the right, and ultimately its mandate caused a historically minded Supreme Court to give the right new life in accordance with its historical meaning. In the United Kingdom there is no comparable text, and the only operative mandate comes from the European Convention and the cases construing it. The path of least resistance would be to obey the commands of that jurisprudence and do nothing more. But perhaps *Crawford*, by effecting a virtual rediscovery of the confrontation right in the former colonies, will eventually lead to a similar phenomenon in the mother country as well.

[39] In a blog post titled *Opportunity for Cross-Examination at Preliminary Proceedings*, http://confrontationright.blogspot.com/2007/08/opportunity-for-cross-examination-at.html (29 August 2007), I posed the question of how often counsel engaged in complete cross-examination at preliminary hearings. The responses suggest that they hardly ever do so and that sophisticated defence counsel avoid later problems by confirming that the judge would not allow them to.

[40] Eg, *Vozhigov v Russia*, App No 5953/02 (ECHR 26 Apr 2007). See also, eg, *Delta v France*, Series A, No 191-A, App No 11444/85, [1993] 16 EHHR 574 (ECHR 1990) (accused should have an 'adequate and proper opportunity' for confrontation 'either at the time the witness makes his statement or at some later stage of the proceedings').

IV

The Challenge for Comparative Scholarship

15

The Good Faith Acquisition of Stolen Art

JOHN HENRY MERRYMAN

The radical defense of ownership is one of the less satisfactory aspects of Roman law. Modern legal systems, and also some ancient ones, have striven to arrive at more equitable solutions.[1]

Whereas most continental legal systems protect the bona fide purchaser, English and American law only exceptionally grant him such protection.[2]

INTRODUCTION

COMPARATIVE LAWYERS KNOW that substantive private law rules in Western legal systems are much alike. Most of the really interesting differences between the civil law and common law appear in the law of procedure, a vast field that Professor Damaška's scholarship has elegantly illuminated. In this tribute I avoid trespassing on his territory and instead consider one of the rare substantive law examples of direct opposition,[3] with particular attention to the world of art.

The glamour of art insures that the theft of a valuable work, if publicly revealed, will be widely reported in the media. It is also likely to be recorded in the Art Loss Register, of which more below. Such publicity significantly contracts the thieves' market. Indeed, in many cases the owner (or the owner's insurer) is the thieves' best market, and much stolen art is held for ransom. Still, stolen art sometimes enters the marketplace and is

[1] R Yaron, 'Reflections on Usucapio' (1967) 35 *Tijdschrift voor Rechtsgeschiedenis* 191, 223.

[2] JG Sauveplanne, 'The Protection of the Bona Fide Purchaser of Corporeal Movables in Comparative Law' (1965) 29 *Rabels Zeitschrift* 651.

[3] I know of only two situations in which substantive civil law and common law private law rules are directly opposed: forced inheritance in the civil law, as contrasted with the freedom to disinherit children and other blood relatives in the common law; and protection of the good faith purchaser against the owner in the civil law, contrasted with 'radical protection of ownership' in the common law.

acquired in good faith by innocent purchasers. This article reconsiders the law applicable to such cases.[4] Our category includes losses during war and occupation: the many thousands of works of art that were seized by the Nazis or otherwise displaced in the disorder and opportunism created by World War II[5] and subsequent conflicts.[6]

THE RADICAL DEFENCE OF OWNERSHIP

In 1946, Edward Elicofon, a Brooklyn lawyer, bought a pair of paintings from 'an American serviceman' returning from Germany. The paintings, which Mr. Elicofon later learned were valuable works by Albrecht Dürer, belonged to the *Kunstsammlungen zu Weimar* (KZW), a Weimar museum. They had been stolen in 1945 from storage in a German castle. In 1969 the West German government, later succeeded as plaintiff by KZW, sued Elicofon in the federal district court to recover the paintings, and the Grand Duchess of Saxony-Weimar, whose family had once owned the paintings, intervened as plaintiff.

Although rich in character, incident and arcane legal issues, the case ultimately became a classic dispute between the foreign owner of stolen property and the American good-faith purchaser. The court, applying the standard American rule concerning the sale of stolen movables to a good faith purchaser, held for the owner, and the paintings returned to Weimar.[7]

[4] Antiquities stolen from private collections and museums are treated as 'works of art' for the purposes of this article. Antiquities 'stolen' from illegally excavated sites in source nations, however, raise a rich group of quite different issues that are not discussed here. For a collection of materials, see chs 3 and 4 of JH Merryman, AE Elsen and SK Urice *Law, Ethics and the Visual Arts* 5th edn (Alphen aan den Rijn, Kluwer, 2007).

[5] In 1994, Lynn Nicholas published *The Rape of Europa*, a systematic historical account of the Nazi looting machine. In 1995, Hector Feliciano published *Le musée disparu*, which appeared in English as *The Lost Museum* in 1997, tracing the whereabouts of works looted in France. Feliciano revealed that nearly 1,000 such works were held in French museums (and a handful were in the collections of American and other museums). In January, 1995, the first international academic symposium on the displacement of art during World War II was held in New York. The publication of the symposium papers appears in E Simpson (ed) *The Spoils of War* (New York, HN Abrams and The Bard Graduate Center for Studies in the Decorative Arts, 1997).

[6] See P Gerstenblith, 'From Bamiyan to Baghdad: Warfare and the Preservation of Cultural Heritage at the Beginning of the 21st Century' (2006) 37 *Georgetown Journal of International Law* 245.

[7] *Kunstsammlungen zu Weimer v Elicofon*, 678 F. 2d 1150 (2d Cir 1982). There is a comment on the decision in (1983) 23 *Harvard International Law Journal* 466. For an interesting attempt by an investigative reporter to reconstruct the theft, see L Maitland, 'From Schwarzburg to Flatbush: The Mysterious Journey of Hans and Felicitas Tucher,' *ARTnews*, Sept 1981, at 78. For a West German comment on the case, see U Drobnig, '*Amerikanisehe Gerichte zum Internationalen Sachenrecht auf dem Hintergrund der Teilung Deutschlands*' (1984) 4 IPRax6l.

Such cases present the Eternal Triangle of movable property law:[8] A owns something valuable that B steals, and C eventually buys it in good faith. B, having played his brief part, has left the stage, and only A and C remain. Can A recover the valuable object from C? In American law the prevailing rule (to which the exceptions need not detain us here) is that A can recover the stolen object and need not compensate C. Even though the good faith purchaser is by definition blameless, he is left to his remedy against B, if he can find him and if B can be made to pay, as to which the odds are not good. A similar rule prevails in some other common-law countries.

In the civil-law world the precise rules vary from nation to nation, but in general the law is significantly kinder to the good faith purchaser and less so to the owner.[9] That is why, in the *Elicofon* case, the American defendant sought to persuade the court to apply German law, while the East German plaintiff successfully argued that the American rule should apply.

In an influential article published in 1987, Professor Levmore pursued his theoretical argument that there will be variety among legal systems' treatment of the good faith purchaser of stolen movables because 'Reasonable people can disagree over whether [the owner or the bfp] is the second-best target of the law-enforcement system' (bfp stands for bona fide purchaser). Levmore briefly examined the solutions in ancient near eastern law, post-biblical Jewish law, Roman and modern French law, American law and Mongolian tribal law and found that the extreme variety of solutions they displayed was consistent with his theory.[10] That article appears to have been misread by Professor Landes and Judge Posner,[11] who, as we shall see below, cite it to support their statement that providing 'complete legal protection of the original owner vis-à-vis the good faith purchaser' is 'the standard legal position in most countries.'[12]

[8] 'Eternal triangles are abundant in the law.': M Mautner, '"The Eternal Triangles of the Law": Toward a Theory of Priorities in Conflicts Involving Remote Parties' (1991) 90 *Michigan Law Review* 95.

[9] The most thorough comparative discussion of the good faith purchaser of movable property is a study by Professor Jean-Georges Sauveplanne of Utrecht: '*La protection de l'acquereur de bonne foi d'objets mobiliers corporels: Etude de droit comparé préparée par M. Jean Georges Sauveplanne, Secretaire général ajoint de l'Institut*' (1961) *L'unification du droit, Annuaire de l'Unidroit* 43. The study was prepared for a project of the International Institute for the Unification of Private Law ('Unidroit') in Rome to prepare a proposed uniform law on the topic and is published in the *UNIDROIT Yearbook* 1961, 43 *ff*. The project is described below. A briefer English language version of his study, covering fewer legal systems, was published by Professor Sauveplanne as 'The Protection of the Bona Fide Purchaser', above n 2.

[10] S Levmore, 'Variety and Uniformity in the Treatment of the Good-Faith Purchaser' (1987) 16 *Journal of Legal Studies* 43–65.

[11] WM Landes and RA Posner, 'The Economics of Legal Disputes Over the Ownership of Works of Art and Other Collectibles,' in VA Ginsburgh and PM Menger (eds), *Essays in the Economics of the Arts* (New York, Elsevier Science, 1996) 177.

[12] *Ibid* 208, citing only Levmore.

In fact, complete legal protection of the owner is the standard legal position only in the United States and perhaps a few other relics of the British Empire. In a far greater number of countries the good faith purchaser receives significantly kinder treatment. As Professor Sauveplanne observed:

> Whereas most continental legal systems protect the bona fide purchaser, English and American law only exceptionally grant him such protection.[13]

Italy provides the sharpest contrast to the American rule: in Italy the good faith purchaser becomes the owner. Italian Civil Code Article 1153 provides:

> He to whom movable property is conveyed by one who is not the owner acquires ownership of it through possession, provided that he be in good faith at the moment of consignment and there be an instrument or transaction capable of transferring ownership. Ownership is acquired free of rights of others in the thing, if they do not appear in the instrument or transaction and the acquirer is in good faith.[14]

The way the Italian statute works is nicely illustrated in the *Winkworth* case,[15] in which Japanese works of art stolen from a private collection in England were taken to Italy, where they were bought in good faith by an Italian collector. The Italian collector later sent them to Christie's in London for sale, and the British collector from whom they had been stolen brought an action to have the works declared his property. The English court held that the legal effects of the sale in Italy were determined by Italian law, under which the good faith purchaser became the owner, and accordingly held for the Italian collector.

The Italian statute was also applied In *Stato francese v Ministero per i beni culturali ed ambientali e De Contessini*,[16] concerning two tapestries that were stolen from a French state museum, taken to Italy and eventually bought in good faith by the defendant De Contessini. In a civil action for recovery brought by the French government, the *Tribunale* (trial court of general jurisdiction) of Rome held, as did the English court in the *Winkworth* case, that Italian law determined the legal effect of the sale to De Contessini and that under Italian law the good faith purchaser became the owner – this even though under French law the tapestries were classified as objects of artistic importance and were 'inalienable.'

More typically, many civil law nations deal separately with the owner's right to recover the object and the right of the good faith purchaser to

13 Sauveplanne, 'The Protection of the Bona Fide Purchaser', above n 2.

14 M Beltramo, G Longo and JH Merryman, *The Italian Civil Code and contemporary legislation*, (Dobbs Ferry, Oceana, 1996) Art 1153.

15 *Winkworth v Christie Manson and Woods Ltd* [1980] 1 All ER 1121.

16 61 *Diritto di autore* 263 (1990).

compensation. Thus Sweden gives the owner the option to recover the object on reimbursing the good faith purchaser, and Finland has a comparable rule.[17] France also permits the owner to recover the stolen work but requires him to compensate the good faith purchaser, as does Belgium.

In Chile, Civil Code art 890 provides that the owner may not recover the object from one who bought it at a fair, a shop, a store or other business establishment in which such things are sold unless he reimburses the possessor for the price he paid for it and for his expense in repairing and improving it. The Civil Code of the Federal District of Mexico art 799 provides that the owner may not recover a stolen object from a good faith purchaser in an auction or from a dealer in such objects unless he reimburses the possessor the price he paid for the object.

In Germany, §935 of the German Civil Code provides that the owner may recover the stolen object, but not if the good faith purchaser acquired it at public auction. Similar rules have been adopted in Greece and Japan. In Swiss law the good faith purchaser who acquired the object at a public auction, a market or from a merchant who deals in such goods is entitled to reimbursement. A similar rule applies in Austria.

Examples of the more generous treatment of the good faith purchaser in the civil law world could easily be multiplied. It is clear that the two major Western legal traditions radically differ on this question. In addition, it is important to note that the two international conventions governing trade in art adopt the civil law position in protecting the good faith purchaser. Thus art 7(b) of the 1970 *UNESCO Convention*[18] requires the state party requesting the return of stolen property to pay 'just compensation' to a good faith purchaser,[19] and art 4 of the 1995 *UNIDROIT Convention on Stolen or Illegally Exported cultural Objects*[20] provides that:

> The possessor of a stolen object required to return it shall be entitled, at the time of its restitution, to payment of fair and reasonable compensation, provided that

[17] Sauveplanne, '*La protection de l'acquereur*', above n 9, at 13.

[18] 'Convention on the Means of Prohibiting and Preventing the Illicit Import, Export and Transfer of Ownership of Cultural Property of 14 November 1970.' On May 30, 2006, Zimbabwe became the 110th State Party to the Convention.

[19] Apparently in reaction to this alien position, when the US ratified the Convention in 1972 it attached the 'understanding' that: 'The United States understands that Art 7(b) is without prejudice to other remedies, civil or penal, available under the laws of the states parties for the recovery of stolen cultural property without payment of compensation.' As a result, plaintiffs in American litigation seeking the recovery of stolen cultural property never rely on the Convention. They sue under state law, which does not require compensation of good faith purchasers.

[20] 'UNIDROIT Convention on Stolen or Illegally Exported Cultural Property' (1995). Nigeria became the 27th State Party when it ratified this Convention on December 10, 2005. The United States has not acceded to the UNIDROIT Convention.

> the possessor neither knew nor ought reasonably to have known that the object was stolen and can prove that it exercised due diligence when acquiring the object.

Finally we should note the fate of a serious international effort to reconcile the irreconcilable. In 1961, UNIDROIT enlisted a Working Committee to draft a proposed uniform law on 'The Protection of the Bona Fide Purchaser of Corporeal Movables' in international trade. As the title suggests, the purpose was to 'protect' the good faith purchaser. The basic working document was a comparative study by Professor Sauveplanne, cited above.[21] In it he had optimistically concluded that: (i) a general rule protecting the good faith purchaser was consistent with the majority of existing laws and 'not contrary to trends in systems that are not based on such a general rule'; (ii) the majority of laws stating that general rule contained an exception allowing recovery from the good faith purchaser if the goods were stolen from the owner; and (iii) that exception was limited in a number of such laws by the requirement of compensation if the good faith purchaser had acquired the object at a public auction or from a dealer.[22]

In 1968 the UNIDROIT Working Committee produced a *Draft Uniform Law on the Protection of the Bona Fide Purchaser of Corporeal Movables* incorporating those principles. When the draft was submitted to member governments for their observations, however, some of them (prominently including the US) strongly objected to it. UNIDROIT then convened a Committee of Governmental Experts to consider and recommend appropriate changes in the draft. The resulting revision was published in 1975 with the significantly altered title: *A Uniform Law on the Acquisition in Good Faith of Corporeal Movables.*[23] It provided in Article 11 that 'The transferee of stolen movables cannot invoke his good faith', thus totally reversing the position taken in the original draft.

It is hardly surprising that no government could be found willing to organise a diplomatic conference to attempt to turn this proposed Uniform Law into an international convention. Eventually, 'consensus on some of the solutions put forward in the draft having proved elusive, the subject

21 Sauveplanne, '*La protection de l'acquereur de bonne foi*', above n 9.

22 *Ibid* 120.

23 The 'Draft Convention Providing a Uniform Law on the Acquisition in Good Faith of Corporeal Movables' is published in (1975) (I) *Uniform Law Review* 66, together with an 'Explanatory Report' by Professor Sauveplanne, in which he noted that this new draft 'received a new orientation which detaches it from the principles which formed the basis of the initial draft.' *Ibid* 87.

was dropped from the UNIDROIT work program in 1985 ...'[24] And so, in its 25th year, Professor Sauveplanne's project joined legal history's catalogue of lost causes.

WHICH IS BETTER?

Since the US rule is less favourable to good faith purchasers, it has been suggested by an influential Italian scholar that civil law nations should adopt the US rule as a way of discouraging theft of cultural property.[25] A similar suggestion was made to the European Economic Community Commission in 1976 by Professor Jean Chatelain of France.[26] Were Professors Rodotá and Chatelain right? Would the legal change they recommend deter art theft? More generally, in a legal world divided on the effect of sale to a good faith purchaser, which is the better (better in what sense?) position? Should the same rule apply to all kinds of movable property, or do works of art call for different treatment? Here are a few ways of dealing with these questions.

Protection of Ownership

This characterisation obviously favours the owner. Its bias – 'the radical protection of ownership' – is built into the common law and is often justified by the maxim *Nemo plus juris transferre ad alium potest quam ipse habet*, or more succinctly *Nemo dat quod non habet*, usually translated as 'No one can transfer better title than he himself has.' In effect, the maxim's legal logic reifies the owner's title, treating it as something separate from the owned object, a thing that the 'holder' can 'pass' or 'transfer' to a donee or purchaser. When the thief steals the painting he acquires the work of art but not the owner's title, which remains with the owner. Accordingly, all the thief is able to 'pass' to the good faith purchaser is possession of the painting itself. Arcane, and mildly interesting, but more a way of stating a conclusion than a reason supporting it.

The protection of ownership argument is also myopic, focused only on the owner and a subsequent good faith purchaser. A rule protecting the

[24] W Rodinó, 'Malcolm Evans and UNIDROIT: A Chronology,' <http://www.UNIDROIT.org/english/publications/review/articles/1998–2&3b.htm> accessed 19 June 2008.

[25] S Rodotá, 'The Civil Law Aspects of the International Protection of Cultural Property' (general report) *Proceedings of the 13th Colloquy on European Law* (Strasbourg, 1984).

[26] J Chatelain, 'Means of Combating the Theft and Illegal Traffic in Works of Art in the Nine Countries of the EEC' (1976) *Commission of the European Communities*, Doc No XII/757/76.

good faith purchaser would, however, provide a different kind of 'protection of ownership.'[27] If the owner had acquired the artwork in good faith, her title would be good against prior claimants. This title cleansing effect would both comfort the owner and produce the benign social effects attributed to settled titles to goods.

Thus the two aspects of 'protection of ownership' work in different directions. Which is the more powerful one? Would a buyer in good faith from a dealer or at an art auction prefer to get a title good against existing claims (but not against a subsequent good faith purchaser from an eventual thief) or a title subject to existing claims (but good against subsequent good faith purchasers from such a thief)? The question is complicated by art market facts, since major American dealers and auction houses generally guarantee the buyer's title against existing claims.

Commercial Necessity

Professor Sauveplanne argued that the needs of commerce require protection of the good faith purchaser because the rapid circulation of movables makes it difficult to trace their legal origin:

> If every purchaser were compelled to investigate his predecessor's title, the circulation of movable property would be seriously impaired. Therefore, as the economic importance of movables increased, the need to protect the purchaser became more urgent, and commercial interests finally outweighed concepts of legal logic.[28]

This argument, which may be persuasive for traffic in other kinds of movable goods, seems unconvincing when applied to works of art, each of which is unique and has its own history. In art transactions, condition, provenance and authenticity often are prominent concerns. The work must be inspected for condition, and research to investigate the seller's title and/or to establish authenticity is not unusual. Buyers and sellers willingly adopt a slower transactional pace in art transactions. Speed may still be desirable, but it ranks low on the list of considerations affecting art transactions.

Deterring Theft

Here the objective is to adopt the rule that more effectively deters theft. Thus Professors Rodotá and Chatelain, as mentioned above, argued that

[27] Richard Craswell contributed this insight, which the writer did not think of and none of the authors cited in this article mention.

[28] Sauveplanne, 'The Protection of the Bona Fide Purchaser', above n 2, at, 652.

the US rule favouring the owner more effectively deterred theft than rules like that in Italy, which favour the good faith purchaser.[29] Were they right? Would placing the loss on the good faith purchaser, rather than the owner, discourage art theft?

It actually might do the opposite. One effective way to deter theft is for the owner to take precautions against it. A rule protecting the good faith purchaser would appear to provide incentive for the owner to increase his precautions against theft, and it would also increase the owner's inclination to insure valuable works of art against theft. Indeed, if theft deterrence were the primary objective, protecting the good faith purchaser rather than the owner would arguably be the better principle. As Professor Levmore put it, '... the more an owner is unable to recover his stolen goods, the more he may guard against theft.'[30]

Economic Analysis

Professor Harold Weinberg[31] also recognised that shifting the loss to owners would lead to 'efficiency gains,' since owners are better positioned to prevent theft and may be superior insurers against risk. He suggested, however, that these increased deterrent effects might be offset by an increase in the demand for stolen art among 'non-innocent shady purchasers' – people who know or suspect that the goods are stolen 'but have a colourable claim of legal innocence resulting from the circumstances of their purchase.' Perhaps so, though it seems more likely that a rule favouring good faith purchasers would in practice lead to a stricter and more rigorously applied definition of good faith. In the end, Professor Weinberg abandoned economics and punted to history:

> Consequently, one cannot conclude that any efficiency gained by shifting the innocent purchaser risk to owners would outweigh the increase in theft-related costs that could result from this shift. One fact suggests that the existing rule of stolen-goods nonnegotiability is efficient; it has survived in the United States for over two hundred years.[32]

This reference to American history, however, actually may cut the other way. Professor Weinberg does not appear to consider, and may have been

[29] In an article critical of statutes of limitation for stolen art, Professor Bibas makes a similar assumption: 'Because statutes of limitation promote maximum marketability rather than optimum marketability, they increase the profitability of art theft and thus encourage more thefts.' SA Bibas, 'The Case Against Statutes of Limitation for Stolen Art' (1994) 103 *Yale Law Journal* 2437, 2452.

[30] Levmore, above n 10, at 46.

[31] HR Weinberg, 'Sales Law, Economics, and the Negotiability of Goods' (1980) 9 *Journal of Legal Studies* 569.

[32] *Ibid* 586.

unaware, that the contrasting civil law position is hardly a modern invention. Rules favouring the good faith purchaser over the owner date back to the revival of commerce in the Mediterranean in the early Renaissance and have long survived in many national legal systems.[33] If survival were the appropriate measure, should those rules displace the US rule?

In an interesting article Professor Landis and Judge Posner[34] specifically address works of art, which 'share several characteristics that make ownership disputes both more likely to arise than in the case of other goods and more difficult to resolve when they do arise.' Their approach to the stolen art problem is summarised in the following way:

> [T]he more rights that the original owner has against a purchaser of a stolen work (even though many transactions may separate the purchaser from the thief), the lower will be the price at which a thief can sell a work of art, thus reducing the incentive for art theft. But the less will be the incentive of the owner to protect his property against theft, which will reduce the cost of stealing to the thief. Analysis of the optimal legal regime is complicated.[35]

The authors describe and pursue the complications, employing an economic model expressed in formidable equations with Greek-letter terms, as well as more familiar forms of argument. They conclude that:

> If our analysis is correct, the costs of favouring original owners ... are probably small, implying that the benefits, which we have no reason to believe are small, outweigh them. This implies in turn that the rule that maximizes social welfare is ... complete legal protection of the original owner vis-à-vis the good faith purchaser. This is the standard legal position in most countries [citing only Levmore, above]. A purchaser, even though he honestly and reasonably believes that he has acquired a good title, does not acquire a good title from a thief; and there is no exception for art.[36]

As we have seen above, Professor Levmore's article does not support the statement that complete protection of the owner is 'the standard legal position in most countries.' On the contrary, Levmore demonstrated the existence of a variety of legal positions, most of which did not provide complete protection of the owner. It is nor clear why Landes and Posner sought support in the 'standard position' generalisation for their conclusion, which seemed to be independently based on their elaborate economic

[33] Sauveplanne, 'The Protection of the Bone Fide Purchaser', above n 2, at 652, n 10.

[34] Landes and Posner, above n 11.

[35] *Ibid* 184. This statement appears to be inconsistent with the authors' later statement that 'the social benefits of deterring theft strengthen the economic argument for returning the work to the owner.' *Ibid* 215.

[36] *Ibid* 208.

argument, that the American rule was the better one. Nor do they explain the basis for their statement that 'there is no exception for art.' These omissions will be considered below.

Professors Alan Schwartz and Robert Scott also offer an economic analysis of the owner/good faith purchaser problem.[37] They first observe that the present American rule appears to be inefficient, but they then inquire whether an economic justification for it can be 'constructed.' They construct one by comparing 'the costs of reducing the risk of theft with the value of the risk.' They assume that the value of recovered goods to the owner is likely to be low (because the goods have been used, and possibly abused, and because the owner may already have replaced them) while the purchasers will place a relatively higher value on the same goods. In a footnote, however, the authors recognise that their constructed argument would not apply to 'goods such as jewels or paintings, which do not depreciate and are not used in the conventional sense.'[38]

Corrective Justice

Professors Schwartz and Scott also consider a 'corrective justice' analysis of the owner/good faith purchaser puzzle: 'A corrective justice theory provides that a plaintiff cannot prevail against a defendant unless the defendant has wrongfully harmed some interest of the plaintiff.' The good faith purchaser, by definition, neither knew nor had reason to know of the theft: 'he merely did what anyone would do–buy goods at a fair price.' The thief was a wrongdoer, but the good faith purchaser was not. Schwartz and Scott conclude:

> Thus, the theft rule is troubling because it seems incorrect on corrective justice notions and at best weakly explicable and justifiable on economic grounds.

And, as they stated in the cited footnote, the US rule would not be even 'weakly explicable and justifiable' on economic grounds if the stolen object were a work of art.

At this point it appears that the case for the American rule favouring the owner of stolen art over the good faith purchaser is, at best, uneasy. 'Protection of ownership' is less a reasoned argument than a statement of a conclusion that the owner wins. Commercial necessity would actually favour the good faith purchaser of many other kinds of traded goods, although it seems less applicable to the art trade. As to theft prevention, protecting the good faith purchaser may encourage more and better

[37] A Schwartz and RE Scott, *Sales Law and the Contracting Process* 2nd edn (Westbury, Foundation Press, 1991) 508–10.

[38] This statement appears *Ibid* 509, n 10.

protection against theft than protecting the owner. Among the economic analyses, Professors Weinberg and Landes and Judge Posner labour to justify the American rule. But Professors Schwartz and Scott find that rule to be 'at best weakly explicable and justifiable on economic grounds' as to some goods and neither explicable nor justifiable on economic grounds when applied to works of art. And when Professors Schwartz and Scott turn to 'corrective justice,' they find the American rule to be 'incorrect.'

Art-specific Considerations

We have seen that a rule favouring the good faith purchaser of stolen movable property may, on theft deterrence, economic and corrective justice grounds, be preferable to one favouring the owner. Are there additional considerations peculiar to works of art that would favour one or the other party?

Elsewhere I have described the special kind and degree of public importance of and interest in works of art and other cultural property[39] and have proposed an ordered triad of art policy objectives that can be summarised as 'preservation, truth and access.'[40] Preservation is of course fundamental; destruction of the work of art destroys the possibility of further study and enjoyment; damage limits it; modification misdirects it. Next comes truth in the broad sense: that is, the valid learning and enjoyment the work of art can provide. Finally, we want the work to be optimally accessible for study and enjoyment.

As to preservation, it is clear that theft is not good for works of art. Reports of the theft of paintings often state that the canvases were 'cut from their frames' by the thieves. The quoted phrase merely illustrates the probability that a stolen work will be damaged in any of a number of ways during its theft and clandestine possession by the thieves. Theft for ransom, a major motive for art theft, may actually contemplate deliberate damage to the work in order to hasten lagging response to ransom demands. Thus the rule that more effectively deters theft more effectively deters possible damage to the work of art. We have seen that the rule favouring the good faith purchaser may more effectively deter theft.

These considerations also argue against the Landes and Posner statement that 'the costs of favouring original owners … are probably small'[41] On the

[39] JH Merryman, 'The Public Interest in Cultural Property,' (1989) 77 *California Law Review* 339; JH Merryman, 'The Nation and the Object,' (1994) 3 *International Journal of Cultural Property* 61, both reprinted in JH Merryman, *Thinking About the Elgin Marbles: Critical Essays on Cultural Property, Art and Law* (The Hague, Kluwer, 2000), 94, 158 (referred to herein as *Critical Essays*).

[40] Merryman, *Critical Essays*, above n 39, at 94.

[41] See above n 36 and related text.

contrary, where works of art are concerned the social costs of favouring owners may be demonstrably high. Society's interest in the preservation of, the truth derivable from, and access to works of art, all of which are threatened by theft, would be advanced by the rule that better deters theft, which appears to be the rule that protects the good faith purchaser.

SPLIT THE LOSS?

If neither the bereft owner nor the good faith purchaser of the stolen work of art is at fault, why should the law allocate the entire loss to one or the other? An action to recover a work of art is, in the words of Jeremy Epstein, a leading New York litigator:

> the classic zero-sum game. At the end of the litigation, one party emerges with the artwork, and the other party leaves with nothing. Although settlements can 'split the baby,' I have seen no judicial decision that apportions the value of a work between the claimants. The harshness of this result does push parties toward a settlement, but there are always cases that cannot be settled.[42]

Right. If both are innocent victims of the theft, why should one emerge whole and the other bear the entire loss? Would it not be fairer to divide the loss between them? Loss sharing certainly is not unknown in the law. Comparative negligence is an obvious example,[43] and there is growing doctrinal and judicial support for loss sharing as a contract remedy.[44] The long-established institution of general average in maritime law provides an additional example.[45] A little reflection quickly produces others.[46]

In their elegant paper-in-progress on windfalls, Professors Parchomovsky, Siegelman and Thel make a general case for loss-splitting in a variety of situations.[47] With specific reference to the good faith purchaser problem they state:

[42] JG Epstein, 'The Hazards of Common Law Adjudication' in K Fitz Gibbon (ed), *Who Owns the Past? Cultural Property, Cultural Policy, and the Law* (New Brunswick, Rutgers University Press, 2005) 123, 127.

[43] G Dari-Matteucci and G De Geest, 'The Filtering Effect of Sharing Rules,' (2005) *34 Journal of Legal Studies* 207.

[44] See LE Trakman, 'Winner Take Some: Loss sharing and Commercial Impracticability,' (1985) 69 *Minnesota Law Review* 471; AM Polinsky, 'Risk Sharing through Breach of Contract Remedies,' (1983) 12 *Journal of Legal Studies* 427.

[45] The leading work on general average is DJ Wilson & JHS Cooke (eds),*Lowndes & Rudolf: The Law of General Average and the York-Antwerp Rules* 11th edn (London, Sweet and Maxwell, 1990).

[46] For example, both judicially encouraged settlements and alternative dispute resolutions often have loss-splitting effects.

[47] G Parchomovsky, P Siegelman and S Thel, 'Of Equal Wrongs and Half Rights,' University of Pennsylvania Law School Public Law and Legal Theory Research Paper, Series No #06–34.

> Saul Levmore's comparison of the treatment of the Bona Fide Purchaser problem across various legal systems provides a kind of anthropological support for our argument. ... The fact that different legal systems offer quite different doctrinal responses to the same problem suggests that no single solution is obviously optimal. It further suggests that nobody should be aggrieved if our judicial system formally comes to this conclusion as well.[48]

To date, however, our judicial system has shown no disposition to soften its radical protection of ownership or weigh it against splitting the loss between the equally innocent owner and good faith purchaser. Should it do so?

Epstein argues that 'there is no insuperable impediment to a more flexible judicial approach. Many cases would benefit from a court-ordered compromise,' and he provides a persuasive illustrative example that would, however, require determination of the artwork's value at two widely separated dates.[49] And there's the rub: establishing the value of a work of art on which plaintiff and defendant will often disagree will itself be a litigious enterprise.

Thus Professor Levmore, in his brief discussion of loss-sharing between the owner and the innocent purchaser,[50] states that one reason it has not been widely adopted in stolen property cases is that a sharing rule generates significant valuation problems for the fact-finder (and attendant legal costs) that all-or-nothing rules typically do not incur. That would certainly be true in art theft cases, where every work of art is unique and there is no convenient, authoritative schedule of art values. Whether the social value of fairness in splitting the loss would outweigh such administrative costs, as Levmore suggests, is an unresolved question.

AS TIME GOES BY ...

We must remember this, as time goes by the good faith purchaser and others come to rely on settled appearances in arranging their lives, and it seems increasingly unfair to upset their expectations. One purpose of the statute of limitations (or in civil law nations 'prescription') is to protect the expectations that grow out of that sort of reliance. If the good faith purchaser acquired the object in the ordinary course of trade there is a distinct but related social interest in promoting the dependability of commercial transactions. Further, as time passes, memories fade, witnesses and principals die or disappear, and evidence grows stale. Another purpose

[48] *Ibid* 40. Levmore describes loss-sharing under a Mongolian rule of 1640 that awarded the better part of a sheep (the head) to the owner and the inferior part (the rump) to the good faith purchaser.

[49] Epstein, above n 42, at 127.

[50] Levmore, above n 10, at 63–65.

of the statute of limitations is to avoid the resulting opportunities for fraud and injustice. Finally, economists tell us that it is socially undesirable for wealth to be immobilised by uncertainty.

Each of these concerns grows stronger with the passage of time, and the gravity of each is independent of the owner's state of knowledge about the circumstances of the theft or about the identity or whereabouts of the stolen object or its possessor.[51] Following this line of thought, it would appear that the statutory period should run from the date of theft.

In the United States, however, consistently with our legal system's radical protection of ownership bias, a strong tendency has grown up to think of statutes of limitations almost as though they were crystallisations of the owner's obligation of due diligence: one who fails to exercise her cause of action within the statutory period loses it for lack of diligence. Following that line of thought, it seems unfair to penalise an owner for lack of diligence in pursuing a cause of action she does not know she has. As a result, in most American states the limitation period does not begin to run until the owner knows, or should with reasonable diligence have known, that her Matisse has been stolen or until she discovers who possesses it. This is the so-called 'discovery' rule, which in practice has tended to become a 'discoverability' rule.

In New York, the center of the art world, which has a 'demand and refusal' rule, the situation is complicated, as is illustrated in the interplay of two cases: *DeWeerth v Baldinger*[52] and *Solomon R Guggenheim Foundation v Lubell.*[53] *DeWeerth* was a diversity action to recover a Monet painting stolen in Germany during World War II. In 1985 DeWeerth discovered that Baldinger, a good faith purchaser, had the painting and demanded its return. Baldinger refused, and DeWeerth sued in the US district court to recover the painting. Applying what it thought to be New York law, the court found: (i) that the action was instituted within the statutory period of three years from the demand and refusal; and (ii) that DeWeerth had met New York's requirement of reasonable diligence in seeking to find and recover the Monet between the time it was stolen and her discovery that Baldinger possessed it. On appeal the Second Circuit

[51] As one might expect in nations that favor the innocent purchaser, time is more likely to begin running sooner than in the US There are an extensive description of the British and briefer descriptions of other European applications of time limits in R Redmond-Cooper, 'Time Limits in Art and Antiquity Cases,' (1999) 4 *Art, Antiquity and Law* 323; R Redmond-Cooper, 'Limitations of Actions and Antiquity Claims Part II' (2000) 5 *Art, Antiquity, and Law* 185. As to the French situation, see T Le Bars, 'La computation des dèlais de prescription et de procédure' (2000) 39 Semaine juridique 1747; M Bandrac, 'Les tendances récentes de la prescription extinctive en droit Français', (1994) 46 *Revue de droit international et de droit comparé* 359. Compare R Zimmermann, *Comparative Foundations of a European Law of Set-off and Prescription* (Cambridge, CUP, 2002).

[52] 658 F Supp 688 (SDNY 1987).

[53] 77 NY2d 311, 567 NYS2d 623 (1991).

reversed, finding that on the facts DeWeerth had not shown the reasonable diligence required by New York law.[54]

In *Solomon R. Guggenheim Foundation v Lubell,* a Chagall gouache was found missing from the Guggenheim Museum's collection in the late 1960s but the Museum did not inform the police or take any other action to publicise the loss. Lubell bought the gouache in good faith from a New York gallery in 1967. In 1985 the Museum learned that Lubell had the work, demanded its return, Lubell refused, and the Museum sued in a New York state court. The trial court found for Lubell, reasoning that by failing to report the theft or take other appropriate measures to find and recover the Chagall the Museum had been insufficiently diligent to postpone the running of the statute of limitations. On appeal, the decision was reversed. The New York Court of Appeals held that, in applying the statute of limitations, the owner had no duty of reasonable diligence (thus also holding that the federal district court in *DeWeerth* had incorrectly stated and applied New York law). The Court, however, added that the defendant could raise the defence of laches on remand.

In 1983, California enacted a form of the discovery rule specifically applicable to art cases: Code of Civil Procedure § 338(c) provides that the three-year limitation period does not begin to run 'until the discovery of the whereabouts of the article by the aggrieved party.' The California statute was applied in *The Society of California Pioneers v Baker*[55] and *Naftzger v American Numismatic Society,*[56] in both of which the defendants were found to be good faith purchasers. Still, the owners prevailed in these cases, as in most art law cases involving the statute of limitations, which for obvious reasons seldom runs against the owner in the US

Thus in the current American climate, concern for the owner dominates, and courts embrace 'notice' and 'demand and refusal' preconditions for the running of the statute of limitations.[57] At the extreme one arrives at Governor Mario Cuomo's statement, when he vetoed a bill that would have tilted application of New York's statute of limitations slightly less strongly against the good faith purchaser, that he would not permit New York to become 'a haven for stolen art.' Thus the substantive vulnerability of the good faith purchaser under our property rules is compounded by the

[54] 836 F2d 103 (2d Cir 1987).

[55] 43 Cal App 4th 774, 50 Cal Rptr 2d 865 (1996).

[56] 42 Cal App 4th 421, 49 Cal Rptr 2d 784 (1996).

[57] For a full discussion and citation of authorities see Merryman, Elsen and Urice, above n 4, at 992–999. For a fervid argument opposing the application of statutes of limitation in art cases see Bibas, above n 29; and compare LE Eisen, 'The Missing Piece: A discussion of Theft, Statutes of Limitations, and Title Disputes in the Art World' (1991) 81 *Journal of Criminal Law and Criminology* 1067.

observable fact that the statute of limitations seldom runs against the owner in American art theft cases: a sort of double whammy.[58]

Since the *Lubell* case, however, New York courts have applied the laches doctrine in favour of good faith purchasers in two cultural property cases. In *Greek Orthodox Patriarchate of Jerusalem v Christie's Inc*,[59] the plaintiff sought recovery of a 10th century palimpsest manuscript of works by Archimedes, and in *Hutchinson v Horowitz*[60] the plaintiff claimed a painting by Theodore Robinson. In both cases, citing *Guggenheim*, the court dismissed plaintiffs' actions on laches grounds. Such cases raise the possibility that the *Guggenheim* doctrine may actually work to protect good faith purchasers by requiring plaintiffs to demonstrate due diligence. This is, of course, a two-edged sword; defendants will also be held to a demanding standard of due diligence, as Epstein explains:

> Since *Guggenheim* the strongest defence available to an owner is often based on the doctrine of *laches*; that is, did the claimant delay unreasonably in asserting his claim, and did that delay prejudice the owner? The lawsuit thus evolves into a diligence contest: if a plaintiff is to overcome a *laches* defence, he must demonstrate that he and/or his ancestor undertook a continuous and diligent search for the work in question. The owner, in turn, must demonstrate that she too was diligent in her scrutiny of the work's provenance at the time of acquisition, and that she did not overlook any title flaws that a careful search would have uncovered. Each side strains in a race to find fault with the other.[61]

WHAT IS TO BE DONE?

The fate of Professor Sauveplanne's project, described above, dampens any expectation that the American rule might be changed to protect the good faith purchaser of stolen art. Nor does there appear to be a bright future for loss-splitting proposals. Radical defence of ownership remains firmly entrenched in American law.

Nevertheless, the pattern for a fairer solution to the stolen art problem already exists in the familiar and widely understood system of real property title security. As all readers know, that system has three essential components:

An accessible, searchable record

The rule that recording puts prospective acquirers on notice

[58] Accord: Landes and Posner above n 11, at 202, speaking of American law: 'The longer the statute of limitations is, the greater the rights of the original owner are … [T]his would argue for setting no deadline for suing a purchaser of art from a thief. In substance though not in form, this is the tendency of the case law.'

[59] *Greek Orthodox Patriarchate of Jerusalem v Christie's Inc* 98 Civ 7664 (KMW), 1999 US Dist LEXIS 13257, 1999 WL 673347 (SDNY 1999).

[60] No 604942/97, slip opinion (S Ct New York County, 8 January 1999).

[61] Epstein, above n 42, at 127.

The rule that good faith purchasers are protected.

In adapting these components to deal with art theft, when a loss is discovered the owner lists the loss in a searchable record of stolen art or risks losing his rights to a good faith purchaser. A prospective purchaser is placed on notice by the record, is bound by it and can rely on it. There are some kinds of cultural property problems (in particular, antiquities removed from undocumented sites) that such a system could not resolve. But it can deal more cleanly, efficiently and fairly with the common run of stolen art cases.

Such a system has in fact been slowly building in the art world for decades. It had its roots in the stolen art records of the Art Dealers Association of America[62] and the International Foundation for Art Research (IFAR)[63] and has grown into the computerised, digitised and widely consulted Art Loss Register (ALR).[64] The ALR includes among its shareholders the major international auction houses and a number of art trade organisations. In addition, 193 insurance companies in Europe, North America, Australia, and New Zealand subscribe to the ALR.[65]

All that would appear to be needed to take the next step, under current New York law, is for the courts to rule that an owner who fails to report a theft to the Art Loss Register is chargeable with laches by a good faith purchaser. Other states could be expected to follow New York, the center of the art world, either by applying laches doctrine or by simply finding that the owner who did not register her loss had failed to be duly diligent.

The adoption of such a system would also affect the application of statutes of limitation/prescription, as shown in *Greek Orthodox Patriarchate of Jerusalem v Christie's Inc*, discussed above. There the plaintiff in

[62] The Art Dealers Association of America (ADAA) began to circulate notices on art thefts to its members in 1962. This service was gradually extended to non-member dealers and auction houses, museums, police departments, insurance companies, the FBI, US Customs Service, and international law-enforcement agencies. In 1986 the ADAA published its last notice, at which time it made its records available to the International Foundation for Art Research (IFAR).

[63] IFAR was founded in 1969 as a not-for-profit organisation. In 1976, it set up an Art Theft Archive and began to collect stolen art reports. Since 1985, the foundation has published IFAR Reports, a valuable journal that provides information about recently reported catalogued stolen art, and carries articles on art theft and authentication. In 1991, IFAR licensed the newly founded International Art Loss Register (ALR) to use its records in that organisation's computerised database of stolen art and antiques.

[64] The Art Loss Register, <http://www.nawcc.org/headquarters/members/alr.htm> accessed 19 June 2008, which was established in 1991, is based in London and New York. It is a private enterprise that advertises itself as 'the world's largest database of stolen art and antiques dedicated to their recovery.'

[65] <http://icom.museum/object-id/final/08-arttrade.html> this site also includes basic information about other sources of information concerning stolen art, including Trace magazine, established in 1988, and the Tracer database, established in 1995, and the Register of Stolen Antiquities, established by the International Association of Dealers in Ancient Art (IADAA) in 1994.

the action to recover the palimpsest argued for application of the New York statute of limitations, rather than prescription under French law. In response Judge Kimba Wood held that:

> Even if the Court were to conclude that New York law applied to determine the rights of the parties, defendants' laches defence bars the Patriarchate's claim to the Palimpsest.

The further development of an Art Loss Register-based solution in stolen art cases faces a variety of questions. Some might wonder, for example, whether it is appropriate for a private, unregulated register of stolen art to serve as the centerpiece of a judicially applied title security system. On reflection, perhaps that is not a real problem. Since the ALR is at present the most publicly available (for a modest fee) and widely used register of lost and stolen art, how could a bereft owner who failed to use it be found to have taken appropriate measures to publish her loss?

Among other questions, who should be considered to be on notice of entries in the Register: auction houses that already routinely consult the ALR, certainly; dealers, probably; major collectors, perhaps; but what of inexperienced collectors and casual buyers with no intention to collect? What should be the 'grace' period – the time within which an entry in the Register should be made in order to have the desired notice effect – and what should be the consequences of sale to a good faith purchaser during the grace period? And so on, sufficient unto the day …

CONCLUSION

The contrasting treatment of good faith purchasers in the US and in the civil law world is an oddity, a rare example of opposing substantive private law rules in the two major traditions of Western law. America's preference for the radical defence of ownership and the civil law's bias toward protection of the good faith purchaser are irreconcilable, as the failure of Professor Sauveplanne's UNIDROIT project amply demonstrates. Perhaps we should not be surprised to have found that the same clash of preferences is evidenced in the rules governing the effect of the passage of time on the rights of the parties.

The difference irresistibly invites evaluation: which is the better system? It is possible that for some kinds of objects one could settle for the proposition that the American position seems to work well enough for Americans, and the civil law position suits civil lawyers. But when we focus on art theft we ask a less provincial question: which approach to the good

faith purchaser problem better supports humanity's interest in the preservation of, the truth obtainable from, and access to these unique, irreplaceable human artifacts that are, in the words of the 1954 *Hague Convention,*[66] 'the cultural heritage of all mankind?'

Even as to ordinary movables, the lawyer-economists and other wise doctors whose views are described in this article appear to agree that legal protection of the good faith purchaser may more strongly deter theft than the American rule, although the differential effect may be small and there may be offsetting social costs. But where artworks are involved the public interest in theft deterrence is magnified and generalised, while the offsetting social costs diminish, and the case for protecting the good faith purchaser becomes stronger. Still, even if there were general agreement among American academics and art world actors that protection of the good faith purchaser is the better rule, the prospective effort required to promote its adoption in the American states is daunting and the probability of success limited. And the result of all that effort would still be an all-or-nothing solution to the problem.

The New York courts' recent revival of the laches doctrine and the growing influence of the Art Loss Register suggest a better, more achievable strategy: encouraging the evolution, already in progress in New York, of a loss registration-based[67] legal regime. Such a regime would more fairly deal with the parties in art theft cases and obviate the necessity of an all-or-nothing choice between the owner and the good faith purchaser of stolen art.

[66] Hague Convention for the Protection of Cultural Property in the Event of Armed Conflict (1954). The quoted language appears in the Preamble. The topic is explored at length in my article 'Cultural Property Internationalism' (2005) 12 *International Journal of Cultural Property* 11.

[67] A register of lost and stolen art is a good start, but it soon becomes apparent that a register that permitted owners of works of art to record their ownership would be a useful addition. The ALR has established such a register. This and other ALR features are described at <http://www.artloss.com/content/history-and-business> accessed 19 June 2008.

16

Faces of Justice Adrift? Damaška's Comparative Method and the Future of Common Law Evidence

PAUL ROBERTS*

INTRODUCTION:
I. FROM *FACES OF JUSTICE* TO *EVIDENCE LAW ADRIFT*

OVER THE LAST three decades, Mirjan Damaška's has been one of the most inventive, incisive, and influential voices in the comparative study of legal process, procedure and evidence. His two major works, published eleven years apart, are sweeping, state-of-the-art reflections on legal procedure at key moments in the evolution of the discipline.

In *The Faces of Justice and State Authority* (hereinafter FoJ),[1] published in 1986, Damaška brilliantly demonstrated the explanatory force of modelling legal processes in terms of their affinity with distinctive styles of government and structures of judicial authority. This compelling exposition made a major contribution to comparative legal studies, and can be credited with helping to inspire contemporary comparative scholars' keen interest in connections between law and (political) culture.[2] FoJ concluded in a tone of serene authorial satisfaction:

* The first drafts of this essay were prepared during my tenure as Professorial Visiting Fellow in the University of New South Wales Faculty of Law, March–May 2007. This visit was generously funded by UNSW Faculty of Law's Visiting Research Scholars Scheme and by the University of Nottingham's School of Law and International Office (U21 Travel Grant). I am very grateful to Dean David Dixon, Professor Jill Hunter and their law school colleagues, academic and administrative, for making me one of their own during my time in Sydney.

[1] MR Damaška, *The Faces of Justice and State Authority: A Comparative Approach to the Legal Process* (Yale UP, 1986).

[2] See, eg, D Nelken (ed), *Comparing Legal Cultures* (Aldershot, Dartmouth, 1997).

> [T]he task set in this volume is largely complete: a framework has been created within which to examine the legal process as it is rooted in attitudes toward state authority and influenced by the changing role of government ... If my scheme contributes to the storehouse of concepts with which the variation of procedural form can be identified and analyzed, and if it suggests new and fruitful lines of inquiry, we can live with the scheme's imperfections.[3]

Published some eleven years later in 1997, *Evidence Law Adrift* (hereinafter ELA)[4] shared its predecessor's preoccupation with models of adversary and inquisitorial procedure, this time concentrated more specifically on the structure and doctrinal details of the law of evidence. But having lulled the reader with these reassuringly familiar themes, the narrative takes a disturbing turn and concludes with this almost apocalyptic prediction:

> [T]he institutional environment appears to have decayed that supplied distinctive features of common law evidence with a strong argumentative rationale ... In its absence, shorn of adequate justification, they face the danger of becoming antiquated period pieces, intellectual curiosa confined to an oubliette in the castle of justice.[5]

It is tempting to characterise this sequential brace of publications as marking a shift from the confident modernism of FoJ to the 'postmodern' anxiety of ELA. Postmodern doubt, uncertainty and scepticism, imported from the humanities and social theory, became two of the *leitmotifs* of legal scholarship in the 1990s, finding expression in various forms and places.[6] These sceptical tendencies have spilled over into the present century, not least regarding the use of models of 'adversarial' and 'inquisitorial' legal procedure as explanatory heuristics, which is now regarded as distinctly passé in certain quarters.[7] Swimming against this sceptical tide, the first sections of this essay reconsider the methodological foundations of FoJ twenty years after its publication, and defend the essentials of Damaška's methodology of comparative modelling against recent critics of orthodox procedural conceptualisations. In the second half of the essay,

[3] FoJ 240, 242.

[4] MR Damaška, *Evidence Law Adrift* (Yale UP, 1997).

[5] ELA 142.

[6] Specifically in relation to procedure, evidence and proof see, eg, C Menkel-Meadow, 'The Trouble with the Adversary System in a Postmodern, Multicultural World' (1996) 38 *William and Mary Law Review* 5; D Nicolson, 'Truth, Reason and Justice: Epistemology and Politics in Evidence Discourse' (1994) 57 *MLR* 726. Cf W Twining, 'Some Scepticisms about Some Scepticisms' (1984) 11 *Journal of Law and Society* 137 & 285 (reprinted in W Twining, *Rethinking Evidence*, 2nd edn (Cambridge, CUP, 2006) ch 4).

[7] See, eg, S Summers, *Fair Trials: The European Criminal Procedural Tradition and the European Court of Human Rights* (Oxford, Hart Publishing, 2007) ch 1; JD Jackson, 'The Effect of Human Rights on Criminal Evidentiary Processes: Towards Convergence, Divergence or Realignment?' (2005) 68 *MLR* 737, 747, suggesting that 'the adversarial/inquisitorial dichotomy has obscured the truly transformative nature of the [European Court of Human Rights'] jurisprudence'.

however, I turn critic myself by arguing, *pace* ELA, that common law evidence is no more 'adrift' than the still securely-grounded methodology of comparative modelling pioneered by Damaška in FoJ.

II. THE METHODOLOGY OF COMPARATIVE MODELLING

Generally speaking, lawyers spend less time reflecting on their basic methodological tools and techniques in comparison to scholars in other disciplines. In consequence, legal method is often not stated as explicitly or understood as widely or profoundly as it ideally ought to be. Method is explicitly addressed to the 'How?' dimension of scholarly inquiry, but it is always also implicitly determined by mutually-conditioning 'What?' and 'Why?' considerations.[8] In order to select a suitable methodology it is necessary to define the parameters of one's inquiry and to clarify the reasons for undertaking it. Subject-matter is determined by motivation, which in turn pre-selects method; but choice of subject-matter is also influenced by available methods (research is the art of the possible), which in turn provide motivation (ought implies can).

Exemplifying these methodological truisms, Damaška simultaneously introduced both his subject-matter and the motivation for his study in FoJ's very first sentence:

> An immense and bewildering subject opens up before one who contemplates the diversity of arrangements and institutions through which justice is variously administered in modern states.[9]

Such pronounced variety in the legal processes encountered across national jurisdictions constitutes a standing provocation to the legal scholar. In matters of such patent social, political and moral significance as legal procedure, adjudication and law enforcement, why have otherwise quite similar western industrialised nations evolved such distinctive forms of justice? Law and justice are not trifling ornaments, like ceremonial national dress or English judges' horsehair wigs, which can be indulged as (mostly) harmless quaint anachronisms. Nor yet are they so obviously features of cultural heritage in which diversity should be positively celebrated, such as national language and cuisine. One senses that there is something strange, if not faintly sinister, in the notion that twenty-first

[8] Expressed somewhat more formally, Questions of Method form one point on an Eternal Triangle of intellectual inquiry, with Questions of Subject-Matter (entailing conceptual taxonomy and definition) and Questions of Motivation completing the timeless geometric triad: see, further, P Roberts, 'Comparative Law for International Criminal Justice' in E Örücü and D Nelken (eds), *Comparative Law: A Handbook* (Oxford, Hart Publishing, 2007).

[9] FoJ 1.

century justice looks quite different in France, Germany and England (to mention only three close European neighbours). Can 'justice by geography' be anything other than an international post-code lottery, with ever declining legitimacy in an increasingly globalised world? There is clearly something here that stands in need of explanation, and – in view of the vital interests at stake – *should* be explained. As Damaška framed the issue:

> Can this stupendous diversity be made intelligible, or reduced to a manageable set of patterns? At a minimum, can a conceptual framework be developed to assist us in tracing similarities and differences in component parts?[10]

Damaška's project in FoJ was therefore characterised from the outset as an exercise in promoting *understanding*, in search of 'new meaning for the previously incomprehensible'.[11] Since 'to know things is to watch them from the outside',[12] comparative methodology was naturally selected for its unrivalled powers of illumination, notwithstanding existential costs for the researcher:

> [T]he illumination provided here will be at best like winter sun: emitting light but little warmth ... [T]he reader should be aware of the unavoidable costs of looking at things from the outside: it is hard to be at once comfortable everywhere and at home anywhere.[13]

Like comparative legal scholars before and since, Damaška found himself in dialogue with an established comparative literature emphasising contrasts between 'adversarial' and 'inquisitorial' legal process. Damaška traced this 'well-trodden path' to a juridical distinction already evident in twelfth century legal thought.[14] However, for reasons that have since become commonplace (partly owing to Damaška's influential writings), the adversarial-inquisitorial dichotomy came to be viewed as an unsatisfactory conceptual prism through which to scrutinise modern legal process in comparative perspective. This conventional dichotomy's principal methodological flaw is traceable to its tendency to confuse normative and descriptive analysis of procedural systems, so that it becomes unclear whether 'adversarial' and 'inquisitorial' characteristics are being defined by the historical evolution of extant, institutionalised legal procedures, or whether existing procedural systems are to be interpreted and evaluated by reference to idealised models of 'adversarial' and 'inquisitorial' process. For example, trial by lay jury has certainly been an historical concomitant of adversarial process in common law jurisdictions, but does this imply that trial by lay

[10] FoJ 3.
[11] FoJ 14.
[12] FoJ 44.
[13] FoJ 15.
[14] FoJ 3.

jury is a definitive characteristic of 'adversarial' trial? An historical interpretation might suggest that it is, whereas a conceptual approach could maintain that the core adversary notion of party-contest does not logically entail trial by jury, or indeed any other particular institutional model of fact-finding. Such ambiguity blunts analytical precision and risks the onset of a vicious circularity: might the adversarial-inquisitorial dichotomy be to historical and contemporary procedural systems as the chicken is to the egg? Basic conceptual confusions are then compounded by florid terminological inconsistency, such that concepts such as 'accusatorial' are routinely claimed for *both* common law *and* modern Continental process.[15] However, exposing the limitations of the adversarial-inquisitorial dichotomy as an analytical device should not automatically be equated with advocating its complete abandonment. Indeed, Damaška worked with and augmented the conceptual models of legal process already to-hand, rather than starting from an analytical Year Zero.

The key to Damaška's reconstruction of the traditional adversarial-inquisitorial dichotomy lies in his realisation that models of legal procedure are intimately related to structures of political authority; a basic insight Damaška freely concedes to Marx.[16] As Damaška himself memorably put it, '[t]o consider forms of justice in monadic isolation from their social and economic context is – for many purposes – like playing *Hamlet* without the Prince'.[17] What Damaška perceived more clearly than his predecessors, however, was that political theorists dealt only in rather sweeping generalities about the law – Marx, indeed, is a case in point[18] – and stopped well short of elaborating any detailed conceptions of legal process and adjudication in terms of their underlying political values, executive ideologies and institutional structures. Recognising that 'most questions relevant to the study of procedural diversity lie beyond the opposition of capitalism, socialism and similar vague socioeconomic concepts',[19] Damaška had discerned the contours of a jurisprudential niche which he proceeded to occupy, furnish and make his own.

The procedural models Damaška elaborated in FoJ were unambiguously ideal-types devised for analytical purposes. Such models were perfectly suited to Damaška's ambition to understand the complexities of existing

[15] If 'accusatorial' refers to the institutional division between prosecution and adjudication, Continental criminal procedure systems became accusatorial when they dispensed with the omni-competent medieval inquisitor by splitting the magistracy into two separate branches – prosecutors and judges – with clearly defined, albeit complementary, roles. See JR Spencer, 'Introduction', in M Delmas-Marty and JR Spencer (eds), *European Criminal Procedures* (Cambridge, CUP, 2002).

[16] FoJ 6.

[17] FoJ 7.

[18] Marx's scattered jurisprudential pensées barely constitute a mature theory of law: see M Cain and A Hunt, *Marx and Engels on Law* (London, Academic Press, 1979).

[19] FoJ 8.

procedural practices in terms of their underlying patterns, logics and values, rather than compiling detailed sociological descriptions of contemporary legal proceedings or scrupulously documented historical exegesis:

> [C]haracteristics of the two archetypes should not be understood as repositories of essential facets of *existing* procedures in civil- and common-law countries. They are meant to be used in seeking to understand the complex mixtures of arrangements, as means to analyze them in terms of their components, as one would study compounds in analytical chemistry.[20]

To the challenge that model-building is an unwelcome distraction from the urgent task of becoming better acquainted with the world around us, Damaška counterposed Weber's powerful retort that it is not possible to understand the real world without constructing abstract analytical models through which to organise and interpret the empirical data which bombard our senses.[21] Meaning is an achievement of 'artificial' (non-empirical) categories of human thought and perception, and generalisation is an inescapable requirement of this human capacity (and existential necessity) to make sense of our physical and social environment and to orient ourselves within it. In this fundamental sense, utilising models of legal procedure is not so much a legitimate methodological preference, as a threshold requirement for undertaking legal analysis of any description:

> [W]ithout a suitable typology, comparative studies of procedural form cannot even begin … [E]xplorations of individuality become possible only after one has first obtained conceptual instruments with which to see and discuss individuality in terms of generic notions.[22]

Damaška was nonetheless at pains to emphasise that his abstracted models should not be taken literally, as faithful depictions of existing legal phenomena. The models were conceived as collections of family resemblances, or artistic genres:

[20] FoJ 12.

[21] 'I believe it is to Weber that we owe the paradoxical dictum to the effect that in order to grasp the real context we have to construct an unreal one': M Damaška, 'Evidentiary Barriers to Conviction and Two Models of Criminal Procedure: A Comparative Study' (1973) 121 *University of Pennsylvania Law Review* 506, 577. See, eg, C Ragin and D Zaret, 'Theory and Method in Comparative Research: Two Strategies' (1983) 61 *Social Forces* 731, 732, noting 'Weber's conviction that social reality is sufficiently complex as to be unknowable in the absence of theoretical interests that guide construction of one-sided type concepts [ie ideal types]'. Also see M Damaška, 'Structures of Authority and Comparative Criminal Procedure' (1975) 84 *Yale Law Journal* 480, 482: 'I concede that there are levels of analysis at which procedural models are generally misleading stereotypes or lifeless clichés. They are also simplifications; but this is precisely their default de qualité, indeed their virtue. They are used to liberate us from the tyranny of details, so that we can discern the overall distinguishing attributes of complex phenomena'.

[22] FoJ 241, 242.

> '[a]ctual Anglo-American and Continental procedures will be seen to belong to one or another mode, as buildings can be said to belong to one or another architectural style ... Of course, one should not expect more from this type of analysis than it can deliver: that a building may be classified as an exemplar of a particular style ... tells us very little about the individuality of the building'.[23]

Damaška's procedural models were constructed along two intersecting axes. The first axis characterises the structure of procedural authority in law, running from 'hierarchical' officialdom at one pole to 'co-ordinate' adjudication at the other. The second axis measures modern styles of government, running from the 'activist' policy-implementation of the social engineers to the 'reactive' *laissez-faire* of the *nachtwächterstaat*. Since, at least in theory (and Damaška argued, in practice as well), these characteristics can be found in any combination, there are four ideal-types to which any actual legal process might most closely correspond: hierarchical-activist, hierarchical-reactive, co-ordinate-activist, and co-ordinate-reactive. The way in which FoJ mapped these analytical categories onto real legal systems traced patterns which are often familiar and predictable, but there were also some unexpected associations and surprising conclusions.

Perhaps the line between idealised-models and empirical reality is always blurred, so that the danger of their confusion is, practically speaking, ineradicable. It is, furthermore, *always* a mistake to think that any single conceptualisation can encapsulate *everything* of potential interest about empirical phenomena. To emphasise particular contrasts and continuities one must always ignore others that might conceivably have been made. But for all the well-known risks of wishful thinking and over-generalisation, in law as in life, it seems that Damaška's use of idealised procedural models was, in principle, methodologically impeccable, as well as exceptionally illuminating.[24]

III. FOUR METHODOLOGICAL STRENGTHS

Damaška's comparative modelling of legal process boasted several notable strengths which, in my opinion, convincingly demonstrate the enduring

[23] FoJ 10, 242.

[24] This was also, broadly speaking, the conclusion of I Markovits, 'Playing the Opposites Game: On Mirjan Damaška's *The Faces of Justice and State Authority*' (1989) 41 *Stanford Law Review* 1313, 1341, who noted that 'by steering our thoughts along one specific path only, we exclude others. But we can always retrace our steps, start anew, try out the road not taken. If the concepts we use impoverish our view by crowding out alternative perspectives, the concepts we did not use, in their different ways, would have done the same. How could we ever chart the globe without a grid, any grid, of meridians? ... Dichotomies create order, not meaning. But do not underrate order as a prerequisite to finding meaning. Like an archeologist's grid of trenches, Damaška's conceptual system has prepared the ground for less formal investigations'.

heuristic value of differentiating between 'adversarial' and 'inquisitorial' procedures, at least as a point of departure for more refined analysis. This section highlights four particular attributes of Damaška's methodology. First, the bridge to political theory constructed by Damaška provides an escape-route from the viciously circular logics of 'adversarial' and 'inquisitorial' conceptual models. Secondly, Damaška's intersecting axes are better able to encapsulate the complexities of real legal processes (albeit still in the relatively abstract conceptualisations of an idealised model) than one-dimensional versions of the adversarial-inquisitorial dichotomy. Thirdly, the modular structure of Damaška's basic conceptual building-blocks facilitates modelling of relatively unusual combinations of features, which brings to light aspects of legal process which tend to be overlooked because they do not meet the normative expectations of orthodox procedural models. Fourthly, when set in comparative perspective, Damaška's models of legal process demonstrate the perspectival nature of all conceptualisations of legal procedure, which are shown to be relative to the standpoint of the observer. This is a novel inflection of the too-little-respected methodological truism that concepts are always ideologically-loaded; or, in the language I introduced earlier, subject-matter is partly defined by motivation. This section elaborates on each of these four strengths in turn.

On reflection, it should always have been patently obvious that the primitive concepts of 'contest' and 'inquest' can only convey a limited amount of information about the workings and values of modern legal systems. If common law trials can plausibly be described as a contest between opposed parties and their advocate-champions, Roman gladiatorial combat, Olympic shot put and the world chess championships are likewise no less properly characterised as 'contests'. Again, it is true to say, broadly speaking, that modern Continental legal procedure is structured around the notion of systematic factual inquiry ('inquest'), but the same could be said for investigative journalism, the researches of professional historians and the intelligence gathering activities of the CIA.[25] As Damaška himself observed elsewhere,[26] Continental legal process in this respect conforms to the precepts for *any* type of rational inquiry into empirical states or events.

[25] See, further, T Anderson, D Schum and W Twining, *Analysis of Evidence*, 2nd edn, (Cambridge, CUP, 2005); W Twining and I Hampsher-Monk, *Evidence and Inference in History and Law: Interdisciplinary Dialogues* (Evanston, Il, Northwestern UP, 2003); DA Schum, *The Evidential Foundations of Probabilistic Reasoning* (Evanston, Northwestern UP, 2001).

[26] 'The officially controlled fact-finding method of Continental procedure – inasmuch as it accords a larger role in the development of evidence to disinterested third parties – comes closer [than adversary process] to the demands of dispassionate, rational inquiry': ELA 101–102.

We can learn much more about the distinctive character of *legal* process, Damaška showed, by situating adjudication within broader styles of government and political authority. A liberal polity wedded to rugged individualism and unencumbered free-markets will tend to regard legal process as a mechanism for dispute-resolution and the maintenance of social peace, especially if – as in the United States – these ideological preferences are ramified by a political culture suffused with deep suspicion of an over-weaning, centralised (federal) government credited with expansionist ambitions:

> [T]he reactive state is first and foremost an adjudicative body. All other state activities are an extension of and subordinated to dispute resolution. Far from being the least dangerous branch of government, the judiciary is – with little exaggeration – indeed the only branch of government ... The verdict in the conflict-solving mode is not so much a pronouncement on the true state of the world as it is a decision resolving the debate between the parties, like a peace treaty putting an end to combat.[27]

A more paternalistic or communitarian polity, by contrast, will easily regard legal process as an extension of official state bureaucracy with an overarching mandate to implement desirable social policies. From this elevated vantage-point, the logic of adversary process in common law jurisdictions is seen to be inspired by a political preference for 'light-touch' conflict-resolution; whilst the logic of inquisitorial legal process in the jurisdictions of Continental Europe (and their (post)colonial satellites) can be explained in terms of a political preference for relatively interventionist policy-implementation through prescriptive legal regulation and a distinctively bureaucratic mode of adjudication:

> In contrast to law in the reactive state, whose stress is on defining forms in which freely chosen goals may be pursued, activist law is directive, sometimes even hectoring: it tells citizens what to do and how to behave ... [A]nimated by its perception of the objective of administering justice, an activist state must seriously consider designing its legal process as an inquiry controlled by state officials. In lieu of privately controlled contest, the idea of officially controlled *inquest* epitomizes the procedural style.[28]

This outline sketch of the affiliations between legal process and alternative conceptions of the point and remit of government acquired greater light and shade from Damaška's intersecting analysis of contrasting structures of legal authority and institutionalised divisions of juridical labour. The attributes of legal officials, the nature of the relationships between them, and the characteristics of their decision-making are the key variables on

[27] FoJ 75, 123.
[28] FoJ 82, 87.

this second interpretational axis.[29] In legal systems corresponding to the 'hierarchical ideal of officialdom', a premium is placed upon bureaucratic audit, consistency and predictability in decision-making, and deference to superiors in the vertically-ordered institutional hierarchy. Legal decision-making is professionalised and depersonalised, in a way which 'promotes institutional thinking',[30] whilst 'official discretion is anathema'.[31] Legal reasoning tends to be relatively formalistic. It is characterised by abstraction from concrete factual particulars, a penchant for normative generalisation and logical-dogmatism in jurisprudential thought.

Essentially the mirror-image of its polar-opposite, Damaška's 'co-ordinate ideal' of legal officialdom embraces lay involvement in legal decision-making, whilst eschewing rigid pyramids of formal legal authority in favour of roughly co-equal decision-makers capable of dominating their own spheres of influence. This combination goes hand-in-hand with an affinity for substantive justice on the particularised facts of the case, and correspondingly less interest in the systematic application of generalised norms. These ideological preferences and institutional functions and competences tend to be mutually reinforcing over time: thus, a preference for substantively just outcomes over formally correct procedures is predictably reinforced by the practical inability of part-time amateur decision-makers (for example, lay jurors) to comprehend technically sophisticated normative standards and to apply them consistently across a variety of factual contexts. The resulting unpredictability and lack of consistency in adjudication, contemplated with horror as elementary and intolerable deficiencies by a hierarchically-ordered legal process, are borne lightly by a legal system in which the co-ordinate ideal of officialdom is embraced:

> [T]he regulation that appeals to logical legalists is alien to laymen. It displays insensitivity to the singularity of human drama, and its capacity to assure principled decision making leaves laymen unimpressed. They are likely to prefer warm confusion to cool consistency … And in this vision of authority, vague standards of substantive justice combine with the absence of hierarchical supervision to ensure that the theme of official discretion becomes the essential accompaniment of co-ordinate judicial organisation.[32]

There are, then, evident affinities between styles of government and structures of legal authority, as well as between Damaška's reconstituted procedural models and the historical evolution and contemporary characteristics of real legal systems. Reactive government, with its focus on dispute resolution, is naturally attracted to the substantively-orientated, broadly participative co-ordinate ideal of officialdom; activist states,

[29] FoJ 16.
[30] FoJ 19.
[31] FoJ 20.
[32] FoJ 28.

meanwhile, will naturally try to establish or co-opt hierarchically-organised judicial bureaucracies into their policy-implementing agendas. Historical and contemporary real-world manifestations of these models are, of course, perfectly familiar. The common law jury trial represents a close approximation to the co-ordinate ideal; the Roman-canon medieval inquisition and its reformed Napoleonic offspring, which colonised the legal procedures of most of Continental Europe during the early decades of the 19th century and remain more or less dominant to this day, exemplify many of the core characteristics of the hierarchical ideal of officialdom.

With these basic contrasts and connections established, it now becomes possible to glimpse the interpretative power of Damaška's comparative modelling over more conventional analyses utilising a one-dimensional adversarial-inquisitorial dichotomy. For example, lay participation in fact-finding favours temporally compressed proceedings and finality in adjudication, whereas bureaucratic fact-finding is more likely to be episodic (so that the sources of information can be thoroughly checked and triangulated against other evidentiary sources) and subject to review and reconsideration by judicial superiors, who are presumptively more skilled and knowledgeable, or at any rate more authoritative, than front-line decision-makers. Episodic, professionalised factual inquiries thrive on extensive record-keeping which encourages a preference for information presented in documentary form, whereas lay involvement in temporally concentrated, 'main event' trials will tend to favour oral testimony. Once a unique adjudicative event has been staged, moreover, it cannot easily be replicated and there is no official record of how the verdict was reached for any hierarchically superior judicial authority to reassess – which goes a long way towards explaining why appeals were so late to develop in common law jurisdictions,[33] and why even today appellate proceedings create tensions in the Anglophone legal world,[34] especially in cases originally tried by juries,[35] which are not experienced by Continental legal systems. None of these distinctive characteristics of modern legal process, nor many more besides, could be deduced from conceptual analysis of adversarial or inquisitorial procedural forms. It was Damaška's pioneering attention to

[33] On the historical evolution of criminal appeals in England and Wales, see R Pattenden, *English Criminal Appeals 1844–1994* (Oxford, OUP, 1996).

[34] R Nobles and D Schiff, 'The Right to Appeal and Workable Systems of Justice' (2002) 65 *MLR* 676.

[35] Cf *R v Pendleton* [2002] 1 Cr App R 441, [6] (Lord Bingham): 'The role of an appellate court reviewing a conviction by a jury can never be the same as that of a court reviewing the reasoned decision of a judge'. Also see JD Jackson, 'Making Juries Accountable' (2002) 50 *American Journal of Comparative Law* 477; JC Smith, 'Is Ignorance Bliss? Could Jury Trial Survive Investigation?' (1998) 38 *Medicine, Science and the Law* 98.

contrasting structures of legal officialdom and their corresponding styles of legal decision-making which supplied 'a key to [unlock] several bizarre comparative law paradoxes'.[36]

It must be stressed, however, that Damaška set out to describe broad tendencies and loose associations, not cast-iron laws of political structure and legal form (and he was thus careful to distance himself from Marx's overly deterministic historicism on this account[37]). Damaška engineered a political theory escape-route from the arid conceptualism of orthodox adversarial-inquisitorial dichotomies. His reformulated procedural ideals could now function as heuristic devices in the study of legal process, purged of any preconceived expectations about the characteristics which legal systems conventionally regarded as 'adversarial' or 'inquisitorial' are supposed to exhibit.[38] The modular flexibility of Damaška's models was a major strength, because real legal systems do not evolve precisely in accordance with the exquisitely-drawn blueprints of procedural ideals. In the empirical world, legal institutions continue to adapt themselves to modern conditions without fully self-conscious or all-encompassing allegiance to procedural heritage. What we observe, in reality, are 'pastiches of procedural form'.[39] Nor is this only a manifestation of predictable variation between the real and the ideal. In certain respects, tensions are already built into what might be regarded, on casual acquaintance, as ideal conjunctions between political morality and structures of legal authority. For example, whereas co-ordinate authority favours substantive justice on the merits, *laissez-faire* reactive government will tend to sponsor formal conceptions of due process – fairness rather than justice – in order to insulate adjudication from substantive political controversies and thus preserve its neutrality and independence.[40] Activist government, for its part, needs to temper its instrumentalisation of law as a technique of political administration with appropriate regard for legal certainty, predictability in adjudication, and a reasonable measure of confidence in the stability of legal entitlements. In conditions of legal and social anarchy, few policies can be implemented successfully or cultivated over time.

Damaška's comparative modelling is arguably at its most illuminating when applied to criminal proceedings. English Crown Court jury trials

[36] FoJ 56.

[37] FoJ 6–8.

[38] It was in order to cast off the blinkers of preconception that Damaška, 'reluctantly', substituted his two neologisms, 'conflict-resolving process' and 'policy-implementing process', for the conventional terminology of 'adversarial' and 'inquisitorial' procedural models: FoJ 80, 88.

[39] FoJ 93.

[40] '[T]he reactive state does not hesitate to place impartiality of process above accuracy of result. If one equates accuracy of outcomes with the attainment of justice, and equal treatment with fairness, one must conclude that the reactive state – and thus the conflict-solving process as well – values fairness above justice': FoJ 136.

(and their American and Commonwealth transplants) represent the acme of adversary process, in popular conceptions of British criminal justice no less than in scholarly exegesis. And yet one would have to delve into the annals of history at least as far back as the Tudor reforms of governmental administration in the sixteenth century[41] to find a time when large tracts of criminality were truly regarded as a private matter between the offender and his victim (and their respective families, clans and supporters). Ever since crime has been apprehended as a threat to public order – an assault on the monarch's peace – the administration of criminal justice has been an increasing preoccupation of government: in Damaška's typology, an arena of policy-implementation. Twenty-first century governments have come to perceive crime control and the formation and implementation of criminal justice policy as amongst their most pressing (and challenging) responsibilities,[42] and at the level of macro-political analysis there is no real difference in this regard between common law and civilian jurisdictions. For example, whilst there are still important structural differences between the organisation of policing in England and France,[43] there is no doubt that – as in every other modern (post)industrial democracy – English and French policing functions are alike discharged by hierarchical, policy-implementing, governmental bureaucracies.[44] In England, criminal investigations have shed many of their informal, 'privatised' trappings and become highly professionalised and extensively regulated by law,[45] whilst the Crown Prosecution Service is gradually acquiring the formal legal powers and *de facto* policy leadership of a Continental-style procuracy.[46] English criminal process, in other words, has come to resemble an

[41] See Sir John Baker, *The Oxford History of the Laws of England: Volume VI, 1483–1558* (Oxford, OUP, 2003), esp. 514–6; Sir William Holdsworth, 4 *A History of English Law*, 3rd edn (London, Sweet & Maxwell, 1945), 492–532. The story is one of progressive development over several centuries from private tort to state crime, in both substantive and procedural law: see Holdsworth, *Ibid* vol viii, ch 5; JH Baker, *An Introduction to English Legal History*, 4th edn (London, Butterworths, 2002) 501–7. The survival of private prosecution in modern English law might be said to demonstrate that the final chapter of this story remains unwritten.

[42] D Garland, *The Culture of Control: Crime and Social Order in Contemporary Society* (Oxford, OUP, 2001).

[43] British policing still retains its county-based structure, although this is increasingly being eroded and supplemented by national policing agencies; French policing is characterised by a more militaristic style: see J Hodgson, *French Criminal Justice* (Oxford, Hart Publishing, 2005) 86–93.

[44] In relation to England and Wales, see RC Mawby and A Wright, 'The Police Organisation' and T Jones, 'The Governance and Accountability of Policing' both in T Newburn (ed), *Handbook of Policing* (Cullompton, Devon, Willan Publishing, 2003).

[45] See, further, P Roberts, 'Law and Criminal Investigation' in T Newburn, T Williamson and A Wright (eds), *Handbook of Criminal Investigation* (Cullompton, Devon, Willan Publishing, 2007).

[46] Cf the illuminating comparative analysis of J Fionda, *Public Prosecutors and Discretion: A Comparative Study* (Oxford, OUP, 1995) which, however, now requires substantial up-dating in relation to the CPS in England and Wales.

instrument of policy-implementation, just as its intimate connection with the maintenance of public order would lead one to expect. However, viewing these developments through the lens of Damaška's procedural models cultivates a considerably more nuanced understanding of this complex – and somewhat conflicted – procedural hybrid.

An enduring allegiance to conflict-resolution has left its indelible mark on criminal proceedings in England and Wales. Thus, English criminal process continues to allow the accused (in effect) to 'privatise' the implementation of criminal policy, through guilty pleas,[47] factual stipulations,[48] and strategic choices (not) to adduce particular sources of information or to develop particular lines of argument (including potentially eligible defences subject to a burden of production).[49] All of these characteristics of Anglo-American law scandalize Continental criminal procedure[50] with its more purist ideological commitment to policy-implementation, conceived as a quintessentially *public* function which cannot be delegated to private litigants under any circumstances. Conversely, by treating the accused who chooses to testify more or less as an ordinary witness, who gives evidence on oath and could at least theoretically be prosecuted for perjury, Anglo-American criminal procedure can be said to tolerate a greater departure from 'pure conflict-solving forms' than Continental process, in which the needs of the accused as a litigant-party are prioritised over his forensic usefulness as a testimonial source of information.[51] In short, whilst 'Anglo-American criminal procedure remains, in the last analysis, a policy-implementing process', Damaška's models illuminate, contextualise and in certain respects qualify 'the comparatively striking fact that more contest forms can be identified in Anglo-American criminal prosecution than in any other contemporary system of criminal justice'.[52]

[47] Recently formalised by the Court of Appeal in *R v Goodyear* [2005] 2 Cr App R 20, CA.

[48] Criminal Justice Act 1967, s.10.

[49] See, eg, *R v Greenwood* [2005] 1 Cr App R 7, CA.

[50] Cf FoJ 113, 119 (footnote omitted): 'That a private individual should decide whether criminal law should use a crude or a refined measure of liability is clearly an idea from the ideological storehouse of laissez-faire government: individuals can themselves decide whether to go to prison or not.... It is thought totally unacceptable, even absurd, in Continental systems to let the prosecution and the defence control the choice or the dosage of the criminal sanction. To let the defendant negotiate with state officials on this score seems to compromise the sovereign prerogative of the government to dispense criminal justice'.

[51] FoJ 130. This particular example is complicated by the thought that an accused with the option of testifying on oath might conceivably be more effective as a party to the proceedings (having been presented with additional strategic options) than an accused who is prohibited from assuming the testimonial status of a non-party witness.

[52] FoJ 222.

At least something of the flavour has now been suggested of FoJ's attributes in terms of establishing a bridge to political theory, the sophistication of its modelling utilising intersecting axes, and the versatility and dynamism of its theoretical components' modular structure. The fourth strength of Damaška's comparative methodology, to which I alluded at the start of this section, is perhaps its most valuable, if somewhat elusive, quality. Damaška demonstrated the perspectival nature of comparative legal studies in two distinct but closely related senses. First, Damaška established that the basic categories of analysis through which legal processes are interpreted, taxonomised and evaluated *are already* laced with idiosyncratic local meanings and significance. For example, the concept of 'adjudication', which in common law countries is treated as synonymous with judicial (lay or professional) decision-making at a decisive 'main event' trial, typically extends over a much broader forensic landscape in jurisdictions with an inquisitorial pedigree. This subtle shift in meaning is nicely encapsulated in the English translation of Kafka's *Der Prozess* as 'The Trial'.[53] Moreover, the different concepts of 'adjudication' which are brought into focus under the microscope of comparative analysis are indicative of fundamentally divergent conceptions of the relationship between legal process and bureaucratic administration – competing conceptions of judicial independence and the separation of powers, as Anglophones would say. They also hint at the relative priority of dispute-resolution and policy-implementation on the activity-roster of good government, as that ideal is comprehended in particular jurisdictions. Theories of law and political administration are in this way reflected in, and reinforced by, juridical taxonomies, terminology and basic concepts, interpreted 'naturalistically' in their local settings:

> Whereas all activities of a radically laissez-faire state, including administration, acquire a flavour of adjudication, all activities of a fully activist state, including adjudication acquire a flavour of administration. But it would be parochial to assume that this narrow concept of adjudication covers activities that are perceived as instances of 'judging' or even activities that are thought to be quintessentially judicial, in all legal cultures of the world ... This is still the prevailing view on the Continent: the idea that to adjudicate need not necessarily imply resolution of contested matters continues to appear natural to lawyer and layman alike ... [I]f in his wanderings from culture to culture, a comparativist were to use the narrow analytical concept of adjudication, many activities widely perceived as instances of adjudication would elude him.[54]

Damaška also brilliantly revealed the inherently perspectival nature of conceptions of legal process by expanding his field of vision beyond the

[53] FoJ 48 (n 1).
[54] FoJ 89, 90 (footnote omitted).

routine contrasts between 'common law' (mostly English and American) and 'Continental' (typically French or German) legal systems which tend to dominate comparative legal studies, to include Soviet law (as it then was) and Chinese conceptions of legality. In this expanded frame, modern Continental process might appear 'inquisitorial' in comparison to common law procedure, yet markedly adversarial and legalistic when set against the inquisitorial jurisdiction of the Soviet *prokuratura*, to say nothing of Mao's China where '[c]riminal justice and administration merged [and] dealing with offenders became part of the broader effort to manage and transform society'.[55] One of the most telling observations to emerge from this analysis is the ease with which defamatory comparisons with the medieval Inquisition – which incidentally libel all parties, including the medieval inquisitors! – can almost effortlessly be recycled and deflected down the legal evolutionary pecking-order. Though Continental jurists might indignantly reject common lawyers' characterisations of modern Continental legal procedure as 'inquisitorial', this did not necessarily prevent Civilians from criticising Soviet law in terms of their own notions of legal form and function. And Soviet lawyers, in their turn, would probably have looked askance at the 'primitive' character of Maoist legal ordering, judged by their own jurisprudential lights:

> In their totality, the features of the Soviet system … appear to Western European lawyers as a partial throwback to Continental inquisitorial procedure after the abolition of judicial torture but before liberals began to leaven it with elements of the contest style. Observe the subtle irony, however: such assessments reproduce almost exactly the impressions which common lawyers regularly express about the conventional Continental amalgam – impressions dismissed as caricatures by classical Continental lawyers, much as the similar impressions just registered are dismissed by officials in the Soviet judicial apparatus … At least to the modern Soviet eye, the blatancy with which the Chinese Communist party interfered in pending cases or justice officials consulted with the party would be repugnant. In short, Soviet lawyers would likely express the same criticisms that are directed against their own criminal procedure by Continental lawyers, accustomed to the conventional pastiche of contest and inquest forms. On the other hand, as seen from Mao's Beijing, Soviet criminal process would reveal a family resemblance with conventional Continental systems.[56]

In these jarring contrasts and disorientating shifts of standpoint we are forced to confront the enormity of the theoretical and practical challenges facing those 'groping toward a legal language common to mankind in the [early twenty-first] century'.[57] The perspectival nature of legal analysis,

[55] FoJ 199. Now also see R Vogler, *A World View of Criminal Justice* (Aldershot, Ashgate, 2005).

[56] FoJ 195, 199 (footnote omitted).

[57] FoJ 199.

which seeps deep into the basic categories of jurisprudential thought, implies not merely that 'lawyers socialised in different settings of authority can look at the same object and see different things',[58] but that their perceptions of reality almost certainly *will* diverge, perhaps radically.

This fundamental epistemological challenge must not be ducked. Measured and unsentimental recognition of the pervasiveness of cultural perspective is an essential first step to overcoming the formidable, but not necessarily insurmountable, obstacles to meaningful communication and mutual understanding across legal institutions, systems and cultures.[59] In FoJ, Damaška supplied powerful and versatile conceptual tools for comparative legal analysis, and his self-consciously reflexive modelling methodology has since served comparative legal scholarship as an exemplary riposte to 'the dogmatism of the untravelled'.[60]

IV. W(H)ITHER COMMON LAW EVIDENCE?

Published a decade later, ELA largely adopted the conceptual framework and modelling methodology pioneered in FoJ, but in this book Damaška focused much more systematically than before on the procedural structure and doctrinal peculiarities of common law evidence and fact-finding. To understand why, on Damaška's account, the common law's complex evidentiary superstructure had by the late 20th century found itself 'adrift', it was necessary for ELA to identify the features of Anglo-American legal process which had hitherto provided common law evidence with secure institutional moorings.

This exercise first called for a note of methodological explanation and some preliminary conceptual clarification. Damaška emphasised that, as in FoJ, his approach would be 'predominantly analytical and interpretive',[61] rather than historical: that is, he set out to explain the meaning and significance of contemporary common law evidence rather than investigating the causal factors responsible for its historical evolution. Frequent recourse to 'the comparative looking glass' to examine features of Anglo-American evidence and proof so basic to our 'procedural architecture that we live by them – and, by the same token, rarely notice them',[62] would be

[58] FoJ 66.

[59] See further, D Nelken (ed), *Contrasting Criminal Justice: Getting from Here to There* (Aldershot, Ashgate, 2000); P Roberts, 'On Method: The Ascent of Comparative Criminal Justice' (2002) 22 *Oxford Journal of Legal Studies* 539.

[60] FoJ 66. I do have further reservations about the methodology of FoJ, in particular regarding its use of normative moral and political theory, but space precludes their elaboration here.

[61] ELA 3.

[62] ELA 5.

another methodological trade mark. Comparative analysis was immediately put to work in qualifying the 'gross exaggeration'[63] that exclusionary rules of evidence are unique to common law procedural systems. In fact, the exclusion of information procured through breaches of rights or other procedural impropriety – those exclusionary standards characterised by Wigmore as 'rules of extrinsic policy'[64] – is commonplace in Continental jurisprudence,[65] which also concedes broad testimonial privileges to potential witnesses.[66] But if analysis is pursued with greater subtlety and sophistication, truly distinctive features of common law evidence and proof do emerge when viewed in comparative perspective:

> To an outsider looking in, three broad tendencies of Anglo-American evidence law appear to express its most distinctive properties. First is the complexity of evidentiary regulation, especially its departure from methods of inquiry that prevail in general social practice. Second is the great sensitivity of the law to the possible misuse of evidence – a sensitivity most prominently manifested in the rejection of probative material on the theory that it might be overvalued or might exert a biasing effect on the decision maker. The last is the pronounced aspiration of Anglo-American law to structure the fact-finders' analysis of evidence.[67]

These, then, are the features which were said to lend common law evidence its distinctive character, and whose institutional logic and alleged recent vulnerability stood in need of explanation.

Thayer popularised the notion that common law evidence is the 'child of the jury system'.[68] Damaška, however, lined up with those contemporary theorists who regard this as, at best, only a very partial explanation.[69] For Damaška, the truly salient feature of trial by jury for the logic of common

[63] ELA 12.

[64] JH Wigmore, 8 *A Treatise on the Anglo-American System of Evidence in Trials at Common Law* 3rd edn (Boston, Little, Brown & Co, 1940; revised by JT McNaughton 1961).

[65] See, eg, D Giannoulopoulos, 'The Exclusion of Improperly Obtained Evidence in Greece: Putting Constitutional Rights First' (2007) 11 *International Journal of Evidence & Proof* 181; EA Tomlinson, 'The Saga of Wiretapping in France: What it Tells Us About the French Criminal Justice System' (1993) 53 *Louisiana Law Review* 1091; W Pakter, 'Exclusionary Rules in France, Germany and Italy' (1985) 9 *Hastings International and Comparative Law Review* 1; CM Bradley, 'The Exclusionary Rule in Germany' (1983) 96 *Harvard Law Review* 1032.

[66] ELA 12–14.

[67] ELA 24.

[68] JB Thayer, *A Preliminary Treatise on Evidence at the Common Law* (Boston, Little, Brown & Co, 1898) 180–81 and 508–9.

[69] To similar effect, see P Roberts and A Zuckerman, *Criminal Evidence* (Oxford, OUP, 2004) 38–9; F Schauer, 'On the Supposed Jury-Dependence of Evidence Law' (2006) 155 *University of Pennsylvania Law Review* 165; W Twining, *Theories of Evidence: Bentham & Wigmore* (London, Weidenfeld & Nicolson, 1985). For historical discussion emphasising mutually reinforcing procedural factors, see JH Langbein, 'Historical Foundations of the Law

law evidence was not so much the infusion of lay standards of decision-making into legal adjudication, but rather the functional bifurcation of the trial court into two separate components. Where legal norms are applied by professional judges but fact-finding is entrusted to lay jurors, the opportunity is created for meaningful exclusion of evidence obtained in breach of evidentiary norms. If, say, an improperly obtained admission or inadmissible hearsay statement is proffered in evidence, the judge can exclude it in *voire dire* proceedings without the jury ever becoming aware of its existence. Tainted or otherwise suspect information is thereby categorically and effectively quarantined and prevented from infecting the jury's ultimate verdict. Setting aside for present purposes the durability of rationales for particular exclusionary doctrines, this institutional separation will tend to support the proliferation of technical legal standards of admissibility to an extent that a unified fact-finding and law applying tribunal cannot plausibly sustain. Once a fact-finding tribunal has already heard (sticking with the same examples) an unlawfully obtained confession or hearsay statements of dubious provenance it makes little sense to talk about such information being 'inadmissible', though the tribunal will probably still want to insist that tainted information has exerted little or no influence on its decision-making in the instant case. In a unified trial court, such as one finds in Continental European jurisdictions utilising collegiate benches of professional magistrates or 'mixed panels' of judges and lay jurors, technical standards of admissibility should be expected to give way to 'naturalistic' precepts of rational inference, proof and fact-finding.

Damaška characterised the bifurcated trial court as the first of three 'pillars' of common law evidence. His second pillar was the concentrated, 'main event' trial which, as we previously learnt in FoJ, is a concomitant of a relatively 'privatised' form of justice with substantial lay input. Owing to the comparative lack of preparation of evidence and testimony prior to trial, and in particular to the absence of any neutral evidence-gathering and fact-checking official inquiry on the Continental model, Anglo-American legal process came to adopt a pronounced sceptical attitude towards proffers of evidence by the litigant-parties.[70] Unless information purporting to bear on the matters in dispute could be authenticated, paradigmatically by the oath of a percipient witness,[71] it was liable to be excluded from the common law trial altogether:

of Evidence: A View from the Ryder Sources' (1996) 96 *Columbia Law Review* 1168; S Landsman, 'From Gilbert to Bentham: The Reconceptualization of Evidence Theory' (1990) 36 *Wayne Law Review* 1149.

[70] Cf EJ Imwinkelried, 'The Worst Evidence Principle: The Best Hypothesis as to the Logical Structure of Evidence Law' (1992) 46 *University of Miami Law Review* 1069.

[71] Hence, 'the principle of orality': see P Roberts and A Zuckerman, *Criminal Evidence* (Oxford, OUP, 2004) ch 6.

> Procedural concentration is thus the strongest rationale for the characteristic demand by common law procedural systems that a secure foundation be laid under the rules for the development of evidence. So long as causes come before the adjudicator without extensive prior investigation, these preludes to proof-taking have strong credentials indeed: they provide an important guaranty of decisional rectitude.[72]

The third pillar of common law evidence identified by Damaška in ELA was adversary process itself, an artefact of reactive government and its preference for legal process orientated towards dispute-resolution, as FoJ had already painstakingly explained. Competitive proof-taking breeds a contentious spirit[73] in which the parties each insist on strict application of the rules against their opponent. And robust procedural rules are urgently required to keep the parties' self-serving evidence-gathering activities and litigation strategies within reasonable bounds, lest a forensic free-for-all should sever any plausible connection with truth-finding in adjudication,[74] which in turn would undermine the predictability and security of legal entitlements and the finality of court verdicts – a vision of Armageddon for the reactive state. In a party-driven legal process 'it is vitally important that each party have an immediate opportunity to challenge sources of information presented by the opponent',[75] since partisan proof is inherently biased and state officials are not equipped, or even allowed,[76] to test its evidential basis thoroughly. Each of these adversarial tendencies is exacerbated when professional advocates come on the scene, in England from the later 18th century onwards, from which point the quantity and complexity of evidentiary norms appears to have increased exponentially.[77] Partisan proof, characterised by the forensic clash of two competing 'cases' unknown to Continental jurisprudence,[78] predictably encourages the development of a normative framework to regulate highly stylised forms of witness examination and cross-examination, which in many respects depart from what would normally be regarded as cognitively optimal fact-finding conditions. 'Attempts to elicit facts in the cross fire of partisan proof-taking', Damaška observed, 'can produce in this confrontational

[72] ELA 64.

[73] S Landsman, 'The Rise of the Contentious Spirit: Adversary Procedure in Eighteenth Century England' (1990) 75 *Cornell Law Review* 497.

[74] Cf C Nesson, 'The Evidence or the Event? On Judicial Proof and the Acceptability of Verdicts' (1985) 98 *Harvard Law Review* 1357.

[75] ELA 79.

[76] ME Frankel, 'The Search for the Truth: An Umpireal View' (1975) 123 *University of Pennsylvania Law Review* 1031.

[77] JH Langbein, *The Origins of Adversary Criminal Trial* (Oxford, OUP, 2003).

[78] ELA 91–93: 'This highly artificial and formalized mode of supplying the fact finder with information is alien to the Continental procedural tradition, according to which the division of proof-taking into two evidentiary versions of the case is unknown: proof-taking is always structured as a single integrated inquiry presided over by the bench'.

context more heat than light'.[79] Notably, in the context of this discussion, the pervasive influence of adversary process on normative development in the common law tradition encourages the Law of Evidence to be conceptualised as a unified whole, transcending the jurisprudential taxonomies and institutional balkanisation which have parcelled out substantive laws into discrete fields of practice and analysis. Somewhat idiosyncratically, 'the law of evidence appears as a subject suitable to be treated as a unified field of regulation and study'.[80]

The main contours of Damaška's argument in ELA can now be discerned. Common law evidence, it was argued, rests on the 'three pillars' of bifurcated trial court, concentrated proceedings and adversary process. The continued vitality of 'the Anglo-American distinctiveness in matters of evidence'[81] would therefore seem to depend upon the support it derives from these architectural features of common law adjudication; and if the pillars should weaken or crumble, the whole elaborate superstructure of common law evidentiary norms might be in danger of tumbling down:

> Erode any of these three pillars, and the rationale for the most characteristic admissibility rule of Anglo-American evidence [ie the hearsay prohibition] is seriously weakened. Erosion of these three pillars has been, however, the central tendency of the twentieth century. If the process advances much further, it could threaten the stability of the whole normative edifice.[82]

There is no shortage of readily-available empirical data to support Damaška's thesis of erosion. Trial by jury rapidly declined across the common law world in the latter part of the twentieth century,[83] even in the United States where jury trial is a constitutional right in *civil* as well as criminal proceedings.[84] The bifurcated trial court has consequently lost ground to institutional variations on the unified law-applying and fact-finding tribunal, such as US bench trials[85] and the 'Diplock' courts in Northern Ireland,[86] not forgetting that most criminal cases in England and Wales are tried by lay magistrates advised by a legally-qualified clerk – a procedural

[79] ELA 100 (footnote omitted).
[80] ELA 109.
[81] ELA 142.
[82] ELA 126.
[83] S Lloyd-Bostock and C Thomas, 'The Continuing Decline of the English Jury' in N Vidmar (ed) *World Jury Systems* (Oxford, OUP, 2000).
[84] The Seventh Amendment to the US Constitution provides that in 'Suits at common law, where the value in controversy shall exceed twenty dollars, the right of trial by jury shall be preserved…' The Sixth Amendment guarantees that '[i]n all criminal prosecutions, the accused shall enjoy the right to a speedy and public trial, by an impartial jury…'
[85] S Doran, JD Jackson and ML Seigel, 'Rethinking Adversariness in Nonjury Criminal Trials' (1995) 23 *American Journal of Criminal Law* 1.
[86] J Jackson and S Doran, *Judge Without Jury: Diplock Trials in the Adversary System* (Oxford, OUP, 1995).

configuration capable of replicating the bifurcated trial court's exclusionary solution to inadmissible evidence only very imperfectly.[87] Visible decline of trial by jury appeared to Damaška to presage the entropy of common law evidence:

> As the tribunal whose peculiar organisation supported classical evidentiary arrangements is thus marginalised, many rules of evidence are now applied in settings where their original raison d'être is no longer certain ... Arrangements and modes of argument that are imbued with pragmatic meaning in jury trials survive in multiplying nonjury contexts mainly by force of habit, dwindled in stature to mere formalities perpetuated by the inertia of the members of the legal profession ... Having ceased to carry most of the structural weight, the oldest prop of common law evidence seems currently in most procedural contexts more ornamental than functional.[88]

The temporal parameters of concentrated trial proceedings have meanwhile been extended through increasingly interventionist judicial trial management (principally motivated by the desire for greater efficiency in litigation)[89] and more demanding pre-trial disclosure obligations.[90] Enhanced opportunities for pre-trial preparation and a more 'episodic' approach to fact-finding go hand-in-hand with declining lay involvement in adjudication.[91] Even party-control of adversary process – the ultimate talisman of Anglo-American legality – is being eroded by the expanding role of trial and appellate judges with a newly-acquired appetite for demanding factually accurate verdicts,[92] particularly in criminal proceedings where the fundamental orientation of adjudication towards policy-implementation (foretold in FoJ) is gradually becoming more evident and influential:

[87] Cf P Darbyshire, 'Previous Misconduct and Magistrates' Courts – Some Tales from the Real World' [1997] *Criminal Law Review* 105; M Wasik, 'Magistrates: Knowledge of Previous Convictions' [1996] *Criminal Law Review* 851.

[88] ELA 127, 129.

[89] J McEwan, 'Co-operative Justice and the Adversarial Criminal Trial: Lessons from the Woolf Report' in S Doran and JD Jackson (eds), *The Judicial Role in Criminal Proceedings* (Oxford, Hart, 2000).

[90] P Duff, 'Disclosure in Scottish Criminal Procedure: Another Step in an Inquisitorial Direction?' (2007) 11 *International Journal of Evidence & Proof* 153; M Redmayne, 'Disclosure and its Discontents' [2004] *Criminal Law Review* 441; R Leng, 'The Exchange of Information and Disclosure' in M McConville and G Wilson (eds), *The Handbook of the Criminal Justice Process* (Oxford, OUP, 2002).

[91] Cf FoJ 52–3: '[U]nless concentrated trials are imposed on judicial bureaucracies, they are likely to adopt the piecemeal style.... Officials argue that observations made at trial must be checked against information methodically assembled over time and preserved in the written record. To decide independently from the file, solely on first impressions, is to decide with inadequate preparation, on flimsy and uncertain grounds'.

[92] Reinforced in England and Wales by the reformed test of 'safety' now applied in determining criminal appeals: see *R v Pendleton* [2002] 1 Cr App R 441, HL; *R v Togher, Doran and Parsons* [2001] 1 Cr App R 457, CA; N Taylor and D Ormerod, 'Mind the Gaps:

> The greater judicial involvement in fact-finding, even if it falls well short of leading to independent investigations, alters the adversary climate of the trial … [T]he court's influence on proof-taking grows and dilutes the adversary flavour of evidentiary arrangements.[93]

With its first supporting pillar greatly diminished in stature and the second leaning heavily on the third,[94] which itself betrayed signs of serious structural stress, Damaška's prognosis for common law evidence concluded on a note of 'crisis and impending doom'. The bleak *denouement* advertised in this essay's introduction can now be quoted in full:

> With jury trials marginalised, procedural concentration abandoned, and the adversarial system somewhat weakened, the institutional environment appears to have decayed that supplied distinctive features of common law evidence with a strong argumentative rationale. As a result, doctrines and practices widely associated with Anglo-American fact-finding style are now often deprived of a convincing theoretical basis. In its absence, shorn of adequate justification, they face the danger of becoming antiquated period pieces, intellectual curiosa confined to an oubliette in the castle of justice.[95]

Then as now, this was an arresting, and doubtless for some alarming, thesis, developed within a magisterial frame of reference and punctuated by Damaška's inimitable stylistic flourishes and pyrotechnic fusillades. But for all its power of shock-and-awe, did the argument presented in ELA really establish that common law evidence was perilously 'adrift' from its institutional moorings? With the benefit of a decade's hindsight, I suggest it did not. There are, moreover, methodological as well as political, moral and pragmatic reasons for challenging the cogency of Damaška's portentous thesis.

The first thing to notice is that Damaška's own analysis was in some ways at odds with his more alarmist conclusions. Indeed, he was careful to qualify his thesis at various key junctures, conceding that '[a]ctivist impulses have so far only sporadically contributed to the relaxation of the litigants' grip on the legal process'[96] such that the crucial

Safety, Fairness and Moral Legitimacy' [2004] *Criminal Law Review* 266; JC Smith, 'Appeals Against Conviction' [1995] *Criminal Law Review* 920.

[93] ELA 135, 138.

[94] ELA 134: 'Once procedural concentration has been abandoned, this pillar no longer carries the weight of the original evidentiary edifice. What prevents it from disintegrating and crumbling in changed circumstances is only the peculiar mode of trial preparation entrusted to partisan lawyers. But since this mode of preparation is an aspect of the contemporary adversary process, the second pillar of the common law evidence rationale has become dependent upon the third'.

[95] ELA 142.

[96] ELA 138.

> third [adversarial] pillar is far from collapsing. In addition to forces of habit and tradition, it is bolstered now by the pressing needs of court systems clogged by swelling caseloads.[97]

Furthermore, on Damaška's own account, adversarial culture had made gains as well as suffering set-backs in recent decades, sometimes as a direct consequence of the erosion of the other two pillars. Less concentrated trial proceedings have extended adversarial litigation styles and strategies into the pre-trial process, for example; and in this connection, Damaška's observations regarding the significance of plea bargaining and negotiated settlements[98] could be compounded by invoking recent developments in English criminal proceedings affecting custodial interrogation,[99] charging practice,[100] pre-trial disclosure,[101] and witness preparation.[102] Once it is conceded that the recent fortunes of adversary culture are marked by gains as well as losses on the balance sheet, we cannot arrive at any final accounting without constructing some appropriate metric for making comparative judgements of aggregate 'adversariness' at different points in time. But this ambitious enterprise was not even attempted by Damaška in ELA.

Perhaps the attempt was never made, moreover, because such an exercise would be insufferably complex, methodologically intractable and, quite possibly, ultimately futile. What would it mean to say that a whole legal culture or system was 'more' or 'less' adversarial than it was at some point in the past? There is an immediate suspicion that making such aggregative judgements would require incommensurable factors to be weighed in the same balance,[103] or at least that crucial distinctions would be submerged in sweeping generalisations. A more fine-grained, empirically-grounded analysis might conclude, for example, that whilst civil proceedings (or some subset of civil process, for example, 'administrative law claims against government bureaucracies') became markedly less adversarial in the closing decades of the 20th century, Anglo-American criminal litigation

[97] ELA 141.

[98] ELA 134.

[99] JD Jackson, 'Silence and Proof: Extending the Boundaries of Criminal Proceedings in the United Kingdom' (2001) 5 *International Journal of Evidence & Proof* 145.

[100] See ID Brownlee, 'The Statutory Charging Scheme in England and Wales: Towards a Unified Prosecution System?' [2004] *Criminal Law Review* 896.

[101] See above, n 90.

[102] Office of the Attorney-General, *Pre-Trial Witness Interviews by Prosecutors – Report* (December 2004): cf L McGowan, 'Prosecution Interviews of Witnesses: What More will be Sacrificed to "Narrow the Justice Gap"?' (2006) 70 *Journal of Criminal Law* 351; L Ellison, 'Witness Preparation and the Prosecution of Rape' (2007) 27 *Legal Studies* 171.

[103] Incommensurability is a sprawling topic which we cannot get to grips with here, but the basic thought is this: if the meaning and value of adversariness are distinctive to particular types of legal proceedings and their related goals and ideals, then trying to measure a gain in adversariness in, say, small claims personal injury actions against a loss of adversariness in, say, criminal litigation may be, not just difficult, but essentially incoherent.

remained, in may respects, as trenchantly adversarial as it ever was. To be sure, Damaška was well-aware of this deviating subplot in his story:

> As arrangements tailored to jury trials are dethroned from their exalted position, common law evidence as we now know it is likely to be *confined to a narrower sphere, perhaps serious criminal cases*, or even completely discarded.[104]

Suppose for the sake of argument that this assessment is broadly correct in relation to national legal process, taken in the round. One might nonetheless still insist that 'the real story' – at least for certain audiences – is the continued vitality of party-dominated process and adversarial culture in (serious) criminal cases. It may be a highly significant feature of recent Anglo-American jurisprudential thought that a sharper differentiation between civil and criminal procedure, so long associated with Continental legal theory,[105] is emerging as a serious rival to the traditional common law orthodoxy of a unified Law of Evidence[106] – and this without challenging the essentially adversarial caste of Anglo-American criminal litigation. Indeed, sharper conceptual differentiation might be regarded as partially insulating criminal process from the declining party-dominance and expanding judicial case-management which today characterise Anglo-American civil proceedings.[107]

This example shows why conceding the continued vitality of pockets of adversarial culture unavoidably complicates, and problematises, an aggregated bird's-eye view of legal process. In order to draw empirically well-grounded conclusions about the character of a particular legal system it would be necessary to try to assess the relative contributions of different types of legal proceedings to the prevailing national scene, particularly bearing in mind that 'serious criminal cases' tend to exert a disproportionate influence on the character and temper of a nation's legal culture. After all, high-profile criminal trials – Louise Woodward; OJ Simpson; Enron – loom much larger in the public imagination, even though they constitute only the very tip of the litigation iceberg, than the dark mass of civil and administrative actions which swells, unobtrusively, below the media-filtered waterline of public consciousness. Damaška did not enter these methodologically turbulent waters, preferring instead to rest his erosion thesis on rough holistic impressions of quantitative legal change.

104 ELA 149 (emphasis supplied).

105 Cf ELA 110: 'Where mainstream Anglo-American thought embraced the idea of a single, over-arching purpose of legal proceedings, Continental thought was in the habit of sharply separating the purposes of civil and criminal justice. The contrast in thinking about the aims of adjudication still affects evidence'.

106 See, further, P Roberts and A Zuckerman, *Criminal Evidence* (Oxford, OUP, 2004) ch 1; but cf J Jackson, 'Taking Comparative Evidence Seriously' in P Roberts and M Redmayne (eds), *Innovations in Evidence and Proof* (Oxford, Hart Publishing, 2007).

107 A Zuckerman, *Zuckerman on Civil Procedure: Principles of Practice* 2nd edn (London, Sweet & Maxwell, 2006).

There is a further methodological difficulty in evaluating Damaška's erosion thesis, relating to the choice of baseline for measuring a legal system's 'standard' or prototypical degree of adversariness. On what non-arbitrary basis could two discrete points in time be selected for the purposes of making a comparison between a legal system's adversariness 'now' and 'then'? When was adversarial legal culture at its zenith in Anglo-American law? Or at its lowest ebb? Is the high-point, or the mean-average, the appropriate baseline for making global comparisons? I do not know how one would even begin to go about answering such questions. Legal change is an inherent feature of legal culture. The law is a living instrument, and when it stops changing to meet the exigencies of the day it tends to atrophy and enter terminal decline. The common law tradition arose in the first place partly because the energies of Roman law were finally dissipated in the cloisters of scholasticism. ELA concludes with this rather enigmatic prediction:

> The new Anglo-American method of establishing facts in adjudication will thus most likely be the product of slow adaptation of traditional institutions to the changing environment. And the cracking pillars of common law evidence examined in the pages of this book will most likely be repaired – or replaced – by domestic masons and by indigenous building material. What lineaments the new construction will assume is of course unforeseeable ...[108]

Damaška presumably regarded these remarks as a suitably open-ended coda to his book's central theme, but it is tempting to read this passage as a moment of revelation tantamount to comprehensively deconstructive auto-critique. If common law evidence is changing through gradual, evolutionary adaptation to prevailing circumstances, as it always has and presumably always will, in what sense is 'the distinctive character of the common law fact-finding process'[109] an artefact of 'decaying institutions'[110] facing 'crisis and impending doom'?[111] Why is common law evidence 'adrift', and not merely adjusting its course in response to the fluctuating demands of political, social and technological influences on modern litigation? Whilst Damaška's diagnosis of procedural change is insightful and in many respects compelling, the pessimism of his prognosis seems to leap beyond any clearly visible signs of pathology.

Damaška did not indicate any temporal limits on the predicted demise of common law evidence, an omission which brings to mind Keynes' bromide that, in the long run, we are all dead. Historical experience teaches that

[108] ELA 152.
[109] ELA 3.
[110] ELA 150.
[111] ELA 142.

procedural law will change dramatically over the course of a century;[112] a fifty year prognosis would be more than sufficiently ambitious. What might English criminal litigation look like in fifty years' time? English law has just undergone the most extensive reform of criminal hearsay and character evidence for at least a century; and some of the provisions of the Criminal Justice Act 2003, the reforming statute in question, are in keeping with Damaška's erosion thesis. There is in general greater receptivity to both hearsay and evidence of the accused's extraneous misconduct,[113] and the common law's studiously-cultivated conceptual dichotomy between (i) facts in issue and (ii) evidence and questions on collateral issues has been substantially denatured.[114] On the other hand, there is no indication of reduced technical complexity[115] – quite the reverse, in several respects – and the determination of admissibility remains a focal point of criminal trials. Even if hearsay or character evidence turn out, on closer inspection, to be admissible, it is still necessary for advocates and judges to conceptualise information correctly as hearsay or non-hearsay, 'bad character' evidence or otherwise, as a prelude to debating its suitability for presentation to the jury. Controversial changes to the privilege against self-incrimination introduced by the Criminal Justice and Public Order Act 1994 paint a similarly contradictory picture. In permitting greater evidential use of testimonial and pre-trial silence the 1994 Act arguably[116] conforms with a policy-implementing (crime control) agenda. But this has been accompanied by a raft of expanding jury directions of almost mind-boggling complexity – the type of forensic reasoning rules which Damaška characterised as uniquely idiomatic to common law evidence.[117] Recent modifications to the ways in which certain witnesses testify in English criminal trials, utilising modern video and digital technologies, do

[112] In 1900, for example, England did not have a criminal appeal court (let alone a Criminal Cases Review Commission), jury service was limited to property-holders, it was unclear whether the Crown bore the burden of proof on self-defence, duress and other denials of constitutive elements of the offence, police impropriety never resulted in the exclusion of evidence, and the accused had only just become generally competent as a witness in his own defence.

[113] See Roberts and Zuckerman, above n 106, chs 11–12.

[114] CJA 2003, ss 119–120.

[115] Cf ELA 12 (footnote omitted): 'Markedly less technical in both [civil and criminal] branches of adjudication, Continental fact-finding presents a stark contrast to the common law. The technical character of evidentiary regulation... is indeed one of the leitmotifs of the present volume...'

[116] Providing that drawing inferences from silence actually does improve the factual accuracy of verdicts in criminal adjudication, at least in the aggregate. This, however, is contested: see M Redmayne, 'Analysing Evidence Case Law' in P Roberts and M Redmayne (eds), *Innovations in Evidence and Proof* (Oxford, Hart Publishing, 2007); R Leng, 'Silence Pre-trial, Reasonable Expectations, and the Normative Distortion of Fact-finding' (2001) 5 *International Journal of Evidence & Proof* 240.

[117] ELA 18–24: 'the Anglo-American repertoire of devices telling the fact finder how to process evidence strikes Continental observers as too rich and even inappropriate'.

represent something of a revolution in common law adjudication, and their implementation could well continue to expand in the coming years and decades.[118] By sanctioning the admissibility of what is technically hearsay, and extending proof-taking deep into the pre-trial process, these 'special measures' undoubtedly depart from common law orthodoxy. On the other hand, they have also introduced greater technical complexity into procedural law, without necessarily diminishing the essentially adversarial structure of common law proof. For as long as 'special measures' are self-consciously reserved for particularly vulnerable categories of witness, and live *viva voce* cross-examination is a normative expectation in all cases,[119] the party-dominated orality of criminal adjudication seems assured, even if proceedings are allowed to become somewhat less concentrated. Perhaps advocates will in future be required to abide by a more stringent code of ethics, emphasising the humane and decent treatment of witnesses alongside traditions of vigorous defence,[120] but this welcome development would be perfectly compatible with the basic structures of adversary process, just as purging criminal adjudication of some of its traditional sexism[121] barely augurs procedural apostasy. Further restricting access to jury trial has been a more or less constant objective of UK government policy – both Tory and Labour – since the major reclassification of indictable offences undertaken in the 1970s entrusted a slew of offences to the exclusive jurisdiction of the magistrates' courts.[122] However, further legislative initiatives in this vein have lately been strenuously resisted both inside and outside Parliament,[123] and even Tony Blair with his sizeable

[118] See P Roberts, D Cooper and S Judge, 'Monitoring Success, Accounting for Failure: The Outcome of Prosecutors' Applications for Special Measures under the Youth Justice and Criminal Evidence Act 1999' (2005) 9 *International Journal of Evidence & Proof* 269; Roberts and Zuckerman, above n 106, 277–289.

[119] It is notable in this regard that the most radical provision, which would have dispensed entirely with live cross-examination at trial in relation to certain witnesses, has never been brought into force: D Cooper, 'Pigot Unfulfilled: Video-recorded Cross-Examination under Section 28 of the Youth Justice and Criminal Evidence Act 1999' [2005] *Criminal Law Review* 456.

[120] On the state's 'duty of humane treatment' in criminal proceedings, see P Roberts, 'Theorising Procedural Tradition: Subjects, Objects and Values in Criminal Adjudication' in A Duff, L Farmer, S Marshall and V Tadros (eds), *The Trial on Trial Volume 2: Judgment and Calling to Account* (Oxford, Hart, 2006).

[121] For example, by reforming the law of corroboration: see Law Com No 202, *Criminal Law: Corroboration of Evidence in Criminal Trials* (HMSO, 1991), implemented by the Criminal Justice and Public Order Act 1994, ss.32–33.

[122] See M Zander, *Cases and Materials on the English Legal System*, 9th edn (London, Butterworths, 2003) 37–46.

[123] See, eg, S Enright, 'A Graceful Withdrawal?' (2000) 150 *New Law Journal* 1560 (27 October); J Straw, 'Changes to Mode of Trial' (2000) 150 *New Law Journal* 670 (12 May); M Zander, 'Why Jack Straw's Jury Reform Has Lost the Plot' (2000) 150 *New Law Journal* 366 (10 March); L Bridges, 'Welcome Conversion' (Letter) (2000) 150 *New Law Journal* 380 (17 March).

parliamentary majority was repeatedly forced to back down or compromise with the jury's defenders.[124] Finally, it is worth mentioning that features of criminal litigation which Americans tend to regard as recent departures from adversarialism, such as extensive pre-trial disclosure by the prosecution[125] and judicial summing-up on the facts,[126] have been routine and, in principle, uncontroversial procedural requirements in England and Wales for decades. All in all, certainly in its application to English criminal litigation,[127] I would wager that Damaška's analysis of 'evidence law adrift' will be about as accurate in 2047 as it was in 1997.

Damaška's final gambit in ELA was to invoke 'the creeping scientisation of factual inquiry'.[128] He predicted that the burgeoning impact of science and technology on all aspects of modern life would be a further nail in the coffin of traditional proof-taking procedures in Anglo-American jurisdictions:

> [T]he Anglo-American procedural environment is poorly adapted to the use of scientific information. If scientific methods continue to creep into the legal process, this feature, presently tolerable, could turn into a major irritant … [B]ecause the law follows the dominant epistemological temper of the historical period – albeit with some time lag – the scientisation of proof is likely to exacerbate the presently minor frictions within traditional procedural arrangements. Their further deterioration should be considered likely on this ground alone.[129]

There can be no question about the vital importance of science and technology in modern life, nor that scientific and other forms of expert testimony present stern challenges, as well as hitherto unimaginable opportunities, for fact-finding in contemporary legal process. But how the march of science buttresses Damaška's erosion thesis is not so easy to discern. Given the vital importance of securing moral and political legitimacy for criminal verdicts, and the intensifying differentiation of procedural forms (which Damaška himself announced[130]), the fact that 'the law

[124] R Taylor, M Wasik and R Leng, *Blackstone's Guide to the Criminal Justice Act 2003* (Oxford, OUP, 2004) ch 4.

[125] For the common law position prior to the enactment of the Criminal Procedure and Investigations Act 1996, see *R v Ward* (1993) 96 Cr App R 1, CA; *Practice Note (Criminal Evidence: Unused Material)* [1982] 1 All ER 734; (1982) 74 Cr App R 302.

[126] *R v Derek William Bentley (Deceased)* [2001] 1 Cr App R 307, CA; *R v Cohen and Bateman* (1909) 2 Cr App R 197, CCA.

[127] American scholars have made similar arguments in relation to US law: see, eg, Ronald J Allen and Georgia N Alexakis, ch 17; SR Gross, 'Law in the Backwaters: A Comment on Mirjan Damaška's *Evidence Law Adrift*' (1998) 49 *Hastings Law Journal* 369.

[128] ELA 143.

[129] ELA 147.

[130] ELA 148: 'The coming differentiation of procedural forms is likely to occur in all dimensions of the institutional environment… In the sphere of court organization, one should anticipate the emergence of a greater variety of both unitary and bifurcated tribunals.'

follows the dominant epistemological temper of the historical period' might be invoked as a significant *constraint* on institutional erosion or evidentiary drift. Society's attitudes towards science and technology are deeply ambivalent, if not self-contradictory, much in the way that nuclear fission might solve the world's energy crisis or just as easily blow us all to Kingdom Come. Within my suggested fifty-year temporal horizon, I do not envisage men and women in white coats replacing the criminal jury's verdict to any appreciable extent, though scientific evidence may well proliferate in criminal trials. And if it does, adversarial defence challenges and 'battles of experts' will proliferate as well.[131] English criminal courts currently show no signs of adopting excessively deferential attitudes towards scientific and other expert testimony.[132]

It seems fatuous to speculate about the future shape of common law evidence beyond a fifty year time horizon, precisely because the pace and magnitude of technological development have become so staggering in our time. For all I know, by 2050 the problems of proof-taking which common law evidence evolved to address may have been solved, conclusively, by androids with the ability to read brainwaves or the discovery of powers of precognition rendering criminal adjudication entirely obsolete.[133] More firmly anchored in the here-and-now, modern law's increasingly cosmopolitan character is another significant factor telling against Damaška's pessimistic prognosis for common law evidence. I will elaborate a little further on this observation by way of conclusion, having first summarised the main lines of argument presented in the preceding pages.

V. CONCLUSION: COMPARATIVE LEGAL METHOD AND COSMOPOLITAN LAW

This essay has contended that the innovative modelling methodology pioneered by Mirjan Damaška in FoJ remains a powerful tool for comparative analysis of legal process. Notwithstanding the inherent limitations of any generalizing method, interpreting legal procedures by reference to their overarching political ideals and distinctive structures of legal authority affords a unique vantage point for comparative scholarship which is

[131] To cite one, admittedly extreme, recent example: in *R v Harris* [2006] 1 Cr App R 5, CA, which involved four conjoined appeals all featuring evidence of 'shaken baby syndrome', the court heard testimony from 11 expert medical witnesses instructed by the prosecution and 10 defence experts in reply.

[132] P Roberts, 'The Science of Proof: Forensic Science Evidence in English Criminal Trials' in J Fraser and R Williams (eds), *Handbook of Forensic Science* (Cullompton, Devon, Willan Publishing, forthcoming).

[133] Actually, there are strong philosophical reasons for doubting even the possibility of any such eventuality, but we do not need to get into that here. The simple point is: who can really say what the future holds two generations down the line?

capable of generating genuinely novel insights. Damaška skilfully demonstrated how procedural form tends to reflect either the policy-implementing agendas of activist government or the conflict-solving orientation of reactive polities, as well as being moulded by hierarchical, vertically-ordered professional legal bureaucracies on the one hand, or co-ordinate, horizontally-ordered judiciaries equipped with extensive discretionary powers and substantial lay involvement in adjudication on the other. Damaška's models breathed new life into the staid dichotomy between 'inquisitorial' and 'adversarial' legal processes and, in my view, have stood the test of time as a persuasive riposte to those commentators who would too lightly dispense with the modelling methodology in general, or the concepts of 'adversarial' and 'inquisitorial' process in particular; provided that it is clearly understood that constructing ideal-typical models should be a starting-point, rather than the ultimate destination, of comparative legal analysis.

Published a decade later, ELA applied FoJ's conceptual framework to the more narrowly-circumscribed topic of evidence and proof, to produce an illuminating commentary on the affinities between particular institutional structures and their characteristic forms and styles of evidentiary regulation. The distinctive characteristics of common law evidence, shorn of some confounding myths, were shown to be related to the bifurcated trial court, temporally concentrated proceedings, and party-dominated adversarial culture, which are today recognised the world over as the hallmarks of Anglo-American legal process. However, where Damaška inferred that noticeable weakening of these 'three pillars' spelled doomed for common law evidence, I suggested that visible symptoms of decline are matched by countervailing indications of continued vitality, at least if we confine our gaze to English criminal adjudication within a realistic 50-year temporal horizon.

I will conclude by drawing attention to a contemporary jurisprudential development of enormous significance which, I believe, lends further support to my more ambivalent reading of empirical trends against Damaška's apocalyptic vision. Ten years on, a striking absence from the analysis presented in ELA, and one crucial determinant of common law evidence's future which Damaška evidently failed to predict, is the increasingly pervasive influence of supra-national norms and decisions by international courts on domestic law and legal process. Law's growing 'cosmopolitanism' is exemplified by the conjunction of an increasingly robust international human rights law implemented by supra-national judicial institutions such as the Strasbourg-based European Court of Human Rights, with the rapid evolution of transnational criminal justice policy-making. Such policies are co-ordinated through the overlapping initiatives of the United Nations and regional organisations such as the Council of Europe and the EU, utilising normal diplomatic channels, and

implemented through international judicial co-operation and mutual assistance at the operational level. (The global 'war on terror' is, of course, a major pretext and motivation for transnational penal policy-making and law enforcement.) Further institutional manifestations of cosmopolitanism in penal law can be seen in the UN's *ad hoc* criminal tribunals for the former Yugoslavia and Rwanda,[134] in proliferating examples of hybrid 'internationalised' tribunals from Sierra Leone to Iraq,[135] and – above all – in the International Criminal Court, now fully operational and running trials at its seat in The Hague.[136] An intriguing feature of such developments, for present purposes, is that the model of criminal adjudication to which all of these international courts more or less subscribe has pronounced adversarial features, in large measure because these characteristics were written into Article 6 of the European Convention on Human Rights (ECHR) (and therefore by extension into Article 14 of the International Covenant on Civil and Political Rights) by their British draftsmen.[137] To the extent that characteristically adversarial procedural guarantees, such as access to effective legal advice and representation and the right to cross-examine opposing witnesses,[138] are being incorporated into a prescriptive international standard of fair trial,[139] the scope for national jurisdictions to depart from adversary norms becomes increasingly restricted, at least for those states wishing to remain part of the law-abiding family of nations welcomed into the 'international community'.

Yet Damaška's analysis in ELA remained cosseted within the statal paradigm of classical comparative law, typified by the over-wrought idiom of 'transplants' between one national legal system and another.[140] Despite

[134] The ICTY and ICTR maintain excellent web-sites: <www.un.org/icty/> accessed 18 June 2008; <www.ictr.org/> accessed 18 June 2008. For a concise introduction, see R Cryer, H Friman, D Robinson and E Wilmshurst, *An Introduction to International Criminal Law and Procedure* (Cambridge, CUP, 2007) ch 7.

[135] See CPR Romano, A Nollkaemper and JK Kleffner (eds), *Internationalized Criminal Courts: Sierra Leone, East Timor, Kosovo, and Cambodia* (Oxford, OUP, 2004).

[136] <www.icc-cpi.int/> accessed 18 June 2008. See Cryer *et al*, above n. 134, ch 8; A Cassese, P Gaeta and JRWD Jones (eds), *The Rome Statute of the International Criminal Court: A Commentary* (Oxford, OUP, 2002).

[137] G Marston, 'The United Kingdom's Part in the Preparation of the European Convention on Human Rights, 1950' (1993) 42 *International and Comparative Law Quarterly* 796, 811. The influential UK draft is reproduced in Council of Europe, *Collected Edition of the 'Travaux Préparatoires' of the European Convention on Human Rights* (The Hague, Martinus Nijhoff, 1976), vol III, 280–88.

[138] ECHR Art 6(3)(c) and (d); ICCPR Art 14(3)(d) and (e); ICC Statute Art 67(d) and (e).

[139] S Trechsel with SJ Summers, *Human Rights in Criminal Proceedings* (Oxford, OUP, 2005); CJM Safferling, *Towards an International Criminal Procedure* (Oxford, OUP, 2001); CM Bradley, 'The Emerging International Consensus as to Criminal Procedure Rules' (1993) 14 *Michigan Journal of International Law* 171.

[140] Cf M Damaška, 'The Uncertain Fate of Evidentiary Transplants: Anglo-American and Continental Experiments' (1997) 45 *American Journal of Comparative Law* 839. For further discussion, see M Langer, 'From Legal Transplants to Legal Translations: the Globalization of

frequently drawing unavoidably transnational contrasts between 'Anglo-American' and 'Continental' laws, institutions and procedures, ELA's implicit unit of analysis for judging the ebbing fortunes of common law evidence was the territorial national state. Thus, in a revealing footnote, Damaška mused:

> It is unlikely that the movement toward new institutional arrangements will proceed evenly or along the same path in all common law jurisdictions. There are many indications that the pace of change may be faster in England than in the United States. For one thing, England has been drawn into the vortex of European integration without a textually fixed constitution. In contrast to the United States, there is no entrenched document in England that can impose serious limits on open departures from existing institutional arrangements.[141]

I have already indicated my reasons for thinking that traditional features of common law evidence will find a secure home in English criminal litigation for at least the foreseeable future. Now viewed in cosmopolitan perspective, it can be seen that the UK's entanglement in 'the vortex of European integration' – reinforced by broader developments in international penal law – is quite likely to produce the opposite effects to those foretold by Damaška. To be sure, the point should not be overstated: for example, neither the ECHR nor the UK's own Human Rights Act 1998 guarantees trial by jury in criminal trials, unlike the US Bill of Rights. But, by the same token, Damaška seems to me to have overrated the significance of a national written constitution for the defence of procedural tradition,[142] whilst simultaneously underrating both the distinctive ideals of criminal justice as an inspiration for procedural design and the tenacity of English legal culture in a time of cosmopolitan law.

Globalisation theorists assure us that international pressures towards homogeneity (inspiring the 'McDonaldisation' of global culture and similar dystopian vistas[143]) are virtually always, in practical experience, subverted by local resistance and adaptive variation,[144] so that globalisation generates as much diversity as sameness in the bazaars of the global village.

Plea Bargaining and the Americanization Thesis in Criminal Procedure' (2004) 45 *Harvard International Law Journal* 1; D Nelken and J Feest (eds), *Adapting Legal Cultures* (Oxford, Hart Publishing, 2001).

[141] ELA 147 (n 10).

[142] In his implicit reverence for the US Constitution Damaška reveals himself more of an acculturated insider to local jurisprudential thought than his self-image as the wandering comparativist would strictly warrant. But what else should one expect? Even the master is occasionally seduced by the normative assumptions of his (adopted) home.

[143] G Ritzer, *The McDonaldization of Society* (Thousand Oaks, CA, Pine Forge Press, revised New Century Edition 2004).

[144] Eg, A McGrew, 'Globalization and Global Politics' in J Baylis, S Smith and P Owens (eds), *The Globalization of World Politics: An Introduction to International Relations*, 4th edn (Oxford, OUP, 2008); U Beck, *What is Globalization?* (Cambridge, Polity, 2000); W Twining, *Globalisation and Legal Theory* (London, Butterworths, 2000).

Likewise, cosmopolitan law – itself conceived as an artefact of globalisation – is caught between the homogenising pressures of an idealistic or market-driven internationalism and the quotidian demands of local conditions 'on the ground', where the ingenuity of human problem-solving in practical contexts (which are always, ultimately, 'local' to the problem-solvers[145]) tends to reinforce the durability of municipal expectations and traditions. These factors together perpetuate, and indeed reinvigorate and extend, the diversity and distinctiveness of national legal cultures.[146] English law, for example, can call upon deeply-rooted institutional and cultural resources in defence of its procedural traditions. Moreover, these indigenous resources have lately been fortified by a supra-national legal framework prescribing elements of adversary process as part of the international community's normative conception of a fair trial. Of course, to the extent that this normative ideal is implemented as well in Continental legal jurisdictions, it will be true to say that Anglo-American legal procedure, and even some aspects of common law evidence, will become less *distinctive* around the world. However, this prospect of global normative transmission, migration and transplantation more naturally conjures up an image of latter-day voyages of discovery and colonisation – sharper critics might call it a new or re-intensified era of Anglophone legal imperialism[147] – rather than Damaška's spectre of common law evidence adrift.

[145] Generally, see D Nelken, 'The Globalization of Crime and Criminal Justice' (1997) 50 *Current Legal Problems* 251; and see AS Godoy, 'When "Justice" is Criminal: Lynchings in Contemporary Latin America' (2004) 33 *Theory and Society* 621 for a particularly extreme version of 'local resistance'.

[146] For cogent demonstration of this thesis in relation to US-style plea-bargaining, see Langer, above n 140.

[147] Cf the critiques of critical comparativists such as U Mattei, 'A Theory of Imperial Law: A Study on US Hegemony and the Latin Resistance' (2003) 10 *Indiana Journal of Global Legal Studies* 383; G Frankenberg, 'Stranger Than Paradise: Identity and Politics in Comparative Law' [1997] *Utah Law Review* 259.

17

Utility and Truth in the Scholarship of Mirjan Damaška

RONALD J ALLEN AND GEORGIA N ALEXAKIS*

I. IN TRIBUTE TO PROFESSOR DAMAŠKA

IT IS A great honour to contribute to this book celebrating the scholarship of Professor Mirjan R Damaška, but it is humbling as well. In his four decades in the academy, Damaška has made substantial contributions to the understanding of western legal systems of the sort to which the rest of us can only aspire. Even for those of whom, like us, comparative scholarship is not a major endeavour, he remains an inspiring figure whose conceptual work has sharpened our understanding of our own institutions.

Damaška has spent his career with both feet firmly planted in a multitude of dichotomous worlds. He is a native of Croatia but has spent close to four decades teaching in the United States. He is a lawyer reared in a system of civil law and Continental procedure but has chosen to make his professional home in a common law country. He has written both about procedure and evidence and has interwoven his interests in these two topics with threads from both civil and criminal litigation.[1] His works are

* Much of the research for this article was done in partial fulfillment of a Senior Research Project done under the supervision of Professor Allen. We are greatly indebted to Steven Bierly, J.D. 2007, Northwestern University School of Law, Alison Buckly, J.D. 2008, Northwestern University School of Law, and Michele Machalani, J.D. 2008, Northwestern University School of Law, for their research assistance. We are also indebted to Professor John Jackson for reading and incisively commenting on an earlier draft of this essay.

[1] See, eg, MR Damaška, *The Faces of Justice and State Authority: A Comparative Approach to the Legal Process* (New Haven, Yale UP, 1986) (hereinafter '*Faces of Justice*'); MR Damaška, *Evidence Law Adrift* (New Haven, Yale UP, 1997); M Damaška, 'Evidentiary Barriers to Conviction and Two Models of Criminal Procedure: A Comparative Study' (1973) 121 *University of Pennsylvania Law Review* 506; M Damaška, 'Structures of Authority and Comparative Criminal Procedure' (1975) 84 *Yale Law Journal* 480; M Damaška, 'Of Hearsay and Its Analogues' (1992) 76 *Minnesota Law Review* 425; M Damaška, 'Propensity Evidence in Continental Legal Systems' (1994) 70 *Chicago-Kent Law Review* 55; M Damaška, 'The

steeped in analytics as well as history and have influenced legal scholars, political scientists, and sociologists alike. And perhaps most revealingly, his English writings are frequently punctuated with choice foreign phrases[2] – a useful reminder that it often takes his uniquely dualistic perspective to communicate an otherwise singular point. As he writes at the close of his introduction to his book *The Faces of Justice and State Authority: A Comparative Approach to the Legal Process*, '[I]t is hard to be at once comfortable everywhere and at home anywhere. *Quisquis ubique habitat nusquam habitat.*'[3]

Throughout his career, Damaška's ongoing struggle to be 'comfortable everywhere' has worked to his advantage and disadvantage. The highwater mark came with his magisterial book, *The Faces of Justice and State Authority*, and thus we concentrate on it here to pay tribute to Damaška's pathbreaking analytical work. In *Faces of Justice*, his familiarity with both the common and civil law systems allowed him to construct a conceptual model of institutional arrangements that has been cited repeatedly in the twenty years since its publication. His analysis culminated in a two-by-two framework (hierarchical versus co-ordinate authority; policy implementing versus conflict resolving state) that has proven useful to scholars, legal and otherwise, searching for a systematic way to organise an almost infinite amount of data concerning systems of justice and governance.

In the latter part of his career, Damaška moved beyond conceptual work – the value of which is measured primarily by utility – and focused instead on propositions with truth value – empirical work, in other words – although Damaška may not so conceive it.[4] Perhaps once again Damaška was acting as a role model for the rest of us, for during this same timeframe American legal scholarship grew increasingly restless with classic forms of conceptual legal analysis, and began importing methodologies from other disciplines, including an increased focused on empirical

Uncertain Fate of Evidentiary Transplants: Anglo-American and Continental Experiments' (1977) 45 *American Journal of Comparative Law* 839.

[2] See D Vagts and M Reimann, Book Review (1988) 82 *American Journal of International Law* 203, 203 (reviewing *Faces of Justices*) (writing that Damaška's 'text is rife with words and maxims in foreign languages (predominantly Latin), mostly without translation'); RD Friedman, 'Anchors and Flotsam: Is Evidence Law "Adrift"?' (1998) 107 *Yale Law Journal* 1921, 1922 (reviewing *Evidence Law Adrift*) ('He sprinkles the page with metaphors and, rather too liberally, foreign language phrases.').

[3] *Faces of Justice*, above n 15 (translating *Quisquis ubique habitat nusquam habitat* into, 'One who lives everywhere lives nowhere').

[4] What we mean by 'empiricism' or 'empirical' is the pursuit of propositions with truth value, using whatever tools are appropriate. See, eg, L Epstein and G King, 'The Rules of Inference (2002) 69 *University of Chicago Law Review* 1, 2–3 (explaining that 'empirical' research can mean more than merely quantitative work, adding that '[w]hat makes research empirical is that it is based on observations of the world – in other words, data, which is just a term for facts about the world').

studies. Here, the best example is Damaška's book, *Evidence Law Adrift*.[5] We thus concentrate on it in this essay as well, although we pay tribute to it differently than we do *Faces of Justice*.

In *Evidence Law Adrift*, Damaška attempts to demonstrate that the common law evidentiary regime is rapidly approaching a state of demise – that it is 'adrift'. Although Damaška's aspirations evolved from utility in *Faces of Justice* to truth in *Evidence Law Adrift,* his methodology did not change. Instead, he relied on the same conceptual approach employed in *Faces of Justice*, replacing that book's signature framework with the three-pillar foundation at the heart of *Evidence Law Adrift*. Moreover, he used a potpourri of anecdotal evidence, selected through no identified methodology, to flesh out those three pillars, to substantiate their existence, and to 'prove' their erosion. *Evidence Law Adrift* thus falls short of its objective of establishing the truth of its central proposition, an outcome almost preordained by the attempt to employ methodologies pertinent to conceptual analysis to the quite different enterprise of empiricism.

Ironically, and this is the deserved tribute to the book, even if *Evidence Law Adrift* does not succeed fully on its own terms, it nonetheless provides important guidance for the rest of us following in its wake, by, just as *Faces of Justice* did before it, sharpening our understanding of our own interests, our own institutions, and most deeply our own commitments to the pursuit of truth. It is also critically important as a cautionary tale to the academy – particularly to younger generations of legal scholars – of the differences between conceptual and empirical work and how the neglect of those differences can lead to difficulties. In that respect, *Evidence Law Adrift* remains a success for, like all of Damaška's work, it points the way for those who follow.

This essay studies the transition from *Faces of Justice* to *Evidence Law Adrift*. In Part Two, we pay tribute to *Faces of Justice* by highlighting its utility. In Part Three, we describe *Evidence Law Adrift*, but with an eye toward discussing its empirical shortfalls. Part Four contextualizes the central themes of this article within a broader discussion of current trends in the legal academy and the rapidly increasing role of empiricism in legal scholarship.

II. THE UTILITY OF *FACES OF JUSTICE AND STATE AUTHORITY*

In *Faces of Justice*, Damaška examines the procedure of common and civil law countries (in capitalist as well as socialist regimes) to develop a systematic understanding of how modern forms of justice manifest in different political contexts. This is not a truth-seeking endeavor. Damaška

[5] Damaška, above n 1.

sets out to prove no specific thesis. He focuses his efforts on developing a 'distinctive analytical framework' that can be used to understand the interplay of legal systems and structures of governmental authority. As he describes his objectives,

> An immense and bewildering subject opens up before one who contemplates the diversity of arrangements and institutions through which justice is variously administered in modern states.[6]

> Can [he asks] this stupendous diversity be made intelligible, or reduced to a manageable set of patterns? At a minimum, can a conceptual framework be developed to assist us in tracing similarities and differences in component parts?[7]

Utility, in other words, is his primary objective.

The scope of Damaška's enterprise in *Faces of Justice* is profoundly complex. Over the course of his book, Damaška touches upon dozens of variables: the legal rules at play in each system, the precise structure and relative rigidity of judicial hierarchies, the manner by which decisions are made, the 'professionalisation' of officials operating in the legal system, and the specific roles that lay people, private attorneys, and government attorneys play in the process. Each variable breaks down into a number of possibilities as a result of the variations that exist across the wide swath of countries that Damaška references – the United States, England, France, West Germany, the Soviet Union, and China. In *Faces of Justice*, in other words, Damaška is an organizer of concepts that in turn lend themselves to the organisation of information:

> Like that great classifier, Carl von Linné,[8] who brought order into the bewildering richness of plant life by devising a consistent hierarchy of plant properties that allows botanists to name and group every conceivable species, Damaška wants to construct procedural archetypes that will allow us to name the components of the most diverse existing procedural styles and group them into recognizable and meaningful patterns.[9]

The test of utility of Damaška's methodological approach is therefore obvious: Does it facilitate the organizing of unruly data? Just as von Linné's task did not call on him to discover new plant and animal species, but merely to organise those already in existence, so, too, Damaška's objective in *Faces of Justice* is not to create something new, but to

[6] *Faces of Justice*, above n 1.

[7] *Ibid* 3.

[8] Carl von Linné (also known as Carl Linnaeus) was an eighteenth century Swedish physician and botanist who developed the system of binomial nomenclature used to classify, organise, and name plants and animals. AE Chudley, 'History of Genetics Through Philately – Carl Linnaeus (Carl von Linné)' (2001) 60 *Clinical Genetics* 104, 104.

[9] I Markovits, 'Playing the Opposites Game: On Mirjan Damaška's *The Faces of Justices and State Authority*', (1988) 41 *Stanford Law Review* 1313, 1315n.9.

categorize that which already exists in a useful fashion. Or as Sean McConville writes: 'Damaška does not claim originality for the insights upon which he draws but rather for the way in which he combines and applies them.'[10]

The best evidence of the book's success is the number of scholars who have found it useful. Inga Markovits, for example, writes:

> [Damaška] has an extraordinarily good eye both for procedural details and for the general traits these details embody ... Thus, long before Damaška fills his four-boxed matrix with specific examples, we have been drawn into his game and have begun to classify procedural species according to his rules.[11]

And, she continues, the power of Damaška's framework is that others 'can easily apply it to phenomena not covered in his book',[12] a point she proceeds to prove by identifying other legal systems that Damaška does not reference but which she can readily place in his taxonomy. Detlev Vagts and Mathias Reimann also write admiringly of Damaška's conceptual scheme, which uses

> complexity and breadth to demonstrate that the traditional adversarial/inquisitorial dichotomy ought to be abandoned in favour of much more differentiated categories.[13]

And Martin Shapiro writes that Damaška does not present his model as 'a rigid set of large pigeon holes', with the expectation that '[a] particular nation's entire legal and political system need ... be put neatly in three and only three boxes.'[14] As a result, he continues

> Damaška's mode of analysis is often most fruitful when it deals with situations in which nations are partially changing from one category to another

or when a 'long established judicial hierarchy' has to be juxtaposed 'with emerging tendencies to reduce levels of state intervention in economic matters.'[15]

In short, we do not have to accept Damaška's framework as 'true'; we only have to accept it for what it is: a useful conceptual scheme that

[10] S McConville, Book Review (1998) 497 *Annals of the American Academy of Political and Social Science* 172, 173.

[11] Markovits, above n 9, 1319.

[12] *Ibid* 1321.

[13] Vagts & Reimann, above n 2, 207. See also GC Christie, *The Influence of Form on the Nature of Authority* (1989) 18 *Contemporary Society* 93, 93 ('Damaška does not deny that there is much truth contained in this traditional distinction; but this dichotomy is not rich enough to capture the complete range of differences between Anglo-American systems and other types of legal systems, let alone to capture the many different nuances in legal systems sharing a common ancestry.')

[14] M Shapiro, Book Review (1987) 35 *American Journal of Comparative Law* 835, 836.

[15] *Ibid.*

succeeds by ordering what was previously chaotic.[16] Damaška never set out to prove that his framework is the uniquely correct way of understanding how legal systems arise; he never sought to fit all empirical data into his two-by-two grid. He simply set out to provide a useful way of organizing the relevant information, a way that is heavily influenced by political context. The framework thus succeeds on its own terms.

The stakes have changed, though, by the time Damaška writes *Evidence Law Adrift*. He is no longer classifying. He is explaining, and predicting the demise of, the common law evidentiary regime by what purport to be accurate appraisals of its current condition. He no longer seeks to provide something useful; he instead articulates a state of affairs that he purports is true. This different enterprise calls for a different methodology, one that relies far less on conceptual analysis and far more on the kind of empirical data of which readers only saw glimmers in *Faces of Justice*.

We now turn to *Evidence Law Adrift* and its success in this brave new world.

III. *EVIDENCE LAW ADRIFT*: A SUMMARY AND CRITIQUE

> This is an accidental book.[17]

With this short, ready admission, Damaška begins *Evidence Law Adrift*, a 1997 book that grew out of a lecture Damaška gave nearly a decade before at a conference on the distinctiveness of common law evidence.[18] With an easy-to-grasp framework (one in which three pillars support the common law system's evidentiary regime) and a bold thesis (that these three pillars are slowly but surely eroding), Damaška's lecture surely entertained conference attendees while educating them on the distinctions between Anglo-American and Continental approaches to evidence.[19] As a fully fleshed out volume, however, *Evidence Law Adrift* disappoints, and our task here is to explain why.

[16] See, eg, G J. Fitzpatrick, Book Review (1987) 81 *American Political Science Review* 1385, 1386 (the value of Damaška's work is that '[i]t places much of what we already know about the administration of justice in a fresher perspective while identifying patterns and suggesting meanings not appreciated before'); McConville, above n 10, 173 ('Damaška ... succeeds in his objective of integrating disparate insights and providing a convincing analytical framework upon which more individualized studies might be modeled.').

[17] *Evidence Law Adrift*, above n 1, ix.

[18] *Ibid.*

[19] Professor Damaška uses the term 'Anglo-American' throughout *Evidence Law Adrift* in contrast to the Continental or civil law system, but his volume is trained on American evidence law. At various points, *Evidence Law Adrift* does discuss English law, but 'there is no discussion of evidence law in other "pure" common law jurisdictions, such as Australia, Canada (other than Quebec) or Ireland'. See N V Demleitner, 'More Than "Just" Evidence' (1999) 47 *American Journal of Comparative Law* 515, 518 (reviewing *Evidence Law Adrift*). We will focus only on the American system and make no claims about other common law jurisdictions.

Damaška's argument is straightforward:

> [A]s the pillars of common law procedure (juries, concentrated trials, party control) are eroded, our rules of evidence will be destabilised and will have to be reassessed,[20]

if not increasingly replaced with alternative approaches to evidence and procedure. Damaška purports to do more, though, than simply hypothesize that erosion could happen. Instead, he argues that 'cracks' already have appeared in the three traditional pillars of evidence law,[21] that this erosion is indeed so far advanced that it has been 'the central tendency of the 20th century',[22] and that if 'the process advances much further, it could threaten the stability of the whole normative edifice'.[23] To support his vision of a common law evidentiary apocalypse, Damaška points to an assortment of trends in the common law, organizing his observations by pillar, examining and dissecting their allegedly crumbling foundations in turn.

As admirably fecund as Damaška's work can be, one simultaneously fights with many of its assertions, wonders what justifies some, and rejects outright others. His too-neat structure invites one to question, for example, whether an analysis of historical, cultural,[24] constitutional,[25] or other factors,[26] or even the sheer force of inertia[27] might prove just as, or even more, telling. The sense unavoidably impinges that, however interesting, much of the discussion in *Evidence Law Adrift* simply is not true.

This, indeed, has been the focus of much of the criticism leveled against *Evidence Law Adrift*, or as Johannes Nijboer writes, 'all the details are true, but the plot is fiction'.[28] Nearly every reviewer of *Evidence Law*

[20] M Redmayne, Book Review (1998) 61 *MLR* 123, 125.

[21] *Evidence Law Adrift*, above n 1, 6.

[22] *Ibid* 126.

[23] *Ibid.*

[24] See JF Nijboer, 'Vision, Abstraction, and Socio-Economic Reality' (1998) 49 *Hastings Law Journal* 387, 393.

[25] For example, 'the Sixth Amendment to the United States Constitution, section 11(f) of the Canadian Charter of Rights and Freedoms, section 25 of the New Zealand Bill of Rights Act, and section 80 of the Australian Commonwealth Constitution act as brakes on any demise of the jury', one of the factors Damaška believes is contributing to the demise of the common law evidentiary regime. JD Jackson, 'Adrift But Still Clinging to the Wreckage: A Comment on Damaška's Evidence Law Adrift' (1998) 49 *Hastings Law Journal* 377, 380.

[26] See Friedman, above n 2, 1923–48 (discussing three factors that are quite different than Damaška's three pillars as the real rationale behind Anglo-American evidence law: Anglo-American countries' 'ideological commitment to individual rights', 'the Anglo-American tendency to legalized evidentiary issues, seeking to the extent feasible uniform results across cases' and 'an intellectual style that values analytical soundness far more than it does theoretical or practical simplicity').

[27] See S Gross, 'Law in the Backwaters: A Comment on Mirjan Damaška's *Evidence Law* Adrift' (1998) 49 *Hastings Law Journal* 369, 373 (citing *Michelson v US*, 335 US 469, 486 (1948)).

[28] Nijboer, above n 29, 390.

Adrift has offered a litany of empirical observations and data to offset Damaška's anecdotes. We add our own below to demonstrate that Damaška does not establish the truth of two of his critical propositions. In the subsequent section, we then generalize this demonstration to the book as a whole.

A. The Myth of the Vanishing Trial

We begin with Damaška's assertion that the American jury is disappearing and with it today's bifurcated courtroom. In its place, Damaška contends, we have an increased number of bench trials, settlements, and plea bargains, all of which have done away with both the common law judge's need to control the jury's verdict through exclusionary rules of evidence (Damaška's first pillar) as well as the common law courtroom's adversarial nature (Damaška's third pillar).

One can understand why Damaška might think that jury trials are a vanishing breed. After all, a veritable cottage industry of scholarship has cropped up around 'the vanishing trial',[29] or what John Lande has termed 'The Phenomenon Known as the Vanishing Trial, or TPKATVT'.[30] Marc Galanter, for example, has emphasised in federal courts the

> long-term and gradual decline in the portion of cases that terminate in trial and a steep drop in the absolute number of trials during the past twenty years.[31]

Brian Ostrom has examined similar jury-trial trends in state courts, concluding that

[29] See, eg, M Galanter, 'The Hundred-Year Decline of Trials and the Thirty Years War' (2005) 57 *Stanford Law Review* 1255; Marc Galanter, 'The Vanishing Trial: An Examination of Trials and Related Matters in State and Federal Courts' (2004) 1 *Journal of Empirical Legal Studies* 459; J Resnik, 'Failing Faith: Adjudicatory Procedure in Decline' (1986) 53 *University of Chicago Law Review* 494, 528–39 (describing the increased judicial enthusiasm for settlement); J Resnik, 'Managerial Judges' (1982) 96 *Harvard Law Review* 374 (describing the rise of managerial judges who negotiate more actively with the parties than did prior judges); BJ Ostrom, SM Strickland and PL Hannaford-Agor, 'Examining Trial Trends in State Courts: 1976–2002' (1982) 1 *Journal of Empirical Legal Studies* 755; MH Redish, 'Summary Judgment and the Vanishing Trial: Implications of the Litigation Matrix' (2005) 57 *Stanford Law Review* 1329.

[30] J Lande, 'Replace "The Vanishing Trial" with More Helpful Myths' (2005) 23 *Alternatives to the High Cost of Litigation* 161, 161 (2005). See also J Lande, 'Shifting the Focus from the Myth of "The Vanishing Trial" to Complex Conflict Management Systems, or I Learned Almost Everything I Need to Know About Conflict Resolution from Marc Galanter' (2005) 6 *Cardozo Journal of Conflict Resolution* 191; J Lande, 'The Vanishing Trial Report: An Alternative View of the Data' (2004) 10 No 4 *Dispute Resoution Magazine* 19.

[31] Galanter, above n 29, 1256.

> the number and rate of state court trials … [for] both jury and bench trials have declined over the last two decades despite substantial growth in the number of state court dispositions.[32]

The problem is that there is much contrary data.[33] For example, in the early and mid-1990s, prior to the publication of *Evidence Law Adrift*, an estimated 150,000–300,000 jury trials occurred annually in the United States,[34] and about 80 per cent of tort claims and 60 per cent of criminal cases that went to trial were tried before a jury.[35] In federal courts, 'jury trials have been a fairly constant proportion of all trials in the last three decades and, in criminal matters particularly, have comprised a majority of all trials.'[36] While Ostrom's study on trial trends in state courts suggests that trials in state courts are experiencing a slight decline, state courts handle a significantly greater number of trials than federal courts, which was the primary focus of Galanter's study.[37] A decline in the rate of trials in the federal system is just a blip in the total scheme.[38] In addition, although civil trial rates dropped by more than half, at least in those 22 states whose data from 1976–2002 was analyzed, that was 'primarily because the number of filings more than doubled during that [same] period'.[39] 'Like Mark Twain's reported death, accounts of the impending demise of the trial are exaggerated.'[40]

And there is more. While the trial may be 'vanishing' today, there was never much to vanish to begin with:[41] trials were never the norm in our system of litigation, as Lawrence Friedman persuasively writes.[42] Criminal

[32] Ostrom *et al*, above n 29, 773.

[33] LC Kirkpatrick, 'Evidence Law in the Next Millennium' (1998) 49 *Hastings Law Journal* (1998) 363, 365. And again, we are only talking of the American system. See above n 19.

[34] Kirkpatrick, *Ibid* 365, n.14-n.18, citing J Abramson, We, The Jury (Cambridge, Mass, Harvard UP, 1994) 251 (obtaining 150,000 estimate from researchers at National Center for State Courts) and JP Levine, Juries and Politics (Belmont, CA, Wadsworth, 1992) 36 (providing 300,000 estimate).

[35] *Ibid* 365, nn 14–18, citing BJ Ostrom and Neal B Kauder, *Examining the Work of State Courts, 1995: A National Perspective from the Court Statistics Project* (National Center for State Courts, 1996) 30, 57 (surveying state courts); Bureau of Justice Statistics Bulletin Pub No NCJ-151167, *Felony Sentences in State Courts, 1992* (1995) tbl 10 (1995).

[36] RC Park, *An Outsider's View of Common Law Evidence*, 96 *Michigan Law Review* (1998) 1486, 1494 and n 16 (1998) (reviewing *Evidence Law Adrift*).

[37] Lande, above n 30, 169–170 ('The lowest state court civil trial rate is substantially higher than the highest federal civil trial rate since 1962, which is 11.5%. Similarly, the number of state court trials dwarfs the largest number of federal civil trials shown in Galanter's report, which was 12,529 trials in 1985.').

[38] Ostrom *et al*, above n 29, 757.

[39] Lande, above n 30, 169, citing Ostrom *et al*, *Ibid.*

[40] *Ibid.*

[41] LM Friedman, 'The Day Before Trials Vanished' (2004) 1 *Journal of Empirical Legal Studies*. 689, 689.

[42] *Ibid.*

trials – and in particular, felony criminal trials – have been declining since 1800, replaced by the guilty plea.[43] By 1926, in Chicago,

> almost 80 per cent of the defendants who pled guilty, pled to a lesser offence – an almost sure sign of a deal;

and in the 1930s, 'in some jurisdictions, plea bargaining accounted for over 90 per cent of all convictions and that remains true today'.[44] The situation for civil cases is 'more or less analogous'.[45] 'Most tort cases have always ended in settlement',[46] and 'what is true of tort cases was also true of other categories of civil cases'.[47] In short, 'trials were the exception, never the rule'.[48] There may indeed be marginal changes occurring today, but neither of Damaška's propositions, the implicit one that trials were once the norm nor the explicit one that they are vanishing, has much empirical support.

Interestingly, it is not even clear whether the existence of jury trial matters for maintaining the rules of evidence. The paucity of such trials throughout history suggests to the contrary, and evidence law serves additional purposes than regulating jury trials. Most cases settle, and as Laird Kirkpatrick points out, '[t]he settlement value of a case may rise or fall depending on whether certain evidence will be allowed', just as the settlement value may hinge on the admissibility of

> evidence of other accidents involving the same product or the implementation of remedial measures by the defendant after the accident.[49]

In the criminal context,

> nothing influences the plea bargaining process more than pre-trial rulings by the trial judge on evidentiary matters, such as whether a defendant's concession or his criminal history will be admitted at trial.[50]

We know from economists that clarity fosters settlement – clarity which is fostered in turn by clear rules of admission and exclusion.[51] The actual implications of rules of evidence and their relationship to different kinds of dispute resolution is thus a marvelously complicated empirical question. Limited by his conceptual approach, Damaška never addresses its intricacies.

43 *Ibid* 691.
44 *Ibid.*
45 *Ibid* 693.
46 *Ibid.*
47 *Ibid.*
48 *Ibid.*
49 Kirkpatrick, above n 33, 366.
50 *Ibid.*
51 See generally GL Priest and B Klein, 'The Selection of Disputes for Litigation' (1984) 13 *Journal of Legal Studies* 1).

B. The Myth of the Managerial Judge

Damaška argues that the Anglo-American system's quintessentially adversarial spirit is being diluted because of a late 20th-century rise in the amount of public interest and class action suits litigated in American courts.[52] Damaška supports this proposition by relying almost exclusively on law review articles dating back to the 1970s,[53] thus mistaking short-term aberrations for true and stable propositions. Since that high-water mark of institutional litigation, the United States judicial system has settled back into long-term status quo, including a declining receptivity for public interest lawsuits in courts; mounting efforts to keep class actions out of state courts and thus to reduce their total number and significance; and an avalanche of state reforms – including requiring proof of malicious intent before awarding punitive damages, setting a cap on the amount of recoverable punitive damages, or even proscribing punitive damages altogether – that are partially motivated by the judicial system having effected too much policy.[54]

Starting in the mid-1980s, the federal judiciary grew increasingly hostile toward the kind of public interest litigation that Damaška claims is partially responsible for the steady demise of the adversarial system.[55] Courts no longer encourage far-reaching 'impact' lawsuits, and judges rarely become involved in the kind of 'institutional litigation'[56] that requires overseeing the operation of public institutions, such as schools, public housing projects, and prisons. Since the 1970s, the federal Legal Services Corporation (LSC), which funds the majority of legal services organisations across the country, has faced a series of funding cutbacks and advocacy restrictions[57]; by 1992, the 'federal appropriation for LSC was down almost one-third from its peak level in 1980',[58] and by 1996,

[52] See *Evidence Law Adrift*, above n 1, 135–52.

[53] *Ibid* 138 n.24, citing A Chayes, 'The Role of the Judge in Public Law Litigation' (1976) 89 *Harvard Law Review* 1281.

[54] See Congress Budget Office, US Congress, *The Effects of Tort Reform: Evidence from the States* 3, *available at* <http://www.cio.gov/ftpdoc.cfm?index=5549&type%20=1>. Thirty-four states have passed statutes limiting punitive damage awards: *Ibid* 7.

[55] See SL Cummings and IV Eagly, 'After Public Interest Law' (2006) 100 *Northwestern University Law Review* 1251, 1264–65.

[56] See generally T Eisenberg and SC Yeazell, 'The Ordinary and the Extraordinary in Institutional Litigation' (1980) 93 *Harvard Law Review* 465; DL Horowitz, 'Decreeing Organizational Change: Judicial Supervision of Public Institutions' (1983) *Duke Law Journal* 1265.

[57] *Ibid*. In 1996, LSC attorneys were prohibited from engaging in lobbying, challenging welfare reform legislation, claiming or collecting attorneys' fees, and participating in class action litigation. See Brennan Center for Justice, *Restricting Legal Services: How Congress Left the Poor with Only Half a Lawyer* (2000).

[58] *Ibid* citing AW Houseman and LE Perle, *Securing Equal Justice for All: A Brief History of Civil Legal Assistance in the US* (2003) 36, *available at* <http://www.clasp.org/publications/Legal_Aid_History.pdf> accessed 18 June 2008.

'funding was reduced to just under one-half of the 1980 level'.[59] Many public interest lawyers have given up pursuing sweeping public interest litigation aimed at promoting broad social change and have chosen instead to focus their efforts on non-legal activities, such as community organizing,[60] which leads to still fewer public interest lawsuits. Equally significant is the increased decentralisation and privatisation of regulatory authority that has occurred since the 1970s, a trend that has given private actors, rather than courts, a greater role in policy formulation and implementation.[61]

Damaška's perspective on class actions similarly lacks empirical support. He writes that judges in class actions and other forms of complex litigation become far more involved in the day-to-day management – an observation that has been corroborated by other legal scholars as well[62] – but he glosses over that a judge's role in supervising a class action is hardly the equivalent of a judge launching an independent inquisition or fact-gathering expedition,[63] and presents no evidence to suggest that the parties and their adversaries take a backseat in the discovery process. Moreover, Damaška's argument assumes that the common law system has few, if any, qualms about the growth of the class action – that this alleged movement toward a more policy-implementing, activist state is one that has been sanctioned by government officials. Dramatic evidence to the contrary is the passage of the Private Securities Litigation Reform Act 1995 ('PSLRA') – codified in both the Securities Act 1933 and the Securities Exchange Act 1934 – through which Congress intended to reduce the number of class actions in the securities area,[64] and the even more recent passage of the

[59] *Ibid* (citing A W Houseman, 'Civil Legal Assistance for Low-Income Persons: Looking Back and Looking Forward' (2002) 29 *Fordham Urban Law Journal* 1213, 1222 tbl 1).

[60] See generally *Ibid*; see also SL Cummings and IV Eagly, 'A Critical Reflection on Law and Organizing' (2001) 48 *University of California Los Angeles Law Review* 443; GP López, *Rebellious Lawyering: One Chicano's Vision of Progressive Law Practice* (Boulder, Colo, Westview Press, 1992); GN Rosenberg, *The Hollow Hope: Can Courts Bring About Social Change?* (Chicago, Chicago UP, 1991); SA Scheingold, *The Politics of Rights: Lawyers, Public Policy, and Political Change* (New Haven, Yale UP, 1974).

[61] See Cummings & Eagly, above n 55, 1285; Joel F. Handley, *Down from Bureaucracy: The Ambiguity of Privatization and Empowerment* (Princeton, Princeton UP, 1996); Jody Freeman, 'The Private Role in Public Governance' (2002) 75 *New York University Law Review* 543; O Lobel, 'The Renew Deal: The Fall of Regulation and the Rise of Governance in Contemporary Legal Thought' (2004) 89 *Minnesota Law Review* 342.

[62] For the classic piece on the relationship between 'managerial judging' and complex litigation, see J Resnik, 'Managerial Judging' (1986) 96 *Harvard Law Review* 374.

[63] Even in class actions where judges have taken on a highly managerial role – see eg, *Dow Chemical Co v Stephenson*, 539 US 111 (2003); *Anchem Products, Inc v Windsor*, 521 US 591 (1997); *Ortiz v Fibreboard*, 527 US 815 (1999) – the judges still did not cross the line into collecting evidence or eliciting testimony from witnesses.

[64] Private Securities Litigation Reform Act of 1995, 15 USC § 77z-1, 15 USC § 78u-4 (1998). The PSLRA operates to limit class actions at the early stages of litigation by staying discovery and other proceedings during any pending motion to dismiss. 15 USC §§ 77z-1(b)(1), 78 u-4(b)(3)(B).

Class Action Fairness Act 2005 ('CAFA').[65] The culmination of many years of debates over the appropriateness of the class action as a litigation device, [66] CAFA adopts the requirement of minimal diversity rather than complete diversity and grants federal courts original jurisdiction in class actions only if the amount in controversy exceeds five million dollars.[67] It thus makes it more difficult for a class action to be heard in state courts where judges may be more willing to certify a class action and to sanction damage awards granted by state-court juries.[68]

C. The Dynamic Generalised

The primary criteria of success for conceptual work are whether it is insightful and stimulating; by contrast, the primary criterion for empirical work is whether it establishes true propositions. The tension between these competing objectives is obvious in Damaška's treatment of jury trials and managerial judging; it also permeates the book as a whole. We give some illustrative examples here.

A scientist approaching the questions that interest Damaška – what are the distinctive features of American evidence law, and what are its prospects for the future? – would first begin by marshalling what we already know about the objects of inquiry. Damaška presents a wooden and bookish description of the American evidentiary process, does not systematically uncover much of the relevant empirical work, presents no empirical work concerning Continental systems, and disregards substantial evidence in conflict with his theses. We take these points in turn.

Damaška's description of the American evidentiary process would have sounded familiar to a law student in the middle of the 20th century. It emphasizes the 'legion' of exclusionary rules[69] designed to weed out evidence of low probative value, and gives special attention to the

[65] Class Action Fairness Act of 2005, Pub L No 109–2, 119 Stat 4 (codified as amended in scattered sections of 28 USC). For an overview of the Class Action Fairness Act, see generally DF Herr and MC McCarthy, 'The Class Action Fairness Act of 2005 – Congress Again Wades into Complex Litigation Management' (2005) 228 *FRD* 673.

[66] The Class Action Fairness Act was, in fact, the sixth attempt to pass legislation on class actions. The first bill was proposed in 1998, suggesting that public sentiment for the curtailment of class action was present at lest some time before then. See A Andreeva, 'Comment: Class Action Fairness Act of 2005: The Eight-Year Saga is Finally Over' (2005) 59*University of Miami Law Review* 385, 385–86.

[67] See Andreeva, above n 66; JM Callow Jr, 'The Class Action Fairness Act of 2005: Overview and Analysis' (2005) 52 *Federal Lawyer* 26, 26.

[68] See 28 USC § 1332(d)(2) and § 1332(d)(6); Callow, above n 67, 29 ('the stated goal of the act is to bring more class actions into federal courts'); JE Pfander, 'The Substance and Procedure of Class Action Reform' (2005) 93 *Illinois Bar Journal* 144, 144 (referring to state court judges as 'certification friendly').

[69] *Evidence Law Adrift*, above n 1, 17.

prohibition on hearsay and the use of character and propensity evidence.[70] The description neglects, however, that the legion of exclusionary rules was one of the prime motivators for the watershed reform of evidence law, as embodied in the Federal Rules of Evidence that has now been adopted more or less whole in over forty states.[71] Indeed, his description neglects that exclusion on relevance grounds now occurs only if the judgment of no reasonable factfinder could be rationally affected by the evidence and on grounds of prejudice only if the prejudicial effect would substantially outweigh its probative value.[72] The description neglects, in short, that at the heart of the transformation of the American evidentiary process that began almost a century ago[73] was the objective of freeing the factfinder from the clutches of that 'legion of exclusionary rules' that form a significant part of the foundation of Damaška's description of the contemporary American evidentiary process.

More telling, perhaps, is Damaška's treatment of the hearsay rule and the character/propensity rules as barriers to the admission of substantial evidence. There is little justification to believe either. Perhaps in some dim past the hearsay rule was a major impediment to the admission of evidence, but from its earliest recorded appearance in the annals of English, and then American, jurisprudence, its prohibitory attributes began transmuting into a rule of admission. The history of the hearsay rule is largely one of stated aspiration – bring witnesses with firsthand knowledge to court to be examined and cross-examined – giving way to the practical demands of a system in need of cheap and reliable information. So, for example, early on deathbed statements were admitted over a wide range of affairs because doing so seemed on balance better than the alternative.[74] The shopkeepers' rules emerged that allowed out-of-court statements contained in shopkeepers' books to be admitted to prove debts in order to

[70] *Ibid* 15–16.

[71] 6 JB Weinstein and MA Berger, *Weinstein's Federal Evidence* 2nd edn (JM McLaughlin, 2007) T-1 (Table of State and Military Adaptations). Federal Rules of Evidence 401, 402 and 403 for example represent an attempt to simplify the rules of evidence by embodying Thayer's notion that the rules of evidence should provide 'the general character of principles, to guide the sound judgment of the judge, rather than minute rules to bind it.' JB Thayer, *A Preliminary Treatise on Evidence at the Common Law* (Boston, Little, Brown, 1898) 530. See also JB Weinstein and MA Berger, 'Basic Rules of Relevancy in the Proposed Federal Rules of Evidence' (1969–70) 4 *Georgia Law Review* 43, 109.

[72] *Federal Rules of Evidence* 401, 403.

[73] See RP Mosteller, 'Evidence History, the New Trace Evidence, and Rumblings in the Future of Proof' (2006) 3 *Ohio State Journal of Criminal Law* (2006) 523, 524; 21 CA Wright and KW Graham, *Federal Practice and Procedure* (St Paul, Minn, West, 1977 & Supp 2001) §§ 5005, 77 n 92.

[74] See 5 *Wigmore, Evidence* 3rd edn (Boston, Little, Brown, Chadbourn rev, 1974) § 1430–36. On the history of the rule, see Kenneth S Broun *et al*, *McCormick on Evidence* 6th edn (St Paul, Minn, Thomson/West, 2006) 514.

counteract the disqualification of interested parties from testifying.[75] Today, virtually any hearsay statement that has probative value can be fitted within one of the exemptions and exceptions in FRE 801(d), 803, and 804, and should that fail FRE 807 permits the court to fashion an ad hoc exception if the need exists. This relentless expansion has never been followed by periods of retrenchment.[76] There are interesting questions concerning the hearsay rule as a form of regulation, why it persists in its present form and so on, but to offer it as an example of a complex rule of exclusion is simply to make a mistake.

This is also largely true of the character and propensity rules as rules of exclusion. Like the hearsay rule's promise of exclusion, the like-minded promise of the character and propensity rules goes largely unredeemed. This is most evident in the long list of 'alternative uses' for prior bad act evidence that are not alternatives at all but quite straightforwardly limits of the primary exclusionary prohibition. For example, FRE 404(b) admits prior bad acts to show motive and identity, yet both necessarily rely on the supposedly prohibited propensity inference, as do many of the other 'alternative uses' listed in the rule.[77] The rules admitting the prior acts of those alleged to have committed sexual or child abuse are direct qualifications of the exclusionary prohibition.[78] And somewhat like the residual exception to the hearsay rule that permits ad hoc admission of reliable information when useful, the courts have created various mechanisms to admit other evidence that might otherwise be excluded. The best example here is the doctrine of chances, which, like much of FRE 404(b), can only be understood as permitting precisely what the prohibition on propensity evidence purportedly prohibits.[79]

The portrayal of the extant empirical data about the American litigation process is likewise curiously sparse. Although Damaška does cite to some of the early work of psychologists in particular, *Evidence Law Adrift* virtually neglects the dramatic impact of the economists on the understanding of the legal system. An entire field has developed that attempts to capture the significance of differing types of private ordering for the outcome of disputes, which goes largely unnoticed in *Evidence Law Adrift*.[80] Nor is there any engagement with the work that examines the

[75] See 5 Wigmore, *Evidence*, *Ibid* § 1517–21.

[76] RJ Allen, 'The Evolution of the Hearsay Rule to a Rule of Admission' (1992) 76 *Minnesota Law Review* (1992) 797, 799 ('[T]here are virtually no examples of hearsay exceptions being eliminated; the dynamic is one of ever-increasing scope for the exceptions.').

[77] *Federal Rules of Evidence* 404(b). See Ronald J Allen *et al*, *Evidence: Text, Problems, and Cases* 4th edn (New York, Aspen Publishers, 2006) 236–57.

[78] *Federal Rules of Evidence* 413–15.

[79] Allen, above n 77, 247–49.

[80] See, eg, RA Posner, *Economic Analysis of Law* 1st edn, (Boston, Little, Brown, 1972); G Tullock, *The Logic of the Law* (New York, Basic Books, 1971); G Tullock, *Trials on Trial: The Pure Theory of Legal Procedure* (New York, Columbia University Press, 1980); W

differing incentive effects of public as compared to private ordering.[81] In his consistently colourful way, Damaška criticises the common law adversarial system for relying on 'two narrow beams of light' – two contrary points of view advanced by trial adversaries – to illuminate the truth, and he praises the Continental system for relying on the inquisitorial, neutral judge who can allegedly shine a more searching, single beacon of light.[82] The American trial lawyer will obfuscate, and the European judge will do her duty fully and faithfully, devoting herself steadfastly to the interests of the parties before her and the larger legal system of which she is a part with nary a thought of her own best interests. The economic prediction would be quite different. The economist would note that the American system locates incentives where they will do the most good, and the broad discovery rules in civil cases provide the tools for optimal investment in search costs, whereas the European judge would be predicted to be, well, a bureaucrat with bureaucratic interests and incentives.

But perhaps the European judge typically rises above the level of humanity posited by the economists. The work in the social sciences over the last fifty years gives one grave doubts, doubts that could only be offset by strong empirical evidence to the contrary, which leads us to the next of these general critiques of *Evidence Law Adrift*. So far as we can tell, in addition to slighting important work about the American system, there is not a single empirical study of any Continental system cited in the book. We are asked to accept Damaška's word about how things actually function. Yet, we know from our own experience that official descriptions and conventional beliefs about the reality of complex systems are often

Landes and RA Posner, 'The Independent Judiciary in an Interest Group Perspective' (1975) 18 *Journal of Law and Economics* 875; RP McAfee and PJ Reny, 'Correlated Information and Mechanism Design' (1992) 60 *Econometrica* 395; P Milgrom and J Roberts, 'Relying on the Information of Interested Parties' (1986) 17 *Rand Journal of Economics* 18; LM Froeb and BH Kobayashi, 'Competition in the Production of Costly Information: An Economic Analysis of Adversarial versus Court-Appointed Presentation of Expert Testimony' (George Mason University School of Law Working Papers in Law and Economics, Working Paper No 93–5, 1993). See also MK Block, JS Parker, O Vyborna and L Dusek, 'An Experimental Comparison of Adversarial versus Inquisitorial Regimes' (2000) 2 *American Law and Economics Review* 170 (reporting the results of a multiyear series of economic experiments comparing the two dominant types of legal procedures used in adjudicating: the adversarial model and the inquisitorial model); TJ Zywicki, 'Gordon Tullock's Critique of the Common Law' (SSRN Elec. Library, Working Paper No 07–13, 2007), available at <http://ssrn.com/abstract=964781> accessed 19 June 2008 (reviewing Tullock's theoretical critique and empirical studies comparing the adversary system of dispute resolution and the common law process of rulemaking with the inquisitorial system and civil law systems).

[81] See, eg, RJ Allen, *et al*, 'A Positive Theory of the Attorney-Client Privilege and the Work Product' (1990) 19 *Journal of Legal Studies* 359, 385 (1990) (the work product doctrine 'mainly protects and encourages … lawyer perseverance'). See also F Easterbrook, 'Insider Trading, Secret Agents, Evidentiary Privileges, and the Production of Information' (1981) *Supreme Court Review* 309; R Posner, *The Economics of Justice* (Cambridge, Harvard UP, 1981) 244.

[82] *Evidence Law Adrift*, above n 1, 100.

false. That is why empirical work is done, but either it has not been done on Continental systems or Damaška has neglected it. In either event, one half of the equation at the center of this book is simply an empirical black hole.

We do not purport to be comparativists, and thus have no basis to assert what is truly distinctive of the American legal system, but our suspicion is that it lies in creating the conditions of optimizing cost and accuracy in dispute resolution. This is precisely why, in a book like *Evidence Law Adrift* that aspires to truth, all data must be considered. This is especially so here because the common complaint about civil law systems is that it is virtually impossible to get efficient adjudication. Germany went through a crisis over the delay in proceedings.[83] It takes upwards of 10 years to get a judgment in an Italian court.[84] By contrast, in the United States, waves of reform are organised over these variables.[85] And of course, the cheapest and most cost effective way to get accurate results is for the parties to work things out themselves. A critical stimulant to the reduction of litigation is the promise that it will occur accurately without too much delay and at an acceptable cost. At the same time, the cost has to be adequate to give parties the incentive to negotiate instead of sue. The rules of evidence in the United States are simply part of this larger dynamic, and perhaps the most fundamental question in the organisation of justice systems is how efficiently their parts coalesce to pursue accurate adjudication.

How well things operate from such a critical perspective is unexamined by Damaška, and thus so too is whether critical differences between Continental and common law systems reside here rather than where he locates them. On that score, there is good reason to think that, as the title of a book published shortly after *Evidence Law Adrift* suggests, many of the civil law systems are in a state of crisis, and one major one that is not is heavily adversarial. France, Italy, Portugal, Brazil and Spain have suffered serious crises.[86] Germany is the major exception among the important economic powers to this dismal picture, but as Adrian Zuckerman points

[83] RJ Allen *et al*, 'The German Advantage in Civil Procedure: A Plea for More Details and Fewer Generalities in Comparative Scholarship' (1988) 82 *Northwestern University Law Review* 705, 725–26 (hereinafter Allen *et al*, 'A Plea for More Details').

[84] M Taruffo, 'Recent and Current Reforms of Civil Procedure in Italy', in N Trocker and V Varano (eds), *The Reforms of Civil Procedure in Comparative Perspective: An International Conference dedicated to Mauro Cappelletti, 12–13 December 2003* (Turin, Giappichelli Editore, 2005) 217, 222.

[85] See, eg, RL Marcus, 'Malaise of the Litigation Superpower', in AAS Zuckerman (ed), *Civil Justice in Crisis: Comparative Perspectives of Civil Procedure* (Oxford, OUP, 1999) 71, 71.

[86] AAS Zuckerman, 'Justice in Crisis: Comparative Dimensions of Civil Procedure' in Zuckerman, *Ibid* 3, 13.

out, 'the German system is largely adversarial'.[87] It also has heavily concentrated proceedings, which by Damaška's criteria make it more like a common law than a Continental system.[88]

There is one other neglected empirical question deserving of mention. The thesis of *Evidence Law Adrift* is, in part, that with its foundation eroded the American approach to litigation is an endangered species. One obvious empirical test of this proposition is how well the endangered species is propagating itself, and rather than being in a state of demise, common law approaches to evidence and procedure are making substantial inroads into Continental legal systems and international tribunals.

Damaška makes brief mention of the Italian experiment with common law approaches.[89] Rather than treat this as an example of the common law's robustness and its appeal to at least a few corners of the Continental community, Damaška editorializes, describing the opposition that has arisen to the changes.[90] But whether or not the Italian experiment has proven controversial has no bearing on the larger issue of whether common law practices are unmoored and on life support. The very fact that the Italian system has chosen to experiment with common law mechanisms suggests more vibrancy than *Evidence Law Adrift* acknowledges.

In fact, Damaška downplays the broader set of changes that Italy adopted with the 1988 Code of Criminal Procedure and which it has since largely maintained.[91] That code 'represented a revolution, inspired by the Anglo-American adversarial system';[92]

[87] *Ibid* 31. Some of the smaller countries, Holland and Switzerland, seem to be doing fine, as well. We wish to be very clear that we are trying to examine the viability of certain features of the American legal system that Damaška has called into question, and more generally his claim that a set of such procedures seems to be falling into desuetude. We are most definitely not making any argument about what constitutes an 'adversarial' or an 'inquisitorial' system; nor are we addressing the common question in comparative law scholarship about 'convergence'. Indeed, we fail to see why that is even an interesting question. Understanding different legal systems is, to us, interesting, as is change in them, but we fail to see any significance to convergence. More importantly, the terms themselves are quite slippery and thus not very useful experimentally or conceptually. For an excellent discussion, see J Jackson, 'The Effect of Human Rights on Criminal Evidentiary Processes: Towards Convergence, Divergence or Realignment?' (2005) 68 *MLR* 737.

[88] See generally Allen *et al*, *A Plea for More Details*, above n 83, 722–26.

[89] *Evidence Law Adrift*, above n 73.

[90] *Ibid.*

[91] For a general overview of Italy's adoption of an adversarial criminal process, see G Illuminati, 'The Frustrated Turn to Adversarial Procedure in Italy (Italian Criminal Procedure Code of 1988)' (2005) 4 *Washington University Global Studies Law Review* 567; M Panzavolta, 'Reforms and Counter-Reforms in the Italian Struggle for an Accusatorial Criminal Law System' (2005) 30 *North Carolina Journal of International Law & Commercial Regulation* 577 (2005); WT Pizzi and M Montagna, 'The Battle to Establish an Adversarial Trial System in Italy' (2004) 25 *Michigan Journal of International Law* 429. See also Luca Marafioti, ch 5.

[92] See Illuminati, *Ibid* 571.

> the break with the past was clear: abolition of the investigating judge; preliminary inquiry conducted by both parties; adversarial presentation of evidence and cross-examination at trial; strong reduction of the judge's ability to introduce evidence.[93]

The goal of the reform was: 'to prevent judicial prejudice founded on knowledge of the investigations conducted by the prosecutor and by the police.'[94] Henceforth, Italian criminal court judges would have to rely on parties to present evidence through the Anglo-American procedures of direct and cross-examination.

Several other civil law countries employ common law approaches that according to Damaška are allegedly peculiarly American: for example, Germany,[95] France,[96] and Spain.[97] Similarly, various modern international tribunals have adopted a 'unique amalgam of civil and common law features' and do not 'strictly follow the procedures of the civil law or common law jurisdictions'.[98] The adoption of common law processes in these courts is particularly striking given that their very creation involves a 'policy implementing' motivation, one that under Damaška's understanding of institutional arrangements would lead to a tribunal far more oriented toward a civil rather than a common law system. And yet the International Criminal Tribunal for the Former Yugoslavia (ICTY) has adopted a largely adversarial process,[99] which calls on the prosecutor – not a judge – to initiate an investigation[100] and the parties to conduct

[93] *Ibid.*

[94] *Ibid.*

[95] See, eg, Allen *et al*, *A Plea for More Details*, above n 83, 722, 726.

[96] See F Ferrand, 'The Respective Role of the Judge and the Parties in the Preparation of the Case in France', in Trocker and Varano, above n 84, 7, 10.

[97] See I Díez-Picazo Giménez, 'The Principal Innovations of Spain's Recent Civil Procedure Reform' in *Ibid* 33, 40 ('[P]arties determine the subject matter and scope of the issues of the proceeding ... , if and when it is initiated, and if it is to be voluntarily terminated ... Within the proceedings themselves, the parties, not the court, usually decide the source of factual proof for the contentions at issue ... . Thus despite Spain's official status as a social State, party autonomy constitutes a general principle in [the new code of Civil Procedure adopted in 2000].'). Further, the new Spanish proceedings are similar to Anglo-American proceedings in that they emphasise oral, rather than written, presentation of evidence and are more concentrated temporally. *Ibid* 42–43, 61.

[98] See R Dixon, 'Prosecuting International Crimes: An Inside View: Developing International Rules of Evidence for the Yugoslav and Rwanda Tribunals' (1997) 7 *Transnational Law & Contemporary Problems* 81, 92.

[99] See JL Falvey Jr, 'United Nations Justice or Military Justice: Which is the Oxymoron? An Analysis of the Rules of Procedure and Evidence of the International Tribunal for the Former Yugoslavia' (1995) 19 *Fordham International Law Journal* 475, 504 ('The Tribunal rules generally provide for public adversarial trials similar to trials in criminal cases in the United States.'). See also John Jackson, ch 12.

[100] *Ibid* 488.

discovery.[101] The same basic approach has been adopted by the International Criminal Tribunal for Rwanda,[102] and the International Criminal Court has adopted some common law approaches to its evidentiary rulings.[103]

Other scholars have noted the apparent distance between Damaška's theoretical account of the American system and reality. For example, critical to Damaška's argument is that the exclusionary rules of Anglo-American law give the judge a mechanism by which to control the jury and, hence, that the rules of evidence are deprived of some of their relevance as the jury vanishes. Speaking of the 'jury control factor', Richard Friedman bluntly writes, 'I do not recognise such a feature of our system'.[104] The implausibility of the assertion, Friedman points out, is highlighted by the nature of jury instructions, which could be used to exert substantial control over juries but are not.[105]

IV. TRUTH AND UTILITY IN COMPARATIVE LEGAL SCHOLARSHIP

Had Damaška presented *Evidence Law Adrift* as yet another intellectual soufflé designed to appeal to the senses and stimulate thought, a book with an interesting argument whose relationship to empirical reality is beside the point, much in the vein of *Faces of Justice*, it would have been a smashing success. It is interesting, parts of it compelling, thought-provoking, stimulating, and all the other adjectives and adverbs typically used to praise a certain style of legal scholarship. In that sense, it might have been the perfect capstone to a wonderful career highlighted by *Faces of Justice*. To his credit, in our opinion, Damaška tried to break out of the mould of conventional legal scholarship dominant during the bulk of his career, and out of the mould of conceptual analysis that, we assume, dominated his education in Europe, and to move in the direction in which modern legal scholarship is going. So, even if our critique of *Evidence Law Adrift* convinces, nonetheless we once more are in Damaška's debt for leading the way. Indeed, *Evidence Law Adrift* succeeds in pointing out the kinds of questions that need to be addressed, and should be read from precisely that perspective by the next generation of scholars.

Evidence Law Adrift is a contribution not only to our field of evidence; it is also and perhaps mainly a contribution to comparative law and –

101 *Ibid* 499–500.

102 The two tribunals share the same Rules of Evidence. See Dixon, above n 98, 84.

103 See generally KD Rutledge, 'Comment: Spoiling Everything – But for Whom? Rules of Evidence and International Criminal Proceedings' (2003) 16 *Regent University Law Review* 151, 186–88

104 Friedman, above n 2, 1929.

105 *Ibid.*

again – in pointing the way forwards in that field. Some think that comparative law is 'in a state of disarray',[106] evidenced by the few law students who enrol in comparative law courses,[107] and that '[w]ithin the intellectual life of the American legal academy, comparative law is a peripheral field',[108] that first-generation comparative law scholars have failed to reproduce themselves;[109] and that law journals and courts pay little attention to comparative legal scholarship.[110] Writing on the occasion of the 50th anniversary of the founding of the *American Journal of Comparative Law*, Reimann writes:

> On the one hand, the discipline has made great progress because it has accumulated huge amounts of valuable knowledge. On the other hand, comparative law has been a serious failure because it has not developed into a coherent and intellectually convincing discipline.[111]

Without an empirical focus to their discipline, comparative legal scholars have been left with 'ridiculously little statistical data about the legal systems [they] study and compare' and are then resigned to rest

> most of [their] conclusions … on personal intuition, anecdotal information, or plain speculation, rather than on systematic observation of hard facts.[112]

Professor Chodosh similarly criticises comparative legal scholars for failing to tell their readers why they are comparing, what exactly is being chosen for purposes of a comparison, what exactly is being left out for purposes of a comparison, and what method – systematic or not – was used in compiling illustrative examples or anecdotes.[113]

[106] See CA Rogers, 'Gulliver's Troubled Travels, or the Conundrum of Comparative Law' (1998) 67 *George Washington Law Review* 149, 150. For more on the problems plaguing comparative law, see A Riles, 'Wigmore's Treasure Box: Comparative Law in the Era of Information', 40 *Harvard International Law Journal* 221, 224 (1999) ('[A] collective crisis of methodological confidence is something of a defining genre of comparative legal scholarship, as each commentator outdoes the next with dire critiques of the field and timid solutions for its reconfiguration.'); M Reimann, 'Stepping Out of the European Shadow: Why Comparative Law in the United States Must Develop Its Own Agenda' (1998) 46 *American Journal of Comparative Law* 637; M Reimann, 'The End of Comparative Law as an Autonomous Subject' (1996) 11 *Tulane European Civil Law Forum* 49.

[107] See JH Langbein, 'The Influence of Comparative Procedure in the United States' (1995) 43 *American Journal of Comparative Law* 545, 546–47.).

[108] *Ibid.*

[109] *Ibid.*

[110] *Ibid.*

[111] See M Reimannn, 'The Progress and Failure of Comparative Law in the Second Half of the Twentieth Century' (2002) 50 *American Journal of Comparative Law* 671, 673.

[112] *Ibid.* See also JH Merryman, *The Loneliness of the Comparative Lawyer and Other Essays in Foreign and Comparative Law* (The Hague, Kluwer, 1999).

[113] See generally HE Chodosh, 'Comparing Comparisons: In Search of Methodology' (1999) 84 *Iowa Law Review* 1025, 104. ('[O]nly a few scholars address the relationship between the questions of why and what one should compare, and still fewer ask how comparisons are or should be made').

For what it is worth, these are exactly the points driving the transformation of legal scholarship in the United States towards empirical legal studies. It is in our judgment both a positive and an inexorable movement. Regardless whether *Evidence Law Adrift* succeeds by these terms, it demonstrates the astonishing success of Damaška's long-term engagement with the law. Not content to simply replicate the tried-and-tested methodologies of a prior intellectual era, toward the end of his career he struck out on a new path, and for that he has our deepest admiration and thanks. From beginning to end, his career has not only advanced understanding but inspired generations of scholars, including ourselves. No one ever gets much of anything truly 'right'; the more important mark of a corpus of work is what it stimulates. As even Sir Isaac Newton said, 'If I have seen farther than others, it is because I have stood on the shoulders of giants'.[114] We are all now standing on Damaška's shoulders, and are seeing farther because of it. At the end of the day, a scholar can offer no stronger tribute to the significance of another's work.

[114] Letter from Isaac Newton to Robert Hooke (5 February 1675).

18

Sentencing and Comparative Law Theory

RICHARD S FRASE

I. INTRODUCTION

HOW AND WHY do nations differ in their approaches to sentencing purposes, procedures, and severity? What accounts for change over time, in these aspects of sentencing? And how well do the comparative theories proposed by Mirjan Damaška and others explain these differences and changes? Damaška only addressed procedural issues, gave little attention to sentencing, and primarily modelled traditional procedures, not recent changes. Comparative sentencing scholars have taken the opposite approach, focusing on recent changes in sentencing purposes and severity, with very little attention given to sentencing procedure and almost no mention of differences in pre-trial and trial procedures; indeed, these sentencing theorists appear to be unaware of the theories of Damaška and other comparative procedure scholars.

How do the core concepts in Damaška's models compare to those found in comparative sentencing literature? What might each of these two literatures learn from the other? Is it helpful – perhaps even essential – to simultaneously model sentencing purposes, procedures (including trial procedures), and severity in traditional and changing systems? And ultimately, how helpful are such models and theories in an era of fast-changing, increasingly hybridised and politicised systems of criminal justice?

Most recent comparative sentencing literature is limited to western nations.[1] Differences in sentencing practices and trends are particularly great between the United States and the Continental countries of Western

[1] See, eg, M Tonry, 'Determinants of Penal Policies' (2007) 36 *Crime & Justice* 1; M Cavadino and J Dignan, *Penal Systems: A Comparative Perspective* (London, Sage Publications, 2006) (also includes Japan); C Tata and N Hutton, *Sentencing and Society: International Perspectives* (Aldershot, Ashgate Publishing Ltd, 2002) (includes China); DvZS Smit and F Dünkel, *Imprisonment Today and Tomorrow* 2nd edn (The Hague, Kluwer, 2001)

Europe, so this essay will focus on those nations. The essay examines both the traditional differences and recent changes on one or both sides of the Atlantic, on the key dimensions of sentencing identified above: purposes, procedures, and severity.

Part 2 of the essay summarises Mirjan Damaška's comparative criminal procedure models, and examines how well his models explain and predict traditional differences and recent changes in sentencing procedures across nations. Although Damaška's models explain or predict some differences and changes, they provide a poor fit on other matters. The reasons seem to be that sentencing procedure is closely related to sentencing purposes and severity, and that all modern systems are complex hybrids which respond to external and internal pressures in unpredictable ways.

Part 3 reviews comparative sentencing literature, most of it focusing on recent changes in sentencing severity and sentencing purposes in developed countries. The most widely-cited theories and models found in this literature are increasingly congruent, but they fail to consider sentencing procedures and procedural models. The concepts underlying Damaška's models may help to explain traditional differences and recent changes in sentencing severity and sentencing purposes.

The Conclusion reflects on the challenges and inherent limitations of global comparative models and theories in the sentencing context.

A preliminary question relates to the function of models – what are they good for? This essay assumes that models can usefully serve one or more of the following purposes: (i) shorthand descriptions of systems – even though models are only ideal types, some systems are close enough to the ideal form that describing them this way conveys useful information about the system's general nature and features; (ii) explanation, showing why certain systems tend to have certain features – this may help those working in or studying a system to better understand it; (iii) prediction, helping policy makers and practitioners foresee how a given system will react to external and internal pressures, and to proposed changes; and (iv) normative functions, articulating underlying policy goals and values, suggesting ways

(includes many non-Western countries); RS Frase, *Sentencing in Germany and the US: Comparing Äpfel with Apples* (Freiburg, Max Plank Institute, 2001); M Tonry and RS Frase (eds), *Sentencing and Sanctions in Western Countries* (Oxford, OUP, 2001); M Tonry and K Hatlestad, *Sentencing Reform in Overcrowded Times: A Comparative Perspective* (New York, OUP, 1997); CMV Clarkson and R Morgan, *The Politics of Sentencing Reform* (Oxford, Clarendon Press, 1995).

a system should be adjusted to make it more consistent with these underlying goals and values, and providing a normative basis to evaluate any proposed change.[2]

II. SENTENCING PROCEDURE AND DAMAŠKA'S MODELS

A. Damaška's Comparative Procedure Models

Mirjan Damaška proposed a two-dimensional theory of comparative criminal procedure.[3] His theory was designed to replace traditional adversary-versus-inquisitorial models, as well as others less widely invoked.[4] The latter include models that are: historically-based (common law versus civil law 'families' of law); socio-political (democratic versus authoritarian); Marxist (capitalist versus socialist) or otherwise ideological ('battle' versus 'family'); and purposive (crime control versus due process models, each defined by its primary objective).

One dimension of Damaška's theory examines the structure of procedural authority, and contrasts 'hierarchical' versus 'co-ordinate' models. The second dimension examines the dominant purpose of the procedural system, and contrasts 'policy-implementing' (or 'activist-state') versus 'conflict-solving' (or 'reactive-state') models. Any given system can be described as tending to one pole or the other on each of these dimensions. When these dimensions are combined into a two-by-two matrix, civil law or 'inquisitorial' systems tend to fall into the box combining hierarchical and policy-implementing traits, whereas most common law or 'adversary' systems tend to combine the co-ordinate and conflict-solving models.

Some of the key features of a hierarchical system are: compilation and heavy reliance upon an official file of documents, permitting adjudication in a series of hearings, written decision-making by career professionals according to formal legal rules and regular review of these decisions by hierarchical superiors. In contrast, co-ordinate systems give greater emphasis to oral testimony taken in a single hearing (the trial), allow key decisions to be made by lay persons or officials exercising discretion without stating reasons, and have limited appellate or other hierarchical review of official or lay decisions.

[2] MR Damaška, *Models of Criminal Procedure* (Zagreb, Zagreb Law School, 2001) 477–78; RS Frase, 'Comparative Criminal Justice Policy, in Theory and in Practice' (1998) in *Comparative Criminal Justice Systems: From Diversity to Rapprochement*, 17 *Nouvelles Etudes Pénales* 112.

[3] MR Damaška, *The Faces of Justice and State Authority: A Comparative Approach to the Legal Process* (New Haven, Yale University Press, 1986); Damaška, above n 2.

[4] *Ibid* 478–94.

On the second dimension, policy-implementing systems seek to manage social problems and achieve defined social or government purposes (including the inquest into and resolution of possible criminal violations). Conflict-solving models are more consistent with a laissez-faire approach to governance in which private parties are left to pursue their interests and the courts merely settle disputes between the parties (including allegations of criminal violations by the police and prosecutor, who are themselves viewed as parties). There is also a tendency to grant defendants more procedural rights, to compensate for the many advantages of the police and prosecution and promote a 'fair balance' between the parties. Policy-implementing systems prefer criminal procedure to be dominated by judges; in conflict-solving systems the 'parties' (including the prosecution) dominate pre-trial and trial proceeding, investigating and presenting their own evidence, invoking or waiving procedural rights, and settling disputes with little or no court intervention.

The next two sections examine how well Damaška's models explain and predict traditional differences and recent changes in sentencing procedures in the US and Europe.

B. Damaška's Models Applied to Traditional Cross-National Differences in Sentencing Procedure

Unlike pre-trial, guilt-determination, and appellate procedures, as to which traditional common law and Continental differences have long been noted, trans-Atlantic differences in sentencing procedure (or indeed, any aspect of sentencing) were not widely studied until the last decades of the 20th century.[5] Accordingly, this essay can do no more than offer plausible working hypotheses as to the probable differences that existed as of the middle of the 20th century, that is, before the revolutionary changes in US sentencing (and the more moderate changes in European sentencing) that occurred in the last half of that century.[6]

My working hypothesis regarding traditional sentencing procedures is that American and European systems shared important similarities at mid-century; highly individualised sentencing procedures generally prevailed on both sides of the Atlantic, and sentencing was often guided by a detailed file (the trial dossier in Europe, the pre-sentence report in the US). However, there were also several important differences. European systems had no separate sentencing hearing; they gave lay jurors or lay judges, as well as crime victims, more substantial sentencing roles; sentences were more often justified by written reasons; and de novo appellate review of

[5] See sources above n 1.

[6] These changes are discussed in the following Section C, below.

sentences was frequently available. In addition, European systems rarely tolerated the common American practice of letting the prosecution and defence negotiate for a recommended or mutually-agreed sentence that the court will normally accept.

Damaška's models would predict the latter differences. The more hierarchical European systems are expected to more often require reasons for sentencing, and grant full appellate review. The policy-implementing nature of these systems is expected to strongly reject sentences that are determined by agreement of the parties. Damaška's models have more difficulty explaining the tendency of European systems to give victims the status of a 'party' and rights to be heard at sentencing and demand that the court issue a compensation order along with the criminal sentence. Such an active victim role seems more consistent with the conflict-solving, party-dominated model characteristic of US systems. Damaška recognised this potential conflict with his models; he explained it by noting that the US party-process is strongly 'bipolar,' which makes US prosecutors and defence counsel very hostile to victims' rights; the more active, policy-implementing European judge is also hostile to 'interference' by the victim, but remains firmly in control of the process.[7]

The other procedural similarities and differences noted above likewise seem inconsistent with Damaška's models, and are harder to explain. Hierarchical European systems would be expected to have more, not fewer separate sentencing hearings; they should have more detailed sentencing files; and they should give lay persons a lesser not a greater role. Finally, the hierarchical, policy-implementing nature of European systems would be expected to produce a more rule-based and less individualised approach to sentencing.

Given that Damaška's models generally provide a good 'fit' with traditional US and European criminal procedures in the pre-trial, trial, and appellate stages, what explains the numerous examples of poor fit noted above, with regard to sentencing procedures? The absence of separate sentencing hearings in Europe seems the easiest anomaly to explain. Such hearings cause delay and possibly added costs; but they were made necessary in American systems by the decision not to give trial jurors a role in sentencing, and also because, given the absence of a trial dossier in the US (or even a trial transcript, in guilty plea cases), sentencing must be delayed pending compilation of information on which to base the sentence. Such information was deemed necessary in otherwise poorly-documented traditional American systems, and (in most jurisdictions) jurors were denied any role in sentencing, because the dominant purpose at sentencing was rehabilitation – a goal which was deemed to require detailed data on

[7] *Faces of Justice*, above n 3, 200–1.

the offender (much of it inadmissible at trial) and expert assessment of his or her needs for and amenability to treatment and/or supervision.[8] Similarly, on the European side, highly individualised rather than rule-based sentencing was deemed necessary to achieve widely-recognised goals of rehabilitation and/or offender reintegration into the community.[9] In short, the 'failures' of Damaška's theory, when applied to traditional US and European sentencing procedures, result from each system's need to accommodate sentencing goals with other features of that system (themselves, consistent with his theory).

C. Damaška's Models Applied to Recent Changes in US and European Sentencing Procedures

Damaška's models were primarily designed to categorise, describe, and explain procedural systems at a given point in time, and gave little emphasis to modelling of change or evolution in these systems. Nevertheless, his models can be used to generate predictions about how systems of a given type (or tending to one pole or the other on each of his two dimensions) should evolve. For example, an essentially hierarchical system would be expected to maintain key features consistent with that model, while eliminating or softening procedures inconsistent with the model.

Unlike the traditional differences discussed above, which must be hypothesised for the sake of discussion, recent changes in sentencing procedures on either side of the Atlantic are easier to examine and summarise, due to the substantial growth of comparative sentencing scholarship in the past two decades.[10] Some of these changes magnify the traditional differences between US and foreign sentencing, hypothesised above, while other changes narrow the gap.

In the final decades of the 20th century and first decade of the 21st, there were several important changes in American sentencing procedures: (i) many US jurisdictions shifted from highly discretionary indeterminate sentencing regimes to some form of sentencing guidelines, parole guidelines, or statutory determinate sentencing, and all jurisdictions adopted mandatory penalties for at least some crimes;[11] (ii) in a series of cases beginning in 2000, the US Supreme Court held that certain facts permitting sentence-enhancement may no longer be informally determined by the trial

[8] See further discussion of sentencing purposes in Part 3C below.

[9] Lay jurors or lay judges did not need to be completely excluded from European sentencing because they deliberate jointly with and tend to be dominated by professional judges.

[10] See sources above n 1.

[11] KR Reitz, 'The Disassembly and Reassembly of US Sentencing Practices' in Tonry and Frase, above n 1.

judge at the sentencing hearing, but must be submitted to the jury and proven beyond a reasonable doubt;[12] and (iii) statutes and constitutions in many jurisdictions gave crime victims the rights to be heard in court and compensated for their injuries, and there was increased use of restorative and/or community justice procedures such as victim–offender mediation.[13]

During these same decades, European sentencing procedures changed very little, and the changes that did occur were mostly in the opposite direction to the major US changes summarised above: (i) sentencing guidelines, mandatory minimums, and other highly structured sentencing regimes remain almost unknown on the Continent – indeed, the individualisation of sentencing may have increased in many countries, due to expanded use of explicit or implicit negotiation by the parties over pre-trial diversion and sentencing dispositions; (ii) the role of lay jurors and lay judges in sentencing did not expand, and in some European countries it contracted, as a result of laws or informal practices which made fewer cases triable to a mixed court containing lay persons; and (iii) restorative justice procedures such as mediation were modestly expanded in some European countries, but most of these countries were already giving victims more rights than were traditionally available in American jurisdictions.[14]

Damaška's models would predict the second US change described above. Jury trial rights would be expected to grow in 'co-ordinate' systems due to their strong emphasis on lay participation; the expansion of reasonable doubt standards would be expected in conflict-solving systems that seek to maintain a fair balance between the parties. And these changes would be more likely to occur if the conditions that previously exempted sentencing from jury trial rights and reasonable doubt standards no longer obtained. The most important change was the dramatic loss of faith in rehabilitation as a sentencing goal.[15] When the dominant purposes of sentencing shifted to retribution, deterrence, and the incapacitation of recidivists, the relevant sentence-enhancement facts became simpler, and thus there was less concern that expanded jury trial and other procedural rights would interfere with sentencing. No similar shift in sentencing purposes occurred in Europe; some countries became more retributive, others became more focused on rehabilitation, and others saw few if any changes in sentencing

[12] RS Frase, 'The *Apprendi-Blakely* Cases: Sentencing Reform Counter-Revolution?' (2007) 6 *Criminology & Public Policy* 403.

[13] RS Frase, 'Historical and Comparative Perspectives on the Exceptional Severity of Sentencing in the United States' (2004) 36 *George Washington International Law Review* 237 (reviewing JQ Whitman, *Harsh Justice: Criminal Punishment and the Widening Divide Between America and Europe* (New York, OUP, 2003).

[14] See discussion in Section B above.

[15] See further discussion in Part 3C.

purposes.[16] Another factor operating in American jurisdictions may have been the rapid escalation in sentencing severity, likewise unmatched in Europe;[17] more severe penalties justify greater procedural safeguards at sentencing.

The third US change – greatly expanded victims' rights – seems inconsistent with the explanation given in Part 2 above for traditionally narrower victims' rights in the US – it does not seem likely that America's party-dominated criminal justice system became less 'bipolar' in recent decades. Again, one reason for expanded victims' rights in the US may have been the decline of the rehabilitative ideal and its replacement with sentencing goals more closely associated with concern for current and future crime victims.

The first US change also seems the opposite of what Damaška's models would predict – highly rule-based, determinate sentencing should be more likely to arise in the hierarchical and policy-implementing systems of Europe. One explanation for this anomaly might be that US sentencing systems are not very 'determinate' in practice, since they are easily manipulated by highly discretionary prosecutorial screening and charge bargaining (and, in relatively flexible determinate-sentence systems, sentence agreements).

But assuming that determinate sentencing laws do make a difference, why were they widely adopted in the US but not in Europe? Again, the answers seem to lie in changing sentencing severity and purposes. More severe maximum and average penalties in the US provide more potential for serious sentencing disparities. And highly discretionary sentencing became much harder to justify when the dominant goal of rehabilitation was replaced with offence-based purposes (retribution and deterrence) and/or sentencing based on prior convictions (incapacitation of repeat offenders). American determinate sentencing reforms may have also been prompted by the greater salience that issues of racial bias have in the US (or at least, the earlier emergence of those issues). Finally, European systems already had some protections against sentencing disparities (highly bureaucratised judges and prosecutors, requirements to state reasons for the sentence, *de novo* appellate review). The wave of determinate sentencing reforms in the US may have been partly a reaction to the extreme lack of procedural protections that characterised traditional US sentencing.[18]

[16] See generally sources above n 1.

[17] See Part B.

[18] MR Damaška, *Evidence Law Adrift* (New Haven, Yale University Press, 1997) 134–42, suggests another development that might explain determinate sentencing reforms in the US by asserting that the dominant purpose of Anglo-American justice systems has shifted toward a more activist, policy-implementation stance. But as noted in Section B above and in text

On the European side, the most significant recent change related to sentencing procedures is the increased frequency of negotiated pre-trial and post-trial dispositions,[19] which seems quite inconsistent with Damaška's hierarchical and policy-implementing models of European procedure. Increased tolerance of negotiated settlements probably reflected systemic needs to process growing caseloads with limited public resources.

To summarise: Damaška's models predict several recent changes in American and European sentencing procedures, but his models are contradicted by other changes. As with the traditional sentencing procedures discussed in Section B, the limited success of Damaška's models in this context reflects the powerful effects which sentencing purposes and severity have on sentencing procedure. Moreover, all modern sentencing systems are complex hybrids, pursuing multiple sentencing goals and responding to external and internal pressures in unpredictable ways.

The second dimension of Damaška's models recognises the close relationship between procedural rules and a justice system's dominant purposes. But Damaška's polar ideals and traditional examples of differing systemic purposes do not coincide with observed differences in sentencing purposes in the same systems. With the possible exception of restorative justice, traditional sentencing purposes would all seem to be examples of policy-implementation by a relatively 'activist' state; yet in traditional and current systems, restorative justice (in the form of victims' rights) is more widely recognised in Europe than in the US, while US governments have 'actively' pursued varied combinations of crime control and retributive purposes. Clearly, the choice of sentencing purposes is driven by factors independent of the dominant systemic purposes identified in Damaška's models. As discussed in the next Part, some recent comparative sentencing scholars have proposed theories to explain why nations adopt differing sentencing purposes.

III. COMPARATIVE STUDIES OF SENTENCING SEVERITY AND PURPOSES

A. Overview of Recent Theories

A number of sentencing scholars have proposed theories and models to explain cross-national differences and recent changes in sentencing severity

below, US systems have always had strong elements of the policy-implementing model, with regard to the choice of sentencing purposes; indeterminate sentencing regimes were created by the state, not private parties.

[19] See, eg, RS Frase, 'France' in C Bradley (ed), *Criminal Procedure: A Worldwide Study* 2nd edn (Durham, Carolina Academic Press, 2007); T Weigend, 'Germany' in C Bradley, above.

and/or sentencing purposes. Some of the most prominent writings are summarised below. None of these writers discusses traditional or changing sentencing procedures, the major cross-national differences in pre-trial and trial procedure, or the work of Damaška or other comparative procedure scholars.

'Modernity' Theories

Anthony Bottoms argued that various aspects of 'modernity' have produced similar sentencing trends in Western countries.[20] The four trends Bottoms emphasised were: (i) human-rights-based principles of desert; (ii) a 'managerialist,' technologically-enhanced focus on systemic analysis, efficient service delivery, and actuarial risk assessment; (iii) the application of community-based sentencing goals and procedures; and (iv) politically-motivated pressures for ever-more-severe penalties for certain offenders (which Bottoms labelled 'populist punitiveness'); however, for both budgetary and principled reasons, increased severity for some offenders (especially violent offenders) is often combined with reduced severity for others, a strategy he called 'bifurcation or the "twin-track" approach.'[21] Bottoms recognised that the assumptions and/or effects of these trends conflict with each other, and he cautioned that specific effects – especially of the fourth trend – would be highly dependent on particular social/political contexts. Nevertheless, his theory implies that sentencing theory and practice in Western countries will tend to converge because, in his view, all countries face the same underlying forces that produce his four trends. In particular, Bottoms felt that the forces of modernity lead to widespread 'dis-embedding' of the individual from traditional kinship relations, local communities, religious cosmologies, and appeals to tradition, with resulting increased emphasis on individual relationships, rights and responsibilities; greater reliance on government to maintain order; increased nostalgia for the lost sense of community; and widespread feelings of insecurity.

Somewhat similar factors were also cited by David Garland,[22] and his theory likewise would seem to predict increasing convergence in punishment theory and practice in Western nations. Garland argued:

[20] A Bottoms, 'The Philosophy and Politics of Punishment and Sentencing' in CMV Clarkson and R Morgan (eds), *The Politics of Sentencing Reform* (Oxford, Clarendon Press, 1995).

[21] *Ibid* 40.

[22] D Garland, *The Culture of Control: Crime and Social Order in Contemporary Society* (Chicago, University of Chicago Press, 2001).

> [L]ate modernity – the distinctive pattern of social, economic, and cultural relations that emerged in America, Britain, and elsewhere in the developed world in the last third of the 20th century – brings with it a cluster of risks, insecurities, and control problems.[23]

In particular, the US and the UK were seen as facing

> the same perceived problems of ineffective social control, the same critiques of traditional criminal justice, and the same recurring anxieties about social change and social order.[24]

At the same time, public officials confronted new practical problems resulting from

> the prevalence of high rates of crime and disorder ... and the growing realization that modern criminal justice is limited in its capacity to control crime and deliver security.[25]

All of these factors contribute to a highly politicised and populist discourse, leading to

> decreased reliance on scholarly and official expertise; reduced support for rehabilitation; increased emphasis on retribution, victims' rights, and public safety; and, following from all of these, massively increased prison populations.[26]

National Culture and Political Economy Theories

The two theorists above focused on recent British and American trends. Michael Tonry's theory is based on his extensive studies of criminal justice on the Continent, as well as in Britain and the US[27] (However, he only addresses cross-national variations in punishment severity, not purposes.) Tonry notes that Western nations, while facing similar patterns of rising (but more recently, falling) crime rates, have had very different recent histories of punishment severity; this, he argues, undercuts the validity of 'modernity' theories since, in Tonry's view, all of these nations are comparably 'modern' or 'late modern.'[28] Tonry then proposes a set of 'risk factors' and 'protective factors' related to the likelihood that a nation will take an unnecessarily punitive approach to punishment. Some of these factors, such as elected versus non-partisan judges and prosecutors, and

23 *Ibid* viii.
24 *Ibid* viii-ix.
25 *Ibid* xi.
26 *Ibid* 8–20.
27 Tonry, above n 1.
28 This view is also shared by JQ Whitman, *Harsh Justice: Criminal Punishment and the Widening Divide Between America and Europe* (New York, OUP, 2003) 5–6.

'conflict' versus consensus-seeking political systems,[29] are essentially structural explanations for national differences, analogous to Damaška's structural (hierarchical-co-ordinate) model. One pair of factors (Anglo-Saxon versus francophone political culture) bears some resemblance to historically-based models (common law versus civil law 'families' of law). Other factors – high degrees of income inequality, and weak social welfare systems[30] – are akin to central elements of Marxist comparative law theory. The remaining factors – sensationalist journalism, perceived legitimacy of and trust in legal institutions, and views as to the desirability of highly politicised, public-opinion-driven versus expert-dominated policy making – are similar to key elements of 'modernity' theory. However, Tonry views these factors as highly variable across modern systems, and thus presumably caused not by modernity but rather by differences in history, other determinants of national culture, or sheer political will (to implement sound policy, or to pursue narrow partisan advantage).

Another recent set of models, proposed by Michael Cavadino and James Dignan, seeks to explain differences in punishment severity and purposes according to four models based primarily on each country's political economy.[31] One model was based on the Japanese system; the three models which apply to the United States and Western Europe are as follows:[32]

Neo-liberalism[33] – These countries are characterised by free-market economic policies; extreme income differentials; minimalist or very limited welfare programs and social rights; strong tendencies toward social and penal exclusion (ghetto-formation, long-term imprisonment, stigmatisation);[34] right-wing political orientation; law-and-order as the dominant penal ideology; and high rates of imprisonment. The US is the archetypal example; other examples are England and Wales, Australia, New Zealand, and South Africa.

Conservative corporatism – These countries are characterised by 'moderately generous' welfare programs and social rights; 'pronounced but not extreme' income differentials; some tendencies toward social and penal exclusion, but also somewhat 'inclusionary';[35] centrist political orientation;

[29] Conflict systems tend to have two major parties, single-party dominance of policy making at any given time, and major policy discontinuities when the other party takes control. Consensus systems tend to have more than two major parties, coalition governments, and policy continuity. See Tonry, above n 1, 18–19.

[30] For further discussion of the direct and indirect effects on sentence severity of variations in the scope of welfare programs, see Frase, above n 13, 235–36.

[31] Cavadino and Dignan, above n 1.

[32] *Ibid* 14–36.

[33] This refers to 'liberal' in the sense of 19th century politically-conservative economic liberalism, not contemporary American (left-leaning) liberalism.

[34] Cavadino and Dignan, above n 1, xiii.

[35] See below n 36.

rehabilitation as the dominant penal ideology; and 'medium' rates of imprisonment. Germany is the archetypal example; other examples are France, Italy, and the Netherlands.

Social democratic corporatism – These countries are characterised by 'generous' welfare programs and social rights; 'relatively limited' income differentials; limited tendencies toward social and penal exclusion, with 'inclusionary' modes of punishment (seeking to maintain the offender in the community and reintegrate him into main-stream society);[36] left-wing political orientation; shifting but relatively non-punitive penal ideologies;[37] and low rates of imprisonment. Sweden is the archetypal example; another example is Finland.

Similarities to Damaška's Theories

Although none of the four comparative sentencing theorists discussed above cites Damaška's work, their theories contain elements of both of his models. All of the comparative sentencing theories point to structural features of a country's legal system, or of the political, economic, or social order. And echoes of Damaška's systemic-purpose models, contrasting activist versus reactive states, can be found in Cavadino and Dignan's contrast between free-market, welfare minimalism and a more activist state providing generous welfare programs and social rights.

How well do these four theories explain and predict cross-national variations in sentencing severity and sentencing purposes? In the separate discussions below of severity and purposes, only the Tonry and Cavadino-Dignan theories will be discussed. This is partly to stay within my allotted page limits, but also because I tend to agree with the Tonry and Whitman critiques of 'modernity' theories – these theories may identify relevant factors, but such factors apparently operate quite differently (or at very different speeds) in different 'modern' countries; we must therefore look to additional factors, such as those identified by Tonry and by Cavadino and Dignan, to explain and predict country-specific patterns.

[36] Cavadino and Dignan, above n 1, xiii.

[37] In the 1980s the dominant Swedish ideology of rehabilitation was replaced by a flexible just deserts model within which rehabilitation goals still operate; the Finnish approach was and remains 'classical' (emphasizing desert limits and general prevention), but in the 1970s a deliberate effort was made to lower the prison population through greater use of shorter terms, conditional sentences, and fines. *Ibid* 154–57, 162–63.

B. The Tonry and Cavadino and Dignan Theories Applied to Sentence-Severity Variations

Cavadino and Dignan explicitly seek to model not only traditional cross-national differences in sentencing severity but also changes over time.[38] Similarly, Tonry's model can be used to generate predicted changes in a given system, to the extent that the factors he cites have changed.

Explaining Traditional Differences in Sentencing Severity

As noted above, it is difficult to neatly summarise traditional (that is, mid-20th century) cross-national differences in sentencing, due to the scarcity of comparative sentencing research prior to the 1990s, so it is necessary to be content with plausible working hypotheses about such differences, based on the limited available sources. But in the case of sentencing severity, there are two, equally plausible competing hypotheses as to the relative severity of US and Continental European penalties in the middle of the 20th century: (i) that average sentence severity was much lower in Europe than in most US jurisdictions; or (ii) that average severity was comparable, particularly if one controls for differences in rates of violent crime.

As suggested by the latter qualification, a threshold problem involves selecting a measure or measures of punitiveness. The most common measure – inmates per 100,000 residents of each country – confounds the effects of sentencing severity and crime rates (and the rate at which offenders are convicted for serious crimes likely to result in a custody sentence). Moreover, total-inmate measures are not available for the US prior to the first federal jail census conducted in 1970, and complete conviction data by offence are still not available today, so one must use adult arrest rates as a proxy.[39] These methodological difficulties and data gaps help to explain why there are two competing hypotheses on this issue. Numerous impressionistic assessments from the 1960s and 1970s assert the first hypothesis.[40] In contrast, Michael Tonry has stated that American and European sentencing severity remained similar until the 1970s,[41] and I

[38] *Ibid* 32.

[39] RS Frase, 'International Perspectives on Sentencing Policy and Research' in Tonry and Frase, above n 1, 283–84.

[40] RS Frase, 'Comparative Criminal Justice as a Guide to American Law Reform: How Do the French Do It, How Can We Find Out, and Why Should We Care?' (1990) 78 *California Law Review* 539, 648; see also Whitman, above n 28 (implying long-standing US-European differences, but providing no statistics).

[41] M Tonry, *Thinking About Crime: Sense and Sensibility in American Penal Culture* (Oxford, OUP, 2004) 22.

have speculated that differences in violent crime rates could explain much of the US-European difference in per capita custody rates as of the early 1970s.[42]

If we assume that US sentencing was already much more severe at mid-century, there is a problem for Cavadino and Dignan's theory, since many of the differences they cite, between neo-liberal and corporatist states, appear to have been much smaller at that earlier point in time. Conversely, if we assume that US sentencing was no more severe at mid-century there is a problem for Tonry's theory, since many of his risk and protective factors were already present back then.

Predicting Recent Changes in Sentencing Severity

Here we are on much more solid ground, empirically. Improved US and foreign statistics permit one to conclude with reasonable confidence that overall sentencing severity (as measured by prison and jail populations relative to resident population, and relative to crime rates and estimated criminal caseloads) has risen substantially in almost all US jurisdictions, whereas European severity has increased only modestly in most countries, and in some has remained flat or even declined.[43]

The rapid US increases would be predicted by adverse changes in several of Tonry's suggested structural 'risk' and 'protective' factors: income inequality, welfare support, sensational journalism, and trust in legal institutions and experts. But his structural factors (elected judges and prosecutors; 'conflict' political systems) have not changed, and US culture is more ethnically diverse, and thus perhaps less 'Anglo-Saxon,' than it used to be. As for Cavadino and Dignan's neo-liberal model of the US, it appears that most of the factors they cite (free market economic policies, extreme income differentials, etc) have grown more conducive to punitive sentencing, in recent decades, as the country's political climate has shifted to the right.

Using Damaška's Models to Help Explain Variations in Sentence Severity

Mirjan Damaška did not seek to model traditional or changing sentencing severity, but his structural and systemic-purpose models might be usefully added to the factors cited by Tonry and by Cavadino and Dignan. Government and professional elites generally prefer to maintain or to lower sentence severity, and the strongly hierarchical structure of European

42 Frase, above n 13, 234.
43 Tonry, above n 1, 2–3.

governments makes it easier for these elites to achieve their goals. Hierarchical structure further promotes moderated sentencing severity by providing bureaucratic and appellate checks and a reinforced sense of professionalism, particularly among prosecutors. Similarly, prosecutors in the typical, 'policy-implementing' European system may be less subject to the extremes of adversary zeal, and they (as well as judges and other officials) may be more attuned to goals of optimizing and rationalizing justice to best serve the public interest in the long-term. However, if the latter hypothesis is valid it implies that European systems may become more punitive as they become more 'adversary' (that is, more party-controlled and rights-based). Recent increases in negotiated justice and human rights protections in Europe do suggest growing adversariness but thus far this change has not produced widespread increases in European punitiveness – perhaps because so many features of the hierarchical model remain in place, restraining adversary excesses and mitigating their punitive tendencies.

Conversely, the less professionalised, more democratically-accountable co-ordinate systems in the US, dominated by the parties rather than judges, might be expected to respond more quickly and dramatically to politically-driven pressures to escalate sanction severity.

C. Cavadino and Dignan's Theory Applied to Sentence-Purpose Variations[44]

Explaining Traditional Differences in Sentencing Purposes

The working hypothesis here is that mid-century Continental sentencing was more diverse in its focal purposes. Whereas sentencing in virtually all American jurisdictions was dominated by the 'rehabilitative ideal', subject to very loose outer proportionality limits,[45] sentencing was 'classical' or 'repressive' (primarily retributive and deterrent) in some European countries,[46] but strongly oriented to rehabilitation and/or reintegration in

[44] Tonry's theory is not discussed in this section because, as noted previously, he did not address cross-national variations in sentencing purposes

[45] Reitz, above n 11, 223; Frase, above n 1, 95–96.

[46] T Lappi-Seppälä, 'Penal Policy in Scandinavia' (2007) 36 *Crime & Justice* 222 (Finland); T Weigend, 'Sentencing and Punishment in Germany' in Tonry and Frase, above n 1, 190 (Germany).

others.[47] Restorative justice also received more emphasis in many European systems, where victims had rights to initiate and participate in criminal prosecutions and obtain monetary compensation awards.[48]

Cavadino and Dignan's three-family model doesn't fit the patterns described above. Jurisdictions with classical-repressive sentencing goals (Finland and Germany) were found in both of the corporatist groups, and all three families had jurisdictions (Sweden, France, and the US) strongly emphasizing rehabilitation. Although the model features of these three families may have grown more distinct in recent decades, most of these features were already in place at mid-century.

Predicting Recent Changes in Sentencing Purposes

In recent decades American sentencing has become more attentive to retributive, public safety, and restorative justice goals, while rehabilitation has been de-emphasised.[49] In Europe sentencing became more retributive in some countries (at least in theory), and more focused on rehabilitation and/or reintegration in other countries; in several countries there was little change in dominant purposes, but restorative justice gained more attention in most countries.[50]

The American changes seem broadly consistent with Cavadino and Dignan's neo-liberal model; most of the factors in that model seem intuitively linked to retributive, public safety, and victim-centered goals, rather than rehabilitation, and these factors have become more pronounced in recent years. But it remains unclear why a 'conservative corporatist' state like France would remain attached to rehabilitation and reintegration, while the more strongly welfare-oriented Nordic states in the social democratic corporatist family became more desert-oriented.[51] However, it is perhaps not surprising that these (or any?) broad theories have difficulty explaining shifts in punishment purposes. The choice of such purposes, like the definition of crimes, defences, and penalties, reflects cultural factors and political conditions which vary greatly over space and time. The anomalous case may indeed be the US, where for much of the 20th century virtually all states subscribed to one goal, rehabilitation. This uniform and stable pattern may have reflected core ideals (hopefulness, belief in scientific progress) that once defined this nation of immigrants, pioneers, and innovators.

[47] Cavadino and Dignan, above n 1 (Sweden); S Roché, 'Criminal Justice Policy in France: Illusions of Severity' (2007) 36 *Crime & Justice* 487 (France).

[48] Frase, above n 40, 669–72; Lappi-Seppälä, above n 46, 226–27.

[49] Reitz, above n 11.

[50] See generally sources above n 1.

[51] Roché, above n 47, 487 (France); Cavadino & Dignan, above n 1, 154–57, 162–63 (Sweden and Finland).

Using Damaška's Models to Help Explain Variations in Sentencing Purposes

Mirjan Damaška did not seek to model traditional or changing sentencing purposes, but his structural and systemic-purpose models might be usefully added to the Cavadino and Dignan models. The hierarchical structure of most European government functions may help to explain why in most countries the public did not lose trust in judges, government officials, and private experts to formulate policy and pursue rehabilitative goals requiring discretion and case-level assessments. And when these elites decided to make major changes in punishment purposes, they were likely to succeed owing not only to the hierarchical structure but also their policy-implementing mindset, which gave them a strong commitment to the reform project.

Conversely, the less elite-dominated co-ordinate systems in the US may have been more susceptible to a major shift away from discretion-based sentencing purposes, resulting from declining public trust in judges and other professionals.

To summarise, comparative sentencing theories are increasingly congruent, pointing to similar socio-political factors which plausibly explain differences in sentencing severity and purposes over space and time. These theories might be improved by incorporating insights from Damaška's structural and system-purpose models. Additional factors, not directly incorporated in these comparative theories, also need to be examined, in particular, the effects of racial and ethnic heterogeneity and rising violent crime rates, especially rapid increases and pronounced spatial concentrations of violent crime, which may have an exponential effect on public fears and punitive pressures.[52]

IV. CONCLUSION

Damaška's models have strongly influenced the ways in which comparative scholars think about criminal procedure, but have not yet had much influence on comparative sentencing theory. This is partly because neither Damaška nor other comparative scholars have addressed cross-national differences in sentencing procedure. But it is also because his procedural models do not seem to work quite as well in the sentencing context, owing to the complex interactions of sentencing procedure, purposes, and severity with each other, and with unique systemic needs and social-political factors. Comparative sentencing scholars have focused on issues of severity

[52] Frase, above n 39, 269; Roché, above n 47, 535–7.

and purpose, but their theories could be improved by explicit incorporation of Damaška's structural and systemic-purpose models. However, modelling cross-national differences and changes in sentencing will remain an extremely challenging task. Sentencing is an organic whole which cannot be fully understood piecemeal. And models are no better than the raw data available for the systems being modelled; critical data is often non-existent or non-comparable. Even with improved data, the value of global models may become increasingly limited; the growing complexity and hybridisation of modern criminal justice systems tends to undercut the simplicity needed for models to serve their descriptive, explanatory, predictive, and normative functions.

19

No Right Answer?

JAMES Q WHITMAN

I. INTRODUCTION

THE TITLE OF this essay is, of course, lifted from one of the most famous articles in the literature of Anglo-American legal philosophy.[1] As we all know, Ronald Dworkin argued, in his 1977 article 'No Right Answer?', that there must indeed always be a right answer to any given question of law, despite the many seemingly intractable disagreements we discover among lawyers and judges. Dworkin's claims have drawn numerous responses, and the 'no right answer?' debate has assumed a central place in the literature of legal philosophy.[2]

Why do I begin an essay celebrating Mirjan Damaška's work in comparative law by invoking a debate among the legal philosophers? Because one of Damaška's many striking contributions is his own analysis of the 'no right answer' problem. Indeed, Damaška has devoted much of his scholarly career to the question of whether legal systems must inevitably be committed to seeking the right answer, starting with his first major article in the pages of an American law review. 'The Continental,' Damaška argued in 1968,

> will seek the right solution; his [American] counterpart will display a liberal agnosticism about "right" answers, coupled with a procedural outlook.

Instead of seeking the right answer, the American lawyer 'will be primarily concerned about good arguments for a case.'[3] In intriguing contrast to Dworkin, Damaška thus argued in 1968 that American law was exceptional among leading western systems in its reluctance to 'seek' right answers. In that 1968 article, and especially in his memorable 1986 book

[1] R Dworkin, 'No Right Answer?' in PMS Hacker & J Raz (eds), *Law, Morality, and Society: Essays in Honour of HLA Hart* (Oxford, Clarendon Press, 1977) 58, 58–84.

[2] See, eg, W Lucy, 'Adjudication' in J Coleman and S Shapiro (eds), *The Oxford Handbook of Jurisprudence and Philosophy of Law* (Oxford, OUP, 2002), 208–221.

[3] M Damaška, 'A Continental Lawyer in an American Law School: Trials and Tribulations of Adjustment' (1968) 116 *University of Pennsylvania Law Review* 1363, 1375.

The Faces of Justice and State Authority, Damaška offered explanations for this peculiarity of American law that were, as I shall argue in this essay, of great philosophical interest. So I begin with an All Hail Damaška!, neglected philosophical voice in the no-right-answer debate.

My aim is not just to praise Mirjan Damaška, though. My aim is to bring together some of the wisdom of comparative law and the wisdom of legal philosophy. Since Damaška's first attack on the problem, comparativists have produced a variety of stimulating studies on the comparative lack of definitive answers (as I will call them) in American law. Indeed, in its own way, the no-right-answer problem has become as important in comparative law as it is in legal philosophy. Yet the two literatures are never read together. Comparatists and philosophers scribble away with no apparent knowledge that their colleagues down the hallway are at work on the same problem. I believe that this is a loss for both fields. A celebration of Mirjan Damaška, the most philosophically adept of comparativists, seems the right occasion to remedy that loss.

Accordingly my main purpose in this essay is to pursue the scholarly lead that Damaška gave us in 1968, writing comparative law in a way intended to interest both comparative lawyers and philosophers. I am not a philosopher, and I will avoid crossing swords with the philosophers on philosophical issues as much as possible. But I *will* argue that legal philosophers have missed some important issues through neglect of comparative law.

To be sure, all legal philosophers understand that legal systems differ from each other, and the problems of comparative law are hardly unknown to them. But when it comes to the no right answer problem they have not tried to work through the comparative law at any depth. This is something that the philosophers themselves acknowledge, let me rush to say, and with admirable frankness. Brian Bix, for example, an advocate of the view that the law is open to multiple answers, has the intellectual honesty to admit that his knowledge is drawn from American law: '[M]y examples,' Bix writes,

> are all drawn from the American legal system, and I do not presume that they exemplify any (necessary or essential) aspect of all legal systems.

There may be non-American systems, he recognises, that do not 'allow one to speak of there being more than one correct – or "acceptable" – answer to a legal question.' Bix speculates that a person trained in such a non-American system might even doubt whether America had law at all – though he can detect no substance in such doubts:

> It is conceivable that someone could put forward an argument that systems … that are structured in such a way that there are *not* always unique correct answers to legal problems, are not 'really' *legal* systems (or not legal systems 'in

> the fullest sense of the term.'). However, as I cannot now imagine how that position might be justified, I will not now concern myself with it.[4]

As these quotes suggest, Bix (and other Anglo-American philosophers, among them Dworkin[5]) have limited themselves to the Anglo-American tradition that they know.

The result, I believe, is that they have missed some data that ought to be of prime philosophical interest. In point of fact, as comparatists well know, there *are* people who believe that legal systems that do not provide 'unique correct answers' are 'not "really" *legal* systems.' In fact, there are many of them. Many legal traditions indeed (notably but not exclusively those of the European Continent) display a strong commitment to the proposition that there must be 'unique correct answers.' But at the same time there are others (notably but not exclusively the American tradition) that display a significantly weaker commitment to that proposition. There is indeed no such thing as 'the' view of 'the' law on whether there must be unique correct answers. Different legal cultures seem to bring quite different attitudes toward that question. This is itself a fact that deserves philosophical reflection.

My purpose, then, is to show that there are such different legal cultures of the right answers. In the effort to describe the differences between these legal cultures, I will propose a classificatory distinction – a distinction that requires us to parse Bix's phrase 'unique correct answers' more finely. All of the systems that I will discuss are committed to the proposition that there are 'right answers' in some sense, I will argue. This is even true of America: Dworkin surely has it right on that score. But what matters, as I will argue, is that different legal cultures tend to conceive of 'right answers' differently. The Continental systems tend to seek answers that are not only *correct* but also *definitive*. They tend to treat the rule of law as requiring that all legal officials will generally produce the same answer to any given question. Other legal traditions, including the American, tend to devote themselves to the search for *correct* answers in a way that largely excludes the possibility that those answers could be *definitive*. I think that the real task of comparative law – and perhaps of legal philosophy – is to explain why this difference in the conception of right answers should exist.

II. NO RIGHT ANSWER: COMPARATIVE LEGAL PHILOSOPHY

The comparative law of right answers begins with Damaška's 1968 article, 'A Continental Lawyer in an American Law School: Trials and Tribulations of Adjustment.' The article was written at a difficult time in Damaška's

[4] B Bix, *Law, Language, and Legal Determinacy* (Oxford, Clarendon Press, 1993), 95.
[5] See, eg, RM Dworkin, *Law's Empire* (Cambridge, Belknap Press, 1986), 88.

life, when he was deciding whether to emigrate from Tito's Yugoslavia. The fact that he was wavering between America and Yugoslavia is more than just a dramatic biographical detail. It is a telling part of the intellectual backdrop to his work. Damaška is the last of a series of immigrant scholars of comparative law who came to America as refugees from the totalitarian countries of Central Europe, most of them from Nazism. But Damaška is a distinctive figure within this remarkable group. This is partly because he was not a refugee from Nazism; but in a deeper sense it is because he is not German. Most of the leading refugee figures were German scholars to the core, who brought German ways of thinking and German approaches to American law. They were insiders to the German system who made intellectual advances by viewing American law from the outside.

Damaška, by contrast, is a Croatian, a man of the Continental periphery. To be sure, as a Croatian he belongs to a nation historically integrated into the Continental tradition, as he has shown better than anyone else through his studies of Croatian jurisprudence in centuries past. Nevertheless, as a Croatian (and one who traveled to distant Paris for part of his legal studies) he has always been able to maintain a kind of emotional detachment from Continental law even as he became an intellectual master of it. The same is true of his mastery of American law. One could say that Damaška is a full initiate of both traditions without ever having become a convert to either. This has always allowed him to write about both with a unique mix of intimate intuitive sympathy and ironic distance, as was manifest in his 1968 lecture.

The subject that this man of the periphery chose for his lecture, the 'no right answer' problem, was one of fundamental philosophical interest, and before turning to his approach it is well to review briefly its place in the history of legal philosophy. The desire for right answers in the law is very old, and so is scepticism about whether right answers can ever be given. The claim that there must be right answers is a claim that can be made with various degrees of subtlety and sophistication. The simplest variation consists in imagining a legal system in which there are unique correct answers to all legal questions, specified with perfect clarity in easily understood legal texts, such that persons who are subject to the law can know in advance, with perfect certainty, the legal consequences of any action they may take. Believers in this simple ideal would insist that without such perfect certainty there can be no meaningful rule of law. But there are very few true believers in this simple ideal, at least among legal philosophers. On the contrary, the history of modern legal thought both on the Continent and in the Anglo-American world has been largely the history of efforts to transcend the simple ideal of a rule of law founded on perfect certainty about right answers.

Before describing those efforts, though, it is wise to make the basic distinction that this essay is intended to pursue. The phrase 'right answer'

is ambiguous. When we speak of answers that are 'right' we may mean two things: we may mean that the answers are what I will call definitive, or we may mean that they are what I will call correct. A system that aims to give *definitive* answers, as I shall use the term, is a system that aims to guarantee that the same answer should always be given by every legal official, leaving no room for variation or discretion. To the extent a system succeeds in providing definitive answers to every possible legal question, it is a system that offers perfect predictability, at least in principle. A system committed to giving *correct* answers, by contrast, is a system that aims to give an answer that is correct according to the dictates of some understanding of legal reason.

It should be obvious that these are two distinct ideals. A system can be fully committed to giving definitive answers without having any particular commitment to giving correct answers, or even accepting the possibility of giving correct answers. Conversely a system can be committed to giving correct answers, while finding the process of determining those correct answers to be so difficult and plagued with uncertainty that no guarantee can be given that its answers will be definitive. (Classical Islamic Law is a prime example: It posits that there is always a unique correct answer, but that since unique correct answers are known only to Allah, while human beings must perpetually struggle to find them, it is impossible to provide definitive answers.[6]) The most naïve form of belief in right answers holds that a legal system can give answers to every possible legal question that are both correct *and* definitive. The distinction between the correct and the definitive is admittedly somewhat rough and ready, but as we shall see it is helpful for understanding the outlines of modern philosophical debate as well as comparative law both in America and on the Continent.

On the Continent the modern debate extends well back into the 18th century. In France, the debate was stimulated by the writings of Beccaria, and by a widespread hostility to judicial discretion.[7] This hostility to judicial discretion is fundamental to the Continental tradition, and it is well to dwell on it for a moment. In the 18th century the French debate turned in part on a technical question in the law of criminal punishment, the question of the judge's 'arbitraire' – that is, the judge's authority to individualise some, but not all, punishments.[8] It also turned in part on

[6] See, eg, K Abou el Fadl, *The Authoritative and Authoritarian in Islamic Discourses: A Contemporary Case Study* 3rd edn (Alexandria, Al-Saadawi Publications, 2002).

[7] For the French debate over Beccaria, see JQ Whitman, *Harsh Justice: Criminal Punishment and the Widening Divide between America and Europe* (Oxford, OUP, 2003) 163, with further citations.

[8] See A Laingui and A Lebigre, *Histoire du droit pénal*, (Paris, PUF, 1979), vol 2, 129–136.

the peculiar tradition of French hostility to the power of the *parlements*, the proudly 'sovereign' courts of the nobility of the robe.[9]

The 18th century debates culminated, in the French Revolution, with a concerted effort to bind judges by creating law sufficiently certain to eliminate their effective discretion. The great instruments for achieving this end were the codes, and in particular the iconic Code Civil, a model both of verbal clarity and of conceptual vagueness. The literature on the Code Civil is of course immense, but I think it is fair to say that the Code aimed to give answers that were both correct and definitive, and that it was largely motivated by a determination to limit judicial discretion.[10] As Germans like to put it, the aim was to make the judge a '*Subsumtionsautomat*,' an automaton who would spit out the right answer just as soda-pop machine spits out the correct bottle when fed the correct change.[11]

Anxiety about judicial discretion has remained a constant of French legal thought down until the present day. Nevertheless by the end of the 19th century scholars like François Gény had come to the conclusion that it was impossible for the law to dispose of all questions in advance with certainty. This led Gény to insist that judges often had to decide cases through 'free scientific research.'[12] Later francophone philosophers have all shared something like Gény's scepticism,[13] and French decisions today are indeed largely made through a kind of 'free scientific research,' which aims to uncover what might be called correct answers even at the cost of introducing some *de facto* uncertainty into French decisional law. Nevertheless, this free research goes on *derrière les coulisses*, as Mitchel Lasser has recently insisted, and French law continues to maintain a kind of public fiction that the law dictates answers that are both correct and definitive.[14]

German law does not maintain the same sort of public fiction, but in its own way the German tradition looks much like the French. In 18th- and 19th-century Germany, the debate turned in particular on the *Allgemeines Landrecht* of Prussia, the immense codification promulgated in 1794 that

[9] B Stone, *The French Parlements and the Crisis of the Old Regime* (Chapel Hill, University of North Carolina Press, 1986).

[10] Classic discussion in JP Dawson, *The Oracles of the Law* (Ann Arbor, University of Michigan Law School, 1968) 374–400.

[11] R Ogorek, *Richterkönig oder Subsumtionsautomat? : zur Justiztheorie im 19. Jahrhundert* (Frankfurt, Klostermann, 1986).

[12] F Gény, 2d (ed), *Méthode d'interprétation et sources en droit privé positif : essai critique* (Paris, LGDJ, 1919).

[13] Eg B Frydman, *Le sens des lois* (Bruxelles, Bruylant, 2005) 588–590.

[14] M Lasser, *Judicial Deliberations: A Comparative Analysis of Judicial Transparency and Legitimacy* (Oxford, OUP, 2004) 27–61.

purported to give definitive answers to every possible legal question.[15] This project was, inevitably, a failure, and thoughtful German jurists, like thoughtful French ones, have understood ever since that it is impossible to resolve all legal problems in advance with certainty. Here again the critical developments came in the later 19th century and the early 20th century. There were even early 20th-century German philosophers who, partly inspired by a kind of Anglophilia, defended some fairly radical views of judicial discretion.[16] Those radical views have had few advocates since 1914 or so, but it is certainly German philosophical orthodoxy that the law cannot specify definitive answers to all, or even most, questions in advance.[17] As we shall see, though, that does not by any means imply that German jurists have given up on the project of attaining certainty within the limits of the possible. The bottom line is that Continental legal philosophers have long since rejected any naïve belief in the possibility of giving definitive answers to all legal questions. (It is more difficult to say whether Continental philosophers believe in the possibility of giving correct answers.)

In the Anglo-American world the modern debate is equally old, and Anglo-American philosophers have come to conclusions that are in many ways similar to those given by their European counterparts. The debate has been especially lively over the last few decades, owing to Dworkin's 1977 intervention, and it includes many ingenious and revealing contributions. This is not the place to review all of the Anglo-American literature. I will take the work of one author, Timothy Endicott, as an example of its depth and perspicacity. Endicott is not content simply to skewer the idea that any legal system could possibly provide a complete set of definitive answers in advance. He goes a step further, arguing that efforts to give definitive answers may in fact *diminish* the level of meaningful certainty in the law. Vagueness is not only inevitable, according to Endicott. It is necessary for proper rule of law.[18] Endicott is one of many such Anglo-American voices. Even Dworkin treats the hunt for definitive answers essentially as at best a kind of necessary aspiration, rather than as a realisable ideal. In this, the Anglo-American is not much different from the Continental.

[15] See, eg, F Wieacker, T Weir (trans), *A History of Private Law in Europe, with Particular Reference to Germany* (Oxford, Clarendon Press, 1995) 264.

[16] For discussion, see W Fikentscher, *Methoden des Rechts in vergleichender Darstellung* (Tübingen, Mohr Siebeck, 1975) vol 3, 365–382; K Muscheler, *Relativismus und Freiheit: Ein Versuch über Hermann Kantorowicz* (Heidelberg, Müller Jur Vlg CF, 1984).

[17] For an authoritative current statement, see W Hassemer, '*Rechtssystem und Kodifikation: Die Bindung des Richters an das Gesetz*' in A Kaufmann, W Hassemer and U Neumann (eds), *Einführung in Rechtsphilosophie und Rechtstheorie der Gegenwart* 7th edn (Heidelberg, Auflage, 2004) 251–269.

[18] TAO Endicott, 'The impossibility of the rule of law' (1999) 19 *Oxford Journal of Legal Studies* 1–18.

The Anglo-American tradition does differ from the Continental, though, in one striking way. Anglo-American philosophers give the impression of being far less concerned with the dangers of judicial authority. For Continentals, especially but not exclusively the French, the problem of right answers has always been, at base, the problem of limiting the scope of judicial decision-making authority. The Continental tradition presupposes a kind of sharp tension between rule of law and rule of men. Correspondingly, for Continentals, any maximalist understanding of judicial discretion smacks of philosophical radicalism.

Anglo-American philosophers, by contrast, are generally relatively untroubled by judicial authority. Dworkin, whose heroic judge Hercules has become a familiar stock figure of the philosophical *commedia dell'arte*, is the obvious example, but he is not the only one. Perhaps precisely because Anglo-American philosophers are less troubled by judicial authority than Continental ones, Anglo-American philosophers are less preoccupied by the pursuit of definitive answers. It is after all the very objective of a system dedicated to definitive answers to limit the scope of the authority of official actors. Here again, Dworkin is the classic example of a philosopher utterly committed to the pursuit of correct answers, while seemingly abandoning the pursuit of definitive ones.

III. NO RIGHT ANSWER: COMPARATIVE LAW

Whatever the differences between Anglo-American and Continental legal philosophers, though, they pale before the similarities. On the one hand, there is a consensus on both sides of the Atlantic, after many generations of debate, that no system can succeed in providing definitive answers to all possible legal questions. On the other hand, there is an absence of consensus on both sides of the Atlantic, after many generations of debate, on the challenging philosophical question of whether it is possible to give correct answers. In the end, the differences are not immense, and we can say that legal philosophy has attained much the same level of sophistication throughout the Atlantic world.

But that does not mean that the philosophically naïve idea that one must hunt for definitive correct answers has vanished from the law. On the contrary, as Damaška argued in 1968, and as he and other comparativists have repeatedly shown since, there remain occidental lawyers who are very much committed to the pursuit of definitive correct answers, whatever philosophers may say. But they are, for the most part, Continental lawyers and not American ones. Indeed, despite the broad agreement among philosophers everywhere, the differences in practice between the functioning of legal orders on either side of the Atlantic can be remarkable.

In part, the differences between the Continental and the American outlook are differences in legal reasoning and legal education, which are elegantly traced in Damaška's 1968 lecture. Damaška's lecture was entitled 'A Continental Lawyer in an American Law School: Trials and Tribulations of Adjustment.' This may seem an unpromising title, the title of the sort of lecture by foreign visitors that one endures rather than enjoys, but in fact Damaška had subtle things indeed to say. He described a kind of astonishment at the culture of American law that many foreign visitors feel.[19] As Damaška explained it, he was the product of a Continental tradition that took it for granted that the law could be studied in an orderly and systematic way, in the effort to find 'right answers.' To such a product of Continental education, it was surprising, and perhaps even shocking, to discover that American law was different.

Now of course, the notion that Continental law is more systematic than American is familiar, and Damaška could easily have presented it in a banal way. He did not. On the contrary, he described the differences with a striking ethnographic detachment, a sample of his admirable ability to describe legal systems without becoming a captive of their basic assumptions. Continental legal education, as Damaška explained, 'involves exposure to … the grammar of law, [and] a panoramic view of the most important fields of law.'[20] He described the 'grammar' and the 'panoramic view' in terms that deserve to be quoted at length:

> In order to gain an understanding of Continental legal grammar, Americans should imagine lawyers of an analytic turn of mind à la Hohfeld at work for a long time, studying the law as it emerged from legal practice. Americans should further imagine that both the analysts' dissection of the law and their generalisations were generally accepted by the legal profession … .
>
> Many rather amorphous American concepts would be subjected to rigorous analysis. An illustration is the concept of jurisdiction, with its bewildering number of meanings. Words and phrases like 'property,' 'standing to sue,' 'security' and 'mens rea' also come to mind. In the process of analysis the twilight zone of the concepts would be somewhat reduced, some of the sub-concepts isolated and separately labeled. A richer and more precise legal terminology would appear. Movement would also proceed in the opposite direction, that is toward the creation of more general, almost cathedral-like concepts. For example, inquiry into what contracts, conveyances and wills have in common would probably result in something similar to the Continental concept of legal transactions (*Rechtsgeschäft, negozio giuridico*). The newly created concepts would become accepted as elements of standard legal terminology. Study would then proceed to the relationships between such legal concepts.

[19] Compare LE Nagle, 'Maximizing Legal Education: The International Component' (2000) 29 *Stetson Law Review* 1091 for similar autobiographical reflections.

[20] M Damaška, see above n 3, at 1364 and 1365 n 1.

> Questions would be raised about the relationship of 'jurisdictional' to 'procedural' issues, of 'mistake' to 'mens rea.' Inquiry into relationships between concepts would be linked to an investigation into the nature or essence of concepts ... Thus, step by step, the conceptual digestion of the law would result in a network of precise interrelated concepts, broad principles and classificatory ideals. This network is the grammar of the law.[21]

The creation of such a grammar belonged to the effort to identify 'right answers':

> There is a significant lack of the argumentative approach towards the law which permeates the atmosphere of law schools in [the United States]. The moving spirit of analysis is not the desire to find the best argument for a proposition, but rather the quest for the 'right' answer to the problem at hand.[22]

As for the 'panoramic view': This offered a general account of the state of any given area of law. 'This comprehensive view of the whole':

> is considered to be of utmost importance. It is feared that if the young lawyer fails to perceive the great contours of private and public law in school, he will seldom acquire an overview later in practice. Entangled in the jungle of practical problems, he will be deprived of the guidance that comes from an awareness of the totality of law in his particular field.[23]

American law, by contrast, had 'no real counterpart to the Continental grammar of the law.'[24] Indeed, Americans were 'sceptical at best of the usefulness of the curious conceptual structure[s]' of the Continent. Instead, they devoted themselves to an argumentative mode, seeking the 'best arguments' for a given case. And panoramic views were nowhere to be found.

Let us pause for a moment to admire the sophistication of what Damaška had to say in this lecture. There are indeed many foreign visitors who experience the kind of astonishment that Damaška describes. I have encountered quite a few, and I can report that most of them, unlike Damaška, simply take the unsympathetic view that American law is primitive. Indeed there are some of them who believe, to return to the passage of Brian Bix quoted above, that American law cannot *really* count as 'legal' system. Such visitors might perhaps admit that American law has an 'argumentative' commitment to finding correct answers, but they are baffled, if not appalled, by the American lack of interest in establishing definitive ones. Damaška, by contrast, came to his lecture with an open mind about American approaches. Moreover, his account of Continental law stands out for its adroitness. He acknowledged that Continental law

[21] *Ibid* 1365–66.
[22] *Ibid* 1364.
[23] *Ibid* 1367.
[24] *Ibid* 1365.

sought answers that were 'right' in the sense that they were both definitive and correct. But he did not defend the naive idea that it is actually possible to arrive at such answers. Instead, he spoke of Continental law, not as *finding* definitive correct answers in fact, but as having a 'grammar,' a coherent method for *seeking* such answers. And he was careful only to describe the Continental tradition as committed to the proposition that the 'twilight zone' of concepts could be 'somewhat reduced.'

At any rate, what Damaška identified in his 1968 lecture as a key theme in comparative law has since captured the attention a number of fine scholars, who have shown that the fundamental contrast described by Damaška can be detected in a wide of range of differences, both substantive and procedural, between the Continental and the Anglo-American traditions. Let me now turn to some of their observations, before adding some of my own.

Robert Kagan, for example, in a book that exploits a large literature of sociological studies, reviews numerous aspects of the American pattern. Kagan's book grew out of a comparative study of harbour management in Oakland and Rotterdam. In the course of that study, Kagan conducted numerous interviews that revealed that parties involved in the business of these two harbors routinely found American law more unpredictable than Dutch law, and he made unpredictability a recurrent theme of his book. In one typically elegant passage, Kagan offered the following observations after discussing the bizarre litigation between Pennzoil and Texaco, which resulted in a multi-billion dollar judgment entirely unforeseen by Texaco's counsel:

> How could a sophisticated company such as Texaco, with its cadre of experienced attorneys and investment bankers, fail by such a wide margin to discern the legal risks to which it was exposed? The answer is that in the decentralised American legal system, constantly being shaped and reshaped by adversarial argument, the legal terrain is often unstable; the ostensibly solid path mapped by one's lawyer can suddenly turn to quicksand. This is not an endemic feature of all legal regimes. When asked about transatlantic cargo damage disputes that reach adjudication, the shipping line and insurance firm representatives whom I interviewed all asserted that results in the courts in Rotterdam are far more predictable than when the litigation occurs in the United States.[25]

Like Damaška, let us note, Kagan thus sees American law as characterised by adversarial 'argument' rather than by a commitment to the quest for right answers. 'In both kinds of legal systems [that is US and European],' Kagan observes at another point, echoing Damaška's account of Europe,

[25] R Kagan, *Adversarial Legalism: The American Way of Law* (Cambridge, Harvard University Press, 2001) 110–111.

'pre-trial settlements occur "in the shadow of the law." But the greater predictability of European adjudication means that the boundary of the shadow is far clearer.'[26]

The boundary of the shadow is clearer in Europe. Europeans are not utter juridical naïfs. They know that not all legal questions can be settled easily and in advance. But they have not abandoned the effort to built systems that seek definitive answers; they are far more committed than Americans to minimising uncertainty to the extent possible; and comparative studies seem to show that they have succeeded. This is an observation that can be made consistently over a wide range of areas of the law. Take the case of divorce, an example highlighted by Kagan. A pair of studies published in 1986, by John Griffiths and Austin Sarat and William Felstiner, revealed striking differences between the Netherlands and the United States. Divorce lawyers in the United States, as anybody who has been involved a divorce of any complexity knows, advise their clients that the results of the litigation will depend on which judge hears the case. American divorce is a world of extreme judicial discretion. Felstiner and Sarat describe the resulting attitude of American lawyers:

> For lawyers, legal justice is situational and outcomes are often unpredictable ... Lawyers are intimately familiar with the human dimensions of the legal process. They know that in most instances the process is not rule governed, that there is widespread use of discretion, and that decisions are influenced by matters extraneous to legal doctrine.[27]

Sarat and Felstiner further describe the consequent frustration and confusion of American clients: 'Where clients want predictions and certainty, lawyers introduce them to the frequently unpredictable reality of divorce.'[28] 'Unpredictable': the word appears again and again in studies of American law. Griffiths, on the other hand, portrays a Dutch system in which most issues are fairly settled, and in which lawyers serve as guides who lead their clients through a system that is, like all legal systems, complex, but that is also quite predictable to those know it. 'The standards by which [child] support is computed by the court,' he writes, for example,

> are clear and detailed. The amount to be paid is therefore usually easy to determine for an expert who knows these standards.[29]

In an area like divorce, we thus see that the comparatively open-ended character of American law can have a direct and powerful impact on the lives of ordinary litigants.

[26] *Ibid* 117.
[27] *Ibid* 126.
[28] *Ibid* 127.
[29] *Ibid* 140.

The same is true of other areas of law as well. Take one example of great importance to contemporary legal life: business contracts. It is a familiar fact of global law that American contracts are far longer and far more complex than contracts produced in countries like Germany or Japan.[30] A stimulating comparative law literature has grown up around this phenomenon, and several explanations have been offered. I will not explore all those explanations here, but at least one has to do with the same differences in the attitude toward right answers we see in so many areas of the law. We can think of a business contract as giving answers to the questions presented by a given transaction. The striking fact, as Hill and King note in a fine recent study, is that German contracts tend to give the same answer all the time, where American contracts are much more varied. In America 'contracts of a particular type of transaction are similar in general coverage, but the specific language varies considerably from contract to contract'; whereas in Germany 'many provisions are quite similar from contract to contract.'[31] The consequence for parties to contracts is the same as the consequence for parties to so many other types of transactions: 'Compared to US law, German law may yield more certain results in litigation.'[32]

Continental law tends to give a single answer more consistently, and the result, as many scholars observe, is that Continental law is generally more predictable. In this we discover one of the 'grand discriminants' dividing American law from Continental.[33]

Let me offer a few more examples, even if only in a cursory way, before turning to the significance of this grand discriminant for legal philosophy. The examples are many and varied – so many and so varied that it is clear that we are dealing with a deep-seated structural difference. The use of expert witnesses is one. On the Continent expert witnesses are appointed by the court, in the expectation that they will give the correct answer on the topic in question. In America by contrast we see the battle of experts offering arguments.[34] Federalism too offers examples of great interest for comparative law. The law in the fifty states of America often gives quite different answers to the most basic questions in the law. Yet Americans

[30] JH Langbein, 'Comparative Civil Procedure and the Style of Complex Contracts' (1987) 35 *American Journal of Comparative Law* 381; C Hill and C King, 'How do German Contracts do as Much with Fewer Words' (2004) 79 *Chicago-Kent Law Review* 889; DH Foote, 'Evolution in the Concept of Contracts' in V Kusuda-Smick (ed), *US/Japan Commercial Law and Trade* (Ardsley on Hudson, Transnational Juris Publications, 1990).

[31] Hill and King, above n 30, at 894–895.

[32] *Ibid* 892.

[33] For this famous phrase, B Kaplan, 'An American Lawyer in the Queen's Courts: Impressions of English Civil Procedure' (1971) 69 *Michigan Law Review* 821, 841.

[34] Eg, M Reimann, 'Liability for Defective Products at the Beginning of the Twenty-First Century: Emergence of a Worldwide Standard?' (2003) 51 *American Journal of Comparative Law* 751, 826–828.

regard all of these different answers as equally valid American law, and efforts to regularise the law on a nationwide basis are quite unsuccessful. This may seem unsurprising to Americans. After all, the 50 states are 50 sovereign entities, even if federated. But it is striking that Continental Europeans do not view matters the same way. The European Union is a federation too. Certainly its member states are least as sovereign as the member states of the US Yet it is a commonplace in contemporary Europe that a functioning federation *must* have a unified system of law, giving the same answer in every case and every place.[35] (Moreover many leading Continental jurists seem to believe that it is possible to provide the federation with answers that are both definitive and correct.)

Nor does the contrast end there. There is not even a fixed system of international private law in the United States. International private law – what we call 'the conflict of laws' – is a hopeless mess in my country. One might have imagined that a federation like ours, with its multiple legal systems, would have at least have developed a dependable doctrine of international private law. Nothing could be farther from the truth: Even in this regard the American system gives no definitive answer. At the same time, our law of jurisdiction permits litigants to file suit in the widest range of jurisdictions – while our corporate law permits firms to choose to incorporate in states with strikingly different corporate regimes. The result is a level of disorder that will often seem, to the Continental jurist, wholly medieval.

Our federal law, similarly, is remarkably varied, with many conflicts among the various circuits that go unresolved for decades. This is inevitable, because of a fact of great significance for comparative law: Our Supreme Court accepts a caseload far too small to permit it regularise jurisprudence on the federal level. The comparison with the French Cour de Cassation is particularly striking. The Cour de Cassation, committed to regularising jurisprudence throughout France, decides tens of thousands of cases each year.[36] The American Supreme Court, by contrast, which 'took control' of its caseload with the Judiciary Act 1925, issues a number of decisions that can only be called miniscule – far too few to regularise American federal jurisprudence.[37] As a result, important differences can persist for long stretches of time among the federal circuits. The Supreme Court may accept enough cases to engage in a quest for correct answers in a few isolated areas of the law, but it makes no meaningful effort to

[35] Eg, R Zimmermann, 'Civil Code or Civil Law –Towards a New European Private Law' (1994) 20 *Syracuse Journal of International Law and Commerce* 217.

[36] See <http://www.courdecassation.fr/IMG/File/pdf_2007/divers/plaquette_statistiques_2006.pdf> accessed 19 June 2008.

[37] Eg, A Hellman, 'The Shrunken Docket of the Rehnquist Court' (1996) *Supreme Court Review* 403.

guarantee definitive answers over the broader legal landscape. Thousands of flowers bloom in the law of the United States. The many federal circuits, like the many states, routinely give different answers to the same questions, and all of their answers are regarded as perfectly valid, or at least un-policeable in their variety.

It is almost needless to remark that the basic forms of judicial decision-making show much the same pattern. American judges render 'opinions' – a very strange term from the French point of view, as Antoine Garapon and Ioannis Papadopoulos observe.[38] Moreover, American judges have a tradition of publishing their dissents in a way that was once deemed completely *outré* on the Continent. Dissents have made some headway in European constitutional law in recent years, but the American culture of dissent has hardly conquered Europe yet. Different American judges cheerfully deliver clashing 'opinions' on questions of law, and lawyers often refer to what judges decide as their 'arguments.' The American Supreme Court, not least, presents what can seem a spectacle of stunning lawlessness to outsiders, as lawyers makes plays for the votes of the justices, trying to 'get to five.' To the Continental eye this of course looks like a baffling, not to say disturbing, acceptance of a rule of men rather than a rule of law – rather like the American system of divorce law. Regularisation of decisionmaking at the first instance is made extraordinarily difficult by the system of jury trial, with its unreviewable fact-finding, and by the use of the 'clearly erroneous' and 'abuse of discretion' standards in reviewing judicial determinations. And on it goes.

At the same time, our basic approach to jurisprudence makes it quite impossible to give what Damaška called the 'panoramic view.' The American common law often looks a caricature of the common law tradition, and this is also true of our jurisprudence. American courts take the case-law approach utterly seriously: We are trained to decide the case before us using the most minimal possible jurisprudential means. This tradition of judicial minimalism has produced, for example, the Ashwander doctrine in American constitutional law, which enjoins courts to avoid reaching constitutional questions if at all possible.[39] The consequence of this American minimalism is that courts scrupulously avoid exploring all the issues presented by any particular area of law. Indeed, it is common for our Supreme Court to 'reserve' questions – that is, to refuse expressly to decide important questions raised by the case before the Court. Because of our minimalism, American courts never give a full conspectus of any area

[38] A Garapon and I Papadopoulos, *Juger en Amérique et en France* (Paris, Odile Jacob, 2003) 199–226.

[39] *Ashwander v TVA*, 297 US 288, 347 (1936) (Brandeis J, concurring).

of law.[40] Meanwhile American scholars devote themselves primarily to various forms of inventive law-and scholarship: law-and-economics, law-and-history, what have you. The great majority of American law professors, at least during the last 20 or 30 years, have even less interest in systematic investigation of the law than American courts do.

In all these respects, American law seems never to have embraced the core Continental commitment to creating a form of rule of law based on the pursuit of certainty to the extent humanly possible. In criminal law in particular, that core Continental commitment goes by a name, the name of 'legality,' and I would like to close this section by speaking for a moment about the concept of legality and what it implies. Americans have a concept called 'legality,' which at first glance looks little different from what we find on the Continent. It holds that criminal liability and punishment can only be imposed on the basis of a clear legislative prohibition.[41] But in practice, the Continental approach differs dramatically from the American, in ways that reveal the powerful grip of the right answer mentality in the Continental world.

The Continental concept of 'legality' derives from the familiar Latin maxim *nulla poena, nullum crimen, sine lege*.[42] In modern times this principle of legality is said to have two basic implications: a ban on retroactivity and a requirement of maximal certainty. The fundamental idea of legality can be found in Article 8 of the Declaration of the Rights of Man and the Citizen 1789: '*La Loi ne doit établir que des peines strictement et évidemment nécessaires, et nul ne peut être puni qu'en vertu d'une Loi établie et promulguée antérieurement au délit, et légalement appliquée.*' Its current form can be found, for example, in the 1983 European Court of Human Rights decision in *Silver v United Kingdom*:

> a norm cannot be regarded as 'law' unless it is formulated with sufficient precision to enable the citizen to regulate his conduct: he must be able – if need be with appropriate advice – to foresee, to a degree that is reasonable in the circumstances, the consequences which a given action may entail.

These statements may seem unexceptionable to most Americans. Do they not correspond to what we think of as legality too? Nevertheless, in Europe they are taken to imply legal prescriptions unimaginable in the United States.

The most important of these have to do with prosecutors. Prosecutors seem like threatening figures to Europeans in a way that is not the case in America. In the United States we tend to think of the arbitrariness of

40 C Sunstein, *One Case at a Time: Judicial Minimalism on the Supreme Court* (Cambridge, Harvard University Press, 1999).

41 PH Robinson, *Criminal Law* (New York, Aspen Law & Business, 1997) § 2.2, 74–75.

42 For the long history, reaching back to Antiquity, see V Krey, *Keine Strafe ohne Gesetz* (Berlin/New York, Gruyter, 1983).

judges as the main threat to rule of law: Most of our discussion of the risks of 'rule of men' as opposed to 'rule of law' in the United States, to the extent we discuss those risks, turn on the problems of judging. Not so in Europe. Europeans certainly regard judicial arbitrariness as a danger. Indeed, by contrast with Americans they can seem obsessed with the danger. But in sharp contrast to Americans, they regard prosecutorial arbitrariness as dangerous too. (The contrast is particularly striking in light of the recent scandals involving the politicisation of the American prosecutorial corps both on the state level in North Carolina and on the federal level). This has significant implications for Continental legality. The Continental concept of legality holds, in a way foreign to American practice, that prosecutors must determine the 'correct' charge in any given case. From the Continental point of view, the application of criminal law is only appropriate if proscribed behavior has been clearly defined in advance. By implication, the prosecutor, if his power is to be properly cabined, must be able to give a single right answer to the question: what clearly forbidden act has the accused committed? Continental legality holds that there must be, at least in principle, a right answer, and that prosecutors must therefore have no charging discretion.

Anglo-American criminal law, by contrast, has historically been entirely innocent of this Continental concept of legality. This has consequences of real importance for comparative law. To begin with, American prosecutors have the widest range of charging discretion. Indeed, they bring the same spirit of inventiveness to their task that American business lawyers bring to the drafting of contracts. The fact that American prosecutors have this inventive discretion is immensely important – particularly when it comes to the practice of American plea bargaining, which notoriously involves charge bargaining rather than sentence bargaining. Indeed, these differences in plea bargaining have become the subject of one most fertile sub-literatures in comparative law – and the subject of one of the great political debates on the global legal scene as well.[43]

Another consequence of the historic difference in concepts of legality is being felt in contemporary England. England faces considerable difficulties, here as elsewhere, under the Human Rights Act 1998: English criminal law must deal with Continental concepts of 'legality' and 'certainty' that have no place in its jurisprudence. English criminal prohibitions are framed in language that fails to meet the Continental test of certainty, and as a result

[43] See generally M Langer, 'From Legal Transplants to Legal Translations: The Globalization of Plea Bargaining and the Americanization Thesis in Criminal Procedure' (2004) 45 *Harvard International Law Journal* 1–64; J Ross, 'Criminal Law and Procedure: The Entrenched Position of Plea Bargaining in United States Legal Practice' (2006) 54 *American Journal of Comparative Law* 717.

England is facing the possible task of producing an entirely new criminal code divorced from its common law traditions.[44]

IV. CONCLUSION

Further detailed examples could be given, but for now I would like to turn to larger questions of interpretation. What should we say about these consistent and wide-ranging differences in attitude toward the pursuit of right answers? One's first temptation in surveying all of this is to ask which of the two approaches is better. Continentals will tend to deplore American law as verging on lawlessness. Americans will tend to dismiss the Continental approach as naïve in its efforts to minimise discretion, and poorly attuned to the economic and social values inherent in letting parties craft their own agreements and settle their own disputes. Each side is likely to exaggerate the failings of the other. My view is that there are advantages and dangers in both. The Continental tradition does provide more certainty, which makes for a more comfortable experience for most litigants, since it shields them from much litigation risk. The Continental approach also contributes to the making of a more humane criminal law. The American tradition, by contrast, requires litigants to accept more risk, just as American life generally requires individuals to accept more risk than individuals do in northern Continental Europe. This is difficult for many people, but it probably permits more innovation and encourages a culture of individual autonomy.

But asking which is the better approach is not the only, or even the best, way to do comparative law. Far-reaching change is not likely on either side of the Atlantic. People in both worlds are much too deeply attached to their way of doing things. We all resist radical critiques of the basic value commitments of our legal traditions; and the differences I have traced in the comparative law of right answers are, in my view, differences in basic value commitments. That is to say, they are not merely 'functional' differences – differences between 'better' and 'worse' methods chosen to achieve a goal shared by actors in all legal systems.[45] They are differences that have to do with fundamental differences in attitude toward questions like the primacy of individual autonomy or the imperative of reducing risk in everyday life. They are differences that grow, not out of different approaches to solving the technical problems of the law, but out of more fundamentally disparate perceptions of what matters in the world.

[44] A Ashworth, 'Human Rights, Criminal Law, and the Principles of Legal Certainty and Non-Retrospectivity' in J Arnold *et al* (eds) *Menschengerechtes Strafrecht. FS für Albin Eser zum 70. Geburtstag* (Munich, Beck, 2005) 48–59.

[45] See the classic discussion of K Zweigert and H Kötz, T Weir (trans), *Introduction to Comparative Law*, (Oxford, Clarendon Press, 1992).

How can we explain the fact that such disparities in basic values divide countries of the Atlantic world? Let me assert as forcefully as possible that the disparities in question are not the product of differences in philosophical analysis of the no-right-answer problem. It is not that Americans have engaged in careful collective reflection over the place of definitive answers in the legal system, weighed the pros and cons, and opted for a maximally open-ended approach. Most American lawyers are utterly unselfconscious about this aspect of their law. Nor is it that Continentals have carefully weighed the pros and cons. Jurists who work in the Continental tradition are certainly the beneficiaries of a superb intellectual tradition, but (contrary to what my friend Bill Ewald has claimed[46]) they do not translate the lessons of philosophy directly into law. Like lawyers everywhere, they spend their time patiently working out the technical legal implications of deeply held, but poorly articulated, beliefs. The only possible explanations for our differences in law have to do with differences in culture, history and social traditions.

So what are the differences in culture, history and social traditions that account for the contrast between American and the Continent? Damaška gave us the single finest answer we possess in his 1986 masterpiece *The Faces of Justice and State Authority*, which famously traced a remarkable range of differences in procedure and legal reasoning to differences in the structure of authority. As Damaška argued, America was characterised by 'co-ordinate' authority, while the Continent was relatively more 'hierarchical.' This had fundamental implications for the shape of legal reasoning. In a hierarchical system, oriented toward to the supervision and control of the behavior of lower-ranking officials by higher-ranking ones, it is essential that the law give a definitive answer to the extent possible. If it fails to do so, the work of lower-ranking officials can not be verified and corrected by their superiors.[47] On this view, the Continental tendency to embrace a single answer has little or nothing to do with the lessons of philosophy. Indeed, the lessons of philosophy would suggest that the hunt for definitive answers is fated to fail. Instead, it has to with a culture of distrust of lower-level officials. It is part and parcel of the Continental tradition of legality, founded not so much on any particular conception of law, but on an extreme suspiciousness toward anything that smacks of the rule of men. American law, by contrast, with its weak hierarchical controls and wide-ranging discretion for trial-level judges and juries, is not the product of a comparable culture of distrust. It is the product of a world that accepts a wide diffusion of authority among legal officials. The forms of legal

[46] W Ewald, 'Comparative Jurisprudence: What Was it Like to Try a Rat?' (1995) 1995 *University of Pennsylvania Law Review* 1889.

[47] M Damaška, *The Faces of Justice and State Authority: A Comparative Approach to the Legal Process* (New Haven, Yale University Press, 1986) 54–56.

reasoning are thus derivative of the structure of authority in the societies that Damaška considered, so he argued.[48]

Now, Damaška's account deserves, and needs, to be both expanded and supplemented. First, it is important to remind Continentals that the open-ended character of American law that he described so well is not unique to America. On the contrary, it is typical of many world systems, especially those that take the form of a *Juristenrecht*. Classical Roman law, for example, did not give a single definitive answer. All the evidence we have shows the classical jurists expressed differing, and sometimes sharply differing, opinions on questions of law. Like the judges of modern America, the classical Roman jurists seemed to have functioned without significant hierarchical oversight, despite what may have been efforts by the Emperor Augustus to restrict opinion-giving to officially sanctioned jurists.[49] The same is true of Talmudic law, and perhaps most notably of classical Islamic law, which is marked by a powerful resistance to the notion that definitive answers can be dictated by any supreme human hierarchical authority.[50] Indeed, Continental law is arguably quite exceptional in insisting on definitive answers. That does not mean that there are no parallels to the Continental pattern. Imperial Chinese law may be one. At any rate, Damaška's analysis can be applied revealingly well beyond the US/Continental contrast that was his subject in *The Faces of Justice*.

Still, revealing though it is, Damaška's analysis does leave some questions unanswered. Damaška leaves us wondering why the United States shows a co-ordinate pattern while the Continent shows a hierarchical one. In some sense, the answer is easy: We all know that relatively strong resistance to hierarchical forms of authority has been a recurrent theme of American history. Nevertheless, one wants more. There are also other factors that deserve more discussion, some of them mentioned by Damaška, some not. The more orderly and 'scientific' Continental approach is the product of a legal tradition that emerged in the medieval universities, while the English common law established itself in the universities only much later. This is a fact of obvious importance for explaining the contrast between the Continent and the Anglo-American world. Perhaps the importance of

[48] The importance of trust and distrust in the structure of legal reasoning is the subject of Scott Shapiro's forthcoming book, *Legality*.

[49] See now the excellent account of K Tuori, *Ancient Roman Lawyers and Modern Legal Ideals*, (Helsinki, University of Helsinki Printing House, 2006) 101–84.

[50] For the 'questioning, pluralistic' structure of Talmud, see, eg, B Lifshitz, 'The Age of the Talmud' in NS Hecht, BS Jackson, SM Passaneck, D Piatelli and AM Rabello (eds), *An Introduction to the History and Sources of Jewish Law* (Oxford: Clarendon Press, 1996), 179. For Islamic law, see, eg, Abou El-Fadl, *The Authoritative and the Authoritarian*, above n 6.

universities in the making of Continental law has some relation to the hierarchical character of authority Damaška describes, but it is not entirely obvious what that relation might be.

Damaška hints that he thinks differences in religious traditions play a role too. In the American pattern he detects the strength of Protestant tradition that lays all the weight on the conscientious decision-making of individuals.[51] Presumably he sees the Continental tradition as more Catholic. I think this explanation is problematic, but one does want to hear more about it. Is it possible that the Continental commitment to right answers is the intellectual offspring of some Christian idea of orthodoxy? After all, Christianity is nearly unique among world religions in its commitment to policing belief.[52] Perhaps the Continental jurists are the inheritors of a Catholic version of the ancient feature of Christianity. As I have indicated, I also believe that there are differences in the attitude toward individual autonomy that may deserve more attention.

But all this is amounts to no more than quibbling over how to characterise the basic values at stake. What matters, as Damaška rightly insisted in *The Faces of Justice*, is that there is no way to explain the comparative differences we discover without acknowledging how much the law is shaped by what are often poorly articulated value commitments – and without acknowledging that those value commitments differ from society to society.

Surely it is those value commitments that must be the topic of any ultimately persuasive legal philosophy of right answers. Surely we must recognise that people do not philosophise carefully about their law, and that therefore careful philosophy cannot offer us full descriptions of how the law works. Of course Brian Bix can not imagine how the position 'might be justified' that

> systems ... that are structured in such a way that there are *not* always unique correct answers to legal problems, are not 'really' *legal* systems.

From the point of view of careful philosophy, such a position cannot be justified. And yet Continental legal systems seem to reflect some level of commitment to exactly that proposition.

Lawyers do not think philosophically, and they do not so for the simple reason that law is not philosophy. Instead it is an effort to remain faithful to certain dearly held values, even when there is no perfectly persuasive or philosophically cogent way of doing so. I think comparative law forces us to recognise that legal systems are value systems of that sort. Of course, to say law is not philosophy is not to insinuate that the philosophers have all

[51] Damaška, above n 47, at 19.
[52] R MacMullen, *Christianity and Paganism in the Fourth to Eighth Centuries* (New Haven, Yale University Press, 1997).

gotten it wrong. On the contrary, I imagine that Dworkin too conceives of the enterprise of the law as an effort to work out the consequences of basic value commitments. Nevertheless even Dworkin, like so many other philosophers, seems, to the eye of the comparative lawyer, all too obviously the product of the values of his own legal culture. The picture that Dworkin paints – the picture of a law that seeks correct answers, but not definitive ones – is, after all, manifestly the picture of *American* law. The broader picture is one that the philosophers have yet to offer us.

Postcript

20

Anglo-American and Continental Systems: Marsupials and Mammals of the Law

RICHARD LEMPERT

WHEN PETER TILLERS invited me to participate in this *festschrift* for Mirjan Damaška, I proposed to write a short concluding essay reviewing the articles in this volume and drawing links between them. Perhaps I should have anticipated that this would be no easy task, and maybe even have foreseen that it was an assignment I would eventually shun. I should have known that there would not be the six to eight articles I anticipated but the 17 that have been submitted. Had I thought more, I would have realised that there would be many people, myself included, who would seek both to honour Professor Damaška and the opportunity to bask in his reflected glory. I certainly should have realised that there would be no easy way to summarise everything submitted, for Professor Damaška's academic *corpus* is too diverse and scholars' views of even the same works are too different to allow for any easy synthesis of contributions commenting on or inspired by Damaška's scholarship. Some see Professor Damaška as a leading comparativist, some admire him for his work on criminal procedure and some, myself included, view Professor Damaška as an outstanding evidence scholar, who has managed the all too rare accomplishment of bringing truly new ideas to the study of evidence and procedure. Fortunately what daunted me did not daunt John Jackson and Maximo Langer, for they have, in their introduction, done a superb job of pulling together the separate themes of this volume's contributions, although I will point out that not even they could unify the articles herein under a single theme.[1]

[1] J Jackson, M Langer, ch 1.

So if I am not to attempt a synthesis, what can I contribute? First, I simply want to add to the chorus of admiration for Professor Damaška. My admiration for him goes back to the first work of his I read, his path-breaking book *The Faces of Justice and State Authority*. I had read nothing like it before, nor, I might add, have I seen its equal since. It is one of those rare works that allows one to see what are familiar issues, in this case differences between Anglo-American and Continental legal systems, in a new light. Once viewed in this light, matters are never the same. In particular, by breaking down what had become fixed and sterile portraits of adversarial and inquisitorial systems, Professor Damaška helped his readers perceive and make sense of variations within and common features across Anglo-American and Continental justice systems. He did so by highlighting features that were either imperceptible or puzzling when viewed from within the confines of the received adversarial-inquisitorial dichotomy.

Professor Damaška first learned law abroad, and English is a second language to him. His work on comparative evidentiary and procedural law thus builds on certain (dare I say 'unfair') advantages Professor Damaška has over most of us who labour in evidence law's vineyards. He has a deep knowledge of Continental legal systems and the contexts in which they function, a level of knowledge to which few Americans even aspire. Also he writes English far better than almost all who acquired the language at a mother's knee. The freshness of his insights is matched, and perhaps enabled, by the freshness of his prose. For example:

> To consider forms of justice in monadic isolation from their social and economic context is – for many purposes – like playing *Hamlet* without the Prince.[2]

and

> Yet because [the opposing lawyer's] accounts are contrary in nature, the initial polarity created by the two evidentiary scenarios is preserved. Thus, as in a car driving at night, two narrow beams continue to illuminate the world presented to the adjudicator from the beginning until the end of trial.[3]

What American-born legal academic would, or could, write this way?

By receiving his initial legal training abroad, Professor Damaška avoided the downside of being taught to 'think like a lawyer'. Rather his thinking has been shaped by what he has observed and not by any ends he has aimed at. His is a Holmesean view of law, based on observation and experience; not logic. One reason Professor Damaška's insights are fresh is that he makes no attempt to fit Continental and Anglo-American legal

[2] M Damaška, *The Faces of Justice and State Authority* (New Haven, Yale University Press, 1986) 7.

[3] M Damaška, *Evidence Law Adrift* (New Haven, Yale University Press, 1997) 92.

systems into any boxes other than those boxes into which they seem empirically to fit best. Indeed, the Damaška who wrote *Faces of Justice* is more of a sociologist than a lawyer. Only those who confuse empirical analysis with quantitative data would not recognise this, for *Faces of Justice* is empirical at its core. It tells a sociological story linking the structure of legal procedure, and especially the trial, with the development of political authority and the goals of states. The theses it advances are not rigorously tested in accord with the canons of social science, but their broad outline so well fits facts we think we know that it is easy to find Professor Damaška's narrative compelling.

I hesitate to tread the fields Professor Damaška has sown, for my knowledge of comparative law and of European legal procedure pales next to his, but the temptation to follow Professor Damaška's example and think sociologically about the structure of the Anglo-American and Continental legal systems is more than I wish to resist. Like Professor Damaška, I shall construct, but cannot rigorously,test a sociological narrative of how Anglo-American and Continental legal systems function, but my starting point will be even further removed from the on the ground details of Anglo-American and Continental legal systems than Professor Damaška's ideal types, and my approach will suggest even more room for contingency in shaping the details of Anglo-American and Continental legal systems than his does. Without any necessary inconsistency with Professor Damaška's theorising, the perspective I shall offer will help explain why, as Professor Damaška recognises, his ideal types break down and overlap in practice. Also, the perspective I offer allows some speculation about how legal systems might develop in an increasingly international and global world.

To speak metaphorically, the Anglo American and Continental legal systems are the marsupials and mammals of the legal world. Because physical separation limited their competition with each other, marsupials in Australia and mammals in most of the rest of the world long ago took separate evolutionary paths. At the same time, despite local dominance, neither reproductive form entirely excluded the other. Viewed in one way marsupials and mammals are profoundly different; after all what is more fundamental than the developmental stage at which the young enter the world and the ways in which they are protected and nourished as they grow to self-sufficiency. Moreover, some life forms are unique to each – compare the kangaroo with any mammal of similar size, and remark on the lack of marsupial elephants. Yet in other ways many marsupials native to Australia are remarkably similar to mammals born elsewhere. Where ecology made the same demands, or offered the same opportunities, for survival, species that mirrored each other, like the marsupial thylacine and the mammal wolf, developed. Despite fundamental differences in reproduction and some surface differences in appearance, where marsupials and

mammals such as these filled the same ecological niche, they adapted in similar ways and shared the phenotypical characteristics most necessary for survival.[4] In similar fashion Anglo-American and Continental modes of trial and legal action have developed, or so I shall argue, to fill similar niches. Despite obvious and in some ways deep differences in premises and appearance, to the extent that similar demands have been placed on them, Continental and Anglo-American legal systems have much of what matters most in common.

Professor Damaška in *Faces of Justice* spotlights differences in Continental and legal systems engendered by differences in the social ecology and histories of the states that spawned them. I shall focus on states more as societies than as political actors and from this perspective point to fundamental similarities in the Anglo-American and Continental systems, with particular attention to how cases are decided. More speculatively, I will question whether the association between state authority and ways of trying cases trials that Professor Damaška *Faces of Justice* illuminates is a necessary one. Perhaps Professor Damaška's more centrally-driven Continental states could have functioned well with a judicial system that looked much like the non-hierarchical conflict resolving Anglo-American approach to trial justice, while the latter states could have coupled their more diffuse vesting of political power with a more hierarchical policy-oriented judiciary. Looking at existing practice one can only say that Professor Damaška tells a powerful story about why the association he posits is the more probable one. It is impossible to prove from the data at hand whether the association is necessary rather than plausible or likely. Indeed, I would not be surprised if a scholar as gifted as Professor Damaška could tell an opposite but equally convincing story were the facts on the ground reversed.

The perspective I shall write from is functionalism, an approach to understanding society that is seen as outdated by many American sociologists, although it has greater currency on the Continent.[5] It is also the perspective most consistent with Professor Damaška's approach to explanation in *Faces of Justice*. Functionalism is teleological in nature because it seeks to explain social norms and structures by the ends they serve.[6]

[4] Wikipedia explains: 'An example of convergent evolution, the Thylacine showed many similarities to the members of the Candidae (dog) family of the Northern Hemisphere: sharp teeth, powerful jaws, raised heels and the same general body form. Since the Thylacine filled the same ecological niche in Australia as the dog family did elsewhere, it developed many of the same features. Despite this, it is unrelated to any of the Northern Hemisphere predators — its closest living relative is the Tasmanian Devil (*Sarcophilus harrisii*).' <http://en.wikipedia.org/wiki/Thylacine> accessed 19 June 2008.

[5] See, eg, N Luhmann, *Social Systems* (Stanford, Stanford University Press, 1995).

[6] See A Stinchcombe, *Constructing Social Theories* (Chicago, University of Chicago Press, 1987) ch 3.

Because it most often seeks to plausibly explain the status quo, functionalism is often regarded as a conservative approach to social analysis, but functionalism is more properly seen as an analytic perspective that entails no normative approval of the status quo, and a functional analysis need not be conservative in its implications. Functionalism is also sometimes regarded as circular, for the persistence of an institution is evidence that it fills an important social function. There is more substance to this claim than to the claim that functionalism is necessarily conservative, but this does not mean the functional perspective is wrong, nor does it exclude the positing and testing of hypotheses about the roles institutions play in society and the implications of change or variation in institutions.

Functional theory is associated most prominently with the work of the American sociologist Talcott Parsons.[7] Parsons posited that there were four basic functions that a society, and the core institutions within a society, had to fill in order to survive. These were captured by the acronym AGIL, which stands for adaptation, goal attainment, integration and latency or, more commonly and more revealingly, pattern maintenance. At the societal level the economy was the core adaptive institution, the polity was core to goal attainment, cultural systems were fundamental to pattern maintenance and value systems, including especially legal institutions, were core to integration. No institution is, however, exclusively concerned with its associated core function. Economic, political and cultural systems also contribute to societal integration just as legal institutions contribute to adaptation, goal attainment and pattern maintenance.

What Parsons' functional perspective implies for the current discussion is that even if approaches to dispute processing on the Continent and in Anglo-American systems appear different, they each must efficaciously achieve similar ends relating to the binding of society together. To the extent that Continental and Anglo-American states exist in similar environments and face similar challenges, their legal systems will have to solve similar problems of social integration, and similarities in how they go about doing this can be expected even if, like marsupials and mammals, structural differences are apparent and in some ways fundamental. The functional perspective also suggests that the role and characteristics of the legal system will turn in part on the degree to which other institutional sectors contribute to social integration because what is crucial is meeting the systems' functional needs and not the particular way these needs are met. Thus, as Stewart Macaulay long ago showed, lawyers seldom play (or played) a major role in resolving business disputes, and litigation between businesses that deal regularly with each other is rare. This is because

[7] For a general statement of Parson's approach see T Parsons, *The Social System* (Glencoe, Free Press, 1951).

economic incentives motivate parties to preserve their relationship, while litigation and its threat are likely to end it.[8] Similarly the rule of law largely disappears in some dictatorships because, for a time at least, brute force and the threat of force can maintain social integration. It is the implications of this functional perspective for comparative legal analysis that I wish to pursue here.

If the Continental and Anglo-American judicial systems play the same functional role in their various societies, one can expect that despite visible differences, there must be important respects, and perhaps the most fundamentally important respects, in which they are similar. For starters, as instruments of adjudication, courts are primarily concerned with resolving disputes in ways that will generally be regarded as legitimate. In post-Enlightenment Western societies this means that disputes must be resolved in accordance with pre-established legal norms by unbiased decision makers who have rationally evaluated the evidence available to them. In both the Anglo-American and Continental legal systems the norms brought to bear on disputes are in principle known in advance. In Continental systems this is obvious because the norms courts apply are embodied in legal codes. In the Anglo-American world the situation has seemed to some observers, particularly Continental observers, less clear, for only some norms that courts apply are embodied in codes while others are embedded in precedent. Moreover, Anglo-American systems assign key law-applying tasks to the jury, which Continental scholars, at least since Weber, have regarded as 'irrational', not in the sense of being crazy but in the sense of not following consistent rules.[9]

The differences between the two systems on these dimensions are, however, more apparent than real. In each system many fundamental norms, particularly norms regarding matters treated by the criminal law, track popular norms about right and wrong behaviour. In each system other norms may be poorly publicised or ambiguous as applied to certain facts, but they are not unknown or unknowable. Rather, professional legal training is thought to allow those so trained to identify and interpret relevant law through the investigation of codes, prior applications of the norms and canonical commentaries, which tend to be treatises in the Continental systems and high court pronouncements, including dicta, in the Anglo-American legal world. Juries, at least in theory, do little to change this situation, for they are not in the business of deciding what the law means. Their task is rather to find facts and state the legal conclusion

[8] S Macaulay, 'Non-Contractual Relations and Business: A Preliminary Study' (1963) 28 *American Sociological Review* 55–69.

[9] M Weber, M Rheinstein (ed), *On Law in Economy and Society*, (Cambridge, Harvard UP, 1954). See also A Kronman, *Max Weber* (Stanford, Stanford UP, 1983) and D Trubek, 'Max Weber on Law and the Rise of Capitalism' (1972) *Wisconsin Law Review* 720.

these facts portend, given what they have been told about the law. While juries can and do leaven the law's commands with their sense of what is moral or just, the evidence since Kalven and Zeisel's path-breaking research[10] is that by and large juries take their legal role seriously and seldom render decisions that are legally indefensible.

A second similarity, also closely tied to concerns for legitimacy, is that both the Anglo-American and Continental systems are concerned with judicial competence and unbiasedness. In the Anglo-American system professional legal training, experience as a lawyer and modes of judicial selection are seen as guarantors of judicial competence, while the common sense of ordinary citizens and the virtues of group deliberation are presumed to make juries capable of rationally judging the facts before them. In Continental systems, judicial competence is guaranteed by extended professional training designed explicitly to produce judges, by the structure of judging as a professional career and by multi-judge and mixed professional/lay judge courts, especially in important cases. Unbiasedness is guaranteed in the American system by norms that separate the judiciary from the 'political' branches of government, by rules for judicial recusal and by allowing litigants to vet jurors and challenge those whose neutrality seems questionable. In the Continental system, making judging a career track separate from prosecution and private lawyering, together with professional judicial training, is thought to promote judicial neutrality along with competence.

In neither system need the assumptions of competent and impartial judging always hold. From a functional standpoint all that matters is that people ordinarily believe they do. If people believe courts are fair and competent, the judicial resolution of disputes will be presumed legitimate, allowing courts and the law to play the integrative role that state and society require.

A third element essential to the legitimacy of court verdicts and hence to the likelihood that legal institutions will fill their integrative function is the requirement that court decisions be based on the rational evaluation of reliable evidence. This too is a demand placed on both Anglo-American and Continental legal systems, but ideas about what evidence is reliable and what it means to evaluate evidence rationally may vary with location and over time. For example, in England before 1215 belief in the reality of divine intervention made trial by ordeal and trial by battle apparently

[10] H Kalven Jr and H Zeisel, *The American Jury* (Chicago, Univ of Chicago Press, 1966). Although the Kalven and Zeisel study was done some years ago, its results have held up well over time. See, eg, N Vidmar and V Hans, 'The American Jury at Twenty-Five Years' (1991) 16 *Law & Social Inquiry* 323; see also T Eisenberg *et al*, 'Judge–Jury Agreement in Criminal Cases: A Partial Replication of Kalven and Zeisel's *The American Jury*' (2005) 2 *Journal of Empirical Legal Studies* 171.

rational ways of determining guilt and deciding legal disputes. After 1215, however, when decrees of the Fourth Lateran Council barred priests from giving ritual blessings as preludes to common ordeals and trial by battle, these modes of resolving disputes fell out of favour in England, although trial by ordeal had surprising persistence on the Continent. The two systems also differed in the weight they were willing to give confessions obtained through torture and hence in their use of torture to secure confessions.

Post-Enlightenment, there has been considerable convergence about what it means to decide a legal claim rationally and, I would argue, for a long while there has been no great difference between Continental and Anglo-American systems on this score. Both systems presume there is a true state of affairs that can be best determined by first collecting reliable evidence that bears on the existence of whatever state legal norms problematise, and then dispassionately evaluating that evidence in light of what is known about how people act and how the world works. The systems do, however, differ somewhat in their judgments of the relative reliability of kinds of evidence, and they differ even more in the processes that they see as most conducive to the marshalling and rational evaluation of evidence.

Hearsay is the iconic example of how systems can differ in their judgment of what evidence is reliable. Hearsay is presumed barred in Anglo-American systems and allowed on the Continent. In practice, however, differences in the treatment of hearsay are not that great. Anglo-American evidence law has proliferated exceptions that admit hearsay, and even where exceptions do not neatly fit statements offered, trial courts will often find some way to admit hearsay that judges think reliable. Continental systems, on the other hand, often treat hearsay with suspicion, discounting it when it is not corroborated by other evidence, and in one Continental system, Italy, theoretical barriers to admitting hearsay appear similar to what they are in the United States and England. This convergence is not surprising, for there is little reason to believe that hearsay is, in fact, more or less probative depending on whether it is gathered in England, in the United States or on the Continent, nor is there reason to believe that experience with hearsay will lead Anglo-American and Continental thinkers to differ substantially in their views of the probative force of particular pieces of hearsay evidence. If the probative value of a hearsay statement is likely to seem similar to Continental and Anglo-American observers, the functional perspective suggests that there will be considerable on-the-ground similarity in how that statement is treated despite different traditions. Giving weight to apparently reliable hearsay and discounting or refusing to consider unreliable hearsay is

impelled by a common rationalist commitment to the evaluation of reliable evidence and by the relationship of this commitment to the legitimacy of judicial verdicts.

When we move beyond issues of fundamental fairness and basic epistemological requirements for rationally evaluating evidence to the procedures that are most likely to promote the fair and rational evaluation of evidence, there is considerable room for historically (that is, path dependent) and culturally rooted differences in how Anglo-American and Continental systems gather and present evidence and adjudicate cases. This is possible because there is 'more than one way to skin a cat'. A variety of different approaches to adjudication may yield results that are in the aggregate sufficiently fair and rational to be accepted by parties and observers and hence to allow legal institutions to play the integrative role that Parsonian systems theory demands. Partisans of one system or the other may present reasoned arguments why their favoured approach to adjudication should be preferred, but to date no one to my knowledge has ever shown empirically that one system produces more accurate verdicts than the other, is less likely to convict the innocent or favour more powerful parties or is more likely to yield verdicts that meet with widespread popular resistance. Indeed, it is the absence of empirical evidence that allows disputes between partisans of the Anglo-American and Continental systems to flourish.

Most commentaries on comparative procedure, including *Faces of Justice,* focus not on the system-level contributions that legal institutions make to social integration but rather on differences in the rules and behavior that govern court cases. These differences appear stark. The Anglo-American system in its purest form believes that a group of unbiased lay people (that is, a jury) exposed to the evidence and arguments that opposing parties think most support their positions is the best means of determining where truth in litigation lies. It also believes that with proper instructions the jury can state the legal implications of the facts they have found.[11] The Continental system in its purest form has treated the truth as unitary and proceeds on the assumption that the judicial discovery of the truth best proceeds in a unitary fashion. Thus the iconic figure in Continental jurisprudence is the investigating judge who himself seeks out evidence and follows it, wherever it leads, to discern the truth.

[11] The belief that juries exposed to conflicting stories can find facts accurately enjoys considerable research support, but faith in the jury's ability to understand the meaning of instructions and to correctly apply the law, as explained in the instructions, to the facts at hand rests on shakier ground. For a synthetic overview of the jury's strengths and weaknesses in finding facts and applying the law see N Vidmar and VP Hans, *American Juries: The Verdict* (Amherst, Prometheus Press, 2007) ch 7.

The usual practice on the Continent is different. In criminal cases, an investigating agency, analogous to the police/prosecution pairing in Anglo-American systems, prepares a dossier setting forth the facts uncovered. The court then uses this dossier, perhaps supplemented by testimony from and questioning of the accused, a complainant and expert or other witnesses, to decide the case. On the civil side yet more is left to the parties. Unlike the Anglo-American system, where the jury has long been a favourite research subject, there has been little empirical scholarship on the ability of Continental courts to reach fair and accurate trial decisions.[12] What little research exists focuses mainly on whether lay judges in mixed court systems have substantial independent influence on the cases in which they sit. The answer with respect to verdicts has been a resounding 'no', although some work has suggested that lay judges may have more of an influence on sentencing decisions than they do on verdicts reached.[13]

Another iconic difference between the Anglo-American and Continental systems is that trial courts on the Continent give reasons for their decisions while Anglo-American courts do not do so when trial is to a jury. In discussing the relative merits of the two systems with Continental scholars and their Anglo-American sympathisers, this difference is often presented to me as trump by those who assert the superiority of Continental-style adjudication by professional judges. Indeed, many Continental observers

[12] This is my impression, but I have not searched the foreign literature, and there may be research on the fairness and accuracy of professional judges I do not know about. Machura touches on this issue in a survey of lay assessors in two German cities: see S Machura, 'Interaction Between Lay Assessors and Professional Judges in German Mixed Courts' (2001) 72 *International Review of Penal Law* 451. He reports that 84% of the lay assessors he interviewed in one city and 79% of those he interviewed in the other thought that the verdicts in the cases they sat on were either 'very' or 'quite' just. I would not give too much weight to survey data of this sort in assessing the competence of professional judge or mixed tribunals.

[13] The first study published in English to document this that I know of is G Casper and H Zeisel, 'Lay Judges in the German Criminal Courts' (1972) 1 *The Journal of Legal Studies* 146–191. Their finding that lay judges on mixed courts almost always have the same verdict preferences as the professional judge or judges has been replicated by a number of other scholars. Indeed, in some courts the lay judges are known as 'nodders' because they seem to do little more than nod their heads in agreement with the professional judge or judges. A recent study based on a survey of lay judges who sat in lower criminal courts in two German cities by the sociologist Stefan Machura presents a more nuanced view of the situation but the study does not seem to differ greatly from the received knowledge in its bottom line: see *Ibid*. Machura documents various structural reasons that serve to limit the influence of lay judges, such as their ignorance of the case before it begins and the ability of the professional judge to negotiate what Americans would call 'plea bargains' without consulting their lay counterparts. He also notes the large degree of agreement between lay and professional judges, but in doing so he cites survey responses that indicate that lay judges feel they have had some influence on proceedings by influencing the professional judge's views. He notes, however, that the influences his lay respondents report may be slight and that professional judges prefer informal proceedings to formal voting. Keeping things informal help a professional judge keep control of the deliberations, making it difficult to know when lay judges have influenced proceeding and, in particular, whether their presence resulted in a verdict different from that which the professional judge or judges sitting alone would have reached.

find it hard to imagine a modern legal system that can pronounce verdicts without giving reasons. The difference seems to me, however, to be overdrawn. First, jury decision-making is not necessarily antithetical to reason-giving. Even though the Anglo-American jury does not provide reasons for its decisions, some countries that have adopted jury systems have required their juries to give reasons,[14] and in the United States the use of special verdict forms that specifically probe the facts the jury found is not uncommon, especially in civil cases. Second, and more importantly, reasons for jury verdicts are often transparent if one cares to look. The jury are told that they can only find for the moving party (plaintiff or prosecution) when certain facts hold. When a verdict is for the moving party, the reason is obvious: The jury believed all the facts necessary for the plaintiff or prosecution to prevail. If, for example, conflicting testimony was given on a crucial point, then the jury must have believed the testimony of the party that had to prove the point to win. Matters are less transparent when verdicts are for defendants, but at least we know that some facts essential to the plaintiff's or prosecution's case were not shown to the requisite degree of proof.

It may be objected that a jury may not have actually found crucial facts in the way their verdict implies, and that if they gave reasons for their verdicts, as judges do on the Continent and in bench trials in the United States, this would be known. The comparison here, however, assumes that judges' reasons accurately reflect how they assessed the evidence and what motivated their decisions. Judges are smart people, familiar with the law. They know what reasons will support a verdict and which will not. Hence, whatever a judge thought of the evidence and whatever motivated a decision, a judge is unlikely to craft an opinion that rests the verdict on an unsupportable ground. Indeed, reason-giving is open to abuse. I recall one conversation with a European judge who told me that on the rare occasions where his opinion did not prevail on a mixed court, he might write an opinion that would lead the appellate court to reverse the decision that he was, in theory, advocating.[15] Jurors, of course, do not have professional legal knowledge, and if they had to specify the reasons for their verdicts, they might well offer unacceptable justifications, sometimes because their reasons were in fact unacceptable and sometimes because

[14] SC Thaman, 'Europe's New Jury Systems: The Cases of Span and Russia' (Spring 1999) 62 *Law and Contemporary Problems* 233. Austria, like Spain, requires its juries to give reasons for their verdicts.

[15] Even when the lay judges' views have prevailed over that of the professional judge on a mixed court the task of laying out the reasons for the verdict is typically assigned to the professional judge. Because mixed courts often strive to reach an informal consensus rather than bring matters to votes, it may be that the lay judges will not realise they have not persuaded the professional judge to their views, so they will not suspect that a judge might try to subvert their verdict through the opinion he writes.

they did not know how to convey clearly what motivated them.[16] The fact that we do not learn when a jury has relied on unacceptable reasons does not mean that juries are less faithful to the law than a judge who might reach a verdict unsupported by the facts or law, but who knows enough to disguise this in an opinion.

The requirement that Continental courts provide reasons does, however, have an important functional implication. Together with the dossier that accompanies the case, written reasons allow an appellate court to overturn a verdict below by rejecting the trial court's reasons and substituting its own judgment. In this sense the Continental system serves well the hierarchical bureaucratic state that Damaška describes in *The Faces of Justice*. But hierarchical control is not something that only Continental governments want or need. Any modern state seeks significant control from the top. Anglo-American courts too have means that allow higher courts to supervise the verdicts of trial courts and ensure that trial court verdicts are acceptable. They can use the rules of evidence to this end. Almost every trial contains some evidentiary error, for shortcuts are often taken in the presentation of evidence, and admissibility decisions are often based on rules of thumb rather than on a close technical analysis of what is and is not admissible. The upshot is that when an appellate court wishes to overturn a verdict below, it can invariably find some justification. Conversely when a higher court does not wish to disturb a verdict, it can ignore evidentiary error or recognise error but find it harmless.

From a functional standpoint it would appear to be no accident that rules of evidence began to arise in England at about the time that other, more direct means of jury control, such as actions of attaint brought against jurors who did not decide as the Crown through its judges wished, were disappearing. No state can afford to trust decisions about the exercise of its coercive power entirely to the masses, and although the jurors who were eligible to sit on cases in the 17th, 18th and early 19th centuries were by no means 'the masses', they were an element beyond direct hierarchical control.[17]

Overturning verdicts for evidentiary error is, to be sure, a clumsier way of exercising hierarchical control than the substitution of judgment which the review of a case dossier in light of a trial court's reasons allows. What makes it inefficient is that the standard remedy for evidentiary error is to remand the case for a trial in which the error will be corrected, and there is no guarantee that a verdict an appellate court wished to reject will be

[16] We see something like this when jurors are given verdict forms that require them to respond to specific questions. Occasionally the answers they give are inconsistent or do not support the verdict they render.

[17] See, eg, *Bushell's Case* (1670) 1 Freem 1, and Vaughan 135.

different because an evidentiary error is avoided on retrial.[18] At least in the United States, however, appellate courts are becoming more adept in substituting judgment even when they are reversing for evidentiary error, most commonly in cases involving scientific evidence where they opine that without the evidence they have found wrongfully admitted, the party proffering the evidence has no case. Moreover, even when an appellate court does not mandate a result, remanding for evidentiary error may predictably result in a party's decision not to pursue the case further or may stimulate a compromise verdict that the appellate court would have found acceptable.

In the United States, however, there is an important exception to the power that appellate courts gain through their ability to reverse for evidentiary error. When an accused criminal is acquitted, he cannot be tried again on the same charge even if the acquittal would not have occurred but for a trial judge's error in admitting or excluding evidence. It might seem that criminal cases are where hierarchical control would most matter to those with state power. This may well be true, but juries have seldom posed substantial obstacles to the exercise of hierarchical control. Most criminal charges have no implications beyond their outcomes, and where charged crimes have a political dimension convictions are often easy to come by because jurors ordinarily share the views and prejudices of the authorities who have ordered the prosecution. Acquittals are most likely in situations where substantial public sentiment, although not necessarily majority sentiment, favours the accused. Acquittals in these cases may, ironically, do more to defuse tensions and allow the peaceful maintenance of state authority than would follow from the convictions the state seeks. In a less democratic society matters might be different, for in such states legitimacy may play a lesser role than minimally disguised power in maintaining the government.

Lest I be misunderstood, let me make state clearly that the fact that appellate courts can exercise hierarchical control by reversing trial verdicts for evidentiary error does not mean that the Anglo-American and Continental systems are equally effective in enabling hierarchical control. Thus, I am not disagreeing fundamentally with Professor Damaška's analysis. Rather, my point is that even if law's contribution to social integration is functionally necessary, a social system can persist with contributions toward this end that fall considerably short of perfection. The degree to

[18] Thus, the United States Supreme Court twice reversed verdicts for Sallie Hillmon in her famous law suit against the Mutual Life Insurance Company, apparently feeling that she was engaged in insurance fraud and that a jury had mistakenly believed her story. But Ms Hillmon eventually received most of what she claimed due. For a fascinating account of this case, and a suggestion that it was the Supreme Court rather than two juries that was mistaken on the facts, see M Wesson, 'The *Hillmon* Case, the Supreme Court and the McGuffin' in R Lempert (ed), *Evidence Stories* (New York, Foundation Press, 2006) 277–305.

which institutional arrangements facilitate particular outcomes may, however, tell us something about how important that outcome is to the system in question. A strong jury system is, for example, not necessary to democratic government just as it is not incompatible with considerable hierarchical control, but at some point system demands may mean that jury justice cannot be tolerated. A likely example is post-Communist Russia. Jury trial was an early and popular reform as Russia moved toward democracy. But allocating real power to juries became less tolerable as the Russian state under Putin became a far more hierarchically directed and authoritarian regime. Thus it is not surprising that since Putin's advent, jury justice has been largely gutted, and in any case where central authorities seek to achieve certain results, they can do so regardless of what a jury might decide at trial.[19]

A third important difference between the Anglo-American and Continental legal systems is the difference between entrusting evidence gathering to an investigating judge or an agency charged with reporting all the relevant evidence it finds (whichever way it cuts) and leaving the gathering and presentation of evidence to adversarial parties. Both systems arguably respond to the same functional requisite: that the collection and presentation of evidence be handled in a way that seems fair and allows for rational judgments based on reliable facts. Seen in this light, the difference between the systems appears small, for each allows considerable evidence to be amassed for presentation to the court. The Continental system not only entrusts evidence gathering to a person or agency that is nominally neutral, but it also provides ways for the parties to add to or influence the information included in the dossier and to add to that evidence in court proceedings. The Anglo-American system[20] is seemingly different, for evidence gathering is entrusted to the parties and they are, with rare exceptions, expected to assemble and present only that information that helps their cases. But the situation on the ground is not the private knowledge situation that exists in theory. Parties commonly agree to or are required to share considerable information. In civil cases by the time a case reaches trial a party through discovery will know the opposing party's legal theories and almost all the evidence that will be offered to support them. Defendants in criminal cases know specifically what they are charged with,

[19] Compare Thaman, above n 12, with SC Thaman, 'The Nullification of the Russian Jury: Lessons for Jury-Inspired Reform in Eurasia and Beyond' (2007) 40 *Cornell International Law Journal* 355. See also Stephen C Thaman, ch 6.

[20] I know far less about what occurs in Britain and her former colonies than I do about how matters proceed in the United States, so what I write below may be truer of the American legal system than of Anglo-American systems in general.

and through preliminary hearing testimony, the receipt of *Brady* material,[21] their own contact with the state's witnesses and informal information sharing with the prosecution often begin trial with considerable knowledge of the case the state will present. At one time, the prosecution had no reciprocal access to the defendant's evidence or planned trial strategy, but increasingly the defendant must reveal information in order to acquire information in the state's possession, and defences most likely to surprise the state or to require advance preparation to counter, like alibi defences or the insanity defence, often must be noticed in advance of trial.

State authority would most likely be undercut if too many criminal defendants were acquitted, for this would cast doubt on the fairness and effectiveness of a state's social control mechanisms and suggest a state was not adequately protecting its inhabitants. But both Anglo-American and Continental systems have mechanisms to ensure that too many acquittals do not happen. Most important is the resource advantage the state enjoys over all but the wealthiest criminal defendants. Thus in both Anglo-American systems and on the Continent criminal cases are typically characterised by such an imbalance of evidence that defendants are persuaded either to plead guilty or, if guilty pleas are technically unavailable, to refrain from mounting substantial defences. Foregoing a meaningful defence is not necessarily bad, for a meaningful defence may not be available. The state's evidence is presumably overwhelming because the defendant is overwhelmingly likely to be guilty.

We can, however, ask whether this presumption necessarily holds. Recent studies in the United States have indicated that in a troublesome proportion of cases where defendants were convicted of rape or murder, which are the most seriously punished ordinary crimes, the defendants were in fact innocent when they stood trial.[22] It would not be surprising if false conviction rates were similar in England and on the Continent.[23]

[21] *Brady* material is significant exculpatory material that the state uncovers in its investigation which it is required to turn over to the accused. *Brady v Maryland* (1963) 373 US 83.

[22] HA Bedau and ML Radelet, 'Miscarriages of Justice in Potentially Capital Cases' (1987) 40 *Stanford Law Review* 21; SR Gross, K Jacoby, DJ Matheson, N Montgomery and S Patil, 'Exonerations in the United States 1989 Through 2003' (2005) 95 *Northwestern Law Review* 529–533; MD Risinger, 'Convicting the Innocent: An Empirically Justified Wrongful Conviction Rate' (16 September 2006), available at SSRN: <http://ssrn.com/abstract=931454> accessed 19 June 2008; SR Gross and B O'Brien, 'Frequency and Predictors of False Conviction: The Problem, and Some Data on Capital Cases' unpublished manuscript on file with the author [2007]. Estimates of the proportion wrongfully convicted range from about to 2% to about 5%.

[23] Anecdotally, support for juries in Japan and the country's eventual move to mixed courts was stimulated by two cases in which defendants sentenced to death were later proven innocent. There is similar anecdotal evidence of wrongful convictions in Great Britain, but I know no systematic attempts to identify the wrongfully convicted in either country or in any other country in Europe.

The kinds of misleading evidence that in the United States result in wrongful convictions, such as mistaken eye witness identifications, faulty forensic science and psychologically coerced confessions, are also likely to play an important role in English and European trials. Other structural problems also conduce to error by diminishing the likelihood that faulty evidence will be refuted. Criminal defence counsel in the United States are often over-worked, under-compensated or simply incompetent; funds for experts to check the state's forensic science evidence are limited if they exist at all; and once the police or prosecution decide to arrest a person they have strong professional incentives to make the arrest stick. I don't know of research that documents similar shortcomings in Continental justice systems, but I would not be surprised if similar systemic biases and deficiencies exist. I say this not just because psychological and organisational limitations are not bounded by the Atlantic Ocean but also because criminal justice systems lose legitimacy when they do not solve crimes and secure the convictions of those who are officially claimed to have 'done it'.

My thesis to this point is that if we focus not on how Anglo-American and Continental legal systems ideally go about their judicial business but on the relationship between legal systems and social integration, we see that the two systems face similar challenges and in large measure operate under similar post-Enlightenment constraints. Although the systems have devised somewhat different mechanisms for meeting those challenges, like the thylacine and the wolf they have evolved to do much the same thing. Seen in this light, Professor Damaška's observation that the pure systems of his ideal types are nowhere to be found is expected rather than remarkable. There is no reason why bench trials should not be common in the United States and Britain or why some judges should not ask their own questions of witnesses, or freely admit hearsay evidence or appoint court experts. Similarly no functional necessity precludes Continental systems from giving parties a role in developing evidence, using juries in some cases or regarding hearsay with such suspicion that it is ignored entirely.

The Anglo-American and Continental systems are not pure manifestations of the ideal types Professor Damaška gives us[24] because they don't have to be. What they do have to be are generally acceptable ways of deciding cases, which in today's world means they should be based on the apparently rationale and unbiased evaluation of reliable evidence. So long as these requisites are met, judicial dispute resolution will contribute to social integration.[25] Nothing about the functional role of courts means there is only one way they can fill their function.

24 This is a fact Damaška not only recognises but highlights.

25 I have in this chapter focused on courts and how their adjudicative activities contribute to social integration. This is by no means the only way in which legal institutions play an integrative role in society. Contract law, for example, is crucial to economic coordination.

Given this functional leeway, it is not surprising that *within* both the Anglo-American and Continental legal worlds, systems of evidence gathering and adjudication have evolved differently and that what seems to be a unitary Continental or Anglo-American tradition when viewed from afar has long dissolved into a set of country or even locality-specific practices when viewed close up. One need only compare Dutch, French, Italian and German legal proceedings now or even 50 years ago to appreciate this. Nor is it surprising that within systems differentiation is ongoing. Italy's adoption of a hearsay rule similar to that of the United States is a Continental example of divergent evolution within a tradition while Great Britain's abolition of once available jury trial rights in cases where they remain available in the United States is a similar example on the Anglo-American side.

Moreover, I expect that the breakdown of the Continental and Anglo-American ideal types will only accelerate. Increased international interchange promotes borrowing across traditions, for such interchange means that legal elites develop a better appreciation of alternative ways of case processing and that ordinary people, through the media, travel and other sources, find that what was once an entirely alien approach to legal action has some familiarity. Taking an evolutionary perspective, I would expect borrowing across traditions to be most likely where aspects of the Continental or Anglo-American tradition seem functionally superior to received ways of doing things. A Continental example of such borrowing may be the increased role for defence counsel in questioning the state's evidence and ensuring that evidence favourable to the defendant is part of the case record. An Anglo-American example is the increased responsibility placed on trial judges to monitor the quality of scientific evidence and an apparent increase in the willingness of judges to appoint neutral court experts. Both examples of borrowed procedure are thought to make for fairer, more accurate verdicts. In this respect, they strengthen the law's capacity to resolve disputes legitimately, which in turn makes the law a more effective agent of social integration.

Globalisation poses special problems for the law as an instrument of integration. Not only do legal norms and cultures compete for authority on the world stage, but also no nation is committed to an integrated global system of government. Yet there is enough global interchange and there are enough situations where countries, organisations and even people must cooperate cross-nationally that some degree of social integration at the global level is necessary for everyone's well-being. If the legal sphere is, from a functional standpoint, the lead institution in promoting social integration at the national and subnational levels, can it play a similar role in global society? Or to put the point more strongly, can we build a globalised society without legal institutions that promote its integration? The Parsonian theory I have built this discussion on would say 'no'.

This problem is not an abstract one, but is faced every day in those spheres where globalisation is most advanced and where close ties across national borders add the most value. Perhaps the best example is multinational commerce. Those engaged in multi-national commerce cannot escape entirely the legal regimes of those countries in which they do business, which means they cannot escape inconsistency in the laws by which they are regulated.[26] However, it seems safe to say that most organisations that do business internationally would prefer regulation under a single legal regime, one that employs similar regulatory and dispute resolution procedures no matter where disagreements arise. Without a world government in place, the functional imperative of integration has led the most active players in the world trade system to try to establish their own legal system. In some measure they have been able to do so through the establishment of a regime of international arbitration[27] that can yield judgments binding under different countries' domestic laws. Commercial forces have also influenced and taken advantage of international treaties, which sometimes establish their own special tribunals. Even when tribunals are not established, treaty law is often binding on and enforceable by court judgments within nations.

What is happening internationally replicates what happened domestically in England and on the Continent centuries ago. Merchants of various sorts as well as labour guilds established their own laws and courts to deal with disputes within their ranks. As national legal systems developed, much of the business of these courts was taken over by national court systems and the norms they enforced were incorporated into official law or replaced by it.[28] Whether something like this will happen on a global sphere is a question I have no way of answering. A related question is what procedures will best serve the function of societal integration at the global level. Arbitration procedure suggests that the procedures that emerge will be a blend of Continental and Anglo-American traditions. One the one hand, rules of evidence are relaxed in arbitration and there is no jury. On the other hand, arbitrators are passive judges and the parties are responsible for developing their cases. Reason giving, which is sometimes seen as the most important distinction between Anglo-American jury trials and Continental judge or mixed-court systems, is sometimes expected in

[26] Witness Microsoft's antitrust difficulties in the United States and the EU and the different resolutions it has had to accede to.

[27] See, e.g., Y Dezalay and B Garth, *Dealing in Virtue: International Commercial Arbitration & the Construction of a Transnational Order* (Chicago, University of Chicago Press, 1997).

[28] Merchants' courts have not entirely disappeared. See, eg, L Bernstein, 'Merchant Law in a Merchant Court: Rethinking the Code's Search for Immanent Business Norms' (1996) 144 *University of Pennsylvania Law Review* 1765.

arbitration proceedings and sometimes forbidden. So if we look to arbitration for a clue as to the procedures that are functionally best suited to promoting social integration, supporters of both the Anglo-American and Continental systems can point to ways in which the procedures they espouse are superior. But it may be a mistake to look to arbitration, international or otherwise, for such a clue. At the core of Professor Damaška's book is a set of arguments that associates ways that legal systems handle cases with the structures and goals of types of governments. The legal forms that might best promote the integration of a mature globalised state are likely to depend on how that state is organised, which from today's vantage point is unknowable.

Professor Damaška's great book, *The Faces of Justice and State Authority,* opened its readers' eyes to how Anglo-American and Continental legal procedures articulate with the societies in which they are found, and it alerted readers to issues that arise in considering this articulation. I have tried to examine the connections of procedural law and society at a yet more abstract level. I have not written a great book, just a short chapter. It is highly speculative, and I do not know if it succeeds as a work of theory. But I do hope it succeeds in its primary purpose, as a tribute to Professor Mirjan Damaška.

Appendix

Interview with Mirjan Damaška

MÁXIMO LANGER*

A COMPLICATED LINGUISTIC STORY

MÁXIMO LANGER [hereinafter **ML**]: First of all, could you tell me where were you born, and about your family background and childhood?

Mirjan Damaška [hereinafter **MD**]: I was born into a Croatian family in what is today Slovenia. My mother stemmed from a very old Croatian family called Tkalčić, which is the Croatian for the German 'Weber'. I find this amusing because many people say I was greatly influenced by Max Weber. As a matter of fact, one of my forebears for whom a street is named in Zagreb – a street very popular among young people – used to call himself Weber-Tkalčić.

On my father's side, my forebears came three generations before my father was born from what is now Germany. They belonged to a Slavic group located at the border between Germany and Poland – the Sorbs. Speaking of streets named for my relatives, there is a long, winding street in Berlin just off Kurfürstendamm – Damaschke Straße – in memory of a distant relative of mine who was an agrarian reformer in 19th century Germany.

The fact that I was born in Slovenia created linguistic problems for me that I think were somewhat unusual. While in primary school, I had to speak Slovenian. Slovenian is a Slavic language, but quite different from Croatian, so that Slovenes and Croats have difficulty understanding one another –they really have to learn one another's languages to be able to communicate. To make matters more complicated, at my parents' home we spoke a dialect of Croatian called 'Kajkavski', a dialect that is spoken by people in Zagreb and the surrounding area. It is quite different from

* This interview took place in Mirjan Damaška's office at Yale Law School on 12 April 2007. I sent Mirjan Damaška an initial version of it, which he edited and revised. I would like to very much thank John Jackson for brainstorming with me about what questions to ask to Mirjan Damaška for this interview. I would also like to thank Karen Mathews and Samantha Luu for writing down a first transcript of the interview.

literary Croatian –almost a separate language. As you know, what is a dialect and what is another language is often a political question. In any event, someone who comes to Zagreb and its environs from other parts of Croatia, or from Serbia, has difficulty understanding 'Kajkavski'.

As a still further complication, my brother and I had an Austrian governess, because both of our parents were very busy professionals. So, as small kids, we also spoke German at home. It was therefore only when I was nine years old, and my family moved to Zagreb, that I began to learn the literary Croatian language. I also had to master the Cyrillic script, which –though used by Serbs rather than Croats – was a mandatory subject of instruction in Croatian grammar schools. I still remember the traumatic experience when I first came to the classroom in Zagreb and could neither understand the language properly, just a little bit, nor read what other pupils were writing.

All in all, I learned to speak my mother's tongue properly only when I was about 10 years old. And thereafter for many years my favorite foreign language was French. Because my mother and father took great interest in their children learning and cultivating foreign languages, I had private lessons in French, and also went for many years to the French Institute in Zagreb. In higher grades of secondary school I had to take Russian and English, and as an elective language course I chose Latin. Russian I did not particularly like, so that it is fair to say that English was the last living foreign language that I seriously studied in school.

COMMUNIST REGIME, ART AND LAW SCHOOL

ML: Why did you decide to study law?

MD: We moved to Zagreb in 1940, and in 1941 the Nazis invaded the Kingdom of Yugoslavia. Then, in 1945, the Communists seized power. The new regime created all sorts of problems for my family, because we belonged to the bourgeoisie. I personally experienced unpleasant things in school because of my family's background.

At that time, I had great interest in drawing and painting. I was actually a sort of infant prodigy, so much so that I was taken by my parents to the studios of some foremost Croatian painters, even to the Academy of Arts in Zagreb. The funny thing about it was that, while regular students draw nudes from life, I was too young to be confronted with naked women and had to work in a separate room with casts – Greek statues, gods and goddesses. This was a period of my life when I just wanted to be an artist. Sometime after puberty, however, I just lost interest. Well, I should not say 'lost interest', because art remains my life-long love. I only gave up the idea of art as a career. I still like to draw. When I am bored at faculty meetings, for example, I am in the habit of making doodles of my colleagues. As a

matter of fact, I recently made one of my Dean, Koh, of Yale. I think he keeps the sketch in his office. But while art is now for me just a hobby, at one point in my life I really took it very, very seriously.

After Gymnasium, I wanted to study medicine. My father was a well-known pharmacologist and most of my friends decided to study medicine. But when, prior to enrollment, I went to a pathology class, and saw a professor's assistant sawing off the head of a cadaver, I said to myself, 'This is not for me'.

In desperation I enrolled in law school. I say in desperation, because at the time, as a result of Red rule, legal education was permeated with simplistic ideology and crude political propaganda. Law studies were to a great extent a refuge for the less talented, or preparatory training for those who contemplated becoming party hacks. Being a scion of a bourgeois family, I was actually misplaced in this milieu. But because in those days whoever had any smarts did not study law, so that there was little serious competition for academic excellence in law schools, it was easy for me to become a stellar student. In the first semester I distinguished myself thanks to my proficiency in Latin. For reasons not altogether clear to me, the Communist regime retained a course in Roman law – a course that was then in the first year curriculum a rare subject unpolluted by politics and propaganda. The regime also retained a professor of Roman law from the pre-Communist days who liked me and asked me at seminar sessions to read from Gaius Institutes. This impressed both the Faculty and the students and I early on established a name for myself.

JOINING THE FACULTY OF THE UNIVERSITY OF ZAGREB LAW SCHOOL

ML: How did you become a faculty member at the University of Zagreb?

MD: Law school lasted four years. When I was a third-year student I wrote a paper for a seminar in public international law taught by Professor Andrassy, a professor from the old guard, who was retained by the regime because of his international reputation. I still remember that the paper discussed the theory of the French professor George Scelle – a theory of *dédoublement fonctionel,* claiming that States can create international law by unilateral practice.

When I submitted the paper, the professor said: 'This is a very good piece. Translate it into French, and I am going to send it to the Academy of International Law in The Hague. Maybe you'll get a scholarship'. I did, and got a scholarship. It seemed to me, then, that my career was going to be in public international law.

Upon graduation, I had to spend nine months in the Yugoslav army. When I came back to Zagreb, eager to devote myself to public international law, Professor Andrassy disappointed me by saying, 'You stand no chance to join the Faculty of Law. You are not a member of the Communist party, you have no political connections, and neither do I. Forget about the career in academia'. In those days it was indeed very hard to join the law school unless you were a Communist or otherwise well connected. Here I was, not only not a Communist, but also from a bourgeois background. So I followed the professor's advice and went into practice.

What happened next was this. A professor of criminal law who had a better opinion of my knowledge than I deserved, gave me a manuscript of a book he was writing and asked me for comments. He was a brilliant Jewish intellectual, who somehow survived the period of Nazi occupation. I respected him tremendously for his learning, especially in German philosophy, and was deeply honoured by his request – although I doubted that I could make any useful suggestions to him. But before I finished reading the manuscript, he suddenly died of a heart attack.

A few days later, a professor of criminal procedure at the Zagreb Law School, the son-in-law of the deceased, found out that the manuscript was with me, and asked me to return it to him. Impressed by the fact that his father-in-law had such a high opinion of me as to request my comments, he invited me to become his assistant. In the Yugoslav university hierarchy, as well as in many continental European countries, this was the first rung on the academic ladder. I let him know that Professor Andrassy told me I had no chance to join the Faculty. 'This is different', he said. 'I am friendly with Vladimir Bakarić, the head of the Croatian Communist party. We studied together and I did him a great favour once, a favour for which he might want to reciprocate. I am going to talk to him, and we shall see. I think that you have a chance'.

A few months later, a meeting was held of the Zagreb Law Faculty Council, a body at which professors sat with a few communist party *apparatchiks* supposed to exercise political supervision. Among the latter was the head of the Zagreb secret police. As the voting on my appointment started, a couple of professors voted against me, thinking that this was the politically correct step. But when the turn came to the police official, he voted in my favour. After that, all remaining members of the Council voted in my favour. I was later told that he was contacted by the Croatian Party boss, whose investigation revealed that I was basically innocuous – ha, ha! – or whatever. This, then, is how I joined the faculty.

I rose very quickly through the ranks. Responsible for my rapid promotions was a person older than I, who became assistant a short while after me. He was a charming, very well connected and ambitious party member. The party was pushing him, so that he rose through the ranks

with unusual speed – from assistant, to 'docent', to extraordinary and finally to full professorship. But because I enjoyed a greater scholarly reputation than he did – both in the country and abroad – the Faculty thought, after each of his promotions, they should also promote poor Mirjan. Thanks to this colleague, I ended up being the youngest full professor in the University.

INTELLECTUAL FORMATION AND PUBLICATIONS IN CROATIA

ML: Due to language barriers, your work in Croatian is not known internationally. Could you tell me about your work before you emigrated to the United States?

MD: My first articles dealt with narrow legal-technical issues of interest to practitioners. For example, one piece explored the question of how many charges prosecutors can legitimately 'squeeze' out of a criminal event. Another suggested ways in which appealable errors of trial courts could more clearly be classified. Yet another discussed technical complications that arise in libel cases when cross-complaints are filed. My colleagues at Yale would turn their noses on such pedestrian stuff.

Gradually I started writing articles with broader theoretical ambitions. For instance, one article examined the question, in the criminal justice system of former Yugoslavia, of when formal criminal procedure begins, so that various procedural safeguards are triggered. I also published a couple of essays on substantive criminal law. One, dealing with the problem of mistake of law, was very well received. Another contained the first attempt by a Yugoslav legal scholar to argue that male homosexuality should be decriminalised. Involved here was also the constitutional problem of equal protection, because being a male gay was a criminal offence, but being lesbian was not.

But all these articles were written in the narrow Continental doctrinal vein. A single exception was a large study I published after I returned from America in the late 1960s. The study discussed the admissibility of evidence obtained by the police, and argued that this evidence should in some situations be excluded. This created quite a stir in conservative legal circles. I was told that some of my proposals infuriated some powerful officials in the federal prosecutor's office.

My first book was to a great extent under the influence of Vladimir Bayer. Bayer was, you will remember, the professor of criminal procedure with a politically powerful friend, the professor who arranged for me to become his assistant. My book was entitled *Defendant as a Source of Evidence in Criminal Procedure*. It discussed quite frankly, I think, the manifold and sometimes latent pressures to which defendants are exposed in the traditional Continental administration of criminal justice. The

discussion was historical, comparative and informed to some extent by political theory. It represented for me a significant step away from narrow doctrinal analysis. The book is still sometimes cited in the scholarly legal literature on the territory of former Yugoslavia.

The other book published in former Yugoslavia was the *Dictionary of Criminal law and Procedure*. I co-authored it with professor Zlatarić, who was then a well known figure in European criminal law circles. The book was not a traditional legal dictionary. It had larger ambitions. An example I can think of is the entry on 'principles of procedure', theoretical constructs first developed by 18th-century German scholars. I did not approach these principles in the conventional dogmatic fashion, but tried to describe their purpose – descriptive, prescriptive, or merely decorative – suggesting which deserve to be taken seriously and which could be discarded.

The book brings to mind my late Yale colleague Arthur Leff, who started writing a Dictionary of American Law, but died before he managed to complete the entries belonging to the first four letters of the alphabet. The fragments published in Yale Law Journal reveal that his ambition was not to write an ordinary legal dictionary, but rather a collection of witty essays. Even jokes can be found in the text. Now, my dictionary was conceived along similar lines –although much more modest, and much less scintillating. I am told that it has still not been forgotten in the old country, although it was published more than forty years ago.

ML: In terms of people who were important in your intellectual formation in Zagreb, you mentioned Professor Bayer, the criminal procedure scholar. Could you tell me a little bit about him?

MD: Speaking of people who affected my intellectual formation, I must say that Bayer was not the only one. The person who sparked in me the love for theorising about the law was Stanko Frank – the professor who gave me the manuscript of his latest book before he died. As I said before, he was a brilliant Jewish intellectual who somehow managed to survive the occupation, and rejoined the Law Faculty after the war. He was primarily a legal philosopher, although he also taught substantive criminal law. Through him, as a second year law student in communist Yugoslavia, I got acquainted with criminological theories like Sutherland's on white collar crime. Frank was very important in my intellectual formation.

Professor Bayer was a highly original thinker. In problems of fact-finding and evidence, for example, his skill was to start from some epistemological phenomenon obvious to everybody –an ordinary perception perhaps – and then build from there to complex evidentiary problems. A great mind, with piercing analytical powers. In criminal procedure he was interested as much in what actually went on in the life of the law as in doctrinal issues. So he published an article in Italy – I cannot remember any more what its precise title was – in which he chastised as ideologically distorting the then

prevailing view in Continental procedural scholarship that the defendant is really not a source of information, but only a party to the proceedings. In many Continental jurisdictions procedural provisions mandated that, at the outset of the trial, the judge ask the defendant what he has to say in response to the prosecutor's indictment. His answers were formally treated as mere allegations, not as evidence. Only after this opening stage of the trial was proof-taking supposed to begin. Professor Bayer pointed out that, in practice, the defendant's initial statement regularly morphed into judicial interrogation of the defendant, and that what he said was actually used as a source of information by the court in reaching its decision. This is an example of how my mentor was breaking out of the conventional scholarly mold. He was also a great Latinist with an interest in history, particularly the history of procedure in Hungary and Croatia. He inspired me to look at the root of things, so to speak. It is through him that I developed a love for historical research. As I look back, it seems to me that I enjoyed writing about history more than writing about anything else.

ML: Did he pass away long ago?

MD: He died in 1990, just before the outbreak of the war that caused the destruction of Yugoslavia. We had problems, he and I, personal problems. I was young, impatient and ambitious, and he was trying to slow me down. And when I stayed in the United States, he was instrumental in my rather brutal and non-ceremonial dismissal from the Law School. But I can now understand his anger: He was nursing me as his successor and I disappointed him by leaving the country. He was important in my life. A remarkable person.

ML: Besides these two professors, did you have a broader intellectual milieu in Croatia to interact with? For instance, seminars at the university or interactions with people of your generation that were intellectually stimulating.

MD: I cannot recall any university seminar worth mentioning. Nor can I think of particularly stimulating interactions with people of my own generation. But I greatly profited from interaction with my maternal uncle, Marijan Tkalčić. It is a good thing you asked me this question, because I would have forgotten it. He was a professor of philosophy at Zagreb University, a superb lecturer, and one of the most popular professors in the University. Students would come from other departments to listen to him. He also wrote beautiful essays in the form of Platonic dialogues. He taught me all kinds of little tricks. So he would say, 'When you read a book, make it truly your own. Make your own indices. When something strikes you as interesting, write it down in the book's margins, or on its blank back pages'. I follow this advice to the present day. So if you look at almost any book in my library, you will find in them my 'private' glossary. He also urged me to keep what he called '*florilegium*' in Latin, or '*Buch der Bücher*' in German. When you like a passage you have read very much,

you write it down in a diary-like book, and can then enjoy rereading it from time to time. This suggestion of his I also follow to this day, and now have many such 'commonplace books'. He shaped my relation to books, and his idea of copying passages proved very useful in my life.

Although he was a specialist in Kant and the neo-Kantians, he is best known for having introduced existentialism in the intellectual circles of former Yugoslavia. Under his influence I was briefly a devotee of this philosophy, although its proponents were far removed from the clear exposition that I always admired. I am not aware of any trace of this philosophy in my writings. But I vividly remember that in the late fifties, during my first stay in Paris, I rushed to *Les Deux Magots*, in the hope of seeing Sartre or Simone de Beauvoir. All in all, when I think of people outside the legal profession who had an influence on my intellectual formation, my maternal uncle stands out.

FIRST OFFER TO STAY IN THE UNITED STATES AND LIBERAL REFORMS IN COMMUNIST YUGOSLAVIA

ML: How did you establish contact with American legal academia?

MD: In 1960 I went to the Salzburg Seminar in American Studies. It was just a few months before I got married. I was quite active in seminar discussions, so one day Professor Louis Schwartz from the University of Pennsylvania Law School asked me whether I would give a lecture on the relation of ethics to law in socialist countries. He was in charge of codifying the special part of the Model Penal Code, and was then quite well known in the American legal academia. I don't remember what I said in this lecture, but a few days after I delivered it, Schwartz invited me to come to the University of Pennsylvania Law School as 'Fellow in Criminal Law'. I accepted the invitation and spent the academic year 1961–62 in America.

Early in 1966 the phone rang in my Zagreb office. The Dean of the Pennsylvania Law School called. Would I come to Philadelphia –this time as a visiting professor of comparative law? In the meantime I had taught a series of lectures at the Faculty for Comparative Law in Luxembourg, and acquired the reputation of a budding comparativist. I said yes and spent the academic year 1966–67 in Philadelphia. A few weeks before I was to return to Europe, I received the offer of a tenured position from Penn. I could not make up my mind so quickly and asked for an extension of the visiting professorship for another year. It was promptly granted.

So it was not until the summer of 1968 that I had to make my final decision. It was a very difficult time for Marija and me. We did not know what to do. Back in Zagreb, we did not even have an apartment, and had to live with my parents. The Communist regime had created a great

housing shortage. In Philadelphia, by contrast, we had a very nice and spacious home. My American salary was also very generous in comparison to what I earned as a professor in Zagreb. Yet, we were both attached to our native land.

At this point, Marvin Wolfgang, a prominent criminologist, offered help. 'Listen', he said to me, 'you should make your decision in a scientific fashion. Make a list of factors in favour of and against staying in America. Bring the list to me, and we shall try to attach rough weight to the factors. Then I am going to figure out what you should decide'. I did as suggested, and after a few days Marvin called me, and announced the result: Marija and I should stay in the United States. So I went to Dean Fordham and accepted the offer. There was a champagne party at his home that evening.

But at night I had a change of heart. I suddenly felt that I could not live with this decision – no matter how rational it might be. I felt like a juror to whom a Bayesian theorist tells what should be his updated estimation of the likelihood of an event, but the juror then feels impelled to change his estimate of prior odds.

Deeply embarrassed, I went back to Dean Fordham in the morning to tell him the news. But he was very gracious and understanding. A major reason for my change of heart were political transformations that were then taking place in former Yugoslavia. Communist parties in republics that comprised the Federation became much more tolerant than they were before. No longer did you have to be a party member to reach important positions or be entrusted with important tasks.

While I was agonising about what to do, a number of politically important people called me from Zagreb and urged me to return. 'Come back', they said, 'we need you. We want to dismantle the police state, liberalise criminal procedure, and proceed with reforms in other areas'. They also played on my national sentiment, disclosing their intent to curb the dominance of Serbia in the Yugoslav Federation. My hope to be in position to contribute to these changes, coupled with the reluctance to leave my ageing parents, prevailed over all countervailing 'variables' that I identified to Marvin.

OUSTING OF THE LIBERAL LEADERSHIP IN FORMER YUGOSLAVIA AND MOVING TO THE UNITED STATES AND YALE LAW SCHOOL

ML: What did happen after you went back to former Yugoslavia in 1968?

MD: When I came back, I was given important responsibilities. I was, among other things, made President of the Commission on Criminal Law Reform of the Croatian Parliament. In this capacity I regularly interacted with the leadership of the liberalising movement. And as acting Dean of the

Law School, I presided over the faculty conference that elected the most important Croatian political figure to a lecturer's position. Then, in December of 1971, Tito sided with Party conservatives and ousted the liberal Croatian leadership on grounds of nationalism and excessive tolerance, capable, he thought, of diluting the rule of the Communist party. The liberal leadership of Serbia and Slovenia was also sacked. In Zagreb, university students staged protests. One night, in the city's main square, they were viciously clubbed and beaten by the police. I witnessed the scene from the window of my mother-in-law's apartment that overlooked the square. I remember saying in disgust to my in-laws, 'I am not going to stay here'. The idea that Communist rule would come to an end in my lifetime did not occur to me. My father, who was already in the twilight of his life, although saddened about the prospect of losing me, unselfishly encouraged me to go. So, four days after the end of the so-called 'Croatian spring' I left the country.

The decision to come to America was relatively easy, because a few months before these political events, I had gotten an offer from the University of Pennsylvania to come again as a visiting professor. At least, I thought, I have a temporary job awaiting me in America! It turned out, however, that in late spring of 1972 the Penn Faculty already voted me tenure.

I soon established a close working relationship with Bruce Ackerman. We also became good friends. But after two years, Bruce, a Yale Law School graduate, went back to his alma mater. This was a blow to me. Another blow was that about that time the then Dean of the Penn Law School neglected to secure my permanent residency papers. Because I came to the US on the wrong visa, I was faced with the prospect of having to leave the country for two years. I had tenure with the University of Pennsylvania, mind you, but not with Uncle Sam. The Dean's neglect made me very upset, although I can understand him now: his wife was dying of cancer and he had other things on his mind. Anyway, upset as I was, I told some colleagues on the Faculty that I was considering leaving the School. The word must have spread through the grapevine for I suddenly got offers to visit Harvard, Berkeley and Yale. I first accepted Yale's offer, because Bruce was teaching there. But Marija and I were thinking of accepting Harvard's offer of tenure – if it were forthcoming. The main reason for this preference was that we both liked life in big cities, and New Haven was no match for Boston. But when I met with Dean Sacks of Harvard, he informed me that they had a policy against directly voting tenure. A rule required that one first spend a year as a visiting professor. 'Do not worry about giving up your tenured position at Penn', he assured me though. 'I have little doubt that you are going to be voted tenure after a year's visit'.

ML: Did you have to give up your tenured position at Penn to be a visiting professor at Harvard?

MD: Yes, because I had already spent a year visiting at Yale. Anyway, if Dean Sacks did not have any doubts, I did. After I had expressed my concerns to him, he told me that he was going to check whether the rule could be waived. I soon learned that a faculty committee decided that my case did not deserve a waiver. Despite this unfavorable decision, I still wondered for a while whether to take the risk of giving up my tenure at Penn, but finally decided against it. Even if Harvard offered me a permanent position after a year's visit, I would have to wait for a total of eight years for my first sabbatical leave. At Yale, by contrast, I already had an offer of tenure and the prospect of a semester of sabbatical leave after two and a half years of teaching. So I declined Harvard's and accepted Yale's offer.

But Marija was very unhappy at New Haven. She wanted us to go to Berkeley. The landscape around San Francisco and the way of life she tasted during a brief visit to Berkeley were much closer to what she was used to in the country from which I uprooted her. To make a long story short, I went to Dean Wellington of Yale Law School, and announced that we were going to the West Coast. But he was very persuasive in outlining to me the professional and financial advantages of Yale.

So Marija and I reached a compromise. I was going to accept Yale's offer, and stay in New Haven for two-and-a-half years. We would then spend the leave in Berkeley and stay there permanently – if Berkeley renewed its tenured offer. And after two-and-a-half years, in execution of this plan, we went to Berkeley. The law school rented a beautiful little house for us in Berkeley's hills, and we started seriously hunting for a home. But as we had almost no savings – we came from Yugoslavia without any money – we could not afford any decent house in the San Francisco area. Crestfallen, we returned to Yale. As time went by Marija got used to the rhythms of life in New Haven. This is the unvarnished truth of how we stayed at Yale.

LEGAL ÉMIGRÉS, INTELLECTUAL MILIEUS AND THE AZORES ISLANDS

ML: A few years ago I participated in a panel on comparative law and émigrés and I studied the life of some of the German scholars who came to the United States escaping from Nazism. One thing I noticed was that most of the scholars who succeeded in the United States, such as Max Rhenstein and Rudolf Schlesinger, came at a relatively young age when they were still in their twenties or early thirties. Most of those scholars who came at an older age did generally not succeed or were ostracised in US legal academia.

MD: Hans Kelsen is a good example.

ML: Exactly. Your case is interesting because you moved to the United States permanently when you were 40 years old, and were already well established in former Yugoslavia and Europe. But you still managed to have a very successful career in the United States.

MD: I actually have had two lives, professional-wise. While I was one of the leading scholars in my field in former Yugoslavia, I was also known in European criminal law circles. I mentioned that I was invited to teach at Luxembourg, for example. I was also part of a group which drafted a code, the Siracuse Code, on the general part of international criminal law. I had close contacts with several French scholars, including Marc Ancel. And in Dubrovnik, in 1969, I was general reporter at a huge international congress on traffic offences. After all that, I started a new life in a country with a very different legal culture. I very often say in conversations 'in my previous life' I did this or that.

ML: How was the adaptation to the United States?

MD Terrible! I had to learn tremendously. It was not just the question of boning up on American law. My knowledge of the larger American culture and history was poor. People would say, 'Founding Fathers would agree with this ... this sounds like Madison ... this is also what Franklin thought'. But I did not know, or did not know sufficiently, what was their point. At faculty meetings, I would often be in a sort of epistemic fog. My colleagues would make references to things I did not understand. In class, I would occasionally say something and everybody would start laughing, while I did not know the reason for their outburst. Maybe I mispronounced something or .... Anyway, it was really painful. I must say that if I had known how hard it would be to adjust, I probably would not have stayed in America. The experience I gathered as a visiting professor was far from sufficient to prepare me for what I was going through. What was expected of me as a visitor was much less demanding and rather different. Had I had a child, I would have never been able to do it. And had I not had Marija who actually took over everything, including balancing the checkbook, I would not have made it. I was just working, and working, burning the candle at both ends.

The fog I mentioned has not totally lifted even now, although I have been here for so long. Now and then, at faculty meetings, my colleagues allude to something which is familiar to American schoolchildren or those who listened to nursery rhymes ... they make this reference and everybody laughs. I am the only one who remains serious, because I do not know what the hell they are talking about.

Serious demands on me stemmed also from a difference in the self-understanding of European and American law professors. In Europe, you are a specialist. If you are, let's say, in contract law, you are not going to engage in a serious debate with a colleague who is not competent in your field. Nor are you going to challenge a colleague who specialises in another

field of law. This is one reason why there were in Zagreb no stimulating professorial seminars. In America, things are different, of course. Here it is a free-for-all. People talk across fields. For this reason, it was not just that I had to become proficient in the counterparts of the discipline I mastered in Europe. I also had to acquire at least a modicum of understanding of all kinds of areas of law, from property law to constitutional law – everything.

How and why I survived is not entirely clear to me. When I first arrived, I was still a compelling lecturer. Students at the University of Pennsylvania loved me. I was witty, sprinkling my lectures with colorful metaphors and jokes.

I also had a very retentive memory, and the capacity, I think, to listen to a great deal of information, manage to get the gist of it, and mould it in a plausible fashion. In casual conversation I would often propound ideas, or made *aperçus,* that would intrigue my interlocutors, even if much of this fluffy stuff could not survive close scrutiny. Let me give you an example. In comparing the concept of real estate property in Anglo-American and Continental law, I would relate the different conceptual armature to different conceptions of order in the two cultures. Because Continentals have a greater need for order, I said, they crafted an overarching concept of ownership, and a limited number or lesser property rights. A hierarchy of sorts. Anglo-Americans, on the other hand, have all these various entitlements, but no overarching concepts of property. A co-ordination of co-equal entitlements.

At the time I was also very self-confident. But all that I just said does not satisfy me as an explanation. There must have been lucky breaks of which I am not aware. Perhaps I gave people the impression that I was smarter than I actually am. I say this without false modesty, because I still don't understand how come that, after just a few years in America, I got offers to teach at Yale, Harvard and Berkeley.

ML: Continental Europe and the United States do not present differences only about the content of law. They also provide different intellectual milieus for legal scholarship. How was the transition in this respect?

MD: This is also a convoluted story. Notice, first of all, that I was raised as a lawyer in the Communist system, with its Marxist twist on law, and its political idiosyncrasies. But early on, still as a student, I got into contact with the Continental variant of Western legal culture in Holland and Luxembourg.

Making sense of this contact did not place great intellectual demands on me. It changed my original approach to law to a very minor extent. I did not find it difficult to get oriented in French, or German law, for example. Linguistically, there were very few obstacles for me. The organisation of law was also similar, and so was the *doctrine*. It is true that Communists managed to make it a little fuzzy, but the underlying conceptual structure of the law was roughly the same. Remember that, as a law student in

communist Yugoslavia, I excelled in seminars on Roman law. It was a required part of the first year curriculum. In property law, students were supposed to be familiar with concepts like *servitudo* or *iura in re aliena*, although the Yugoslav political leadership boasted that it invented a novel form of 'social property'. The fabric of legal sensibility, so hard to define, was also similar. René David, whose lectures I attended in Luxembourg, once used a metaphor that I found very apt. Within the civil law system, he said, when you go from country to country, you know the furniture, and you know which drawer to open, you just don't know what is in the drawer. In many respects, Yugoslav law belonged to the civil law system, and my main difficulty was only to figure out what was in the drawers.

Coming to America was quite another story. Suddenly, a new world of law opened to me. I was now unsure about the legal furniture and its drawers as well. But this was not the most frustrating thing: the way of thinking about legal problems and the weight of legal arguments also differed. It often happened to me that I would advance a logical argument in discussions, an argument which I thought was a clincher, only to find that it left my colleagues totally unimpressed. Whereas my mode of approaching problems was more concept-driven, that of my colleagues was more fact-driven.

As I started reflecting on the foundation and the reasons for these differences, the doctrinal style to which I was accustomed gradually appeared to me as deeply contingent and possibly too narrow. And when Bruce Ackerman and I began our long exchanges, and as he enticed me to read widely in political theory, I began to drift away from the legal culture in which I was raised.

The final result of this process is that I live between two worlds. I am not completely at home in American law: There are many things here that I find alien. On the other hand, when I go back to Continental Europe, the local conception of lawyering often looks to me overly technical and narrow. I am no longer at home there either. Mine is a strange perspective on law: I look at things as if I were located in the Azores Islands, somewhere in the middle of the Atlantic Ocean.

DEBTS OF GRATITUDE IN THE UNITED STATES

MD: In this country there were several people to whom I owe a debt of gratitude. I said already that I profited greatly from my decades long conversations with Bruce Ackerman. But before I met Bruce – we met only in the early seventies – I had a close relationship with Louis Schwartz, the man who arranged for me to come to Philadelphia in the early sixties. If it were not for him, I would most likely never have had my second life. He passed away a few years ago.

Then there was Paul Mishkin, my colleague at the University of Pennsylvania who moved to Berkeley and recently retired. In my opinion, he is one of the sharpest constitutional lawyers. When I came to this country I was hungry for information, but often tired of doing research on my own. Paul had an encyclopedic knowledge of the law, and I was brazen enough to take advantage of it. So I would walk into his office and say, 'Paul, I do not understand this. Could you help me?' It was a rare occasion when he did not have an immediate answer. A remarkable man.

At Yale, and in the same role, I owe a tremendous debt to the late Arthur Leff, whom I mentioned in connection with the law dictionary I published in former Yugoslavia. He was not only one of the greatest intellectuals at Yale Law School, but also a delightful person. I still vividly remember the joy of reading his article 'Law and' that appeared in the Yale Law Journal about thirty years ago. Unfortunately he died relatively young. I still miss him.

But let me return to Bruce Ackerman, who understood my adaptation difficulties better than anybody else, and who encouraged me to persevere in some of my pursuits when most people thought they did not make much sense. He was ideal for bouncing ideas against. I would come to him and say, 'Listen, what do you think about this half-baked theory of mine?' He had a blackboard in his office and would start drawing diagrams illustrating conceptual relationships. It was useful to talk to him even in areas about which he knew little or nothing. He would quickly understand things and was able to spot weaknesses and strengths in argumentation.

He was also helpful to me in seeing that my mental children see the light of the day. Take my *Evidence Law Adrift* as an example. It was originally an article rejected by *Yale Law Journal*. Bruce said, 'Listen, why don't you turn it into a book. Write an additional chapter'. I did, but then worried who would be interested in publishing it. 'Don't' you worry', Bruce said, 'I have friends at Yale University Press'. He made a few phone calls, and – to make a long story short – the book came out in a year or so. He was helpful in other ways as well. In buying my first car in America, for example, I refused to negotiate the price. In the country I came from, cars had fixed prices, and dickering was considered fit only for Oriental bazaars. So I found haggling below my dignity. When Bruce learned about my attitude he said, 'I will negotiate for you'. So he went with Marija to the Ford dealer. When they emerged from his office, Bruce triumphantly announced that the deal was closed and that he had saved me a bundle.

WORKS IN ENGLISH, INTELLECTUAL INFLUENCES AND THEORETICAL TRADITIONS

ML: Regarding your work in English, what has been the influence of Max Weber on it?

MD: The answer may require a little prelude. I do not belong to geographical specialists in comparative law, people who make themselves experts, say on Russian or French legal system. I could not even write meaningfully about all areas of the legal system in which I was originally trained – except at a very superficial level – let alone compare this system to a foreign one. From my first attempts to study law from a comparative and historical perspective, I was therefore drawn to focus on areas in which I was domestically proficient, areas that related to social practices whose problems were well known to me. So I concentrated on foreign judicial procedure, court organisation, evidence and criminal law. The influence of Max Weber on these studies may easily be exaggerated. In many of my publications you will find no trace of his ideas. But he was obviously an inspiration to me in the part of my opus devoted to the relationship between administration of justice and types of authority. And I continue to think that his 'ideal types' are very useful as a tool to those engaged in the comparative study of law.

ML: Are there other intellectual traditions you would consider your work part of?

MD: One reviewer of my book *Faces of Justice* discovered parallels between my method and the then fashionable theories that evolved from literary criticism. This came as a surprise to me, for I read the *coryphaei* of this movement much later and found myself in deep disagreement with them. I am quite frankly not aware of following any particular school of thought, especially not the grand theoreticians of comparative law. Let others, if they want, place me in a particular niche. Personally, I always wanted to be able to say to myself that what I wrote was concocted on my own. 'It may be wrong, but it is original, and it is mine'. This conceit is a mild form of a more extreme attitude I picked up from Professor Bayer. 'In approaching a problem', he used to say, 'I first read in a rather perfunctory fashion what others said on the topic. Then I think things through on my own'. Only after he would come up with his own answer or was unable to find one, he would read others in a systematic fashion. And he would do so mainly to discover whether what he came up with on his own held water.

There are people who come to subjects they write about from above, from some larger theoretical standpoint. I think that most of my work went in the opposite direction. I preferred that my theories bubble up from the ground, from 'little things' I observe in the life of the law. And because

of my marginality, or my perspective from the Azores, I developed a certain alertness of observation in regard to these little things – the raw material for my abstractions.

I am aware that my reluctance to follow established theoretical approaches can be considered a weakness, or a predicament. It may be that for this reason some of my publications appear to the critics as a sloppy mixture of the historical and the theoretical, with much of the theoretical being a little shaky because of the injection of the historical. If I may compare myself to really important people who may be vulnerable to this sort of criticism, Hannah Arendt and Isaiah Berlin come to mind.

ML: Why can the reluctance to follow established intellectual traditions be considered a weakness?

MD Because you are not standing on the shoulder of giants. You must develop your own conceptual instruments and your own method. By way of contrast, consider the example of scholars who have adopted the powerful micro-economical methodology for the study of legal problems. In a sense they have it easy: They have at their disposal sophisticated concepts, and a widely accepted methodology. Give them 'institutional knowledge' of law, and they will provide you with interesting solutions with relative ease. Another problem with following your own path is that it gets time consuming. For this reason – and also because I use a borrowed tongue – I write very, very slowly. At this stage in my life's journey this is quite frustrating. To give you an example, one of my remaining ambitions is to publish a study on a more recent change in the traditional Continental conception of judicial office and on the transformation in traditional Continental perceptions of the desirable degree of order in the law. At the speed at which I work, the completion of this ambition will take years. And even though I am not yet affected by the indolence of old age, I wonder whether I will be able to complete this project before I go *ad plures*.

ML: You referred to your work and Hannah Arendt's and Isaiah Berlin's work as sloppy. Why did you use that adjective?

MD: I did not mean to disparage their work. From the standpoint of analytical rigour and discipline, what I called sloppiness stems from tensions between historical explanation and analytical theory. History is messy and replete with contradictions. Theory, on the other hand, tolerates neither. I experienced this tension especially as I was writing, long ago, my Yale essay *Structures of Authority*. I recall how often I was torn between historical description and the reductionist impulse to develop a theory. Trying to combine the synchronic reductionism and the richness of diachronic exposition easily results in a work in which neither your theory nor your history are at their best.

Look at Hannah Arendt's *The Origins of Totalitarianism*. No doubt, it is an impressive book. There is theory in it and also history. But neither is the

history beyond reproach, nor is there much rigour in theorising. In a sense her work is quite disheveled. Or, take Isaiah Berlin's hedgehogs and foxes. They do not stand for models which would satisfy social scientists. Besides, Berlin was too much drawn to life's complexities and contradictions to be a systematic philosopher. This is all the more remarkable since, in Oxford, he was surrounded by analytical philosophers.

ML: Going back to the creation of the co-ordinate ideal as a theoretical category opposed to the hierarchical ideal. Could you tell me a little about their conception?

MD: The idea of these two structures of authority came to me as I tried to theorise about 'little things' I observed after I came to America, things that were strikingly different from those I was familiar with in my native legal culture. Let me give you an example to illustrate what I mean. At the time, some federal district judges attempted institutional reforms in prisons and school systems by issuing what my colleague Owen Fiss termed 'structural injunctions'. In light of what I knew about Continental judiciary, this was astonishing. In most Continental countries, trial judges were modest bureaucrats, waiting for signals from the judicial top for any bold move. Moreover, structural injunctions seemed from my perspective more of an administrative than of a judicial genre. Are these federal judges not grossly uninhibited, I wondered, acting with abandon like fauns in Debussy's *Afternoon*? It was contrasts like this that I tried to stylise and capture in constructing the co-ordinate and hierarchical ideals.

ML: And what about the policy-implementing and conflict-solving models?

MD: They were also a distillation of my experience. Remember that I was raised in Communist Yugoslavia which was initially as avid in its totalitarian ambitions as Stalin's Soviet Union. Notionally, everything was then fair game for policy implementation. To imagine criminal procedure, for example, as an instrument to resolve conflict between the state and the individual would have been a sort of blasphemy in this political climate. In America, however, this was the accepted view.

ML: Do you see *Evidence Law Adrift* very different as an intellectual enterprise from *The Faces of Justice*?

MD: Oh yeah, it is different. You will find very little of Max Weber in the book. Which is not to say, however, that you might not be able to detect some family resemblance between the hierarchical and the co-ordinate model, on the one hand, and holistic and atomistic approach to evidence, on the other.

LAW ENFORCEMENT, DEFENDANT'S RIGHTS AND THE FUNCTIONS OF PROCEDURE

ML: One of the traditional divides among criminal procedure people is between those that are more pro-prosecution and those who are more pro-defence. When you were in former Yugoslavia, where did you situate yourself in this divide?

MD: You might say that I was someplace in between these two opposite camps. In teaching law to my students in Zagreb, I developed a Freudian metaphor to describe inherent tensions in the administration of criminal justice. This metaphor expresses well my middle-of-the road position. By the way, I wonder whether I ever used this metaphor in any of my writings in English.

ML: I believe you used it in a footnote in *Evidentiary Barriers to Conviction*.

MD: Did I? Let me then reuse it now. The crime control, or pro-prosecution urge, I associated with the system's *id*, and the pro-defence, or human rights impulse, with the system's *super ego*. A healthy criminal justice system, I maintained, requires that neither of these contrary impulses become too strong. The pro-defence orientation, no matter how laudable and attractive to academics, can also go too far. An overly strong *super ego* may generate neurotic symptoms in the justice system, of which hypocrisy is only the most obvious example. I still think that our humanist impulses should not make us blind to the crime-control needs. We should try to civilise them, but the obstacles to their satisfaction should not be set too high.

Lately I have advocated this *via media* approach for international criminal courts. Although I have been critical of them in my writings, I realise that they are driven by their special needs to depart somewhat from the due process of national courts. Protection of witnesses, for example, is one of their special needs. It is much more pronounced than in typical domestic cases. Witnesses, mind you, also have rights. One can be unfair to them just as one can be unfair to defendants. Some departures from domestic due process forms may also be warranted by the social-pedagogical goal of international courts. It looms larger than domestically, because international courts have no endogenous enforcement powers and cannot rely on deterrence to the same degree as their national counterparts. And if pedagogy is so high on the totem pole of their aspirations, international criminal courts can be driven to adopt arrangements preventing defendants from using trials as a platform for propagating their views. I hope you see that I remain somewhere in the middle.

A SLAVIC SOUL: ROOTS, HOMELESSNESS AND FAILING TITO'S SON

ML: We already talked about your two professional lives and the fact that you have lived in two different legal cultures. You have been able to speak to both of them.

MD Yes. But I paid a price for it: I'm not completely at home in America, and I'm no longer completely at home in my native Croatia. To purloin Heidegger's phrase, I am struggling 'to be at home in homelessness' – *Heimischwerden in Unheimischsein*.

ML: You make a reference to this in *The Faces of Justice*.

MD I do not want to sound melodramatic, but I find something sad in living between cultures. May be this is just because I am a Dostoevsky's Slavic soul. Although I would have professionally achieved much less if I stayed in the old country, I am not so sure that I would not have been on the whole happier. I would not experience the feeling of belonging everywhere and nowhere. As it is, I am often visited by nostalgia. My thoughts of the old country are inseparable from the experience of first things – first loves, first successes, the joy of being young.

ML: But is this nostalgia a result of leaving your country?

MD I would put it this way. My ancestors lived in Croatia, in a country with a rather unfortunate history. Some of them worked unstintingly to improve its lot. I myself played a little part in attempts to make things better. And by leaving the country I feel a little bit like I betrayed my country, my ancestors. I remember how deeply satisfying it was for me to be able to make a difference in the brief period when I was entrusted with important responsibilities. Here, in the academy, I write articles and books. Of course, it is satisfying when a publication is a success – if only a *succès d'estime*. But it is much more satisfying when you do something that really makes a difference or say something that really counts. Let there be no doubt: America, my adopted country, has been very good to me. I am a professor in a distinguished university and in one of the country's top law schools. This is an honour that I do not want to belittle. But it does not come close to positions of influence I could have expected in my former life. To paraphrase Caesar, it is easy to be among the first in an Alpine village I sometimes wonder where I would be if I had stayed. Some of my colleagues were, or are now, in very influential positions. Who knows how much I could have helped the Alpine village if I stayed in it?

ML: Yes, this is one possible scenario. But another possible scenario could have been becoming ostracised after 1971. Then you would have been an ostracised professor in Zagreb without political impact and with nothing happening until 1991. Those 20 years were the most important years of your second professional career, right?

MD: Well, you may be right. It is conceivable that I would have been rejected. I was somewhat inflexible, well-known to take risks in acting on principle. I do not know if I ever told you: I once did something which was very risky.

ML: What did you do?

MD: It was sometime in late spring of 1969, I believe. The Zagreb Law School had more than 800 regular students, and only oral examinations back then. I would have to give exams to more than 20 people a day. It was like torturing the examiner rather than the defendant with long interrogations.

ML: Yes, I am familiar with this type of oral examination. We have them in law schools in Argentina too.

MD: So you know how it is. As I came to the school, two Communist party activists on the faculty announced that Tito's son was one of the candidates that day. This was supposed to put pressure on me. I still remember that I examined five students before it was Tito's son turn. I quickly realised that he was bright, but spoiled rotten by special treatment he regularly received. He talked a blue streak to give the impression to the large audience that he was well prepared. But what he said was nonsense. When the exam was over I said to the assembled students, 'I am interrupting the examination, and will give the grades to the group that I examined after a short break'.

Then I desperately ran next door to the office of Professor Bayer. 'What shall I do?', I asked him. 'I would have to fail six people whom I examined so far. One of them is Tito's son, who – unlike the rest – talked all the time to give the impression that he was well prepared. But he did not really know anything. It was rather insulting to me. I do not know what to do'. The old professor said only, 'Do what your conscience directs you to do'. I went back to my office and spent a few minutes in what the French would call *recueillement*. Letting the impertinent fellow pass would have been very unethical. I felt that I would betray the principles I lived by so far if I buckled under pressure. So I opened the door to the hallway where a large group of students was standing. When I announced to them that Broz – Tito's family name – did not pass there was a hush. Complete silence.

That evening my father was very upset, and so was Marija. 'What is going to happen to you now?', they lamented. Nothing happened. Someone told me much later (whether it's true I have no way of knowing) that Tito found out about it and was not cross at all. He apparently felt it was good for his son to learn about getting along in life without special treatment. But I was worrying more that some lesser party official might try to prove his loyalty to the regime by harming me.

So you outlined a possible scenario. Had I stayed in Zagreb, I might have gotten into trouble, especially after the old Communist guard took over in the early seventies. Looking back, it seems to me that what I did

was really risky. But I always hated compromising ethical principles. This flows from the mode of sensibility related to my spiritual side.

ML: Your parents were Catholic. Were you raised Catholic? Did you go to church?

MD: Not during the Communist regime. As a matter of fact, Marija and I were married in Church only recently, courtesy of the Catholic Chaplain at Yale. But life to me always possessed a religious dimension, and Catholicism is my spiritual home. It sustained me in difficult situations and prodded me in pursuit of excellence. It is part of my roots. As you can well imagine, some of my friends think that my full-hearted love of a good beyond life is an irrational streak in me. I usually respond by invoking Niels Bohr's idea of two parallel worlds and their complementarity. Or, I direct them to read Charles Taylor's recent book on the secular age.

ML: Continuing with the question about roots, although you have lived in the United States since 1971, you have stayed in touch and have done many things for Croatia, haven't you?

MD: After I settled in America, I was at first a little nervous about going back to the old country. But people assured me that preventing me from returning to America would create a diplomatic problem for Yugoslav authorities and that I should not worry. Since I badly wanted to see my ageing parents, I went back next summer. Nothing happened. So, until they died, I would spend summers with them in Croatia. Parting with them was always agony. But for almost a decade I did not have any relationship with the university there. Many former colleagues were avoiding me.

Sometime in the mid-80s, the President of the World Victimological Society, a former colleague of mine at the Zagreb Law School, organised an international congress in Zagreb, and invited me to give a keynote address. That was the beginning of my rehabilitation.

With the onset of the Yugoslav crisis I got involved in events surrounding the disintegration of the country. In September of 1990, the then President of Croatia (Yugoslavia still existed, but was decentralised and each republic had its president) asked Yale Law School to comment on the draft of an international treaty that would convert Yugoslavia from a federation into a confederation. The transformation was supported by the Croatian and Slovenian governments. Dean Calabresi accepted the request and charged me with forming a group of experts to do the job. Not all of them were from Yale: The most prominent outsider was Professor Joseph Weiler, then of Michigan, now of New York University. The group quickly came up with suggestions for improvement, and I sent them to Croatia. But the most powerful actor in the crisis, the Serbian leader Milošević, rejected the idea of confederation out of hand. He wanted just the opposite: greater centralisation of Yugoslavia around Belgrade. Or, in the alternative, the destruction of the state, and the creation of greater Serbia. The slide toward war began.

A few months before its outbreak, I attended an international conference in Atlanta, sponsored by President Carter. I took advantage of this opportunity to ask him to take the initiative and offer the services of his Center for Reconciliation in resolving the crisis. The idea for this request was suggested to me by the Yugoslav Mission at the United Nations. But President Carter refused, explaining that his Center takes a reconciliation job only if officially asked.

After Croatia became independent, my connections with the old country intensified. The first 'big fish' to be tried by International War Crimes Tribunal for former Yugoslavia happened to be a Croatian general, Tihomir Blaškić. I was asked to represent him, but there was no way for me to get a leave of absence from Yale for the required period. Thereupon the Croatian ambassador to the Netherlands asked me to help finding an American law firm to defend the general. I did, and remained of-counsel during the pre-trial and trial proceedings.

A few years later, I was asked to join a Croatian Government's Council charged with relations to The Hague Court. As a result, I got involved in international criminal law and most of my writing is now in this field. I also became involved in Croatian public life, through television appearances and interviews in newspapers, but mainly in connection with events surrounding war crime trials.

This involvement culminated last year, when Zagreb Law School celebrated the 230th anniversary of its founding. As part of the program, an international meeting was organised in my honour, and the President of the Republic awarded me a medal of merit.

ML: Could you tell me more about this celebration?

MD: It took place in the lovely setting of the National Opera House in Zagreb – a small replica of the Viennese Opera House. Yale Law School Dean Koh and I sat in the government booth, along with the Croatian Prime Minister and his Deputy. There was a musical programme. I was, of course, informed that the President of the Republic would come and award me a prestigious medal, but nobody told me that I was expected to prepare a speech. Only at the last moment a woman from the President entourage told me so. So the President marches in, and starts expatiating about my achievements, real and imagined. I am not really listening, trying frantically to think of what to say in response. Fortunately I managed to come up with a few words people must have liked, because what I said appeared in the evening press. The centrepiece of this little speech was that, in receiving the medal, I feel like a prodigal son whom mother Croatia gave a kiss. I used the old 'Kajkavski' term for kiss – 'pusu' – which warmed the hearts of older people in the audience. The moment was caught by a photographer. It shows the President holding my hand, smiling and gesturing to the public. It was a very emotional moment for me.

Speaking of emotional moments, I was deeply touched when I spotted a very old professor from the University of Ljubljana in the audience, a man whom I greatly admired because of his courageous defense of freedom during the Communist regime. We were close in the old days, but had not seen each other since the 1970s. I rushed to embrace him, thinking of old times when talk was not cheap. Easy on the tear, I had to struggle hard to contain my emotions.